BOLOGNA & EMILIA-ROMAGNA

'a fervent insistence on the plain truth sets Bologna apart. The city's handsome centre disdains imported marble or ornate stucco, preferring honest red brick. In the 11th century it was the desire for truth and law that led to the founding of the University. And it is Bolognese sincerity and honest ingredients that has made la cucina bolognese *the best in all Italy.'*

Dana Facaros & Michael Pauls

About the Guide

The **full-colour introduction** gives the author's overview of the country, together with suggested **itineraries** and a regional **'where to go' map** and **feature** to help you plan your trip.

Illuminating and entertaining **cultural chapters** on cultural chapters on history, food and drink and local heroes give you a rich flavour of the country.

Travel covers the basics of **getting there** and **getting around**, plus entry formalities. The **Practical A–Z** deals with all the **essential information** and **contact details** that you may need, including a section for disabled travellers.

The **regional chapters** are arranged in a loose touring order, with plenty of public transport and driving information. The author's top **'Don't Miss'** **sights** are highlighted at the start of each chapter and there are also **short-tour itineraries**.

A **language and pronunciation guide**, a **glossary** of cultural terms, ideas for **further reading** and a comprehensive **index** can be found at the end of the book.

Although everything we list in this guide is **personally recommended**, our authors inevitably have their own favourite places to eat and stay. Whenever you see this **Author's Choice** icon beside a listing, you will know that it is a little bit out of the ordinary.

Hotel Price Guide

Luxury	€€€€€	€230 and above
Very Expensive	€€€€	€150–230
Expensive	€€€	€100–150
Moderate	€€	€60–100
Inexpensive	€	€60 and under

Restaurant Price Guide

Very Expensive	€€€€	over €60
Expensive	€€€	€40–60
Moderate	€€	€30–40
Inexpensive	€	under €30

About the Authors

Dana Facaros and Michael Pauls are professional travel writers. They spent three years in a tiny Italian village, where they suffered massive overdoses of food, art and wine, and enjoyed every minute of it. They reckon they could whip 98 per cent of the world's non-Italian population at Trivial Pursuit (except for the sports questions). They now live in southwest France.

4th Edition Published 2007

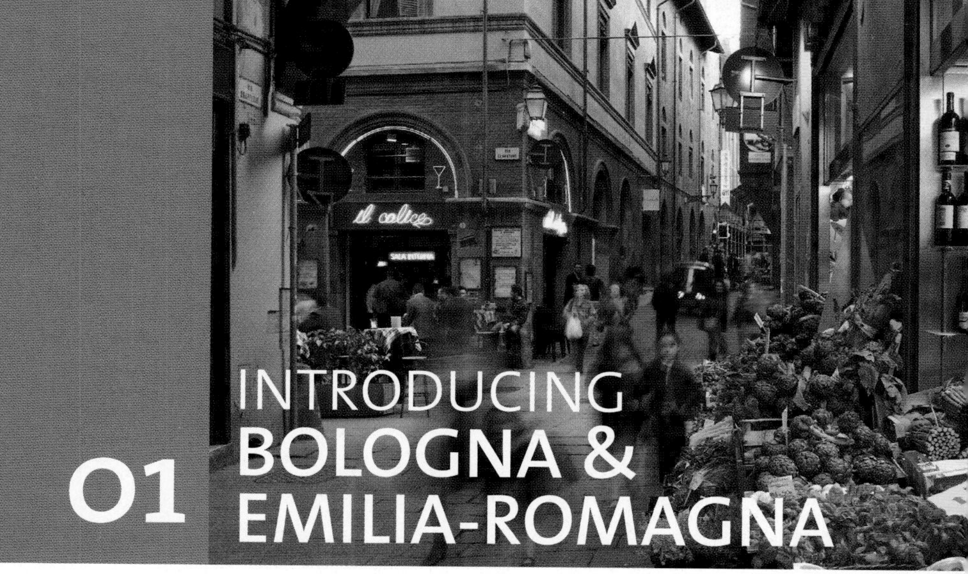

01 INTRODUCING BOLOGNA & EMILIA-ROMAGNA

Above: A street market in Bologna, p.223

The stupendous wealth of art, architecture, history and gastronomy combine to make Emilia-Romagna the most civilized of treats. It is also an area of extraordinary contrasts: its layout seems to have been designed by a government committee. Start with a road that runs almost perfectly straight for 320km (200 miles). String all the cities along it, at regular intervals. Put all the hills on one side of the road, and all the flatlands on the other. Sprinkle the whole thing liberally with red bricks, (former) Communists and tortellini, and you couldn't get anything else but Emilia-Romagna.

The joke is, it probably was designed by a committee. Sometime near the close of the Second Punic War, no doubt, some Roman senators, engineers and military men sat down together and came up with the plan for developing this newly acquired territory. The biggest expanse of flat land in Italy gave them a chance to put the Roman passion for rationalism into practice on a massive scale, and their hard-nosed pragmatism has marked everything in the region's life for the last 2,200 years: its politics, its ways of thinking, and even at times its art. That straight-as-an-arrow Roman high road that ties everything together, the *Via Aemilia*, gave the land its character along with its name.

After their orderly and efficient start as Roman colonies, the towns along the Via Emilia went their separate ways in the Middle Ages. Each one picked itself up from the rubble of the Dark Ages and built itself into a prosperous free city, and each had a busy career battling popes, emperors and each other. Eventually each one fell under the rule of city bosses, and as these *signori* turned

Opposite: Organ at the Duomo, Parma, pp.131–2

into aristocratic dynasties, they added mightily to an already impressive hoard of castles and cathedrals, palaces, churches and frescoes.

Since then, the region's accomplishments have been many. Emilia-Romagna is the cradle of many of Italy's most innovative film directors, Fellini, Bertolucci and Antonioni. Before cinema, almost every town, large and small, built an ornate theatre-concert hall as a proud civic centrepiece, and a testimony to its devotion to the arts. So it shouldn't be surprising that the region is also the home of many of the nation's musical greats, from Verdi and Respighi to Toscanini and Pavarotti.

'Emilia-Romagna' is a slightly artificial region, given official status only in 1970 when Italy began decentralizing power to local governments. Another committee decided to lump together Emilia, the stretch from Piacenza to Bologna, with the Romagna to the west, a territory with a history shaped by centuries of rule by the pope. But it does hang together. One feature that all its towns have in common is their radical politics, born over a century ago, and surviving two wars and Mussolini to blossom after 1945 as 'Red' Emilia-Romagna, where Communism with a human face gave the region Italy's most efficient and enlightened government, and at times even made the businessmen happy.

Along with radicalism, this region's other claim to fame is a well-established reputation as the home of Italy's finest cooking. When you begin to see how these two contradictory passions fit together, you'll understand the odd brand of earthy pragmatism that sets Emilia-Romagna apart. It helps to notice how simple this famous cuisine really is – all you need are the right ingredients, which the patient farmers of the region have had centuries to perfect. Here, even a *piadina* sandwich from a street-corner stand can be a strangely transcendent experience.

Yet, whether the food comes from the street or the serious five-toque temples of tortellini that turn up in the most out-of-the-way villages, dukes and revolutionaries agree that living well is the best revenge. It all seems paradoxical at first. Emilia-Romagna is the place where plain brick churches conceal preposterously fancy *quadratura* ceiling frescoes, where everybody knows the lyrics to at least one Verdi aria and one old socialist anthem, where platoons of women in mink coats pedal bicycles through the town centres, on their way to the grocer or the theatre. Stay around for a while, and it will all start to make sense.

Where to go

This book is arranged by cities – in Emilia-Romagna, that is where the main attractions lie; you'll seldom be tempted to spend too much time outside them, except perhaps to bake on a beach or to visit the **Apennines**. These mountains, touching the borders of Tuscany and the Marches, are a seldom-visited corner of Italy; they have some nice surprises, but you won't be touring them end-to-end. The main roads run along parallel valleys that descend towards the plain, and it isn't always easy getting across from one to the other. Most likely, you'll be seeing the mountains as side trips from the towns.

As for the **plains** north of the Via Emilia, perhaps a little rude candour is required. These are the most dolorous, dismal landscapes in Italy: flat, intensively farmed and densely populated, a panorama of drainage ditches, power lines and hardscrabble farmhouses and villages that have somehow totally escaped the Italian obsession with *bella figura*. Only in the wetlands and *valli* near the Adriatic coast, decorated with groves of umbrella pines by the ancient Romans, does the Po plain take on a romantic and quite attractive loneliness. For the rest, this curious land is a place where paradoxically the oases of beauty and tranquillity aren't to be found in the countryside, but right in the centre of town.

Below: Parma ham

Opposite: Ghetto Ebraico, Jewish quarter, Bologna, p.196

For convenience's sake, this guide takes the cities in a straight march down the Via Emilia from west to east, following in the footsteps of Caesar marching from Gaul to the fateful banks of the Rubicon. Seven immaculately maintained historic centres, each with its own personality, cultivated over the centuries: each one of these has its own story to tell, and offers its own particular delights.

Piacenza, the Medieval, a town that had its best days as a trade and banking centre in the 1200s, the crossroads of northern Italy. Though Piacenza gradually fell under the shadow of Milan and Parma, its exceptional Romanesque cathedral and churches and museums make this city more than just a day trip. In the hinterlands are frescoed castles, the venerable abbey of **Bobbio**, founded by Dark Age Irish monks, the Art Nouveau spa of **Salsomaggiore Terme** and the delightful hill town of **Castell'Arquata**.

Parma, the Mannerist, a city of lightness and grace that it must have learned from its greatest painter, Correggio. In truth Parma is as level-headed and stalwartly socialist as any city in the region, though its pretty head may seem full of operatic melodies and thoughts of what's for dinner – the latter, of course, is a weighty question, in this culinary capital, famous for

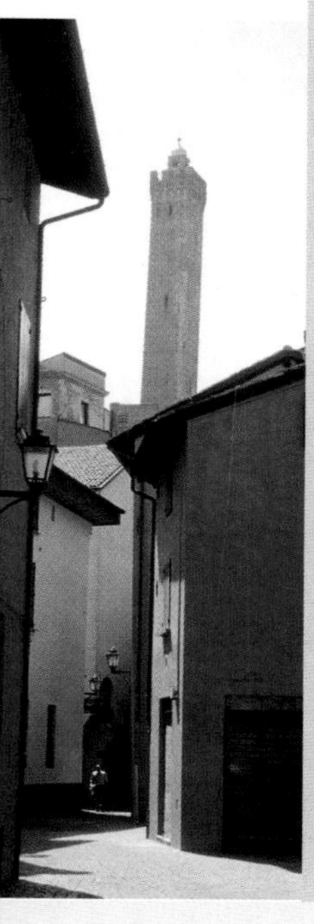

its hams and cheeses and so much more. Parma may be one of Italy's great art towns, but even the church frescoes come in cake-frosting colours to help your appetite along. Parma's countryside, besides its rich farmlands, carries an aristocratic note with a wealth of villas and castles, including the old ducal palace at **Colorno**, the 'Versailles of Emilia'.

Modena, sleek and refined, once the capital of the Este dukes and now better known for its Ferraris and Maseratis. For all its Baroque churches and palaces, the city's heart still belongs to the Middle Ages, exemplified by one of Italy's greatest cathedrals and the soaring tower called the Ghirlandina. Just a few minutes away are other estimable art towns, **Reggio Emilia** and **Carpi**, while to the south lies a particularly attractive patch of Apennines and the cherry orchards of Vignola.

Bologna, the Metropolis, resists all capsule characterizations. It spreads beneath two bizarrely leaning towers. This is Italy's most serious big city, brick-built and earnest, devoted to science and scholarship. For almost a thousand years, the great University has set Bologna's tone, and filled it with curiosities like the ornate tombs of its medieval legal doctors and museums of wax anatomical models. But its presence has also

Chapter Divisions

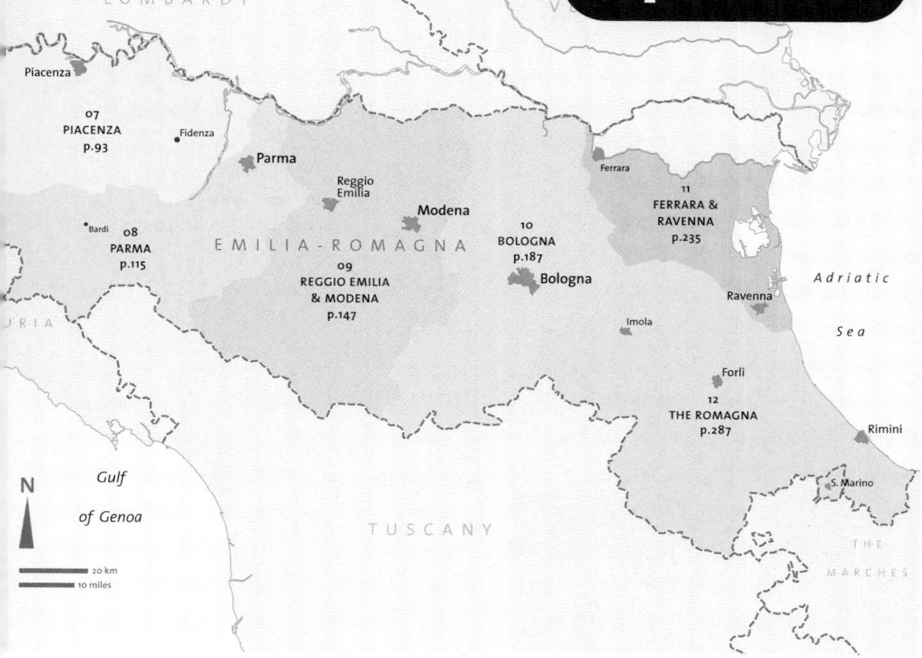
LOMBARDY
Piacenza
07
PIACENZA
p.93
Fidenza
Parma
Reggio Emilia
Modena
Ferrara
11
FERRARA &
RAVENNA
p.235
Bardi
08
PARMA
p.115
EMILIA-ROMAGNA
10
BOLOGNA
p.187
09
REGGIO EMILIA
& MODENA
p.147
Bologna
Adriatic
Sea
Ravenna
Imola
Forlì
12
THE ROMAGNA
p.287
Rimini
S. Marino
N
Gulf
of Genoa
TUSCANY
THE
MARCHES
20 km
10 miles

Above: Fontana Netuna, Bologna, p.199

Below: Palazzo Archiginnasio, Bologna, p.203

helped keep Bologna modern and alive. The city of quiet porticos, culture and celebrated cuisine is also one of the most progressive and forward-looking in Italy. Hills are close at hand: from the edge of the old centre, you can walk up to them shaded by the world's longest portico, with wonderful views over the city. Further afield are the lovely villages and scenery up the valley of the Reno.

Ferrara, where the springtime brilliance of the early Renaissance shines through the mists from the Po, is the eccentric in this bunch, a city designed and embellished according to the new ideas in the air of the quattrocento; the refined sensibility of its aristocratic court found its highest expression in the magic frescoes of the Palazzo Schifanoia. From Ferrara the delta of the Po spreads out to the Adriatic in marshes and lagoons that are home to a wide variety of waterfowl, even flamingos. Also here are **Comacchio**, the Romagna's 'Little Venice', and the medieval art treasures of the **Abbey of Pomposa**.

Ravenna, another exotic bloom of the coastal wetlands. Ravenna is a modern industrial town, but its centre holds some of Italy's most unforgettable artistic treasures, evoking the faraway world of Rome's fall, and the beginnings of Byzantium. Its brief but remarkable spell as capital of Italy a millennium and a half ago left it with the greatest collection of Byzantine mosaics anywhere, sparkling in green, blue and gold.

Rimini, Federico Fellini's town and the cosmopolitan beach Babylon of the Adriatic, welcomes visitors in their thousands, whether they come from Middlesbrough or Moscow. There's more to Rimini than just seafood and fun fairs, including one of the jewels of Renaissance art, the Malatesta Temple, while the surroundings include a number of pretty hill towns, one of which is the sovereign Republic of **San Marino**. Before you get to Rimini the Via Emilia will take you through three more cities: **Imola**, with a modest helping of art and some great restaurants; **Faenza**, famous for painted ceramics since the Renaissance; and Mussolini's city of **Forlì**. The real attractions here are up in the hills to the south, including the lovely village of **Brisighella** and some others nearly as good, in the part of the mountains known as the 'Tuscan Romagna'.

Piazzas for Walking

A dozen or so of Italy's most refined towns and cities, and all of them perfect for a stroll. Cities in Emilia-Romagna took the lead in making their centres into car-free zones, and now we can see them the way they were meant to be seen. Peaceful streets, with beautiful things to look at, amply provided with parks and cafés when you need a rest. Besides walking, the bicycle is the preferred city-centre mode of transportation here, and you can rent one anywhere without bother.

Bologna, the metropolis, is a special case, with over forty miles of streets under graceful stone arcades, or *portici*. Other towns adopted the habit too – here, you can do your strolling in the rain and not even get wet.

Renaissance Magic

The cradle of the Renaissance might be over the mountains in Tuscany, but when it crossed into Emilia-Romagna it took a turn towards the exotic and strange. In an age when princes wore amulets and consulted astrologers, they had their artists build esoteric lessons into their works – some of the greatest art of the Renaissance. You can puzzle out their meanings in the Camera di San Paolo in Parma, or Rimini's Malatesta Temple, or the *Triumphs of the Months* in Ferrara's Palazzo Schifanoia.

The Renaissance is everywhere in Emilia-Romagna, though the best places to see it are Parma, city of Correggio and Parmigianino, and Ferrara, where the Dukes of Este tried to create the perfect Renaissance city.

Above from top: Two portici on Piazza Santo Stefano, Bologna, pp.206–8; Ferrara Cattedrale façade, pp.243–4

Music in the Air

They like to sing here (yes, sometimes even in restaurants and on buses), and more often than not the melody will be from one of Emilia-Romagna's great names. Busseto, near Parma, has become a shrine to its native son Giuseppe Verdi, while Parma honours the conductor Arturo Toscanini. Every city has its grand old theatre, with concert and opera seasons in winter and festivals in the summer. It isn't only classical. Ravenna does jazz, Ferrara puts on Europe's biggest buskers' fest, and Modena even has a contest for military bands. The Modenese take their fingers out of their ears when hometown favourite Luciano Pavarotti gives his concert every September in the Piazza Grande.

Above: Verdi's statue, Busseto, p.112

Right and below: Rounds of Parmesan cheese and handmade pasta

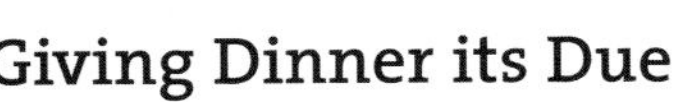

Giving Dinner its Due

It's the most renowned food region in Italy, perhaps in the entire galaxy. Emilia-Romagna gives the world Parma ham, tortellini, Parmesan cheese, balsamic vinegar, and ever so much more. Its people found culinary academies, and argue for hours over the proper way of folding a *tortellino*. You'll find colourful street markets here, and some of the finest restaurants in the world, in city centres and little country towns. Never believe it's limited only to formidably expensive temples of cuisine. This is a famously democratic region, with a cuisine to match. You'll eat well everywhere, in every price range; even a mere sandwich (called a *piadina*) can be transcendent.

Seafront, Rimini,
pp.321–2

Along the Adriatic

Emilia-Romagna has a seacoast and, while it might not be the Côte d'Azur or the Amalfi Drive, it does have its charms. Our region's stretch of the good grey Adriatic comes in two distinct parts. Rimini is the centre of Italy's biggest resort, a forty-mile strip of built-up beach. It's a surprisingly civilized scene, and a good bargain, especially out of season. The northern part is a delight to explore: the delta of the Po, home to flamingoes, storks and white Camargue horses. Comacchio, with its canals, is the Romagna's 'Little Venice', while just down the coast waits the most exotic of the region's art towns, Ravenna, full of glittering Roman and Byzantine mosaics.

Dining room, Grand Hotel, Rimini, p.305

High Life

After all, this is the land of mink coats and sports cars, one of the wealthiest corners of Europe and a grand place for putting on the ritz. There are classic Belle Epoque cafés to lounge in, elegant spas, or you can swan around the Grand Hotels of the Adriatic coast (including the one that obsessed little Federico Fellini when he was growing up in Rimini). Have a look at the Ferraris at the factory in Maranello, even if you can't afford one.

The high life here can also mean a trip through the aristocratic past, perhaps a visit to the haunts of Napoleon's Queen Marie Louise, who ended up Duchess of Parma. The well-groomed countryside around that city contains her palace at Colorno, the 'Versailles of Emilia', among many others such as Soragna, with fine frescoes and an English garden, or Renaissance Sanvitale and Torrechiara. For dead posh, you can't beat the Castello Estense in Ferrara, where the dukes kept an orange grove on their roof garden.

The Modenese Apennines near Sassuolo, p.182

A Touch of the Vertical

Italy's flattest region isn't the place to go if you're mad for hills, or hill towns, but when you get tired of wide-open spaces it can offer a modest sprinkling of both. The northern slopes of the Apennines do run through here, and as for Tuscan-style hill towns, there are at least two perfect ones: Castell'Arquato, near Piacenza, the background of a Renaissance painting come to life, and Brisighella, south of Faenza, with a memorable skyline of medieval towers.

South of Modena, there's Vignola, famous for cherries, and a little higher up, on Monte Cimone, you can even go skiing. Some of your best chances for an escape up into the hills will come south of Forlí, in a corner of the Apennines that used to be part of Tuscany. Amidst lovely scenery in a national park, you'll find such delightful villages as Portico di Romagna and Bagno di Romagna.

Above from top: Palazzo del Podestà, Bologna, p.199; The Due Torri in Piazza Porta Ravegnana, Bologna, pp.204–5

Hometown Spirit

Emilia-Romagna's first springtime came in the Middle Ages. It arrived in a world of battling city-states, competing in war and in art. Each of these was a little world in itself, and the traditions and habits established nine centuries ago continue today. These towns have personality, and much of the pleasure of a visit here lies in getting to know them and their quirks.

In each, the medieval heritage is a collection of monuments that have become city symbols. Like modern American cities, with their competing skyscrapers, the medieval Italians were crazy for towers, like La Ghirlandina in Modena, or the endearingly preposterous leaning towers of Bologna. You'll see some remarkable sculpture – Benedetto Antelami's on the baptistry in Parma, or Wiligelmo's on Modena cathedral – and get to know some excellent painters, such as Vitale da Bologna and Pietro da Rimini.

Above: San Luca, Bologna, p.206; San Stefano, Bologna, p.220

Itineraries

A Two-Week Art Tour – By Train

A car would be pointless, and you'd have no place to put it anyhow. But Emilia-Romagna's great art towns are strung out like pearls along the VIa Emilia and the main railroad line, each an hour apart at the most. Since it's so convenient, why not see them the old-fashioned, civilized way?

Day 1 If you're starting from Piacenza, take a day looking through the paintings and Etruscan curiosities of the Musei Civici, and a walk around to see the city and its collection of fascinating churches.

Days 2–3 Just down the road is Parma. There's lots to see: medieval sculpture in the famous Baptistry, Correggio in the Duomo and the Camera di San Paolo, Parmigianino at the Madonna della Steccata, the collections of the Galleria Nazionale and the grandiose Teatro Farnese, the charming Glauco Lombardi Museum. There may be time for a trip out to the palace at Colorno.

Days 4–5 Modena will take two days too, between the tremendous cathedral, the Galleria Estense and the host of smaller museums. For one afternoon, it's an easy half-day trip out to Carpi for more art (or venture to Maranello to see the Ferraris).

Days 6, 7 and 8 Save three days (at least) for the Big Tortellino. Bologna is a subtle city, one that takes some effort to know, and besides the well-known monuments there are plenty of surprises to hold your attention. Don't miss the Medieval and Renaissance Museum and do make the climb up to San Luca.

Days 9–10. Leave the Via Emilia, finally. Tell the train to branch out to the left and head out for Ferrara. Besides the Castello Estense, the Pinacoteca Nazionale and the wonderful frescoes in the Palazzo Schifanoia, this bicycle-friendly city has some real surprises, as in the Cathedral Museum and Sant'Antonio in Polesine.

Days 11–12 After all this, we leave the Renaissance and go back a thousand years in Ravenna, with the spectacular mosaics of San Vitale and the other churches, more exceptional museums, and a short suburban trip out to the basilica of Sant'Apollinare in Classe.

Day 13 Wind it up in Rimini, with a look at the magical Tempio Malatestiana and some more good museums.

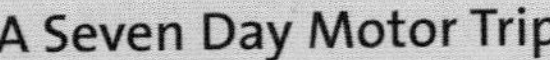

Above: San Marino, pp.330–32

Below: Brisighella, p.296; Panorama, Bologna, pp.187–230

A Seven Day Motor Trip

After you've seen the cities, you might wish to spend some additional time touring the Apennine slopes and foothills, and some of the lonely open spaces of the Romagna. If you've already done the first itinerary, you can round out the trip by going back the other way from Rimini.

Day 1 The proud, very tiny Republic of San Marino may have turned itself into a funny tourist trap, but it still deserves to be seen. There will be time for some castles and hill towns in the surroundings, such as Santarcangelo, Torriana or Verrucchio.

Day 2 Find your way over the back roads to Bagno di Romagna and the other pretty hill towns in the Apennines south of Forlí; end up in the most attractive of them all, Brisighella, with its 12th-century Rocca.

Day 3 Stop at Faenza, for a look at the faïence, and then head north into the marshlands. The attractions here are the Romagna's 'Little Venice', Comacchio, wildlife in the National Park at the Po delta, and great medieval frescoes at the Abbey of Pomposa.

Day 4 Now it's a longish drive westwards, through some empty spaces to the refined little town of Carpi, with its castle and museums. Continue on to Correggio.

Day 5 From here, head south around Reggio to the most dramatic part of the Emilian Apennines, around the Rocca di Bismantova. When you're through sightseeing, end up towards Parma, around Torrechiara.

Day 6 Spend a day in the Parma foothills, where there are plenty of interesting castles, as at Bardi or Montechiarugolo, as well as Collecchio with its natural park; you may find your way north of the city for Colorno and its imposing palace and gardens.

Day 7 Between Parma and Piacenza, there's a choice of routes and attractions: more palaces, at Soragna and Fontanellato, Giuseppe Verdi's Busseto, a fine Romanesque cathedral in Fidenza and, to finish, the loveliest hill town in the region, Castell'Arquata.

CONTENTS

The Guide

Reference

Maps and Plans

History and Art

02

History

History in these parts goes back over 3,500 years, but the 'region' of Emilia-Romagna is a political newborn, created only in the 1970s when all of Italy was divided into regions in a long-overdue move towards decentralization. Some of Italy's regions have an obvious historical or geographical identity – Tuscany, the Veneto or Sicily for example. This one doesn't. Until relatively recently, the 'Emilian' part of the Po valley was considered part of Lombardy, while the Romagna followed a different destiny, first as part of the Byzantine Exarchate of Ravenna after the breakup of the Roman Empire, and then in the Papal State. The 'border' between Emilia and Romagna is generally considered to be the little river Santerno that flows by Imola – but ask the question of a few Italians and you're likely to get a few different answers.

BC

Finds of tools and statuettes of fertility goddesses testify to the occupation of the Po plain in Palaeolithic times, and small farming settlements existed all through the Neolithic, but the first accomplished culture in the area was that of the remarkable Terramare people, who made the soggy plain habitable by digging the first drainage canals.

16th century arrival of the Terramare people in the Po valley
12th century disappearance of the Terramare
***c.* 1000** Villanova people settle the area around Bologna, and the Apennine foothills around Rimini
9th century coming of the Etruscans

The Etruscans, arriving most likely from Asia Minor, imposed themselves as rulers on the existing Villanovan peoples, and the new hybrid culture, organized in confederations of city-states, became the most powerful and advanced nation in Italy. From their first centres in Tuscany and northern Lazio, the Etruscans expanded over the Apennines. From their new towns of Bologna and Spina, near Comacchio, the Etruscans gradually expanded to occupy the entire Po plain by the 6th century. Already, though, they were facing a new enemy: the Celts.

***c.* 510** Etruscans found Velzna (Bologna)
5th century expansion of the Celts over the Alps
475 defeats by the Greeks in southern Italy and by the Celts in the Po plain signal the decline of the Etruscans
390 Celts sack Rome
***c.* 350** Celts take Bologna

Even in Caesar's time, the part of Italy north of the Apennines was not 'Italy' at all, but called by the Romans Cisalpine Gaul, an area dominated by two main tribes, the Insubri in the west and the Boii around Bologna. Roman historians described a Celtic world in northern Italy that sounds a good deal like medieval Ireland. From 343 to 290 Rome fought its climactic battle for the rule of Italy – the Samnite Wars, in which that powerful southern Italic people was allied with the Celts and some

Etruscans. Roman victories on all fronts opened the Po plain to Roman conquest and colonization.

295 victory of the Romans over the Celts at the Battle of Sentinum
268 founding of Ariminium (Rimini), the first Roman colony north of the Apennines
223 Romans achieve final conquest of Cisalpine Gaul

The historian Polybius called the fight between Romans and Celts 'unsurpassed by any other war in history' in terms of the size and courage of the armies involved. The Romans built their great roads and established Latin colonies in the Po plain, but even after their defeat the Celts weren't done, and the struggle in Gaul became part of an even bigger conflict, the Second Punic War, in which the Celts allied themselves with Carthage and served in great numbers in Hannibal's army.

220 opening of the Via Flaminia, from Rome to Rimini
218 opening of the Via Aemilia, founding of Placentia (Piacenza)
Hannibal crosses the Alps, defeats the Romans at Trebbia, near Piacenza, winters at Bologna
202 defeat of Carthage, end of the Second Punic War
189 founding of Latin colony at Bononia (Bologna), conquered from the Celts
187 opening of the Via Postumia, connecting Genoa with Heracleia via Piacenza
183 founding of Parma
175 founding of Reggio Emilia
132 opening of the Via Popelia, the Adriatic coastal road through Rimini
115–102 last Celtic raids into Italy

Roman surveyors, as relentless and methodical as the soldiers, carved the entire Po plain into a grid of straight roads, rectilinear towns and rectilinear land parcels called centuriae. Most of the land was expropriated from Celtic farmers and built into large estates (latifundiae) to enrich the Roman élite, though considerable areas around the new towns were granted as smallholdings to the colonists: Latins and army veterans.

49 Caesar crosses the Rubicon, ceases Rome expansion of Roman citizenship to all inhabitants of Cisalpine Gaul

AD
98–180 the height of the Roman Empire, in which an unbroken line of good emperors (Trajan, Hadrian, Antoninus Pius and Marcus Aurelius) preside over a period of peace and prosperity

The decline began directly afterwards. In an empire increasingly oppressive and costly, run by and for the army, commerce and cities decayed greatly. After an unsettled period in the 3rd century that saw Germanic raids into the peninsula, Italian towns began building walls.

310 legendary founding of San Marino by Christians fleeing Diocletian's persecutions
330 Constantine orders the closing of the pagan temples

364 final division of the Empire into eastern and western halves
402 Ravenna becomes capital of the Western Empire

The Vandal general Stilicho defended Italy (with a mostly German army) against German invasions. After his treacherous murder by Emperor Honorius, the army had no chance of holding the Western Empire together. For its last two decades, western emperors were puppets while German generals held the real power; after 476 Italy was a German-run kingdom, with its capital at Ravenna. It enjoyed a period of recovery under the strong and enlightened rule of King Theodoric.

408 murder of Stilicho
409 invasion of the Visigoths, followed by their sack of Rome
450 death of Galla Placidia
452 Attila the Hun invades Italy
476 end of the Western Roman Empire
476–93 *Odoacer, King of Italy*
488 Ostrogoths cross the Alps into Italy
493–526 *Theodoric*
525 San Vitale (Ravenna) begun by Theodoric; execution of the philosopher Boethius
529–53 Greek-Gothic Wars

The greatest disaster in the history of Italy, the result of the ambition of Emperor Justinian to reconquer the lost lands of the west, led to a long, terrible war in which the flourishing Gothic Kingdom of Italy was destroyed, the Eastern Empire gravely weakened, and Italian civilization dealt a near death blow. As Italy lay in ruins, a Germanic tribe heretofore quiet and backward, the Lombards, migrated over the Alps to fill the vacuum.

539 widespread famine
540 Ravenna falls to the Byzantines under the great General Belisarius
567–8 the Lombards under King Alboin overrun most of Italy
c. 590 creation of the Exarchate of Ravenna

This period initiated the political divide between the two parts of our region, as the western half under Lombard control began to be considered part of 'Lombardia', while the east, still under the rule of the empire, was known as 'Romania'. Here some important centres got their start: the Abbey of Pomposa, and the cities of Ferrara (originally a Byzantine fort) and Comacchio, protected like Ravenna and Venice by its lagoons. Elsewhere, the devastation of the wars and invasions and the decrease of population had created a wasteland. In the 6th and 7th centuries most rural areas in the plain of the Po, which had depended on the upkeep of their drainage canals, once again became largely deserted, though none of the old cities except Velleia near Parma died completely.

612 St Columbanus founds the Abbey of Bobbio
727 Lombards capture Bologna; Ravenna revolts against Byzantine rule
751 Lombards capture Ravenna
752 Lombards found abbey of Nonantola

754–6 Frankish invasion of northern Italy

As the Lombard Kingdom finally consolidated its power, and threatened papal rule in Rome, the papacy was alarmed enough to invite in King Pepin and the Franks, whose military superiority made short work of the Lombards. The origins of the Papal State came about with the 'Donation of Pepin' – the Franks, upholding their end of the deal with Rome, ceded the Romagna (and much of central Italy) to the temporal rule of the popes. Though they held on to this dubious claim tenaciously, they were in fact rarely able to wield much authority over these regions until the 1500s.

800 Charlemagne crowned Emperor
952 Otto the Great occupies northern Italy, is crowned Emperor the same year; creation of the Marquisate of Canossa

In this complex, feudal north Italy, the new house of da Canossa was not the only great power in the region. Another was the Obertenghi, a family of Lombard origins. They ran much of northwest Italy in the 10th century and held substantial lands in Germany too. Branches of the Obertenghi eventually grew into the houses of Este, Malaspina and Pallavicini, three of the most powerful families of medieval Emilia-Romagna. Meanwhile, the rule of Otto and his successors, in the new Holy Roman Empire centred in Germany, restored order after the decay of the Carolingian Empire, and cities and culture throughout Italy started to revive.

After 1000 the revival gained speed, inaugurating three centuries of nearly constant economic expansion. The booming cities organized themselves into free comuni; *their efforts to increase their freedom from imperial or papal control provide most of the plot of Italian medieval history.*

1055 birth of Irnerius, first of Bologna University's *glossatori*
1071–1115 *Matilda, Countess of Tuscany*
1073–80 *Pope Gregory VII*
1077 penance of Henry IV at Canossa, settling the investiture conflict between popes and emperors
1088 traditional date of the founding of the University of Bologna
1095 First Crusade proclaimed at Piacenza
1099 Modena Cathedral begun, consecrated 1184
1115 Ferrara gains its independence from Canossa
1119 building of the Two Towers of Bologna
1122 Piacenza Cathedral begun
1135 Ferrara Cathedral begun
1152–90 *Emperor Frederick I Barbarossa*
1167 founding of the Lombard League, an alliance of the *comuni* to uphold their rights against Frederick
1178 Parma Cathedral completed; baptistry begun in 1196
1198 Peace of Constance between the Emperor and the Lombard League
1212–46 *Emperor Frederick II*
1221 death of St Dominic in Bologna
1226 death of St Francis of Assisi

1236 founding of the Second Lombard League
1240 Guelphs under Azzo d'Este control Ferrara, begins three centuries of Este rule
1248 siege of Parma, defeat of Frederick II; Guelphs under Malatesta da Verucchio take control of Rimini
1249 Guelph victory of Fossalta (Modena), capture of the emperor's son, King Enzo

The cities had won the first round, against Barbarossa; against his grandson Frederick II they had another hard fight, full of dramatic reverses of fortune. By now all Italy was divided into two factions, the pro-imperial Ghibellines and the Guelphs, supporters of the free cities and their ally, the pope. Of course, one of the rights most important to the comuni *was the right to battle each other, and in the shifting course of events 'Guelph' and 'Ghibelline' were often merely labels of convenience in purely local struggles.*

After 1248 the Guelphs were victorious almost everywhere in north Italy, and the cities were generally free from imperial interference. But the factional fights within them continued, and nearly every city found the only solution was rule by a single boss, a signore, *whose family often continued in power as a dynasty.*

1255 destruction of the castle of Canossa by the *comune* of Reggio
1256 Bologna abolishes feudalism in the communal territory
1275 Guido da Polenta establishes his family's rule in Ravenna
1278 Rudolph of Habsburg cedes sovereignty over Bologna and the Romagna to papacy
1295 Malatesta da Verucchio becomes *signore* of Rimini; San Marino adopts its Statutes and becomes an independent Republic
1307 Este rule in Modena
1314 Dante completes the *Commedia*; the poet dies in exile in Ravenna in 1321
1325 the 'Rape of the Bucket' by the Modinesi from Bologna
1331 beginning of the rule of the Pio family in Carpi; they last until 1525
1346 the Visconti seize Parma, beginning a century of Milanese rule there
1348–9 the Black Death wipes out one third of the Italian population

The plague returned throughout the region in 1361, in Bologna, Ferrara and Forlì in 1362, in Bologna and the Romagna in 1374 and again in 1382 and 1383. Much of Italy had a similar fate, and the plagues marked the first interruption of the medieval economic expansion. The cities recovered, and in the 15th century, Ferrara, and to a lesser extent Rimini and Bologna, became important centres of Renaissance art.

1360s campaigns of Cardinal Albornoz to establish papal control in the Romagna; Cesena taken in 1357, Bologna in 1360
1376 Bolognese throw out papal legate, establish oligarchic rule of the 'Sixteen Reformers of Liberty'
1377 bloody repression of revolt against papal rule in Cesena
1385 building of the Castello Estense at Ferrara
1390 Basilica di San Petronio begun in Bologna
1401 the Bentivoglio gain control of Bologna
1441 Venice establishes rule over Ravenna
1446 Malatesta Temple begun at Rimini

1462 excommunication of Sigismondo Malatesta, who loses most of his lands in the Romagna and Marches to the popes the following year
1470s first printing presses in Ferrara and Bologna
c. **1475** frescoes of the Palazzo Schifanoia at Ferrara
1482–3 War of Ferrara, prelude to the Wars of Italy
1494 Wars of Italy begin with the invasion of Charles VIII of France

After 1494, the delicate equilibrium of the small and wealthy Italian states was wrecked once and for all by the intervention of the ambitious nation-states France and Spain. The popes did as much as the foreign powers to keep the pot boiling in the decades of confusing and bitter war that followed. There was a string of calamitous popes – Alexander VI, Julius II, Leo X, Clement VII and Paul III – all intelligent men and patrons of learning and the arts, but their egomania, devotion to their families' interests, and constant intrigues with foreign powers resulted in the end of Italian liberty and the subjection of nearly all of the nation to the eventual victor, Charles V, who was both King of Spain and Holy Roman Emperor. For its part, the papacy won undisputed direct control of the lands of the Papal State, including the Romagna and Bologna, for the first time.

1495 Battle of Fornovo, demonstrating the ineffectuality of the Italians against the foreigners
1499 campaigns in the Romagna of Cesare Borgia, son of Pope Alexander VI; captures Imola, Forlì and Rimini
1501 marriage of Lucrezia Borgia and Alfonso I of Ferrara; Cesare Borgia's conquests dissolve on the death of his father and the transfer of the papacy to his enemies
1506 the Bentivoglio deposed in Bologna, papal rule established
1509 Pope Julius II raises a powerful coalition against Venice (League of Cambrai), which loses all its possessions in the Romagna
1519 Correggio paints the Camera di San Paolo in Parma
1527 Sack of Rome by Imperial troops
1530 coronation of Charles V in Bologna
1532 publication of Ariosto's *Orlando Furioso*
1534 Alessandro Farnese becomes Pope Paul III
1539 famine and plague in the Romagna
1545 Paul III creates the Duchy of Parma and Piacenza for his son, Pier Luigi
1547–63 Council of Trent

While Italy was subject to the unholy alliance of pope and Spaniard, the Reformation in northern Europe and the reform of the Church at Trent brought the liberal, humanistic culture of the Renaissance to an end in Italy. The new totalitarian Church that emerged from the council wiped out free thought and put severe strictures on art and the conduct of everyday life. Even the independent small states of Parma and Modena were seldom able to resist the pressure.

1553 Inquisition installed at Bologna
1559 treaty of Cateau-Cambrésis confirms Spanish control over most of Italy
1564 Duke Cosimo of Florence builds Terra del Sole in the Tuscan Romagna
1593 Jews expelled from Bologna and Romagna
1598 Pope Clement VIII ousts the Este from Ferrara

As if Italy did not have enough troubles, after 1600 the economy began a rapid decay, caused partly by the shift of the richest trade routes from the Mediterranean to the Atlantic, and partly by papal and Spanish misrule and the loss of initiative in the merchant cities. Some agricultural prosperity remained, especially from silk and hemp cultivation around Bologna, but in this period the region was best known as a source of soldiers for the wars of northern Europe; opportunities at home were scarce. In the Baroque era Italy became a backwater, and no part of it suffered more than the Papal State, in which by 1650 the only thriving trades were church-building and banditry.

1618 Farnese Theatre begun in Parma
1630–1 great plague in Emilia and most of Italy
1672 earthquake at Rimini
1713 the close of the War of the Spanish Succession leaves Austria as the guarantor of the existing order in northern Italy
***c.* 1720** introduction of maize as a food crop; Emilians discover polenta
1731 extinction of the House of Farnese in Parma, rule passes to Charles of Bourbon
1735 founding of the *Gazzetta di Parma*, Italy's oldest newspaper
1759 Enlightenment reformer Guillaume du Tillot transforms Duchy of Parma
1796 Napoleon enters Italy, creation of the 'Cispadane Republic' at Modena
1797 Cispadane Republic merged into a new 'Cisalpine Republic'
1813 Giuseppe Verdi born
1814 end of French rule
1815 Austrian garrison installed at Ferrara to protect the Papal State from revolts

The Congress of Vienna re-established the Papal State, gave the Duchy of Parma to Napoleon's estranged wife Marie Louise and restored the Este to Modena, in the person of the reactionary Francesco IV. In reality, all Italy was to be managed by Austria, but after the big Napoleonic shake-up things would never be the same. In the decades of the 'Risorgimento', liberal thought and Italian nationalism were reborn. The secret societies called the Carbonari and revolutionaries such as Mazzini and Garibaldi led the fight for a united, democratic Italy, while conservative patriots hoped for unification under the Kingdom of Sardinia (Piedmont); the Bolognese poet Giosué Carducci and composer Giuseppe Verdi also played important roles.

1830–1 Revolution in Bologna, followed by Modena, Parma and the Romagna. Government of the 'United Italian Provinces' set up; the revolt is soon crushed by Austrian troops
1843 beginnings of Rimini as Italy's first beach resort
1845 short-lived revolt in Rimini against papal rule
1847 death of Marie Louise
1848 revolutions across Europe, and Italy; Carlo Alberto of Piedmont wars against Austria, and loses
1849 collapse of revolutionary regimes; Garibaldi flees across the Romagna to Venice
1858 railway reaches Bologna
1859 revolt in Modena throws out the Este after 553 years; revolt in the Romagna. Both join Piedmont by plebiscite

1860 Parma incorporated into Piedmont, whose King Vittorio Emanuele II becomes King of Italy in 1861
1867 Arturo Toscanini born in Parma

Italian unity proved a disappointment to many under the oppressive and corrupt governments of the following decades; their liberal economic policies, while building modern industry, caused considerable hardship and dislocation in rural areas. Emilia-Romagna, where a large class of landless agricultural labour existed, became the most radicalized section of the nation, the birthplace of the Italian Socialist and co-operative movements.

1869 severe riots in Parma and elsewhere against the Grist Tax, designed to build up the new Italy's army
1872 large land-clearance and drainage programmes in the Romagna
1874 socialist-anarchist revolt in Bologna
1881 Andrea Costa founds the Revolutionary Socialist Party of Romagna, and a year later becomes the first Socialist deputy in Parliament
1889 Imola elects Italy's first Socialist administration
1895 Guglielmo Marconi of Bologna sends the first radio signal
1896 first consumers' co-operative founded at Molinella, near Bologna

After the First World War, and Italy's disappointment at Versailles, the nation became polarized between the revolutionary movements and unions of the left, and the frightened propertied classes, who turned to the new Fascist party, led by the Romagnolo and former Socialist Mussolini, for salvation. In the years before Mussolini's assumption of power, Emilia-Romagna was the key battleground.

1918–20 the 'Red years', waves of strikes throughout industrialized northern Italy
1921–2 wave of violence by Fascist gangs against leftist institutions, co-operatives and municipal governments
1922 Mussolini's March on Rome; he becomes head of the government
1925 planning of the *Città del Duce* at Forlì
1926 murder of defiant Socialist leader Giacomo Matteotti (from Fratta Polesine)
1937 hundreds of Emilia-Romagna men escape Italy to fight with the International Brigades in Spain
1940 first Ferrari built in Modena
1943 the Allies invade Italy

The Allies' concentration on opening a new front in France led to stagnation on the Italian front. A failed offensive in August 1944 against the German Gothic Line, which extended across Emilia-Romagna, let the Germans and Fascist militias mop up Resistance groups, while allowing more time for Allied bombers to wreak havoc on the region's cities. Rimini was perhaps the most heavily bombed city in Italy. Bologna and Ravenna were also hit hard, and artistic monuments like the Teatro Farnese in Parma were destroyed.

1943 the partisans set up a short-lived free zone in the Apennines, the 'Republic of Montefiorino', and then conduct pitched battles with the Germans in Bologna

1944 the 'march of death'; SS massacres in several villages, notably Marzabotto, in reprisal for partisan activities
1946–8 the first post-war elections give Italy a Christian Democrat government, while Emilia-Romagna votes solidly Communist in local elections
1947 massive, successful strikes by tenant farmers in the Po plain

After liberation, the Americans saw to it (quite understandably, in the context of the Cold War) that the new Italian Republic was a limited democracy at best. But while Italy was manipulated to ensure permanent control by the centre-right Christian Democrats, Emilia-Romagna bucked the trend by becoming a bastion of enlightened Communism. Their government did business no harm at all, and the region paradoxically also became a bastion of the 'third Italy' of small, successful, often family-run manufacturing firms.

Recovery was rapid, especially in agriculture (while the percentage of workers in that sector fell from over 50 per cent of the work force to 10 per cent), so much so that the Po plain saw extensive deforestation. A quarter of Italy's pigs called Emilia-Romagna home. A big chemical industry grew up in Ravenna and Ferrara, metals and machinery thrived in Bologna and Modena, along with ceramic products and textiles in several centres, and beach tourism in Rimini.

1956 Khrushchev's revelations about Stalin and the Hungarian revolt cause a split and serious soul-searching among the Communists
1964 death of painter Giorgio Morandi
1970 region of Emilia-Romagna created, with elections for a regional assembly
1970s the *Anni di Piombo*, a decade of political crime and right-wing terrorism climaxing in the Bologna rail station bombing, killing 85 people
1974 Fellini's *Amarcord*
1998 election of conservative Mayor Giorgio Guazzaloca in Bologna
2004 election of Mayor Sergio Cofferati, a former trade unionist, in Bologna

Art in Emilia-Romagna

In art, Emilia-Romagna defies generalizations: look at it not as a matching pearl necklace but rather as a charm bracelet, with charms that evolved in various cities at various times in history. Influences came from every direction and, when the patronage was there, the efforts often merged into a coherent school. The region's talent for making pretty things goes back to the Villanovans and at various times in history it set the standard of excellence in Italy – in late Roman–Byzantine mosaics, in medieval illumination, in Baroque theatre and stage sets, and in painting during the late 16th and 17th centuries, when paintings by the Bologna school were in demand throughout Europe.

As much art as Emilia-Romagna has to offer today, an extraordinary amount of it was destroyed or is now in museums outside the region: for instance, nothing remains in the region by the major Renaissance painter Melozzo da Forlì. On the other hand, the region has a whole cast of lesser-known artists, local obsessions and talents. Faenza gave the world **faience**, but the whole region, like anywhere

Etruscans once lived, has a knack with **terracotta**, and used it to produce mournful statue groups of the Deposition of Christ, as well as the decorative friezes of its simple brick churches and palaces. The Renaissance brought a mania for **intarsia** (wood inlay), employed most in choir stalls – every church had to have a set, and most depict townscapes and simple everyday objects, both meant to show the artists' skill in perspective. Emilia-Romagna's **castles**, especially around Parma and the Romagna, are among the most striking in Italy, and often have lavish interiors added in or after the Renaissance, when they were converted into stately residences.

Except for the castles, **architecture** is a subject that Emilia-Romagna people do not often choose to bring up. In fact, the region has always been strangely allergic to architectural achievement of any kind. On the rare occasions when they cared to build ambitiously, they were usually content to find their inspiration, or their builders, from somewhere else. Parma, Ferrara and Piacenza, to an extent, are exceptions, but Bologna, for all its attractive porticoes, is unquestionably the most architecturally deprived great city of Italy.

Ancient and Medieval

The finds from **Villanovan** and **Etruscan** cemeteries are scattered in the archaeology museums of the region, with the biggest concentrations in Bologna and Ferrara. Special mention must go to Verucchio near Rimini, where a Villanovan cemetery yielded unusually well-preserved artefacts, including textiles and wood from the 7th century BC. Like their compatriots to the south, the Etruscans of the Po valley made beautiful bronzes, ceramics and jewellery, and had a taste for ancient Greek pots (Ferrara has an extraordinary collection of red figure vases), besides making copies of their own. Unlike the Etruscans of Tuscany, however, they did not bury their dead in *tumuli* or painted tombs, but often under remarkable large circular tombstones carved with reliefs. The region was neither particularly wealthy nor accomplished in **Roman** times; the best collections of art and artefacts from that period are in Parma, Bologna and Rimini, and at the lost city of Velleia.

In the so-called Dark Ages, the Greek heirs of the Roman Empire in **Constantinople** gave the region one of the most dazzling charms on its bracelet in **Ravenna**. Although its 6th-century churches and splendid **mosaics** exerted more immediate influence on Byzantium's protégé Venice (which could afford such fancies), you'll find echoes of Ravenna throughout the region, in the bell towers of its churches and mosaic pavements, and Byzantine miniatures.

Outside Ravenna, you'll find early medieval traces in Bologna's Santo Stefano complex, the Abbey of Nonantola near Modena, and Bobbio, a great centre of learning in the Dark Ages. Among the Romanesque churches, the brightest jewels are Modena Cathedral, decorated by the sculptor Wiligelmo, his followers and the Campionese Masters of Lombardy, and Parma Cathedral and Baptistry, with fine sculptures by Antelami. A favourite subject of sculpture in the Middle Ages was the Allegories of the Months, at Modena (Duomo), Parma (Duomo and Baptistry), Ferrara (Duomo and the Palazzo Schifanoia), Argenta (San Giorgio), Bobbio (San Colombo) and Piacenza (San Savino).

Other notable **Romanesque** churches include Piacenza's San Savino, Castel l'Arquato's Collegiata, Fidenza's Duomo and the **Abbey of Pomposa**, the region's greatest shrine of trecento art, with beautiful frescoes by Emilia-Romagna's two medieval schools of painting, Bologna and Rimini.

The **Bolognese** school grew up alongside the university. The city's artists excelled in illuminated manuscripts, Bibles and religious texts, but also legal codices and books of guild statutes or poetry (Biblioteca Estense in Modena, Biblioteca Comunale in Bologna). Although Byzantine influences were initially strong, by the late 13th century Giotto's more naturalistic, volumetric style led to a wealth of invention, foreshortening, movement and the individualization of characters. Although most works are anonymous, Jacopino da Reggio, Bernardino da Modena and Franco Bolognese (highly praised by Dante) are among the names that have come down to us. The only important Bolognese artist of the trecento to work on a larger scale was Vitale da Bologna.

The often charming **Rimini School** blossomed in the early 14th century, initially inspired by Byzantine miniatures from Ravenna, and later by the frescoes in Assisi by Giotto and the finest Roman and Umbrian artists of the day. Little is known of its artists beyond their names (if that): the 'Pseudo Jacopino', Pietro da Rimini, Giuliano da Rimini and Giovanni Baronzio are among the identified, each with their individual quirks, joy in decoration, genre details and tendency to exuberant narrative.

Renaissance and Mannerism

In the quattrocento, the **Ferrara school** was the first in Emilia-Romagna to shine, thanks to the unflagging enthusiasm and deep pockets of the Este. They founded a university to attract leading scholars to their city, commissioned works from the greatest painters, and did all they could to encourage the talents of local artists. Cosmè Tura, their court artist, had a style unto himself – a very nervous and elegant line, creating highly energized dreamlike scenes, reflected to varying degrees in the work of the other great quattrocento Ferraresi: Francesco del Cossa, Dosso Dossi, Lorenzo Costa and especially Ercole de' Roberti.

By the early 1500s the **duchy of Parma** joined Ferrara among the leading artistic centres of northern Italy, where sophisticated patrons had an insatiable appetite for the luxurious and for precious art, especially if it came with scholarly allusions, visual puns and illusionistic effects. Art no longer imitated life, but life imitated art, in the costumes and spectacles and the striving for a refined, artificial air. In Parma, Correggio and Parmigianino were the men of the hour: Correggio's Camera di San Paolo has as many mysterious allusions as the region's other great Renaissance shrine, Rimini's Tempio Malatestiano; his proto-Baroque domes are full of illusionistic effect, and his mythological paintings among the most sensuous. He inspired Parma's two great painters, the exquisite Mannerist Parmigianino, with his elongated hyper-elegant and sensuous forms, and the early Baroque master, Lanfranco.

High Renaissance and Baroque

In the late 16th century, Bologna became a cradle of reaction against the exaggerations and distortions of Mannerism, a fight led by the Carracci brothers Annibale and Agostino and cousin Ludovico, who started off together painting palaces, and in the 1580s founded a school of painting with the startlingly inaccurate name of the *Accademia degli Incamminati* ('the progressives'). Their success was not necessarily due to any change in Italian tastes. The **Council of Trent**, which concluded its reform of the Church in 1563, decreed that religious art was to fall under the close supervision of the clergy, and clear rules were set down for it. Painting and sculpture must be simple and intelligible, realistic, and filled with emotional appeal to encourage piety. The Carraccis' genius was to hit on a formula that the Counter-Reformation Church could approve. They emphasized draughtmanship, life drawing, perfect polish and the restoration of classicism; their approach discouraged thinking, vision and imagination, which made their followers in the Bolognese school exceedingly popular and gave the region's museums and churches their acres of virtuoso wallpaper.

There were some notable exceptions. The most gifted of the Carracci, Annibale, revived interest in the then-neglected art of Correggio before moving off to Rome to paint the ceiling of the Galleria Farnese, his masterpiece and a fundamental point of departure for Baroque painting. He is also credited with the invention of the 'ideal landscape', an art perfected by Poussin, and was the first to draw caricatures. Many graduates of the *Accademia* followed Annibale to Rome. The most accomplished, Guido Reni, soon returned to Bologna, where his huge studio sent religious paintings to patrons around Europe. Domenichino and Giovanni Lanfranco of Parma became rivals in Rome; Lanfranco surpassed Domenichino with his more dynamic, illusionistic work, full of the dramatic foreshortening he had learned while growing up and looking at Correggio's domes. The much younger Guercino, a great draughtsman, flirted with a more exuberant Baroque style before returning to Bologna in 1624 to take over Reni's studio, and spent the next thirty years churning out sleeping pills. As Rudolf Wittkower wrote:

> *The tradition of the Carracci 'Academy' had an extraordinary power of survival, and through all vicissitudes Bolognese classicism, even in a provincial and, sometimes, debased, feeble and flabby form, continued to be a power which for good or evil made itself felt in many other centres.*

In the 19th century, the Bolognese school fell dramatically from favour, attacked by Ruskin in 1847 as having 'no single virtue, no colour, no drawing, no character, no history, no thought', which sums up the worst of it.

But Bologna had more up its sleeve: from the time of the Carracci it was the European centre of ***quadratura*** painting, illusionist decoration that makes a room appear to extend into imaginary space – a technique invented by the ancient Romans and revived by Mantegna in nearby Mantua. Specialist *quadraturistas* were used by other artists around Italy to paint backgrounds: the first leaders in the field were Girolamo Curti, 'Il Dentone', followed by Michele Colonna and Agostino Mitelli, who invented *quadratura* with multiple vanishing points. Even when demand for Bologna's hackneyed Grand Manner petered out in the 18th century, the imaginative *quadraturistas* were still in high demand: one of the most famous was Gerolamo Mengozzi Colonna of Ferrara who worked with Giambattista Tiepolo. This reflected the region's importance in theatre building – the reconstructed Baroque Teatro Farnese in Parma is considered the first modern theatre, and the Bibbiena family of Bologna were in demand around Europe for theatre designs.

18th–21st Centuries

Ducal Parma is well endowed with 18th- and 19th-century **neoclassical** architecture and art. The Glauco Lombardi Museum, the Teatro Regio and Biblioteca Palatina, the ducal palace at Colorno and the Teatro Municipale in Reggio Emilia are highlights; another centre of the neoclassical was Faenza. Painting in Bologna and elsewhere in the region had run out of ideas, and almost nothing of value was produced. The low ebb of art in the 1700s did not prevent churches and cathedrals from being demolished (Ravenna and Rimini) or redecorated in the worst possible taste, no doubt destroying much earlier work in the process (Ferrara, Imola, San Mercuriale at Forlì).

Almost all of the region's museums end with a section of **19th-century painting**, and though the names are obscure, and the styles and subject matter not especially original, these are always worth a look. **Liberty Style** (the Italian Art Nouveau, named after the London department store) found its greatest expression in the region's spas (especially Salsomaggiore) and in the grand hotels and villas built in the newly fashionable seaside resorts along the Adriatic. If you see anything in Emilia-Romagna's cities that looks too medieval to be true, with Gothic mullioned windows and carved coats of arms, it probably dates from the period 1890–1930, which saw a fad for romantic and imaginative restorations of genuine medieval buildings (Alfonso Rubbiani's transformation of the palaces of Bologna's Piazza Maggiore is a good example). In Forlì, there's a fair amount of **Fascist architecture** provided by Il Duce.

In 1917–19, Ferrara witnessed a brief revival of its Renaissance affinity for dreamlike, atmospheric art when Futurist Carlo Carrà and poet Filippo de Pisis (both natives of Ferrara) met up with De Chirico, who was in the city for his military service, and in contact with Giorgio Morandi of Bologna. Rebelling against the Futurist doctrines of machines, motion and modernity, the **Metaphysical School** was based on the 'eternal, passionless and unalterable' ideal, which the painters tried to depict while evoking its magical, mysterious quality. At first all experimented like De Chirico with dressmakers' dummies and other hermetical subjects, and by 1919 all had moved on in other directions, although Morandi didn't move too far.

You'll find collections of contemporary art in Ferrara and Bologna. The province of Reggio has a special affinity for **naïve art**: the well-known naïve painter Antonio Ligabue was born at Gualtieri; nearby at Luzzara, there's a charming Museo Comunale dei Pittori Naïf.

Artists' Directory

dell'Abate, Niccolò (1512–71). Painter and sculptor of Modena, influenced by Correggio and Parmigianino; spent the years 1548–52 in Bologna, then went to the court of Henri II where he and Primaticcio founded French Mannerism, the 'Fontainebleau style' (**Modena**, San Pietro).

Agostino di Duccio (1418–81). With Donatello and Ghiberti, one of the three great Florentine sculptors of the quattrocento, known for his great elegance of line and originality in subject matter (**Rimini**, Malatesta Temple; **Modena**, Cathedral).

Aleotti, Giovan Battista (1546–1636). Innovative early Baroque architect of Parma, where he designed the 'first modern theatre' for the Farnese in the Palazzo della Pilotta, and the church of S. Maria del Quartiere (**Ferrara**, University and other buildings; **Gualtieri**, Piazza Bentivoglio).

Antelami, Benedetto (active 1150–1200). Italy's first great medieval sculptor; probably studied in Provence. His trademark black niello-work borders add an elegant touch to his reliefs; his Parma Baptistry, neither ancient nor medieval, has been called 'proto-Renaissance' (**Parma**, Baptistry and Cathedral pulpit; **Fidenza**, Cathedral).

Il Bastianino (Sebastiano Filippi, c. 1532–1602). Ferrarese Mannerist with a soft touch (**Ferrara**, Cathedral, San Paolo, Sant'Antonio in Polesine, Pinacoteca).

Begarelli, Antonio (16th century). Sculptor of fine terracotta groups in **Modena** (Cathedral, San Domenico).

Bianchi Ferrari, Francesco (*d.* 1510). Modenese lesser light of the quattrocento, noted for canvases full of colour and emotion (**Modena**, Galleria Estense).

Bibiena, Ferdinando (1657–1743). One of the elder members of a family of Bologna, famous for their stagings of theatre, opera and Baroque public spectacles, also talented as architects and painters. Most of the family's works are elsewhere (**Colorno**, Palazzo Ducale; **Parma**, Sant'Antonio Abate). Another Bibiena, Antonio, built **Bologna**'s Teatro Comunale.

Bonone, Carlo (1569–1632). A late Ferrarese painter critics like to dismiss as a 'provincial eclectic', and not without reason; you'll see echoes of the Carracci, Correggio, Schedoni and Guercino in his work, but little else (**Ferrara**, Pinacoteca).

Cagnacci, Guido (1601–63). Bolognese classicist and follower of Guido Reni, with a penchant for unusual colours; became court painter to the Habsburg emperor in Vienna (**Rimini**, Museo della Città).

Carracci, Agostino (1557–1602), **Annibale** (1560–1609) and their cousin **Ludovico** (1555–1619). Of Bologna, devoted to rescuing the classicism in art from the caprices of Mannerism. Annibale went to Rome and, until the 19th century, his reputation was as high as those of Michelangelo and Raphael; his engravings of lower-class scenes, the *Arti di Bologna*, would influence painters in the 18th century. Agostino was more academic and less imaginative; Ludovico, a more personal, expressive artist, stayed in Bologna as head of the school (**Bologna**, Museo Civico Medioevale, Palazzo Comunale, Pinacoteca; **Cento**, Pinacoteca; **Parma**, Ducal Palace).

Cavedoni, Giacomo (1557–1660). From Sassuolo, a close follower of Ludovico Carracci; developed a richly coloured palette. Never went to Rome (**Bologna**, Pinacoteca).

Correggio (Antonio Allegri; 1494–1534). No intellectual, but a daring master of foreshortening in large works (his virtuoso frescoes in the cupola of Parma Cathedral, where the saints soar into a miasma of leggy angels, were called 'a hash of frogs' by a contemporary), and painter of emotional nuances, charming gesture, and smoky Leonardo-esque shadowing in his more intimate scenes. His lofty reputation in the 18th century was based largely on his voluptuous mythological fancies, the inspiration for so much of this kind of art in the centuries that followed; for these you'll have to travel to Berlin, Rome, Dresden and Paris (**Parma**, Cathedral, Camera di Correggio, San Giovanni Evangelista, Galleria Nazionale).

Cossa, Francesco del (1436–78). Early protagonist of the Ferrarese school, influenced by miniaturists and Tura. His best-known work is his contribution to the frescoes of the Palazzo Schifanoia in **Ferrara** – original, energetic and good-humoured. Miffed at being paid by the square foot, he went to Bologna, where his most important works were lost or broken up (the Griffoni altarpiece); the best survivor is the *Madonna with SS. Petronius and John* in the Palazzo Comunale in **Bologna**.

Costa, Lorenzo (*c.* 1460–1535). A leading artist of the Renaissance Ferrarese school, along with Cosmè Tura and Ercole de Roberti; in 1485 he went to Bologna where he became a favourite of the Bentivoglio and gradually adopted a softer, sappier style more pleasing to Bolognese tastes, bland and lifeless at its worst, graceful and tenderly melancholic at its best (**Ferrara**, Palazzo Schifanoia; **Bologna**, S. Petronio, S. Giacomo Maggiore, S. Maria dei Servi).

Crespi, Giuseppe Maria (called *Lo Spagnuolo*, 1665–1747). Late Baroque painter of Bologna, and one of its few real talents in that era, with a rare depth of feeling and sincerity (**Bologna**, Pinacoteca, Palazzo Pepoli Campogrande, Galleria Davia-Bargellini; **Finale Emilia**, Collegiata).

Domenichino (Domenico Zampieri, 1581–1641). Pupil of Annibale and Ludovico Carracci who followed them to Rome, where by the 1620s he became the city's leading painter. A dignified classicist like Guido Reni, he held an immensely high reputation in the 18th and 19th centuries (**Bologna**, Pinacoteca).

Dossi, Dosso (Giovanni di Lutero, *c.* 1490–1542). One of the great late Renaissance Ferrara painters, influenced by the romanticism and rich colours of the Venetians Giorgione and Titian. Equally at home in many genres, he excelled in landscapes and mythological subjects that renewed the spirit of magic and fantasy that characterized the earlier Ferrara school; all his best works are outside Emilia-Romagna (**Modena** Cathedral; **Ferrara**, Pinacoteca).

Fontana, Lavinia (1552–1614). Bolognese, daughter of the painter Prospero Fontana who herself became a rare woman painter of the Renaissance, and was elected to the Roman Academy; noted for portraits of prominent people as well as religious works (**Bologna**, Pinacoteca; **Imola**, Pinacoteca).

Franceschini, Marcantonio (1648–1729). One of the more accomplished late Baroque painters of the Bolognese school; a light touch, and a gift for landscapes in conventional religious scenes (**Modena**, San Carlo; **Reggio**, San Prospero).

'Il Francia' (Francesco Raibolini, 1450–1517). Bolognese, began as a goldsmith, jeweller and maker of medallions, and didn't paint until he was over 40, but soon became the most fashionable painter in the city. He was identified with the Bentivoglio family, and many of his works were destroyed after they lost power. A follower of Raphael, although the two never met (**Bologna**, Pinacoteca).

'Il Garofalo' (Benvenuto Tisi, 1481–1559). Ferrarese High Renaissance, heavily influenced by Raphael; cranked out polished but imaginatively numb religious scenes by the dozen before going blind; held in high esteem by critics from Vasari to the 18th century (**Ferrara**, Pinacoteca, Palazzo del Ludovico il Moro; **Argenta**, San Domenico).

Giovanni da Modena (1396–1451). The great quattrocento painter that nobody knows; a tremendous *Last Judgement* in Bologna's San Petronio (also **Bologna**, Pinacoteca).

Girolamo da Carpi (1501–56). Important Mannerist painter, influenced by Giulio Romano and Parmigianino, and a keen student of Roman antiquities (**Bologna**, San Salvatore, San Michele in Bosco; **Ferrara**, San Paolo, Pinacoteca).

Guercino (Giovanni Francesco Barbieri, 1591–1666). 'Squinty-eye' was born in Cento, near Bologna, but initially rebelled against the Carraccesque classicism, and painted powerful, expressive atmospheric Baroque works in Rome. Ran the studio of Guido Reni after that artist's death in 1642, and succeeded him as the most popular painter in Bologna (**Modena**, Galleria Estense; **Cento**, Pinacoteca and Chiesa del Rosario; **Parma**, Galleria Nazionale; **Piacenza**, Duomo; **Bologna**, Pinacoteca, San Luca; **Reggio Emilia**, Duomo, Madonna della Ghiara; **Ferrara**, Cathedral).

'Pseudo Jacopino' (fl. 1320–30). Unknown Riminese artist, notable for often breaking the boundaries of conventional, stylized religious works with a precocious realism (**Bologna**, Pinacoteca).

Lanfranco (fl. 1100–37). Architect of **Modena** Cathedral, built according to the basic principles of the northern Lombard style, with allusions to the classical basilican form. His work inspired the architects of Ferrara's cathedral.

Lanfranco, Giovanni (1582–1647). Born in Parma and trained under Agostino Carracci. Became one of the first great Baroque painters in Rome and Naples, inspired by his childhood familiarity with Correggio.

Lendinara. Family of quattrocento artists, especially known for their skill in creating intarsia wooden choir stalls; the most noteworthy is Cristoforo da Lendinara (**Modena**, Cathedral, Galleria Estense).

Lombardo, Pietro (1435–1515). Leading Venetian sculptor with an interest in antiquities. Pietro sculpted Dante's tomb in **Ravenna**; his son Antonio made Alfonso d'Este's 'marble study' but his reliefs are now in the Hermitage, St Petersburg.

Magnasco, Alessandro (1667–1749, known as *Il Lissandrino*). Worked mostly in Milan; one of the greatest and most eccentric late Baroque painters, specializing in macabre scenes of monks and convents (**Castell'Arquato**, Museo della Collegiata).

Mastelleta (Giovanni Andrea Danducci, 1575–1655). Bolognese, a master of ethereal poetic landscapes in a manner well in advance of his time, inspired by Correggio and Nicolò dell'Abate (**Modena**, Galleria Estense; **Bologna**, Pinacoteca).

Morandi, Giorgio (1890–1964). Of Bologna; generally considered the greatest Italian painter of the 20th century. An artist of geometry and tonal intimatism, a few everyday objects formed his contemplative and lyrical 'personal alphabet' (**Bologna**, Museo Morandi; **Traversetolo**, Fondazione Magnani Rocca).

Morazzone (Pier Francesco Mazzucchelli, 1573–1626). Milanese fresco painter, a transitional figure between the late Renaissance and Baroque whose cool, precise line and love of contrast often harks back to the quattrocento (**Piacenza**, Duomo).

Nicolò dell'Arca (Nicolò da Bari, fl. 1462–94). Sculptor from Puglia who spent most of his career in Bologna, where he earned his name and his reputation from his work on the Arca di San Domenico in San Domenico church (also, **Bologna**, Palazzo Comunale, Santa Maria della Vita).

Orsi, Lelio (*c.* 1511–87). Born in Novellara, a distinctive Mannerist painter with a touch of the bizarre and dramatic lighting effects (**Novellara**, Museo Gonzaga; **Modena**, Galleria Estense).

Palma Giovane (Jacopo Negretti, 1544–1628). Trained by Titian, and spent early career in Central Italy before returning to his native Venice to become the city's leading painter (**Reggio Emilia**, Pinacoteca).

Parmigianino (Girolamo Francesco Mazzola, 1503–40). The 'little Parmesan' started his precocious career under the influence of Correggio, with a keen interest in unusual spatial effects from the start. He went off to Rome and later returned to Bologna and Parma. According to Vasari, he became an alchemist. The word *imparminigiare* came to mean to paint elegance at the expense of the subject. Was a major influence on Niccolò dell'Abbate and many others (**Parma**, Madonna della Steccata, San Giovanni Evangelista; **Fontanellato**, Castello di Sanvitale).

de' Pasti, Matteo (*fl.* 1441–72). Painter, sculptor, medallist and architect of Verona; the collaborator of Agostino di Duccio on the interior of **Rimini**'s Tempio Malatestiano.

Pietro da Rimini (*fl.* early 14th century). Gifted member of the Rimini school, at his best capable of painting figures of delicate beauty; he is one of the few whose work remains in the region (**Ravenna**, Museo Nazionale di San Vitale; **Abbey of Pomposa**).

de Pisis, Filippo (Luigi Filippi Tibertelli, 1896–1956). Poet of Ferrara, where he met De Chirico; turned to painting in 1919. Best works are his marine still lifes, of incongruous objects on a beach, in dreamlike relationships with the surrounding seascapes (**Ferrara**, Musei Civici d'Arte Moderna e Contemporanea).

Pordenone (Giovanni Antonio de Sacchis, 1483–1539). Self-taught painter who followed Titian and Michelangelo; dramatic and slightly uncouth; died in Ferrara while designing tapestries for Ercole II (**Piacenza**, Madonna di Campagna).

Preti, Mattia (1613–99). Calabrian Baroque painter, influenced by Caravaggio. Worked all over Italy including a short spell in Emilia-Romagna (**Modena**, San Biagio); most of his best work is in Malta, for the Grand Master of the Knights of St John.

Procaccini: brothers, **Camillo** (1560–1629) and the younger and more gifted **Giulio Cesare** (1574–1625). From Bologna, where they studied under the Carracci; they later moved to Milan, where they collaborated with Marazzone and Crespi, becoming key figures in the new art of the Counter-Reformation, under the influence of San Carlo Borromeo (Camillo: **Piacenza,** Duomo; **Reggio Emilia**, S. Prospero; Giulio Cesare: **Modena**, Galleria Estense).

Quercia, Jacopo della (*c.* 1374–1438). Sienese, one of the greatest sculptors of the early Renaissance; died while working on the reliefs of the portal of San Petronio, **Bologna** (also **Ferrara**, Museo della Cattedrale).

Reni, Guido (1575–1642). The 'maximum exponent of the classical ideal of the seicento', and a fastidious fellow, 'generally believed to be a virgin', his reputation peaked in the 18th and early 19th centuries, when many (such as Joshua Reynolds) considered him the greatest painter of all time, the 'divine Guido'. Those may have been the opinions of an artistically retarded age, but his reputation survives as one of the greats of his period, especially notable for his refined colouring, graceful line and curious lighting. Most of the dull works with his name on them are by his studio. Most of his best ones are in Rome (**Bologna**, Pinacoteca, San Bartolomeo; **Modena**, Pinacoteca; **Castelfranco Emilia**, S. Maria Assunta).

Ricci, Sebastiano (1659–1734). Venetian late Baroque painter who studied at Bologna and Parma and adapted the lessons to his own brilliant, virtuoso style (**Piacenza**, Musei Civici; **Parma**, Galleria Nazionale).

de' Roberti, Ercole (*c.* 1450–96). One of the most powerful and inventive painters of the Ferrara school, with a very nervous line, refined colouring and metallic harshness that lends his work an unusual lyricism; followed del Cossa to Bologna, then became court artist to the Este in 1486. Some of his later works go beyond the dramatic to the ferocious; few remain in the region (**Ferrara**, Palazzo Schifanoia, Pinacoteca; **Bologna**, Pinacoteca).

Rossetti, Biagio (1447–1516). Court architect to Ercole I of **Ferrara** who planned the layout of the 'Herculean addition'; designed the Palazzo dei Diamanti and many of the city's palaces and churches.

Scarsellino (Ippolito Scarsella, 1551–1620). One of the last important painters in Ferrara, noted for his romantic treatment of landscapes in both religious and mythological scenes (**Ferrara**, Pinacoteca, Palazzo Schifanoia).

Schedoni, Bartolomeo (1578–1615). Born in Modena, pupil of Annibale Carracci, influenced by Correggio and the Roman Baroque; known for his dramatic use of light, sculptural forms bordering on abstraction and metallic Mannerist colours. After 1607 became court painter to the Farnese in Parma (**Parma**, Galleria Nazionale; **Modena**, Palazzo Comunale).

Simone de' Crocefissi (*fl.* 1355–99). Painter of Bologna, well within the International Gothic style, though his works become increasingly naturalistic in his later years (**Bologna**, Pinacoteca).

Spada, Leonello (1576–1622). Born in Sassuolo near Modena; went to Malta with Caravaggio; in Bologna they called him 'Caravaggio's ape' (**Bologna**, San Domenico; **Modena**, Galleria Estense; **Reggio Emilia**, Madonna della Ghiara).

Spolverini, Ilario (1657–1734). Court painter of the Farnese, creator of the genre of 'ceremonial painting', capturing the staged processions and ceremonies of the Baroque age; also known for Biblical and battle scenes (**Piacenza**, Galleria Farnese).

Tiarini, Alessandro (1577–1668). Bolognese, a follower of the Carracci noted for large, dramatic compositions; later fell under the influence of Caravaggio (**Parma**, S. Alessandro; **Bologna**, San Domenico; **Reggio Emilia**, Madonna della Ghiara).

Tibaldi, Pellegrino (1527–96). Mannerist painter, sculptor and architect inspired by Michelangelo (**Bologna**, Palazzo Poggi; also S. Giacomo Maggiore).

Tommaso da Modena (*c.* 1325–79). One of the most celebrated painters of his day, from the Bolognese miniaturist tradition, who individualized his subjects and moved towards a more natural, objective style. Most of his work is elsewhere: commissioned by Dominicans in Treviso, and the German Emperor in Prague (**Modena**, Galleria Estense, Sant'Agostino).

Tramello, Alessio (*c.* 1455–*c.* 1535). Architect of Piacenza, builder of many of the city's churches, including San Sisto and the Madonna della Campagna.

Tura, Cosmè (*c.* 1430–95). Son of a shoemaker, became court painter in Ferrara for over thirty years. Equally influenced by Mantegna and Piero della Francesca, he turned the one's precise line and the other's infatuation with geometric volumes in dreamlike space into one of the most intense and eccentric styles of the quattrocento (**Modena**, Galleria Estense; **Ferrara**, Museo del Cattedrale).

Vignola, Giacomo Barozzi da (1507–73). Innovative Mannerist architect, a favourite of the Farnese and Pope Julius III; but you'd never guess he was one of the greats of his day from his work in his native Emilia, where his most important building, **Piacenza**'s Farnese Palace, was never finished (**Parma**, Palazzo Ducale; **Bologna**, Palazzo dei Banchi).

Vitale da Bologna (Vitale d'Aimò de' Cavalli, *c.* 1309–61). The most noteworthy painter of the Bolognese trecento, whose delicate, decorative art was influenced by the International Gothic art of Siena (**Bologna**, San Francesco, Pinacoteca, Galleria Davia-Bargellini, Madonna dei Servi; **Pomposa**).

Wiligelmo (active 1106–20). Perhaps of German origin, one of the greatest and most influential of Romanesque sculptors, whose heavy stocky forms were based on medieval Ottonian manuscripts (**Modena** Cathedral).

Magic, Mayhem and Mortadella

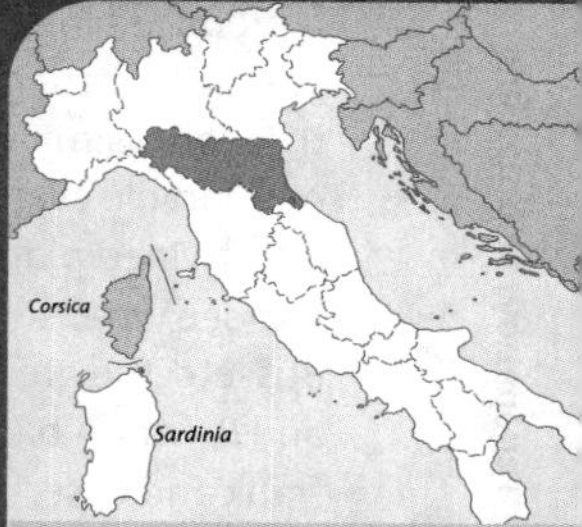

03

The New Boss

By God, why shouldn't I rule this city?

Uberto Pallavicini, addressing the Capitano del Popolo Ghiberto da Gente and the people of Parma

Italian medieval history may be a brilliant pageant of great men and great women, of stirring tales that would put any novelist to shame, but its study does require just a modicum of masochism. In its endless infernal complexity, it resembles one of those fractal pictures generated from the Mandelbrot set, where you can focus on any tiny corner of the image and see the whole pattern reproduced in all its twists and turns. While Guelphs and Ghibellines battled in an unending struggle for mastery of Italy, every city and every town was going through a similar drama of its own, with its own cast of characters, its own memorable events and moral fables – not so much a novel as a soap opera, full of intertwined plots, sudden reverses of fortune and surprises.

To see what sort of actor thrived in these potboilers, consider Uberto Pallavicini of Busseto, the great Marchese who built the family's little empire between Piacenza and Parma. A baron of the old school, regarded by his contemporaries as generous, frank and wise, Uberto had only one eye; the story went that a crow had pecked out the other one while he was a baby. He signed on early with the Ghibellines and never changed sides, serving Frederick II as *podestà* in several Italian cities. In the 1240s he was 'Imperial Vicar' in three regions of northern Tuscany, and by 1251 he was 'Captain General and Vicar of the Empire', the main military man looking out for the Emperor's interests. With Frederick's death, things got hot for his partisans, and especially for him, top Ghibelline in an area where the Guelphs were victorious almost everywhere.

Think of it as a game of Monopoly, where the players circle around a board in which the stops are walled merchant towns – some cheap properties, and some quite choice ones. In 1254 Uberto held the titles to four *comuni*, Piacenza, Pavia, Cremona and Vercelli. On that turn he landed on Chance and picked up a card that said 'You have been excommunicated by the Pope; other players may jump you and help themselves to your money and properties.' (This was the worst card in the pack; Frederick himself got it twice.)

Uberto had always been a staunch anti-cleric, and a protector of the area's numerous Cathars. The Pope found this a convenient excuse not only to excommunicate him, but to preach a crusade against him. This was largely a matter of politics, lining up a string of Uberto's enemies and promising them whatever of his lands they could capture. Uberto lost his four prize properties, but the 'crusaders' soon fell out in quarrels among themselves, and by 1259 Uberto came out stronger than before. He got Brescia for a while, before his ally Ezzelino da Romano tricked him out of it, and he won a share in the rulership of Milan and its dependent towns. Cremona fell in his lap, and finally Piacenza came back, when the *comune* granted him a four-year term of rule in 1261. He also picked up three cities in Piedmont: Asti, Tortona and Alessandria. Fortune then turned on him again, as the Guelphs came once more to the ascendant, and he lost nearly all his cities before his death in the late 1260s.

If you didn't follow all that, it doesn't matter, no more than the plot of any soap opera or game of Monopoly. Thirteenth-century Italy produced a score of men whose careers were just as colourful and complex. The times were fluid, and all the commotion and seemingly constant war did little damage to the sophisticated and wealthy life of the cities. It was in fact the presence of the cities that made the medieval chronicles so interesting. Emilia-Romagna's were surrounded by three great ones, each a power on a European scale: Florence, Milan and Venice. There was also an Emperor, who claimed authority over them all but was rarely able to enforce it, a Pope, whose pretensions were even greater, and whose power might vary from the overwhelming to the laughable and back again overnight, and plenty of old-fashioned feudal barons up in castles, especially in the Apennines, where the economic revolution of medieval Italy hadn't quite arrived.

The cities themselves, however, were the important part. After 1000 they had formed republican *comuni*, electing their own officials and running their own affairs. They stood up for their rights, forming the Lombard League against Emperor Frederick I, and they won. The *comuni* had all of the money, and most of the brains, and in their heyday in the 1100s they carved the territory of northern and central Italy into a patchwork quilt of city-states, each a compact and well-ordered economic unit of *città* and *contado*. They had wrested control away from the rural nobles, and often they forced them to live in town where they thought they wouldn't get up to any mischief.

What the cities could not do was evolve a fair and orderly way of governing themselves. The nobles still had plenty of money and influence. They usually monopolized the *comune*'s offices, and their vassals, clients and retainers made up private armies that often put them beyond the reach of the *comune*'s justice. They remained addicted to factionalism and vendettas, and by the 1200s the old feudal quarrels of the past had turned into civil wars within the *comune*'s walls. Most cities saw their middle classes organize as the *popolo* to make a stand against noble power and violence, but this usually only added another complexity to the game: nearly always they would choose a noble to lead them as *Capitano del Popolo*. Uberto himself held that office in several towns.

The titanic battle that occurred between Frederick II and the popes was the time when the weaknesses of the *comuni* started to unravel them. Local factional fights, between city and city or baron and baron, folded neatly into the greater struggle of Guelphs and Ghibellines, and the Pope and Emperor were always ready to give a prod and a push whenever any pair of local opponents looked like settling their differences peacefully.

Every noble with an armed force became, quite simply, a politician. He had a party to answer to, clients to support, allies to plot with (or against), and divided cities to overawe or seduce. The stakes were high: as the conflict got hotter, any leader or faction that gained control of a city might exile the opponents and burn down their houses; that is how Dante Alighieri ended up in Ravenna.

The cities couldn't take the strain. The strongest, Florence, Siena and Venice, held on to their republican institutions for centuries more, but most of them, including every *comune* in Emila-Romagna, sooner or later succumbed to the lure of boss rule. Uberto Pallavicini was one of the prototypes for the *signori* who would soon be ruling everywhere; only, unlike Uberto's, their rule would be permanent, often hereditary, and the interests of the city and its ruling family would become one – the Este in Ferrara and Modena, the da Polenta in Ravenna, the Malatesta in Rimini, and less enduring families in the other towns. Sometimes the old offices and laws of the *comuni* were maintained for a while, but eventually even that pretence was dropped.

The precocious republican experiment of the Middle Ages had failed, and dictatorship had taken its place. As a chronicler of Ferrara put it on the assumption of power of Obizzo II d'Este: 'The new ruler has more power than God eternal, who is not able to do unjust things.'

Magic in the Air

tempus loquendi, tempus tacendi

inscription in the Malatesta Temple, Rimini

'A time to speak, and a time to be silent.' This enigmatic motto is repeated in small letters throughout the decoration of Sigismondo Malatesta's Temple in Rimini, carved on banners entwined with the trunks of Sigismondo's omnipresent stone elephants. These elephants have been faithfully keeping their secrets now for over 500 years. But if they ever decide it is time to speak, they could tell us things about the Renaissance we never imagined.

In 1438, only 14 years before the fall of Constantinople to the Ottoman Turks, a solemn Ecumenical Council was held at Ferrara and Florence to discuss the reunion of Eastern and Western Christianity, with the hope of raising support in the west for military aid against the Turks. In fact a union of the churches was proclaimed in 1439, though the haughty Byzantines, whose 'empire' by then consisted of nothing beyond part of the Peloponnese and Constantinople itself, scornfully dismissed it.

But the Council was a momentous event nonetheless, if only for bringing some of Greece's most learned men to an Italy thirsting for the knowledge of classical antiquity. Among the delegation from Constantinople was Bessarion, who became a cardinal in the western Church and brought the important collection of Greek books that became the nucleus of the new library in Venice. Another was the 82-year-old George Gemistos Plethon, the last philosopher of Byzantium. Not much is known for certain about what Gemistos Plethon was really up to, courtesy of the Patriarch of Constantinople, who burned all his manuscripts after he died, but his presence must certainly have livened up the Council, for Gemistos Plethon was a thoroughgoing pagan.

His stay in Italy was one of the principal causes for a profound influx of Neo-Platonic thought, the undercurrent to so much that happened in the Renaissance. In the late Roman Empire, many Platonic ideas had got mixed up with Orphic religion, elements from Pythagoreanism, eastern mystery cults and magic, and it was in this form that Gemistos Plethon brought them back to Italy. By this time, a few surviving late Roman mystical texts were erroneously assumed to be much older. Renaissance scholars saw them as the fount of all philosophy and religion, dating back to the Egyptians and the mythical figure of Hermes Trismegistus, 'Thrice-great Hermes', founder of letters and science and the most ancient of prophets, in fact the teacher of Moses.

Marsilio Ficino, doctor, priest, philosopher and magus of Florence, was the man chiefly responsible for the dissemination of these ideas in Italy. His patron Lorenzo de' Medici had him translate some of these Hermetic books in 1471 – bidding him hold off on his translations of Plato until this more important work was finished. Ficino also translated the *Enneads* of Plotinus, the mystical philosopher of 3rd-century AD Alexandria, who contributed more to what came to be known as Neo-Platonism than Plato himself. While all this work was under way, Ficino led the informal 'Platonic Academy' in its discussions at the country villa of Lorenzo de' Medici. After Ficino came Pico della Mirandola, lord of that small town in the Po valley. Pico, who wrote the famous manifesto of Renaissance humanism, the *Oration on the Dignity of Man*, was also a cabbalist and Hermetist. His magical 900 *Conclusiones* so shocked Rome in 1486 that Lorenzo had to intercede with the Pope to get him out of jail.

Willing neither to dispose of Christianity entirely, nor to let their thought be subjected to its dogmas, these philosophers concentrated on what they saw as a 'natural religion' that lay beneath the surface of all faiths. Its origin was in ancient Egypt, with Hermes Trismegistus (or in Iran, with Zoroaster, according to Gemistos Plethon), and it reappeared in different forms through Moses, Orpheus, Pythagoras, Plato and finally Christ. Along with the natural religion went a 'natural magic'. The gods of the old religion, along with their planetary counterparts, the seven 'Governors of the sensible world', and the constellations, were considered as Platonic forms, ideas in the mind of God. To each corresponded elements in nature, stones and plants, as well as symbols, places and times. The natural magic of the Neo-Platonists consisted in manipulating these to capture the virtues of the forms in an image, constructing it of the proper materials, at the proper astrologically determined time. Such an image could be a talisman – or it could be a work of art.

We will probably never know how many Renaissance paintings and sculptures were specifically made as magical images. The famous mythological allegories of Botticelli certainly were. In the *Primavera*, for example, the three main figures represent the three 'good' planets, Jupiter, Venus and the Sun; Ficino recommended their healthy influence to counteract the gloomier side of scholarly, Saturnine natures like his own. Something similar is likely to be behind the two ambitious Neo-Platonic works of Emilia-Romagna, the Malatesta Temple and the frescoes of the Palazzo Schifanoia at Ferrara; both of these are astrologically comprehensive images of the universe as a whole. The decoration of the Malatesta Temple is particularly fascinating; it seems to draw us on, inviting us to try and solve its puzzle. Some have claimed that the Temple provides a complete exposition of Neo-Platonic doctrines, readable only to initiates, and that it was a site for secret rites of Sigismondo Malatesta and his court.

Such things could not be fully laid out in plain sight. Persecution of the humanist scholars by the Church had already appeared, in a mild form, in the 1460s under Pope Paul II, though they were encouraged under his successor Sixtus IV. There was indeed a time to speak, and a time to be silent. Less than 20 years after Pope Pius II condemned the 'pagan' Malatesta Temple, Hermeticism was at work in the Pope's own city of Siena, where artists covered the cathedral pavement with inlaid stone figures of Hermes Trismegistus himself, along with the sibyls of antiquity and philosophical allegories that cannot be interpreted today.

Of all the curious baggage that came along with Neo-Platonism, none perhaps was curiouser than a book called the *Picatrix*, which was probably written by the last pagans of the Middle East, the star-worshipping Sabeans of Harran, and transmitted through the Muslim world to Spain. The *Picatrix* is a book of magic that deals with the making of talismans and star images, and it is based on the 36 asterisms (star groups) called the *decans*. These originated at least 4,000 years ago in Egypt, where they often appear on coffin lids and the ceilings of tombs. Each decan was a daemon, a spirit something less than a god. Each one ruled a 10-day 'week' of the 360-day Egyptian calendar, and each had its moment when its stars were seen to rise just before the sun. Sirius, whose 'heliacal rising' promised the annual flooding of the Nile, was the first and most important of them.

The decans lost their everyday importance in Egypt after the conquest of Alexander, and the introduction of the zodiac and a new calendar. But they lived on in magic, and their great antiquity gave them special power and mystery. The decans were condemned by St Augustine and Origen, and as the Christians turned daemons into mere demons, the whole business began to have a whiff of the infernal about it. In the Middle Ages, though astrology was widely accepted, any old books that mentioned decans would have been the sort that monks kept locked away in a special place.

Ficino, in his book *De vita coelitus comparanda*, 'On capturing the nature of the stars', touched on the decans, but it was probably through some other channel that their images found their way into Renaissance art, in the magnificent frescoes planned by Cosmè Tura for Borso d'Este in the Palazzo Schifanoia at Ferrara. Under the Este that city was an important centre of the new philosophy and mysticism. In the 1470s a chair of Platonic philosophy was established at the University of Ferrara, held by the philosopher Francesco Patrizi. Decans were still dangerous, and in all Italy they only appear in one other place, in the frescoes by Niccolò Miretto in the Salone of the Palazzo della Ragione in Padua.

Sigismondo Malatesta died in 1468, just after his return from an expedition to the Peloponnese. What was he doing in Greece, with his city almost bankrupt and threatened by enemies on all sides? Trying to make a little money, of course, and at the same time working on his last grand gambit – that successes in Greece would restore his power and reputation, and perhaps even lead to western enthusiasm for a Crusade against the Turks to reconquer Constantinople. The Turks were too strong, and Sigismondo came home empty-handed – except for the body of Gemistos Plethon, which he had dug up from Mistra and transferred to his temple at Rimini, where it is buried under a Greek inscription that proclaims him the 'Greatest of the Philosophers'.

Reds

Mezzanotte in fondo
Si sente un gran rumor'
Ecco gli scariolanti
Chi vengano da lavor'

(In the deepest midnight,
what noise is this?
Here they are, the wheelbarrow men,
coming home from work)

folksong from Ferrara province

The *scariolanti* pushed their wheelbarrows home so late because their villages were often many miles away from the unhealthy marshes of the Po where they worked. In the decades after Italian unification in 1860, times when men were glad to get any kind of work at all, they worked hard and long for pennies, raising levees and digging hundreds of miles of ditches and drainage canals, all by hand. They came not only from Emilia-Romagna, but from across northern Italy. Slightly luckier ones became farm hands on new estates created by the vast land reclamation projects, or on older farmlands that were being transformed by the economic changes of the 19th century.

For both, life was as nasty, brutish and short as in any part of Italy; to their horrific working conditions were added chronic malaria from the marshes, and pellagra from a diet overdependent on corn polenta. These men and their families were a new phenomenon, a desperate rural proletariat with no roots in the soil, no heritage of village life and traditions and deference to the local lords – no old habits at all, in fact, to keep them from becoming the most thoroughly radicalized rural population of Europe.

The new Italian state was proving a disappointment, especially for working people. Its extreme centralism meant inscrutable decrees from Rome, enforced by foreign prefects. The landless and illiterate were excluded from voting. The politicians promised land reform, and they did try to follow through, but while this created a new class of peasant proprietors in Lombardy and other northern regions, in Emilia-Romagna it had little effect, even though two of Italy's first prime ministers, Farini and Minghetti, came from Emilia. In parts of the region feudal conditions still prevailed; Ferrara province, for example, had twenty families owning 60% of the land. Only eight years after unification, a widespread revolt against high taxes on grain, particularly severe in Parma, had to be put down by the army.

Already, the rural workers were starting to organize themselves, at first in 'mutual aid societies', and a region that had distinguished itself in the revolts against Austrian and papal rule before 1861 proved fertile ground for the new ideas of anarchism and socialism. 1872 saw the first meeting of the Italian branch of the First International at Rimini, where workers sat in on the arguments between the followers of Marx and those of Bakunin. The anarchist theorist himself, after his escape from Siberia, turned up in 1874, just in time to participate in the anarchist revolt of that year in Bologna.

The revolt was not a serious threat, and Bologna was hardly the place to try it. While other parts of Europe opposed radicalized industrial cities with a conservative hinterland, here the bourgeois cities felt besieged by a countryside full of Reds. In those days the metropolis of Emilia was called *Bologna rossa* only for the colour of its bricks. Before 1900, despite its large working-class population, the city was still a centre of reaction, home to Church-sponsored right-wing organizations like the Italian Catholic Association and the Opera dei Congressi. Along with the new proletariat came a new class of antagonists. Some of the old noble families had managed to hold on to parts of their estates, but the rest, along with the lands that had once belonged to the Church, fell into the hands of investors from the towns, or foreign corporations. It was these new men who reaped the big profits that came from the land reclamation schemes. They founded a *Consorzio* to look after their interests, and used every legal means, and most of the tried and true illegal ones, to keep their hold on the farm labourers.

For the rest of the century the Reds built their movement pragmatically and carefully, step by step, with the police looking over their shoulders all the way. Italy's first Socialist party, the Socialist Party of the Romagna, appeared in 1881; its leader Andrea Costa of Imola became the first Socialist parliamentary deputy in the next elections. It became a national party in 1884, the same year its newspaper *Avanti!* was founded in Imola. The rest of the decade witnessed the first big agricultural strikes, in Emilia-Romagna and across the Po in Mantova province, and the split between the revolutionary anarchists and the more practical Socialists. For most radicals in this region, the revolution could come later; for now the party worked on practical concerns such as universal suffrage, labour rights and welfare issues. They also founded their first co-operatives, and made the region the strongest co-op centre south of Scandinavia. Urban industrial trade unions were growing too; the first appeared in Piacenza in 1891.

In the years up to the First World War, the movement had its ups and downs. The strikes and fierce repression of 1898, especially rough around Ferrara, were followed by over a decade of sympathetic government under the moderate Giovanni Giolitti, in which labour rights were extended and the co-operatives even got a share of government contracts. Agricultural strikes like the huge one around Parma in 1908 usually ended in failure, but the co-ops, the unions and the Socialist Party grew a little stronger every year. A sharp recession caused the fall of Giolitti, and not long after came a spontaneous uprising called 'Red Week', when 100,000 troops had to be sent to the Romagna. This put such a scare into the powers that be that it helped convince them to drag Italy into the First World War.

As soon as the war was done, the Socialists rose up again, and with a little leadership they might easily have accomplished the revolution. Instead, this time the powers raised up Mussolini and his blackshirts to beat them into the ground once and for all (see below). Or so they thought. All through the dictatorship, the leftist organizations, increasingly led by the Communist Party, continued to organize underground, and some even got their newspapers out on a fairly regular basis.

The movement was reborn in the resistance of the Second World War, and here too the Communists took the lead; two-thirds of the *partigiani* were Party members. Resistance here was as strong as any part of Italy, and the fighting was undoubtedly the fiercest. At first the *partigiani* tried to make a stand in the mountains, establishing the free zone of the 'Republic of Montefiorino' in 1943. That strategy was a failure, and they soon learned that, paradoxically enough, their guerrilla war worked better in the flat Po valley and in the cities, where they proved such a bother that the Germans responded with horrific massacres of civilians, at Ferrara in 1943 and Marzabotto in 1944. The British didn't like them any better than the Nazis. Winston Churchill (who said in the 1920s that if he were an Italian, he would join the Fascists) inspired the declaration of late 1944 asking the *partigiani* to cease their operations. But the Allies and the Communists did manage to come together in the coordinated effort of April 1945 that liberated the region without wrecking its cities.

New explosions on the level of 1914–22 were avoided after the war by an increasing maturity on both sides. In 1947, one in five adults in Emilia-Romagna was a Party member. Together, the Communists and Socialists could command over 60% of the vote at any election. The rightists in Rome finally realized that Emilia-Romagna radicalism was utterly unkillable; they were content to run Italy and leave the region to the Reds. The Communists, for their part, had learned the hard way what happened when they tried revolution, and instead of trying to bring the system down they learned to work with it, while evolving the most humane and constructive brand of Communism the world has ever seen – ironically, with Stalin's blessing.

The old streak of Emilia-Romagna pragmatism led to a remarkable political cohabitation. The Communists took over the co-operative movement, quite democratically, and ran it well. Their local governments, of which Bologna was the showcase, were by far the best-run, most honest and most efficient in all Italy. Public transport, housing development and social services became models for Europe. In the 1960s, the Reds even won support from many of the region's employers. Emilia-Romagna was spawning large numbers of successful small manufacturing businesses, and the Communists demonstrated how such businesses were as much disadvantaged by monopoly capital as the workers. Whenever a businessman needed something done, he found a sympathetic Communist mayor ready to lend a hand.

Nowadays the Reds of Emilia-Romagna are to a certain extent victims of their own success. Their region has climbed to the top in average income for Italy, and some of the co-operatives have grown so posh they are quoted on the stock market. When Italians think of Emilia-Romagna, visions of *tortelli* and truffles, Ferraris and Maseratis are likely to dance in their heads, not agitators and picket lines. In two thousand years, the region has metamorphosed from Cisalpine Gaul to Cisalpine Scandinavia: well-organized, intelligent and conspicuously caring, pink and plump, and (as some Italians might tell you) perhaps a little bit dull.

The great social experiment survives, however, and builds on its successes, and whatever the future has in store for Emilia-Romagna it seems that the region will be able to adapt and evolve and stay true to its principles. The question remains though, why should this region, out of all the world, be the one where socialism really makes sense? Perhaps the answer goes back to the *scariolanti*, and the land-reclamation programmes dating back to the Middle Ages. Like the Dutch, the people of this region have a quiet sense of solidarity and a proprietary feeling about their land. After all, they built it.

The Bully Boy from Predappio and the Emilia-Romagna Civil War

Our program is simple. We wish to govern Italy. They ask us for programs, but there are already too many.

Benito Mussolini, in an article he wrote on Fascism for the *Enciclopedia Italiana*

Mussolini was born on 29 July 1883 at Verano di Costa, a hamlet near Predappio in Forlì province. His father Alessandro, a blacksmith by trade, was an ardent and somewhat thuggish Socialist activist, his mother a pious Catholic schoolteacher. Their house, like many others in Italy, had two pictures on the wall, one of Garibaldi and the other of the Madonna. Alessandro named his first-born son Benito Amilcare Andrea, for three of his revolutionary heroes: Benito Juarez of Mexico, Amilcare Cipriani, a Romagnolo who had fought with Garibaldi and in the Paris Commune, and the Romagnolo Socialist leader Andrea Costa.

Little Benito was a prize student in the Catholic boarding school where his mother sent him, a boy with a passion for books. He also had a reputation as a bully, one who especially picked on girls (it was to be a lifelong habit). At the age of 11, he got expelled for stabbing a schoolmate in the hand with a knife. At 15, in another school, he stuck another classmate in the bum, but this time he got off with a short suspension. At 17 he was already well known in the bordellos of Forlimpopoli, and he was chosen by his school to give an oration to the town for a ceremony on the death of Giuseppe Verdi.

Reality, as it will do, was breaking in on this charmed life. Benito was 18, and a graduate, faced with the unpleasant prospect of earning a living. The best he could do was a job as schoolteacher in the woebegone village of Gualtieri on the Po, teaching seven-year-olds to conjugate verbs and pronounce their double consonants. The girlfriends he picked up and the company of fellow radicals – for Benito was as much a revolutionary as his father – held few thrills, and reality had another dirty trick to play, the prospect of two years in the Army. To avoid conscription, he fled to Switzerland in 1902. At the time, his father was on trial back home for trying to steal an election by intimidating non-Socialist voters at the polls.

Among the Swiss, Mussolini carried loads of bricks to the bricklayers, bummed his way from town to town, learned French and occasionally slept under bridges. Switzerland provided a refuge, if a precarious one, for radicals from all over Europe in those days, and Mussolini spent most of his time with them, attending political meetings and writing poems and articles for socialist papers. He started to make a name for himself, and the Swiss police started to make half-hearted attempts to deport him back to Italy; their failure, an odd lapse in Swiss efficiency, might be explained by later allegations that he had been in their pay, spying on his friends.

There was only one way he could ever return to Italy. It was either life in Switzerland or the Army, and in 1904 Mussolini made the only intelligent choice. Amazingly, they sent this nearly useless revolutionary tramp to the elite corps, the *Bersaglieri*, and he seems to have thoroughly enjoyed it. With typical Mussolinian bombast, he later wrote of his 21 months as a soldier that 'a man must learn to obey before he can learn to command'. After the Army came three more wasted years, but in 1909 Mussolini finally found his calling, as the editor of a socialist newspaper in Trento, then under Austrian rule. He also found his style, blunt and rough, typically Romagnolo, and seldom did he ever again write or speak a paragraph that did not impugn someone's virtue or intelligence, or scream for their blood.

1909 was the height of *Italietta*, the 'little Italy' of a booming economy, ice cream, motorcars and modest bourgeois happiness, presided over by the liberal Prime Minister Giovanni Giolitti. Never before had Italy been so contented and prosperous; even the working classes were making impressive gains. All the intellectuals hated it. An odd change came over Benito Mussolini, as if he was emerging from a cocoon. Now wearing a decent suit, he began to write a bit dismissively about the common man; the word *gerarchia*, the hierarchy, started to figure prominently in his articles on the elite that would be necessary to create a 'new Italy'. He began to acquire odd habits. Like Hitler, the new Mussolini was a vegetarian, a nonsmoker and a teetotaller. Even worse than Hitler, he became a fitness nut and an amateur violinist. Since he was going bald anyhow, he started shaving his head.

Mussolini was still enough of an internationalist in 1911 to oppose the imperialist war against Turkey, which was designed to steal Libya and take people's minds off an economic recession. He wrote fierce editorials, and organized demonstrations against the departing soldiers. Some Socialists had supported the war, including the editor of the national party newspaper *Avanti!* So Mussolini got him kicked out of the party, and took his job. His talents for demagoguery soon made him the most successful editor the paper ever had; its circulation tripled within a year.

Mussolini was now somebody. His next metamorphosis came, like so many other unexpected and unpleasant things, with the outbreak of the First World War. Leftists were divided over whether Italy should join in. Mussolini threw away his old principles to call for war: this time it was his turn to get thrown out of the party and lose his job. He started a new paper in Milan, *Il Popolo d'Italia*, with a little help from some new friends – the French and Belgian governments, who financed both the paper and Mussolini's campaign to bring Italy into the war.

The perfection of the former Socialist's sellout came right after the armistice. When the Allies at Versailles broke all their promises to Italy, it wasn't only the Socialists who were pointing out that 600,000 Italians had just died for nothing. Accounts that had been put off for four years were now being settled. The Socialists convulsed Italy in a wave of strikes and factory occupations; they swept the local elections, and the propertied classes were gripped by a chilling fear that Italy was going the way of Russia. How Mussolini felt is only too easy to imagine. He had guessed wrong about the war. He was politically dead, and the revolution was happening without him. His rapid conversion into a gangster boss at the service of the rich was one of the cleverest political comebacks in history. Already during the war, Mussolini had been making contacts with the Milan industrialists and the big landowners of his home region. Tellingly, the first meeting of the *Fasci di Combattimento* in 1919 was held at the Milan Chamber of Commerce.

The next four years, when the Fascist *squadristi* terrorized the nation and forced their will on it while the police turned a blind eye, can look very much like an Emilia-Romagna civil war. Socialist and democratic opposition to the Fascists was strongest here, but paradoxically the region also gave Mussolini some of his strongest supporters, from the middle classes and especially among the class of landlords, who finally saw a chance to get back at the socialist and anarchist farmers with their agitation, their strikes and their co-operatives. Many of the top Fascist leaders came from the region: not only Mussolini, but Count Dino Grandi, from Mordaro near Bologna, and Italo Balbo, from Ferrara. Balbo, who was Jewish, and would die early in the war before he got a chance to regret what he had helped create, was the roughest and smartest of the *squadra* chiefs.

While the Fascists began their terror campaign bashing Slavs in Trieste, it was clear that the Red heartland, Emilia-Romagna, would have to be their prime objective. Their weapons were clubs and pistols, torches and petrol, and bottles of castor oil to pour down the throats of opponents – small-time stuff, compared to what Europe would be seeing in the 1930s and 40s, but in Italy it had just the desired effect. Mussolini sent Balbo to begin the campaign in 1920 with a raid on Bologna. He spent most of 1921 destroying the co-operatives in the region by violence and intimidation, and the next year led many of the attacks on Emilia-Romagna's cities, including his home town, where he assembled some 60,000 Fascists to seize control of the city government. Two weeks later they did the same in Bologna, though they were nearly stopped by a brave prefect named Cesare Mori, who barricaded himself inside his office until the government in Rome ordered him to let the Fascists have their way. Ironically, the same Mori would later become a Fascist and work for Mussolini as prefect in Sicily, where he did his job so well he nearly drove the Mafia out of business.

In one day, 29 July 1922, Balbo's *squadri* torched the buildings of every Socialist and Communist organization in Ravenna and Forlì provinces. Only Parma held out against the Fascists, thanks on one occasion to the working men of the Oltratorrente, who built and defended barricades across the city, and on another to a democratic army commander who refused just to stand by, the only time such a thing happened. All through their subjugation of Emilia-Romagna, the small numbers of *squadristi* had the near-total support of the army, the police, the King and the Church. Still, they never would have succeeded if the Socialists and democrats had not not proved so totally bereft of courage and leadership. Despite Parma, the war in Emilia-Romagna was over, and the *squadri* moved on to bully the rest of the country; the King made Mussolini Prime Minister in October.

The rest of the story is familiar enough. Cynical opportunism is such a feature of Italian politics that there's even a name for it – *trasformismo*. Even so, the blacksmith's boy from Predappio is a truly special case: the Socialist who wrecked the unions and outlawed the Socialist Party, the atheist who signed the Concordat with the Church, the man who had briefly gone to jail for opposing one Italian imperialist war in Africa, and later started one himself, the implacable foe of the Germans and Austrians who became Hitler's best pal. His story would make a marvellously squalid historical novel or film, though it might not sell in Italy; the average Italian of today would never be convinced that such things actually happened.

Food, Glorious Food

Enough of politics, you say. And five million people in Emilia-Romagna, including the Communists, are only too happy to agree. Fifteen years ago, the tourist offices of the region handed out a 50-page booklet with a complete Marxist-orientated history of class struggle and capitalist contradictions in the region to entertain you on your holiday. Now you'll get brochures full of colour photos of hams, truffles and pasta. Search for 'Parma' on the Internet, and what do you get? A six-page recipe for *anolini in brodo*, with theoretical discussions on why each ingredient must go in at a certain time, and a chemist's explanation of why to make a proper broth you must put the meat in while the water is still cold, not when it's boiling. The cursed 20th century with all its dialectics and heroic seriousness is dead. Let's eat.

Tortellini

If the first father of the human race was lost for an apple, what would he not have done for a plate of tortellini?

an old saying in Bologna

The Bolognese are not an excitable race, but they go as gaga as Neapolitans on the subject of tortellini. For many, even the University pales before plump rings of pasta as Bologna's culminating cultural achievement. Men have fought for the honour of tortellini; in the 1920s, when a visiting Venetian dared to insult them, a postman beat him up so badly that one ended up in the hospital and the other in jail (sentenced to six months *without* tortellini). They may even be as old as the University; the first reference to *turtlein*, as they are known in Bolognese dialect, goes back to the 12th century when they were given to priests at Christmastide, and to this day no Christmas table in Emilia is complete without a bowl of tortellini in capon broth. A recipe discovered in a 14th-century manuscript prescribes a stuffing similar to the one used today, although with the addition of medicinal herbs. It has also been revealed that a certain Adelaide, wife of a Bolognese notary, produced in the year 1821 the first canonical tortellini filled with minced ham, veal, mortadella, Parmesan cheese and nutmeg. In 1963, the *Accademia del Tortellino* was founded to pursue perfection in Adelaide's recipe. Although tortellini machines have simplified the lives of countless Bolognese chefs, connoisseurs disdain them; a handmade tortellino contains 20 to 30 per cent more filling, which is why they cost more.

In Bologna, tortellini have passed beyond the realm of culinary science into myth. Their shape in particular makes the Bolognese go all dewy-eyed, for they are supposedly modelled on a woman's navel, a navel so beautiful that it could only belong to Venus herself. In the 17th century, a Tuscan poet named Ceri imitated the satirical *Rape of the Bucket* (*see* pp.168–9) with a poem telling how the goddess of love stopped at an inn, disguised as a mortal; the cook there had a glimpse of her naked, and was moved to model his pasta on the shape of her navel. In 1925 a play called *The Man Who Invented Tortellini* in Bolognese dialect follows the same theme, only the navel in this instance belonged to the wife of the cook's employer. The cook had been discovered in the wife's bedroom, and he invented tortellini as a love letter.

Tagliatelle

Feminine pulchritude was also behind tagliatelle, invented in Bologna in 1487 on the occasion of Lucrezia Borgia's wedding to the Duke of Ferrara. The pope's daughter had long golden hair, and a chef named Zafirano from the village of Bentivoglio, called on to help prepare the wedding feast, created the long fair strips of pale golden egg pasta in her honour. It must be rolled out until a person holding it up can be seen through the dough. The Academy of Italian Cuisine, based in Bologna, has solemnly decreed that for pasta to be called tagliatelle, the width of the ribbons must be precisely 1/1,270th of the height of the Torre Asinelli, i.e. 9mm, no more, no less. It takes about 15 years of practice to get it exactly right.

Mortadella

Mortadella, 'the most noble of all pork parts' according to a proclamation of 1661, was so prized in the 14th and 15th centuries that it was used for currency, as noted in the contracts of the Cathedral Chapter of Bologna. The word comes from the mortar (*mortaia*) used by friars to grind the pork into a smooth paste, before kneading it with whole peppercorns and stuffing it tightly into its casing: the exact rules for its making were established with the Corporazione dei Salaroli (the sausage-makers guild) founded in 1367. The Americans, who loved it, are responsible for much of the confusion over the name, after 1899 calling any kind of sausage 'mortadella' or just plain Bologna sausage, or baloney. A lot of sausage made elsewhere that's labelled mortadella might as well be baloney. A good mortadella must be eaten sliced as thinly as possible; in the days before slicing machines, there were contests to see who could slice it thinnest and fastest.

Parmesan Cheese

'Poets have been mysteriously silent on the subject of cheese,' observed Chesterton, but Parmesan is an exception. It appeared in Boccacio's *Decameron*; although the description is about the Basques, it sounds very much like Emilia-Romagna:

> *...in a region called Cornucopia, where the vines are tied up with sausages. And in those parts there was a mountain made entirely of grated Parmesan cheese on whose slope there were people who spent their whole time making macaroni and ravioli.*

Parmesan cheese is officially *Parmigiano-Reggiano*, and is produced in a delimited area around Parma, Modena and Reggio Emilia. A true one tastes nothing like the pre-grated packaged stuff you often get at home. Each great wheel is made of 100 litres of rich milk solids, given by cows grazed on the lushest meadows in Italy, and heated to 40°C while being stirred. The solid lump that forms is sieved through cloth, placed in a cylindrical container and mixed with brine. A month later a brown crust forms, and the cheese is stamped with its place of origin. After another seven months or so it is tapped with a hammer; a hollow sound means troublesome bacteria has formed within, and surgery is performed to preserve the cheese. A year is the minimum ageing period, but the longer it sits in the cheese vaults, the sweeter and fuller the taste. A two-year-old cheese is called *vecchio*, at three years *stravecchio*, and at four years *stravecchione*. This makes an excellent dessert cheese, and comes with a sprinkling of balsamic vinegar.

Parma Ham

Every country in Europe, every region in Italy makes ham, but very few would dare to rival the subtle, glamorous, velvety, paper-thin slices of *prosciutto di Parma*, which owes its greatness to a variety of unique conditions that the Parmigiani swear cannot be reproduced anywhere else on the planet. The fresh hams, made from porkers fed on a special diet of whey left over from the making of Parmesan cheese, are boned, rounded into a fine shape, pounded with paddles until smooth, then brushed and polished. After spending a few days out in the cold, they are laid in a bed of rock salt and turned once a week – unlike other hams, Parma hams can get by with only a minimum of salt because of the uniquely preservative and anti-bacterial qualities of the air where they are dried. Air, indeed, is perhaps the most important factor in the whole process. Ideally the ham should first hang in the sweet air of the hills in the Magra valley, where it acquires the scent of pine and olives; then taken to the Cisa Pass, where it is subtly flavoured with the chestnut-breezes of the Apennines, before being brought down the valley of the river Parma to dry from September to March, specifically at Langhirano, a town entirely devoted to curing Parma hams. The finished product is stamped with the five-pointed ducal symbol and the motto, in case you have any lingering doubt: *quello dolce è il crudo di Parma*, 'the sweet one is Parma ham'.

Balsamic Vinegar

In 1944, when the frantically clanging bells of the Ghirlandina warned Modena that American bombers were approaching, thousands took to bicycles and pedalled desperately out of the city. Many of them had taken time to scoop up money, jewels and other easy-to-carry valuables; and on dozens of luggage carriers small kegs were securely strapped. They contained vinegar.

Waverly Root

Modena's famous balsamic vinegar, now exported all over the world, is first documented in 1046, when Countess Matilda's dad gave a keg of it to the emperor; in those days it was prized as much for its supposed medicinal qualities – hence its name – as for dressing vegetables. Now manufactured commercially, it is made according to strict rules from the cooked and fermented must of Trebbiana grapes, to which a squirt of aged 'mother vinegar' has been added. Then it is kept in a red oak barrel. Over the next 10 years, the vinegar will be diligently poured from one barrel to another in a specially prescribed sequence, each made of a certain wood, including mulberry and juniper, which give the vinegar its perfume, until it achieves its distinctive glowing coffee colour, delicate aroma and a taste between sweet and tart. The most prized vinegars are over 50 years old. One company, Acetaia Malpighi, makes not only traditional balsamic vinegars but also caramels and chocolates filled with the stuff (Vin Drop and Vin Royal respectively), designed for people who think they've tried everything.

The 'Swan of Busseto'

To Italians Verdi is not just another great composer, but the genius who expressed the national spirit of the Risorgimento in music: Italy's equivalent of Richard Wagner (the two were both born in the same year, 1813). As a national icon in his own lifetime, Verdi could have played a role in the unification of Italy without even trying. In the 1850s, crowds at the opera screamed *Viva Verdi!*, but not just as a tribute to the composer – everybody knew it was also a not-too-subtle demand for ***V**ittorio **E**manuele, **R**e **D'I**talia*!

But he did try. Right from the beginning, Verdi was a sincere patriot and progressive, though he was forced to work political themes into his operas in the most careful ways to get them past the ever-present censors. At a discouraging phase in his early career when he was considering giving up composing altogether, he was inspired anew by a lament of the captive Jews in Babylon in a libretto someone had offered him; this became *Nabucco*, his first big success, and his rendition of the lament reminded audiences, as he intended, of Italy's fight for political freedom. Through themes like these, and works based on distant periods of Italian history such as *I Lombardi* and *I Due Foscari*, Verdi was able to insert a little politics into every opera season. The censors nevertheless did their best to annoy. In an absurdity of truly operatic proportions, they forced him to transfer the setting of *Un Ballo in Maschera* from the royal court of Sweden to, of all places, Puritan Boston, since the original libretto dealt with the taboo subject of regicide.

Next to music, Verdi's greatest talent seems to have been carrying grudges. The experience of losing his first chance at a job, as musical director of his home town, when the local priests proposed their own candidate, made him an anti-cleric for life. He never forgave La Scala for the poor reception its audiences gave to some of his early works, and his feuds with collaborators were legendary. He never really forgave Busseto either, although after a brief spell as a member of the first Italian parliament he retired to an estate nearby, which he tended with particular care, while making himself a generous benefactor of the poor, and the local hospital and school.

Food and Drink

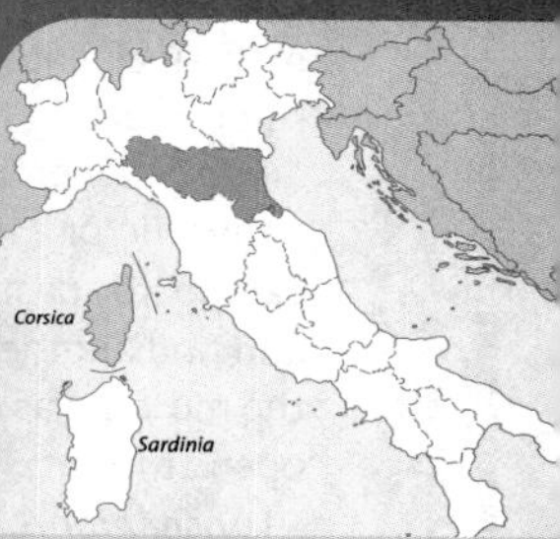

04

There are those who eat to live and those who live to eat, and then there are the Italians, for whom food has an almost religious significance. Here in Emilia-Romagna, the 'Food Valley' of Europe, it also fuels a good part of the economy, so it's taken very seriously indeed (*see* 'Food, Glorious Food', pp.51–4).

Restaurant Generalities

Although many hotels now serve morning buffets, **breakfast** (*prima colazione*) in Italy is traditionally no lingering affair, but an early morning wake-up shot to the brain, with few pretensions to nutrition: a *cappuccino* (espresso with hot foamy milk – incidentally, first thing in the morning is the only time of day at which any self-respecting Italian will touch the stuff), a *caffè latte* (white coffee) or a *caffè lungo* (a generous portion of espresso), accompanied by a croissant-like *cornetto* or *brioche*, or a fancy pastry. Beware of the increasingly prominent factory-made cardboardy pastries with great lumps of sugar on top; stand up for civilization and find another bar. This repast can be consumed in any bar and repeated during the morning as often as necessary until the *pizza al taglio* and snack stands open at 10am.

Lunch (*pranzo*), served around 1pm, is traditionally the most important meal of the day, with a first course (*primo piatto*: any kind of pasta dish, broth or soup, or rice dish or pizza), a second course (*secondo piatto*: a meat dish, accompanied by a *contorno* or side dish – a vegetable, salad, or potatoes usually), followed by fruit or dessert and coffee. You can, however, begin with a platter of *antipasti*, ranging from warm seafood delicacies to raw ham and cured meats in a hundred varieties, savoury toasts (various *bruschette* and *crostini* – especially good with truffles on them), olives, pâté and many, many more. All of this is accompanied by wine and mineral water – *acqua minerale*, with or without bubbles (*con gas/frizzante* or *senza gas*), which supposedly aids digestion. Many people conclude their meals with an espresso coffee, or maybe a *caffè corretto* (a 'corrected' coffee, with a squirt of brandy or grappa in it), or else a *digestivo*, Fernet Branca and so on, which invariably tastes like medicine but can be weirdly addictive. Then, in an ideal world, one has a nice long nap.

Although people in rural areas often maintain the classic big lunches, the pace of modern urban life has made them a strictly Sunday affair for many. Office workers frequently now behave much as their counterparts elsewhere in Europe and consume a rapid snack at lunchtime; restaurants serve special express lunches, and bars often double as *paninoteche*, which make hot or cold sandwiches to order; outlets selling pizza by the slice (*al taglio*) and *piadina* sandwiches are common in city centres.

Cena, the **evening meal**, is usually eaten around 8pm. This can be much the same as *pranzo* although lighter, without the pasta; a pizza and beer is a favourite. In restaurants, however, they offer all the courses, so if you have only a sandwich for lunch you have the full whack in the evening. Pizza is extremely popular in the evening, and rare in the afternoon, so if you want one for lunch look for a pizzeria that advertises *pizza anche a pranzo*.

In Italy the various terms for types of **restaurants** – *ristorante, trattoria* or *osteria* – have been blurred. A *trattoria* or *osteria* can be just as elaborate as a restaurant, although rarely is a *ristorante* as informal as a traditional *trattoria*. Unfortunately the old habit of posting menus and prices in the windows has fallen from fashion, but as a general rule, the fancier the fittings, the fancier the bill, though neither of these points has anything at all to do with the quality of the food. If you're uncertain, do as you would at home – look for lots of locals.

In Emilia-Romagna, the best restaurants are often hidden away on alleys or on the edge of town, where you normally wouldn't come across them (this book should help); the Italian mania for motoring means that many are out of town altogether, where it's easy to park.

The Specialities of Emilia-Romagna

Food

The cuisine of Emilia-Romagna holds a special place in Italy: this great and wealthy agricultural region produces the nation's favourite ham, its favourite cheese and most heavenly vinegar; cherries, asparagus, tomatoes, much of its finest wheat, and other fruit and vegetables; with lots of seafood as an added bonus.

The diversity of this doubled-barrelled region is perfectly reflected in its kitchen, which has been called gastronomically the most complex in Italy. Every province, not to mention every town, has its own specialities and variations on the classics, which increasingly appear on menus in dialect to complete the bewilderment of the innocent diner. Many Italians, however, say you eat better here than anywhere else; the locals certainly believe it and show it with their reputation as the nation's greatest trenchermen and biggest drinkers. *A panzu pina u s'ragiona mej*, 'You think best with a full belly', they say, flying in the face of the usual Italian prohibition on mental activity during digestion. In other words, if you love to eat, you've come to the right place.

Salumi

Salumi means cured pork products – cold cuts, if you will – and Emilia-Romagna is the cold-cut capital of Italy, where the most typical *antipasto* is a selection of *salumi*. This usually includes thin slices of the world-famous Parma ham (*prosciutto di Parma*), and, if you're lucky, *culatello di Zibello*. Even more revered and expensive than the famous ham of Parma, this is pork loin cured like prosciutto, prepared only in the humid lowlands of the Po Valley. Connoisseurs say the real thing, properly matured, is hard to find but worth looking out for.

But that's only the tip of the *salumi* iceberg. Bologna has been making *mortadella* since the Middle Ages (the 'baloney' of American kid lunches is a dumbed-down imitation), and *lardo stagionato*, which sounds like 'seasoned lard' but isn't. There's the rare and excellent *salame di Felino*, the *spalla cotta di San Secondo* (baked shoulder, cured like ham, a favourite of Verdi), and *coppa di Carpaneto* (sausage); in Reggio it's *fioretto* (made from the shoulder).

There are more elaborate concoctions as well. Ferrara makes *zia* and *zentil* salami, the latter strongly flavoured with garlic, but most famously *salama da sugo*, a favourite of Greta Garbo apparently, prepared with pork and liver mixed with Vino di Bosco, pepper, cinnamon and cloves, hung in a cool dark room for a year, and then boiled for four hours and often served cold as *salumi* or hot as a main course with mashed potatoes. Modena is especially famous for its *zampone*, or pig's trotter, hollowed out, deboned, and filled with a special concoction of minced pork, salt, pepper, nutmeg, cinnamon and cloves, crushed into a smooth paste. It is then cooked for hours until it has the consistency of soft butter, then served hot and sliced.

Piadina and Other Obsessions

What goes with your plate of *salumi*? A hot and savoury pancake. All of the Romagna is the realm of the *piadina* (also known as the *piê*, *pjida*, *pieda*, *piaden* or *piadéna*), a soft round savoury pancake. The main source of carbohydrates for the poor in the area for at least a thousand years, the essential ingredient of any festa, they are served in the traditional *osterie*, where someone will be flipping them out fresh and hot. They (and a thinner version known as *guscioni*, *cassoni* or *crescioni*) have also enjoyed a Renaissance and spread even into neighbouring regions as street food, split like a sandwich and filled with whatever you fancy – ham, salami, mozzarella, aubergines, tomatoes, fontina, anchovies, wild herbs, etc. A *piadina* with sausage and onions can be transcendent. Always remember this bit of Romagnolo folk wisdom: *Con la piadina è meglio* ('it's better with a *piadina*').

Each province in Emilia also has its own savoury pancake or focaccia, although these tend to be more elusive. Otherwise sane folks will drive an hour just to eat them (many places only prepare them on weekends or evenings). In Reggio, it's the *gnocco fritto* or sometimes the *chizza*, the latter being flaky and served with butter and cheese; in Piacenza, the *burtléina*; in Parma, the triangular *torta fritta*; in Ferrara the *pinzini*. In Modena and Bologna, the *crescentina*, similar to focaccia, is traditionally cooked between chestnut leaves and two stone discs in the hot ashes of the hearth.

Throughout Emilia you'll find the *tigelle*, made with yeast and lard, or the *borlengo*, a huge crêpe made with eggs and milk, prepared out of doors in the Apennines because the pan is too big to fit over any indoor fire. When a *borlengo* or any of these fried cakes are hot out of the pan, they are rubbed with bacon, rosemary and olive oil and sometimes garlic, or folded over ham or soft cheese.

Pasta Pasta Pasta

Pasta is the classic among the *primi* (or *minestre*, as this first course is often called in Emilia-Romagna). Many of Italy's favourite forms of pasta originated here, and still taste better here than anywhere else. Several of the forms of pasta for which the region is renowned come from the word *torta*, or twist, which describes how they're made: the pasta is rolled and cut, the filling is spooned on, and sealed in a ring with a twist. *Tortellini*, or *tortelli*, the classic, are part of the region's mythology (*see* pp.51–2). In Bologna they are filled with pork, ham, mortadella and Parmesan; in Parma, they prefer *tortellini d'erbetta* filled with herbs (spinach usually) with ricotta, served with melted butter and freshly grated Parmesan. Bigger ones are *tortelloni*. The *cappelletti* are made from a square rather than a circle of pasta, so that they form a little peak or 'hat'; in Ferrara they like them big, *cappellacci*, filled with pumpkin, Parmesan and nutmeg, served either with a pork ragout or melted butter and sage. *Anolini*, 'rings' filled with stewed beef, Parmesan, eggs, breadcrumbs and nutmeg, come in a chicken and beef broth. *Panzerotti* are like tiny stuffed pancakes.

Another regional classic, tagliatelle, should be ideally served with a *ragù* – the original of the 'spag bol', a dish as bastardized in the UK as mortadella has been baloneyed in America. The original *ragù* is a smooth sauce of very finely minced pork and veal, prosciutto, onions, carrots, celery, butter and tomato; in general when a dish is labelled *alla Bolognese* it means with *ragù* (one exception is *maccheroni alla bolognese*: macaroni baked with truffles and chicken livers and doused in fresh cream).

The third great pasta dish claimed by Bologna is lasagne, although even the Bolognese acknowledge that the dish goes back to the Romans who called it *laganum*. In most places you'll find it as *lasagne al forno*, layered with *ragù* and cheese and topped with bechamel, which is recorded as being served in Cesena in the 14th century – long before it was supposedly invented by Louis XIV's *maître d'hôtel*, the Marquis de Béchameil. Bologna claims to be the mother of green lasagne, made with spinach; a proper *lasagne alla bolognese* has prosciutto, chicken livers, bacon and bechamel. In autumn look for lasagne with truffles or wild mushrooms.

Ferrara is home of the almost overwhelming *pasticcio di maccheroni*, which was invented by nuns in the 17th century; it has a sweet crust, filled with macaroni, veal ragout, truffles, mushrooms, chicken, beef, butter, garlic, milk, white wine, marsala, onion, celery and bechamel, and baked in the oven. Other common pasta forms you will come across are *garganelli* (rolled and cut with a device resembling a loom card), *strozzapreti* ('priest-chokers') and *passatelli in brodo*, which features little dumplings made of spinach or beef marrow, breadcrumbs, eggs and Parmesan. As a reaction to all the pasta discipline, a favourite form is *maltagliati* ('badly cut'). When cooked with beans, it is known as a 'chin sprinkler'. In the restaurants along the coast, almost any form of pasta is a likely candidate to be stuffed or covered with seafood.

Other First Courses

Rice dishes (the paddies of Lombardy are just across the Po) have long been popular, especially in Emilia, where the classic preparation is the *bomba di riso* – boiled rice in a mould, with a rich mushroom sauce and pieces of boned pigeon, topped with butter and breadcrumbs and baked in the oven. *Risotto al sugo* incorporates minced chicken and cheese. Comacchio, the land of eels *extraordinaire*, popularly serves a risotto cooked in eel broth. In Reggio they make a soup called *erbazzone*, with spinach, cheese and butter, that goes back to Roman times, when it was called *moretum*.

In Piacenza and Parma a favourite dish is *pisarei a faso* (borlotti bean stew, with bread dumplings); you may also find a *fritā cui bavaron* (leek omelette), or truffle omelette, or *melanzane alla parmigiana* – fried aubergine slices, with ham and ripe tomatoes.

Secondi

Meat courses in Emilia-Romagna tend to be on the hearty side as well. One of the heraldic dishes of the region is *stracotto*, topside of beef, ideally cooked for hours (or days, by some extremists) in wine with herbs and vegetables until it becomes incredibly tender; sometimes it has sausage and will come garnished with mushrooms or even truffles. Another classic is *bollito misto*, a variety of boiled meats served with a range of sauces, which generally comes on a cart (*carrello dei bolliti*) in restaurants, allowing diners to pick and choose. *Coppa arrosto*, a speciality of Piacenza, is pork cooked in butter, oil, garlic and rosemary, then doused with wine and roasted in the oven. Stew or roasted poultry dishes are popular – roast duck and goose, or *anitra* or *faraona alla creta* (duck or guinea fowl cooked in a terracotta dish).

In Bologna they make a tasty concoction called *canestrelli di pollo* – chicken fillets stuffed with smoked ham and onions on a bed of puréed spinach. Tripe (*buzeca*) is popular, often cooked *alla parmigiana*, and various veal dishes, among them *cima ripiena* or *picaja* (stuffed breast of veal). Horse and even donkey meat have their aficionados in the winter months (especially in Piacenza); the former is often served raw and minced, or cooked with diced vegetables (*picula ad cavàll*). In the Apennines game dishes are popular in season; at many trattorias, the simply grilled meats are delicious.

Seafood is plentiful along the coast, although there are few special regional recipes: much of it is simply grilled or fried up in a fritto misto. The local fish stew is usually known as *brodetto* or simply *zuppa di pesce*. Inland, traditional seafood dishes are *baccalà* and trout and other freshwater fish, but most valued by gourmets are frogs (*rane*), either fried or stewed.

Cheese and Sweets

Besides Parmesan and its various *grana* cousins (*see* pp.52–3), Emilia's cheeses include provolone from Piacenza, *stracchino* (a kind of soft cheese) and creamy *ribiòla* in Piacenza and Parma, made from pure ewe's or ewe's and cow's milk, eaten fresh or ripened in jars covered with a layer of olive oil. In Romagna, a favourite is *formaggio di fossa*, made by leaving cheese to mature in pits or underground cellars, which gives it a special taste and strong smell.

The region produces abundant fruits – peaches, cherries, pears, apricots, grapes, apples, kiwis, melons, watermelons, strawberries and more, which go into a wide range of jams, cakes and *crostate* (pies). Among the most traditional desserts are *torta di riso*, a delicate cake of rice, sugar, almonds and milk; *zuppa inglese*, the Italian version of trifle; *ciambella* or *buslàn*, a ring-shaped cake flavoured with lemon rind, ideal for dunking in wine at the end of a meal; and *spongata*, a dense cake filled with honey, nuts and candied fruit. Then there are *croccante di nocciole*, crunchy, caramelized hazelnut bars, and *buslanêi*, ring biscuits. *Amaretti* are a speciality of Modena, while in Reggio Emilia they make *erbazzone dolce*, a curious sweet pie with ricotta and chard.

The dense, rich Christmas-New Year cake, *pampapato*, invented by Ferrara's nuns of Corpus Domini in the 17th century, is made with almonds, cocoa, orange peel, lemons, cinnamon, cloves and candied fruit; it must sit for about ten days after baking, and is then topped with more chocolate; the *panspeziale* in Bologna is similar. *Sfrappole* (or *crespelli*), twisted ribbons of dough deep fried and dusted with vanilla sugar, are carnival favourites; in the summer look out for chilled *semifreddo* or ice cream with custard doused in chocolate sauce.

Wines and Liqueurs

De vein bon s't' bivrè
e' tu sang t'arnurvarè.
(Drink good wine
and rejuvenate your blood.)

an old Romagnola saying

Stretching from north of Genoa to the Adriatic, Emilia-Romagna does more than its share to contribute to the European wine lake, producing over seven million hectolitres a year – more than any other region in Italy – much of which ends up as cardboard boxes of supermarket plonk. It also produces some gems among its 77 wines of DOC status (*Denominazione di Origine Controllata*), although three dominate the list. Lambrusco, a light-bodied – 10–11.5 per cent – slightly sparkling red wine (the bubbles disappear after the first foamy froth), is the totem wine of Emilia, and although the locals will swear till they're blind that it's perfect to drink with their hearty food and rich pasta dishes, you wouldn't be the first to disagree. This is when the ruby-red, fuller bodied Sangiovese (the 'blood of Jove') of Romagna may come in handy; this is one of the main grapes of Tuscany's Chianti, although the results are usually lighter and fresher, making it a popular lunchtime tipple. The finest Sangiovese, however, can take some ageing and can hold its head as high as the noble Tuscans. The third by sheer volume is straw-coloured Trebbiano, the most common if rather ordinary white wine, best drunk young.

Piacenza and Parma

The traditional white wines from the Colli Piacentini are Monterosso Val D'Arda and Trebbiano Val Trebbia – the grape, as Pliny the Elder acknowledged in his praise of *trebulanus*, is indigenous to Piacenza's River Trebbia, where Hannibal first defeated the Romans, although nowadays most of the Trebbiano from the region is grown in Romagna. Sauvignon and Pinot Grigio are also popular.

There are a variety of reds, especially from Barbera and Bonardo, which here are best blended into the province's finest and most generous red wine, DOC Gutturnio, famous since Roman times, when it was *Gutturnium*. For something different, try Ortrugo, native to the area.

The hills of Parma (Colli di Parma) produce two white wines, a Sauvignon and Malvasia, either dry or *amabile*, and nearly always sparkling or *frizzante*, and a red from Barbera and Bonarda.

Reggio-Emilia and Modena

These are the home provinces of frothing fresh Lambrusco, a grape native to the region. There are four DOC varieties: Lambrusco Salamino di Santa Croce, Lambrusco di Sorbrara (generally considered the best) and Lambrusco Grasparossa di Castelvetro, all from the hills surrounding Modena, and Lambrusco Reggiano, from Reggio. It traditionally comes either *secco* (dry) or *amabile* (sweet), which is vile. Best drunk slightly chilled, if at all. In Reggio, the Colli di Scandiano e di Canossa produces a *frizzante* white Lambrusco, Bianco di Scandiano, as well as Cabernet, Chardonnay and Pinot.

Besides enormous quantities of Lambrusco, Modena is the centre of the region's distilleries. The most famous liqueur is walnut *nocino*, made according to hallowed tradition from green walnuts picked on St John's Day, 24 June, in the foothills of the Apennines between Sassuolo and Formigine: pure alcohol is poured over the crushed nuts, and sugar, cinnamon, cloves and lemon rind are added; the mixture sits with its walnuts, their empty shells and the spices for two years, then is transferred to oak casks for another year of ageing. The result is a chocolate-brown liqueur, smooth and sweet but with an underlying touch of walnutty bitterness. Other common liqueurs are *Sassolino* (made from star anise, at Sassuolo), *alchermes* (made with cloves, cinnamon, nutmeg and other spices), *laurino* (made from bay leaves), raspberry *lamponcino*, lemon *limoncino*, and *grappa*.

Imola and Bologna

DOC Colli di Imola produce fine wines: blood-red Sangiovese, Cabernet Sauvignon, Chardonnay and Pignoletto. The energetic Pignoletto, a native of the province, has recently been the focus of special attention among wine growers and is worth a try, with seafood and even cheese; the same grapes are used to make a fragrant grappa. The hills south of Bologna, the Colli Bolognesi, produce similar varieties, as well as a fine Riesling Italico, and reds Cabernet, Barbera and Merlot. The Reno valley, around and north of Bologna, is known for its Montuni del Reno and Pignoletto.

Ferrara and Ravenna

The coastal areas of Ferrara and Ravenna provinces are the home of DOC Vino di Bosco or Bosco Eliceo, introduced here in 1528 by Renée of France, who brought some vine cuttings from Burgundy's Côte d'Or with her when she wed Ercole II d'Este. Still known as the *uva d'oro* (a bit confusing, as it's black and produces a very black wine) it grows in the sand dunes around Comacchio and produces a slightly bitter wine when young. It's supposedly good with eels, but again you may not agree.

Faenza, Forlì-Cesena and Rimini

Much of this area is encompassed by DOC Vini di Romagna, producing Sangiovese di Romagna, Trebbiano and Albana (dry, sweet or sparkling), a native varietal and Italy's first white wine raised to the status *Denominazione di Origine Controllata e Garantita*, DOCG, although it's rare that it measures up to its letters of nobility; the best is often the sweet slightly nutty *amabile* version. Others are Pagadebit ('pay the bill') and Cagnina, a fragrant purple-red dessert wine, recommended with roast chestnuts or a *ciambella*. Within the Vini di Romagna area are the smaller districts of Colli di Faenza and the Colli di Rimini.

The most comprehensive place to try the regional wines is inside the 13th-century fortress of **Dozza**, near Imola, which was converted in 1970 to house the **Enoteca Regionale Emilia-Romagna**. Completely restructured in 1990, it stocks 800 wines from the region's 67,500 wine-producers. For a preview, check their website, *www.enotecaemiliaromagna.it*, **t** 0542 678089.

Italian Menu Vocabulary

Antipasti (Starters)

antipasto misto mixed *antipasto*
bruschetta garlic toast (with olive oil and sometimes with tomatoes)
caponata mixed aubergine, olives, anchovies and tomatoes
carciofi (sott'olio) artichokes (in oil)
frutti di mare seafood
funghi (trifolati) mushrooms (with anchovies, garlic and lemon)
gamberi ai fagioli prawns (shrimps) with white beans
mozzarella (in carrozza) soft cow/buffalo cheese (fried with bread in batter)
prosciutto crudo (con melone) Parma ham (with melon)
salsicce sausages

Minestre (Soups) and Pasta

agnolotti meat-stuffed pasta parcels
bomba di riso baked rice in mushroom sauce
bucatini thin pasta tubes
cacciucco spiced fish soup
cappelletti small stuffed pasta, often in broth
crespelle crêpes
crespolina pancake
frittata omelette
insalata di mare seafood salad
insalata di riso rice salad
minestra di verdura thick vegetable soup
orecchiette ear-shaped pasta
panzerotti crescent-shaped pastry filled with tomato and tuna or mozzarella
pappardelle alla lepre pasta with hare sauce
pasta e fagioli soup with beans, bacon and tomatoes
pastina in brodo tiny pasta in broth
penne all'arrabbiata quill-shaped pasta with tomatoes and hot peppers
polenta yellow cornmeal that is boiled in salted water, left to set and then cut into pieces
ravioli flat, stuffed pasta parcels
risotto (alla milanese) Italian rice (with stock, saffron and wine)
spaghetti all'amatriciana with spicy bacon, tomato, onion and chilli sauce
spaghetti alle vongole spaghetti with clams
stracciatella broth with eggs and cheese
tagliatelle flat egg noodles
tortellini stuffed crescents of pasta filled with meat, cheese or vegetables
tortellini al pomodoro/con panna/in brodo tortellini served with tomato sauce/with cream/in broth
vermicelli very thin spaghetti

Carne (Meat)

agnello or ***abbacchio*** lamb
anatra duck
animelle sweetbreads
arista pork loin
arrosto misto mixed roast meats
bistecca steak
bocconcini veal mixed with ham and cheese and fried
bollito misto meat stew
braciola chop
brasato di manzo beef with vegetables
bresaola dried raw meat
carne alla pizzaiola beef in tomato and oregano sauce
carne di castrato/suino mutton/pork
carpaccio thinly sliced raw beef
cassoeula pork stew with cabbage
cervella brains
cervo venison
cima ripiena stuffed breast of veal
cinghiale boar
coniglio rabbit
costoletta or ***cotoletta*** chop
fagiano pheasant
faraona guinea fowl
fegato liver
fegato alla veneziana liver with onions
guanciale pork cheek
involtini sliced, stuffed slices of meat
lepre (in salmì) hare (marinated in wine)
lingua tongue
lumache snails
maiale (al latte) pork (cooked in milk)
manzo beef

osso buco braised veal knuckle
pajata calf's/lamb's intestines
pancetta bacon
pernice partridge
petto di pollo boned chicken breast
petto di pollo alla Fiorentina/Bolognese/ Sorpresa boned chicken breast fried in butter/with ham and cheese/stuffed and deep fried
piccione pigeon
pollo chicken
polpette meatballs
quaglie quails
ragù meat sauce
rane frogs
rognoni kidneys
salami cured pork in sausage form
saltimbocca veal, prosciutto and sage, in wine
scaloppine thin slices of veal sautéed in butter
spezzatino pieces of beef or veal, stewed
spiedino meat on a skewer or stick
stracotto slow-cooked beef with wine, herbs and vegetables
stufato beef and vegetables braised in wine
tacchino turkey
trippa tripe
uccelletti small birds on a skewer
vitello veal
zampone pig's trotter

Pesce (Fish)

acciughe or ***alici*** anchovies
anguilla eel
aragosta lobster
aringa herring
baccalà dried salt cod
bonito small tuna
branzino sea bass
brodetto fish stew
calamari squid
cape sante scallops
cefalo grey mullet
coda di rospo angler fish
cozze mussels
datteri di mare razor (or date) mussels
dentice sea bream
dorato gilt head
fritto misto mixed fried fish
gamberetti shrimps
gamberi prawns
granchio crab
insalata di mare seafood salad
lampreda lamprey
merluzzo cod
nasello hake
orata bream
ostriche oysters
pesce azzurro various types of small fish
pesce di San Pietro John Dory
pesce spada swordfish
polipi or ***polpi*** octopus
riccio di mare sea urchin
rombo turbot
rospo monkfish
sampiero John Dory
sarde sardines
seppie cuttlefish
sgombro mackerel
sogliola sole
squadro monkfish
stoccafisso wind-dried cod
tonno tuna
triglia red mullet (rouget)
trota trout
vongole small clams
zuppa di pesce fish soup

Contorni (Vegetables)

aglio garlic
asparagi asparagus
broccoli (calabrese/romana) broccoli (green/spiral)
capperi capers
carciofi artichokes
carciofini artichoke hearts
carote carrots
cavolfiore cauliflower
cavolo cabbage
ceci chickpeas
cetriolo cucumber
cicoria green chicory
cipolla onion
fagioli white beans
fagiolini French (green) beans
fave broad beans
finocchio fennel
funghi (porcini) (cep) mushrooms
insalata mista mixed salad
insalata verde green salad
lattuga lettuce
lenticchie lentils
melanzane aubergines
patate (fritte) (fried) potatoes
peperonata stewed peppers
peperoncini hot chilli peppers
peperoni sweet peppers
piselli (al prosciutto) peas (with ham)
pomodoro tomato
porri leeks
radicchio red chicory
radice radish
rapa turnip
rucola rocket
sedano celery
spinaci spinach
verdure greens/vegetables
zucca pumpkin
zucchini courgettes

Formaggio (Cheese)
bel paese soft white cow's cheese
cacio/caciocavallo pale yellow, sharp cheese
caprino goat's cheese
fontina rich cow's cheese
groviera mild cheese (gruyère)
parmigiano Parmesan cheese
pecorino sharp sheep's cheese
provolone sharp, tangy cheese
stracchino soft white cheese

Frutta (Fruit, Nuts)
albicocche apricots
ananas pineapple
anguria watermelon
arance oranges
banane bananas
ciliege cherries
cocomero watermelon
composta di frutta stewed fruit
datteri dates
fichi figs
fragole strawberries
frutta di stagione fruit in season
lamponi raspberries
limone lemon
macedonia di frutta fruit salad
mandarino tangerine
mandorle almonds
melagrana pomegranate
mele apples
melone melon
more blackberries
nocciole hazelnuts
noci walnuts
pera pear
pesca peach
pesca noce nectarine
pinoli pine nuts
pompelmo grapefruit
prugna/susina prune/plum
uva grapes

Dolci (Desserts)
amaretti macaroons
cannoli crisp pastry tubes filled with ricotta, cream, chocolate or fruit
coppa gelato assorted ice cream
crostata fruit flan
gelato ice cream
granita (con panna) flavoured ice, usually lemon or coffee (with cream)
panettone cake with candied fruit and raisins
panforte dense cake of chocolate, almonds and preserved fruit
semifreddo refrigerated cake
spumone a soft ice cream
tiramisù sponge fingers, mascarpone, coffee and chocolate
torrone nougat
torta cake, tart
zabaglione egg yolks and Marsala wine, hot
zuppa inglese trifle

Bevande (Beverages)
acqua minerale mineral water
acqua gasata/frizzante fizzy water
acqua non gasata still water
aranciata orangeade/orange soda
bicchiere glass
birra beer
birra alla spina draught beer
bottiglia bottle
caffè coffee
caffè freddo iced coffee
caffè macchiato espresso with a drop of milk
caraffa carafe
cioccolata calda hot chocolate
ghiaccio ice
granita iced drink (with fruit or coffee)
latte milk
latte macchiato milk with a drop of coffee
latte (intero/scremato) milk (whole/skimmed)
limonata lemonade/lemon soda
litro litre
mezzo half
quarto quarter
selz soda water
spremuta fresh fruit juice
spumante sparkling wine
succo di frutta fruit juice (from concentrate)
tè tea
tè freddo (sweet, iced) tea
tisana herbal tea
tonica tonic water
vino wine
vino rosso red wine
vino bianco white wine
vino rosato rosé wine

Snacks
biscotti biscuits
caramelle sweets, candy
cioccolato chocolate
grissini bread sticks
patatine crisps/potato chips
pizzetta small pizza with cheese and tomato

Cooking Terms (Miscellaneous)
aceto (balsamico) (balsamic) vinegar
affumicato smoked
aglio garlic
ai ferri grilled without oil
alla brace barbecued
alla milanese fried in egg and breadcrumbs
al dente cooked, but still firm
al forno baked
al sangue rare

alla griglia grilled
allo spiedo cooked on the spit
arrosto roast
ben cotto well done
bollito or ***lesso*** boiled
brasato cooked in wine
burro butter
coltello knife
conto bill
cotto cooked
crudo raw
cucchiaio spoon
filetto fillet
forchetta fork
forno oven
fritto fried
ghiaccio ice
griglia grill
grattugiato grated
in bianco plain, without tomato
in umido stewed
magro lean meat; pasta without meat
maionese mayonnaise
marmellata jam
menta mint
miele honey
olio oil
olio di oliva olive oil
olive olives
pane bread
pane tostato toasted bread
panini sandwiches (in roll)
panna cream
pepe pepper
piadina hot, savoury pancake
piatto plate
pizzaiola cooked with tomato sauce
prezzemolo parsley
ripieno stuffed
rosmarino rosemary
sale salt
salsa sauce
salvia sage
stracotto braised, stewed
tartufi truffles
tavola table
tazza cup
toast toasted sandwich
tovagliolo napkin
tramezzini sandwiches (in sliced bread)
uovo (uova) egg (eggs)
zucchero sugar

Planning Your Trip

When to Go

Climate

Emilia-Romagna is a year-round destination. In **summer** millions come from around the world to fry in Rimini and the other seaside Babylons; the high Apennines stay fairly cool, while the great cities along the Po may be somewhat less inviting in the heat and humidity. In August prices are at their highest, the coasts are packed and the cities (and all the best restaurants) are abandoned to hordes of tourists while the locals go elsewhere.

As in most places in Italy, **spring** and **autumn** are the loveliest times to go for general touring. The weather is mild, places aren't crowded, and you won't need your umbrella too often, at least until October. In many ways the cities are at their best in **winter**: although the valley of the Po is cold, eternally foggy and often blanketed in snow, opera season runs from December to March, museums are rarely crowded, hotels are cheaper, and the hearty food of the region tastes best. The snow lingers on the highest Apennines until May.

Average Temperatures °C (°F)

	Day	Night
January	7 (44)	0 (32)
February	9 (48)	2 (35)
March	12 (53)	4 (39)
April	17 (62)	7 (44)
May	21 (69)	11 (52)
June	25 (77)	15 (59)
July	27 (81)	17 (62)
August	27 (81)	17 (62)
September	24 (75)	14 (57)
October	19 (66)	11 (52)
November	13 (55)	6 (43)
December	8 (46)	2 (35)

Festivals

On the whole, Emilia-Romagna isn't the most exciting Italian region when it comes to festivals. The regional obsession with fast cars finds its highest expression in the Imola race track, but this is a rather staid and decorous region, not one of wild merriment, at least outside the discos of Rimini.

Food-related events tend to dominate in the region, although you will find a few events such as *palii* and other similar excuses to indulge in the favourite Italian pastime of swanning about in medieval or Renaissance costumes.

Check at the local tourist office for exact dates, which alter from year to year, and often slide into the nearest weekend.

See also the 'Calendar of Events' below for a diary of major local festivals throughout Emilia-Romagna.

National Holidays

See p.88.

Calendar of Events

January

Modena: *Fiera* and *Corrida di San Geminiano* (31).

February

Bellaria-Igea Marina: *Fiera di Santa Apollonia* (7–9).

Cento: Carnival. Historical carnival with lots of floats.

San Giovanni in Persiceto, Bologna: Carnival. Parade of satirical floats.

Borgo Tossignano: *Maccheroni* Mardi Gras. Carnival.

Imola: *Sfilata dei Fantaveicoli*. Carnival with bizarre floats (or first days of March).

March

Ponticelli: *Maccheroni* festival (early March).

Forlimpopoli: *Segavecchia*. Gastronomy and burning of the effigy of Old Woman Winter in mid-Lent.

Casalfiumanese, Bologna: Ravioli festival (2nd or 3rd Sun).

Cavriago: *Fiera del Bue Grasso*. Cattle fair, with crafts demonstrations and food stands (25–7).

Rocca San Casciano, Forlì: Bonfire festival (last weekend of month).

Around Easter

Sarsina: *Pagnotta di Pasqua* (Palm Sunday). Dedicated to the traditional Easter cake.

Ravenna: Mister Jazz. Seminars and concerts during February–April.

Tredozio, Forlì: *Sagra e Palio dell'Uovo*. Egg-cracking contests and the Italian hard-boiled egg eating championship, on Easter Sunday.

Fontanelice: *Sagra della Piè fritta*. Festival of *piadine*, Easter Monday.

Gambettola: Float races. A humorous procession, on Easter Monday.

April

Vignola: Cherry Blossom Festival (4–18).

Ferrara: *Vulandra*. Kite and kitemakers' festival (3rd or 4th weekend of the month).

May

Ferrara: Events all month in the lead-up to the *Palio di San Giorgio*.

Borghi, Forlì: Bustreng Festival. Traditional cake and *palio* (2nd weekend).

Quattro Castella: Investiture of Matilda of Canossa; in period costume (2nd Sun).

Predappio: *Bruschetta e Sangiovese* (2nd Sun).

Cervia: 'Marriage to the Sea'. Ceremony on Ascension Day.

Guiglia, Modena: *Sagra del borlengo*. Pancake festival (2nd–3rd weeks).

Riccione: TTV, Festival of TV, Theatre and Video (3rd–4th weeks; next held 2008).

Roncofreddo, Forlì: Pea festival (3rd Sun).

Malabergo, Bologna: Asparagus festival (3rd Sun).

Modena: *Balsamico*. Vinegar festival with exhibitions, special menus in restaurants, and cookery classes (late May/early June).

Ferrara: *Palio*. Horse races between the eight *contrade* and Renaissance pageantry (last Sun; moved to 1st Sun in June if it rains). The oldest *palio* event in the world.

Busseto: Verdi Voice Competition (May/June).

June

Faenza: *Palio del Niballo*.

Marinara, Ravenna: International rally of vintage boats.

Imola: Music festival (2nd weekend). Rock festival (3rd weekend).

Ravenna: Ravenna Festival. Opera, classical music and ballet in the churches (mid-June to mid-July).

Cervia: Festival of the Feinda Dance (19–27).

Spilamberto: *Fiera di San Giovanni*. With a balsamic vinegar competition (23–7).

Cesena: San Giovanni (24).

Modena: Pavarotti and Friends. Opera and pop duets; *Settimana Estense*. Historical tournaments and spectacles (24 June to early July).

Castel del Rio: Renaissance Festival (last weekend).

Civitella: Cherry festival (last Sun).

July

Porretta: Soul Festival (June and July).

Ferrara: *Ferrara sotto le stelle*. Rock festival.

Gatteo Mare: *Festa della Micizia*. Cat festival.

Santarcangelo: Theatre festival.

Pomposa: Music at Pomposa abbey throughout July and Aug.

Brisighella: Medieval Festival (1st week).

Codigoro: Melon festival.

Cervia: VIP Master Tennis competitions (mid-month).

Modena: International Military Bands festival (mid-month).

Ravenna: Ravenna Jazz Festival (2nd half).

Nonantola: *Palio dell'Abate* and *Palio delle Due Torri* (last two Suns).

August

Casina, Reggio Emilia: Festival of Parmesan cheese.

Cesenatico: *Festa di Garibaldi* (1st Sun).

Casalborsetti, Ravenna: San Lorenzo. Fair with fireworks (10).

Premilcuore, Forlì (10).

Cervia: Fireworks and fair (10).

Mondaino: *Palio del Daino* (mid-month).

Comacchio: St Cassino Fair (13).

Pievepelago: Traditional festival (15).

Lido delle Nazioni: Lake festival; fireworks (15).

Bagno di Romagna: Food, music and fireworks (15).

Verghereto: Donkey *palio* (2nd Sun).

Rimini: Meeting *per l'amicizia fra i popoli*. Events on a different theme every year, dedicated to international friendship (late in month).

Ferrara: Buskers' festival. The largest of its kind in Europe (last week).

Meldola: *Madonna del Popolo* and *palio* (4th Sun).

San Benedetto Val di Sambro: *Palio storico* (end of month).

Terra del Sole: *Palio di Santa Reparata*. Medieval *palio* (end Aug to early Sept).

September

Castel San Pietro Terme: Honey fair.

Ravenna: *Settembre Dantesco*. Readings and events dedicated to Dante throughout the month, culminating on the 10th.

Langhirano: Parma ham festival (1st week).

San Marino: *Palio delle Balestre*. Crossbow competitions (3).

Bertinoro: Hospitality festival. Wine and *piadine* (1st Sun).

Terra del Sole: *Palio della Fune* (1st Sun).

Gaggio Montano, Bologna: Sausage festival (1st Sun).

Argenta, Ferrara: Big fair.

Cervia: Festival of salt.

Castelfranco, Modena: *Festa del tortellino* (2nd Sun).

Sorbara, near **Bomporto**: *Festa del Lambrusco* (3rd weekend).

San Pietro in Vincoli, Ravenna: *Festa dell'Uva*. Wine festival with a parade (late in month).

October

Goro: *Ottobre d'Oro*. Cultural events and films all month.

Casola Valsenio, near **Ravenna**: *Festa dei Frutti Dimenticati*. Celebrating forgotten fruits.

Fragno, Parma: Truffle festival.

Santerno: *Sagra paesana di Santerno*. Country fair, with music, food, stands, games and fireworks (end Sept–early Oct).

Portico di Romagna: *Frutti del Sottobosco*. Autumn food feast/festival (2nd Sun).

Comacchio: Eel Feast (last two Suns).

Dovadola: White truffle festival (last two Suns).

San Mauro Pascoli: *Festa di San Crispino*. Patron saint of cobblers (25).

Porto Corsini: Hallowe'en and Tree Festival (31).

November

Fanano: Chestnut festival (1st Sun).

Cusercoli: *Sagra di tartufo*. Truffle festival (1st two Suns).

Imola: Sangiovese wine week (2nd week).

Modena: Huge antiques fair (2nd week).

Brisighelle: Truffle festival (3rd Sun); olive oil festival (last Sun).

Sogliano (Forlì): *Formaggio di fossa*. Festival (3rd and 4th Suns, and 1st Sun of Dec).

December

Imola: International short film festival (end Nov–early Dec).

Forlì and **Savignano**: *Santa Lucia* (13).

Sestola: Live Christmas crib, traditional bagpipes and old crafts, at Christmas.

Ravenna: Big *presepi* (crib) displays at Christmas.

Brisighella: Olive oil festival (4th Sun).

Tourist Information

The best tourist offices are in the city centres, and Emilia-Romagna has some of the best-run examples we have ever seen. Known under various initials as EPT, IAT, APT or AAST, tourist offices are usually open 8am–12.30 or 1pm, and 3–7pm, possibly longer in summer. Few open on Saturday afternoons or Sundays. Information booths can also be found at major railway stations and provide hotel lists, town plans and terse information on local sights and transport. Queues can be maddeningly long. Nearly every city and province now has a web page, but it may not provide much useful information. For general travel advice to Italy see *www.fco.gov.uk* (UK Foreign Office) and *http://travel.state.gov* (US Department of State).

Before you go: The main Emilia-Romagna Tourist Agency is **APT Servizi**, Piazzale Fellini 3, 7900 Rimini, **t** (0541) 438 211, *info@aptservizi.com*, *www.emiliaromagnaturismo.it*. Tourist and travel information is available from **Alitalia** (Italy's national airline) and **CIT** (Italy's state-run travel agency); the main website is *www.italiantourism.com*.

Italian Tourist Offices Abroad

Australia: Level 26, 44 Market Street, Sydney, NSW 2000, **t** (02) 92 621 666.

Canada: 175 Bloor Street East, Suite 907, South Tower, Toronto ON M4W 3R8, **t** (416) 925 4882/925 3725.

UK: 1 Princes Street, London W1B 8AY, **t** (020) 7408 1254, *www.enit.it*; Italian Travel Centre, 30 St James' Street, London SW1A 1HB, **t** (020) 7853 6475; Italian Embassy, 14 Three Kings Yard, Davies Street, London W1K 4EH, **t** (020) 7312 2200, *www.embitaly.org.uk*.

USA: 630 Fifth Avenue, Suite 1565, New York NY 10111, **t** (212) 245 5095/4822; 12400 Wilshire Boulevard, Suite 550, Los Angeles CA 90025, **t** (310) 820 0098; 500 N. Michigan Avenue, Suite 2240, Chicago IL 60611, **t** (312) 644 0996.

Embassies and Consulates

In Italy

Australia: Via Antonio Bosio 5, Rome, **t** (06) 852 721.

Canada: Via G. Carducci 29, Naples, **t** (081) 401 338.

Ireland: Largo del Nazarenos, Rome, **t** (06) 678 2541.

New Zealand: Via Zara 28, Rome, **t** (06) 440 2928.

UK: Via dei Mille 40, Naples, **t** (081) 423 8911. Via Terribile 9, Brindisi, **t** (0831) 568 340, *www.britain.it*.

USA: Piazza della Repubblica 2, Naples, **t** (081) 583 8111.

Abroad

Australia: Level 45, The Gateway Building, 1 Macquarie Place, Circular Quay, Sydney, NSW 2000, **t** (02) 9392 7939, *www.conssydney.esteri.it*.

Canada: 1100–510 West Hastings St, Vancouver BC V6B 1L8, **t** 1-604 684 7288, *http://consvancouver.esteri.it*.

Ireland: 63–5 Northumberland Rd, Dublin, **t** (01) 660 1744; 7 Richmond Park, Belfast BT9 5EF, **t** (02890) 668 854, *www.ambdublino.esteri.it*.

New Zealand: PO Box 463, 34 Grant Rd, Thorndon, Wellington, **t** (04) 473 5339, *www.italy-embassy.org.nz*.

UK: 38 Eaton Place, London SW1X 8AN, **t** (020) 7235 9371; 32 Melville St, Edinburgh EH3 7HA, **t** (0131) 226 3631; *www.embitaly.org.uk*.

USA: 690 Park Ave, New York NY, **t** (212) 489 8600, *www.italconsulnyc.org*; 12400 Wilshire Boulevard, Suite 300, Los Angeles, CA, **t** (310) 820 0622, *http://sedi.esteri.it/losangeles*.

Entry Formalities

Passports and Visas

To get into Italy you need a valid passport. EU citizens do not need visas in order to enter Italy. US, Canadian and Australian nationals do not need visas for stays of up to 90 days. If you mean to stay for longer than 90 days in Italy you will have to get a *permesso di soggiorno*. For this you will need to state your reason for staying, be able to prove a source of income and have medical insurance. After a couple of days at some provincial Questura office you should walk out with your permit.

According to Italian law, you must register with the police within eight days of your arrival. If you check into a hotel this is done automatically. If you come to grief in the mesh of rules and forms, you can get someone to explain it to you in English by calling the Rome Police Office for visitors, **t** 06 4686, ext. 2987.

Customs

EU nationals over the age of 17 can now import a limitless amount of goods for their personal use. Arrivals from non-EU countries have to pass through Italian Customs.

Duty-free allowances have now been abolished within the EU. For travellers entering the EU from outside, the duty-free limits are 1 litre of spirits or 2 litres of liquors (port, sherry or champagne), plus 2 litres of wine, 200 cigarettes and 50 grams of perfume. Much larger quantities – up to 10 litres of spirits, 90 litres of wine, 110 litres of beer and 800 cigarettes – bought locally and provided you are travelling between EU countries, can be taken through customs if you can prove that they are for private consumption only and taxes have been paid in the country of purchase. Under-17s are not allowed to bring tobacco or alcohol into the EU. Pets must be accompanied by a bilingual Certificate of Health from your local Veterinary Inspector. Note that you cannot bring meat, vegetables or plants into the UK.

Residents of the USA may each take home US$400-worth of foreign goods without attracting duty, including the tobacco and alcohol allowance. Canadians can bring home $300 worth of goods in a year, plus their tobacco and alcohol allowances.

Disabled Travellers

Italy has been relatively slow off the mark in its provision for disabled visitors. Cobblestones, uneven or non-existent pavements, appalling traffic, crowded public transport and endless flights of steps are all disincentives. Progress is being made, however. Emilia-Romagna is well above average, and access in most public buildings and major museums should be no problem.

A national support organization in your own country should have some specific

Specialist Organizations for People with Disabilities

In Italy

Accessible Italy, Piazza Pitagora 9, 10137 Turin, **t** 011 301 8888, *www.mondopossibile.com*. Travel agency which provides valuable, detailed help and information on access in Italy, including detailed coverage of accessible tourist spots, transport and accommodation in Tuscany.

Centro Studi Consulenza Invalidi, Via Gozzadini 7, 20148 Milan, **t** (02) 4030 8339. Publishes an annual guide, *Vacanze per Disabili*, with details of suitable accommodation in Italy.

CO.IN (Consorzio Cooperative Integrate), Via Enrico Giglioli 54a, 00169 Rome, **t** (06) 2326 7504, toll free in Italy **t** 800 271 027, *turismo@coinsociale.it*, *www.coinsociale.it* (in English too). Their tourist information centre (*open Mon–Fri 9–5*) offers advice and information on accessibility. They also offer **COINtel**, **t** (06) 2326 7695, a 24-hour information line in English, and can assist with bookings for guided tours with suitable transport, **t** (06) 7128 9676.

Vacanze Serene, toll free in Italy, **t** 800 271 027. Gives information on accessible travel throughout Italy (*open Mon–Fri 9–5*).

In the UK and Ireland

Holiday Care Service, The Hawkins Suite, Enham Place, Enham Alamein, Andover, Hampshire SP11 6JS, **t** 0845 124 9971, *www.holidaycare.org.uk*. Holiday Care can give up-to-date information on destinations both in the UK and abroad, on transportation and on suitable tour operators.

Irish Wheelchair Association, Blackheath Drive, Clontarf, Dublin 3, **t** (01) 818 6400, *www.iwa.ie*. An organization with services for disabled travellers; they also publish guides with advice for disabled holiday-makers.

RADAR (Royal Association for Disability and Rehabilitation), 12 City Forum, 250 City Road, London EC1V 8AF, **t** (020) 7250 3222, *www.radar.org.uk*. RADAR publish several useful books, including *Access to Air Travel*, as well as holiday fact-packs.

Royal National Institute for the Blind (RNIB), 105 Judd Street, London WC1H 9NE, **t** (020) 7388 1266, *www.rnib.org.uk*. Offers 'Plane Easy', on audio cassette, advising the blind or partially sighted on travelling by plane. They also advise on accommodation.

Royal National Institute for the Deaf (RNID), 19–23 Featherstone Street, London EC1Y 8SL, Infoline **t** 0808 808 0123, textphone **t** 0808 808 9000, *informationline@rnid.org.uk*, *www.rnid.org.uk*. Call their information line for help and advice.

In the USA and Canada

Access America, *www.disabilityinfo.gov*. Provides information on facilities for disabled people at international airports. The US government website, *www.dot.gov/airconsumer*, also has some useful information.

American Foundation for the Blind, 11 Penn Plaza, Suite 300, New York NY 10001, **t** (212) 502 7600, toll free **t** 800 232 5463, *www.afb.org*. The best source for information in the USA for visually impaired travellers.

Federation of the Handicapped, 211 West 14th Street, New York NY 10011, **t** (212) 747 4262. Organizes summer tours for members; there is a nominal annual fee.

Mobility International USA, 132 East Broadway, Suite 343, Eugene OR 97401, **t** (541) 343 1284, *info@miusa.org*, *www.miusa.org*. This international nonprofit organization, based in the USA, provides information and a range of publications for the disabled traveller. $35 annual membership fee.

SATH (Society for Accessible Travel and Hospitality), 347 5th Avenue, Suite 610, New York NY 10016, **t** (212) 557 0027, *www.sath.org*. Offers advice on all aspects of travel for the disabled, for a small charge, or unlimited to members. Their website is a very useful resource.

Travel Information Service, MossRehab Hospital, 1200 West Tabor Road, Philadelphia PA 19141-3099, **t** 800-CALL MOSS, *www.mossresourcenet.org/travel.htm*. Advice and information on all aspects of accessible travel.

Tour Operators for Disabled Travellers

In the UK

Assistance Travel Service, 1 Tank Lane, Purfleet, Essex RM19 1TA, **t** (01708) 863198, *www.assistedholidays.com*. Organizes tailor-made trips all over the world, for people with any disability.

Can Be Done, 11 Woodcock Hill, Harrow HA3 0XP, **t** (020) 8907 2400, *www.canbedone.co.uk*. Cruises, city breaks, self-drive holidays.

Chalfont Line Ltd, 4 Providence Road, West Drayton, Middlesex UB7 8HJ, **t** (01895) 459540, *www.chalfont-line.co.uk*. A large range of accessible international holidays, which can be tailored to suit. They also have adapted vehicles for hire.

Travelability, Avionics House, Naas Lane, Quedgeley, Gloucestershire GL2 4SN, **t** 0870 241 6127, *www.travelability.co.uk*. International tailor-made holidays.

In the USA and Canada

Alternative Leisure Co., 165 Middlesex Turnpike, Suite 206, Bedford MA 01730, **t** (781) 275 0023 *www.alctrips.com*. Vacations abroad for people with disabilities.

Accessible Journeys, 35 West Sellers Ave, Ridley Park PA 19078, **t** 1-800 846 4537, or (610) 521 0339, *www.disabilitytravel.com*. Individual travel in Italy.

Flying Wheels Travel, 143 W Bridge Street, Owatonna MN 55060, **t** (507) 451 5005, *www.flyingwheelstravel.com*. Escorted tours and custom itineraries.

The Guided Tour Inc, 7900 Old York Rd, Suite 114-B, Elkins Park PA 19027-2339, **t** 1-800 783 5841, *www.guidedtour.com*. Accompanied holidays.

Nautilus Tours and Cruises, 22567 Ventura Blvd, Woodland Hills CA91364, **t** 1-800 797 6004, or 818 591 3159, *www.nautilustours.com*. Accessible Italian tours.

Stay and Visit Italy, 4971 Ringwood Meadow, Sarasota FL 34235, **t** (941) 308 6020, toll free 877 782 9878, *www.stayandvisit.com*. Organizes tailor-made tours throughout Tuscany and Umbria. Florence, plus a wide range of customized vacations.

Useful Websites

www.access-able.com. Information for aged and disabled travellers.

www.access-ability.org/travel.htm. Information on travel agencies.

www.emerginghorizons.com. International on-line travel newsletter for people with disabilities.

Disability World, *www.disabilityworld.org*. On-line network for disabled travellers, with links to other websites, archives and information on travel guides.

information on facilities in Italy, or will at least be able to provide general advice. Any provincial tourist office or CIT (travel agency) can also advise on hotels, museums with ramps and so on; some of the provinces, notably Modena, have excellent, detailed information in print to send you. If you book rail travel through CIT, you can request assistance.

Insurance and EHIC Cards

You can insure yourself for almost any possible mishap – cancelled flights, stolen or lost baggage and ill health. Check any current policies you hold to see if they cover you while abroad, and under what circumstances, and judge whether you want a special **traveller's insurance policy** for the journey. Travel agencies sell them, as well as insurance companies.

Citizens of **EU countries** are entitled to **reciprocal health care** in Italy's National Health Service and a 90 per cent discount on prescriptions: bring a valid **European Health Insurance Card (EHIC)** with you. The EHIC is free but does not cover all medical expenses (no repatriation costs, for example, and no private treatment), and it is advisable to take out separate travel insurance for full cover. Citizens of non-EU countries should check carefully that they have adequate insurance for any medical expenses, and the cost of returning home. Australia has a reciprocal healthcare scheme with Italy, but New Zealand, Canada and the USA do not. If you already have health insurance, a student card, or a credit card, you may be entitled to some medical cover abroad.

No specific **vaccinations** are required or advised for citizens of most countries before visiting Italy; the main health risks are upset stomachs and the effects of too much sun. Take a supply of medicaments with you (insect repellent, anti-diarrhœal medicine, sun lotion and antiseptic cream), and any drugs you need to take regularly.

Maps

The maps in this guide are for orientation only and, if you want to explore in any detail, you should really invest in a good, up-to-date regional map before you arrive. The green **Touring Club Italiano** map of Emilia-Romagna (1:200,000) is good but enormous, and requires some deft folding to make it manageable. It's available in most Italian bookshops or sometimes on newsstands. Try the following bookshops before you go:

Stanford's, 12–14 Long Acre, London WC2 9LP, **t** (020) 7836 1321.

The Travel Bookshop, 13 Blenheim Crescent, London W11 2EE, **t** (020) 7229 5260.

The Complete Traveller, 199 Madison Avenue, New York, NY 10016, **t** (212) 685 9007.

Italian tourist offices are also helpful and can often supply good area maps as well as town plans.

Money

The currency of Italy is the **euro** (€). There are 7 euro notes: 500, 200, 100, 50, 20, 10 and 5; and 8 coins: 2 euros, 1 euro, 50 cents, 20 cents, 10 cents, 5 cents, 2 cents and 1 cent. It doesn't hurt to order a wad of euros from your home bank to have on hand when you arrive in Italy, the land of strikes, unforeseen delays and quirky banking hours. Take great care how you carry it, however (don't keep it all in one place).

Most larger businesses in Emilia-Romagna will accept **credit cards**, but some smaller places will not. **ATMs** (Bancomats) will spout cash with your bank card and PIN, albeit for the price of a significant commission.

Otherwise, obtaining money is often a frustrating business involving much queuing and form-filling. The major banks and exchange bureaux licensed by the Bank of Italy give the best exchange rates for currency or traveller's cheques. Hotels, private exchanges in resorts and exchanges run by rail operator FS at railway stations usually have worse rates, but are open outside normal banking hours. Most large cities and airports have exchange offices that are open at weekends.

You can have money transferred to you through an Italian bank but this process may take over a week, even if it's sent urgent, *espressissimo*. You will need your passport as identification when you collect it. Don't send cheques by post.

Getting There

By Air from the UK and Ireland

Bologna is the big regional airport, linked to London Gatwick by daily flights operated by **British Airways**. Booked in advance, these can be very inexpensive (and fares quoted on the website include taxes, unlike many others), although at peak season prices rise considerably. Cheap scheduled flights are offered by **Ryanair** from London Stansted to Forlì and Parma; they also fly to Ancona and Pisa, which have quick train links into the region.

MyTravel operates flights from London and Manchester to Rimini and San Marino, and **easyJet** flies from Luton to Bologna and other cities in north Italy.

Milan is a straightforward 2-hour train journey from Bologna, via Modena, Parma and Piacenza. There are several **Alitalia** and **British Airways** flights to Milan from London Heathrow or London Gatwick. BA also have flights from Manchester to Bologna, and to Milan via Heathrow.

Also worth considering are **Meridiana**'s flights to Florence.

From Ireland and Aberdeen, **Aer Lingus** operate direct flights to Bologna, and from Dublin or Belfast to Milan or Rome, while

Airline Carriers

UK and Ireland

Aer Lingus, Dublin, **t** 0818 365 000; or Belfast, **t** 045 084 4444, *www.aerlingus.com*.

Alitalia, London, **t** 0870 544 8259; Dublin, **t** (01) 677 5171, *www.alitalia.co.uk*.

British Airways, **t** 0870 850 9850, *www.ba.com*.

easyJet, **t** 0905 821 0905, *www.easyjet.com*.

KLM Direct, **t** 0870 243 0541, *www.klm.com*.

Lufthansa, **t** 0845 773 7747, *www.lufthansa.com*.

Meridiana, **t** (020) 7839 2222, *www.meridiana.it*.

MyTravel, **t** 0870 241 5333, *www.mytravel.com*.

Ryanair, **t** 0871 246 0000, *www.ryanair.com*.

USA and Canada

Air Canada, **t** 1 888 247 2262, *www.aircanada.ca*.

Alitalia (USA), **t** 800 223 5730, *www.alitaliausa.com*.

British Airways, **t** 800 AIRWAYS, *www.ba.com*.

Continental, **t** 800 231 0856, or hearing impaired **t** 800 361 8071; Canada **t** 800 525 0280, *www.continental.com*.

Northwest Airlines, **t** 800 447 4747, *www.nwa.com*.

Delta, **t** 800 241 4141, *www.delta.com*.

United Airlines, **t** 800 433 7300, *www.ual.com*.

Discounts, Special Deals, Student and Youth Fares

UK and Ireland

Budget Travel, 134 Lower Baggot Street, Dublin 2, **t** (01) 631 1079, *www.budgettravel.ie*.

Italy Sky Shuttle, 227 Shepherds Bush Road, London W6 7AS, **t** (020) 8748 1333, *www.travelshop.com*.

Italflights, 125 High Holborn, London WC1V 6QA, **t** (020) 7405 6771.

Trailfinders, 215 Kensington High Street, London W8S 6BD, **t** (020) 7937 1234, *www.trailfinders.com*. Additional branches in other major cities.

United Travel, 2 Old Dublin Road, Stillorgan, County Dublin, **t** (01) 215 9300, *www.unitedtravel.ie*.

Besides saving 25 per cent on regular flights, young people under 26 have the choice of flying on special discount charters.

STA, 1 Campden Hill Road, London W8 7DU, **t** 0870 166 2608, *www.statravel.com*. With other branches around the UK.

USIT Now, 19–21 Aston Quay, Dublin 2, **t** (01) 602 1904, and other branches in Ireland, *www.usitnow.ie*.

Websites (UK and Ireland)

For a useful directory of inexpensive flights, visit *www.whichbudget.com*. For some of the best last-minute bargains, try the following:

www.cheapflights.com
www.icelolly.com
www.lastminute.com
www.thomascook.com
www.travelocity.com

USA and Canada

Airhitch, 481 Eighth Avenue, Suite 1771, New York NY, 10001-1820, **t** 247 4482, 1-877-247 4482, *www.airhitch.org*.

Last Minute Travel Club, 132 Brookline Avenue, Boston, MA 02215, **t** 800 527 8646.

Now Voyager, 74 Varick St, Suite 307, New York NY 10013, **t** (212) 431 1616, *www.nowvoyager.com*. For courier flights, plus gay and lesbian travel.

STA, 205E 42nd Street, New York NY 10017, **t** (212) 822 2700 or 800 781 4040 *www.statravel.com*; ASUC Building, 1st Floor, University of California, Berkeley, CA 94720, **t** (510) 642 3000. Also with branches at universities.

TFI, 34 West 32nd Street, New York, NY 10001, **t** (212) 736 1140, toll free **t** 800 745 8000, *www.lowestairprice.com*.

Travel Cuts, 187 College St, Toronto ONM5T 1P7, **t** (416) 979 2406, *www.travelcuts.com*. Canada's largest student travel specialists, with branches in most provinces.

Websites (USA and Canada)

You could also try some of the US cheap flight websites, which include:

www.air-fare.com
www.eurovacations.com
www.expedia.com
www.flights.com
www.orbitz.com
www.priceline.com (bid for tickets)
www.smartertravel.com
www.travelocity.com

Ryanair usually offers the best deal to Emilia-Romagna, to Forlì via London Stansted.

Return fares vary greatly, depending on the season. The best-value deals include **APEX** or **SuperAPEX** fares: you must book 14 days ahead, and stay a Saturday night in Italy, and no alterations or refunds are possible.

By Air from North America

From the United States there are direct **Alitalia** and **British Airways** flights to Rome and Milan, the former connected by flights to Parma, Rimini or Bologna; Alitalia also fly from New York to Parma. Your travel agent may find a significantly cheaper fare from your home airport by way of London, Brussels, Paris, Frankfurt or Amsterdam. Alitalia flies direct to Italy from both the USA and Canada.

To be eligible for low-cost or **APEX** fares you'll have to have fixed flight dates and spend at least a week in Italy, but no more than 90 days. **SuperAPEX**, the cheapest normal fares available, must be purchased at least 14 days (sometimes 21 days) in advance.

There are penalties to pay if you change your flight dates. At the time of writing the lowest midweek SuperAPEX between New York and Milan off season is around $500, rising to the $900 zone in summer.

To sweeten the deal, Alitalia in particular often has promotional perks like rental cars (Jetdrive), or discounts on domestic flights within Italy, on hotels, or on tours. Ask your travel agent. Children under the age of two usually travel for free and both British Airways and Alitalia offer cheaper tickets on some flights for students and the under-25s.

By Train

From London Waterloo it's about 15 hours to Bologna (changing in Paris: the Eurostar arrives at the Gare du Nord, and trains to Italy depart from Paris Bercy or the Gare du Lyon). The fare is from around £170 second-class return, £271 first class, travelling by Eurostar on the London– Paris leg of the journey, and includes reservations and *couchettes*.

Discounts are available for senior citizens, families and for children, and anyone under 26. Get them from Rail Europe or RailChoice (*see* below) and throughout Europe at student offices (CTS in Italy) in main railway stations. The **Trenitalia Pass** is valid from 4 to 10 (consecutive or non-consecutive) days within a 2-month period. You can get it at the main Italian stations, or request it in travel agencies abroad. Three kinds of pass are available: Basic, 1st or 2nd class, for adults; Youth for 12–26 year-old customers travelling in 2nd class; and Saver, 1st or 2nd class, for small groups (2–5 people). Prices vary accordingly. An **Inter-Rail Pass** (available to EU residents only; see *www.interrail.net*) offers unlimited travel for all ages throughout Europe for up to a month. Prices vary according to how many countries you are visiting and over what time period you are travelling; the pass is cheaper for the under-26s. The **Eurail Pass** is a similar pass for those living outside Europe and North Africa (and is cheaper if bought outside Europe): see *www.eurail.com*.

Various youth fares and inclusive rail passes are also available within Italy, and if you're planning on doing a lot of train travel solely in Italy you can organize these before leaving home at Rail Choice, or log on to *www.trenitalia.it*.

Useful websites for planning rail trips in Europe are *www.bahn.de* (the German rail website, which you can use for planning journeys between any European countries; it gives times, platforms and in some cases actual fares) and *www.seat61.com*.

Rail Agencies

Rail Choice, UK: 15 Colman House, Empire Square, High Street, Penge, London SE20 7EX, **t** 0870 165 7300, *www.railchoice.co.uk*; USA: 1-800 361 RAIL (Eurostar tickets and Inter-Rail passes), *www.railchoice.com*.

Rail Europe, UK: 178 Piccadilly, London W1V 0BA, **t** 08708 371371, *www.raileurope.co.uk*; USA: **t** 1-877 257 2887, *www.raileurope.com*.

CIT (agents for Italian State Railways), UK: The Atrium, London Road, Crawley, West Sussex, **t** 0870 901 4013; USA: 875 3rd Ave, mezz. level, New York NY 10022, **t** 1-800 CIT-TOUR; Canada: 80 Tiverton Court, Suite 401, Markham, Toronto ON L3R 094, **t** 800 387 0711, *www.cittours-canada.com*.

By Coach

Usually more expensive than a charter flight, the coach is the last refuge of plane-phobic bargain-hunters. The journey time from London to Bologna is around 27 hours, changing in Paris and/or Milan; the return fare starts from around £69.

Eurolines UK Ltd, Ensign Court, 4 Vicarage Road, Edgbaston, Birmingham B15 3ES, **t** 0870 580 8080, *www.eurolines.co.uk*. Bargain bus travel across Europe.

By Car

Driving to Italy from the UK is a lengthy and expensive proposition, and if you're only staying for a short period, figure your costs against an airline's fly-drive scheme. No matter how you cross the Channel, it is a good two-day drive, about 1,300km.

Ferry information is available at any travel agent or direct from the ferry companies. You can avoid some of the driving by putting your car on the train (although again balance the sizeable expense against the price of hiring a car for the period of your stay). There are Motorail links from Denderleeuw, in Belgium, to Bologna, Rimini and Rome (infrequently

Drivers' Clubs

For more information on driving in Italy, contact the AA, RAC or, in the USA, the AAA:

AA, General enquiries, **t** 0870 600 0371, *www.theaa.com*.

RAC, General enquiries, **t** 0870 572 2722, *www.rac.co.uk*.

AAA (USA), **t** 800 222 4357, *www.aaa.com*.

in winter: for further details contact Rail Choice, **t** (020) 8659 7300, *www.railchoice.co.uk*). The **Italian Auto Club** (ACI), **t** 06 4477, 06 491 115 (information for foreigners), 800 116 (from Italy only), *www.aci.it* (in Italian only), offers motorists reasonably priced breakdown assistance.

To bring a GB-registered car into Italy, you need a **vehicle registration document**, **full driving licence** and **insurance papers** (a Green Card is not necessary, but you'll need one if you go through Switzerland), which must be carried at all times when driving. If your driving licence is of the old-fashioned sort without a photograph you are strongly recommended to apply for an **international driving permit** (available from the AA or RAC). Non-EU citizens should preferably have an **international driving licence**, which has an Italian translation incorporated. Your vehicle should display a nationality plate indicating its country of registration.

Before travelling, check everything is in perfect order. Red hazard triangles, a phosphorescent orange jacket (for breakdowns) and headlight converters are obligatory; also recommended are a spare set of bulbs, a first-aid kit and a fire extinguisher. Spare parts for some non-Italian cars are difficult to come by. Before crossing the border, fill your car up; fuel is very expensive in Italy.

Getting Around

Emilia-Romagna has an excellent network of railways, highways and byways, and you'll find getting around fairly easy – until one union or another takes it into its head to go on strike. However, by law, unions are not permitted to strike during the high holiday season, or over Christmas and New Year. Just in case, learn to recognize the word in Italian: *sciopero* (SHO-pe-ro).

By Train

FS information from anywhere in Italy, ***t*** *89 20 21 (from Italy only), www.trenitalia.com (in English too)*

Emilia-Romagna is a perfect place to base a trip on public transport. Most of the attractions are in the cities, and you can hop from one to the next on very frequent trains – usually a trip of an hour or less – and then walk out of a station that is surrounded by hotels. After a while it will all seem wonderfully civilized. At any station you can pick up the free booklet *In Treno Emilia-Romagna*, with a full list of regional schedules.

Italy's national railway, the FS (*Ferrovie dello Stato*), is well run and often a pleasure to ride. There are also several private rail lines around cities and in country districts. We have tried to list them all in this book. Some, you may find, won't accept Inter-Rail or Eurail passes.

Train **fares** have increased greatly over the last couple of years and only those without extra supplements can still be called cheap. On Friday nights, weekends and in the summer, **reserve a seat** in advance (*fare una prenotazione*). The fee is small and can save you hours standing. For the upper echelon trains and the Eurostars, reservations are mandatory. Do check when you purchase your ticket in advance that the date is correct; tickets are only valid the day they're purchased unless you specify otherwise.

Tickets may be purchased not only in the stations, but also at many travel agents, and it's wise to buy them in advance as the queues can be long. Be sure you ask which **platform** (*binario*) your train arrives at; the big boards in the stations are not always correct.

Always remember to **stamp your ticket** (*convalidare* or *obliterare*) in the not-very-obvious machine at the head of the platform before boarding the train. Failure to do so may result in a fine. If you get on a train without a ticket you can buy one from the conductor, with an added 20 per cent penalty. You can also pay a conductor to move up to first class as long as there are enough places available.

There is a strict hierarchy of **trains**. A *Regionale* travels shortish distances, and tends to stop at all the stations. There are only a few *Espresso* trains left in service, but they are in poor condition, and mostly service the long runs from the south of Italy. No supplement is required. *Intercity* trains whoosh between the big cities and rarely deign to stop. Some carry an obligatory seat reservation requirement (free in this case), and all have a supplement. The true Kings of the Rails are the super-swish and super-fast *Eurostars* (Rome–Florence in 1½ hours; not related to the Channel Tunnel trains of the same name). These make very few stops, have 1st- and 2nd-class carriages, and carry a supplement which includes an obligatory seat reservation. So the faster the train the more you pay.

For details of **special offers and discounted tickets** check *www.trenitalia.com*.

Refreshments on routes of any great distance are provided by bar cars or trolleys; you can usually get sandwiches and coffee from vendors along the tracks at intermediary stops. Station bars often have a good variety of takeaway travellers' fare; consider at least investing in a plastic bottle of mineral water, since there's no drinking water on the trains.

Besides trains and bars, Italian stations offer other **facilities**. Most have a *deposito*, where you can leave your bags for hours or days for a small fee. The larger ones have porters (who charge about €2.50 per piece) and some even have luggage trolleys; major stations have an *albergo diurno* ('day hotel', where you can take a shower, get a shave and haircut, etc.), information offices, currency exchanges open at weekends (not at the most advantageous rates, however), hotel-finding and reservation services, kiosks with foreign newspapers, restaurants, etc.

You can also arrange to have a rental car awaiting you at your destination – Avis, Hertz, Autotrans and Maggiore are the firms that provide this service.

The Parma–Suzzara Rail Line

The only other railroad in the area is the little **Ferrovia Parma-Suzzara**, the *Trenino di Don Camillo*, which crosses the Po valley from Parma to Comacchio, by way of Brescello, Gualieri, Guasalla, Suzzara, Bondeno, Ferrara and Osellato; for information and schedules, **t** 800 915 030 (free number; only from Italy).

A second line (run by the FS) is **La Faentina** from Florence to Faenza to Ravenna, an old trans-Apennine line that was destroyed by the Germans in the war. It was reopened in 1999, and the locomotives (sometimes the old steam ones) chug along in leisurely fashion through the quiet countryside, offering a chance to drink in the scenery. For further information, contact local tourist offices or Stazione di Borgo San Lorenzo, **t** (055) 845 9116.

By Coach and Bus

Inter-city **coach** travel can be quicker than train travel, but also a bit more expensive. The system really comes into its own for that small minority of people who want to see the country without the hassles of a car. Italy's system is admirable; coaches reach even the smallest villages; they're reliable and services are usually arranged to make connections possible to more distant points. In rural regions they are the only means of public transport and are well used, with frequent schedules. Coaches, generally painted blue, almost always depart from the vicinity of the train station, centralized in a *Stazione Autobus, Stazione Autolinee* or *Autostazione*, and tickets usually need to be purchased before you get on; if there isn't a ticket booth, they'll be on sale in one or more of the nearby bars. If you can't get a ticket before the coach leaves, get on anyway and ask the driver for one. Note that the bases for all country bus lines are the provincial capitals.

City buses, which are almost always painted orange, are the traveller's friend. Most cities label routes well; all charge flat fees for rides within the city limits and immediate suburbs, at the time of writing around €1.

Bus tickets must always be purchased before you get on, either at a tobacconist's, a newspaper kiosk, in bars, or from ticket machines near the main stops.

Once you get on, 'obliterate' (validate) your ticket in the machines in the front or back of the bus, so that your ticket is stamped with the date or time of travel; controllers stage random checks to make sure you've punched your ticket. Fines for cheaters are about €40.

By Taxi

Taxi meters start at €2.33 plus extras, and add €0.78 per km. There is a minimum charge of €4. Each piece of baggage will cost €1.04 extra, and there are surcharges for trips outside the city limits, trips between 10pm and 6am, and trips on Sundays and holidays.

By Car

In the cities, a car is the last thing you want or need, but for dipping into the Apennines and touring the local castles it's the most convenient way to go if you want to see a lot in a hurry. As Italy becomes a more car-orientated society, more and more hotels and restaurants are located on the outskirts of towns or in the country. In Emilia-Romagna, though, the city centres still have plenty.

In all the major cities, a car is only a liability. First of all, in town centres, **parking** is always a problem. Some areas are marked *zona disco blu* for the blue time discs, obtainable in many shops and fixed inside the windscreen, where you set the hour of your arrival and get an hour or two of parking. Elsewhere an old gent with a book of receipts will shamble up to your car and hit you for €1 or so, or there may be a parking ticket machine; blue stripes on the pavement instead of white always mean pay parking. Worse than parking, sometimes, can be simply driving. The Italian *centro storico* was just not made for cars. Often, sensibly, it is closed to them; all the cities of Emilia-Romagna have extensive **ZTLs** (*zona traffico limitato*, pronounced 'zittle') and completely pedestrianized areas inside these. The red circle sign at the entrance will have a notice underneath explaining hours and vehicles forbidden, which are usually complex. Though they are well respected, enforcement isn't very strict, and exceptions are usual if unloading at a hotel.

Even when you can get into the centre, finding that the main street soon funnels into a 12ft passage full of pedestrians makes driving lose much of its charm. One false move in smaller towns, especially in the mountains, and you'll be driving through an alley where your car gets stuck between the walls. Give these fine old towns, and their residents, a break, and leave your beast in the car parks thoughtfully signposted around the walls. Another feature of motoring life in towns with too many cars and too little space (in effect, all of them), is the early **evening rush hour**, a daily festival of immobility even in villages of 5,000 people. It lasts from about 4.30 to 7 or 8pm, or even later. On the other hand, if you want to look around a town from your car, do it at 1–3pm, when the Italians are dining and digesting. Make sure you watch out for kids on scooters; they don't watch out for themselves.

Third-party **insurance** is a minimum requirement in Italy. Obtain a Green Card from your insurer, which gives proof that you are fully covered. Also, get hold of a **European Accident Statement** form, which may simplify things if you are unlucky enough to have an accident. Always insist on a full translation of any statement you are asked to sign.

Fuel (petrol or gasoline is *benzina*, unleaded *benzina senza piombo*, and diesel *gasolio*) is still expensive in Italy (around €1.30 per litre), although at the time of writing, prices are comparable to France or Germany. Many filling stations close for lunch in the afternoon, and few stay open late at night, though you can usually find a 'self-service' where you feed a machine nice smooth notes. Motorway (*autostrada*) tolls are quite high. Rest stops and filling stations along the motorways stay open 24 hours.

Italians are famously anarchic behind a wheel, at least when they can find an open road (very few drive dangerously in a town centre). The only way to beat the locals is to join them by adopting an assertive and constantly alert driving style. North Americans used to leisurely speeds and gentler road manners may find the Italian interpretation of the highway code stressful. **Speed limits** (generally ignored) are 130kph on motorways, 110kph on main highways, 90kph on secondary roads, and 50kph in built-up areas. Speeding fines may be as much as €250, or €50 for jumping a red light.

The **Automobile Club of Italy** (ACI) is a good friend to the foreign motorist. Besides having useful information and tips, they can be reached from anywhere by dialling **t** 116 – also use this number if you have to find the nearest service station. If you need major

Major Car Hire Companies

Avis, UK **t** 0870 010 0287, *www.avis.co.uk*; USA **t** 1-99 100 133, *www.avis.com*.
Hertz, UK **t** 0870 844 8844, *www.hertz.co.uk*; USA **t** 800 654 3001, *www.hertz.co.uk*.

repairs, the ACI can make sure the prices charged are according to their guidelines.

Hiring a Car

Hiring a car (*autonoleggio*) is simple but not particularly cheap – Italy has some of the highest car hire rates in Europe. A small car (Fiat Punto or similar) with unlimited mileage and collision damage waiver, including tax, will set you back around €85 per day although, if you hire the car for over three days, this will decrease slightly pro rata. The minimum age limit is usually 25 (sometimes 23) and the driver must have held their licence for over a year – this will have to be produced, along with the driver's passport and credit card, when hiring the car. Most major rental companies have offices in airports or train stations, though it may be worthwhile checking prices of local firms. If you need a car for longer than three weeks, leasing may well be more economical.

Taking all things into account, it probably makes quite a bit more sense to arrange your car hire with a domestic firm before making your trip and, in particular, to check out fly-drive discounts. This is usually the cheaper option. Prices tend towards the €35 per day mark, often with large discounts for a second week of hire. The deposit is also usually waived.

By Motorbike or Bicycle

Mopeds, Vespas and scooters are the vehicles of choice for a great many Italians. You will see them everywhere. In the cities this is an ubiquity born of necessity; when driving space is limited, two wheels are always better than four. However, in Italy, riding a two-wheeler often seems to be as much a form of cultural and social expression as it does a means of getting from A to B.

Watch the traffic on a busy town corner for any length of time and certain trends will become apparent. For one thing, there is a clear generational control at work over the individual's choice of machine. The young prefer chic Italian lines, Vespas, Lambrettas and the like, which they parade self-consciously through the town's main drags. Older members of society plump for mopeds, the type you can actually pedal should you feel so inclined.

Choosing your machine, however, is only the first stage of this cultural process; it then becomes necessary to master the Italian way of riding. This almost invariably means dispensing with a crash helmet, despite the fact that they are compulsory, so as to be able to perfect the method of riding in as laid-back a style as possible while still achieving a positively alarming rate of speed. Riding sidesaddle, while on the phone, while wearing sunglasses, while smoking, while holding a dog or small child under one arm: all of these unnerving methods have their determined and expert adherents.

Despite the obvious dangers of this means of transport (especially if you choose to do it Italian-style), there are clear benefits to moped-riding in Italy. For one thing it is cheaper than car hire – costs for a *motorino* (moped) range from about €30 per day, Vespas (scooters) somewhat more (from about €50) – and can prove an excellent way of covering a town's sites in a limited space of time. Furthermore, because Italy is such a scooter-friendly place, most car drivers are more conditioned to their presence and so are less likely to hurtle into them when taking corners. Nonetheless, you should only consider hiring a moped if you have ridden one before (Italy's alarming traffic is no place to learn) and, despite local examples, you should always wear a helmet. Also, be warned, some travel insurance policies exclude claims resulting from scooter or motorbike accidents. You must be at least 14 to hire one.

In many of the cities in Emilia-Romagna, everyone, including coiffed and bejewelled women in fur coats, gets around by bicycle: it helps them work off some of the tortellini, and the flat terrain makes pedalling a doddle. It's usually easy to join them; if your hotel doesn't give or rent them out, they can tell you where to find one. Hire prices range from about €10 per day; to buy one costs upwards of €150. Many cities, such as Modena, run municipal bike rentals – some even offer them free to tourists. There will often be a cycle depot at the train station; bikes can easily be transported by train, either with you or within a couple of days. Apply at the baggage office (*ufficio bagagli*).

Where to Stay

Accommodation in Italy is classified by the Provincial Tourist Boards. Price control, however, has been abandoned since 1992. Hotels now set their own tariffs, which means that in some places prices have rocketed. At the top end of the market, Italy has a number of exceptionally sybaritic hotels, often in historic buildings, furnished and decorated with real panache. Good-value, interesting accommodation in cities can be hard to find, but there are plenty of simple, older-style hotels and *pensioni*. In many cases, you can now book your hotel online.

Hotels and Guesthouses

Italian *alberghi* come in all shapes and sizes. They are rated from one to five stars, depending on the facilities they offer (not their character, style or charm). The star ratings are some indication of price levels, but for tax reasons not all hotels choose to advertise themselves at the rating to which they are entitled, so you may find a modestly rated hotel just as comfortable (or more so) than a higher rated one. Conversely, you may find a hotel offers few stars in hopes of attracting budget-conscious travellers, but charges just as much as a higher-rated neighbour. *Pensioni* are generally more modest establishments, though nowadays the distinction between these and ordinary hotels is becoming blurred. *Locande* are traditionally an even more basic form of hostelry, but these days the term may denote somewhere fairly chic. Other inexpensive accommodation is sometimes known as *osterie*, *alloggi* or *affittacamere*, rooms over bars in small towns. You'll never find them by looking; ask around or at the tourist office (they can give you a list of b&bs and *affittacamere*). There are usually plenty of cheap dives around city railway stations; for something more salubrious, head for the town centre or the fringes near a motorway. Asking locals about hotels is hardly foolproof (they have their own beds; they don't need hotels). The tourist office does know, and if they're not open ask a cop (a local cop, not a Carabiniere; they don't know anything about anything).

If you're picky about hotels and prices, stop in at any tourist office and ask for an *elenco degli alberghi*. Nearly every province publishes a complete list of accommodation, with all the necessary information and correct prices – they'll usually only cover that province, so while you are travelling make sure you know where the boundaries are.

Price lists, by law, must be posted on the door of every room, along with meal prices and any extra charges, such as air conditioning. Many hotels display two or three different rates, depending on the season. Low-season rates may be about a third lower than peak-season tariffs. Some resort hotels close down altogether for several months a year, while in August city hotels may close; we've tried to note them all. During high season you should always book ahead to be sure of a room (an email reservation may be less frustrating to organize than one by post). If you have paid a deposit, your booking is valid under Italian law, but don't expect it to be refunded if you have to cancel.

Tourist offices do not generally make reservations although major railway stations often have accommodation-booking desks; inevitably, a fee is charged. If you arrive without a reservation, inspect the room (and bathroom) before you book, and check the tariff carefully. Italian hoteliers may legally alter their rates twice a year, so printed tariffs and tourist board lists (and prices in this book) may be out of date. Hoteliers who wilfully overcharge should be reported to

Accommodation Price Ranges

This guide lists hotels according to these ranges, for a double room with bath in high season:

luxury	€€€€€	over €230
expensive	€€€€	€150–230
moderate	€€€	€100–150
inexpensive	€€	€60–100
budget	€	up to €60

the tourist office. You will be asked for your passport for registration; they should give it back as soon as they fill out the form for the police.

Prices listed in this guide are for double rooms; you can expect to pay about two-thirds the rate for single occupancy, though in high season you may be charged the full double rate in a popular beach resort. Extra beds are usually charged at about a third more of the room rate. Rooms without private bathrooms generally charge 20–30% less, and most offer discounts for children sharing parents' rooms, or children's meals (many older posh hotels still have a room or two without a full bath at cheaper rates; you can always ask about these). A *camera singola* (single room) may cost anything from about €25 upwards. Double rooms (*camera doppia*) go from about €40 to €150 or more. If you want a double bed, you will need to specify a *camera matrimoniale*.

Breakfast is usually optional in hotels, though sometimes it's included in the rates. You can usually get better value by eating breakfast in a bar or café.

In high season you may be expected to take half-board in resorts, and one-night stays may be refused.

Hostels and Budget Accommodation

There aren't many **youth hostels** (*alberghi* or *ostelli per la gioventù*) in the region covered by this book, but they are generally pleasant and sometimes located in historic buildings.

Having an international membership card will enable you to stay in any of them. You can obtain these in advance from youth hostel associations (*see* box above). Cards can also usually be purchased on the spot in many hostels if you don't already have one. Rates are usually somewhere between €7 and €10, normally including breakfast.

Discounts are available for senior citizens, and some family rooms are available. You generally have to check in after 5pm, and pay for your room before 9am. Hostels usually close for most of the daytime, and many operate a curfew. During the spring, noisy school parties cram hostels for field trips. In the summer, it's advisable to book ahead. Contact the hostels directly.

Youth Hostel Associations

For a list of 'official' European hostels, see *www.iyhf.org*) or *www.hostels.com* (which also lists private ones); the Italian body is the **Associazione Italiana Alberghi per la Gioventù**, *www.ostellionline.org*.

Australia: Australian Youth Hostel Association, 422 Kent Street, Sydney, NSW 2000, **t** (02) 9261 1111, *www.yha.com.au*.

Canada: Hostelling International Canada, 205 Catherine Street, Suite 500, Ottawa ON K2P 1C3, **t** (613) 237 7889, *www.hihostels.ca*.

UK: Youth Hostels Association of England and Wales (YHA), Trevelyan House, Dimple Road, Matlock, Derbyshire DE4 3YH, **t** 0870 770 8868, *www.yha.org.uk*.

USA: Hostelling International USA, 8401 Colesville Road, Suite 600, Silver Spring,MD 20910, **t** (301) 495 1240, *www.hiusa.org*.

Villas and Flats

If you're travelling in a group or with a family, self-catering can be the ideal way to experience Emilia-Romagna. There are literally thousands of holiday apartments in the coastal resorts, and any of their tourist offices would be happy to send you a list of agencies.

The National Tourist Office has lists of UK and USA firms which rent places on a weekly or fortnightly basis. If you have set your heart on a particular area, write to its tourist office for a list of agencies and owners, who will send brochures. Maid service is included in the more glamorous villas; ask whether bed linen and towels are provided.

Some larger operators are listed on p.84.

Rural Accommodation: *Agriturismo*

For a breath of rural seclusion, the Italians tend to head for a spell on a **working farm**. *Agriturismo*, as they call it, is an idea that has grown tremendously in the last decade. Most feature bed-and-breakfast arrangements that range from the basic to rooms in restored medieval towers – some of the more interesting places are listed in the text. Sometimes the real pull is a restaurant in which you can sample some home-grown produce. Outdoor activities may include riding, fishing and mountain biking. Staying on such properties can also be a good way to meet Italians, especially if you speak Italian.

This branch of the tourist industry is run by **Agriturist**. It has grown in recent years, but prices are still reasonable. Local tourist offices have details of *agriturismo*.

Agriturist, Corso V. Emanuele 101, 00186 Rome, **t** (06) 685 2337, *www.agriturist.it*.

Turismo Verde, Via Mariano Fortuny 20, 00196 Rome, **t** (06) 324 0111, *www.turismoverde.it*.

Camping

The coast of Romagna concentrates the campsites in the region, and in August they are at bursting point. A list of local sites is available from any regional tourist office, but for a complete list with full details for all of Italy, pick up the Italian Touring Club's *Campeggi e Villaggi Turistici*, available in Italian bookshops.

You can also obtain an abbreviated list free from the Centro Internazionale Prenotazioni Federcampeggio, Casella Postale 23, 50042, Calenzano (Firenze), **t** (055) 882 391, *www.federcampeggio.it* (Italian only); request their booking forms as well to reserve a place – note that this is essential in the height of summer.

Camping fees vary according to the facilities, but will usually be around €3–10 per adult and €2–8 per child; €4–20 per tent/caravan and €2–7 per car. A car-borne couple could therefore pay as much at a well-equipped campsite as in an inexpensive hotel.

Unofficial camping is not really recommended, and if you attempt it, you may well attract a stern rebuke from the local police.

Tour Operators

In the UK

Abercrombie & Kent, St George's House, Ambrose Street, Cheltenham, Glos GL0 3LG, **t** 0845 070 0610, *www.abercrombiekent.co.uk*. City breaks in all major cities.

Ace Study Tours, Babraham, Cambridge CB22 3AP, **t** (01223) 835 055, *www.study-tours.org*. Cultural tours in Bologna and the Marches.

Arblaster & Clarke Wine Tours, Farnham Road, West Liss, Petersfield, Hants GU33 6JQ, **t** (01730) 893 344, *www.arblasterandclarke.com*. Annual 'Gourmet Northern Italy' tour in November, staying in 4–5-star accommodation in Reggio Emilia with wine- and food-tasting excursions to Bologna, Parma and Modena.

ATG Oxford, 69–71 Banbury Road, Oxford OX2 6PJ, **t** (01865) 315 678, *www.atg-oxford.co.uk*. Walking and cycling holidays along continuous routes.

Brompton Travel, 3 Hinchley Way, Hinchley Wood, Esher, Surrey KT10 0BD, **t** (020) 8398 3672, *www.bromptontravel.co.uk*. Organizers of tailor-made trips, city breaks and opera tours.

The Caravan Club, East Grinstead House, East Grinstead, West Sussex, RH19 1UA, **t** (01342) 326 944, *www.caravanclub.co.uk*. Arranges advance booking and pitch reservation at caravan sites throughout the area.

Fine Art Travel, 15 Savile Row, London W1S 3PJ, **t** (020) 7437 8553, *www.fineartravel.co.uk*. Recreates the spirit of the Grand Tour, staying in private villas and palazzi.

Italiatour, 9 Whyteleafe Business Village, Whyteleafe Hill, Whyteleafe, Surrey CR3 0AT, **t** (01883) 621 900, *www.italiatour.co.uk*. Options include fly-drive holidays between the cities of Emilia-Romagna.

Italian Institute, 39 Belgrave Square, London SW1X 8NX, **t** (020) 7235 1461, *www. icilondon. esteri.it*, or 686 Park Avenue, New York NY 10021, **t** (212) 879 4242, *www.iicnewyork. esteri.it*. The main source of information on courses for foreigners in Italy.

Kirker, 4 Waterloo Court, 10 Theed Street, London SE1 8ST, **t** 0870 112 3333, *www. kirkerholidays.com*. Short breaks in Bologna and tailor-made tours.

Magic of Italy, 227 Shepherds Bush Road, London W6 7AS, **t** 0870 888 0288, *www. magictravelgroup.co.uk*. Tailor-made breaks in 3–5-star luxury hotels, self-catering villas and converted farmhouses.

Martin Randall Travel, Voysey House, Barley Mow Passage, Chiswick, London W4 4GF, **t** (020) 8742 3355, *www.martinrandall.com*. Offering a 7-day tailor-made cultural tour of the Via Emilia in groups.

Prospect Music and Art Tours, 94–104 John Wilson Park, Whitstable, Kent CT5 3QZ,

t (01227) 773 545, *www.prospecttours.com*. Offers specialist holidays devoted to figures such as Dante and Piero della Francesca.

Ramblers, Box 43, Lemsford Mill, Lemsford Village, Welwyn Garden City, Hertfordshire AL8 7TR, **t** (01707) 331 133, *www.ramblersholidays.co.uk*. Walking holidays. **Simply Tuscany and Umbria**, Kings Place, Wood Street, Kingston-upon-Thames, Surrey KT1 1SG, **t** (020) 8541 2222, *www.simplytravel.com*. Offers tailor-made itineraries and a range of courses on art, architecture and vegetarian cookery, as well as balloon flights and painting holidays.

In the USA and Canada

Abercrombie & Kent, Suite 212, 1520 Kensington Rd, Oak Brook IL 60523 2156, **t** 800 554 7016 *www.abercrombiekent.com*. City breaks and walking holidays.

Bike Riders' Tours, PO Box 130254, Boston, MA 02113, **t** 800 473 7040, *www.bikeriderstours.com*. Organizers of 'Roman Roads in Emilia-Romagna', a 5-day cycling tour.

Butterfield & Robinson, 70 Bond Street, Suite 300, Toronto ON M5B 1X3, **t** 866 551 9090, 1-800 678 1147, *www.butterfield.com*. Six-day biking holiday down the Po valley.

CIT Tours, 875 3rd Ave, mezz. level, New York NY 10022, **t** 1-800 CIT-TOUR, *www.cittours.travel.com*; and, in Canada, 7007 Islington Avenue, Suite 205, Woodbridge ON L4L 4T5, **t** 800 387 0711, *www.cittours-canada.com*. Custom tours.

Europe Train Tours, 2485 Jennings Road, Olin NC 28660, **t** (USA) 800-551-2085; (Canada) 800 361-RAIL. Escorted tours by train and car.

Italiatour, 666 5th Avenue, New York NY 10103, **t** 800 845 3365 and (Canada) 888 515 5245, *www.italiatourusa.com*. Fly-drive holidays and tours organized by Alitalia.

Maupintour, 2688 South Rainbow Boulevard, Las Vegas NV 89146, **t** 800 255 4266, *www.maupintour.com*. Escorted 12–18-day tours through the whole of Italy.

Travel Concepts, 191 Worcester Road, Princeton MA 01541, **t** (978) 464 0411. Tours offering appreciation of wine and food.

University Vacations, Writer's Corner, 3660 Bougainvillaea Road, Coconut Grove FL 33133-6505, **t** (305) 567 2904 or 800 792 0100, *info@universityvacations.com*. Courses on history, philosophy, art history and literature.

Worldwide PO Box 1166, Milwaukee, WI 53201, *www.worldwide.edu*. Database listing educational organizations around the world.

In Italy

Cook Italy, t 00 39 (from outside Italy) 349 007 8298, *www.cookitaly.com*. Culinary tours and one-day cookery courses in Bologna.

Self-catering Tour Operators

In the UK and Ireland

There is no shortage of choice. Try studying the small ads in the Sunday papers or magazines, or search on the Internet.

Inghams, 10–18 Putney Hill, London SW15 6AX, **t** (020) 8780 4400, *www.inghams.co.uk*.

Interhome, 383 Richmond Road, Twickenham, Middlesex TW1 2EF, **t** (020) 8891 1294, *www.interhome.co.uk*.

Italianvillas.com, *www.italianvillas.com*.

Magic of Italy, 227 Shepherds Bush Road, London W6 7AS, **t** (020) 8748 7575, *www.magictravelgroup.co.uk*.

The Individual Travellers, Spring Mill, Earby, Barnoldswick, Lancashire, BB94 0AA, **t** 08700 780 193, *www.indiv-travellers.com*.

In the USA

At Home Abroad, 405 East 56th Street, Suite 6H, New York NY 10022-2466, **t** (212) 421 9165, *www.athomeabroadinc.com*.

CIT Tours, 15 West 44th Street, New York NY 10036, **t** 4-800 CIT-TOUR, *www.cit-tours.com*. Also fly-drive rental car packages.

Rentvillas.com, t 1-800 726 6702, *www.rentvillas.com*.

Hideaways International, 767 Islington Street, Portsmouth NH 03801, **t** 877 843 4433, *www.hideaways.com*.

Homeowners International, 1133 Broadway, New York NY 10010, **t** (212) 691 2361.

RAVE (Rent-a-Vacation Everywhere), 135 Meigs Street, Rochester, New York NY 14607, **t** (716) 246 0760.

Practical A–Z

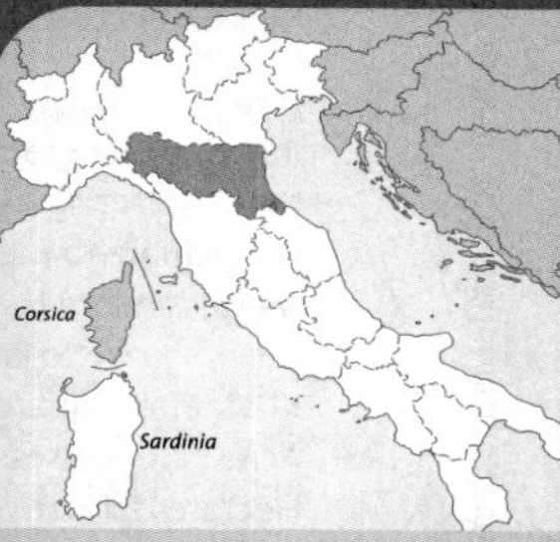

06

Imperial–Metric Conversions

Length (multiply by)

Inches to centimetres: 2.54
Centimetres to inches: 0.39
Feet to metres: 0.3
Metres to feet: 3.28
Yards to metres: 0.91
Metres to yards: 1.1
Miles to kilometres: 1.61
Kilometres to miles: 0.62

Area (multiply by)

Inches square to centimetres square: 6.45
Centimetres square to inches square: 0.15
Feet square to metres square: 0.09
Metres square to feet square: 10.76
Miles square to kilometres square: 2.59
Kilometres square to miles square: 0.39
Acres to hectares: 0.40
Hectares to acres: 2.47

Weight (multiply by)

Ounces to grams: 28.35
Grammes to ounces: 0.035
Pounds to kilograms: 0.45
Kilograms to pounds: 2.2
Stones to kilograms: 6.35
Kilograms to stones: 0.16
Tons (UK) to kilograms: 1,016
Kilograms to tons (UK): 0.0009
1 UK ton (2,240lbs) = 1.12 US tonnes (2,000lbs)

°C	°F
40	104
35	95
30	86
25	77
20	68
15	59
10	50
5	41
-0	32
-5	23
-10	14
-15	5

Volume (multiply by)

Pints (UK) to litres: 0.57
Litres to pints (UK): 1.76
Quarts (UK) to litres: 1.13
Litres to quarts (UK): 0.88
Gallons (UK) to litres: 4.55
Litres to gallons (UK): 0.22
1 UK pint/quart/gallon = 1.2 US pints/quarts/gallons

Temperature

Celsius to Fahrenheit: multiply by 1.8 then add 32

Fahrenheit to Celsius: subtract 32 then multiply by 0.55

Italy Information

Time Differences

Country: + 1hr GMT; + 6hrs EST

Daylight saving from last weekend in March to end of October

Dialling Codes

Italy country code 39

To Italy from: UK, Ireland, New Zealand 00 / USA, Canada 011 / Australia 0011 then dial 39 and the full number including the initial zero

From Italy to: UK 00 44; Ireland 00 353; USA, Canada 001; Australia 00 61; New Zealand 00 64 then the number without the initial zero

Directory enquiries: 12

International directory enquiries: 176

Emergency Numbers

Police: 112/113
Ambulance: 118
Fire: 115
Car breakdown: 116

Embassy Numbers in Italy

UK: 081 423 8911; **Ireland** 06 678 2541; **USA**: 081 583 8111; **Canada** 081 401 338; **Australia** 06 852 721; **New Zealand** 06 440 2928

Shoe Sizes

Europe	UK	USA
35	2½ / 3	4
36	3 / 3½	4½ / 5
37	4	5½ / 6
38	5	6½
39	5½ / 6	7 / 7½
40	6 / 6½	8 / 8½
41	7	9 / 9½
42	8	9½ / 10
43	9	10½
44	9½ / 10	11
45	10½	12
46	11	12½ / 13

Women's Clothing

Europe	UK	USA
32	6	2
34	8	4
36	10	6
38	12	8
40	14	10
42	16	12
44	18	14

Crime and the Police

Police: t 113

In a recent EU study on the incidence of crime, Italy came in 11th of the 15 nations, well below Britain and most north European lands. And political terrorism, once the scourge of Italy, has nearly disappeared in recent years. There is a fair amount of petty crime – purse-snatching, pickpocketing, minor thievery of the white-collar kind (always check your change), car break-ins and theft – but violent crime is rare. Nearly all mishaps can be avoided with adequate precautions. Scooter-borne purse-snatchers can be foiled if you stay on the inside of the pavement and keep a firm hold on your property (sling your bag-strap across your body, don't leave it dangling from one shoulder). Remember that pickpockets strike in crowded buses or trams and gatherings; don't carry too much cash, and split it so you won't lose the lot at once. In cities (especially Bologna) and popular tourist sites, beware groups of scruffy-looking women with babies or children with pieces of cardboard, apparently begging. They use distraction techniques to perfection. The smallest and most innocent-looking child is generally the most skilful pickpocket. If you are targeted, grab hold of any vulnerable possessions or pockets and shout furiously. (Italian passers-by or plain-clothes police will often come to your assistance if they realize what is happening.) Be extra careful in train stations, don't leave valuables in hotel rooms, and always park your car in garages, guarded lots or on well-lit streets, with portable temptations well out of sight. Purchasing small quantities of soft drugs for personal consumption is technically legal in Italy, though what constitutes a small quantity is unspecified, and if the police don't like you to begin with, it will probably be enough to get you into trouble.

Small towns and rural areas are the preserve of the black-uniformed national police, the *Carabinieri*. Local matters in cities are usually in the hands of the *Polizia Urbana*; the nattily dressed *Vigili Urbani* concern themselves with directing traffic and issuing parking fines. If you need to summon any of them, dial **t** 113.

Restaurant Price Categories

This guide divides restaurants into the following categories (for full meal, per person, but not including wine):

very expensive	€€€€	over €60
expensive	€€€	€40–60
moderate	€€	€30–40
inexpensive	€	below €30

Eating Out

The bill (*conto*) will include the bread and cover charge (*pane e coperto*, between €1 and €2.50), and maybe a 15% service charge. This is often included (*servizio compreso*); if not, the bill will say *servizio non compreso*, and you'll have to do your own arithmetic. Additional tipping is discretionary. In many places you'll find restaurants offering a *menu turistico* – full, set meals of usually meagre inspiration for €10–15. More imaginative chefs often offer a *menu di degustazione* – a set-price gourmet meal that allows you to taste their daily specialities and seasonal dishes. Both of these are cheaper than if you had ordered the same food *à la carte*.

When you leave a restaurant you will be given a receipt (*scontrino* or *ricevuta fiscale*) which by law you must take with you out of the door and carry for at least 60m. There is a slim chance the tax police (*Guardia di Finanza*) may have their eye on you and the restaurant, and if you don't have a receipt they could slap you with a heavy fine. There was a wave of this bureaucratic silliness in the early 1990s, which ended when the police tried to prosecute an eight-year-old boy who bought an ice cream on the beach and didn't take away his *scontrino*. To the applause of the Italian nation, the courts ruled in his favour, as his swimming trunks didn't have any pockets.

See also **Food and Drink**, pp.55–66.

Electricity

Italy uses 220 volts. Travellers from some countries, including the UK, will need to take an adaptor to use their own electrical gear; these are easily found at airports and shops back home; some Italian plugs and sockets are non-standard however. For details of which plug to use, see *www.kropla.com*.

Health and Emergencies

Ambulance: t 118
Fire: t 115

In an **emergency**, dial **t** 115 for fire and **t** 118 for an ambulance (*ambulanza*) or to find the nearest hospital (*ospedale*). Less serious problems can be treated at a *Pronto Soccorso* (casualty/first-aid department), at any hospital clinic (*ambulatorio*) or at a local health unit (*Unità Sanitaria Locale* – USL).

Airports and main railway stations have **first-aid posts**. If you have to pay for any health treatment, make sure you get a receipt, so that you can make any claims for reimbursement later. Most Italian doctors speak at least rudimentary English, but if you can't find one who does, contact your embassy or consulate for a list of English-speaking doctors. Standards of health care in the north are generally higher than in the deep south.

Dispensing **chemists**, or pharmacies (*farmacia*), are generally open 8.30–1pm and 4–8pm, at the resorts until 10pm in the summer. Pharmacists are trained to give advice for minor ills. Any large town will have a *farmacia* that stays open 24 hours; others take turns to stay open (the address rota is posted in the windows).

For information about doctors, health insurance, the European Health Insurance Card (EHIC), vaccinations and other health matters you need to know before you travel, *see* **Planning Your Trip**, p.73.

Internet

You can find Internet cafés even in smaller towns. There is also Internet access in many hotel rooms and main rail stations. Most email accounts have a webmail facility so you can log into a website and pick up your mail as you travel: if you do not know the web address (URL) of your webmail, ask your Internet Service Provider.

National Holidays

Banks and shops are closed on the following national holidays; the museums tend to stay open Sunday hours, except for Christmas and New Year and 1 May. In addition to these general holidays, many towns also take their patron saint's day off.

1 January New Year's Day, *Capodanno*.

6 January Epiphany; better known to Italians as the day of *La Befana* – a kindly witch who brings the *bambini* the toys Santa Claus (Babbo Natale) somehow forgot.

Easter Monday Usually pretty dull.

25 April Liberation Day – even duller.

1 May Labour Day – lots of parades, speeches, picnics, music and drinking.

2 June Festa della Repubblica.

15 August Assumption, *Ferragosto*; the biggest of them all – woe to the innocent traveller on the road or train!

1 November All Saints' Day, *Ognissanti*; liveliest at the cemeteries.

8 December Immaculate Conception of the Virgin Mary – a dull one.

25 December Christmas Day.

26 December *Santo Stefano*, St Stephen's Day.

Opening Hours

Most of Emilia-Romagna closes down from 1pm until 3 or 4pm, to eat and properly digest the main meal of the day. Afternoon hours are 4–7, often 5–8 in the hot summer months. Bars are often the only places open during the early afternoon. In any case, don't be surprised if you find anything unexpectedly closed (or open for that matter), whatever its official stated hours.

Banks

Banking hours vary, but core times in large towns are usually Mon–Fri 8.30am–1pm and 3–4pm, closed weekends and on local and national holidays (*see* opposite). Outside normal hours, you will usually be able to find somewhere to change money, and there are plenty of ATMs.

Churches

Italy's churches are a prime target for art thieves and as a consequence the smaller or more remote ones are usually locked when there isn't a sacristan or caretaker to keep an eye on things. We do not list hours for most churches, since they tend to be rather informal, but all churches close in the afternoon at roughly the same hours as the shops (*12 or 1 to 4 or 5pm*), and the little ones can be closed permanently. Emilia-Romagna is a region of badly lit churches full of good frescoes; always have a pocketful of coins for the light machines in churches, or whatever work of art you came to inspect will remain clouded in ecclesiastical gloom.

Don't do your visiting during services, and don't come to see paintings and statues in churches the week preceding Easter – you will probably find them covered with mourning shrouds.

In general, Sunday afternoons and Mondays are dead periods for the sightseer – you may want to make them your travelling days. Places without specified opening hours can usually be visited on request – but it is best to go before 1pm. We have listed the hours of important sights and museums, and specified which ones charge admission.

Entrance charges are not exorbitant; few will be over €3, and others may be completely free. EU citizens under 18 and over 65 get free admission to state museums, with identification.

Museums and Galleries

With two or three works of art per inhabitant (accounts differ), the Italians have a hard time financing the preservation of their national heritage. However, they made a truly impressive effort to get old monuments and museums fixed up and ready for the Jubilee Year of 2000, and you'll see the fruits of this everywhere you go.

Monday is the usual closing day. Note that opening hours on public holidays are usually the same as those on Sundays, though at Christmas and New Year every place is shut.

Offices

Government-run dispensers of red tape (e.g. visa departments) receive supplicants for quite limited periods, usually during the mornings, Mon–Fri, and Thurs afternoons. It pays to get there as soon as they open (or even before) to spare your nerves in an interminable queue. Anyway, take something to read, or write your memoirs.

Shops

Shops usually open Mon–Sat 8am–1pm and 3.30–7.30pm, though hours vary according to season and are shorter in smaller centres. In some large cities hours are longer. Some supermarkets and department stores stay open throughout the day. During summer, shops in seaside resort areas are open daily 7am–midnight.

Post Offices

Dealing with *la posta italiana* has always been a risky, frustrating, time-consuming affair. It is one of the least competent and slowest postal services in Europe, and although it has improved in recent years, it's easy to understand the Italians' love affair with fax machines and email.

Post offices are usually open Mon–Sat 8am–1pm, or until 6 or 7pm in a large city. To have your mail sent poste restante (general delivery; in Italian *Fermo Posta*), have it addressed to the central post office *Fermo Posta* and expect it to take three to four weeks to arrive. Make sure your surname is very clearly written in block capitals. To pick up your mail you must present your passport and pay a nominal charge. Stamps (*francobolli*) may be purchased in post offices or at tobacconists (*tabacchi*, identified by their blue or black signs with a white T). Prices fluctuate. Don't try to mail packages at all, if you value your sanity; take the thing home with you if you can. One alternative, in cities, is to look for stationers' of the *Registri Buffetti* chain. Some of these, and a few other business-oriented shops, are drop-off points for DHL or other private carriers.

You can also have money telegraphed to you through the post office; if all goes well, this can happen in a mere three days, but expect a fair proportion of it to go into commission.

For further information, visit *www.poste.it*.

Shopping

'Made in Italy' has become a byword for style and quality, especially in fashion and leather, but also in home design, ceramics, kitchenware, jewellery, lace and linens, glassware and crystal, chocolates, bells, hats,

Weekend Flea Markets

Weekend flea markets/antique fairs take place on the following monthly schedule:

Wednesday evenings (May–Sept): Cervia.

Friday nights (mid-June to mid-Sept): Brisighella.

First Saturday in the month: San Pietro in Casale.

First Sunday: Budrio (exc Aug); Santarcangelo di Romagna (exc Aug).

First Saturday and Sunday: Ferrara (exc Aug).

Second Saturday and Sunday: Bologna (Piazza Santo Stefano; exc Jan, July and Aug).

Second Sunday: Savigno (exc July and Aug).

Third Saturday and Sunday: Ravenna.

Third Sunday: Fontanellato (exc Jan); Casalecchio (exc July–Aug).

Fourth Saturday and Sunday: Modena; Imola (exc June–July).

Fourth Sunday: Pieve di Cento; San Giovanni in Marignano (July and Aug at night).

art books, Christmas decorations, engravings, hand-made stationery, gold and silverware, bicycles, sports cars, woodworking, liqueurs, aperitifs, coffee machines, gastronomic specialities, and antiques (both reproductions and the real thing). Emilia-Romagna is packed with things to buy and take home: perhaps a Ferrari, Maserati or Lamborghini from Modena province, ceramics from Faenza, Ferrara or Sassuolo, mosaics from Ravenna, olive oil from Brisighella, leather or wrought iron from Bologna, traditional hand-printed linens from Santarcangelo and Gambettola, and lace or wicker baskets throughout the region. But nothing sums up this area so well as food: cheese, the wide variety of *salumi*, pasta, dried *porcini*, wine and liqueurs. Non-EU citizens should save all receipts for Customs on the way home. If you spend over a certain amount in one shop you can get a tax rebate at the airport; participating shops have details.

Sports and Activities

Cycling

In Emilia-Romagna, nearly everyone has a bike, at least on the flat Po plain. Many hotels lend them out to guests, or can tell you where you can hire one. Although the traffic would make general touring between the cities a dismal proposition, there are bike paths laid out through the coastal wetlands. Serious cyclists may like to try the two-week **Coast to Coast** (*Da Costa a Costa*) tour laid out by the regions of Emilia-Romagna and Tuscany, designed to take in the best scenery and sights (and leave time to see them) whether you have a touring or mountain bike: write to the regional tourist office for the detailed map and guide.

Fishing

You don't need a permit for sea-fishing (without an aqualung), but Italy's coastal waters may disappoint. Commercial fishing has depleted stocks to such an extent that the government has declared two- and three-month moratoria. Many freshwater lakes and streams are stocked. To fish in fresh water buy a three-month type D licence for tourists (around €40) from the **Federazione Italiana della Pesca Sportiva**, which has an office in every province, and can tell you about local conditions and restrictions.

Football

Soccer (*calcio*) is a national obsession. All major cities, and most minor ones, have at least one team of some sort. Big-league matches (Bologna and Parma are both in the first division) are played on Sunday afternoons from September to May. Rugby and baseball are also played increasingly.

Golf

Italians are catching on fast to appreciate the delights of biffing a small white ball into a hole in the ground. Write or ring beforehand to check details before turning up at a golf course (*see* list opposite). Most take guests and hire equipment. Emilia-Romagna has 16 courses, ranging from simple par-3 layouts to championship-level links.

Hiking and Mountaineering

These sports are becoming steadily more popular every year. The Apennines now have a good system of way-marked trails and mountain refuges run by the **Italian Alpine Club**, CAI (local branch Via Cesare Battisti 11/a,

Bologna, **t** (051) 234 856, *www.caibo.it*). Walking in high altitudes is generally practicable between May and October, after most of the snow has melted; all the necessary gear – boots, packs, tents, etc. – is readily available in Italy but usually for more money than you'd pay at home.

The major trail in Emilia-Romagna is the **Grande Escursione Appenninica**, a 25-stage trek from the Due Santi Pass to Bocca Trabaria. Shorter, less strenuous walks include the **Grande Circuito della Romagna** (13 stages) or the **Sentiero dei Ducati**, a 9-stage walk from Canossa to Luni.

Riding Holidays

They are now widely available, particularly in the Apennines and Po Delta National Park, often connected to *agriturismi*. For more information, contact the local tourist offices.

Skiing and Winter Sports

Italy has a better reputation for skiing than it once did, though erratic snow cover is always a problem. Emilia-Romagna has 18 ski stations in the Apennines, many with new facilities and extras such as ice rinks, cross-country ski routes and indoor pools. Equipment hire is generally not too expensive, but lift passes and accommodation can push up the cost of a winter holiday, although here it never hits Alpine levels. Keep your eyes open for special deals: for instance Lizzano in Belvedere, **t** (0534) 51052, offers a special deal on a ski pass that includes train and bus transport from Bologna direct to the pistes. Prices are highest during Christmas and New Year holidays, in February and at Easter. Most resorts offer *Settimane Bianche* (White Weeks) – off-season packages at economical rates.

Major Golf Courses

See *www.golfing.it* for a complete list of courses in Italy.

Rimini Golf Club, Via Tenuta Amalia 109, Villa Verucchio, Rimini: **t** (0541) 678 122, *www.riminigolf.com*. Championship course, 6,729 yards, par 72. Lots of water.

Adriatic Golf Club Cervia, Via Jelenia Gora 6, Milano Marittima, (Ravenna): **t** (0544) 992 786, *www.golfcervia.com*. 6,830 yards, par 72. Lots of pines but a little bit cramped.

Golf Club La Torre, Via Limisano 10, Riolo Terme (near Ravenna), **t** (0546) 74035, *riologolf@telez.it*. 6,737 yards, par 72. One hazard is the *calanco*, a curious eroded limestone formation.

Golf Club Argenta, Via Poderi 2, Argenta, Ferrara, **t** (0532) 852 545, *www.argentagolf.it*. 6,889 yards, par 72. On the banks of the Po di Primaro, flat, lots of water and dunes.

C.U.S. Golf Ferrara, Via Gramicia 41, Ferrara, **t** (0532) 708520, *http://web.unife.it/centro/cus/golf*. 9 holes, 2,706 yards, par 33.

Golf Club Cento, Via dei Tigli 4, Cento, **t** (051) 683 0504, *www.golfcento.com* (in Italian only). 9 holes, 2,899 yards, par 3. Double starts optional to make 18 holes.

Golf Club Molino del Pero, Via Molino del Pero 323, Monzuno, Bologna, **t** (051) 677 0506, *molinogolf@tin.it*. 9 holes, 2,854 yards, par 35. Picturesque.

Golf Club Bologna, Via Sabattini 69, Monte San Pietro, Bologna (between Crespellano and Ponte Ronca), **t** (051) 969 100, *www.golfclubbologna.it*. 6,505 yards, par 72. Hilly, wooded.

Golf & Country Club Modena, Via Castelnuovo Rangone 4, Colombaro di Formigine, Modena, **t** (059) 553 482, *www.modenagolf.it*. Championship course, 27 holes, deeply wooded.

Golf Club Matilde di Canossa, Via del Casinazzo 1, San Bartolomeo, Reggio Emilia, **t** (0522) 371 295, *web.tiscali.it/golfcanossa*. 6,814 yards, par 72. Pretty and varied course.

Golf Club La Rocca, Via Campi 8, Sala Baganza, Parma, **t** (0521) 834 037, *www.golflarocca.com*. 6,618 yards, par 71. 8 kilometres from Parma.

Salsomaggiore Golf & Country Club, Case Carancini 105, Loc. Contignaco, **t** (0524) 574 128, *www.salsomaggioregolfclub.com*. 6,334 yards, par 72. Hilly and rough, but a fairly easy course.

Country Club Croara, Croara Nuova di Gazzola (near Bobbio), Piacenza, **t** (0523) 977 105, *golf.croara@ntt.it*. 6,632 yards, par 72. Pretty scenery and lots of variety.

Golf Club Castell' Arquato, Alseno, Piacenza, **t** (0523) 895 544, *golfclubcastellarquato@hotmail.com*. 6,618 yards, par 73. Challenging, with steep narrow fairways.

Golf Club Castello La Bastardina, Agazzano, Piacenza, **t** (0523) 975 373, *www.golf-bastardina.com*. 9 holes, 3,390 yards, par 36. A varied, hilly course on the former grounds of a castle.

Spas

From Salsomaggiore Terme near Piacenza to Brisighella in the Romagna, Emilia-Romagna has a great underground current of hot mineral water that has given rise to a large spa industry, with some 18 spa towns and hundreds of hotels. In Rimini, there's a thalassotherapy centre, **t** (0541) 424 011, *www.riminiterme.com*.

Tennis

Every *comune* has public courts for hire, especially resorts. Private clubs may offer temporary membership, and hotel courts can often be used by non-residents for a fee. Contact local tourist offices for information.

Water Sports

Eighty per cent of all tourists to Emilia-Romagna come to hit the beach, and if you join them you'll find plenty to do. All the usual watersports are popular along the Adriatic – sailing, windsurfing, water-skiing, scuba diving – along with swimming pools, big waterparks for the kids and many other beach activities, especially volleyball.

The seaside resorts are plagued (or blessed, according to your point of view) by that peculiarly Italian phenomenon, the *bagnaio* or *stabilimento balneare*, who parks rigid ranks of sunbeds and brollies all the way along the best stretches of coast, and charges all-comers for the privilege of clean sand and watching your neighbours. You can often find a public beach amidst the concessions, but it will probably be strewn with rubbish. No one bats an eye at topless bathing.

Telephones

Public telephones for international calls may be found in the offices of **Telecom Italia**, Italy's telephone company. They are the only places where you can make reverse-charge calls (*a erre*, collect calls) but be prepared for a wait, as all these calls go through the operator in Rome. Rates for long-distance calls are among the highest in Europe. Calls within Italy are cheapest after 10pm; international calls after 11pm. Most phone booths now take phonecards (*schede telefoniche*), available at tobacconists and newsstands – snap off the small perforated corner or they won't work. In smaller villages, you can usually find *telefoni a scatti*, with a meter on it, in at least one bar (a small commission is generally charged). Try to avoid telephoning from hotels, though this is less of a major rip-off than it used to be: small hotels will usually do it without a mark-up, but others might add 25% to the bill or lots more.

Direct calls may be made by dialling the international prefix (for the UK 00 44, Ireland 00 353, USA and Canada 00 1, Australia 00 61, New Zealand 00 64). If you're calling Italy from abroad, dial 00 39 and then the whole number, including the first zero.

Mobile or cell phones are very widely used. If you are going to make a lot of calls in Italy it might be worth buying a Simcard locally.

Time

Italy is on Central European Time, one hour ahead of Greenwich Mean Time and six hours ahead of Eastern Standard Time. From the last weekend of March to the end of September, Italian Summer Time (daylight saving time) is in effect.

Tipping

If you are in a bar, you can leave small change in the form of copper-coloured coins (1, 2 or 5 cents) if you are standing, and around 30–50 cents if seating. For restaurants, if service is included you do not need to tip; if it isn't, then tip around 10%. For taxis, 10% is the norm.

Toilets

You will only find public toilets in places like train and bus stations, museums and bars. You can always use the toilets in a bar (assuming they have one in the first place); by law they are not permitted to refuse you. Ask for the *bagno*, *toilette* or *gabinetto*; in stations and the smarter bars and cafés, there may be washroom attendants who expect a tip for keeping the place decent. Don't confuse the plurals: *signori* (gents), *signore* (ladies).

Piacenza

Competing with the more famous charms of Parma, Cremona and Milan, Piacenza is the unassuming wallflower of Renaissance art cities, with one of northern Italy's finest cathedrals, a memorable museum, two of the most gallant horses in Italy, and the world's most famous bronze liver.

Unlike most of the provinces in this book, Piacenza's has a wealth of attractions to tempt you out into the countryside. Venerable Bobbio was once the headquarters of Irish monasticism on the continent, a candle in the Dark Age. On the way to Parma are Castell'Arquato, a perfect Tuscan hill town that somehow sneaked over to this side of the Apennines, and the miniature Renaissance cities of Fontanellato and Cortemaggiore. There are plenty of castles, and opera-lovers can trace the career of Giuseppe Verdi around his home town of Busseto.

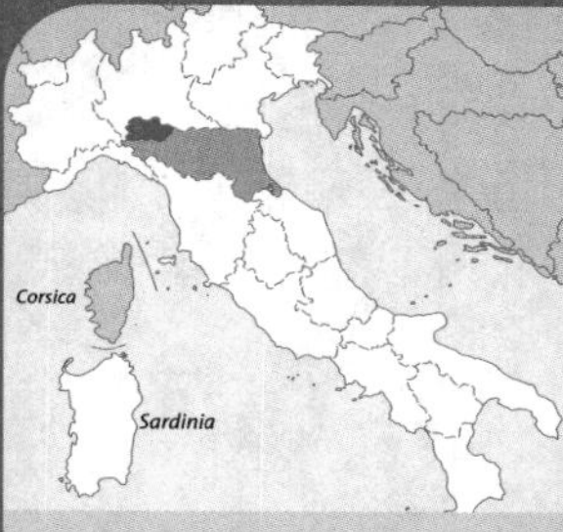

07

1 A Romanesque masterpiece
Piacenza cathedral p.99

2 Four museums in one
Palazzo Farnese museum, Piacenza p.101

3 Medieval hill-top perfection
Castell'Arquato p.107

4 Memories of Giuseppe Verdi
Busseto p.112

5 A miniature Ferrara
Fontanellato p.114

See map overleaf

Around Piacenza

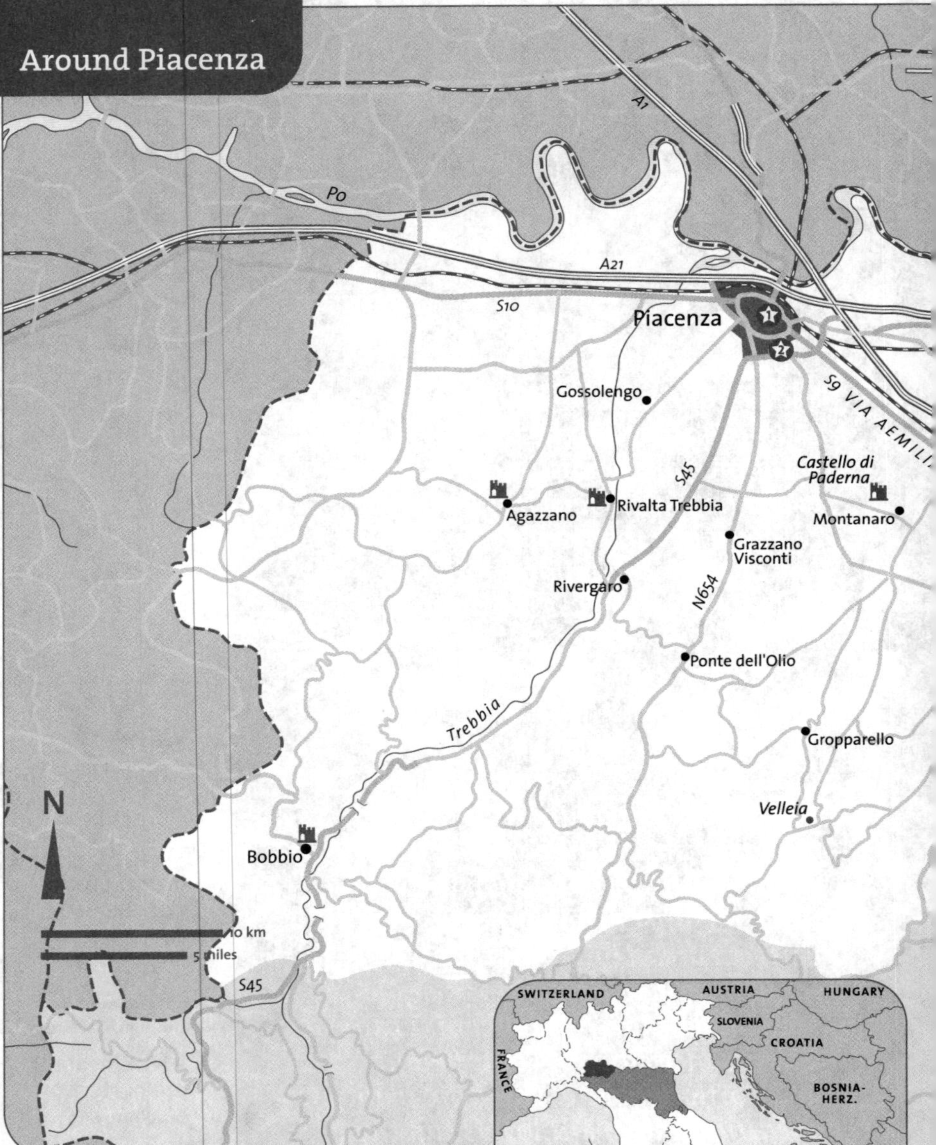
A1
Po
A21
S10
Piacenza
S9 VIA AEMILIA
Gossolengo
S45
Castello di Paderna
Agazzano
Rivalta Trebbia
Montanaro
Grazzano Visconti
Rivergaro
N654
Ponte dell'Olio
Trebbia
Gropparello
Velleia
N
Bobbio
10 km
5 miles
S45

p.143

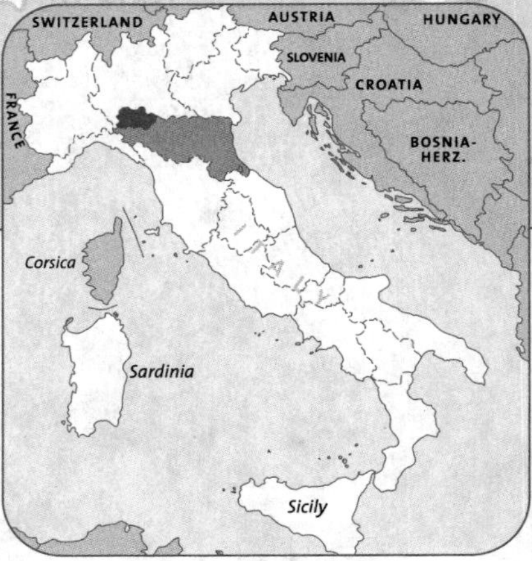
SWITZERLAND
AUSTRIA
HUNGARY
SLOVENIA
CROATIA
FRANCE
BOSNIA-HERZ.
Corsica
Sardinia
Sicily

Don't miss

1. Piacenza cathedral **p.99**
2. Palazzo Farnese (Musei Civici) **p.101**
3. Castell'Arquato **p.107**
4. Busseto **p.112**
5. Fontanellato **p.114**

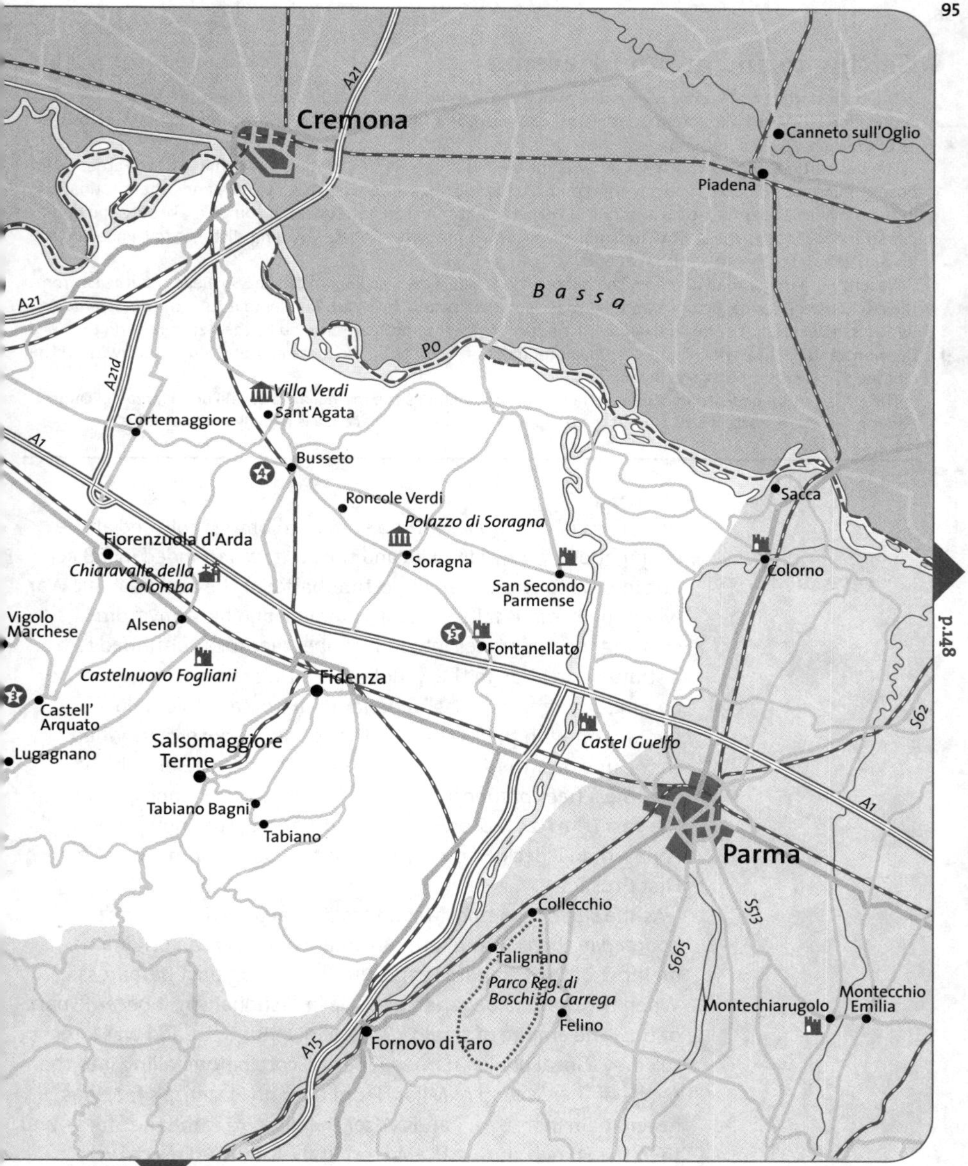

p.148

p.143

Piacenza

'Nobody ever comes to see us', the Piacentini wistfully complain. It's a quiet old town, with a large medieval centre from the days when Piacenza competed with the more famous cities in the North Italian big leagues. After that good start, it fell into the shadows when first Milan and then Parma came to rule it.

Getting to and around Piacenza

The **train station**, on Piazzale Marconi, is about a 10-minute walk from the centre. There are frequent connections to Milan (1hr 40mins) and Parma (40mins), and further afield to Bologna and points west, as well as to Cremona, Turin and Genoa.

The **bus station, t** 800 211173, *www.tempi.piacenza.it*, is in the Piazza Cittadella, near the Palazzo Farnese, with buses to Cremona, Bobbio (10 a day, 1hr 15mins), Grazzano Visconti, Castell'Arquato (1hr) and other destinations in the province. Buses to the excavations in Velleia (1hr 40mins) are infrequent; if you go make sure you don't get stranded. Besides these, **STAT Turismo**, *www.statturismo.com*, will take you long-distance to Genoa and the Riviera, Bolzano or Trento, **t** (0142) 781 660.

Piacenza is a major **road** junction. The historic Via Emilia, now also known as the SS9, heads southeast from the city towards Parma, Bologna and the coast, and northwards to Milan. Parallel to it runs the *autostrada* A1, which is, however, not quite as straight. Just north of Piacenza both are crossed by the A21 from Turin to Cremona and Brescia, which is accompanied for most of its route by the more peaceful SS10. Southwest of the city the SS45 leads off towards Bobbio and Genoa.

The city's central **pedestrian zone** is rather small, but includes the main Piazza Cavalli and Piazza del Duomo. **Parking** areas are scattered all around the periphery, and traffic in Piacenza is usually not too fierce.

History

Piacenza began as *Placentia*, a Roman colony established at the conjunction of the Via Emilia and the Po. It was founded in 218 BC, just in time to witness an important battle of the Second Punic War, when the Romans failed to stop Hannibal and his army from crossing the Apennines into Italy proper. Piacenza continued to be a strategic location in the Middle Ages; under the Holy Roman Empire, emperors such as Frederick Barbarossa would hold a parliament with their vassals in the spring of those years when they came over the Alps to Italy – not in the town itself, which became a free *comune* in 1126, but on the plains of Roncaglia just to the east (the A24 motorway runs through the spot now). In 1095 Pope Urban II decided on Piacenza as the place to proclaim the First Crusade.

As the site of an important international trade fair, Piacenza boomed in the 12th and 13th centuries, and it was an original member of the Lombard League in the fight against Barbarossa. When the *comune* began to dissolve in factionalism, it became part of the little empire of Ubaldo Pallavicini of Busseto, and was later ruled by a local banker named Alberto Scoto before falling into the hands of the Visconti of Milan. From then on Piacenza's fate was never again in its own hands. After the Visconti came the Sforza, and then the French, during the Wars of Italy. After the French were kicked out, Piacenza was grabbed by the Papacy, and in 1545 Paul III made it part of the Duchy of Parma and Piacenza he had created for his son Pier Luigi Farnese.

It remained something of a backwater, under the Farnese and later the Bourbons, until the revolutions of 1848. After a plebiscite, in which the vote went 37,089 to 496, Piacenza became the first city to unite with Piedmont in the new nation of Italy, earning itself the nickname of *Primogenita* or 'first-born'.

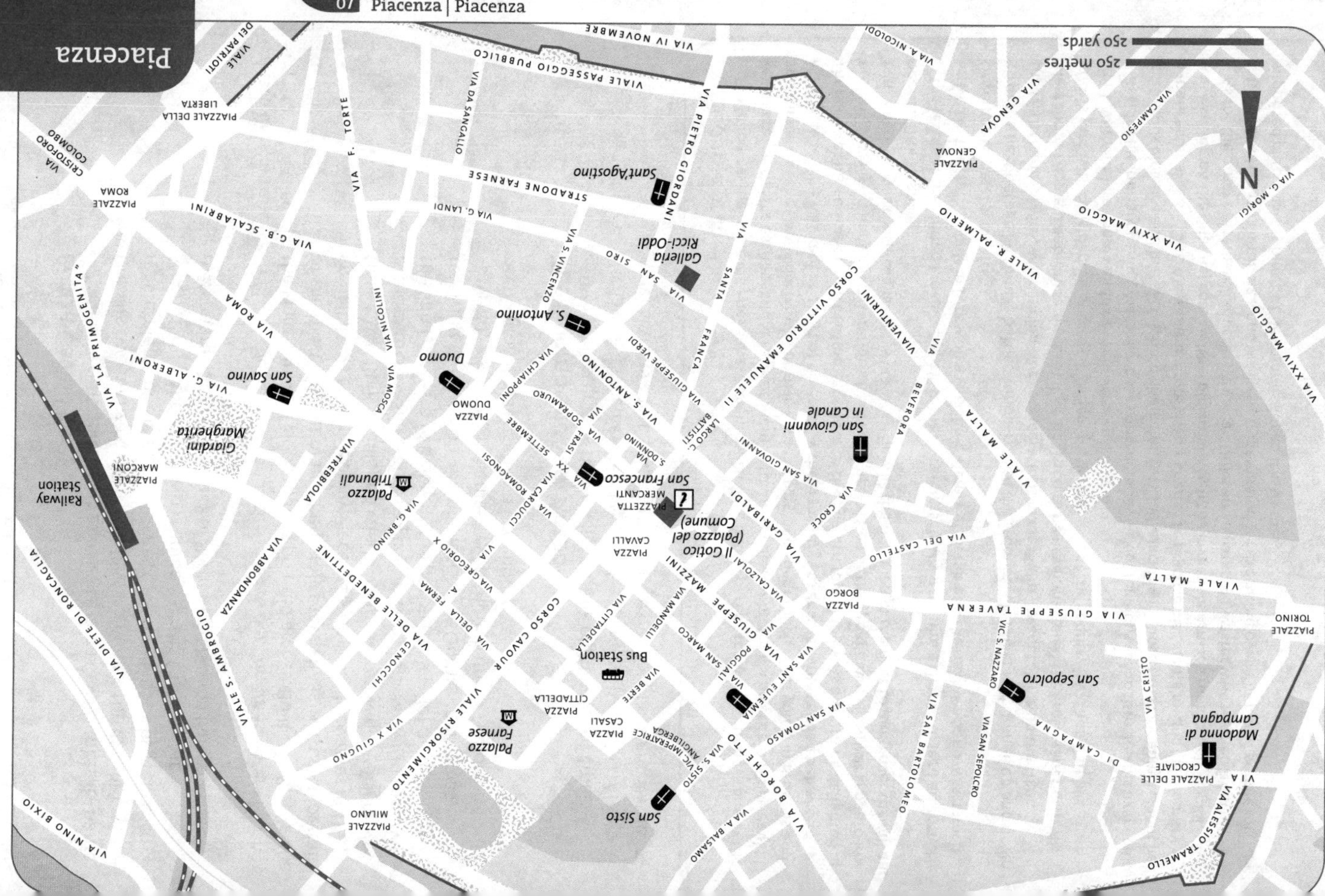
Piacenza
Railway Station
Piazzale Marconi
Giardini Margherita
San Savino
Palazzo Tribunali
Duomo
Piazza Duomo
S. Antonino
Sant'Agostino
Galleria Ricci-Oddi
San Francesco
Piazzetta Mercanti
Il Gotico (Palazzo del Comune)
Piazza Cavalli
San Giovanni in Canale
Bus Station
Piazza Cittadella
Piazza Casali
Palazzo Farnese
San Sisto
San Sepolcro
Madonna di Campagna
Piazzale delle Crociate
Piazzale Torino
Piazza Borgo
Piazzale Milano
Piazzale Roma
Piazzale della Liberta
Piazzale Genova
Via Nino Bixio
Via Diete di Roncaglia
Viale S. Ambrogio
Via Abbondanza
Via Trebbiola
Via "La Primogenita"
Via Cristoforo Colombo
Via G. Alberoni
Via Roma
Via G.B. Scalabrini
Via F. Torte
Via Nicolini
Via Mosca
Via G. Bruno
Via delle Benedettine
Viale Risorgimento
Via X Giugno
Genocchi
Via della Ferma
Via Gregorio X
Corso Cavour
Via Romagnosi
Via Carducci
Via XX Settembre
Via Chiappone
Via Sopramuro
Via Frasi
Via S. Donnino
Via S. Antonino
Via Giuseppe Verdi
Largo C. Battisti
Via S. Vincenzo
Via G. Landi
Stradone Farnese
Via da Sangallo
Viale Passeggio Pubblico
Via IV Novembre
Via Pietro Giordani
Via San Siro
Via Santa Franca
Corso Vittorio Emanuele II
Via Venturini
Via Beverora
Via San Giovanni
Via Croce
Via Garibaldi
Via Calzolai
Via Giuseppe Mazzini
Via Mandelli
Via Cittadella
Via Berte
Via San Marco
Via Poggiali
Vic. Imperatrice Angilberga
Via S. Sisto
Via A. Balsamo
Via Borghetto
Via Sant Eufemia
Via San Tomaso
Via San Bartolomeo
Via San Sepolcro
Vic. S. Nazzaro
Via Giuseppe Taverna
Via del Castello
Viale Malta
Viale R. Palmerio
Via XXIV Maggio
Via Genova
Via Campesio
Via G. Morigi
Via A. Nicolodi
Viale dei Patrioti
Via di Campagna
Via Cristo
Via Alessio Tramello
N
250 metres
250 yards

Piazza Cavalli

Piacenza's centrepiece, the excellent Piazza Cavalli, takes its name from its two bronze horses with flowing manes, the **Cavalli**, masterpieces of the early Baroque, cast in the 1620s by Francesco Mochi. Riding them are two members of the Farnese clan: Alessandro, the second Duke of Parma, and his son Ranuccio (*see* box, below).

Palazzo del Comune
open to visitors during temporary exhibitions

Behind the Cavalli stands the **Palazzo del Comune**, better known to the Piacentini as Il Gotico for its pointed arches. Built in 1280, it's one of the most elegant of northern Italy's town halls, with swallowtail crenellations that give away Piacenza's Ghibelline loyalties at the time it was built, mullioned windows and a rose window. Here also is the church of **San Francesco**, begun two years earlier, in the style of the San Francesco in Bologna; the portal has a relief of St Francis receiving the stigmata. Behind it the fine Gothic interior has survived relatively unchanged, even though under Napoleon's occupation it was used as a warehouse.

The Duomo and Sant'Antonino

Though Piacenza is the smallest of the eight cities of Emilia-Romagna, its medieval historic centre is larger than most. After a great start as a free city, its importance dwindled under the rule of

The Scourge of the Dutch

The fellow on the horse may never have spent much time in this part of the world, but he is one of the key figures of the 1500s. Alessandro Farnese, named for his great-grandfather, who became Pope Paul III and carved out the family duchy, was born in Rome in 1545, and spent much of his youth in Brussels and Madrid, where he was kept as a sort of hostage by the Habsburgs to ensure Farnese good behaviour. There he got his education and became very close to the Spanish royal family. As a youth he delighted in nothing more than hunting and warfare; he saw his first action at the great naval victory at Lepanto in 1571, where he was conspicuous for his bravery – he was the first man in the fleet to jump over the rail and board a Turkish galley.

The revolt of the United Provinces against the Habsburgs finally gave him a chance to lead an army. He arrived in the Netherlands in 1577, won a smashing victory at Gembloux the next year, and was named Governor-General soon after.

For the next decade his armies battled furiously with the redoubtable William of Orange up and down the Netherlands. Twice, when diplomatic considerations made Philip II want to give up the fight, Alessandro's dogged determination kept it going. Though he never mastered the Protestant north, his efforts met with considerable success in the south, where he kept the country loyal and Catholic – just think, without him there would never have been a Belgium.

Besides his military genius, Alessandro was noted for his lack of religious fanaticism and his aversion to gratuitous violence and massacres, both characteristics sadly lacking in those times. Tyranny seldom had a more estimable servant. Alessandro almost had a chance to practise his talents on another country. He was waiting on the Channel coast with a big army when the Invincible Armada met its end in 1588.

As for the other horseman, Ranuccio was a bad Duke and a paranoid waster who reigned from his father's death in 1592 until 1622, and was best remembered for executing over a hundred people for supposed plots against him. But he commissioned the statues.

Milan and the Farnese dukes and, walking its long quiet streets, laid out in a businesslike grid that has not changed much since the Romans planned them, you might feel a sense of great expectations that were never fulfilled.

Duomo
open daily 7.30–12.30 and 4–7.30

From Piazza Cavalli, the main Via XX Settembre takes you to one of the finest works of Lombard-Romanesque architecture, the **Duomo** (1122–1233). This imposing pile was begun only four years before the declaration of the *comune*; an earlier church on this site had just been knocked down by an earthquake. Viewed from the side and apse it's a picturesque confusion of columns, caryatids and galleries in the shadow of an unusual octagonal cupola and the mighty campanile (1333), crowned by one of the landmarks of Piacenza, the golden 'big angel', or *Angilon*. Though the central portal was rebuilt in the 1500s, the two on the side still have their original reliefs by the followers of Wiligelmo, the master of Modena cathedral.

The transitional interior (from Romanesque to Gothic) features a striking striped marble floor and some good 15th-century frescoes; note the reliefs on some of the columns in the nave, showing the work of cloth-makers, merchants, bakers and the other guilds; all helped in the building of the cathedral. The cupola has frescoes of *Old Testament Prophets* by the Milanese painter Morazzone – his last work; he died before they were completed, in 1626, and most of the dome, and the figures of the *Sibyls* below, were done by Guercino. Among the Duomo's other frescoes are works by Ludovico Carracci and Camillo Procaccini. Piacenza's inability to keep up with its rival neighbours after the Middle Ages may be due to its unfortunate choice of patron saints – the best the city could come up with was the obscure 4th-century martyr Santa Giustina; her relics are kept down in the impressive crypt, with its 108 columns.

In front of the cathedral, **Piazza del Duomo** was originally a proper asymmetrical medieval square. Pope Paul III had the area around the cathedral redesigned, creating a simple rectangular piazza that was more pleasing to Renaissance tastes; the Pope wanted to get Piacenza looking a little more up to date before he made a present of it to his son Pier Luigi.

Sant'Antonino
open Mon–Sat 8–12 and 4–6.30, Sun and hols 8–12 and 8–9.30pm

From here Via Chiapponi leads to **Sant'Antonino**, Piacenza's most ancient church and its original cathedral, with an 11th-century octagonal tower believed to be the first of its kind built in Italy, and a lofty Gothic porch called the *Paradiso*, added in 1350; under this is a portal with a relief of Adam and Eve. The plan is unusual: the tower rises over the crossing, which is in the rear of the church, not in front of the altar. Note too how the walls of the aisles are tilted inwards towards the altar, creating a disorienting effect if you see it from the right angle. Most of the church was rebuilt before 1000; it replaced earlier incarnations going back to the 4th century.

Ricci-Oddi Gallery
t (0523) 320742, www.riccioddi.it; open 10–12 and 3–6; closed Mon; adm; free last Thurs of month

Giuseppe Nicolini Conservatory
Via S. Franca 35, t (0523) 384345, www.conservatorio.piacenza.it; concerts, Oct–June

Just southwest on vias San Siro and Santa Franca, across the street from a picturesque but derelict Art Nouveau theatre, is the **Ricci-Oddi Gallery**, a huge collection by a local collector with a keen eye that offers an excellent idea of what Italian artists were up to between the years 1800 and 1930. Near the Ricci-Oddi Gallery, you can find the small-scale **Giuseppe Nicolini Conservatory**, which organizes classical concerts during the academic year; most of the concerts are hosted in the Conservatory.

A Constellation of Churches

San Savino
Via G. Alberoni, t (0523) 318 165; open daily 7.30–12 and 4–7

Piacenza does have an exceptional collection of parish churches – more than it ever needed, perhaps; at least three big Baroque confections stand abandoned and crumbling around the town. One that isn't, **San Savino**, just east of the Duomo, hides one of the town's best Romanesque churches, completed in 1107, behind a late Baroque façade. Inside, beyond some fancifully carved capitals, the main attraction is two remarkable original mosaics, discovered during restoration work in this century. One, in the presbytery, shows a classically allusive Time, or Fate, spinning, surrounded by the cardinal virtues: Justice, Fortitude, Temperance and Prudence – the last represented by a pair of chess players. The other, in the crypt, depicts the signs of the zodiac and the labours of the months. If the church is closed, try phoning.

Palazzo Costa
t (0523) 306 137 or 305 073, mobile 3387 451 756, marcohorak@virgilio.it; open daily; visits by appointment only

Nearby on Via Roma are two imposing palaces, the rococo **Palazzo Costa** and, next door, the Renaissance **Palazzo Landi**, now housing the provincial courts.

San Sisto
open Mon–Fri 7–10 and 4.30–6.30, Sat 7–10 and 3–6, Sun 7–12 and 3–6

San Sisto, looming at the end of Via San Sisto, north of Piazza Cavalli, was a Benedictine monastery church since Charlemagne's time; the present building was the first work of the prolific Piacentino Alessio Tramello (1499). Behind the imposing façade, so perfect for its time (though it was altered somewhat in the 1600s) that it could be a stage set in a late Renaissance theatre, there is an unusual interior with domes at either end, set over columned drums. Besides the chiaroscuro decoration, a feature of many of Piacenza's churches (as in Parma), there is plenty of good painting, including works by Zuccari and Palma Giovane. The real prize, an altarpiece by Raphael, is missing and has been replaced by a copy; the monks sold it off cheap long ago to a king of Poland. Fortunately the king did not have room in his suitcase for the excellent intarsia choir stalls (1514) of architectural scenes and perspectivist objects.

Santa Eufemia
open only for mass: Sat 6pm, Sun and hols 8am and 11am, Mon–Fri 5.15pm and 6pm

Backtracking down Via San Sisto takes you to **Santa Eufemia** (*c*. 1100), which possesses one of the region's most elegant Romanesque façades, incorporating an arcaded portico, and some good capitals inside.

San Giovanni in Canale
open Fri and Sat 7.30–12 and 5–6, Sun and hols 8.30–12 and 5–7, other days 7.30–12 and 3.30–6; closed pm July and Aug

San Sepolcro
open daily 7.30–12.30 and 3–6.30

Continuing in the same direction, south of the main Corso Garibaldi on Via Beverora is **San Giovanni in Canale**, a Dominican church with some good medieval and Renaissance tombs inside; it was built outside the original walls, on the banks of a small stream (now long vanished), hence the name. Corso Garibaldi, which becomes Via Campagna, leads off to the western gate, passing **San Sepolcro**, another work of Alessio Tramelli (1513) that has never really recovered from its occupation by Napoleon's men.

Santa Madonna di Campagna

Santa Madonna di Campagna
open Mon–Sat 9–12 and 3–6, Sun 9.15–10 and 3–6

Just before the gate itself, Tramelli's Santa Madonna di Campagna (1522) replaced an ancient pilgrimage chapel outside the old walls, built for a miraculous image of the Virgin Mary. A large field surrounded it; Pope Urban II proclaimed the First Crusade at a Church Council here in 1095 (in most histories the Council of Clermont in France, held later the same year, is given as the site of the proclamation – only because the news made a much bigger stir among the French, who were to supply most of the crusaders).

Renaissance Tuscany and Umbria developed a habit of building architectural showpiece churches just outside a town, usually in a centralized Greek-cross plan following the architectural theories of the day, as at Todi or Montepulciano. Piacenza is one of the few places in northern Italy to have one, though, as at Sant'Antonino, the Piacentini eventually modified it to fit their odd penchant for backwards churches; Tramelli began the Madonna di Campagna as a Greek cross, but in the 1790s the nave was extended not to the west front, but behind the altar. The unusual plan gives this church tremendous presence; instead of looking out towards the focal point of the building one is standing in it upon entering, while the arches and columns recede towards the altar under a coffered ceiling, an effect like the architectural fantasy in Raphael's *School of Athens*.

Piacenza was fortunate in finding just the man to decorate this dramatic interior. Pordenone, an artist who was influenced equally by the Venetian painters and Michelangelo (and the arch rival of Titian), contributed the colourful, intense frescoes (1529–31) covering the two domed chapels on the left, the Cappella di Santa Caterina and Cappella della Natività, as well as those on the dome, where God and the prophets share space with figures from classical mythology.

(2) Palazzo Farnese (Musei Civici)
t *(0523) 492 661, www.musei.piacenza.it; open July–15 Sept Tues–Thurs 8.45–1, Fri–Sat 8.45–1 and 3–6, Sun 9.30–1 and 3–6; 16 Sept–June Tues–Thurs 9–1, Fri–Sat 9–1 and 3–6, Sun 9.30–1 and 3–6; guided tours available in summer, Tues–Fri at 10am, Sat and Sun 9.30am, 11am, 3pm and 4.30pm; adm; joint tickets available for Musei Civici, Galeria Ricci-Oddi and Pinacoteca Alberoni, and for Musei Civici and Galeria Ricci-Oddi*

Palazzo Farnese (Musei Civici)

From Piazza Cavalli, Corso Cavour leads to the pachydermic Palazzo Farnese, local headquarters of the ducal family, begun in 1558 by Vignola, the High Renaissance's most accomplished architect, but never finished. Inside is the Musei Civici, a complex of four museums including a **Pinacoteca**. The Farnese may never have got around to tacking on the stone façade Vignola designed, but there are some lavishly decorated rooms inside, with precious stuccoed trim framing scenes of the family's favourite subject: themselves. These are impressive paintings, mostly done in the 1680s: Giovanni Draghi gets the job of glorifying Alessandro Farnese, while the Venetian Sebastiano Ricci takes on Paul III: *The Pope reconciling Emperor Charles V and François I* – visitors should note the artful pose, taken from Velazquez's famous *Las Lanzas*, and the Pope floating up in heaven on the ceiling.

Further on, there is some excellent 14th-century painting, mostly detached frescoes from the long-deconsecrated church of San Lorenzo. Bartolomeo and Jacopino da Reggio, and the 'Maestro di Santa Caterina', so called for the cycle on the *Life of St Catherine* here, are all masters of the precise and virtuous line, precursors of the Tuscan quattrocento. The Hall of Sculptures contains terracotta decoration from local churches, and five good Renaissance reliefs of the Apostles from San Sepolcro, as well as a gruesome wood *St Augustine* from the 1700s (how one might imagine the old bigot really looked). They share the space with the most famous Etruscan bronze of them all: the *Fegato di Piacenza*, a model of a sheep (or some say human) liver, designed for apprentice *haruspices*, or augurs, diagrammed and inscribed with the names of the Etruscan deities. The Etruscans regarded the liver as a microcosm of the sky, divided into 16 houses (not 12, as in the zodiac), each ruled over by a god. The augurs looked in the liver for blemishes to see which deity had anything to communicate. The Etruscans were renowned throughout the ancient world for augury, and Roman emperors consulted their haruspices until the coming of Christianity; they were the last speakers of the lost Etruscan language.

More paintings follow upstairs. Botticelli's lovely *Tondo* is a work of the 1480s, the time when the artist was coming under the influence of Savonarola and trading in his mythological fancies for Christian piety; his Madonna is still the familiar Venus, though a little older and wiser. Later paintings are few, but big ones fit for a Duke. Pride of place goes to the inimitable Ilario Spolverini, a specialist in Farnese-flattering ceremonial scenes and tremendous battle paintings and biblical extravaganzas worthy of Cecil B. de Mille: Joshua makes the sun stand still, and the Hebrews are led through the desert by Moses and Aaron. Note also the Second Antechamber, painted with *trompe-l'œil* walls and the *Chariot of the Sun* on the ceiling by the Venetian Pietro della Vecchia.

The other parts of the Musei Civici include an **Archaeological Museum**, not of much interest, a **Museum of the Risorgimento**, and a **Museum of Carriages**, with one that belonged to King Vittorio Emanuele and a wonderful piece of folk art, a Sicilian cart painted with scenes from the operas of Verdi. Across the courtyard from the main part of the palace stand the scanty remains of its predecessor, the 14th-century **Cittadella** built by the Visconti. The Farnese pulled most of it down while planning its replacement; no doubt the place was an embarrassment to them. Pier Luigi, the first Duke, met his end here in 1547 when rebellious Piacentini nobles murdered him and threw his corpse out of a window into the moat. After that they moved the capital of the duchy to Parma.

Collegio Alberoni
Via Emilia Parmense 77, **t** *(0523) 577 011, www.piacenzamusei.it; open April–June and Oct on Sun; guided tours at 4pm, by appointment only, call* **t** *(0523) 609 730 to book; adm*

About 2km southwest of the city, out towards Parma, is the **Collegio Alberoni**, founded as a college of theology for poor boys by Giulio Alberoni, a gardener's son who became a Cardinal and then Spanish prime minister in the reign of Philip V. This college contains a fine collection of Flemish tapestries and, among its 16th–18th-century Flemish and Italian paintings, a rare work of Antonello da Messina, a Sicilian who was the greatest southern painter of the 1400s, and probably the first Italian to take up oil painting; he would be better known if his works were not so few. This is an *Ecce Homo* – an unusual composition, and the Renaissance's most sorrowful Christ.

Where to Stay in Piacenza

ⓘ Piacenza >
Piazza Cavalli 7, **t** *(0523) 329 324, iat@comune.piacenza.it, www.comune.piacenza.it, www.provincia.pc.it, www.piacenzamusei.it, www.piacenzaturismi.ne; open Tues–Sat 9–1 and 3–6*

Piacenza ✉ 29100

Expensive (€€€€)

****Grande Albergo Roma**, Via Cittadella 14, **t** (0523) 323 201, *www.grandealbergoroma.it*. Piacenza's most prestigious hotel is just off Piazza Cavalli. Completely refurbished in 1996, this 72-room hotel is equipped with soberly elegant woodwork and furnishings, old-fashioned service, comfortable air-conditioned rooms, a garage, a gymnasium and sauna, and a pair of good restaurants; one, the **Ristorante Piccolo Roma**, has pretty views over the city.

***Nazionale**, Via Genova 35 (south of the centre), **t** (0523) 712 000, *www.hotelnazionale.it*. For modern rooms with TV and air conditioning near the *centro storico*. In business since 1932 and totally refurbished; private parking garage, rooms in a variety of shapes and sizes, satellite TV, and friendly owners.

Moderate (€€€)

***Hotel City**, Via Emilia Parmense 54, **t** (0523) 579 752, *www.hotelcitypc.it*. Southeast of town on the Parma road (on the extension of Via Colombo), this modern hotel has 60 quiet and businesslike rooms.

***Milano**, Piazzale Milano 7 (north of Piazza Cavalli), **t** (0523) 336 843, *www.hotelmilano.it*. Near the *centro storico*, with all mod cons, this sober businessman's hotel has comfortable rooms in a quiet part of town near the station.

***Ovest**, Via 1 Maggio 82, **t** (0523) 712 222, *www.hotelovest.com*. A big collection of newer hotels is spread around the cheerless suburbs. West of the centre (near the Piacenza Ovest exit), new, stylish, this offers good-value creature comforts, including air conditioning, satellite and pay TV, minibar, modem hook-ups, big bathrooms, excellent buffet breakfast, private car park and garage.

***VIP**, Via Cipelli 41 (off Via Giuseppe Manfredi), **t** (0523) 712 420, *www.viphotel.it*. South of the centre, linked to the centre and station by bus no.6; rooms are simple but cosy (some may be *inexpensive*).

Inexpensive (€€)

Il Bagatto, Via C. Colombo 126, **t** (0523) 614 228. South of the station near Piazzale Roma, with seven en suite rooms and a restaurant.

Budget (€)

Ostello Don Zermani, Via Zoni 38/40, **t** (0523) 712 319, *www.ostellodipiacenza.it*. Youth hostel.

Eating Out in Piacenza

As part of the same duchy, Piacenza follows Parma closely in the kitchen: *coppa* and *pancetta* are its cold meats, and its *tortelli caudati*, filled with ricotta, Parmesan and herbs and topped with butter and Parmesan, are not unlike its neighbour's classic. *Pisarei e faso*, which appears on some menus, is a dish of dumplings in saucy beans. In none of Piacenza's restaurants are you likely to discover this town's dark secret – the Piacentini are inordinately fond of donkey (*asino*). If you have a kitchen, though, you can cook up your own from one of the numerous horse-and-donkey butcher shops around town.

★ Antica Osteria del Teatro >

Antica Osteria del Teatro, Via Verdi 16, near Sant'Antonino, **t** (0523) 323 777, *www.anticaosteriadelteatro.it* (€€€€). What Piacenza has that Parma hasn't is one of Italy's very best restaurants. At this exceptional gourmet pleasure dome local recipes merge delectably with French nouvelle cuisine under chef Filippo Chiappini Dattilo's magic touch: the *tortelli del Farnese* with butter and sage are as light as a summer's breeze; *secondi* include sea or land food, including heavenly *foie gras* in pastry, layered with honey and Calvados, or a bit of Sardinia in the roast suckling pig perfumed with myrtle; for dessert, splurge on one of the heavenly chocolate concoctions. There's a choice of two *menus di degustazione. Be sure to book. Closed Sun and Mon, 10 days in Jan and 3 weeks in Aug.*

Vecchia Piacenza, San Bernardo 1, **t** (0523) 305 462, *www.ristorantevecchiapiacenza.it* (€€€). Just west of the centro, off Via Taverna, this little place has tasty *antipasti* (try the *porcini* if they're on the menu), and a constantly changing list of first and second courses, based on the market and the chef's whim. *Closed Sun and all July. Booking advisable.*

La Carozza, Via 10 Giugno 122, north of the station off Viale S. Ambrogio, **t** (0523) 326 297, *arturoramelli@tiscali.it* (€€). Offers typical Piacenza cooking with fixed price menu at lunchtime.

La Pireina, Via Borghetto 137, **t** (0523) 338 578 (€). A traditional trattoria located near the old city walls, serving typical local dishes in a simple, unpretentious way: *tortelli d'erbetta* (stuffed with spinach and ricotta), *tagliolini al ragù*, or *faldia* (a type of schnitzel made with horse steak). *Closed Sun, Mon eve and first 3 weeks Aug.*

South of Piacenza

The rarely visited hills and mountains south of Piacenza offer several possibilities for excursions or road stops. The celebrated monastery at Bobbio is the main attraction, and Castell'Arquato is one of the prettiest smaller towns in the entire region.

Rivalta and Grazzano Visconti

Castello di Rivalta
t (0523) 978 104, www.castellodirivalta.it; open Feb–Nov; guided tours Feb–Nov exc Aug Sun 3–5pm, Mar–Nov Sat 11am and 3–6pm, Sun 9–12 and 3–6; Aug Wed–Fri 4.30pm, Sat 11am, 3–6pm, Sun 9–12 and 3–6pm; adm

There is certainly no lack of castles south of Piacenza. The **Castello di Rivalta**, overlooking the river Trebbia in a grove north of Rivergaro, goes back in parts to the 11th century, though the whole presents a stately Renaissance aspect; its round tower was built by an architect named Solari, who also designed parts of the Kremlin in Moscow. Inside are period furnishings and art, frescoes of country life, and a room of armour with three of the battle flags that were carried by

Agazzano Castle
t (0523) 975 171, corradogonzaga@tin.it; open April–Oct Sun and hols, guided tours 11, 3, 4.15 and 5.30; adm

La Bastardina
open Mar–Nov Sun 9–12 and 3–6.30; adm

Castello di Paderna
t (0523) 511 645, fontanellato@tin.it; open Mar–Oct Sat and Sun exc 2 weeks in Aug, guided tours 10–12; other days by prior booking only; adm

the Christians at Lepanto in 1571. Just to the west, the square castle of **Agazzano** is mostly from the late 15th century, with a U-shaped 18th-century palace added on the side, the two linked by a large French garden; it contains period furnishings and some frescoed rooms. The grounds of Agazzano's other castle, **La Bastardina**, have been converted into a nine-hole golf course; this castle too has some frescoes, here from the 1660s.

Due south of Piacenza on the N654, the village of **Grazzano Visconti** was rebuilt a century ago in the medieval style by a descendant of the Visconti. The result is more than a bit of a tourist trap (there's a museum of antique cars), but it has its charms, and the village is a good place to purchase ornamental wrought iron. The **Castello di Paderna**, east of Grazzano, is a different sort of castle, a rectangular walled manor of the sort that was once common on the Piacentino plain, a fortified farm in a style introduced by the Byzantines, defended by a tower and surrounded by a moat; a Greek-cross chapel from the 11th century made up of Roman fragments is the oldest section. In the second half of June, the Castello di Paderna hosts a traditional music festival, with instruments ancient and modern. Most of the concerts are free.

Bobbio

The main SS45 to Genoa follows the valley of the Trebbia, a wild meandering stream that has carved the hills into odd-shaped cliffs and bowls. This will take you to **Bobbio** (46km), where St Columbanus founded a monastery in 612, shortly before his death. Columbanus, one of several scholarly Irish monks who came to the illiterate continent as missionaries in the Dark Ages, was also the founder of the great abbey of Luxeuil (Vosges), which he had been forced to leave because of his outspoken views on the local Frankish barons, and the Celtic observances followed in his church. The same thing happened in Switzerland, but Columbanus found a home here by the good graces of the Lombard King Aistulf.

Bobbio became one of the most important monastic centres in Italy, renowned for its library and scriptorium; it was the first monastery in the West to be free of the control of its local bishop. Its most celebrated abbots were Saint Wala, a cousin of Charlemagne, and Gerbert of Aurillac, a friend of Emperor Otto III, who had studied science and philosophy in Muslim Spain. Gerbert was the most learned Christian of his day, so much so that his enemies accused him of sorcery (it didn't help that he spent much of his time constructing planetary spheres and mechanical clocks). Gerbert ran afoul of the nobles in the Val de Trebbia when he tried to collect the abbey's rents, but he went on to become Pope Sylvester II in AD 999.

Bobbio began to decline in the 1400s, and the abbey was suppressed by Napoleon.

The abbey was largely rebuilt in the 15th–17th centuries, and not much remains of its medieval splendours, but the **Basilica** retains its campanile and apse from the 800s. Inside are frescoes of Columbanus' life and miracles, and another fine Renaissance carved choir, but the ancient treasures are in the **crypt**: the Renaissance tomb of Columbanus (1480) and the original tombs of his Frankish followers (and successors as abbot) SS. Attala and Bertulphus, the latter covered in carved arabesques in a style called 'langobardic' (Lombard), though they look as if Columbanus had brought them down with him from Ireland. To the right is a marvellous, intricate wrought-iron screen from the 12th century. In 1910, parts of the medieval church's **mosaic pavement** were discovered behind the crypt; these are also 12th-century, with a wealth of medieval fancy in their labours of the months and astrological signs. Better preserved are scenes from the Second Book of Maccabees: the wars of Judas Maccabeus (with elephants), the city of Antioch and the prophet Eleazar, along with some mythological beasts, including a dragon and a 'quimera' (chimera). This one has three heads, one on its back and one on the tail, just like the famous Etruscan bronze in the archaeology museum of Florence. Where did the medieval artists get the idea?

Museo dell'Abbazia
t (0523) 936 018; open Sept–June Sat 3-4.30, Sun 11–12 and 3–5; July–Aug Tues–Sat 5–7, Sun 11–12 and 4–7; adm; joint ticket available with Museo della Città

Museo della Città
t (0523) 962 804; open Nov–Mar Sat and Sun 11.30–12.30 and 3–5; April–June and Sept–Oct Sat and Sun 11.30–12.30 and 5–7; July and Aug Wed–Fri 5–7, Sat and Sun 11.30–12.30 and 5–7; adm

Castello di Bobbio
t (0523) 936 069; open Apr–Sept Tues–Fri 8–2, Sat and Sun 8–4.30; Oct–Mar Mon–Sat 8–3

In the cloister, the **Museo dell'Abbazia** contains a famous 4th-century *teca*, an ivory urn with reliefs, and Romanesque statuary and painting; the same cloister also has a small **Museo della Città**. In the town of Bobbio, clustered around the monastery and castle, there are many fine old stone houses. The **Castello di Bobbio** is open to visitors though there isn't a lot to see: at the time of writing only the garden and tower are open to visitors. Bobbio's inimitable landmark is its 'hunchback bridge', the Ponte del Gobbo, a lumpy, eccentric construction all of whose arches are of different sizes; though it's mostly medieval, parts of it are as old as the Romans.

Roman Velleia

Antiquarium
t (0523) 803 091; open 1 Mar–4 Nov daily 8–7, 5 Nov–28 Feb daily 9–3; closed Mon; adm free

Gropparello Castle
t (0523) 855 814, www.castellodigropparello.it; open 12 Mar–12 Nov Sun and hols 10–6.30, till 5 in autumn; adm

Emilia's best-preserved Roman town, prettily situated on a hillside, is **Velleia**, 33km south of Piacenza between Bobbio and Salsomaggiore. It was never very large, but retains at least the foundations of an interesting forum, temple, amphitheatre and some mysterious large carved stones that resemble bathtub plugs. Most of the items excavated are in Parma, including the famous *Tabula Alimentaria* (*see* p.123); bits and pieces remain in Velleia's **antiquarium** on the site. North of Velleia, beware the attractive medieval castle at **Gropparello**, once the home of honest robber barons, it now houses the Parco delle Fiabe, or 'Fairytale Park',

…*tivo* in Italy', where underemployed … witches, Celtic druids, knights, damsels an… their best to amuse you and your offspring. They say the cas… haunted, too.

Castell'Arquato

Castell'Arquato

Drivers can cut over the hills from here to Lugagnano and lovely Castell'Arquato, the closest to a Tuscan hill town this region can offer. Starting out as a Roman military camp, the home base of the VIIIth Legion, it metamorphosed into the fortified village of a Lombard baron by the 8th century, and later fell into the hands of the bishops of Piacenza. Around 1200, Castell'Arquato was able to declare itself a free *comune*. It couldn't last. Alberto Scoto, boss of Piacenza (and, as his name implies, of Scotch or Irish descent), seized control in 1290; he in turn lost it after a siege by Galeazzo Visconti of Milan, and ended up languishing in the Visconti dungeons. From them it passed to the Sforza, and finally to the Farnese dukes.

It's a stiff climb up to the town centre, but the reward is the elegant ensemble of the Piazza del Municipio, or Piazza Alta, little changed since the days of the *comune*. The highlight, which you can view from the outside only, is the asymmetrical **Palazzo del Podestà**, completed after Scoto took power, with picturesque loggia and covered stairs (Scoto was a leading Guelph, so someone else must have added the Ghibelline swallowtail crenellations). The basement now holds an **Enoteca Comunale** where you can try out the area's wines.

Collegiata di Santa Maria
open daily 9–12 and 2–6

Opposite, the **Collegiata di Santa Maria** turns its back to the piazza, but that is its best side, an elaborate composition of Lombard apses, gables and blind arcading. The church was last rebuilt in 1122, following an earthquake; on the side is a portico called the *Paradiso*, like Sant'Antonino's in Piacenza. Inside this sweet little church are some good carved capitals, including a few nice barbaric ones recycled from the 8th-century pre-earthquake church. The original baptismal font survives too, a big one for immersion baptisms, with a curious relief of the Trinity, represented as three equal persons, on the side. On and around the altar are some excellent 12th-century reliefs, including symbols of the Evangelists: these probably formed part of a pulpit when the church was built. There are two decorated chapels, one a sumptuous work of 1630, the **Cappella di San Giuseppe**, with paintings by the Piacentino Giacomo Guidotti; but as usual the Baroque is upstaged by a simpler frescoed chapel from the early days: the **Cappella di Santa Caterina**, covered with a lively cycle on the Passion and the Life of Catherine of Alexandria by an unknown artist, probably Tuscan, *c.* 1400. Outside the church, in the tiny, delightful timber-roofed cloister, the **Museo della Collegiata** has

Museo della Collegiata
***t** (0523) 805 151; open daily April–Sept 9–12 and 3–7, Oct–Mar 9–12 and 2.30–6, till 7 on Sun and hols; adm free, donation requested*

a collection of paintings in which the star is undoubtedly a magnificently disturbing work by the master of late Baroque macabre, Alessandro Magnasco: Burial of a Carthusian. There is also a 15th-century altarpiece, and a rare Byzantine silk pallium from the 900s.

Rocca
t (0523) 803 091, www.castellarquato.net; open Mar–Oct Tues–Sun 10–7, Nov–Feb Sat, Sun and hols 10–1, 3–5 June Tues–Fri 10–12 and 3–5, Sat–Sun 10–12 and 3–6; 15 June–30 Sept Tues–Fri 10.30–11.30 and 3.30–5.30, Sat–Sun 10–12 and 3–6; 1 Nov–28 Feb Sat–Sun 10–12 and 3–5; adm

To complete the ensemble, there is the **Rocca**, built by the Visconti in 1345. Though an impossibly picturesque toy castle at first glance, it did the job; the Rocca comes in two parts, this citadel at the top, and a connected lower one to control the slopes. There's also a virtual museum with three-dimensional animation about medieval life, military techniques, legends and history of Castell'Arquato. Adjacent, Piazza del Municipio opens into a shady belvedere, with views over the surrounding hills.

Another pretty park with an avenue of trees lies beneath the lower castle, near the entrance of the town. Here too is a medieval fountain, which reveals the big drawback of living in Castell'Arquato in the old days: until the 20th century this was the town's only source of water, and people who lived at the top had to carry their supplies all the way up.

Just north of Castell'Arquato, Vigolo Marchese has a Romanesque church and a rare 11th-century circular baptistry; inside it are some rare bits of frescoes from the same period.

Where to Stay and Eat South of Piacenza

The first 20km or so south of Piacenza has a large number of good restaurants the Piacentini like to visit for their Sunday lunch.

Rivergaro ✉ 29029

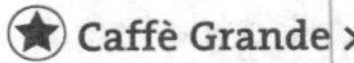

Caffè Grande, Piazza Paolo 9, **t** (0523) 958 524, *www.caffegrande.it* (€€). Dating from the mid-19th century, a local institution on the main square where Piacentini cuisine is taken very seriously indeed. Classic dishes include the fried biscuit called the *burtléina* that accompanies the *salumi*, also *tortelli di ricotti*, 'with a tail', as well as succulent grilled meats. Garden in the summer. *Booking essential in the summer; closed 5–30 Jan and two weeks Aug–Sept.*

ⓘ Grazzano Visconti
Cortevecchia 7, t (0523) 870 997, www.grazzano.it; open Apr–Oct Tues-Sun 9.30–12.30 and 3–6; Nov–Mar Tues–Fri 9.30–12.30, Sat–Sun 9.30–12.30 and 2.30–5.30

Ponte dell'Olio ✉ 29028

Ponte dell'Olio has long had a gold star on the Piacentini gourmet map, and it can make a particularly rewarding stop while you are visiting the castles.

Riva, Via Riva 16, **t** (0523) 875 193, *aradelli.carla@libero.it* (€€€€). This famous place is located in a little *frazione*, and run by one of Italy's top female chefs, Carla Aradelli. Her elegant, imaginative cuisine is based on the freshest locally sourced ingredients, and you'll have to make a substantial journey to find better stuffed courgette (zucchini) flowers with mushrooms, tortellini with black truffle, ravioli filled with a delicate mix of peppers and rice, or pheasant with hazelnuts. Desserts are just as lovely (try especially the *fondente di cioccolato* with hazelnut mousse); excellent wine list too. *Closed lunch Mon and Tues.*

Bellaria da Trecordi, at Biana 17, **t** (0523) 878 333 (€€). Another good choice on the outskirts of Ponte dell'Olio, this is a pretty mid-19th-century *osteria* that has been beautifully restored. A perfect setting for traditional Piacentina cuisine, from *salume* (including the local *pancetta* and *coppa*) and other items such as gnocchi with pumpkin to its renowned two-tailed *tortelli* to succulent roast duck. *Closed Thurs and 3 weeks in Sept.*

ⓘ **Bobbio >**
*Piazza San Francesco 1, **t** (0523) 962 815, www.comune.bobbio.pc.it; open Jan–Mar Tues–Sat 9–1, 4–7; April–15 June and 15 Sept–Dec Wed–Sat 9–12.30, 4–7, Sun 8.30–12.30; 15 June–15 Sept Wed–Sat 9–12.30, 4–6, Sun 8.30–12.30, 4–6*

Bobbio ✉ 29022

****__Albergo Le Ruote__, Via Emilia Parmense 204, Roveleto di Cadeo, **t** (0523) 500 427, *www.hotelleruote.it* (€€€€). Located a few kilometres from Piacenza, near Bobbio, this sleek modern glass block makes the ideal stop on the Via Francigena. The bedrooms are comfortably appointed and provided with cable TV (international channels), sound-proofing, minibar and air conditioning with temperature control. There are six suites too, with Jacuzzis. The restaurant offers a selection of Emilian traditional recipes and innovative cuisine.

***__Piacentino__, Piazza San Francesco 19, **t** (0523) 936 563, *www.hotelpiacentino.it* (€€). Facing the tree-lined square, this has 20 functional but very adequate rooms, some of which benefit from air conditioning, and a restaurant that features some good home cooking.

***__Ridella__, Via Giarrone 13, **t** (0523) 933 130, (€). Situated some way above Bobbio at Santa Maria, on the slopes of Monte Penice, this peaceful hotel has 18 rooms and is placed in a leafy park. It benefits too from an excellent restaurant with an enormous and impressive list of *primi* (try for example the *tortelli piacentini* with cheese) and grilled *involtini*. In the summer and on weekends, it's essential to book. *Closed Wed and 2 weeks Nov.*

San Nicola, not far from the abbey at Contrada San Nicola 11, **t** (0523) 932 355 (€€). The old abbots would have been a mite shocked perhaps to find that the old church has been stylishly converted into a restaurant with a superb cellar of wines and spirits from around the world. There is a good choice of well-prepared seasonal dishes to accompany them, with delicious mushrooms and home-made pasta as well as game, boar stewed with juniper and a good selection of cheeses. Also four comfortable rooms. *Closed Mon.*

ⓘ **Castell' Arquato >>**
*Viale Remondini 1, **t** (0523) 803 091, www.castellarquato.com; open Tues–Sat 9.30–12.30; summer also Sun 10–12 and 3–4.30*

Castell'Arquato ✉ 29014

Conservatorio Villaggi, Via Villaggi 27, **t** (0523) 805 245 (€). Get thee to a nunnery: the place to stay here is this 15th-century convent, beautifully restored and with a splendidly historic atmosphere. The ten rooms come in all sizes, from singles to quads, and while modern creature comforts may be somewhat lacking, many of the rooms are decorated with their original frescoes, fireplaces and lovely panelled ceilings. The restaurant, which is only open to guests who reserve in advance, serves an array of delicious and well-presented Piacentini cuisine. *Closed Oct–May. Evenings only.*

__Leon d'Oro__, Piazza Europa, **t (0523) 803 651, *leondoro72@hotmail.com* (€). Basic accommodation, but this is conveniently located at the entrance to the old town.

__San Giorgio__, Piazza Europa 12, **t (0523) 805 149, *p.sticchi@libero.it* (€). Also situated at the entrance to the old town, and also tending towards the very basic, with an inexpensive restaurant.

Maps, Piazza Europa 3, **t** (0523) 804 411 (€€€). A straightforward but distinctly elegant restaurant, with some seafood among its specialities; try for instance *pisarei e faso. Booking advisable. Closed Mon and Tues.*

From Piacenza to Parma

North of the Via Emilia between Piacenza and Parma is the flat countryside of the Po Valley known as the *Bassa*, often featured in Italian films. For five centuries, this territory made up a cohesive and remarkably long-lived feudal state; the Pallavicino family of Busseto, who ruled it, were often major players in medieval Italy's factional wars (*see* pp.40–2).

Cortemaggiore

In 1479 Gianludovico Pallavicino decided to build a new capital for this little state, and the result was Castel Lauro, now called Cortemaggiore, between the Via Emilia and the Po. **Cortemaggiore** is often touted as one of the planned 'ideal cities' of the Renaissance, but this would be giving too much credit to an age that, for all its artistic talents, cared little for town design. With its neat rectangle of walls and grid plan, with an arcaded square and church at the centre, Cortemaggiore was only following what had been Europe's accepted practice for laying out new towns since the early Middle Ages; the plan is the spitting image of a medieval French *bastide*.

Cortemaggiore has suffered a strange fate since the last war, with the discovery of northern Italy's biggest gas deposits and the industrialization that followed, but the old town preserves some of its Renaissance graces. At its centre is the **Collegiata di Santa Maria**, designed by Gilberto Manzi, who also laid out the town; it contains the tomb of Gianludovico Pallavicino and a number of paintings by Filippo Mazzola, the father of Parmigianino. Most of the other Pallavicini are buried in SS. Annunziata, in elegant Renaissance tombs accompanied by frescoes and paintings by Pordenone.

Abbey of Chiaravalle della Colomba
t (0523) 940 132; open Mon–Sat 8.30–11.30 and 2–6; book for guided tour; adm free, donation

Castelnuovo Fogliani
t (0523) 947 112; open by appointment

Down the Via Emilia itself, 4km north of Alseno, the **Abbey of Chiaravalle della Colomba**, the first Cistercian monastery in Emilia-Romagna, has a Romanesque church, with a chapel frescoed in the manner of Giotto and a beautiful brick cloister; all was rebuilt after the original abbey was destroyed by the troops of Frederick II in 1248. Also near Alseno, **Castelnuovo Fogliani** is a medieval stronghold that was reshaped into an up-to-date palace with sumptuously decorated rooms and a large park by Luigi Vanvitelli, 18th-century court architect to the King of Naples and builder of the 'Italian Versailles' at Caserta.

Fidenza

More elaborate Romanesque awaits at **Fidenza**, the Roman *Fidentia Iulia*, known for centuries as the Borgo San Donnino until Mussolini resurrected its old, more imperial-sounding name. For 600 years, beginning in the 9th century, the town belonged to the Pallavicini, and its history consists only of brief interruptions bound up with turmoil in nearby Parma; whatever faction was exiled from there often took up residence here, and on two occasions the Parmigiani sacked the town. Fidenza is a large and lively town, but its artistic interest is limited to its 13th-century **Duomo** dedicated to the town's martyr and patron San Donnino, begun in 1162. The porch is adorned with statues by followers of the great Antelami, the master of Parma's Baptistry. The impressive, lofty interior, with matroneum and clerestory, contains a number of frescoes, including a scene of *St George* by a trecento artist called 'Mangiaterra' ('eat-up-the-ground') for the speed of his painting; there is more Antelamian sculpture around the altar and in the crypt.

Salsomaggiore Terme

South of Fidenza, Salsomaggiore Terme with its 109 hotels, is the largest and best-known of a cluster of saline water spas specializing in arthritic and rheumatic cures. It was popular with Italian royalty at the turn of the 20th century, and is now sometimes favoured by operatic celebrities. Its main baths, the **Terme Berzieri**, are concentrated in an intriguing half-baked Liberty-style palace. Better, stop in at the **Palazzo dei Congressi** on Viale Romagnosi. Once this was the town's grandest hotel, built in Salsomaggiore's pre-First World War golden era and owned by Cesar Ritz; past clients have included Caruso, Toscanini and Queen Margherita of Italy. The lobby is still one of the grandest in Italy – a Liberty-arabesque fantasy with fabulously colourful frescoes by Italy's Art Nouveau master Galileo Chini. Another important spa nearby is **Tabiano Bagni**, with stinky sulphur springs.

Tabiano Bagni
t (0524) 564 111, or toll free from Italy only 800 860 379, www.termeditabiano.it

Where to Stay and Eat in Fidenza and Salsomaggiore

ⓘ Fidenza >
Piazza Duomo 16, t (0524) 83377, www.comune.fidenza.pr.it; open Tues–Sun 9.30–12.30 and 3–5

ⓘ Cortemaggiore
Piazza Patrioti 8, t (0523) 832 711; open Mon–Sat 8–1 and 2–4

Fidenza ✉ 43036

*****Astoria**, Via G. B. Gandolfi 5, **t** (0524) 524 314, *www.hotelastoriafidenza.it* (€€). In the centre and fine for a night. Just beside the hotel is the Ristorante Pizzeria Astoria, refurbished in 2003, offering regional and traditional cuisine (closed Mon).

****Ugolino**, Via C. Malpeli 90, **t** (0524) 522 422 (€). Also in the centre, this has simple rooms and a good, reliable no-frills trattoria (€), serving *anolini* in a rich broth, *bollito misto* and chicken *alla cacciatora. Closed Mon and early Aug.*

ⓘ Salsomaggiore Terme >
Galleria Warowland, Piazzale Berzieri, t (0524) 580 211, www.portalesalsomaggiore.it; open May–Oct Mon–Sat 3–12.30 and 3.30–6.30, Sun 10–12.30; Nov–April Mon–Fri 3–12.30 and 3–6, Sat 3–12.30

Salsomaggiore ✉ 43039

*******Grand Hotel et de Milan**, Via Dante 1, **t** (0524) 572 241, *www.demilan.it* (€€€€€). Large 19th-century country villa once owned by the Dukes of Parma. The public rooms have retained their old-fashioned charm, while the air-conditioned bedrooms have been completely modernized, and many equipped with private spas. There's a heated pool in a pretty garden, a solarium and beauty farm; the restaurant serves regional cuisine and meals for guests on special diets.

******Grand Hotel Porro**, Viale Porro 10, **t** (0524) 578 *221,www.grandhotel-porro.it* (€€€€). Liberty style and peacefully placed in a 12-acre park, the Porro is dedicated to life in the slow lane, with extremely comfortable rooms to relax in after visits to the spa, sauna and fitness centre. It has menus for special diets, and is open all year.

******Valentini**, Viale Porro 10, **t** (0524) 578 251, *www.hotel-valentini.it* (€€€). Another old hotel, with its own spa and swimming pool in a quiet park setting.

*****Elite**, Viale Cavour 5, **t** (0524) 579 436, *www.albergoelite.it* (€€€). Comfortable, quiet, modern and stylish, set in a green meadow; rooms here are air-conditioned and are equipped with satellite TV. Good buffet breakfasts.

****Vittoria**, Via Roma 14, **t** (0524) 578 239, (€€). One of the classic old spa hotels that has come down in the world a bit, though it's still well kept. *Open April–Nov.*

***Florida**, Viale Fidenza 40, **t** (0524) 565 572, *www.florida-tabiano.it* (€). A pleasantly tranquil little place to stay and close to the spa, this has a restaurant offering a characteristic choice of Emilian cuisine. Minimum 3 nights' stay. *Closed Dec–Feb.*

***Livia**, Vicolo Concordia 6, **t** (0524) 573 166 (€). Plain but centrally located. *Open May–Oct.*

***Villa Berardinelli**, Viale Romagnosi 15, **t** (0524) 573 300 (€). One of the cheapest in town and very basic, this occupies a remarkable turn-of-the-20th-century villa up on the hill. *Open Mar–Oct.*

Antica Torre, Case Bussandri 197, **t** (0524) 575 425, *www.anticatorre.it* (€). Located some 3km above Salsomaggiore at Cangelasio, this retreat allows you to enjoy a stay in agreeably peaceful surroundings. The tower in question is from the 1400s and once belonged to the Pallavicini; now in the centre of the large Pavesi family farm, it guards the swimming pool. There are eight doubles, and good home-cooked meals made with farm-fresh ingredients. *No credit cards. Open Mar–Nov.*

Osteria Bellaria, Via Bellaria 14, **t** (0524) 573 600 (€€). When the locals want to dine well, they leave town and venture out here. To the west, on the Piacenza road, the Bellaria puts *porcini* mushrooms and truffles in as many dishes as possible – *sott'olio* as an *antipasto*, in the tortelli, in the *tortino*, on the grill, by a steak. All the dishes are simply prepared and delicious. There is also a choice of home-made desserts and local wines. *Booking advisable. Closed Mon, 10–30 Jan, and 20 July–10 Aug.*

Trattoria Predosa, Via Contignaco 83, **t** (0524) 578 246 (€€). Located just outside Salso-maggiore at Predosa, this unpretentious trattoria serves a range of fresh home cooking under a pergola: there is a wide range of *secondi* (roast duck, *osso buco*, etc.) as well as the typical delicious pasta dishes you would expect to find in Emilia, with truffles and mushrooms in season. *Booking essential. Closed Mon and July.*

Busseto

Verdi's birthplace
t (0524) 97450, www.bussetolive.com; open April–mid-Oct 9–11.45 and 2.30–6.45; Jan–Mar and mid-Oct–mid-Dec 9.30–11.30 and 2.30–4.30, closed Mon and last half Dec; adm

Teatro Verdi
t (0524) 92487; open Tues–Sun 10–12 and 3–6.30; adm

Museo Civico
t (0524) 92487, www.bussetolive.com; open Feb–Oct Sat–Sun 9.30–12.30 and 3–7; adm

Villa Verdi
t (0524) 830 000, www.villaverdi.org; open Mar–Sept Tues–Sun 9.30–11.30 and 3–6.30; Oct–Nov Tues–Sun 9.30–11.30 and 2.30–4.30; adm

Busseto

Lying some 15km north of Fidenza on the road to Cremona, Busseto is the attractive walled town that gave the world Giuseppe Verdi (*see* p.54). Opera buffs can have a field day in this area and take in the complete Verdi tour, beginning in **Verdi's birthplace**, the simple house at Roncole, 9km southeast of Busseto, where the composer was born in 1813, son of a grocer and tavern-keeper. While in Roncole, you may also like to pay a visit to the parish church where little Giuseppe was baptized and played the organ.

In Busseto proper a statue of Verdi relaxes in an armchair near the medieval castle, or Rocca, built by the Pallavicini lord, Oberto, who became the subject of Verdi's first and seldom-heard opera, *Oberto*. The Rocca contains the **Teatro Verdi**, modelled after La Scala, built in the composer's honour in 1845; Verdi frequently attended performances here. The Rocca's Palazzo Pallavicino is now the **Museo Civico**, packed full of Verdian memorabilia. With the proceeds from his immortal opera *Rigoletto*, the composer built the **Villa Verdi** just outside Busseto in Sant'Agata. It is privately owned, but there are guided tours of the house and a replica of the hotel room in Milan where Verdi died in 1901 at the age of 87.

You can also purchase a joint ticket covering Teatro Verdi, the birthplace house at Roncole and Salone Barezzi in Sant'Agata di Villanova, 3km north of Busseto.

Where to Stay and Eat in Busseto

ⓘ **Busseto >**
*Piazza Giuseppe Verdi 10, **t** (0524) 92487, www.bussetolive.com*

Busseto ✉ 43011

****Palazzo Calvi**, Loc. Samboseto 26, **t** (0524) 90211, *www.palazzocalvi.it* (€€€€, *restaurant* €€€). Just outside the centre, six welcoming rooms in the guesthouse of an 18th-century villa, in a lovely garden setting with a pool. Friendly management; an added bonus is the excellent restaurant and *enoteca*. *Booking advisable.*

★ **I Due Foscari >**

***I Due Foscari**, Piazza Carlo Rossi 15, **t** (0524) 930 031, *www.iduefoscari.it* (€€, *restaurant* €€). The finest place to stay in Busseto is, naturally enough, named after one of Verdi's operas, and is owned by the family of a tenor who often performs in them, Carlo Bergonzi. This neo-Gothic, neo-Moorish building is small, comfortable (the public rooms have lovely ceilings and furnishings) and will probably have no vacancies unless you book in advance; air conditioning is not the least of its charms. Here, too, you can find one of Busseto's best restaurants (€€€). *Closed Mon and 3 weeks Aug.*

Campanini, Via Roncole Verdi 136, Madonna Prati, **t** (0524) 92569, *www.culatelloandwine.it* (€€€). Just outside Busseto, this place has been in the same family for generations. One of their concerns is producing *culatello*, made from the finest hind cuts of pork; the humid environment essential for its curing is supplied in spades by the winter fogs (the famously misty, moisty *culatello* capital, Zibello, is situated just a short distance up the road). Try it, and the other cold meats made by the family, as well as their exquisitely prepared home-made pasta. In spring they serve sturgeon in parchment, at other times *bolliti* and roast duck. *No credit cards. Booking essential. Evenings only, except Sun and hols. Closed Tues–Wed and 20 July–20 Aug.*

Alle Roncole, Viale della Processione 179, **t** (0524) 930 015, *www.alleroncole.it* (€€). In the town of Verdi's birthplace, this restaurant offers four different kinds of *tortelli*, stewed rabbit, and a choice of tempting home-made desserts. Try the home-made *salumi* and the green pasta. *Closed Wed eve and Thurs, 2 weeks in Dec, and Jan.*

Osteria Sant'Ignazio on the main street near the Due Foscari, **t** (0524) 91258 (€€). Offers a range of experimental cuisine. *Closed Wed, 10 days Aug, and 1 week Jan.*

The Castles of Parma

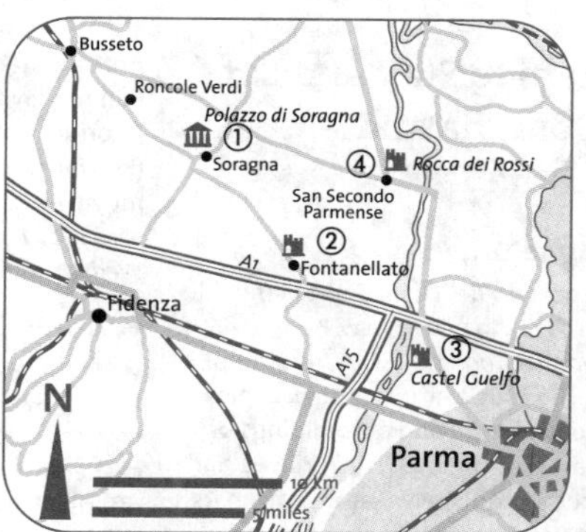

The province of Parma is known for its beautiful castles. Some of the choicest examples lie in the country between Busseto and Parma. Fontanelatto is perhaps the most perfect corner of all.

Rocca of Soragna
t (0524) 597 978, www.roccadisoragna.com; open Mar–Oct Tues–Sun 9–11 and 3–6, Nov–Feb 9–11 and 2–4; adm

The **Rocca of Soragna** ① was begun in the 8th century as a castle and converted into a palace ten centuries later by its current owners, the Meli Lupi. It contains original furnishings from the 16th century and opulent frescoes. The English garden, planted in the early 1800s, has fine old trees and 18th-century statues around the lake.

Fontanellato

Castello di Sanvitale
t (0521) 822 346, www.fontanellato.org; open April–Oct daily 9.30–11.30 and 3–6; Nov–Mar Tues–Sat 9.30–11.30 and 3–5, Sun 9.30–12 and 2.30–5; adm

The village of **Fontanellato**, just east of Soragna, seems rather like a charming miniature Ferrara, spreading around the moated Renaissance **Castello di Sanvitale** ②. The castle was rebuilt in its present form after 1404 by a little dynasty of counts that got its start serving the Visconti of Milan and only died out in 1951. The interior is adorned with frescoes; the rich, sensuous *Diana and Actaeon* in the boudoir, heavily influenced by Correggio's Camera di San Paolo in Parma, is by Parmigianino (1524). Other frescoed rooms include the Sala delle Armi and the dining room, and there is an unusual *camera ottica* built a century ago that allows you to spy on Fontanellato's piazza through a complex arrangement of mirrors. Also in Fontanelatto, in Viale IV Novembre, the church of the **Santuario della Beata Vergine** possesses a perfectly elegant Baroque façade – tacked on in 1913; all the art inside is guaranteed 17th-century.

Another imposing fortress nearby, **Castel Guelfo** ③ can be viewed from the outside only. It once belonged to the Ghibelline Pallavicini family of Busseto, but was renamed as an insult by its Guelph captors in 1407.

Rocca dei Rossi
t (0521) 873 214 or t 3382 128 809, www.cortedeirossi.supereva.it; open Feb–Nov Tues–Sun, guided tours 10–5; April–Sept daily 10–6; Dec–Jan Sat–Sun 10–5; adm

One other castle you can (and should) visit is the **Rocca dei Rossi** ④, located to the northeast at San Secondo Parmense. A bastion of the Rossi, one of the most powerful families of Parma, it became the family's chief residence in the 15th century. Pier Maria Rossi built the castle and, in 1502–21, Troilo Rossi I made it into an elegant pleasure dome, commissioning the frescoes of the 'Wolf Room' and others, but most notably an original cycle on the *Golden Ass* of Apuleius. Troilo Rossi II, an astute politician who enabled the family to coexist convivially with the Farnese, restored the castle and added more frescoes in the rooms he built, on mythological themes and, most grandly, 12 scenes on the glory of the Rossi family.

Where to Stay and Eat in Soragna and Fontanellato

Soragna ✉ 43019

****__Locando del Lupo__, Corso Garibaldi 64, **t** (0524) 597 100, *www.locandadellupo.com* (€€€€, *restaurant* €€€). The 18th-century Lupo occupies the coach house and outbuildings of the castle of the Meli Lupi princes, and has been exquisitely restored, from its terracotta floors to its old oak beams. Baroque paintings hang on the walls, and special pride is taken in the wrought-iron beds. The excellent restaurant serves regional and international dishes. Bike hire.

Antica Osteria Ardenga, at Via Maestra 6 in nearby Diolo, **t** (0524) 599 337 (€€). A former possession of the Meli Lupi. (Bertolucci shot several scenes of the movie *La Luna* here.) All of the *salumi* is made *in casa*. *Closed Tues eve and Wed, 2 weeks Jan and 3 weeks Aug.*

Fontanellato ✉ 43012

Locanda Nazionale >>

Locanda Nazionale, Via A. Costa 7, **t** (0521) 822 602 (€). A small hotel with six simple rooms overlooking the castle; the restaurant (€€) is excellent, offering Parmigiano home-cooking. All the pasta is home-made (try the *maltagliati*, *tortelli* with herbs); typical hearty second courses are roast duck and *stracotto* (beef braised in red wine and stewed), and steak cooked in balsamic vinegar. *Closed Mon.*

Parma

One of Italy's great art cities, and the second city in Emilia-Romagna after Bologna, Parma is admired for her splendid churches and elegant lanes, her artworks and antiquities, the lyrical strains of grand opera that waft from her Teatro Regio – a house that honed the talents of the young Arturo Toscanini – and for the glories of her famous cheese and ham at table – reasons not only to visit, but to return again and again.

08

See map overleaf

200 metres
200 yards
N
Centro Sportivo
Via Giovanni Lanfranco
Via Enrico Sartori
Viale Piacenza
Palazzo Ducale
Viale Piacenza
Viale Pasini
Via Marchesi
Parco Ducale
to Via Aemilia
Via Kennedy
Via Gramsci
Piazzale Santa Croce
Casa di Toscanini
Ospedale Vecchio
Borgo Santo Spirito
Piazza Serventi
Borgo R. Tanzi
Santa Croce
Via Massimo D'Azeglio
Via Cocconcelli
Borgo P.A. Bernabei
Borgo P. Cocconi
Via A. Ferrari
Viale dei Mille
Viale Vittoria
SS. Annunziata
Piazza Corridoni
Pon
Strada Imbriani
Piazza Picelli
Strada D. Quartiere
S. Maria del Quartiere
Strada Costituente
Borgo Paglia
Piazza Matteotti
Via T. Gulli
Borgo S. Giuseppe
Strada Bixio
Via Della Salute
Via Luigi Musini
Viale Vittoria
Viale dei Mille
Borgo S. Domenico
Piazza Rondini
Ponte
Via Monte Santo
Viale Maria Luigia
to Cimitero Villetta
to Cimitero Villetta
Viale Gorizia

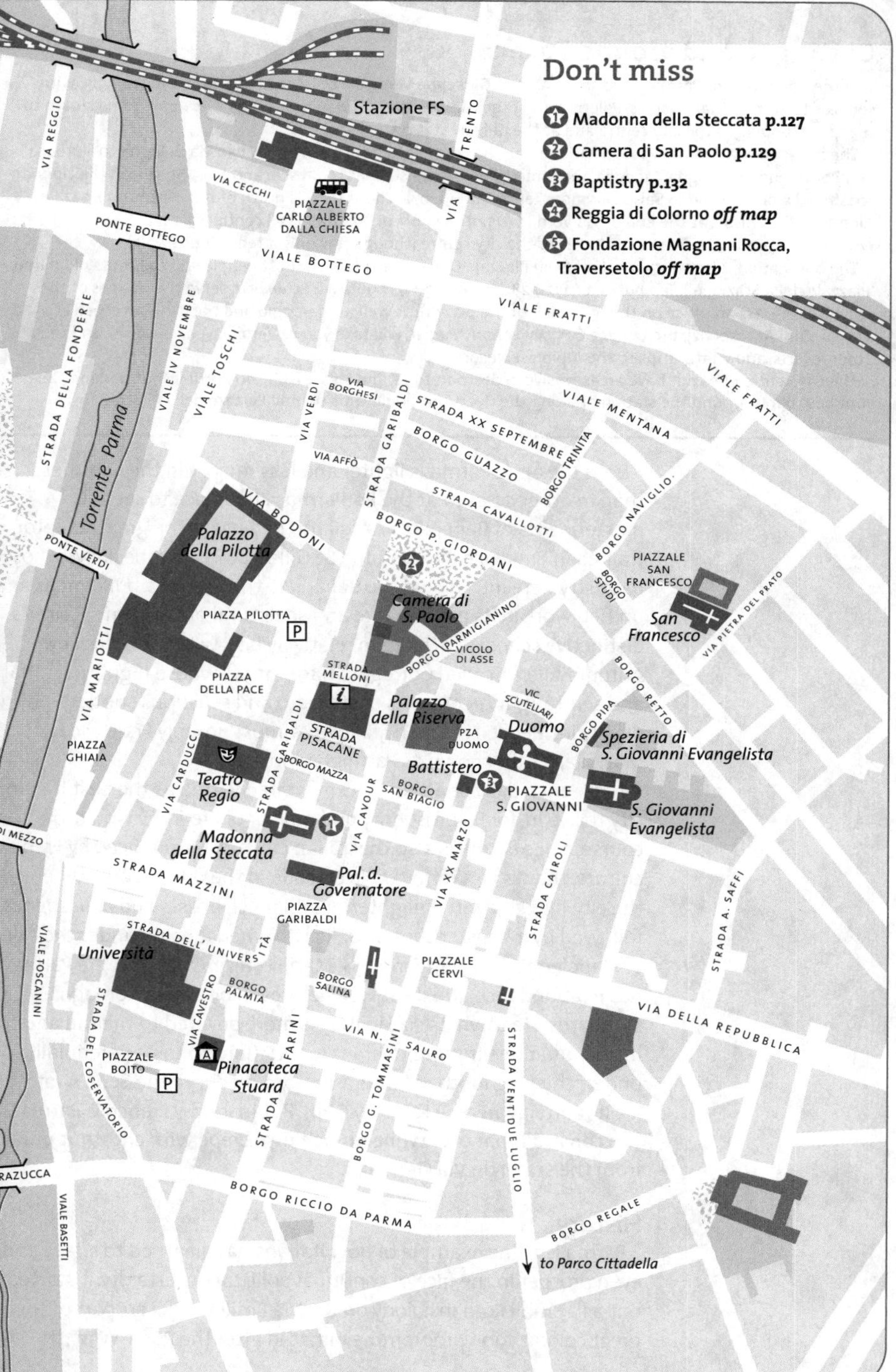
Don't miss
1 Madonna della Steccata p.127
2 Camera di San Paolo p.129
3 Baptistry p.132
4 Reggia di Colorno off map
5 Fondazione Magnani Rocca, Traversetolo off map
Stazione FS
VIA REGGIO
VIA TRENTO
VIA CECCHI
PIAZZALE CARLO ALBERTO DALLA CHIESA
PONTE BOTTEGO
VIALE BOTTEGO
VIALE FRATTI
STRADA DELLA FONDERIE
VIALE IV NOVEMBRE
VIALE TOSCHI
Torrente Parma
VIA BORGHESI
VIA VERDI
STRADA GARIBALDI
STRADA XX SETTEMBRE
VIALE MENTANA
BORGO GUAZZO
BORGO TRINITÀ
VIA AFFÒ
STRADA CAVALLOTTI
BORGO NAVIGLIO
VIA BODONI
BORGO P. GIORDANI
PONTE VERDI
Palazzo della Pilotta
PIAZZALE SAN FRANCESCO
BORGO STUDI
Camera di S. Paolo
BORGO PARMIGIANINO
PIAZZA PILOTTA
San Francesco
VIA PIETRA DEL PRATO
VICOLO DI ASSE
VIA MARIOTTI
STRADA MELLONI
PIAZZA DELLA PACE
BORGO RETTO
VIC SCUTELLARI
Palazzo della Riserva
PZA DUOMO
Duomo
BORGO PIPA
Spezieria di S. Giovanni Evangelista
PIAZZA GHIAIA
VIA CARDUCCI
STRADA PISACANE
BORGO MAZZA
Teatro Regio
Battistero
BORGO SAN BIAGIO
PIAZZALE S. GIOVANNI
S. Giovanni Evangelista
VIA CAVOUR
Madonna della Steccata
E DI MEZZO
VIA XX MARZO
STRADA CAIROLI
STRADA MAZZINI
Pal. d. Governatore
PIAZZA GARIBALDI
STRADA A. SAFFI
STRADA DELL' UNIVERSITÀ
Università
VIALE TOSCANINI
BORGO PALMIA
BORGO SALINA
PIAZZALE CERVI
VIA CAVESTRO
STRADA DEL CONSERVATORIO
VIA DELLA REPUBBLICA
STRADA FARINI
VIA N. SAURO
BORGO G. TOMMASINI
STRADA VENTIDUE LUGLIO
PIAZZALE BOITO
Pinacoteca Stuard
PRAZUCCA
VIALE BASETTI
BORGO RICCIO DA PARMA
BORGO REGALE
to Parco Cittadella
08 Parma

Getting to and around Parma

In the northwest of Parma is the small **Airport Giuseppe Verdi**, Via dell'Aeroporto 44/a, **t** (0521) 9515, with services to Rome, Milan, Naples, Palermo and other destinations. The **Aerobus** runs every day from 5.20am to 11.30pm, stopping in the city centre and at the railway station.

The city is easy to reach by **rail**, positioned on the main lines from Turin and Milan via Bologna to Florence and Rome, and to Bologna, Modena and Rimini. There are also lines to Brescia and to La Spezia on the Ligurian coast, and a branch line to Salsomaggiore Terme via Fidenza. The station is north of the centre, on Piazzale Alberto Dalla Chiesa, at the end of Via Verdi, **t** (0521) 783 960, or **Trenitalia** call centre 892021, *www.trenitalia.com*; buses 1 and 8 link it to the city centre (though it is only a ten-minute walk).

The **bus station**, **t** (0521) 273 251, is also on Piazzale Dalla Chiesa (which most people still call by its old name, 'Piazzale della Stazione'). Tep buses, **t** (0521) 282 657 or 800 977 966, *www.tep.pr.it*, serve the villages of the province (there is an office on the west side of the piazza), as well as Viareggio and the Ligurian coast, **t** (0521) 273 251. Zani Autoservizi, **t** (0521) 242 645, *www.zaniviaggi.it*, will take you to Verona, Venice, Rimini and the other resorts, and winter trips to the Alpine ski resorts.

The city centre does not have an extensive pedestrian zone, and traffic isn't too horrible, but **parking** can be; your best bet is around the station or along the riverfront boulevards behind Palazzo della Pilotta.

Even the air in Parma is lighter and less muggy in the summer than in other cities near the Po. Parma is the place to see the masterpieces of Benedetto Antelami (1177–1233), the great sculptor trained in Provence (in Arles and St Gilles-du-Gard especially) whose baptistry here introduced the Italians to the idea of a building as a unified work in its architecture and sculptural programme. Parma's distinctive school of art began relatively late, with the arrival of Antonio Allegri, called Correggio (1494–1534), whose highly personal and self-taught techniques of sfumato and sensuous subtlety deeply influenced his many followers, most notably Francesco Mazzola, better known as Parmigianino.

The French daily *Le Monde* recently rated Parma as the best Italian city to live in, for its prosperity and quality of life. They would, of course, since Parma is also the Italian city most influenced by French culture, thanks to a remarkable episode in the 18th century when the city filled up with Enlightenment French artists and *philosophes*, followed by a booster shot of Gallicism when it came under the rule of Napoleon's forsaken Empress, Marie Louise. Quality of life Parma has in abundance. You'll eat well here, even by Emilia-Romagna standards. No town its size in Italy is more devoted to theatre and music, and none is more tolerant (or indifferent) to its perennially underachieving football team, a bottom-feeder of the Serie A (at least it often wins the Fair Play Cup). But just how French is Parma? You can mull that over while munching a crêpe with chestnut purée from the stand on Via Garibaldi.

History

Parma is a fine example of how Italians have learned to adapt and even prosper in the face of continual political uncertainty. It started out as a small Roman colony on the Via Emilia in 183 BC, part of the great colonization programme initiated after the Punic Wars; its name means 'shield'. Parma passed the Roman centuries as a fat and happy provincial town without distinguishing itself in any way. Though it took some hard knocks from the invading Germans and Huns in the 5th century, it never was abandoned completely, unlike Modena. Under the short period of Byzantine rule that followed the Greek-Gothic Wars, Parma seems to have been the seat of the army treasury, and acquired the perhaps mocking nickname of Chrysopolis, the 'city of gold'. The Lombards and Franks kept it as an administrative centre, though throughout the Dark Ages the power of the local bishops was growing stronger; at some unknown date, probably in the 11th century, they took control of the town's affairs.

By this time Parma, like most of its neighbours, was booming; a *comune* was established, the cathedral and the famous baptistry were begun, the walls were expanded, and the old cathedral school began developing into a university. Parma played its role in the struggles against the Hohenstaufen; its men helped the Lombard League defeat Barbarossa at the Battle of Legnano in 1176, and in 1248 they dealt a crushing blow to Frederick II's hopes of subjugating northern Italy. The Emperor was besieging the city, and had vowed to raze it to the ground and move its people to a new town, which he would call Vittoria. Instead, the Parmigiani made a clever sortie while Frederick was off hunting, capturing his camp and forcing him to end the siege. Through all this, the quarrels of pope and emperor were echoed internally by the factions of the Da Correggio and Rossi families, and the popolo began to assert itself. In 1250, when the Ghibelline exiles were allowed back into the city, they immediately began to plot against the *comune*. A tailor named Barisello, with 500 armed men behind him, went to visit them all, and convinced them to behave themselves. Barisello retained influence in the government for the next 14 years, much to the dismay of all the nobles of Emilia. Such an early outbreak of populism could not last, but under a noble *capitano del popolo* named Gilberto da Gente the commoners ran the town until 1259.

From then on, however, like its neighbours, Parma solved its addiction to factionalism by turning to boss rule. Various *signori* included Da Corregios and Rossis, and even a della Scala from Verona. The Visconti of Milan grabbed Parma in 1346, and held it until 1447, followed by the Sforza. Francesco Sforza's death in 1466 led to a bloody civil war, and Parma was in utter confusion for a century after; the Wars of Italy made things even worse, bringing numerous campaigns through the *contado* and almost two decades of French occupation. Yet all the troubles did not keep Parma from developing into one of the important artistic centres of the High Renaissance. During the period of confusion San Giovanni Evangelista and the Steccata were built, and Correggio and Parmigianino were painting their most celebrated works.

The Farnese

Parma's disarray made it an easy plum to pick for the mightiest grafter ever to sit on St Peter's throne. Alessandro Farnese, born in 1468, came from an obscure noble family north of Rome. His clerical career was made with the help of his sister Giulia (there's a nude statue of her on his tomb in St Peter's, now discreetly covered up); Alessandro set her up as mistress to the Borgia pope, Alexander VI, and soon he was collecting the revenues of no fewer than 16 absentee bishoprics, serious swag even by Renaissance standards. When he became pope in 1534, as Paul III, he fostered learning, promoted church reform (though he also instituted the Papal Inquisition), cultivated the greatest artists of his generation, including Michelangelo, and always kept one eye on the main business of building his family an empire any way he could. The final settlement of the Wars of Italy, in which a system of Papal-Habsburg control was constructed across nearly all of the nation, gave him a chance to create a new duchy in Emilia, which in 1545 he bestowed upon his son Pier Luigi.

Pier Luigi's own ambitions, and the favour he showed towards the urban *comuni* of Parma and Piacenza, led shortly to his assassination, plotted by the Spanish King and Holy Roman Emperor Charles V and carried out by local aristocrats. His son, Ottavio, who ruled 1547–86, moved the capital from Piacenza to Parma and presided over a long period of prosperity and calm. The next in line, Alessandro, ruled only by correspondence, preferring to spend his time fighting in the Netherlands for the King of Spain (*see* p.98); Parma did not seem to miss him, and the city might have been happier if it had never seen his successor, Ranuccio I, either. Ranuccio (1592–1622) had one quality of the ideal Baroque prince, a sense of grandeur, expressed in the building of the ponderous new ducal palace, the Pilotta, and its famous theatre, meant only for elaborate court spectacles. Otherwise he was a morose and distrustful ruler, who executed over a hundred people for a plot against him in 1612.

Next came Odoardo (1622–46), who wished to emulate his grandfather, the great general Alessandro, but instead compromised the duchy's independence and nearly bankrupted it in a series of futile wars. Ranuccio II (1646–94) was a useful ruler who did his best to repair the damage, but the family that the papacy had built was now facing implacable papal enemies, out to steal their lands and titles. The first were the Barberini, who started their own family empire when one of them became Urban VIII, and warred constantly against the Farnese in both Parma and Lazio during Odoardo's reign. Even worse was Innocent X, a fellow most famous for painting pants on Michelangelo's nudes (and installing a metal dress on Giulia Farnese). This pope, as grasping as Paul III but without the talent and culture, came from a rival Lazio family, the Pamphili. On a trivial pretext, he made war against the Farnese, seizing their southern Duchy of Castro in north Lazio and razing its capital to the ground.

Innocent also did his best to destroy the Duchy of Parma. Ranuccio held out, but his successor, Francesco Maria (1694–1727), found himself in such a weak position that he was eventually obliged to seek papal protection. His Duchy, the second-smallest state in Italy after Lucca, had become an inconsequential Ruritanian backwater, ruled by dukes who have been described as 'tolerant more from laziness than virtue' and dominated by an equally decadent rent-collecting nobility. The city shared in the general collapse of the Italian economy after 1600, though the intensive agriculture of the Parma countryside developed new techniques and was, like nearby Lombardy, able to remain one of the few relatively prosperous rural areas in Italy; those famous Parmesan cheeses, exported since the Middle Ages, were still finding markets.

Like the Medici in Florence, the Farnese line sputtered to a pathetic end. Francesco Maria left no heirs, and the Duchy passed to his useless glutton brother, Antonio (ruled 1727–31). After Antonio ate himself to death, Parma's fate was in the hands of the Great Powers, who were busily rearranging the map of Europe after the War of the Spanish Succession. They gave it to the talented but unemployed Charles of Bourbon, the son of Philip V of Spain and Elisabetta Farnese, niece of Francesco Maria. Charles soon afterwards became Carlo III of Naples, and he carted the Farnese's entire library and picture collection down south with him, along with all of the palace furniture (Parma and Piacenza got many of the paintings back in the 1920s).

The French Invasions

Charles, or Carlo, ruled Parma through a regent for 14 years until the Powers reconsidered and bestowed the Duchy on his younger brother Phillipe, Filippo to the Parmigiani. When Filippo got to Parma, he found that his brother had not even left him a bed to sleep on, so he sent off to Paris for a whole new kit. His wife Babette (Louise-Elisabeth), who was the daughter of Louis XV of France, sent home for Frenchmen to keep her company, and they came in such numbers that within a few years they made up an eighth of the city's population: artists, writers, architects, cooks, *philosophes*, court dandies, *gaveurs de volaille* (to make the *foie gras*), and, most importantly, the very useful M. Guillaume du Tillot.

This gentleman, who had started out as a manservant to the King of Spain, became the Duke's minister in 1759, and immediately began transforming the little Duchy into the ideal Enlightenment state with Filippo's blessing. Du Tillot kicked out the Jesuits and appropriated their vast wealth, reduced the privileges of nobles and clergy, taxed church lands, put taxation on a more equitable basis, closed convents, reformed the university and started primary schools for the people. The French intellectuals, who enjoyed greater freedom here than back in Paris, founded academies, museums and libraries, while the Duke's favourite architect, Ennemond-Alexandre Petitot, transformed the face of the city. The new Accademia delle Belle Arti, with its all-French staff, disseminated the works of Voltaire and Diderot in editions made by one of the great printers and type-designers of all time, Giovanbattista Bodoni. Parma had become one of the cultural capitals of Italy.

It was too good to last. Filippo died in 1765, leaving as successor a son, Ferdinando, who was weak, pious and entirely under the control of his wife Maria Amalia, one of the great harridans of Italian history. Shrill, reactionary, ignorant (and remarkably ugly, if the writers of the time are to be believed), this daughter of Austrian Empress Maria Teresa devoted her life to small dogs, and to slandering du Tillot; in 1171 she finally succeeded in getting Ferdinando to dump him. The Jesuits came back, as did the Inquisition, and all the other reforms were carefully undone. Most of the French went back home.

Many came back in 1796, only this time the invasion was led not by Enlightenment intellectuals, but by Napoleon's army. As long as the French were allied with Spain, the Duchy remained under Spanish protection, and things continued unchanged. Napoleon passed through again to sort out Italian affairs in 1802, and this time the Duchy was united with Tuscany in the 'Kingdom of Etruria'. While Napoleon squeezed the economy with heavy war taxes, he did give Parma a first-rate governor, Moreau de Saint-Méry. This man proved a second du Tillot, reorganizing the laws and the government while promoting culture and trade. In 1814, as Napoleon fell, the allies installed another enlightened governor, this time an Italianized Irishman named Francesco Magawly-Cerati. The reforms of these two men lasted, and contributed much to the happiness of the Parmigiani in the decades to follow.

As in 1731, the Great Powers at the Congress of Vienna had determined to use the Duchy to accommodate a notable in need of a throne. This time, however, the new ruler was to be no less a personage than Marie Louise, Napoleon's second wife and late Empress of the French (*see* p.129). Parma returned to its cosy Ruritanian life, and rather enjoyed being ruled by an attractive woman with a romantic past – at least until the Austrians, who pulled the strings, started forcing oppressive and unpopular policies on her. Parma became a stronghold of the secret patriotic society, the Carbonari, and Austrian troops had to put down a rebellion in 1831. The Parmigiani let Marie Louise live out the rest of her reign in peace. After her death in 1847, however, the Duchy reverted to the Bourbons who had ruled it before the wars. The new Duke, Carlo II, was a reactionary rotter, and the people of Parma forced him to flee a year later. Carlo abdicated in favour of his son Carlo III, who was even worse; he was stabbed to death in 1854. The handwriting was on the wall; a child Duke, Roberto I, and his well-intentioned mother and regent, the Duchesse de Berry, held on for five more years until a revolt during the second Piedmontese-Austrian War put an end to the Duchy for ever. In 1860, after a plebiscite, Parma was incorporated into the Kingdom of Italy.

Piazza Pilotta and Piazza della Pace

Arriving by train or bus in Parma, one of the first buildings you notice is also, unfortunately, the most pathetic: the ungainly, never-completed and, since 1944, bomb-mutilated **Palazzo della Pilotta**, built for the Farnese. Begun in 1602 by the gloomy Duke Ranuccio, it was named after *pelote*, a ball game once played in its courtyard. Big as it is, it seems the Pilotta was never intended as a residence, but only to house the dukes' officials, soldiers and horses. Yet looks are deceiving – for within this patched-together shell, half of it reconstructed since the war, are Parma's greatest treasures.

Museo Archeologico Nazionale

Museo Archeologico Nazionale
t (0521) 233 718; open Oct–Mar Wed–Sat 9–1, Sun and hols 3–5; April–May Wed–Sat 9–1, Sun and hols 3–6; June–Sept Sun and hols only 9.30–12.30 and 4–7; adm

From the palace courtyard, a grand staircase leads to this first-floor museum, founded in 1760 during the rule of du Tillot and containing finds from the excavations at Roman Velleia and elsewhere. The single most important exhibit is the *Tabula Alimentaria*, a large bronze tablet that records the contributions of private citizens to a special dole. The story is an example of the Roman world at its best in the enlightened days of Emperor Trajan. The fund was established to provide relief for small farmers being pushed out of business by the large estates; the tablet also mentions how the government was attempting to encourage them to diversify into other crops, such as vines. When the *Tabula* was discovered in 1747, the local priest had it broken into pieces to sell it as scrap; an educated nobleman saved it from the forge almost at the last minute.

Beyond this, there are Egyptian sarcophagi, Greek vases from Etruscan tombs at Vulci in Lazio, and some Roman statues, including one of Nero as a boy. Exhibits detail Emilia's prehistory, which is pretty dull except for the accomplished and mysterious Terramare culture (*see* p.157), covered here in great detail.

The Teatro Farnese

Teatro Farnese
t (0521) 233 309; open Tues–Sun 8.30–2; adm; joint ticket for Galleria Nazionale available

To reach the part of the Pilotta that houses the Galleria Nazionale you first pass through the Teatro Farnese, built in a hurry in 1618–19 by Palladio's pupil Giambattista Aleotti to honour the planned visit of Duke Cosimo of Florence, who then changed his mind and never

That's Entertainment!

All this effort is devoted to rebuilding a theatre that was used exactly eight times, one that is totally impractical for either drama or music. Indeed impracticality seems here to be refined into a divine principle; originally there was a line of statues around the rail, effectively blocking the view from the best seats. Today such a theatre, with its vast U-shaped gallery, would be fit for nothing but a political party convention, but its purpose was something we can scarcely imagine today: the Baroque court spectacle, in which the new art of opera was combined with musical *intermezzi*, dance, equestrian shows, masques and elaborate allegorical tableaux involving sumptuous props designed by the court artists. Stage machinery was employed to create spectacular effects: monsters rose from the sea, gods descended from above, and clouds rolled in to cover a change of scene.

With a modicum of Italian exaggeration, the Teatro Farnese has been called the 'first modern theatre'. Unlike his master Palladio's famous Teatro Olimpico in Vicenza, which had a fixed set of a Renaissance street scene, Aleotti created a living theatre, with an empty stage where sets could be created and rearranged for each spectacle (something already done on a much smaller scale in London's Globe Theatre, and in Spain). The huge space between the stage and the U of seats, the *platea*, was designed for the horses, for dancing and for mobile tableaux on floats. It could even be flooded for mock naval battles, which became popular in the Renaissance when people read in Vitruvius how they were enjoyed by the ancient Romans. The general theme of a spectacle would be drawn from classical mythology, or medieval romance; the first performance here was entitled 'The Tournament'. While trying to imagine all this, consider also that the tremendous wood backdrop of columns and arches was originally covered with stucco and painted. Stage and forecourt would be illuminated by thousands of candles or oil lamps, while Jove and the Olympian gods looked down from the blue heavens on the painted ceiling.

Such Baroque spectacles, invented here and perfected at Louis XIV's Versailles, were the most expensive entertainments between ancient Rome and the Hollywood of D. W. Griffith and Cecil B. de Mille. Understandably, even a duke could only afford to mount one for a very special occasion: the visit of a king or emperor, or a wedding, such as that of Elisabetta Farnese and Philip V of Spain in 1714. By 1732, when the last of them was presented, such colossal undertakings were already out of fashion. The theatre stood abandoned and forlorn ever after.

showed up. Unfortunately, Aleotti built it entirely of wood, for economy and for acoustics, and an incendiary bomb burned it to the ground in 1944. The Parmigiani have been painstakingly reconstructing it ever since, according to the original plans and using the original methods and fragments of materials wherever possible. Today most of the seating has been restored, and they're working on the stage area, with an impressive proscenium flanked by statues of Alessandro and Ottavio Farnese, and a florid inscription honouring Ranuccio, Duke of Parma and Castro, dedicating the theatre oddly to 'Bellona [the goddess of war] and the Muses'. Almost all of the lavish painted and sculptural decoration was lost. The Italians have a succinct proverbial rule to describe their feelings about their damaged monuments: *dov'era, com'era* – they like things where they were and as they were. We shouldn't be surprised if, with their admirable doggedness, they restore the decoration too, even if it takes another fifty years or even more.

Galleria Nazionale
t (0521) 233 309, www.artipr.arti.beniculturali.it; open Tues–Sun 8.30–1.45; adm; joint ticket with Teatro Farnese available

Galleria Nazionale

The rest of the Pilotta houses the Galleria Nazionale, founded in 1752, even earlier than the Archaeology Museum. As the Accademia

Parmense delle Belli Arti, it was far more than just a museum: part school, part meeting place for intellectuals of all kinds, in imitation of the Academy in Paris, it has played a major role in the city's cultural life for over two centuries.

The museum is divided into two parts, with separate entrances off the Teatro Farnese. *Percorso A*, reached from backstage, starts in the Middle Ages with noteworthy sculptures from Benedetto Antelami and some excellent paintings by little-known local artists: panels showing *Male and Female Saints* by Puccio di Simone (*fl.* 1320–53) and a *Dormitio Mariae* of Nicolo di Pietro Gerini (*d.* 1415). The early Renaissance collection features works by the Tuscans Agnolo Gaddi, Spinello Aretino, Giovanni di Paolo, Starnina and Fra Angelico, and the Emilians Simone de' Crocifissi and Jacopo Loschi (whose charming *St Jerome* holds a toddler of a lion paternally by the paw). Loschi (*d.* 1503) was top dog in the Parma quattrocento, and you can compare his approach with that of younger painters such as Cristoforo Caselli and Filippo Mazzola who ran off to learn their trade in Lombardy or Venice just to escape his influence.

As in Venice, museums in Emilia-Romagna often feature surprising works from the Cretan-Venetian painters of this era, Orthodox Greeks working in a half-Byzantine, half-Italian style. Here the outstanding works are an anonymous *Pietà* and a *Madonna* by Andrea Rico of Candia (Herakleion). Further on is the *Guarigione del Cieco* (Healing of the Blind Man) from the greatest figure to come out of this exotic world, El Greco.

From the Renaissance Tuscans, there's a lovely portrait sketch by Leonardo, *La Scapigliata*, four fine works by the Venetian Cima da Conegliano, works by Bronzino and Giulio Romano, and a portrait by Sebastiano del Piombo of the handsome, foolish Medici pope, Clement VII. Local talent of the late Renaissance is represented by Gerolamo Bedoli, Giovanni Battista Tiuti and Bartolomeo Schedoni (*d.* 1615), the court painter to Ranuccio I, whose striking use of colour and contrast shows up in his *Ultima Cena* (Last Supper) and the dreamlike *Le Marie al Sepolcro*.

Among the non-Italian pictures are works by Peter Brueghel the Younger, Van Dyck, and one of Holbein's famous portraits of the sharp-featured Erasmus. A Frenchman, Giovanni Sons, uses the story of *Adam and Eve* as an excuse for six wonderful Edenic landscapes with a cast of characters that includes Adam's pet cat, an ostrich, a unicorn and one of European art's first turkeys. From the Italian seicento, there are huge mythological canvases of Sebastiano Ricci, including a *Rape of Helen* that spent a couple of centuries entertaining the nurses of Parma's Foundlings' Hospital. This section closes with a sentimental touch – 19th-century paintings, views and prints of Parma by various artists.

Percorso B, on the ground floor, contains gigantic classical statues of *Hercules* and *Bacchus*, looted by the Farnese from the emperors' palace on the Palatine in Rome while Paul III was pope. Besides various portraits and sculptures of the Farnese, Bourbons and Marie Louise, including a statue of her by Canova, there is the complete collection of the Academy's prize paintings. For over a century a prestigious annual competition was held here, and the winning entries offer a lesson in what passed for taste in the late Baroque; few of the winners were ever heard from again, though the 1771 prize went to a young fellow from Spain named Goya. To show how the Baroque sensibility lived on even into Napoleonic times, there is the impressive *Trionfo da Tavola* of 1803 – a table setting for grand banquets, with accompanying sculpture and metalwork. Such dining room extravaganzas were a minor genre of the time. This one, made for the Spanish ambassador to Rome, is one of the few anywhere to survive intact. The next rooms are devoted to Parma's own: Correggio and Parmigianino. Correggio weighs in with the 1530 *Madonna della Scodella*, a seminal work for the simple humanity expressed in its portrayal of the Holy Family at rest during the return from Egypt, and the 1523 *Madonna di San Gerolamo*, a *sacra conversazione* with the most unlikely grouping of the Virgin, St Jerome and Mary Magdalene (what could those three have been conversing about?). Parmigianino's contributions are the *Marriage of St Catherine* and the flirtatious *Turkish Slave*.

Biblioteca Palatina
t *(0521) 220 429, www.bibpal.unipr.it; open Mon–Fri 8.15–7.15, Sat 8.15–1.45*

On the same floor as the gallery, the **Biblioteca Palatina** was one of Europe's first great public libraries, another part of the heritage of Duke Filippo and du Tillot. It contains some 700,000 volumes, including a vast collection of incunabula, codices and manuscripts, in neoclassical halls designed by Ennemond Petitot; like the rest of the palace, it suffered greatly from the bombings in 1944.

Museo Bodoniano
t *(0521) 220 411, www.mb-museobodoniano.it; open Mon–Sat 9–1 by appointment only; closed last 2 weeks of Aug*

The **Museo Bodoniano** is devoted to Parma's great 18th-century printer and type-designer, with examples of his work, as well as his presses and tools, and exhibits on bookmaking and typography.

Piazza della Pace

Once a car park, the piazza facing Palazzo della Pilotta has become the subject of a controversial planning project, providing Parma with an interminable soap opera for most of the 1990s while the politicians argued over various plans and counter-plans for its redevelopment. More complications were added when the builders – inevitably – uncovered some important archaeological remains, and the piazza spent years closed off behind an ugly board fence. The new design is now completed, trees are planted, and the piazza has been officially inaugurated. Facing Via Garibaldi is the cinematic **Monumento al Partigiano**, designed by the 'painter of the Resistance' Renato Mazzacurati.

Teatro Regio
*Via Garibaldi, **t** (0521) 233 309, www.teatroregioparma.org; open Tues–Sat 10.30–12; booking advisable; adm*

The south side of Piazza della Pace is occupied by the celebrated **Teatro Regio** entrance in Via Garibaldi, built by Marie Louise in 1829. This austere neoclassical pile is one of operatic Italy's holy-of-holies, and the best place to hear the region's favourite son, Verdi. Its audiences are legendarily contentious and demanding, and each year tenors and sopranos from all over the world submit either to avalanches of flowers or catcalls from the upper balconies, the *loggioni*. Toscanini began his career here playing in the orchestra, which has since been renamed in his honour. Walking south from the palace along Viale Mariotti or Via Carducci will take you to the excellent daily **market** in Piazza Ghiaia, where a cornucopia of the region's gastronomic delicacies can be found on sale, along with clothes and trinkets; the Farnese planned this space as a vast monumental square, and the façade of the Pilotta would have faced towards it.

The Madonna della Steccata

Madonna della Steccata
open daily 9–12 and 3–6

Across from the Teatro Regio, the church of Madonna della Steccata was built on the site of a miracle-working image of John the Baptist painted on a wall. So many people pressed in to see it in the 1300s that a wooden fence (*steccata*) had to be built to protect it. Eventually a small oratory covered the site, to be replaced in 1521 by the present church. It is sometimes claimed the Steccata was built on Bramante's original design for St Peter's. Don't believe it, but its massive, Greek-cross plan does sum up one of the architectural ideas that were in the air in the High Renaissance. Various local architects worked on the building during its long construction – the final exterior decorations were not added until 1697, and the choir in 1730 – but one great one, Antonio da Sangallo the Younger, suggested the design for the dome while passing through Parma in 1521. Having so many cooks didn't spoil this dish; despite its great bulk, and the lack of a proper piazza to show it off, the church has great dignity and presence.

The chapels in its sumptuous interior are covered with 16th-century frescoes by many of the same artists who worked on the Duomo and S. Giovanni: Mazzola, Bedoli and Gatti. As the city's fashionable church, the Steccata also became the shrine of the city's rulers. Marie Louise's consort Count Neipperg is buried here, and the crypt is full of Farnese and Bourbons. For all the art in this church, the real attraction is the frescoes by Parmigianino on the arch leading to the sanctuary. Parmigianino had painted here early in his career (some of the work on the big organ doors is his), but he was a changed man after his sojourn in Rome among the works of Michelangelo and Raphael, and the hyper-elegant Mannerist frescoes of the *Wise and Foolish Virgins* on the arch, pictured along with *Adam and Eve*, *Aaron* and *Moses*, are his finest work in his home city. Parmigianino never finished all the painting he promised to do here, and the church canons briefly had him jailed for breach of contract; gossips said the artist's obsession with his alchemical experiments was taking up all his time.

Virtually nobody ever looks into the church right across the street, completely overshadowed as it is by the Steccata, but

Sant'Alessandro
open 9.30–12 and 3–5.30

Sant'Alessandro (1527, with a neoclassical façade added in the 1780s) is yet another colourful treasure-house of Parma painting, performed by the city's usual late Renaissance cast of characters, including Gerolamo Bedoli Mazzola and Alessandro Mazzola. Some time after this came Alessandro Tiarini, who frescoed the dome and pendentives (1627).

The Glauco Lombardi Museum

Glauco Lombardi Museum
*Via Garibaldi 15, **t** (0521) 233 727, www.museolombardi.it; open Tues–Sat 9.30–3.30, Sun 9.30–6.30; adm*

Back towards Piazza della Pace, just one block north of the Steccata is the **Palazzo della Riserva**, a graceful Baroque palace that covers an entire block, with enough room to house the main post office, shops, and several cultural institutions including the Glauco Lombardi Museum. The 'Riserva', as its name implies, was the spare palace of the Duchy, used for visiting guests. Part of this 'Casino of the Nobles, Courtiers and Foreigners' was revamped by Petitot, including the severe façade of the part that holds this museum. Glauco Lombardi, a wealthy scholar and collector, assembled this collection of art and objects relating to the time of the Bourbons, the Napoleonic era and the reign of Marie Louise. Most visitors to Parma don't find the time for it, which is a pity; few museums anywhere are so successful in summoning up the spirit of a distant age.

And it was a strangely attractive age, at least seen from tranquil, refined Parma. The main room of the museum is the gorgeous *Grande Sala delle Feste*, designed by Petitot in pastel blue with great chandeliers. Among the paintings on display are works by Nattier, Fragonard and Mignard (*Portrait of Mme de Sévigné*), and portraits of Marie Louise, Napoleon and their child, the 'King of Rome'. There is bric-a-brac aplenty, from Marie Louise's sewing kit and some of her dresses to the ornamental, golden, very French Empire *Corbeille de Mariage*, a wedding present from Napoleon. The most surprising item is the collection of drawings of Ennemond Petitot; this seemingly dry classical architect was never given a chance to follow his fancy, but he left plans for bizarre buildings, such as a water tower that looks like a modern American skyscraper, and incredible designs for masquerade costumes and festival decorations that juggle the ancient Greek with the Aztec and Egyptian. Letters to the Duchess from various Bonapartes and celebrities of the day are placed in glass cases – most touchingly, in excruciatingly correct French schoolboy handwriting, from her son in Vienna, and from her nephew who would one day be Napoleon III.

A Bird in a Gilded Cage

After a visit here, you might suspect that Glauco Lombardi intended this museum as something of a shrine to Parma's great lady. The Parmigiani were always fond of her, even though they once chased her out of town. Maria-Luisa Leopoldina Franziska Theresia Josepha Luzia von Habsburg-Lothringen was born in 1791 at the imperial court in Vienna. A shy, introverted girl with a certain talent for art (some of her sketches and watercolours of romantic landscapes can be seen in the museum), this emperor's daughter grew up well aware that her life would be determined according to the purposes of the dynasty.

She did not, however, imagine that she would be offered up as a sacrifice to someone her people saw as the 'Ogre of Europe', especially after what had happened in France to her Aunt Marie Antoinette. In 1809 Napoleon was master of Europe, and starting to be concerned with his succession. He did love Josephine, as much as he was capable of loving anyone, but she was never able to come up with an heir. Napoleon knew it wasn't his fault – there were already two of his offspring crawling around the apartments of his mistresses – and he decided suddenly on a divorce. Josephine found out when she returned home one day to find that the door between their rooms had been walled up.

The logical place to look for a wife was the Habsburg court in Vienna; such a match would cement France's alliance with her most important potential rival. Count von Metternich, the Austrian foreign minister who had first suggested the idea to Napoleon, talked the Emperor into accepting it by pointing out it would give defeated Austria time to recover her strength, and before long the 18-year-old Marie Louise found herself on a coach bound for France. They were married in a civil ceremony at St-Cloud on April Fool's Day, 1810, and did it all over again for the priest the next day in the Tuileries.

Marie Louise found she was pregnant about three months later. Life as Empress of France proved pleasant enough, especially since her husband was hardly ever at home. Napoleon's charms were lost on her. Once from a battlefield he had written a one-line letter to Josephine: 'I arrive in Paris in three weeks. Don't wash', an approach unlikely to make a favourable impression on a Habsburg princess. They last saw each other, briefly, while the allied armies were closing in on Paris in 1814. She flatly refused to follow him to Elba, and after he threatened to have her abducted she stopped answering his letters, leaving the diplomats with the delicate problem of what to do with her. The vacant Duchy of Parma proved a perfect choice; she moved in with her new lover, the Austrian General Count Neipperg, and made him prime minister. He did an excellent job, and the Parmigiani were quite content until his death in 1829.

After that, however, Metternich – who by now was making all the big decisions in Europe – decided the Duchy needed a less tolerant ruler. He forced one of his minions, Josef von Werklein, on Marie Louise as the new prime minister, and Werklein proved such a good Austrian that Parma rebelled two years later. Marie Louise was forced to flee to the protection of the garrison at Piacenza. The troops there soon had her back on her throne, but from then on it was only as a figurehead.

The great tragedy of Marie Louise's life was her son Napoleon-François, the 'King of Rome', now reduced to a mere Duke of Reichstadt. In 1814 she had allowed Metternich to talk her into bringing the three-year-old child to Vienna. For obvious reasons of state, he had to be watched closely; the Napoleonic partisans in France were already referring to the child as 'Napoleon II'. The Austrians never let him go; Metternich kept him in Vienna as a virtual prisoner. In his teens he contracted tuberculosis, and Marie Louise was able to visit him only once, just before his death in 1832.

Camera di San Paolo (Camera di Correggio)

27 Camera di San Paolo (Camera di Correggio)
t (0521) 233 309; open Tues–Sun 8.30–1.45; adm

Just off the Via Melloni, bordering the northern side of the Palazzo della Riserva, is the Camera di San Paolo, one of the most remarkable sights of Parma, contained in two little rooms. In the 1510s its worldly abbess, Giovanna Piacenza, rebuilt the convent and hired Alessandro Araldi and Correggio to fresco its refectory and an adjoining chamber. At the time, the abbess was the centre of a learned circle of humanists; whatever they were up to may have worried the church, for Giovanna had a long battle with the popes to avoid the cloistering of her convent. Finally in 1524 the pope had his way and the nuns were shut in, one small, early step in the slow strangulation of Italy's intellectual life by the Counter-Reformation Church. The frescoes were eventually forgotten, and no one but the sisters saw them again until the 18th century.

In 1519 Correggio had just returned from a visit to Rome, and the abbess's commission was his first chance to practise his mature style in Parma; he turned the vaulted ceiling of the **refectory** into a delightful green arbor, with the philosophical scheme of Giovanna's devising discreetly limited to the edges. Various interpretations of its meaning have been attempted, most of them concluding that the theme is the 'conquest of moral virtue'. Correggio portrayed the abbess herself (some say) as the *Goddess Diana* over the fireplace, with the enigmatic inscription *Ignem Gladio ne Fodias*, 'Do not use the sword to poke the fire'. The rest of the scheme involves sixteen putti set over sixteen lunettes of mythological emblems, painted in elegant chiaroscuro that gives them the illusion of depth. The interpretation of many of the figures is an open question, but the cycle was probably meant to be read from the entrance door, beginning with the god *Pan*, making a great noise on a conch shell to create 'panic' (as he did at the battle of the Olympians and Titans); this is followed by allegorical figures representing perhaps *Integrity* and *Chastity*. Next, over the fireplace wall, come the goddess *Fortune*, *Minerva* (or *Bellona*), the *Three Graces* and *Adonis* (or *Virtue*). On the next wall, the four elements, water, earth, air and fire, are represented respectively by an obscure figure called the *Bonus Eventus* or *Genius of the City of Rome*, *Tellus* or *Africa*, *Juno* and *Vesta*. Opposite the fireplace is a *Philosopher*, or maybe the god *Saturn*, then the *Temple of Jupiter*, the spinning *Fates* and *Rhea Silvia* (mother of Romulus and Remus), or else *Ino* and *Bacchus*. Returning to the beginning, the cycle is closed with the goddess *Ceres*, or perhaps *Diana*.

Much of the charm of Correggio's ceiling comes from the putti above the lunettes, bearing attributes of Diana's hunt and pictured behind what seem to be windows into the heavens. But the putti too are part of the allegorical scheme. Each is a playful comment on the figure below it: above Pan, a putto blows into another shell while a second one puts its fingers in its ears. Some of the others are more obscure; scholars have been arguing about them, as they have about everything else in this room, for the last two centuries.

Correggio gets all the attention, but the **second chamber**, with frescoes painted in 1514 by Alessandro Araldi, is quite the equal of the first in the singularity of its subject matter. Here too the subtle abbess dictated the scheme, which has been interpreted as representing the 'conquest of spiritual virtue', with a series of scenes on the lunettes around the cornice complemented by Biblical and mythological vignettes set in the beautiful blue *grottesco* decoration of the ceiling. The inscription over the fireplace perhaps gives a key: *Transivimus per ignem et aquam et eduxisti nos in refrigerium*, 'We passed through fire and water, and you led us to a cool place'.

Whatever sort of mysticism inspired this, it does seem that Abbess Giovanna imagined it with a decidedly feminist slant. In the main series, the first scene, *Roman Charity*, records the legend of a daughter who saved her father by nursing him. Next comes a *Burning Triumph*, from the Roman story of Paulus Emilius, whose sons all died on the same day, and then the *Lady and the Unicorn* and *Judith and Holofernes*. On the next wall, three lunettes tell the classical story of *Cleobi and Bitone*, sons of a priestess, who pulled the cart of Juno to the temple when the sacred oxen died, and were rewarded with eternal life. The third wall begins with a pair of feet walking on water, said to be an ancient Egyptian symbol for the impossible, followed by two scenes of women sacrificing. The triumph of virtue on the last wall is represented by the goddess *Ceres*, a woman killing an ape, and another despatching a dragon.

Piazza Duomo

Strada Pisacane connects the Piazza della Pace to the Piazza Duomo, the strangely quiet heart of an otherwise lively city and the site of its Romanesque cathedral and baptistry.

The Duomo

Duomo
open daily, outside Mass times, 9–12.30 and 3–7; free guided tour Sat 3pm

The exterior of the Duomo is angular Romanesque, completed in 1178. The façade is embellished with rows of shallow arches; three tiers of them across, creating an illusion of depth around the central arched window, and the pattern continues in the rich decoration of the sides, apses and dome. The central portal of the façade, with a pair of lions added in 1281, has reliefs of the *Labours of the Months*, starting with March (in much of medieval Italy, the New Year came in with the Annunciation, at the spring equinox). The Gothic campanile, completed in the late 1200s, was originally surmounted by a gilded statue of the *Archangel Raphael*; this is now kept inside on a pillar on the left side of the nave.

There are plenty of lighting machines inside, but come on a sunny morning to get the full effect of one of the most ambitiously frescoed cathedrals in Italy. They completely cover the tall nave, a collaborative effort of the local Mannerist painters Lattanzio Gambara, Alessandro Mazzola, Gerolamo Bedoli Mazzola, Bernardo Gatti and Orazio Samacchini, done between 1555 and 1574. They've fitted most of the Bible on these walls, arranged according to the theological doctrine of typology; each scene from the Gospels, on the upper band, is accompanied below by the Old Testament event that in some way prefigures it. Besides these, some of the side chapels have good medieval and early Renaissance frescoes.

The most important fresco, however, is in the dome, Correggio's *Assumption* (1526–30), a work of art celebrated since the days of Vasari for its almost three-dimensional portrayal of clouds, angels and saints, with masses of pink virtuous flesh getting vacuumed up into heaven. One of the first and greatest of illusionistic dome frescoes, anticipating the Baroque, it had an important influence on artists for the next two centuries – even though the Parmigiani originally gave it such a poor reception that Correggio left town in disgust.

Don't let this pastel ocean of fresco keep you from noticing the cathedral's other attractions: the medieval capitals, some by Antelami and his men, are excellent. Some of the best are up in the *matroneum*, the women's gallery, where you can't often get to see them; an odd one portrays a *School for Wolves*. In the choir is something no Emilian cathedral can do without, an extravagant set of carved intarsia choir stalls, made by Cristoforo da Lendinara in 1473. Nearby, under a rich Renaissance ciborium, is a bishop's chair sculpted by Antelami (1196) with stories of St Paul and St George. It sits under a fresco of the *Last Judgement* by Gerolamo Bedoli Mazzola, where Jesus and the cross looming out with 3-D effect come uncomfortably close to the Salvador Dalí kitsch barrier. There is more Antelami in the north transept, a fine relief of the *Deposition from the Cross* (1178). In the crypt are fragments of Roman mosaics moved here from a site excavated in the piazza, where they formed the pavement of Parma's first Christian basilica.

The Baptistry

3 Baptistry
open daily 9–12.30 and 3–6.30; adm

There is a big firm in Parma that makes *panettone*, Italy's inevitable Christmas cake; they ship them out in boxes that are little models of this building – Parma's symbol, as much as Pisa's leaning tower or Milan's cathedral. The octagonal Baptistry is one of the jewels of Italian Romanesque, constructed of pale rose marble from Verona. It was designed in 1196 by Benedetto Antelami, who also carved the remarkable ribbon frieze of animals and allegories that encircles the lower part of the exterior. The meaning behind all the winged cats, archers, griffins and sea serpents is as elusive as that of San Paolo's ceiling; many are repeated in mirror images elsewhere in the frieze.

Why are Italian baptistries nearly always octagonal? To mystics, this geometric form is said to represent the 'marriage of the earthly and the spiritual', though it may be simply a matter of tradition, following the original free-standing baptistry Constantine built at St John Lateran in Rome. A better question would be how baptistries became an architectural genre of their own in the early Middle Ages;

Parma's joins those of Florence, Pisa and Ravenna as the most glorious examples of their kind. Antelami planned it with a decorative scheme worthy of a cathedral, a *summa theologica* meant to represent everything on earth and in the heavens.

Antelami is also responsible for the two great **doorways**, the *Portale della Vergine* (north door) with reliefs of the Three Kings, the baptism of Christ, Herod's banquet (with the devil himself present, behind Salome) and the decapitation of John the Baptist; and the *Portale del Giudizio* (west door), an ambitious scene that includes the twelve Apostles, the separation of the saved and damned souls, and on the door jambs the *Six Ages of Man* and the *Parable of the Vineyard*. The remarkable south door, a later work, illustrates an episode from the legend of Barlaam, originally a Buddhist story from India that became popular in late Roman and medieval Europe. The scene represents a moral fable originally told by the Buddha himself; the Tree of Life appears, with two mice, one black and one white (representing night and day) gnawing at its root. The man in the tree was attracted by the honey in the beehive there (sin), but awoke the sleeping dragon (the devil), which consumes him in its fire.

The interior, in which each side of the building is doubled to create a sixteen-sided space, is almost entirely covered with paintings, one of the most complete ensembles of Italian medieval art. Those in the upper portion, from the 1200s, are tempera, not true fresco. The vault is divided into six distinct zones, with a starry heaven, *Christ in Glory*, flanked by the Virgin and John the Baptist, and in the lower two zones the *Life of St John the Evangelist* and the *Life of Abraham*, with the *Four Elements*, the *Four Seasons* and the *Four Rivers of Eden*. Below these, the works are by various hands of the 14th and 15th centuries, a tremendous grab-bag of saints and figures from Old Testament and New. You might pick out the two musicians: David with his harp, and St Genesius (a Roman actor who converted and was martyred) playing the violin. The fresco of the two dragon-killers, St Michael and St George, is attributed to Buffalmacco, the Tuscan painter who did the great, lost *Triumph of Death* in Pisa's Campo Santo. Also inside are Antelami's famous reliefs of the *Twelve Months*, with the *Labours* and zodiacal signs, and the *Seasons*, of which only *Spring* and *Winter* survive. Also present, at floor level, are a number of statues that once held places in the niches outside, including *Michael and Gabriel*, *David*, *Habbakuk*, *Solomon* and the *Queen of Sheba*.

San Giovanni Evangelista, and the Neighbourhood Pharmacy

San Giovanni Evangelista
t (0521) 235 311; open daily 8–12 and 3–7.45; guided tours by appointment

Save some coins for the lighting machines in **San Giovanni Evangelista**, the church just behind the cathedral. Behind its Baroque façade (1607) it shelters one of the masterpieces of the

High Renaissance, Correggio's *Vision of St John* fresco in the dome. There's more art here than appears at first sight; this is one of the most carefully planned ceiling frescoes ever. Start from the door, and see how the composition gradually reveals itself as you walk down the nave.

Unfortunately, when the church was remodelled in 1587 Correggio's reputation was at a low point and all of his other ceiling decorations were lost, though a fresco of St John writing down his vision survives over the door north of the altar. Other frescoes here are early works of Parmigianino: figures of saints on the first, second and fourth chapels on the left. There is another fine intarsia choir, and three stately cloisters outside.

Spezieria di San Giovanni
Borgo Pipa; open Tues–Sun 8.30–1.45; adm

San Giovanni was originally part of a Benedictine monastery, one with roots on this site going back to the 10th century. Nearby you can visit another part of the monastery, the historic **Spezieria di San Giovanni**. Herbs and medicines were always a Benedictine speciality, and this pharmacy was in operation from 1298 up to 1881. After that it sat untouched until the 1950s, when its grand Renaissance-Baroque interior was restored and reopened as a museum. It's a fascinating place, with paintings of the great doctors of antiquity, both real and mythological: Mercury and Apollo, Hippocrates and Galen, Averroes and Avicenna. There are herbals and alembics, old jars, pots, 16th-century carved wood cabinets and medieval pharmaceutical instruments. A 16th-century Venetian painting stands over the altar in the back room, for prayer to help the cures.

North of the cathedral complex, on Borgo degli Studi, **San Francesco** is one of the finest examples of the Emilian approach to Gothic, built entirely in brick (1240–50). The church has taken some hard knocks, especially during the Napoleonic occupation when it was used as a prison. The interior was once entirely covered with 14th- and 15th-century frescoes; now only a few fragments remain. The church is now part of Parma University.

Piazza Garibaldi

In company with the rest of the old gents of Parma, Garibaldi and Correggio (or at least their statues) spend their day in the modern centre of the city, Piazza Garibaldi. Here too stands the yellow **Palazzo del Governatore**, with its intricate sundials, which will tell you not only the day and the time of sunrise, but when noon comes in various towns from Quebec to Constantinople. The façade, along with the piazza, was redesigned by Ennemond Petitot in 1759 to modernize a space that has been Parma's civic centre since it was the Roman-era forum. Opposite stands the **Palazzo del Comune** (1623), a contemporary of the Palazzo della Pilotta built in the same blank, gloomy late Farnese manner.

Palazzo del Comune
open Mon and Thurs 8.30–1 and 2.30–5.30; Tues, Wed and Fri 8.30–1; adm

Via Mazzini/Via della Repubblica, which passes through the square, is the old Via Emilia, running as inflexibly straight a course through Parma as it did when the Romans laid it out. Just south of it, on Strada dell'Università, Parma's **University** is one of Italy's oldest, growing out of a cathedral school of the 11th century. This building, however, was created as a Jesuit college in 1654, and given to the University only after the Jesuits were finally kicked out in 1768. An indignant plaque on the entrance records how the building was taken over as a prison and torture centre by the Fascist militias near the end of the war. Inside, you can visit the **Museo di Storia Naturale e Etnografia Africana**, a collection of mostly African plants and zoological trophies, collected in the last century while the Italians were out empire-building. Nearby on Borgo Palmia is the forlorn, deconsecrated **San Tiburzio** (1720), a late Baroque jewel box in the Roman manner, sadly in need of some care.

Museo di Storia Naturale e Etnografia Africana
***t** (0521) 234 082 or 236 465, musnat@unipr.it; open Thurs 3–6, Sat 10–12; adm free*

Across from the University on Via Cavestro, the **Pinacoteca Giuseppe Stuard** is the bequest of an artist and collector who died in 1834. It's an eclectic collection, with a good selection of trecento Florentine and Sienese paintings, works of Uccello, Guercino, Jan Brueghel, Schedoni and Sebastiano Ricci, and some interesting but little-known 19th-century Parma painters, such as Edoardo Raimondi.

Pinacoteca Giuseppe Stuard
***t** (0521) 231 286, www.servizi.comune.parma.it/stuard; open Wed–Mon 9–6.30, Sun and hols till 6; adm*

If you wander out to the southern edge of town, you'll come to traffic-clogged Viale Martiri della Libertà, which gives no indication that it was one of Italy's first proper boulevards. After the city's walls were demolished, Petitot laid out this stretch as the **Stradone** in the 1760s, lined with horse-chestnut trees and marble benches, a place for the gentry to parade in their carriages following the fashion of Paris. To close the view at the end, he built the severe, neoclassical **Casino** as a café for the elite (casino, or 'little house', incidentally, did not imply gambling until the green tables were set up in Venice in the late eighteenth century). At the opposite end is the city's small **Botanical Garden**.

Botanical Garden
***t** (0521) 233 524, www.biol.unipr.it/ortobot/orto.html; open daily 8–12 and 2–5.30; tours by appt*

South of the Stradone, the **Cittadella** was Alessandro Farnese's only gift to Parma. The absentee soldier-duke may never have cared to reside in his duchy, but he did spend much time and care on the planning of this new-model fortress, a prototype of the sprawling, low forts of the Baroque era, designed to withstand artillery. This one, which had a twin in Antwerp, Belgium, was roughly the size of Parma's city centre, but Alessandro must have missed something, for the Cittadella was never attacked without falling almost immediately. Nearly all of it has been demolished and converted into a city park. A soccer pitch occupies the old *place d'armes*, but you can still see the impressive monumental **gateway** (1596).

South of the Cittadella, the **Museo Cinese ed Etnografico** has a collection of Chinese art and various ethnographic items collected by missionaries.

Museo Cinese ed Etnografico
*Viale San Martino 8, **t** (0521) 990 011, www.museocineseparma.org; open Thurs–Sat, Mon and Tues 9–12 and 3–6, Sun 3–6; appt recommended; adm by donation*

East of Piazza Garibaldi

From Piazza Garibaldi, a walk down Via della Repubblica will take you to the east end of Parma, passing **Sant' Antonio Abate**, an eccentric church by Ferdinando Bibiena, greatest of the famous Bolognese family of theatre architects and stage designers (his *scena per angolo* opera sets inspired Piranesi's *Carceri*). While designing operas for Ranuccio II, he found time to give this church its unusual cross vaulting and false ceiling, set with windows to expose the heavenly scenes frescoed on the real one. Further on, **San Sepolcro** is an honest Gothic church (1257) bushwhacked by the Baroque, with a bizarre leaning campanile (1616) and an ornate interior, including the lavish Capella dell'Addolorata and a carved wood ceiling. In the first chapel on the right is a sunny blue *Polyptych of St Ubaldo* by Alessandro Araldi.

Certosa
open Mon–Fri 9–12 and 2–4, Sat 9–12; adm free

Stendhal aficionados will be glad to know that there really is a Charterhouse of Parma, the **Certosa**, though it bears no resemblance to the novelist's invention in atmosphere, architecture or history. Located 4km east of town on Via Mantova (bus no.10), it was founded in 1281 but totally rebuilt in the 17th century, and now serves as a military school. The cloister is out of bounds, but you can visit the church's frescoed interior.

L'Oltratorrente: Parma across the River, and the Parco Ducale

From the market in Piazza Ghiaia, in the shadow of the Pilotta, the **Ponte di Mezzo** will take you across the Torrente Parma to the city's west end. This is the most recent incarnation of the Roman Via Emilia bridge; if you take the underground passage near the market you'll see some arches of a rebuilding job by the Gothic King Theodoric. The name *Torrente* is an admission that the Parma is rather less than a river; for most of the year you'll see only a grassy flood plain with a trickle down the middle.

SS. Annunziata
open daily 7.30–12 and 3–7.30

Ospedale Vecchio
open Mon–Sat 9–12 and 4–7

Santa Croce
open daily 8–12 and 3.30–7

On the other side of the bridge, **SS. Annunziata** (begun 1566) is a genuine surprise, a Baroque building that went up long before the Baroque was even dreamed of. The architect G. B. Fornovo conceived this experimental work, an elliptical domed church with ten radiating chapels. The new plan brought some tricky architectural problems; Fornovo's dome collapsed in 1626, but was immediately rebuilt. Nearby, on the Oltratorrente's main street, Via Massimo d'Azeglio, the **Ospedale Vecchio** was one of Europe's first, founded in 1201 by a knight of the Teutonic Order; the building (1476) now houses the state archive. At the end of the street, at Porta Santa Croce, the church of **Santa Croce** (1210) contains some extremely peculiar medieval capitals amidst the Baroque redecorations. There is one more late Renaissance experiment among the churches of the Oltratorrente, **Santa Maria del Quartiere**, south of S. Croce in Piazza Picelli. This tall, hexagonal pile (1604) was by Gian Battista Aleotti, architect of the Farnese Theatre; inside is a dome fresco by Pier Antonio Bernabei in imitation of Correggio, the *Paradiso*.

Santa Maria del Quartiere
open Mon–Sat 9–12

North of Strada d'Azeglio is Parma's largest park, the **Parco Ducale**, laid out for Ottavio Farnese in the 1560s. In its day this was one of the renowned gardens of Italy, with a spectacular sculpted fountain facing the residence of the dukes. By the time the Farnese trundled off to extinction, however, the park had become neglected and overgrown. In the 1760s Duke Filippo and du Tillot brought in French landscape designers and sculptors for a total makeover, under the direction of Ennemond Petitot. The result is what you see today, a reflection of the gardens of Versailles with a touch of informality. The graceful statues – satyrs and shepherdesses, naiads and classical gods – are by a sculptor named Jean-Baptiste Boudard. There is a classical ruin, built to celebrate the arrival of the horrible Maria Amalia, and a large lagoon with islands and a 'Trianon Fountain'.

Parco Ducale
open winter 7am–8pm, summer 6am–12am

The hodgepodge **Ducal Palace**, begun by Vignola in 1561, suffered additions and remodellings by half a dozen architects, including Ferdinando Bibiena and Petitot, over the next two centuries. The palace is now the home of the Parma police, but they'll let you in to see the surviving frescoed rooms, including the *Sala di Amore*, the last work of Agostino Carracci. Agostino was sent here by the Farnese after the success of the fresco cycle he and his brother Annibale produced for the Palazzo Farnese in Rome, but he died before it was finished. Other rooms contain more frescoes by artists on the theme of love, mythological scenes from the story of Orpheus, and illustrations from Tasso's *Gerusalemme Liberata*.

Ducal Palace
***t** (0521) 537 678; open Mon–Sat 9.30–12; adm*

The **Centro Studi Archivio della Comunicazione** is an institute (due to move to the Certosa di Villa Serena di Paradigma) founded by the University of Parma. Although it mainly contains documents relating to the media, photography and dramatic arts, it includes many interesting paintings and sculptures by contemporary Italian artists.

Centro Studi Archivio della Comunicazione
*Via Palermo 6, **t** (0521) 270 847, www.unipr.it/arpa/csac; closed for restoration*

Paganini and Toscanini

There are two musical pilgrimages to make on this side of the river. The first is to the **tomb of Paganini**, a 15-minute walk from the centre of Parma to Viale della Villetta on the southern edge of town, the embalmed wizard of catgut and bow (1867–1957), who lies decked out in virtuoso splendour in Villetta cemetery.

Tomb of Paganini
***t** (0521) 963 565; open Mon–Sat 8–5, Sun 8–12.30 and 2.30–5; later in summer*

The **birthplace of Arturo Toscanini** is a modest house at Borgo Rudolfo Tanzi 13, between the Ponte di Mezzo and the Parco Ducale; it contains memorabilia and a copy of every record he ever made. Toscanini was one of the first cultural notables to become an enthusiastic Fascist; in 1919 he stood as a candidate for parliament

Birthplace of Arturo Toscanini
***t** (0521) 285 499, www.museotoscanini.it; open Tues–Sun 9–1 and 2–6; adm*

from Milan on the same ticket as Mussolini. The violence of the *squadri* and the creation of the dictatorship turned him against the movement. In 1931 he was beaten up during a concert for refusing to play the Fascist anthem *Giovinezza*, and he moved to the USA.

ⓘ **Parma >**
Strada Melloni 1/b, www.turismo.comune.parma.it, just off the main Strada Garibaldi, **t** *(0521) 218 889; open Mon–Sat 9–7, Sun 9–1.*

Shopping in Parma

There are plenty of **antique shops** in Parma, mainly to be found along or around Via N. Sauro, and on the third Sunday of every month (*exc Jan*), a huge antiques fair, the **Mercatino dell'Antiquariato**, takes place at Fontanellato, 15km to the west; another antiques fair, the **Mercante in Fiera**, is held twice yearly in Parma, in spring and autumn.

Fashion shops are clustered around Borgo Angelo Mazza, along with **perfume shops** that will sell you a bottle of *Violetta di Parma*, the essence of violets worn by Marie Louise, who had commissioned her hairdresser Borsari to come up with something nice. For the next century or so the fragrance was the rage in Paris, and Borsari was launched on a career as one of Italy's most eminent perfume makers; along with the original Parma violets, the firm now produces 300 different scents.

And then there's **food**; after all, this is the city that hosts a biennial world food fair, the **Cibus**, held in even-numbered years. The main market in Piazza Ghiaia, by the river, is the most convenient place to stock up for a picnic or pick up some local specialities to take home. Otherwise, try **Specialità di Parma**, Via Farina 9/c, a magnificently stocked emporium supplying all the regional delicacies. For tours of the establishments making Parma's prime gastronomic products – *prosciutto*, wine and Parmesan cheese – ask at the Parma tourist office, or at one of the cooperatives: the Consorzio Prosciutto, **t** (0521) 243 987, *www.prosciuttodiparma.com*, and the Consorzio Parmigiano, **t** (0522) 307 741, *www.parmigiano-reggiano.it*.

Where to Stay in Parma

Parma ✉ 43100

Parma's trade fair grounds are bustling in May and September, when you may well find no room at the inn if you haven't reserved a couple of months in advance.

Luxury (€€€€€)

******Palace Maria Luigia**, Viale Mentana 140, **t** (0521) 281 032, *www.sinahotels.it*. A large and luxurious palace handily situated in the centre, with a discreet air and designer rooms – try to get one with a view out over the *centro storico*. Its restaurant **Maxim's** is well known in Parma.

******Star Hotel du Parc**, Viale Piacenza 12/c, **t** (0521) 292 929, *www.starhotels.it*. Overlooks the Parco Ducale; the public rooms are Liberty-style, full of lovely furniture, and the quiet modern rooms have every possible convenience down to heated towel rails. Restaurant serving local and international cuisine.

******Hotel Villa Ducale**, Via del Popolo 35/a, Moletolo, **t** (0521) 272 727, *www.villaducalehotel.com*. Located 2km from the centre of Parma, this is an 18th-century country villa that once belonged to Marie Louise. A quiet haven set in its own park of lawns and trees, it deftly combines old and new; rooms are well equipped, with Internet access. Car park and restaurant.

Expensive (€€€€)

******Hotel Verdi**, Via Pasini 18 (facing the Parco Ducale), **t** (0521) 293 539, *www.hotelverdi.it*. The Verdi is refined and intimate. Located in an elegantly refurbished Liberty-style building, it's steeped in the well-being that the city is known for, complete with marble floors, Murano lamps and marble baths, and lovely linen sheets. Facilities include a garage, free bicycles for guests, and an adjacent gourmet restaurant, the **Santa Croce**. *All closed 2 weeks Aug.*

******Park Hotel Stendhal**, Via Bodoni 3, **t** (0521) 208 057, *www.hotelstendhal.it*. Right in the heart of town alongside the Piazza Pilotta, an older hotel with good facilities and a pay-parking garage. Restaurant **La Pilotta** offers local specialities and seafood. *Closed lunch Sun and Mon.*

***Astoria Executive**, Via Trento 9, **t** (0521) 272 717, *www.piuhotels.com*. Located near the station, a short walk to the centre. Comfortable, sound-proofed rooms and a good breakfast buffet make for a comfortable place to stay; residents dine for less at the hotel's restaurant.

Moderate (€€€)

***Button**, Borgo Salina 7, **t** (0521) 208 039, *hotelbutton@tin.it*. In the knot of small streets behind the Duomo, this hotel is almost as cute as its name. Rooms are distinctly on the small side but very comfortable; no restaurant but an excellent buffet breakfast. *Closed 10 days Dec–Jan and 20 days in summer.*

Inexpensive (€€)

***Brenta**, Via G. B. Borghesi 12, **t** (0521) 208 093, *www.hotelbrenta.it*. In the same area as the Astoria, this little family-run hotel has the least expensive rooms in this category, simple and fairly quiet.

★ Torino >

***Torino, Borgo A. Mazza 7, **t** (0521) 281 046, *www.hotel-torino.it*. Centrally located, this hotel has ample, comfortable rooms and very friendly staff. You can have your morning coffee in a Liberty-style breakfast room or in the flower-filled courtyard. Free bicycles for residents will get you about town, Parma-style.

Moderno, Via Cecchi 4, **t** (0521) 772 647, *moderno@century.it*. Ancient, somewhat mouldering and vaguely Art Nouveau in character. Most of the rooms are en suite.

***Lazzaro**, Via XX Marzo 14, **t** (0521) 208 944 or 333 319 5395. Near the Cathedral and Baptistry, an old-fashioned *locanda*: a good solid trattoria with well-kept rooms upstairs, the only cheap ones in the centre.

***Leon d'Oro**, Viale Fratti 4, **t** (0521) 773 182, *www.leondoroparma.com*. You won't find en-suite rooms here.

Budget (€)

Really low-cost rooms are pretty hard to find in this city, and most of them are located near the station.

Ostello Cittadella, Parco Cittadella 5, **t** (0521) 961 434, *ostellocittadella@libero.it*. Parma's 25-bed youth hostel is housed in the Farnese's 17th-century pentagonal fortress, which now serves as a municipal park (bus no.9 from the station gets you to within 400 metres; the rail station is 1.5 kilometres away). IYHF card required. *Open April–Oct.*

Eating Out in Parma

Music and food are the Parmigiani's ruling passions; a perfect aria is greeted with the same rapt silence as a perfect dish of pasta, dusted with freshly grated Parmesan cheese. Dishes particularly to look out for, besides the city's famous ham and cheese, are *stracotto* (stewed beef), *carpaccio* (raw beef), the various methods of serving *carciofi* (artichokes) – in fritters, pasta dishes and in crêpes – and the famous pasta dishes: *tortelli d'erbetta* (stuffed with ricotta and spinach, and served with melted butter and Parmesan), or *di zucca* (with pumpkin), or with potato.

Very Expensive (€€€€)

Il Cortile, Borgo Paglia 3, **t** (0521) 285 779, *www.parmacucina.com/web/ita-r-ilcortile.html*. Stylish and intimate, located in a covered interior courtyard, and serves a delicious mix of traditional and modern dishes – pasta with asparagus tips, pistachios or shellfish, sea bass cooked in salt and sturgeon grilled with chives. Good list of wines. *Closed Sun and Aug. Booking advisable.*

La Greppia, Via Garibaldi 39/a, **t** (0521) 238 686. Although this is housed in a former stable, it presents some of Parma's most modern and innovative cuisine, based on local traditions. There's a delicious selection of *pasta di verdure* (made with spinach or tomatoes) and other original vegetable dishes, exquisite pasta, and good second courses, all prepared before your eyes in the glass kitchen. *Tortellini* with chestnuts, apples and grapes is an ancient local recipe. *Closed Mon, Tues and July. Booking advisable.*

Parizzi, Via Repubblica 71, **t** (0521) 285 952, *parizzi.rist@libero.it*. Another great place to dip into Parma's specialities, this is a large, cheerful restaurant with delicious *antipasti* of *prosciutto di Parma* and salami, followed by *crêpes alla parmigiana*, asparagus in pastry, or

Trattoria dei Corrieri >>

I Tri Siochètt >>

cappelletti, Parma's favourite shape of pasta. Try for instance the *ricotta tiepida con verza* (warm ricotta with cabbage) or the innovative fish dishes. *Book. Closed Mon and part of Aug.*

Expensive (€€€)

Al Tramezzo, Via del Bono 5/b (on the east side of town, at San Lazzaro Parmense), **t** (0521) 487 906, *altramezzo@libero.it*. This wine bar started life selling sandwiches, and has kept its friendly atmosphere. Try the ricottina with shrimp and bacon, fish dishes or scampi with asparagus and mayonnaise. Excellent list of wines and spirits. *Closed Sun, and the first half of July.*

Angiol d'Or, Vicolo Scutellari 1, **t** (0521) 282 632, *www.angioldor.it*. Located near the Duomo, this eaterie has seating outside that allows you to contemplate the Baptistry while enjoying a steaming plate of *tortelli d'erbetta, tortellini di zucca*, pasta with sea bass and peas, or tripe with *parmigiano*. For dessert, try the *tortino di riso* with grape must. *Closed Sun evenings, Mon and Aug.*

Antica Cereria, Borgo Tanzi 5, **t** (0521) 207 387, *anticacereria@libero.it*. Near the Parco Ducale, occupying an old candle factory. The Antica serves one of the region's famous dishes, *bomba di riso con il piccione* (a moulded round of rice around boned pigeon in mushroom sauce, baked in the oven). *Closed Mon, Sun in summer, and Aug. Booking advisable.*

Cocchi, Via Gramsci 16/a, **t** (0521) 981 990, *www.hoteldaniel.biz*. Elegant but not fussy, dedicated to bringing out the finest in Parma's fine ingredients: *culatello di Zibello* and *prosciutto*, rich minestrone, various *bolliti*, delicately stewed *baccalà*, stuffed veal, and old-fashioned home-made ice cream. *Closed Sat, all Aug and 1 week Dec. Booking advisable.*

Moderate (€€)

Osteria della Gatta Matta, Borgo degli Studi 9/a, **t** (0521) 231 475. Come here to sample local cuisine such as parmesan pudding with ham and vegetable and wonderful desserts such as *pasticcio di mele* (apple pie). *Closed Sun and Mon, and Aug.*

Il Trovatore, near the station, Via Affò 2/a, **t** (0521) 236 905, *www.iltrovatoreristorante.com*. An elegant restaurant which serves the usual classics along with an interesting choice of less traditional dishes, which might include venison with forest fruits, rabbit with tomato and olives or turbot *involtini* with lemon and potatoes. Dessert wines by the glass; good value four-course menu with wine. *Closed Sun, 2 weeks Aug and 1 week Jan.*

Trattoria dei Corrieri, Strada del Conservatorio 1, **t** (0521) 234 426, *www.trattoriacorrieri.it*. Traditional Parma cuisine at reasonable prices is served in a former postal relay station, near the university, where the walls are a veritable museum of old Parma photos and memorabilia. This is certainly the place, and everybody knows it; get in early for a seat at lunch. *Closed Sun in summer.*

Trattoria del Tribunale, Vicolo Politi 5/a, **t** (0521) 285 527. In the heart of the historic centre, next to the Tribunale (Court House), this family-run restaurant is one of the most beloved by Parma cuisine lovers. *Closed Mon and Tues, 2 weeks between Dec and Jan, 2nd part of Aug.*

I Tri Siochètt, Strada Farnese 74, **t** (0521) 968 870, *itrisiochett@virgilio.it*. A few kilometres southwest of the centre (take a taxi). An old *osteria* with a lovely summer veranda, and it has become so popular that reservations are essential. The reason is simple: delicious innovative cuisine based on tradition, that won't break the bank. The *salumi* is delicious as always, and in the evening comes with *torta fritta*. Pasta lovers shouldn't miss the *tris di tortelli*, featuring three different kinds. *Osso buco* and other traditional dishes make up the *secondi*; among the desserts, the *amaretti* ice-cream cake with a hot chocolate sauce is a favourite. *Evenings only, except Sun (open all day). Closed Mon, 1 week in Aug, and 1 week in Dec.*

Inexpensive (€)

Antica Osteria Fontana, Via Farini 24a, **t** (0521) 286 037. This has been here for donkey's years. Although wine is the main focus, with over 700 on offer, there's a small menu of typical dishes at lunchtime. In the evening it becomes a wine bar, with a good selection of sandwiches and *charcuterie* to make up a light meal around a bottle. *Closed Sun and Mon, and most of Aug.*

Bottiglia Azzurra, Borgo Felino 63/a, **t** (0521) 285 842. In the evening, this popular place draws a young crowd. It offers creative and ethnic cuisine on a changing menu, a wide choice of Italian and French cheeses, and a big wine list. *Stays open late, but closed Sun, July and Aug.*

Gelateria Caraibi, Via Emilio Lepido 9. This has the widest selection of flavours, including many exotic ones.

Gelateria K2, by the cathedral in Via Cairoli. One of two places which rival each other for the best ice cream in Parma. Try the *bacio*.

Lazzaro, Borgo XX Marzo 14, **t** (0521) 208 944 (with rooms, *see* p.139). Has all the *tortelli* and the usual favourites, and for a light lunch there are big salads (*insalatone*) and crêpes. *Closed Sun evenings in July–Aug.*

Entertainment and Nightlife in Parma

Opera has a more enthusiastic local audience here than just about anywhere else in Italy, and Parma is also one of Italy's most devoted theatre towns. Parma also hosts two **music competitions**, one at the end of August for conductors, and another in October for operatic singers. In May–June there's the **Verdi Festival**; for information, contact Fondazione **Verdi Festival**, Via Farini 34, **t** (0521) 289 028, *www.giuseppeverdi.it*. Throughout the summer concerts are held in the nearby **castles** – the tourist office provides a list of events. **Busseto,** Verdi's home, has its own philharmonic and chorus, and puts on its own small opera season in December and January; for tickets contact the tourist office, Piazzale Verdi 10, **t** (0524) 92487. Listings are in a weekly free magazine called *Parmagenda*.

Nuovo Teatro Pezzani, Borgo San Domenico, **t** (0521) 200 241, *www.nuovoteatropezzani.it*.

Teatro al Parco e delle Briciole, Parco Ducale, **t** (0521) 992 044, *www.briciole.it*. Try out classics in Italian, and shows for children.

Teatro Europa, Via Oradour 14, **t** (0521) 243 377, *www.europateatri.it*. Experimental performances and cabaret.

Teatro Farnese, in the Palazzo della Pilotta, **t** (0521) 039 399.

Teatro Lenz, Via Pasubio 3/e, **t** (0521) 270 141, *www.lenzrifrazioni.it*. A modern experimental company.

Teatro Regio, Via Garibaldi 16/a, **t** (0521) 039 399, *www.teatroregioparma.org*. The season at this theatre runs through winter, from December to March. *Box office open weekdays 10–2 and 5–7, Sat 9.30–12.30 and 4–7. Closed Sun, Mon and hols.*

Teatro Stabile, Viale Basetti 12/a, **t** (0521) 230 242, *www.teatrodue.org*. Contemporary theatre and dance. *Box office open Mon–Fri 9.30–1 and 5–7.30.*

Cinema d'Azeglio, Via d'Azeglio 33, **t** (0521) 281 138.

Cinema Edison, Largo VIII Marzo, **t** (0521) 967 088.

Around Parma

Reggia di Colorno
t (0521) 312 545, reggiadicolorno@tiscali.it; open for guided tours only Mar and Nov Tues–Sat 11 and 3, Sun 10, 11, 3, 4 and 5; April–Oct Tues–Sat 10, 11, 3 and 4, Sun 10, 11, 3, 4, 5 and 6; closed Dec; adm

North of Parma: Colorno

North of Parma, at Colorno on the road to Mantua, in 1660 Duke Ranuccio II converted an old castle into a summer villa called **Reggia di Colorno**. Later architects Ferdinando Bibiena and Ennemond Petitot perfected its stately arcaded façade into what was often called a 'miniature Versailles'. The Bourbon rulers of Parma spent much of their time here, as did Marie Louise. After Italian unification, Colorno became the property of the king, who stripped it of most of its works of art to embellish his own palaces. Nevertheless, its neoclassical interior is worth a visit, a bright and airy residence more habitable than the average 18th-century palace. Among the highlights are Petitot's Sala Grande, the ducal chapel and the 'astronomic observatory' of Duke Ferdinando. Outside, the dukes had gardens with canals, an orangerie – and tunnels; the later Bourbon rulers must have been nervous, for they installed escape hatches leading all over the countryside, one supposedly running all the way to Parma. The **gardens**, once laid out in the French style, but converted by Marie Louise into an informal English park, suffered neglect for decades, but are now being restored according to the original plan.

If you've got the time, just 12km over the Po in Lombardy is **Sabbioneta**, the 'ideal Renaissance city' founded by Vespasiano Gonzaga of Mantua in the 1580s. Though this experiment never thrived, it retains some attractions: a frescoed Ducal Palace and one of the first Renaissance theatres.

The Parma Foothills

The foothills south of Parma are the source of much happiness – almost all of the famous Parma hams are produced here, as well as plenty of Parmigiano cheese, DOC *Colli di Parma* wines, and even truffles, from around the village of Calestano. There are buses to each of the villages from Parma, but not between them, so to do a full tour you need a car.

Castello di Torrechiara
***t** (0521) 355 255; open Oct–Mar Tues–Fri 8–3.15, Sat–Sun 9–4.15; April–Sept Tues–Sun 8.30–6.45; adm*

On the main road south, the SS665 for Langhirano, you'll pass the magnificent **Castello di Torrechiara**, a castle of brick and fantasy almost unchanged since the 15th century, when it was built by Pier Maria Rossi (1413–82), a humanist, linguist, astronomer and military captain who was a great friend of Milan's Francesco Sforza. Visible from miles around, and defended by a double set of walls and four mighty towers, each surrounded and linked by covered walkways, it has an elegant courtyard with ornate terracotta tiles and good frescoes on the ground floor by a quattrocento artist named Cesare Boglione, who also painted the delightful cycle of acrobats performing impossible feats with hoops on the backs of lions. The castle's best frescoes, however, are by Bonifacio Bembo in the beautiful 'Golden Bedchamber', where Pier Maria brought his young lover Bianca Pellegrino, and where he died in her arms. Bembo covered the walls with gold leaf (now gone) and a fresco cycle dedicated to their love and pictures of the Rossi family's forty castles.

Fondazione Magnani Rocca
***t** (0521) 848 327, www.magnanirocca.it; open Mar–Nov Tues–Sun 10–5; adm*

East of Torrechiara at **Traversetolo**, the **Fondazione Magnani Rocca** is a small but surprising collection of art housed in a country villa. The writer Luigi Magnani (*d.* 1984) assembled works by painters from Gentile da Fabriano, Carpaccio, Lippi, Titian, Dürer and Fuseli to Cézanne, Goya, Monet and De Chirico, with a special emphasis on

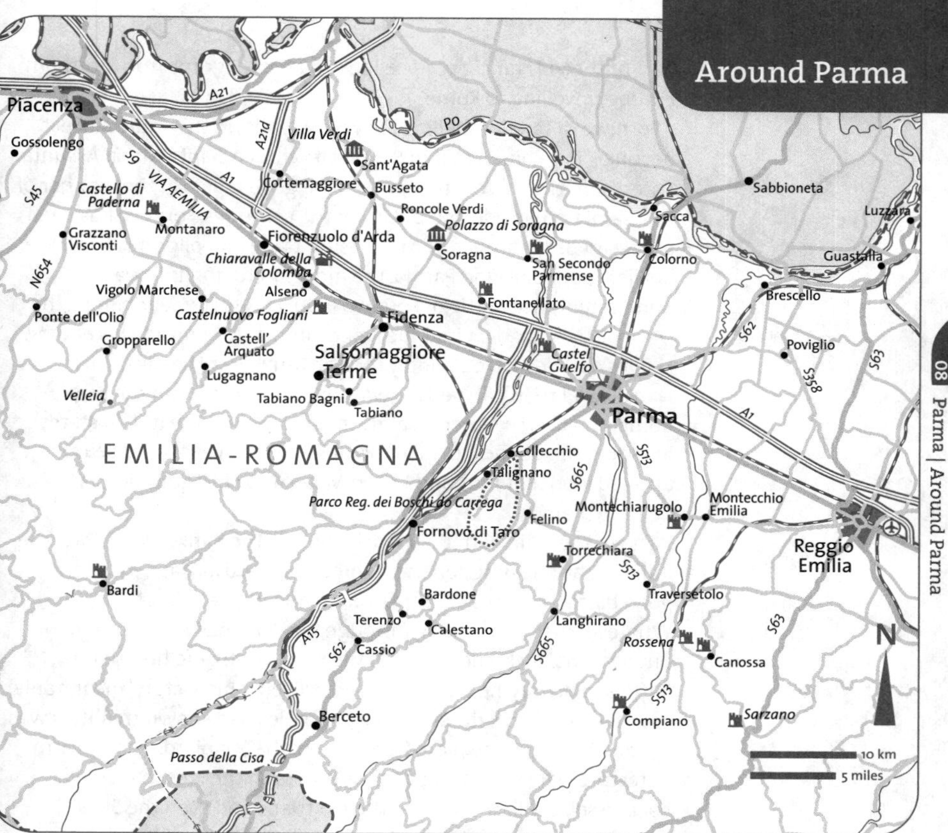

the drawings and engravings of Giorgio Morandi, and the whole is now open to the public. It also has an excellent restaurant.

To the west, a lovely ancient forested area bordering the village of **Collecchio** has been set aside as the **Parco Regionale dei Boschi di Carrega**. Once the hunting reserve of Ranuccio Farnese and a summer retreat of the dukes, the area still has two of their villas inside: the Casino dei Boschi, designed by Petitot, and the Villa del Ferlaro built for Marie Louise. There is a visitors' centre in the Casinetto next to the casino. At the western edge of the park, the village of **Talignano** has a well-preserved Romanesque country church, the Pieve di San Biagio, with a rare relief on the portal of St Michael weighing souls at the Last Judgement.

Around the Valley of the Taro

Since the time of the Romans this has been the main route through the northern Apennines. It branches at Fornovo, one road (now the SS308) following the river over the mountains to Liguria, and another (now the SS62, paralleled by the A15 motorway) taking a more tortuous path over to Tuscany. In the Middle Ages, this was part of the Via Francigena, the high road for pilgrims from northern Europe travelling to Rome.

Fornovo di Taro has been a busy crossroads on this route since it began as the Roman *Forum Novum*. Its church, **Santa Maria Assunta**, dates from the 11th century, with some good reliefs in the manner of Antelami both inside and out. Over the centuries, Fornovo has been a crossroads for armies as much as for trade and pilgrims. Of all the battles fought around Parma, the most fateful for Italy was undoubtedly the Battle of Fornovo in July 1495. The year before, the Duke of Milan had invited the French into Italy to invade his enemy, Naples. Charles VIII obligingly took an army over the Alps, seized Naples, and then pillaged his way up the peninsula on the way home. Venice and Florence, almost alone among the Italian states in seeing the danger to Italy from foreign intervention, raised an army to intercept him, and talked Milan into changing sides and helping them.

They caught up with the French here, on the banks of the Taro. The Italians had the best general, a three to one advantage in men, a good battle plan, and a simpleton for an opponent in Charles. Whatever his shortcomings, though, the king had a reputation for phenomenal luck, and in one of the most confusing hour-long battles in history, he managed to win. Even if his 'victory' meant only escaping Italy with his army intact, Charles had shown that Italy was a plum waiting to be picked. Soon after, the Spaniards sent an army to restore Naples to its rightful king; in 1499 the French would be back to seize Milan, and later the Austrians and even the Swiss would be looking for bits of Italy to grab. The Wars of Italy had begun, and four decades later when it was all over Italian liberty would be dead, and the entire nation subject to the pope or foreign powers.

Bardone, in the hills southeast of Fornovo, has a similar Romanesque church, the Pieve di Santa Maria. South, **Cássio** has a modest building called the 'Ospedale' that may be the only surviving medieval pilgrims' hostel of the Via Francigena. Near the Passo della Cisa, the mountain pass that marks the border with Tuscany, **Berceto** is a picturesque village under a ruined castle; the 12th-century **Duomo di San Moderanno** may no longer be a cathedral, but it has a fine Romanesque portal and medieval relics inside that go back as far as the time of the Lombards.

Bardi
t (0525) 71626, www.diasprorosso.com; open Mar–April and Sept–Oct Sat 2–6, Sun/hols 10–6; May–June Mon–Fri 2–7, Sat, Sun and hols 10–7; July daily 10–7; Aug Mon–Fri 10–7, Sat–Sun and hols 10–8; Nov Sat 2–5, Sun and hols 10–5; Dec–Jan by appt; adm

Such a strategic area naturally has sprouted plenty of castles, and one of the most impressive, the 15th-century **Bardi**, perches atop its own hill southwest of Parma. It retains its beautiful beamed ceilings and 16th-century frescoes; now it also contains a rather unusual Museum of Traps and Poaching. On the local road to Reggio Emilia via Montecchio lies the old village of **Montechiarugolo** and its

Montechiarugolo Castle
t (0521) 686 643, biancamarchi@tin.it; open Mar–May Sat 3–6, Sun 10–12 and 3–6; June–Nov Sun only; adm

Castello di Compiano
t (0525) 825 541, www. castellodicompiano.it; open Mar–April Sun and hols 10–12 and 2.30–6.30; May–July and Sept Sat, Sun and hols 10–12 and 2.30–6.30; Aug daily 10–12 and 2.30–6.30, Oct Sat–Sun 2.30–6.30; Nov Sun and hols 10–12 and 2.30–5.30; appt essential for groups; adm

castle. Originally an 11th-century fort that took plenty of knocks during the Guelph and Ghibelline struggles, it was rebuilt by the Visconti in 1313. The main tower resembles Torrechiara, but otherwise it presents a rather austere face to the world. Inside, however, it contains antiques and frescoes from the 15th and 16th centuries, mythologies on the *Four Elements*, and a lavish bedchamber with allegories and scenes of human industry (farming, study, navigation and war).

Compiano, further up in the mountains on the SS513 road, was the capital of a little state encompassing Bardi and Borgotaro, ruled from 1275 by the Landi family, who were granted the title of prince and the right to mint their own coins by Emperor Charles V in 1532. In 1682 they died out, and their **Castello di Compiano** was forgotten until Marie Louise made it into a prison. Now carefully restored (also with accommodation and a restaurant), it contains a curious museum on English freemasonry as well as coins from the local mint.

Where to Stay and Eat Around Parma

Felino ✉ 43035

Cantinetta, Via Calestano 14, **t** (0521) 831 125, *lacantinetta@libero.it* (€€€€). Felino, 17km south of Parma, may be synonymous with its tasty salami, but it's also the place where the Parmigiani come for a blow-out seafood feast, all superbly fresh and superbly prepared and served in a superb setting or out in the summer garden. *Booking advisable. Closed Sun eve, Mon and Aug.*

Fornovo di Taro ✉ 43045

Azienda Agrituristica di Zanetti Maria, Loc. Coste 47, **t** (0525) 2924 (€, restaurant €€). A family-run *agriturismo* with a particularly welcoming atmosphere, this has five rooms in rustic style and a good restaurant. Try *tortelli di patate*, lasagne, gnocchi and game from the farm. *Open all year; restaurant open weekdays and hols only in Nov–Jan.*

★ **Baraccone >**

Baraccone, Piazza Mercato 5, **t** (0525) 3427 (€€€). This restaurant has been in the centre of Fornovo for over a century; the charming country atmosphere and antiques, and the delicious traditional cooking (*salumi* with the classic *torta fritta*, *tortelli* and home-made tagliatelle, pork and rosemary) will hit the spot. *Closed Sun eve, Mon, Aug and Dec.*

Trattoria di Cafragna, at Loc. Cafragna di Talignano (ask for directions in Talignano), **t** (0525) 2363 (€€€). In a pretty setting in the Boschi di Carrega park, this elegant restaurant is a favourite of the Parmigiani, who come in summer to linger on its summer terrace over the delights prepared by chef Giancarlo Camorali: excellent *prosciutto* and *salame di Felino*, unforgettable risotto with truffles, and roast lamb or beef in a creamy mushroom sauce. Home-made desserts, great wine cellar. *Closed Sun eve, Mon, Aug and Christmas–15 Jan.*

Berceto ✉ 43042

Ristorante Vittoria-Da Rino, Piazza Micheli 12, **t** (0525) 64306, *www. darino.it.* (€€€). Excellent country cuisine is served here; this establishment is particularly, renowned for its mushrooms. There are also 15 comfortable rooms (€€). *Closed Mon and 20 Dec–6 Jan.*

Compiano ✉ 43053

******Castello di Compiano**, Via Marco Rossi Sidoli 15, **t** (0525) 825 541, *www. castellodicompiano.it* (€€€€–€€€).

Owned by the town council, and part converted into a guesthouse.

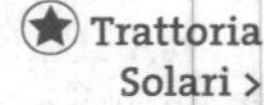

Trattoria Solari >

Trattoria Solari, Loc. Cereseto, **t** (0525) 824 801, *www.trattoriasolari.it* (€€). Prettily positioned among the hills above town, in the *frazione* Cereseto, this trattoria gets a steady procession of local customers who come here for the consistently good food, especially its aromatic wild mushroom dishes served between July and November; in season boar *alla cacciatora* holds pride of place. They also offer bed and breakfast. *Closed Mon exc in summer.*

Sacca di Colorno ✉ 43052

Stendhal-Da Bruno, Via Sacca 80, **t** (0521) 815 493 (€€). in Sacca, north of Colorno on the bank of the Po. The perfect complement to a visit to the Farnese Palace, inhabited in Stendhal's time by Marie Louise. Fish is the speciality here – eels and small fry from the Po, and denizens of the deep; also try mixed *salumi* and risotto with truffles. Great home-made charcuterie, desserts and wine, all served in a serene setting. *Closed Tues, 3 weeks Aug and 1 week Jan.*

Reggio Emilia and Modena

Two cities, almost twins, occupy the heart of Emilia. Reggio Emilia has its modest charms, though since the Middle Ages it has always found itself upstaged by Modena, now known for mink coats and Ferraris, and centuries ago, for one of Italy's greatest cathedrals and the lofty tower called the Ghirlandina.

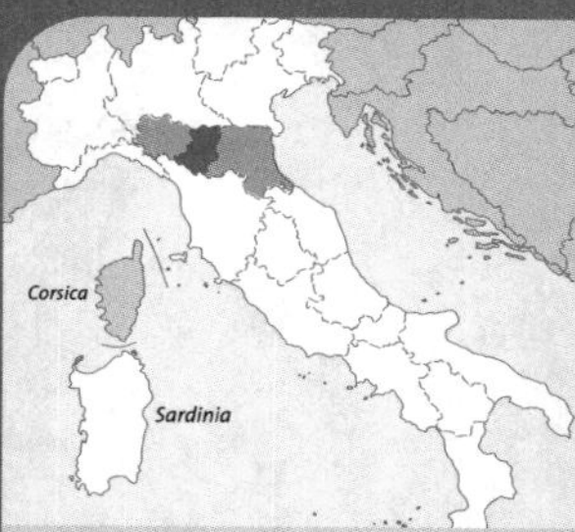

09

1 Castle country
Canossa and the Rocca di Bismantova **p.159**

2 A proud symbols
Duomo di San Geminiano and La Ghirlandina **pp.164–68**

3 Renaissance masterpieces
Galleria Estense, Modena **p.172**

4 Treasures around a huge piazza
Carpi **p.178**

5 Mountain hideaways
Around Sestola **p.185**

See map overleaf

Reggio Emilia and Modena

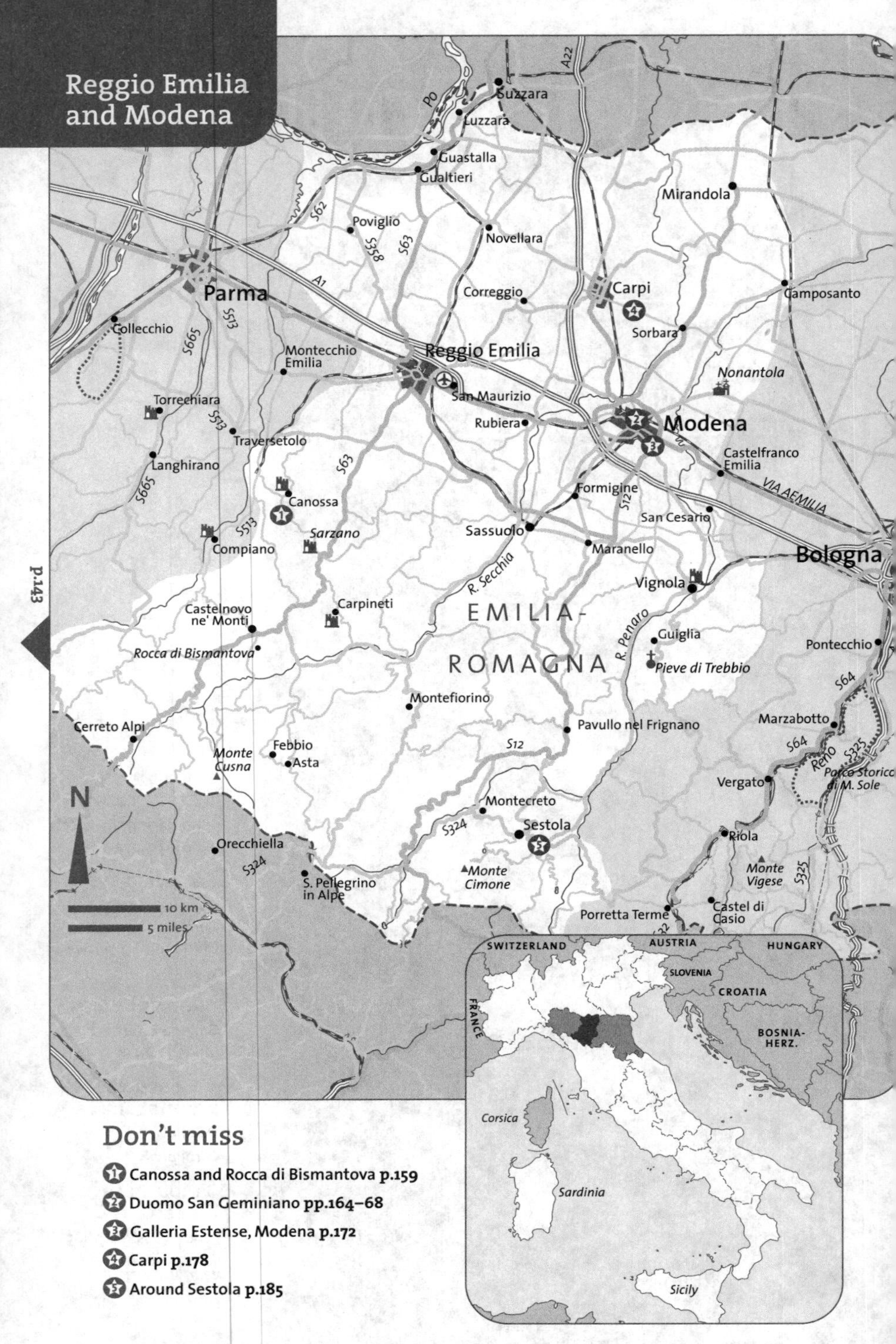

Don't miss

1. Canossa and Rocca di Bismantova **p.159**
2. Duomo San Geminiano **pp.164–68**
3. Galleria Estense, Modena **p.172**
4. Carpi **p.178**
5. Around Sestola **p.185**

Reggio Emilia

The people of Reggio all agree that they don't care if you call their town Reggio nell'Emilia, Reggio di Emilia or simply Reggio Emilia, as long as you do call them. Long the odd man out among the region's art cities, Reggio lacks the compelling attractions of Parma, Bologna or the others. Nevertheless, it is a handsome, well-organized and likeable city, and you won't regret stopping over.

Reggio's hinterlands include a clutch of Baroque memories around the Po in towns like Guastalla, Gualtieri and Correggio. To the south is one of the more attractive stretches of the Emilian Apennines, home to the famous Castle of Canossa (or what's left of it), a bit of skiing, a bit of scenery, and the outlandish Rocca di Bismantova.

History

Reggio started out as the Roman *Regium Lepidi*, a fortified camp town on the Via Emilia founded in 175 BC. When Emilia was a newly founded Roman colony, this frontier area was still troubled by Celtic bandits up in the mountains and it was good to have some legionaries around to keep the peace. As things grew more settled, Reggio developed into a flourishing commercial town, then contracted in the Dark Ages into a tiny *castrum vescovile*, a walled compound that enclosed little more than the cathedral and the bishop's palace. The city started booming again in the early Middle Ages, becoming one of the first towns to found a *comune* in the 12th century, and then commencing one of medieval Emilia's most ambitious sets of city walls, the tidy, hexagonal circuit still traceable on the map in the ring of boulevards that replaced them in the 19th century. Medieval Reggio was famous for violent factionalism, even by the standards of the day. On more than one occasion in the 1200s, this broke out into bloody civil war. The two contending parties were called the 'Uppers' and' Lowers'; in 1287 the Uppers expelled their rivals and demolished all their houses; their leader, Matteo da Fogliano, used the materials to build himself a great palace. After a year of wasting the countryside and burning villages, the Lowers got back in, and served the Uppers the same way. By 1290 both exhausted parties had had enough, and they offered the city to Obizzo II d'Este as *signore*.

This sort of anarchy was followed by the rule of various *signori* in the 1300s, and in the end the city lost its independence once and for all. From 1409 to 1796 Reggio was ruled by the Este family of Ferrara, during which time its most famous sons, Matteo Maria Boiardo (1440–91), author of *Orlando Innamorato*, and Ludovico Ariosto (1474–1533), who continued the epic in *Orlando Furioso*, were born. In the dismal 1600s Reggio managed to keep its head above water thanks to a new industry, silk manufacture. Nowadays it makes a

Getting to and around Reggio Emilia

The FS **rail** station, just east of the hexagon of boulevards on Piazza Marconi, is a port of call for all the trains on the main Rimini–Bologna–Parma–Milan line; there is another line for Mantova and the north, and local ACT lines to Novellara and Guastalla in the north, and San Polo d'Enza and Scandiano to the south; these leave from the ACT station west of the centre on Viale Trento e Trieste, **t** (0522) 431 667, *www.actre.it*.

For Correggio, Carpi and other provincial destinations, as well as Guastalla, there's the **bus**, from the Autostazione on Viale Allegri, next to the Giardini Pubblici.

Traffic can be fierce in Reggio, and most of the centre is closed to traffic. Most of the **parking** areas are located around the ring of boulevards, though you might be able to find a spot on the street in the centre around Corso Garibaldi, Via Roma or the Giardini Pubblici.

---

good living from manufacturing (aircraft, among other things), and the city is noted for its numerous ballet schools, its balsamic vinegar and its Parmigiano-Reggiano cheese (*see* pp.52–3), which, after all, is the real thing.

Piazza Prampolini

The Piazza Prampolini, just south of the Via Emilia, is the civic and ecclesiastical heart of Reggio, and the site of the busy outdoor **markets** on Tuesdays and Fridays; locals like to save a few syllables by calling it simply 'Piazza Grande', as they have since the Middle Ages. The main feature is Reggio's peculiar **Duomo**, topped by a single octagonal tower. Most of its original Romanesque features were remodelled away in the 16th century and replaced by an unfinished façade with fine statues of *Adam and Eve* by Prospero Sogari lounging on the cornice of the portal; in the tower niche is a gilded copper *Madonna* flanked by the cathedral donors. There are Renaissance tombs and paintings by Guercino, among others, in the gloomy interior. Across the piazza is the **Palazzo del Monte di Pietà**, with its lofty Torre dell'Orologio. The 18th-century façade conceals Reggio's original town hall; after a new one was built on the other side of the square, it became the headquarters of the municipal pawn shop, a worthy institution in all old Italian cities. These developed into savings banks, the average man's only source of credit; Reggio's Monte di Pietà has been in business at this location since 1494.

Duomo
open daily 7.30–12.30 and 3.30–7

Palazzo del Monte di Pietà
t (0522) 451 152; visits by appointment Mon–Fri

The **Palazzo Comunale**, begun in 1414 and often restored and rebuilt, occupies the southern side of the piazza. The red, white and green *Tricolore*, later adopted as the Italian flag, first appeared here in 1797 during the second congress of Napoleon's Cispadane Republic, a very short-lived entity that covered the area between Reggio, Mantua, Ferrara and Bologna. Anyone feeling empathetically patriotic may visit the **Museo del Tricolore** inside. This piazza has another surprising distinction; the Polish national anthem (*Poland is not lost, as long as we are living...*) was written here, also in 1797, two years after the last partition wiped Poland from the map, by an

Museo del Tricolore
t (0522) 456 477; open Tues–Fri 9–12, Sat 9–12 and 3–7; July–Aug Tues–Sun 9–12; adm free

exiled poet named Jozef Wybicki who was serving in Napoleon's army and quartered in the Episcopal Palace next to the Duomo.

Next to this, a covered arcade called the **Broletto** connects Piazza Prampolini to another market square, **Piazza San Prospero**, which holds markets on Tuesday and Friday mornings. The Broletto itself is usually full of produce stands, fittingly enough, since the name is an old word for a vegetable garden. Besides affording the best view of the Duomo – from behind, revealing the elegant dome and towers invisible from Piazza Prampolini – this piazza is home to the 16th-century **Basilica di San Prospero**, noted for its fine choir with inlaid stalls, and the cycle of frescoes by the Milanese early Baroque painter Camillo Procaccini, including the *Last Judgement*.

North of Piazza Prampolini and San Prospero, the Roman Via Emilia is today Reggio's pedestrianized main shopping street, passing through Piazza Cesare Battisti, roughly the site of Roman Reggio's forum. Here is the 13th-century **Palazzo del Capitano del Popolo**, now a hotel after a Hollywoodish 1920s restoration that made it look more medieval than the Middle Ages ever dreamed of being.

North of the Via Emilia

Medieval Reggio was never nearly large enough to fill the space inside its ambitious hexagon of walls. The old centre never extended far north of the Via Emilia; this area developed mostly over the last 200 years, and now is home to some fine palazzi and most of the city's cultural institutions. At its heart is the vast **Piazza Martiri del VII Luglio** and the renowned **Teatro Municipale** (1852), the town's opera house, crowned by a surplus of musing statuary. This is one of the most lavish theatres in Italy; built to upstage the Teatro Regio in Parma, it largely succeeds. Performances (all year) of opera, concerts and plays are of a high quality, if not quite as prestigious as Parma's. The site was originally part of the Cittadella, built by the Este to keep an eye on the Reggiani. After the castle was demolished in 1848, the rest of the area behind the new theatre was turned into the shady Giardini Pubblici, embellished as one would expect with statues of Boiardo and Ariosto, but also containing a Roman tomb, the 1st-century AD Tomb of the Concordii, moved from its original location outside town.

Teatro Municipale
t (0522) 458 811, uffstampa@iteatri.re.it; box office open Mon–Fri 4–7, Sat 10–1 and 4–7; performances all year

The **Musei Civici**, a block east of the Teatro Municipale, is a charmingly old-fashioned museum with everything laid out in the musty and scholarly fashion of a century ago. At the entrance is a room of mosaics, both Roman and some fascinating 12th-century ones from a demolished church, including fragments from a *Labours of the Months*: a two-faced Janus and Aquarius for January. Beyond that, in various collections, local pedants assembled the souvenirs of African and Amazonian explorers (a stuffed crocodile and a mounted giraffe head, neck and all), a Neolithic Venus, American Indian

Musei Civici
*Via Secchi, **t** (0522) 456 477, http://musei.comune.re.it; open Mon–Fri 9–12, Sat 9–12 and 3–7, Sun 10–1 (9–12 July–Aug) and 3–7*

ceremonial costumes, a huge collection of Roman coins, mounted fish, the model of the unfinished cathedral façade, and more foetuses in formaldehyde than you have perhaps ever seen: humans, armadillos, a piglet, snakes and several kittens.

Upstairs, the **Pinacoteca** has works of various obscure Emilian artists, notably Paolo Emilio Besenzi and Reggio's Luca Ferrari, along with a fine work of Palma Giovane, the *Compianto su Cristo Morto*. A painting friar, Fra Stefano da Carpi, adds a merry *Self-Portrait* from the 1790s, when he was 82. One room is dedicated to Renato Mazzacurati (1907–69), the 'painter of the Resistance' who did the monument to the *partigiano* in Parma. Mazzacurati was a good socialist influenced by Picasso who also had a sense of humour; besides his serious paintings commenting on the Spanish Civil War and Fascism, there are some caricatures of his friends, including De Chirico, and a series of capitalists and generals made into useful wine pitchers.

Galleria Parmeggiani
Corso Cairoli 2, ***t*** *(0522) 451 054; open Mon–Fri 9–12, Sat 9–12 and 3–7, Sun 10–1 (9–12 July–Aug) and 3–7*

Across the piazza from the Teatro Municipale is the **Galleria Parmeggiani**, a very eclectic and somewhat eccentric collection, brought here from France on the sly by its owners in the 1920s. On display are furniture, paintings, jewellery, costumes, fabrics, arms and armour, from the Middle Ages to 1900. Equally eclectic and eccentric is the building itself; note the 15th-century Moorish-style doorway brought over from Valencia.

Corso Garibaldi and the Madonna della Ghiara

Emilia-Romagna's most elegant boulevard, the tree-lined **Corso Garibaldi**, winds around the southern end of the city's ancient nucleus. It follows the original course of the Torrente Crostolo, a stream that was rechannelled in the Middle Ages when Reggio's walls were built. Beginning at Via Emilia S. Stefano, it passes the **Palazzo Ducale** of the Este, with a neoclassical remodelling of the 1780s, and, across the street, Reggio's greatest artistic monument, the **Santuario della Madonna della Ghiara**. The church commemorates a miracle of 1596, when a deaf-mute recovered his hearing and speech while praying to an image of the Virgin on the site. The church, begun the following year, was designed by Alessandro Balbi, with a certain influence from St Peter's in Rome. With a Greek cross plan and an extended choir, its vaulting is entirely covered by frescoes of Old Testament scenes that complement the main theme, the *Exaltation of the Virtues of Mary*. The frescoes are the work of various artists, notably the Bolognese Alessandro Tiarini and Leonello Spada. All of them take their cue from Correggio and his followers in Parma, with lush pastel colouring and sophisticated graphic sense. Also present, on one of the altarpieces, is a *Crucifixion* by Guercino.

Further down, at No.29, the Palazzo Magnani bears a Reggio landmark, a Renaissance sculpture of two-faced *Janus*, looking into the past and future from his post on a corner of the palace. The Corso ends in Piazza Roversi, where the view is skilfully closed by the delightful rococo façade of the little **Chiesa del Cristo** (1761).

Il Mauriziano
t (0522) 456 527; open by appointment

In San Maurizio, 3km east of Reggio, the 16th-century villa **Il Mauriziano** was the home of Ariosto's family, and some of the rooms in the east wing have been restored to the appearance they had when the poet came to visit from his new home in Ferrara. They have just what a poet's house should have: charming frescoes of love scenes, landscapes and literati.

Where to Stay in Reggio Emilia

ⓘ **Reggio Emilia >**
Piazza Prampolini 5/c, next to the cathedral, **t** *(0522) 451 152, www.municipio.re.it/turismo; open Mon–Sat 8.30–1 and 2.30–6, Sun 9–12*

Reggio Emilia ✉ 42100

****__Mercure Astoria__, Viale L. Nobili 2, **t** (0522) 435 245, *www.mercurehotelastoria.com* (€€€€€). This hotel offers fine views over the municipal gardens. Garage, comfortable air-conditioned rooms with wireless Internet access and restaurant.

****__Delle Notarie__, Via Palazzolo 5, **t** (0522) 453 500, *www.albergonotarie.it* (€€€€). Discreet luxury and lovely wooden floors in an old refurbished palace, a short walk from the cathedral; bedrooms are air-conditioned and well equipped, and there's an excellent restaurant. *Closed 1st 3 weeks Aug.*

****__Posta__, Piazza del Monte 2, **t** (0522) 432 944, *www.hotelposta.re.it* (€€€€). For a historic stay in the heart of Reggio, you can't beat this. Housed in the 14th-century Palazzo del Capitano del Popolo, which later became home to Francesco d'Este. In the 1500s the palace with its swallow-tail crenellations became an inn; the rooms are very comfortable, and the public rooms still have some of their frescoes. There's a bar with a splendid tea room but no restaurant; free bikes available.

***__Park__, Via de Ruggero 1/b, **t** (0522) 292 141, *www.parkhotel.re.it* (€€€). A delightfully small, comfortable and friendly hotel, 4km from the centre of town, in a tranquil setting with garden and restaurant, and a minibus service into town.

For something *inexpensive*, the place to look is around Via Roma, northeast of the centre.

__Saint Lorenz__, Via Roma 45–47, **t (0522) 451 242 (€€–€). Works hard to provide a pleasant stay; although the rooms are on the small side, most have baths.

Ostello Ghiara, Via Guasco 6, **t** (0522) 452 323, *www.ostellionline.org* (€). The youth hostel is modern, well equipped and near the station.

Eating Out in Reggio Emilia

Like Parma, Reggio is a major producer of Parmesan cheese (properly called *Parmigiano-Reggiano*); in fact, the cheese as we know it today had its origins here, in the verdant Enza valley between Reggio and Parma, where the pastures are so lush that cows produce the richest milk in Italy. Food historians assure us that the Etruscans made it, and to this day the finest Parmesan comes from the valley, and in particular from the town of Montecchio. The hard, grainy cheese first became popular abroad in the 17th century, in large part due to Molière, who practically lived on the stuff: it was sold by merchants from Parma, so he asked for 'Parmesan cheese', and the name stuck. Like Modena, too, Reggio distills *aceto balsamico*, or balsamic vinegar, as valuable as frankincense in the Middle Ages (*see* pp.53–4).

Other specialities of Reggio are lasagne, *cappelletti in brodo*, a loaf called *polpettone di tacchino*, made of minced turkey, herbs, nutmeg and cloves, and a savoury vegetable tart called *erbazzone*, sold at the local baker's and ideal for a picnic lunch; good ones are available from Forno Katia, Via Terrachini 35/c.

Morini, Via Passo Buole 82, **t** (0522) 323 986, *www.ristoranteenotecamorini.it* (€€€€). Elegant restaurant just outside the historic centre, offering four menus: fish, meat, vegetarian and *degustazione* (tasting menu). Booking strongly advised. *Closed Sat lunch, Sun, and 2 weeks Aug.*

La Brace, Via C. Teggi 29, Loc. Codemondo, **t** (0522) 308 800, *www.ristorantelabrace.it* (€€€). Six km west of town, this place lures hungry diners with its exquisite grilled (*alla brace*) Florentine steaks, but also offers a wide selection of pasta dishes that vary according to the season, with mushrooms and truffles starring in the autumn: try the risotto with *porcini*. Save room for the grilled cheeses and delicious desserts such as the classic *torta di riso*, with chocolate. *Booking advisable.Closed Sat lunch, Sun, 2 weeks Dec–Jan and all Aug.*

★ Da Arnaldo >>

Cinque Pini da Pelati, Viale Martiri di Cervarolo 46/c, **t** (0522) 553 663, *mapelat@tin.it* (€€€). The place to dine in Reggio, where Marisa Pelati and Camilla Brunesi prepare perfect meals based on prime basic ingredients. Try the shrimp and sole salad in *balsamico*, gnocchi in basil, sea bass with capers and potatoes or the classic *bollito misto* in the winter. *Menu degustazione available. Booking advisable. Closed Tues eve, Wed, 1 week Jan and 3 weeks Aug.*

Trattoria della Ghiara, Vicolo Folletto 1/c, **t** (0522) 435 755 (€€€). Near Piazza Roversi, a bastion of tradition but one where the heavier dishes are given a light modern touch so you can walk rather than waddle out. *Salumi*, delicious *cappelletti in brodo* and main courses according to the season; there's a small but good selection of regional wines. *Closed Sun and Aug.*

Canossa, Via Roma 37, **t** (0522) 454 196 (€€). A fine place to try the various hams of this area, served together as an *antipasto*, and the local Lambrusco wine; other specialities include *cappelletti* in broth and *tortelli* made on the premises. *Closed Wed and all Aug.*

La Casseruola, Via S. Carlo 5/a, **t** (0522) 453 837 (€). For pizza, paella and tagliatelle, at tables on the street. *Booking advisable. Closed Tues and Oct.*

Sotto Broletto, Via Broletto 1/n, **t** (0522) 452 276 (€). In an arcade leading off Piazza Prampolini, a thriving pizzeria. *Closed Thurs.*

Rubiera ✉ 42048

*****Da Arnaldo**, Piazza XXIV Maggio 3, Rubiera, **t** (0522) 626 124, *www.clinicagastronomica.com* (€€). Midway between Reggio and Modena is the site of this quattrocento building, housing atmospheric rooms, wrought-iron beds, marble bathrooms and lovely breakfasts, and the restaurant is very competent. *Restaurant closed all day Sun and Mon lunchtime.*

Reggio's Province

North of Reggio

Correggio and Novellara

Some 15km northeast of Reggio, **Correggio** is a pretty town with old arcaded streets, which suffered an earthquake in October 1996; all the damage seems to have been repaired. It was the birthplace of the painter Antonio Allegri, better known as Correggio (*d.* 1534); his home on Borgo Vecchio was reconstructed in 1755. The brick

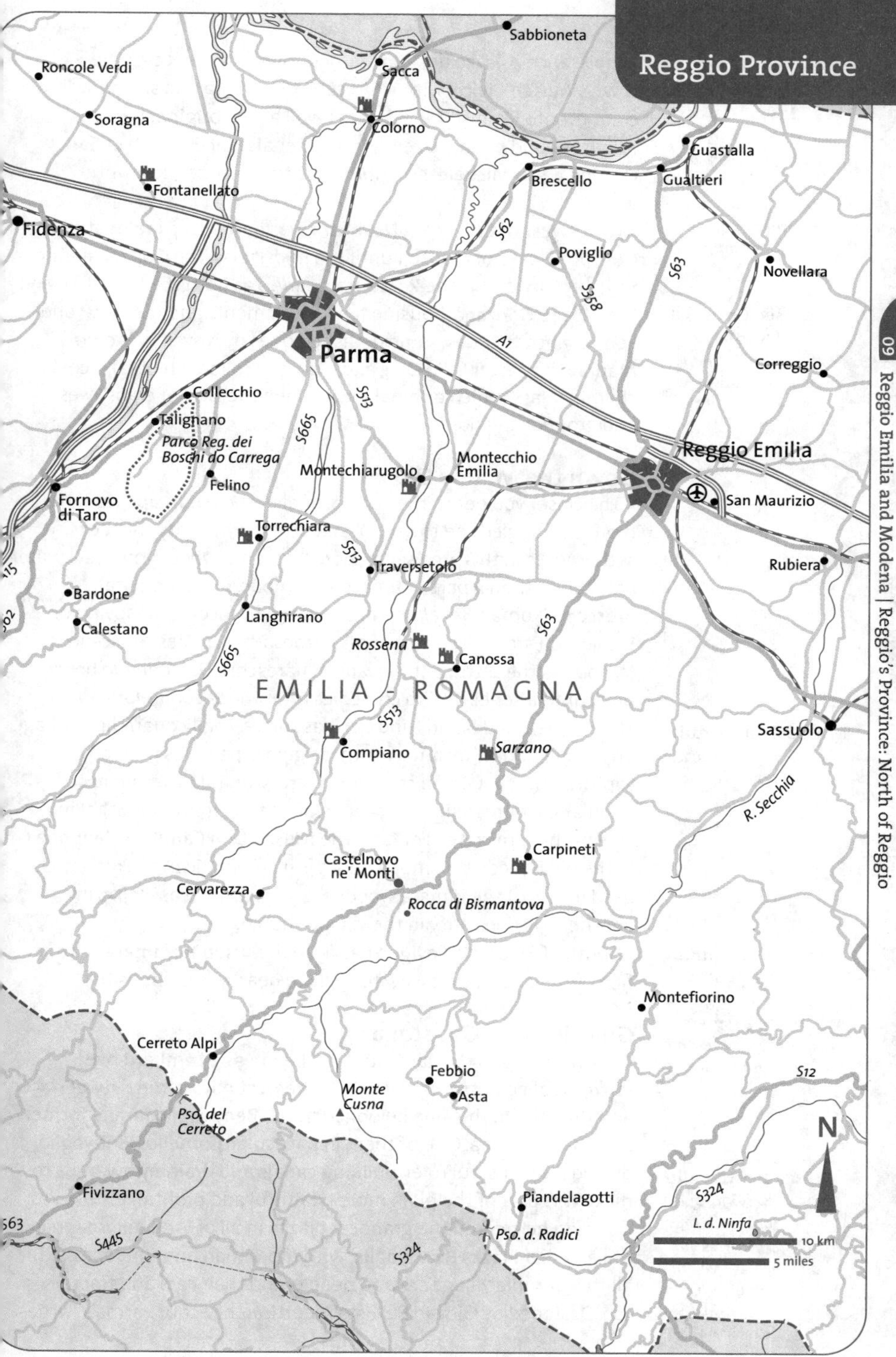

Sabbioneta
Roncole Verdi
Sacca
Soragna
Colorno
Guastalla
Fontanellato
Brescello
Gualtieri
Fidenza
S62
Poviglio
S63
Novellara
S358
A1
Parma
Correggio
S513
Collecchio
Talignano
S665
Parco Reg. dei
Boschi do Carrega
Montecchio
Emilia
Reggio Emilia
Montechiarugolo
Felino
San Maurizio
Fornovo
di Taro
Torrechiara
S513
Traversetolo
Rubiera
Bardone
Langhirano
Calestano
Rossena
Canossa
S63
S665
EMILIA - ROMAGNA
S513
Sassuolo
Compiano
Sarzano
R. Secchia
Carpineti
Castelnovo
ne' Monti
Cervarezza
Rocca di Bismantova
Montefiorino
Cerreto Alpi
Febbio
S12
Monte
Cusna
Asta
Pso. del
Cerreto
N
Fivizzano
Piandelagotti
S324
S63
L. d. Ninfa
S445
Pso. d. Radici
10 km
S324
5 miles

Renaissance Palazzo dei Principi, begun in 1506, contains the town's **Museo Civico**, with a *Christ* by Mantegna and some lovely cinquecento Flemish tapestries as well as the original frescoes, fireplaces and panelled ceilings. The Renaissance church of **San Quirino e San Michele** is attributed to the Farnese's favourite architect, Vignola.

Museo Civico
t (0522) 693 296, http://museo.comune.correggio.re.it; open Sat 3.30–6.30, Sun 10–12.30 and 3.30–6.30; adm free

Northwest of Correggio, **Novellara** was part of the realm of the Gonzaga dukes of Mantua until the mid-1700s. The Gonzagas' fine 14th-century castle, the **Rocca**, now serves as both the town hall and the **Museo Gonzaga**, housing farm implements and medieval and Renaissance frescoes, some detached ones by Novellara's own Mannerist master Lelio Orsi, and a unique collection of faïence chemists' jars, which originally contained the likes of crabs' eyes and ground stag horn.

Museo Gonzaga
t (0522) 655 426, biblioteca@comune.novellara.re.it; closed for restoration

Down the Muddy Old Po

The closer you get to the Po, the lonelier the landscapes and the more bedraggled the towns. Despite their prosperity, most of the settlements in this area seem more like some woebegone backwater of Calabria than a part of prosperous, modern northern Italy. **Brescello** (Roman *Brixellum*) has a statue by Jacopo Sansovino of Ercole II d'Este in the guise of his namesake Hercules. Brescello is famous as the setting of Giovanni Guareschi's *Don Camillo* books, made into a series of film comedies after the Second World War. Starring Fernandel and Gino Cervi as the eternally quarrelling village priest and Communist mayor, these gentle parables perfectly captured the mood of a recovering post-war Italy. They were so popular that Brescello spent much of its time in the 1950s taking care of the film crews. For fans, the **Museo Don Camillo e Peppone** is in the old Benedictine monastery, with an American tank that was used in one of the films; a wooden crucifix carved as a prop in another still does duty in the village church.

Museo Don Camillo e Peppone
t (0522) 962 158, www.museodoncamilloepeppone.it; open Mon–Sat 10–12 and 3–6.30, Sun and hols 9.30–12.30 and 2.30–6.30; donation

South of Brescello, Poviglio has a small **Museo Terramara**, with finds from a recently excavated village nearby (*see* opposite).

Museo Terramara
t (0522) 960 426; usually open Tues and Wed 9–12.30, Thurs and Fri 3–6, Sat 9–12.30 and 3–5.30, but ring ahead

Gualtieri and Guastalla

Down the Po to the east, Gualtieri began as a Lombard river fortress called *Castrum Walterii*. Its greatest days came between 1567 and 1634, when the area belonged to the Bentivoglio family, former bosses of Bologna. One of them in particular, Cornelio Bentivoglio, proved a very useful ruler, building canals and draining swamps to make this part of the plain more healthful and profitable. In Gualtieri he created the grandest piazza in all of Emilia-Romagna, the arcaded **Piazza Bentivoglio**, with more than enough room to fit all this humble village's 6,000 people, and their cars and tractors too. Designed by Giovan Battista Aleotti, architect of Parma's Farnese

Piazza Bentivoglio
t (0522) 828 696; open Mon–Sat for groups only by appt; 15 Mar–July and Sept–15 Dec, Sun and hols 9.30–12.30 and 2.30–6.30

Theatre, the Piazza is a unified ensemble, seemingly a single building on three sides, crowned by a tall clock tower with the Bentivoglio arms. The fourth side, for which the façade was never completed, is the **Palazzo Bentivoglio** (closed for restoration). Inside it has some fine frescoes, particularly those in the *Sala dei Giganti*. Cornelio Bentivoglio was a friend of the poet Torquato Tasso, and the frescoes portray episodes from his *Gerusalemme Liberata* as well as mythological fancies and scenes from the Bentivoglio court. Another part of the palace contains a collection of the works of Emilia-Romagna's best-known naïve painter, in the **Museo Antonio Ligabue**.

Museo Antonio Ligabue
t (0522) 221 851; open Mon–Sat by appointment only, Sun and hols 10–12.30 and 3–6.30; closed Jan, Feb, Aug; adm

Another Po-faced town with Lombard origins, **Guastalla** (originally *Warstal*) was a strategic point for the control of the river, and attracted a lot of attention over the centuries; even in the Dark Ages, the Po was an important trade route, along which salt from the lagoon of Venice was brought up to Lombardy. At times Guastalla belonged to the Canossa, the Visconti, the da Correggios and the Gonzagas; after 1748 it became part of the Duchy of Parma – or to give it its proper name from that point, the 'Duchy of Parma, Piacenza and Guastalla'. Ferrante I Gonzaga gave the town its present shape in 1550, an unimaginative Renaissance grid centred on the 'noble street', Via Gonzaga. Ferrante's statue in bronze dominates the main Piazza Mazzini, facing the sad, abandoned **Ducal Palace**,

Terramare Mysteries

In the 19th century, farmers around the Po valley knew of patches of land with an unusually rich peat-like soil. Called *terra marre*, it was dug up and sold as garden fertilizer. The farmers paid little attention to the potsherds and bits of metal that turned up in these sites, but eventually these attracted the attention of archaeologists, leading to the discovery of one of the most unusual and enigmatic cultures of ancient Italy. They're still putting together the pieces of this puzzle, but so far it is certain that the 'Terramare people' migrated down from the region of Lake Garda around the 16th century BC, and settled most of the Po valley.

Another thing we know for sure is that they were some of the busiest beavers of antiquity. The Terramare people lived in carefully constructed wooden houses raised on piles, like the lake-dwellers of Switzerland (and the Italian lakes, and central Italy; they were probably all closely related). In this soggy valley such houses had to be rebuilt every 20 years or so; it was all this wood, piling up and rotting away over the generations, that made the soil under the villages so rich. A thousand years before the Romans turned Emilia-Romagna into an endless web of right angles, these people built villages that were neatly rectangular, with precise, straight streets. Around the villages they dug networks of canals for irrigation and drainage. It seems they had little time for art, though they did leave a wealth of little ceramic items that seem to be ex voto offerings to their gods – miniature vases and wagons. Although they had the use of metal, their culture gives no evidence of any sort of social hierarchy. They probably held their fields in common, though not their livestock.

At first, Terramare life appears to have been peaceful. Weapons were few, and the earliest villages had no fortifications. Later, however, they are surrounded by elaborate moats and defensive embankments. Were the villages fighting each other, or some foreign raiders? That isn't yet known, but something – war, invasion, disease or soil exhaustion and consequent migration – brought the Terramare world to an abrupt end in the 12th century BC. In one of history's great disappearing acts, the population of the Po valley went from *c.* 120,000 to zero in little over a generation; it would stay that way until the coming of the Etruscans three centuries later.

Biblioteca Maldotti
*Via Garibaldi, **t** (0522) 826 294; open Mon, Tues, Thurs, Fri 2–6, Wed 8.30–12 and 2–6*

Museo Comunale dei Pittori Naïf
***t** (0522) 977 283, www.naives.it; open Tues–Fri by appointment only, Sat 10–1 and 3–7, Sun 10–7; adm*

★ **La Tavernetta del Lupo** >

which is currently undergoing restoration. Other relics of better days include the **Teatro Ruggeri** on Via Verdi (1671, rebuilt 1814), the Baroque **Chiesa dei Servi** on Corso Prampolini, and the **Biblioteca Maldotti**, which includes a small museum that often puts on exhibits of art or history.

Outside Guastalla are two Romanesque churches, the **Basilica della Pieve**, at loc. Pieve, and the **Oratorio San Giorgio**, just over the railway from the centre.

Further down the Po, on the outskirts of **Luzzara**, the former convent of San Felice has been converted into the **Museo Comunale dei Pittori Naïf**, with a permanent collection of naïf art, including more works by Antonio Ligabue of Gualtieri. There are also frequent temporary exhibitions held here, and a competition and show that last through the spring. The museum was founded by Cesare Zavattini, a great *cinema verità* director, and collaborator of Vittorio De Sica.

Where to Stay and Eat North of Reggio

Correggio ✉ 42015

******Dei Medaglioni**, Corso Mazzini 8, **t** (0522) 632 233, *www.albergodei medaglioni.com* (€€€€). This hotel is housed in a converted palace, with up-to-date, comfortable and stylish rooms. *Closed much of Aug and for Christmas.*

Brescello ✉ 42041

***La Tavernetta del Lupo, Piazza M. Pallini at Loc. Sorbolo Levante, **t** (0522) 680 509 (€€€; rooms €€–€). Well worth beating a path here to sample the skilfully done Italian *cucina nuova* that will surprise your tastebuds with dishes such as gnocchi made from carrots with basil and pine nuts, or salmon with raspberry vinegar and poppy seeds. There's also an unusual selection of Italian and foreign cheeses and fruity desserts, and a huge wine and spirits list. *Closed Mon, 1 week Jan and all Aug.*

Guastalla ✉ 42016

*****Old River**, Viale Po 2, **t** (0522) 838 401, *oldriverhotel@pragmanet.it* (€€). Offers excellent air-conditioned rooms (crucial in August) in a pleasant green setting. It also has a restaurant (*closed Tues*) and garage parking.

*****Hotel Carolina**, Via Pegolotti 3, **t** (0522) 830 405, *info@albergocarolina.it* (€€). In the town centre. Rooms have TV and minibar, and there's a restaurant. *Closed Aug.*

Ostello della Gioventù, Viale Po 11, **t** (0522) 824 915, *lunetia@tin.it* (€). The youth hostel is located outside town. *Open Mar–Oct.*

Rigoletto, Piazza Martiri 29, Reggiolo (east of Guastalla), **t** (0522) 973 520, *www.ilrigoletto.it* (€€€€). The best restaurant to be found in these parts, and perhaps in the whole province, this occupies a lovely late 18th-century villa which is endowed with a pretty garden. The very talented chef works wonders with the finest ingredients and makes sure that every detail is correct. Raisin and gorgonzola bread, *tortelli* filled with catfish in a buttery dill sauce, stuffed baby squid in a salad of toasted almonds and crispy bacon, lamb in grape must, or a delicious crayfish and shellfish soup, followed by sublime desserts. Superb wine list. Two *menus di degustazione* are on offer, one featuring land food, and the other seafood. *Booking advisable. Closed Sun eve and Mon in winter, Sun all day and Mon eve in summer, 1 week Jan and all Aug.*

South of Reggio

Canossa and the Rocca di Bismantova

1 Canossa and the Rocca di Bismantova

It's a spot that everyone's heard of, without knowing exactly where it is: one full of history, without much left to see. **Canossa**, where an emperor once humbled himself before a pope, kneeling in the snow and praying for three days begging forgiveness, lies south of Reggio off the SS513, in a place where the Apennines rise abruptly up from the plain. Canossa's importance began with the remarkable career of a knight named Atto Adalbert, a son of Baron Siegfried of Lucca who went to the wars in the service of the Bishop of Reggio and was rewarded with the territory of Canossa. Atto built the castle there, and in 951 he was lucky or plucky enough to manage the escape of Adelaide, rightful Queen of Italy, from her island prison on Lake Garda, where she had been put by a usurper, Berengar of Ivrea. After she took refuge with Atto, she asked Otto I of Germany to help her regain her throne. Before the year was over he had sorted out Berengar and married Adelaide; 12 years later they were crowned Emperor and Empress in Rome by Pope John XII – and the Holy Roman Empire was born, or at least the post-Charlemagne, German version, with a claim to overlordship in Italy that provided the mainspring of Italian history for the next 700 years.

As for Atto, as the Emperor's right-hand man south of the Alps, he did well. Otto made him Marquis of 'Canossiana', a territory that included Modena, Mantua, Reggio and Ferrara. He accumulated an enormous treasure, and his descendants, thereafter known as the di Canossa, became Counts of Tuscany and remained a power in Italy for generations. The most famous member of the family was the mighty, charismatic, warlike Countess Matilda, who would occasionally don armour and lead her men into battle. In 1077 the long pan-European battle over the control of investitures led the great reforming Pope Gregory VII to do something no pope had ever dared before – excommunicate an emperor. His timing was perfect; the German barons used the excommunication as a pretext for revolt, and Matilda, a partisan of the popes who spent most of Atto's treasure financing their cause, was instrumental in bringing Henry IV to Canossa in the snow to apologize to Gregory. Though Henry got his revenge soon after, as Gregory had to witness a sack of Rome and died in exile, it was a turning point; for the next two centuries, popes held the moral high ground over the kings and barons of Europe.

Canossa is a rarity in Italy, a rural *comune* that covers several villages on the hills overlooking the Torrente Enza. The territory is rugged, with sharp peaks and the strangely eroded hillsides the Italians call *calanchi*. When you finally make it up to the **Castello di Canossa** you'll see why the medieval barons found it such an attractive place. A nearly impregnable eyrie, with three circuits of walls, it dominated Emilia until the militia of Reggio captured and razed it in 1255. Later rebuilt as a mountain retreat popular with the Dukes of Parma, Canossa met its definitive end when the powder house inside blew up in 1576. Today the castle is a scenic and tranquil ruin with a small **museum**.

Castello di Canossa museum
t (0522) 877 104, www.comune.canossa.re.it; open 9–12.30 and 3–7; closed Mon

Matilda's capital, more than just a single strong castle, was a whole network of them, spread throughout the *comune* of Canossa and in the surrounding areas; locals call this whole region the Terre di Matilde. On a nearby peak, the picturesque 11th-century **Castello di Rossena** guarded the approaches to Canossa; now restored, it belongs to the Bishop of Reggio and houses an institute devoted to the study of Matilda and her time. To the north, the village of **Quattro Castella** is overshadowed by four more castles on the hills to the south (three in ruins, one turned into a villa), while another, guarding the Enza valley road, is now the town hall of **San Polo d'Enza**. Two more impressive castles complete Canossa's defensive array: one at **Sarzano** to the southwest, and a large one on the summit of Mount Antognano in the mountain resort village of **Carpineti** further south. This was a favourite residence of Matilda, and went through many hands afterwards, most notoriously those of Domenico Amorotto, who received the castle in fief from Pope Julius II and so terrorized the neighbourhood that Julius' successor Leo X had him beheaded, and then ordered that his head be taken through the area to assure locals the villain was dead. The castle was bombed by the Germans in the Second World War, but has been restored. Next to it is the Romanesque church of **Sant'Andrea**.

Castello di Rossena
t (0522) 242 009, www.castellorossena.it; open April–Sept, Sat 3–7, Sun 11–7, closed Sat in July; Nov–Feb Sun and hols 2.30–5.30; adm

Castello di Carpineti
t (0522) 611 335; open Sat and Sun 10.30–12.30 and 2.30–6.30, other days by appointment (groups only); adm

By this point you'll have noticed something odd on the horizon, a looming shape to the south that looks like a titanic squashed top hat. The inimitable landmark of this part of the Apennines (Dante mentions it in passing in the *Purgatorio*), the **Rocca di Bismantova** from closer up resolves into a long, limestone outcrop with a flat top 3,402ft high, overlooking the town of **Castelnovo ne' Monti**. Bismantova may have been a holy place in ancient times. Castelnovo's parish church originally stood on top of it; the villagers got tired of making the long climb and moved it down to the valley stone by stone in the 1600s. Villanovan (pre-Etruscan) remains have been found on top, and both the Romans and Byzantines used it as a fortress. There is still a hermitage chapel up there, reachable in an hour or so on a path from Castelnovo, along with spectacular views over the mountains and the Po plain.

Further south, the highest reaches of the Apennines, bordering Tuscany, are around the 6,890ft **Monte Cusna**, known locally as *Il Gigante*; on the slopes is a small ski resort, the Alpe di Cusna at **Febbio**. There's another at **Cerreto dell'Alpi** to the west, with a pretty mountain lake near the Passo di Cerreto.

Where to Stay and Eat South of Reggio

Canossa ✉ 42026

Pietranera, Via Pietranera 187/188, **t** (0522) 870 420 (€€). Hearty lunches and dinners, with home-made pasta. This includes the classic pappardelle with boar in season, and succulent grilled lamb as a follow-up. Traditional cuisine and fish dishes on Fri. *Closed Mon eve, Wed, and Jan.*

La Cueva, Loc. Giarretta 7, **t** (0522) 876 316, *www.ranchlacueva.it* (€€). Just south of Canossa at Currada, an old country mill converted into a lovely restaurant, featuring *gnocco frito* with *salumi*, *tortellini* and grilled meats. *Closed Mon, Tues and Jan.*

San Polo d'Enza ✉ 42020

Mamma Rosa, Via XXIV Maggio 1, **t** (0522) 874 760, *www.mamma-rosa.it* (€€€). For something a bit surprising in this neck of the woods – the freshest of seafood – try to organize a stop by at this refined little specialist fish restaurant, where the chef certainly knows how to bring out the best flavour in a scampi, oyster or scallop. There is a good wine list, too. *Booking advisable. Closed Mon, Tues, 2–20 Jan and 25 Aug–5 Sept.*

Quattro Castella ✉ 42030

****Hotel Ristorante La Maddalena**, Via L. Pasteur 5, **t** (0522) 887 021 or 887 135 (restaurant), *www.albergolamaddalena.it* (€). In the natural, historic area of 'Colli Matildici'. Recently renovated, it has 11 comfortable rooms and offers country cuisine (€€).

Carpineti ✉ 42033

Le Scuderie, Via San Donnino 77, Loc. Regigno, **t** (0522) 618 397 (€). Handsome stone *agriturismo* overlooking a meadow. The friendly owners offer delicious evening meals. *Closed Nov.*

Modena

Modena puts on a class act – 'Mink City' they call it, the city with Italy's highest per capita income, a city with 'a psychological need for racing cars' according to the late Enzo Ferrari, whose famous flame-red chariots compete with the shiny beasts churned out by cross-town rival Maserati. Sleek and speedy, Modena also has a lyrical side of larger-than-life proportions: Luciano Pavarotti was born here, and its scenographic streets take on an air of mystery and romance when enveloped in the winter mists rising from the Po. Though it grew up as a feisty free *comune* in the Middle Ages, when it built one of Italy's finest cathedrals, Modena learned its graces and style in a more aristocratic age, under the House of Este. The city's formative years came between 1598 and 1859, when it stood among the capitals of Europe – if only as the capital of the Este's little duchy. In that period Modena was transformed into a model Baroque city, and its elegant streets filled up with churches, palaces and porticos in the new style. All this Baroque fussiness, however, is only a stage for a people as devoutly socialist as Bologna's. Italy's richest city is also one of its most progressive; Modena has the largest car-free centre in Emilia-Romagna, making it a delight to walk around. The serene old capital of the Este comes back to life, and the Baroque effect is made perfect by the cadets of the National Military Academy, who live in the old Ducal Palace, and never go out without their hats and capes.

Getting to and around Modena

There are frequent **rail** connections with Bologna (30mins), Parma (35mins) and Milan (2hrs), and also to Mantua (50mins), via Carpi. The station is on Piazza Dante, a 10-minute walk from the centre. There's another station, the Stazione Ferrovie Provinciali, south of the centre on Piazza Manzoni, with a small line that serves Formigine and Sassuolo.

The **bus station** (ATCM) on Via Bacchini 1, **t** 800 111 101 (6am–8pm), *www.atcm.mo.it*, has frequent connections to Bologna, Ferrara and destinations in Modena province and the Apennines (to Vignola every hour; to Fanano and Sestola six times a day; to Fiumalbo, via Pievepelago, eight times a day); and a shuttle service to Bologna airport.

The home of Ferrari is a major **road** junction. Just to the west of Modena the A22 leaves the A1 from Verona, Trento and the Brenner Pass. The Via Emilia runs through the city but there is also a bypass to the north, linking with the SS12 (north, to Verona) and the SP3/SS12 south. The centre is a *zona traffico limitato*. Street **parking** around the periphery is difficult but not impossible, and there are garages on Viale Trento Trieste, east of the centre, in Piazza Roma and in Viale C. Sigonio to the south.

There is a municipal **bike rental** at Parco Novi Sad (*open 7am–7pm; closed Sun*).

History

Known in ancient times as *Mutina*, the city began as a settlement of the Celtic Boii. The Romans took it in 183 BC, and it made little account of itself until the end of the empire, when it had the honour of being sacked by both the Huns and the Lombards. Medieval Modena grew back to prominence as part of the 'Canossiana', the state founded by Atto Adalbert in the 10th century and made glorious by Countess Matilda, powerful ally of the pope; under her rule the city began its great cathedral (1099). When it became an independent *comune*, however, Modena's Ghibelline party was to dominate in response to the Guelph politics of the city's chief rival, Bologna. Throughout the long campaigns of Frederick II in the north, Modena was to remain one of the emperor's most faithful allies. In 1288, after a long spell of fierce factional conflict, the city came under the control of Obizzo II d'Este, the powerful *signore* of Ferrara. A revolution of the *popolo* seized control of the city in 1306, but it lasted only a year. So frightened were the nobles by this outbreak that they put aside their differences and decided to put an end to the *comune* forever. With only a few brief interruptions, the Este would rule Modena for the next 553 years.

After the Este were thrown out of Ferrara by the pope (*see* pp.237–41), Cesare d'Este was allowed to keep Modena and Reggio Emilia. The Este Duchy of Modena endured, though it no longer played a prominent role in Italian history or culture. Not that the Este didn't try. Francesco I (1629–58) was a fervent patron of the arts (Velázquez and Bernini left memorable portraits of him), and he successfully kept his little state afloat in the treacherous currents of the Thirty Years' War, finally dying on the battlefield against the Spanish. (Francesco's daughter Maria Beatrice, or 'Mary of Modena', married James II in 1673, and played a small role in British history simply by being Catholic and thereby increasing James' subjects'

Modena

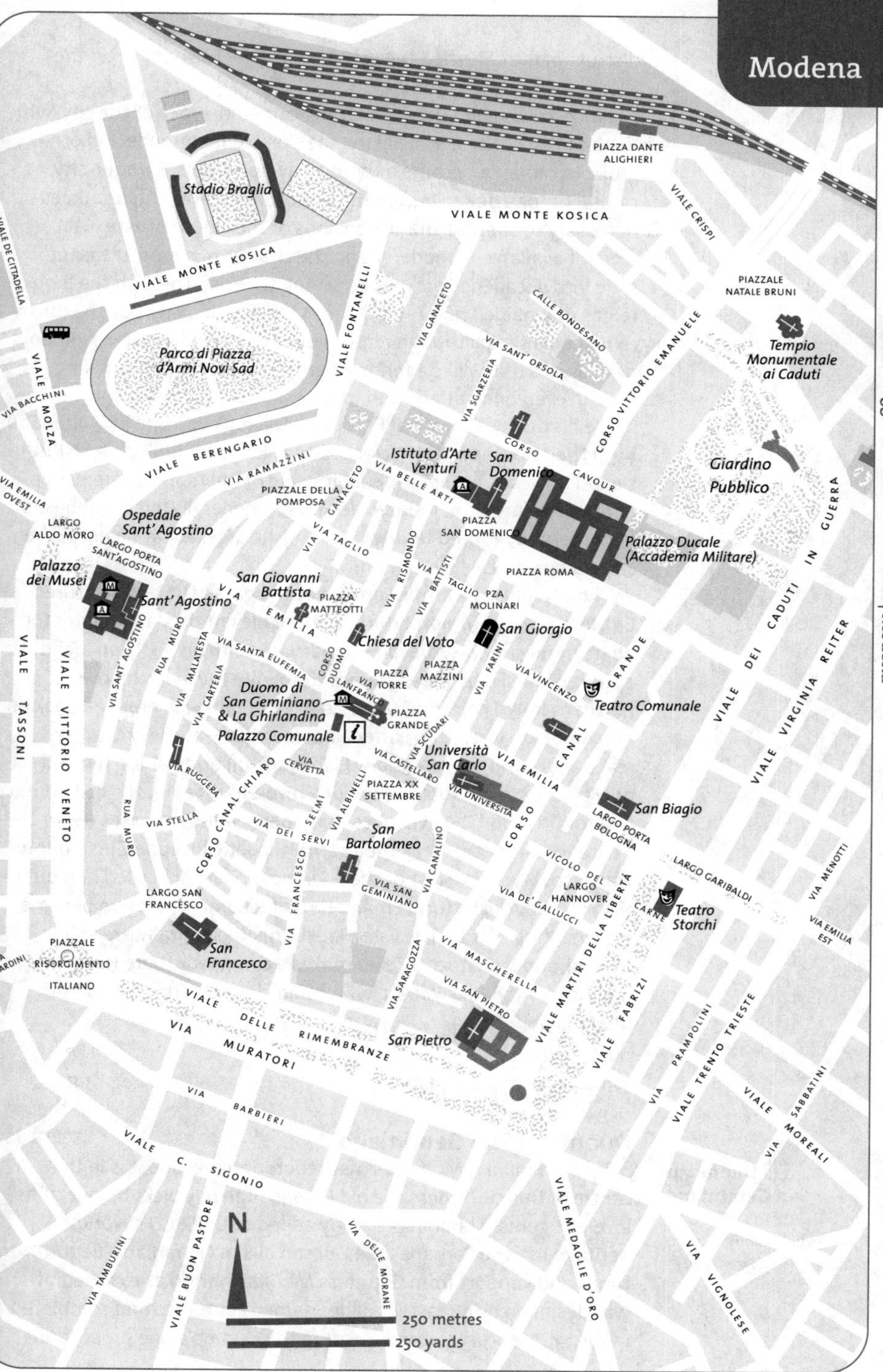
Piazza Dante Alighieri
Viale Monte Kosica
Viale Crispi
Stadio Braglia
Viale de Cittadella
Viale Monte Kosica
Piazzale Natale Bruni
Calle Bondesano
Via Ganaceto
Viale Fontanelli
Via Sant' Orsola
Corso Vittorio Emanuele
Tempio Monumentale ai Caduti
Parco di Piazza d'Armi Novi Sad
Viale Molza
Via Bacchini
Via Sgarzeria
Corso Cavour
Viale Berengario
Via Ramazzini
Istituto d'Arte Venturi
San Domenico
Giardino Pubblico
Via Emilia Ovest
Piazzale della Pomposa
Via Ganaceto
Via Belle Arti
Largo Aldo Moro
Ospedale Sant' Agostino
Piazza San Domenico
Via Taglio
Palazzo Ducale (Accademia Militare)
Largo Porta Sant'Agostino
Via Rismondo
Via Battisti
Piazza Roma
Palazzo dei Musei
San Giovanni Battista
Via Emilia
Piazza Matteotti
Via Taglio
Pza Molinari
Sant' Agostino
Viale dei Caduti in Guerra
Chiesa del Voto
San Giorgio
Viale Tassoni
Viale Vittorio Veneto
Via Sant' Agostino
Rua Muro
Via Malatesta
Via Santa Eufemia
Corso Duomo
Piazza Torre
Piazza Mazzini
Via Farini
Via Vincenzo
Canal Grande
Viale Virginia Reiter
Via Carteria
Via Torre
Duomo di San Geminiano & La Ghirlandina
Via Lanfranco
Teatro Comunale
Piazza Grande
Palazzo Comunale
Via Scudari
Via Cervetta
Via Castellaro
Università San Carlo
Via Emilia
Via Ruggera
Corso Canal Chiaro
Via Albinelli
Piazza XX Settembre
Via Università
San Biagio
Largo Porta Bologna
Rua Muro
Via Stella
Via dei Servi
Via Selmi
San Bartolomeo
Via Canalino
Corso
Vicolo del Carmine
Largo Garibaldi
Via Menotti
Via Francesco
Via San Geminiano
Largo Hannover
Via de' Gallucci
Teatro Storchi
Via Emilia Est
Largo San Francesco
Viale Martiri della Libertà
Piazzale Risorgimento Italiano
Via Giardini
San Francesco
Via Mascherella
Via Saragozza
Via San Pietro
Viale Fabrizi
Viale delle Rimembranze
Via Muratori
San Pietro
Via Prampolini
Viale Trento Trieste
Via Barbieri
Via Sabbatini
Viale Moreali
Viale C. Sigonio
Viale Medaglie d'Oro
Via delle Morane
Via Vignolese
Via Tamburini
Viale Buon Pastore
N
250 metres
250 yards

distrust of him. She fled the country with her husband after the Glorious Revolution of 1688.)

Francesco and his successors transformed the face of the city; with the building of the Ducal Palace, the Corso Canalgrande and other projects, Modena became a thoroughly up-to-date Baroque city, a capital fit for a duke. Despite their efforts, however, the resources necessary to support the pretensions of the House of Este just weren't available in Modena, and the charms of a long, pleasant slide into decadence proved too strong to resist. Through the long reigns of Rinaldo I (1694–1737) and Francesco III (1737–80), the duchy remained a sleepy though reasonably well-run backwater. Rinaldo oversaw his duchy like a fond but grumpy paterfamilias, poking his nose in everyone's affairs and tossing adulterers into prison; he made his duchy the joke of Europe by forcing everyone in Modena to be in their houses by ten o'clock so that they wouldn't disturb his sleep. Francesco, except for building one of Italy's most impressive poorhouses (now the Palazzo dei Musei), generally left his subjects in peace, and devoted his life to eating; he grew so fat he had to be carried upstairs.

When Napoleon's armies arrived at the gates, the good-natured Ercole III (1780–96) simply left town. Ercole left only a daughter for an heir, and she was forced into marriage with an Austrian archduke as part of the Habsburg schemes to solidify their control over northern Italy. Their son Francesco IV (1814–46) was propped back on his throne by Metternich after Napoleon's defeat. He proved as reactionary and useless as any Habsburg, distinguishing himself only by the bloody suppression of a revolt in 1831. His subjects found comfort in food. 'The existence of Modena sausage makes up for the existence of the Duke,' as their satirical poet Giuseppe Giusti put it. Francesco V was the last of the line; the Modenesi booted him out in 1859 in favour of Vittorio Emanuele II of Piedmont, soon to become the first King of Italy. The Este-Habsburgs, incidentally, are still around, and if aristocracy ever makes a comeback there is a pretender, Archduke Robert, who could claim the thrones of both Modena and Parma.

Piazza Grande

Duomo di San Geminiano

2 Duomo di San Geminiano
t (059) 216 078, www.duomodimodena.it; open 7–12.30 and 3.30–7

The Via Emilia is Modena's main thoroughfare, and it is in the centre of this city where the old Roman highway picks up one of its loveliest gems, a building recently added to UNESCO's world heritage list: the Romanesque Duomo di San Geminiano. Begun with funds and support from Countess Matilda in 1099, the cathedral was designed by a master builder named Lanfranco and completed in the 13th century. Complementing the Duomo's fine proportions are the magnificent carvings by the 12th-century sculptor Wiligelmo above the three main entrances and elsewhere around the church. Wiligelmo's followers, and after them the anonymous Lombard sculptors and architects known as the Campionese Masters, carried on the work, making this cathedral a living museum of medieval sculpture.

The **façade** is topped by the strange figure of the *Angel of Death* grasping a lily. Below this are figures of the *Four Evangelists* and *Samson and the Lion* by followers of Wiligelmo, and in the centre the *Redeemer*, by a Campionese sculptor, directly over the great 24-sided rose window, with four panes of 15th-century stained glass created after designs of Giovanni da Modena. Below is a loggia, with capitals carved with imaginary beasts and monsters. Some of the more unusual subjects on this façade are carved on four small panels underneath this: an angel with a reversed torch and an ibis, symbolizing *Death and Sin*; next, a hart with one head and two bodies, taking a drink and symbolizing God knows what; a lion and lioness with lion-headed serpents coming out of their mouths; and on the right another *Angel of Death*. Wiligelmo's four great **relief panels** of *Genesis* come next: over the left portal Adam and Eve in Paradise and the Original Sin; to the left of the main portal the Flight from Paradise and the labour of Adam and Eve; to the right of the main portal the sacrifices of Cain and Abel and the murder of Abel; and over the right portal the murder of Cain and Noah's Ark. These reliefs are believed to illustrate scenes not so much from Genesis directly, but from the medieval mystery play

The Art of City-Building

Few people notice it, but Modena's cathedral and its surroundings also make up an exceptionally skilful ensemble of medieval urban design. Don't think for a minute there is anything accidental in the cathedral's seemingly random placement. People in the Middle Ages built cathedrals as the maximum expression of their faith and art. They were outrageously expensive, but their designers had the ability to combine aesthetics with practicality in ways that made the investment go as far as possible to embellish the town. Like so many in medieval Europe, and particularly in Italy, this cathedral is sited to define and dominate three separate piazzas: the small one at the end of Corso Duomo in front of the façade, the Piazza Torre to the north, where the Ghirlandina is on display, and the Piazza Grande. To reduce the total cost, one or more sides of a cathedral would usually be set into a block of buildings, as in Parma or Modena, or else a side would run along a little alley, as in Ferrara. Either way, the town would save by cutting down the costly sculptural decoration required, and at the same time their cathedral would appear more an organic part of the city, woven into its fabric, instead of just a pretty *objet d'art* isolated in the middle of a square.

The two keys to medieval urban design are *asymmetry* and *surprise*. Any open space in a town was conceived as an aesthetic composition in three dimensions; a good piazza presents constantly changing aspects as one walks around it, any one of which could be the subject for a painting. The dramatic effect, however, comes when one first encounters the composition. Walking towards the centre down Via Castellaro, the Corso Canal Chiaro or the Via Emilia, there is no hint of what lies ahead.

Even in the Middle Ages, the aesthetics of town design were often defeated by practical considerations. Medieval new towns were customarily laid out in simple grids, a practice proven from ancient

Greece to frontier America to be the cheapest and easiest for surveyors (and for land speculators). In the Renaissance the subtleties of medieval design were forgotten, replaced by a mania for the straight line and the right angle perfected in Baroque Rome and Paris, with their broad vistas and strict symmetrical building ensembles. Medieval design reclaimed some popularity in the Romantic era, when painters and tourists learned to appreciate its 'picturesque' qualities without any understanding of the principles that governed them.

Those principles were rediscovered a century ago by a Viennese architect named Camillo Sitte. Sitte's method was to take a taxi from the station to the best bookstore in town, and there to ask three questions: the best map of the town, the hotel with the best dinners, and the tower with the best views. The result, after thirty years studying the cities of Italy and Europe, was a book published in 1889 called *Der Städtebau nach seinen künstlerischen Grundlage – The Art of Building Cities*.

Sitte's ideas were immensely popular in the decades that followed, influencing the design of new towns and suburbs throughout Europe. Then came the Great War, and in its wake the grim cult of architectural Modernism. 'The street must be abolished!' declared Le Corbusier, and a triumphant new ideology proclaimed that modern people must live in tower blocks joined by motorways. The Modernists did not completely succeed in their goal of destroying the old convivial town centres, except in parts of Britain and Romania, and both Europe and America are gradually recovering from this brief attack of madness. Now that we're back at square one, with little notion of how to build correctly, it might be a good idea to look at Sitte's sophisticated medieval compositions once again. Take a walk around old Modena with your eyes open, and see if there's anything that strikes your fancy.

on it, the *Jeu d'Adam*. All the reliefs in the **Portale Maggiore** are Wiligelmo's too: twelve *Prophets of Israel*, and the familiar medieval subject of the *Labourers in the Vineyard*, where the grape harvest prefigures the harvest of souls in the last days. At the top, note the unusual intruder in this Christian scene: the two-headed Roman god *Janus*, still performing his ancient function as guardian of doors and gates. The lions supporting the portal's columns were recycled from a Roman building.

Wiligelmo also carved the inscription above and to the left of the portal recording the building of the cathedral, on a tablet supported by Enoch and Elias: '*As Cancer overtook the Twins, five days before the Ides of June in the year of Our Lord eleven hundred minus one, this house was founded for the great Geminiano*.' Later hands added another message at the bottom: '*From your work here, O Wiligelmus, it is clear how worthy you are to be honoured among sculptors*.'

The south wall, with its conspicuous position facing Piazza Grande, has almost as much good sculpture as the façade. Of the two portals, the one on the right is the **Porta dei Principi**; its reliefs, by followers of Wiligelmo, were damaged by an Allied bomb in the war. On the lintel, the scenes from the *Life of San Geminiano* detail the legend of how the saint voyaged to Constantinople to exorcise a demon that was inhabiting the body of Emperor Jovian's daughter. Above it, to the right, is an inscription of 1184 detailing the consecration of the cathedral, and above that, on the roofline, the builders inserted two sculptures from Roman times, heads of Jupiter and Matrona. The right portal, the **Porta Regia**, was added after the completion of the cathedral by the Campionese Masters, who also designed the gabled false transept to the right. Beneath this is another relief of the *Life of San Geminiano*, the earliest known work of Agostino di Duccio (1442), and a pulpit carved with the *Evangelists* by Jacopo da Ferrara (1500–11). Around the back, the slightly listing **apse** was the first part of the cathedral to be completed. Around the lower, central window, where a figure of the Medusa hides amidst the foliage, medieval Modena carved its standard measures – lengths and brick sizes – to keep the merchants and tradesmen honest.

Wiligelmo's contemporary, the 'Master of the Metopes', executed the fascinating **metopes**, reliefs of mythological creatures and allegorical subjects, on top of the buttresses – monsters relegated to the ends of the cathedral just as they are relegated to the ends of the earth. Exactly what they represent is anyone's guess. The first, on the left, includes an upside-down figure that some believe is an inhabitant of the antipodes. Next comes a hermaphrodite, then a bird-headed creature eating a fish, and finally a nude woman with a dragon.

The north wall was originally built up with the episcopal offices (Via Lanfranco, which runs along this side now, was cut through only in 1898), and consequently there is little decoration. The other four metopes, on the north roofline, show a three-armed woman, a bearded crouching man, a giantess with an ibis and a sphinx, and, last, a fork-tailed siren – one of the most common, and most mysterious of all Romanesque images, found on churches all over Italy, especially in Puglia. In the famous mosaic floor of Otranto Cathedral, she sits enthroned next to King Solomon, surrounded by an Arabic inscription that no one can read. (All the metopes on the cathedral are copies; the mid-12th-century originals, which deserve a much closer look, are in the **Museo Lapidario** in Via Lanfranco. At the same address, the **Museo del Tesoro del Duomo** contains a good deal of church clutter, but also 16 fine Flemish tapestries. Also on the north wall is the Porta della Pescheria, with carvings by Wiligelmo's followers of something else not quite canonical – King Arthur. Stories of Arthur and his knights were familiar in medieval Italy, especially in the south. The Normans brought them down originally, and soon Italians were creating Arthurian stories of their own (in Sicily he sleeps eternally not in Avalon but under Mount Etna). This portal, meant to be seen only by the clergy as they entered the church, pictures him with two of his knights coming to the aid of Guenevere, imprisoned in Modroc's castle surrounded by the sea. Beneath this are fine reliefs of the *Labours of the Months*, along with other strange medieval fancies.

Museo Lapidario and Museo del Tesoro del Duomo
t (059) 439 6969, www.duomodimodena.it; open Tues–Sun 9.30–12.30 and 3.30–6.30; joint adm

The Campionesi masters also added the final touches to Lanfranco's charming **interior**, with its rhythm of arches supported by slender columns and ponderous piers. The floor level is split in the Lombard style, the altar and choir raised above the rest of the church. To decorate the wall, the Campionese masters created the great **Pontile**, carved with lion pillars and polychromed reliefs of the life of Christ, and incorporating the *ambone*, a pulpit with pillars in the shape of telamones with excellent capitals. Behind the altar are intarsia choir stalls by Cristoforo and Lorenzo da Lendinara, and in the left aisle a polyptych by Serafino dei Serafini. Underneath it all is a **crypt** of 32 columns with capitals carved by Wiligelmo and his followers, with more lions, Evangelists and strange devices from the Romanesque bag, including a chimaera and another fork-tailed mermaid. San Geminiano is buried here, in a Roman sarcophagus, and to the right is a terracotta *Holy Family* (Guido Mazzoni, 1480).

In the right aisle of the Cathedral is a terracotta *presepe*, made by Antonio Begarelli (1527), and to the right of that an altar with frescoes by Cristoforo da Lendinara, an artist better known for his work in wood intarsia. Among the altars of the left aisle are one with fragments of frescoes by Tommaso da Modena, and another with an altarpiece by Dosso Dossi.

La Ghirlandina, and the Stolen Bucket

La Ghirlandina
open end April–end Oct daily 9.30–12.30 and 3–7; closed Aug; adm; joint ticket with Palazzo Comunale available

Modena's pride and symbol is the mighty, if slightly askew, campanile called the Ghirlandina. This too is a creation of the Campionese masters. They got the lower part up in a single year (1169), and then left their grandsons the job of finishing the octagonal spire (completed 1319), which accounts for almost half the tower's 282ft – the third-tallest campanile in Italy, after Cremona and Venice. The tower's name is often explained as referring to the 'garland' of arcading around the base of the spire, though another version says that the tower was originally *La Ghiraldina*, and that the Modenese were comparing their work to the most famous tower of the medieval world: La Giralda, the minaret of the Great Mosque of Seville.

The Campionese sculptors were able to follow their fancy in medallions at the corners, and in the capitals of the tower windows, where few would ever see them: more fantastic beasts and mysterious figures, along with the story of a corrupt Modenesi judge and scenes of King David with dancers and musicians. Of the four great bells, one goes back to the year 1350; they still ring it. At the base of the campanile is a photo memorial to Modena's martyred *partigiani*, as in Bologna.

The Ghirlandina houses a famous trophy – an ancient wooden bucket stolen from the town well of Bologna, during a raid on that city in 1325, when the two cities were at war. It is the subject of Alessandro Tassoni's mock-heroic epic, *La Secchia Rapita* (1622), in which every episode starts out in total seriousness and gradually deteriorates into total absurdity, while the gods of Olympus take sides and interfere, as in Homer. The Bolognesi make periodic attempts to steal back their bucket; according to rumour, they have it now, and the one you see is only a replica. Actually, it is a replica; the real one is in the Palazzo Comunale, where it is kept safe from the evil Bolognesi. There's a statue of Tassoni in the Piazza Torre, next to the tower.

Around Piazza Grande

The cathedral turns its back on the heart of Modena, **Piazza Grande**, a spacious and lovely square that is also home to the **Palazzo Comunale**. Though the façade is early 1600s, it conceals a complex of no fewer than ten buildings behind it, the oldest of which, the Palazzo Urbis Mutinae, goes back to 1046. Besides the sacred Bucket, kept in the Camerino dei Confirmati, you can see a painting by Bartolomeo Schedoni, the *Sposalizio della Vergine*, in the same chamber, and in the Sala del Consiglio Vecchio a set of peculiar paintings by Schedoni and Ercole dell'Abate on the theme of patriotism and government. Modenese *campanilismo* finds its apotheosis in the **Sala del Fuoco**, with a series of frescoes by Nicolò dell'Abate on the history of Modena in Roman times.

Palazzo Comunale
t (059) 206 660; open Mon–Sat 8–7, Sun and hols 3–7, closed Aug; joint adm with La Ghirlandina on Sun, otherwise free

Outside the Palazzo, the enormous slab of red Verona marble in the angle of the façade is the **Preda Ringadora**, a speakers' platform in use since the 1200s (an *arringadore* meant an orator; that's where we get our word 'harangue'). Another of Modena's civic icons stands on a pedestal on the corner of the building, where the Piazza meets Via Castellaro: **La Bonissima**, a marble lady documented to have been on this spot at least since 1268. According to one story she is the image of a noblewoman famous for her charity in a time of famine; another one says she was the symbol of the *Buona Stima*, the municipal office that watched over dealings in the markets and among the moneylenders to make sure everything stayed on the level.

South of Piazza Grande

Modena keeps its city **markets** south of the Piazza Grande: an open-air market for clothing and household goods in Piazza XX Settembre, and an absolutely delightful food market adjacent to that, the **Mercato Coperto**, built in 1931 – a miniature glass-roofed Covent Garden, bright and airy, that makes the produce and seafood look even fresher. The streets south of the Piazza Grande, around Corso Canal Chiaro and Via Canalino, are some of Modena's oldest. **Corso Canal Chiaro** in particular is a lovely, winding medieval street, lined with porticoed palazzi. These include the **Palazzo Levizzani**, from the 1500s, and the next-door Palazzo Fogliani (1491); further down at Via dei Servi is the Renaissance **Case Morano**.

San Bartolomeo
open Mon–Sat 9–12 and 4.30–7

A block east, down Via dei Servi, is the Jesuit church of **San Bartolomeo**, begun in 1607. The main feature here is something without which no Jesuit church would be complete, a ceiling covered with *trompe-l'œil* frescoes; the works are by various hands, from the fake dome to the *quadratura* buildings that seem to rise above the roofline and offer parishioners a secret passage between them straight up to heaven. Grandiose Jesuit piles like this one were the fashionable churches of their day and, as in the public squares and the palaces, theatricality was everything.

All these 'canal' street names recall a curious feature of Modena's past – like Venice, this was once a city full of canals. There's plenty of water about, spilling down from the Apennines into the marshy countryside around the city. To get rid of it the medieval *comune* built no fewer than nine canals through its streets to channel the water towards the Po, of which the oldest was the 9th-century Canale Chiaro. All of them led to the moat around the original castle, and from there down the navigable Canale Naviglio, which connected the city to the Po down what is now Corso Vittorio Emanuele. Modena's dukes started bricking over the canals in the 1600s, and the last of them was gone by 1800.

San Pietro
open daily 5–12 and 3–8

Just inside the ring of boulevards, on Via San Pietro, the church of **San Pietro** has a harmonious Renaissance façade (1530) with a strange terracotta frieze of winged satyrs and serpent-horses, perhaps inspired by some of the medieval carvings on the cathedral. The interior is one of the most sumptuous in Modena, with ornate *pietra dura* altars, a painted organ case of 1524, stuccoed decoration and a wealth of painting by local artists of the 16th and 17th centuries, including works by Francesco Bianchi Ferrari and Scarsellino. Outside the church, note the little medieval column topped by a cross. In old Emilia these were common monuments at crossroads or market squares; this one is Modena's only survivor.

Along the Via Emilia

The Via Emilia, Modena's elegant main street, runs just behind the Ghirlandina. Heading east, it passes **Piazza Mazzini**, the site of the Jewish ghetto, instituted by Francesco I in 1638 in a quarter where Jews had already lived since at least the 11th century. After Italian unification, ghettos like this one were closed all over the nation. The oldest and most densely packed part was demolished for reasons of hygiene and made into this square, and a big new **synagogue** was built on one side in 1873.

Like Bologna, Modena is a city of porticos. The longest, on the south side of Via Emilia, is the gracefully curving **Portico del Collegio di San Carlo**, built in the late 17th century. Behind the portico, on Via

Università, is the main building of the **University**, one of Italy's oldest (1175). This complex of buildings, occupying the entire block, includes the portico and the Collegio di San Carlo, a school for young noblemen of the 17th century, and its church of **San Carlo** (1664–1766), with a painting inside by Marcantonio Franceschini commemorating the plague of 1576 in Milan.

San Carlo
t (059) 421 204; open by apt, groups only

San Biagio
open 7.30–11.45 and 3.30–7.15

Farther down the Via Emilia, the medieval church of **San Biagio** was thoroughly Baroqued in 1638, with paintings by a great south Italian Baroque master, Mattia Preti. His greatest works are in Naples and on Malta, where he worked for the Grand Master of the Knights of St John, but before he went back down south Preti left a sweet *Concerto di Angeli* in the choir here, and a host of saints plus *Evangelists* and *Adam and Eve* in the dome. The old city ends at the Porta di Bologna. In place of the old gate is the **Fountain of Two Rivers**, representing the Secchia and the little Panaro. It took Modena thirty years to demolish its walls, starting in 1882, and the city replaced them with a ring of tree-lined boulevards. The best part starts here, with Viale Martiri della Libertà and Viale delle Rimembranze, bordered by parks as they wind around the eastern and southern edges of the centre.

Palazzo dei Musei

Chiesa del Voto
open 10–12 and 4–6

San Giovanni Battista
open for temporary exhibitions only

From the cathedral, the western stretch of Via Emilia will take you to Modena's other main attraction. On the way it passes the **Chiesa del Voto**, built as a promise to the Virgin Mary during the great plague of 1630, and the small and elegant late Baroque **San Giovanni Battista**, with a terracotta tableau of the Deposition by Guido Mazzoni (1476). At the old western entrance to the city, the street opens up into Largo Porta Sant'Agostino, part of a major building scheme of the 18th-century Este dukes. On the right is their Ospedale Sant'Agostino (1753), and facing it across the square the huge Palazzo dei Musei, originally the Albergo dei Poveri – the poorhouse. All over Europe in those days it was considered progressive to lock up the unemployed, disabled and orphans in buildings like this (and profitable too; usually they were subjected to forced labour); stately façades like the one here (1764) served to maintain the decorum of the city and to keep respectable folk from worrying too much about what went on inside.

Musei Civici
t (059) 200 100, www.comune.modena.it/museoarte; open Tues–Sat 9–12 and 3–6, Sun and hols 10–1 and 3–7; adm; joint ticket for three local museums available

In 1884 the complex was converted to house the Este picture collections, and the **Musei Civici**. The museum, another charming old north Italian institution where nothing has changed since it first opened, comes in two parts. First is the **Museo Civico d'Arte**, with a collection of medieval paintings from the city's churches, including a work by Tommaso da Modena and some by his followers; and a room of antique musical instruments – psalteries, cembalos, on up to Neapolitan mandolins, all looking rather sad to be locked up in museum cases. Next comes a room of scientific instruments and early machines, and a huge collection of old Modenese crafts and industrial products – a fascinating and peculiar atticful of everything under the sun, from lace to greeting cards; the display of bridle bits takes up an entire wall. The other part is the **Museo Archaeologico-Etnologico**, rich in potsherds, with exhibits on the Terramare people and the Etruscans, the 'Venus of Savignano', a fertility goddess some 20,000 years old, and the finds from a Lombard tomb. The ethnological section is a mixed bag from all over the world, from pre-Columbian figurines from Central America to Samurai costumes from Japan.

Biblioteca Estense
t (059) 222 248, www.cedoc.mo.it/estense; open Mon–Sat 9–1; adm

Another floor of the Palazzo holds the **Biblioteca Estense**. Among its famous collection of illuminated manuscripts is the Bible of *Borso d'Este*, made for the Duke of Modena, a gorgeously coloured 1,200-page marvel illustrated in the 15th century by the Emilians Taddeo Crivelli and Franco Rossi. Also on display are maps made by the great Catalan cartographers of the Age of Discovery, including one of the New World made shortly after Columbus' voyages, and the *Canzoniere Occitano*, the single most important surviving collection of troubadour poetry.

Museo Civico del Risorgimento
t (059) 200 100; closed for restoration

Museo Lapidario Estense
t (059) 439 5711; open Tues–Sun 8.30–7.30; adm

Besides these, the Palazzo dei Musei has room for a **Museo Civico del Risorgimento**, with objects and exhibits on the history of Modena in the 19th century, and the **Museo Lapidario Estense** houses Duke Francesco IV's collection of Roman and medieval stone carvings, tombs and inscriptions.

Galleria Estense

3 Galleria Estense
t (059) 439 5711, it, www.galleriaestense.it: open Tues–Sun 8.30–7.30; adm; joint ticket for three local museums available

By now, you might expect every city of Emilia-Romagna to have a grand aristocratic picture gallery, and Modena does not disappoint. On the upper floor of the Palazzo dei Musei, the Galleria Estense is a well-arranged collection founded by Francesco I d'Este. The dukes didn't bother much with anything before the 1400s (this is one of those museums that still calls them 'primitives') but there is one work by medieval Modena's greatest painter, Tommaso da Modena, as well as some other good early Emilian works.

A room of quattrocento works shows that in the Renaissance Modena could play too (Bartolomeo Banascia's *Pietá with symbols of the Passion*, and an animated *Crucifixion* by Francesco Bianchi Ferrari). Still, the Florentines steal the show, with works by Francesco Botticini and Andrea del Sarto, and especially Botticelli's ripe Technicolor *Madonna con il Bambino*. Other highlights include Lelio Orsi's dramatic *Martyrdom of St Catherine*, with sword-bearing angels descending through the gloom, bronzes by Il Riccio of Padua, a good Flemish collection, an unusual portable altar painted by El Greco, and several works by Venetian Renaissance artists (Palma Vecchio, Tintoretto, Cima da Conegliano and Veronese). For all that, the painting you can't stop staring at will be the masterpiece and last known work of the great quattrocento eccentric Cosmè Tura, the cadaverous, beautiful, horrific *St Anthony of Padua* (1484), a life-sized vision of spiritual and anatomical deformity, captured in a garish pink sunset, which will send any good Catholic out in search of a stiff drink.

For another curiosity, there is the *Camera delle Meraviglie* of the later Este dukes. Like the later Medici in Florence, these Este cared less about serious art than exotic knick-knacks; most of them have been preserved here, including tiny working pistols, ostrich eggs and minuscule carved ships. The Este got to keep their Ferrara residence, the Palazzo dei Diamanti, after the pope took over the city in 1598, and one of the palace's finest embellishments ended up here: a set of ceiling paintings by various Emilian artists including the Carracci; Ludovico Carracci's winsome *Flora* stands out. Another set of ceiling paintings called the *Ottagoni*, scenes from Ovid's *Metamorphoses* by Tintoretto, was brought here from Venice in 1658. The museum is especially rich in Emilian and other works of the 1600s: two notable canvases of Guercino (a *Martyrdom of St Peter*, and *Venus, Cupid and Mars*), Velázquez' Portrait of *Francesco I d'Este* and Salvator Rosa's *Veduta di una Baia* with a shipwreck, as well as works by Lionello Spada, Guido Reni, Annibale Carracci, Carlo Bonone and Charles le Brun.

Sant'Agostino
open 7–12.30 and 3–7.30

The Palazzo dei Musei had to be built around an existing church, the 14th-century **Sant'Agostino**, also facing the square. For a while, the Este considered making this their dynastic 'pantheon', and in 1660 they hired architect Giovanni Monti and theatre designer Gaspare Vigarini to remodel the interior into something more fitting for the grandiose ceremonials of a Baroque funeral. The Este later dropped the idea, but Sant'Agostino was left with a quite impressive interior, with rich stucco decorations and plenty of forgettable painting and sculpture. Surviving from the original church is a rare work of medieval Modena's greatest painter, the *Madonna della Consolazione* of Tommaso da Modena.

North of Piazza Grande

Palazzo Ducale

Palazzo Ducale
t *(059) 206 660; open Sun only, exc Aug or when the Sun is also a holiday; guided tours at 10 and 11; booking necessary; adm*

From the centre, Via Battisti and Via Farini lead to the huge Baroque Palazzo Ducale, once the headquarters of the Este and now the National Military Academy. After the Este were forced out of Ferrara, they took up residence in the original castle on this site, built by Obizzo II in 1288. Perhaps it was a little too medieval and drafty, or else it reminded Duke Francesco I too much of his lost home in Ferrara (which it resembled, in a smaller version); whatever, the castle was gone and work on a new up-to-date palace under way by 1635. Despite the tiny confines of their state, the Este and their architect Luigi Bartolomeo Avanzini made a home that few princes of Europe could match. The façade, with its elegant window cornices and corner towers flanking an impressive entrance, makes a perfect picture of the aristocratic Renaissance ideals of gravity and refinement. Look closely, though, and you can see how hard-pressed the Este were to keep up their pretensions in their little capital while lacking resources: some of the window cornices and trim are just painted on, and half of the balustrade on the cornice is painted cement, not marble. The stone statues on the roofline were only added in the 1920s – in the originals the Este had to settle for wood.

The army takes good care of its landmark schoolhouse. If you're around for the Sunday tours, they'll show you some of the restored rooms, including the *Salone d'Onore*, with frescoes by Marcantonio Franceschini (1696) and the gorgeous golden *Salottino d'Oro*, done in the 18th century in the style of Versailles. They might also take you downstairs to see the huge underground reservoir, the *Casa delle Acque*, that the dukes built to hold the water flowing from Modena's medieval canals.

Around the Palazzo

After the palace was built this part of Modena took on a decidedly aristocratic air, as Baroque palaces and 'scenographic' churches went up on the surrounding streets. These include **San Domenico** (1707), next to the palace, with a fine terracotta group of Jesus in the House of Martha by Antonio Begarelli inside, and the smaller **San Giorgio** on Via Taglio (1647). To the east of the palace, **Corso Canal Grande** was the 'noble street'. Like the dukes, the great ones who buzzed around their court were often strapped for cash to keep up with the Baroque Joneses; in places you can see where the plaster 'stonework' has chipped away, revealing the bricks beneath. The street is dominated by the long 18th-century **Scuderie Ducali**, the arsenal and stables of the Este and now a barracks of the Military Academy. Just to the south is the 1841 **Teatro Comunale**. The street closes at the dukes' old gardens, given to the people of Modena in 1739 by Francesco III and now the lovely **Giardini Pubblici**. Inside is the **Orto Botanico** and the 1634 Palazzina dei Giardini, built for summer balls and concerts. The city now uses it for exhibitions of contemporary art; a prestigious annual photography show is held here.

San Domenico
open Mon–Sat 8.30–11.30 and 5.30–7, Sun and hols 8.30–12 and 3–4.30

San Giorgio
open 7–12 and 4–7.30

Teatro Comunale
***t** (059) 206 993, www.teatrocomunalemodena.it*

Orto Botanico
***t** (059) 205 6011, www.ortobot.unimo.it; open April–July and Sept daily 9–1*

Corso Vittorio Emanuele, once the Canale Naviglio, is another street of imposing palaces, notably the 1772 **Palazzo d'Aragona**. This street ends at Modena's northern gate, its main landmark the neo-Romanesque **Tempio Monumentale dei Caduti**, built in the 1920s as a memorial to the dead of the First World War.

Istituto d'Arte Venturi
t (059) 222 156, www.isaventuri.191.it; open weekdays 8.30–1.30 by appointment

Museo Astronomico e Geofisico
www.museoastrogeo.unimo.it; closed for restoration

Museo del Presepe
*Via Nova 692, **t** (059) 849 921; open end Dec–Feb 3–6.30; adm by donation*

Archivio Capitolare
t (059) 217 130; open by appointment

Museo della Figurina
*Palazzo Santa Margherita, Corso Canalgrande 103, **t** (059) 203 3090; open by appt*

Museo dell'Auto e Moto d'Epoca e Collezione Maserati
*Azienda Agricola Hombre, Via Corletto 320, **t** (059) 510 660; open by appointment, Mon–Fri 10–12 and 4–6*

Museo dell'Auto De Tomaso
*Viale Virgilio 9, **t** (059) 848 102, www.detomaso.it; open by appointment Mon–Fri 8.30–12.30 and 2–5*

Hidden Treasures

Besides the famous sights, Modena offers a rather surprising collection of specialized museums and curiosities that few visitors ever see; even the Modenesi are unaware of the existence of most of them. Next to the Palazzo Ducale on Via Belle Arti, the **Istituto d'Arte Venturi** has a large collection of 19th- and 20th-century paintings. Across Piazza Roma in the Accademia, the **Museo Astronomico e Geofisico** waits to remind us that Modena under the Este dukes was an important centre of astronomical observations; there are early instruments, and a famous early map of the moon. North of the city centre at Villanova, there is a **Museo del Presepe**, with a collection of figurines for Christmas cribs.

At the **Archivio Capitolare**, next to the cathedral on Via Lanfranco, you can get a guided tour of a notable collection of incunabula, documents, papal bulls, missals and hymnals going back to the 8th century. Possibly the biggest museum collection in Modena, the **Museo della Figurina** in Palazzo Santa Margherita has vast hoards of cigarette cards and every other kind of collectors' cards (*figurine* in Italian), as well as matchboxes, menus, calendars, and 43,000 19th-century letter seals.

Modena University has about seven separate museums, but they don't care to let anyone see them. If you can prove you're a medical student, they'll give you a peek at their 18th-century wax anatomical models and 'obstetric terracottas' (such things were once Italian artistic specialities; you'll get a chance to see some in Bologna). They aren't so strict about their collections of mathematical instruments and machines, scientific instruments, chloroformed vertebrates and dinosaur fossils; all you need to get in is written permission from the directors. If you came to see sports cars, besides the Ferraris at Maranello (*see* p.182), you'll also be interested in the Maseratis at the **Museo dell'Auto e Moto d'Epoca e Collezione Maserati** and maybe even the **Museo dell'Auto De Tomaso**, dedicated to a pre-war Modena marque.

ⓘ Modena >
*Piazza Grande 14, **t** (059) 206 660, www.comune.modena.it/infoturismo; open Mon 3–6, Tues–Sat 9.30–12 and 3–6, Sun and hols 9.30–12.30*

Tourist Information in Modena

Modenatur, Via Scudari 10, **t** (059) 220 022, (*open Mon 3–6, Tues–Sat 9–1 and 3–6*). This agency offers bookings for hotels, restaurants, shows and a range of other events.

Shopping in Modena

Modena sponsors an **Antiques Fair** on the 4th Saturday and Sunday of every month in the Parco Novi Sad (*exc July and Dec*). The big weekly **food and clothes market** is there too (*Mon morning*), while the market in the city centre, in Piazza XX Settembre, is held *Mon–Sat*. An **organic foods market** is held in Piazza S. Agostino (*Tues morning*). There are *consorzi dei prodotti tipici* for balsamic vinegar, Lambrusco, cherries, chestnuts, cheeses and hams (quite as tasty as Parma's). It's often possible to visit the farms around the city where they're made;

tours can be booked through the tourist office or Modenatur.

Where to Stay in and near Modena

Modena ✉ 41100

Luxury (€€€€€)

****Canalgrande**, Corso Canalgrande 416, **t** (059) 217 160, *www.canalgrandehotel.it*. In the centre, this palatial hotel is named after Modena's long-gone medieval canal. Once the palazzo of the Marchesi Schedoni, it has richly decorated and stuccoed 18th-century public rooms, with crystal chandeliers, ceiling frescoes and plush, air-conditioned bedrooms, and a restaurant serving Emilian cuisine. Ancient trees grace the hotel's pretty inner garden.

****Rechigi Park Hotel**, 5km from the centre on Via Emilia Est 1581, **t** (059) 283 600, *www.rechigiparkhotel.it*. Another noble residence, elegant, spacious and packed with mod cons. Some rooms have their own Jacuzzis; there's a park and gym.

Expensive (€€€€)

****Mini Hotel Le Ville**, Via Giardini 1270, in Baggiovara, 7km south of town off the A1, **t** (059) 510 051, *www.minihotelleville.it*. Peaceful hotel with three buildings centred around an old villa in a large park with a pool and sauna.

***Europa**, Corso Vittorio Emanuele 52, **t** (059) 217 721, *www.hoteleuropa.it*. Occupying a 19th-century palazzo, with a restaurant.

Moderate (€€€)

***Centrale**, Via Rismondo 55, **t** (059) 218 808, *www.hotelcentrale.com*. Located close to the cathedral, this useful place has comfortable modern rooms.

***Cervetta5**, Via Cervetta 5, **t** (059) 238 447, *www.hotelcervetta5.com*. Right in the city centre, with TV, air-conditioning, Internet and hi-fi. No smoking.

***Daunia**, Via del Pozzo 158, **t** (059) 371 182, *www.hoteldaunia.it*. East of the centre, near the Zona Universitaria and hospital. This benefits from a pleasant terrace, as well as elegantly appointed and comfortable air-conditioned rooms, and a car park.

***Milano**, Corso Vittorio Emanuele 68, **t** (059) 223 011, *www.modenahotel.it*. Modern and functional, soundproofed, with posh bathrooms; air conditioning for a fee.

***Principe**, Corso Vittorio Emanuele 94, **t** (059) 218 670, *www.hotelprincipe.mo.it*. Bedrooms vary but most are well equipped; air conditioning extra, but good breakfast.

Inexpensive (€€)

San Geminiano, Viale Moreali 41, **t** (059) 210 303, *www.hotelsangeminiano.it*. Just east of the centre off Trento e Trieste. Parking.

Budget (€)

Ask about the rooms without baths at the Centrale, the Milano and the Europa (*see* above).

*Sole**, Via Malatesta 45, **t** (059) 214 245. A clean, old-fashioned *locanda* in a small, ancient street. Basic, spacious rooms without baths.

San Cesario ✉ 41018

****Rocca Boschetti**, Via Libertà 53, t (059) 933 600, *www.roccaboschetti.it* (€€€€€). Once the home of the local lords, built in the 19th century on the site of their medieval castle, this three-storey palace around a courtyard maintains much of its original splendour, with elegantly presented rooms with modern accessories (air conditioning is available for a supplement). Ask to visit the old vaulted wine cellars, and don't miss visiting the 11th-century chapel in the grounds.

Castelfranco Emilia ✉ 41013

Villa Gaidello, Via Gaidello 18, **t** (059) 926 806, *www.gaidello.com* (€€€). An enchanting oasis of greenery, part of which is an organic farm. You can choose between six delightfully done apartments in the beautifully restored early 19th-century farmhouse, and there is a restaurant too (*see* 'Eating Out in Modena', below).

Eating Out in Modena

Modena's kitchen has a long and notable tradition. As well as the famous balsamic vinegar, Modena, in the heart of Emilia's pig country, prides itself on its variety of *salumeria* and *prosciutto*; minced pork fills its *tortellini* and its famous main course, *zampone* (pig's trotter, which is boiled and sliced). It is also the best place to taste true Lambrusco, which must be drunk young to be lively and sparkling; the test is to see if the foam vanishes instantly when poured into a glass.

Very Expensive (€€€€)

★ Cucina del Museo >

Cucina del Museo, Via Sant'Agostino 7, **t** (059) 217 429. A charming, intimate restaurant serving a range of lovely dishes – artichoke ravioli, succulent boned pigeon with rosemary, melon and ginger sorbet. *Closed Mon, July, Aug and last week Dec. Booking advisable.*

Fini, Rua Frati Minori 54, **t** (059) 223 314, *www.hotelrealfini.it*. The cathedral of Modenese cuisine. Founded in 1912, Fini has an almost endless menu of hearty regional pasta (lasagne and *tortellini* prepared in a variety of ways – the *pasticcio di tortellini* is exceptional), meat dishes (the famous *zampone* or *bollito misto*), and appetizers, all deliciously prepared. *Closed Mon, Tues, 2 weeks Dec–Jan and 2 weeks in Aug.*

Osteria Francescana, Via Stella 2, **t** (059) 210 118. One of Modena's more innovative places, offering delicious food served in arty décor, with a constantly changing menu. Artichoke lovers should not miss the *mousseline di carciofi* and dessert enthusiasts will love the fabulous *torta bazozzi* with chocolate and hazelnuts; great wine list. *Closed Sat lunch, Sun, Aug and early Jan. Booking advisable.*

Expensive (€€€)

Vinicio, Via Emilia Est 1526, **t** (059) 280 313, *www.ristorantevinicio.it*. A short drive out of the centre, does an excellent job of adapting the rather heavy local cooking to modern tastes – try *tortelli* with ricotta and spinach. There are very fine salads and vegetables, meat courses prepared with balsamic vinegar, and an wine list. *Closed Mon, 2 weeks Dec–Jan and all Aug.*

Moderate (€€)

Osteria Ruggera, Via Ruggera 18, **t** (059) 211 129. This 150-year-old establishment near the cathedral has delicious daily specials – try the gnocchi with gorgonzola and walnuts, pasta dishes and chops made with balsamic vinegar, and the famous and enormous *cotoletta alla Ruggera*. *Closed Tues and Aug.*

Stallo del Pomodoro, Largo Hannover 63, **t** (059) 214 664, *massimilianotelloli @tim.it*. Takes its name from the former tomato market held here; the menu varies with the market and season. List of over 1,000 wines. One of the springtime specialities is smoked goose breast with asparagus. Outdoor tables. *Closed Sun, and Sat lunch.*

Inexpensive (€)

Aldina, Via Albinelli 40, opposite the Mercato Coperto, **t** (059) 236 106. Resolutely old-fashioned but good, traditional family-run trattoria which attracts a wide range of customers, all happy to plonk down around €20 for a plate of fresh pasta, roast meat, dessert and a bottle of Bruschetteria il Lambrusco. *Open for lunch only; closed Sun, Aug and end Dec.*

Compagnia del Taglio, Via Taglio 12, **t** (059) 210 377. A classy wine bar in the *centro storico* where you could easily make a light dinner of the delicious nibbles and salads. Open Tues 9.30am to 9.30pm, Wed–Sat 9.30am to 12.30pm. *Closed Sun, Mon and mid-July–mid-Sept.*

★ Ermes >>

Ermes, Via Ganaceto 89, **t** (059) 238 065. A simple family-run place with a fixed-price menu, which includes a dish of home-made pasta, a main course (*bollito misto* always on Sat), a side dish, Lambrusco and coffee. *Booking advisable. Open Mon–Sat lunch; closed Sun, hols and mid-July–end Aug. No credit cards.*

Morsichino, Piazza Roma 5, **t** (059) 243 482. Opposite the Palazzo Ducale, and very elegant. Prepares every kind of *bruschetta*, *piadine* and pizzas; live music too. *Open until 2pm. Closed Thurs.*

Castelfranco Emilia ✉ 41013

Villa Gaidello, Via Gaidello 18, **t** (059) 926 806, *www.gaidello.com* (€€€). See p.176 for accommodation. Superb traditional cuisine, such as wine-basted rabbit, prepared with a light and delicate touch; fixed-price menu (€38) includes *antipasto*, three *primi*, main course, *contorno* and dessert. Open to non-guests; reservations a must. *Closed Sun eve, Mon, and Aug.*

Entertainment and Nightlife in Modena

Modena is nearly as mad for culture as Parma. and you are likely to find there is a full schedule of plays, ballet and concerts. The main venues are **Teatro Comunale**, Corso Canal Grande, **t** (059) 206 993, *www.teatrocomunalemodena.it*, the historic **Teatro Storchi**, Largo Garibaldi 15, **t** (059) 213 6011, *www.emiliaromagnateatro.com*, the **Teatro Michelangelo**, Via Giardini 255, **t** (059) 343 662, *www.cinemateatromichelangelo.com* (*closed July and Aug*) and the **Teatro delle Passioni**, Via Carlo Sigonio 382, **t** (059) 301 880, *www.emiliaromagnateatro.com*, as well as at other venues around town.

A weekly hand-out called *News Spettacolo, www.newspettacolo.com*, which also covers Reggio, has all the listings as well as restaurants and night clubs.

For the past few years in mid-September Pavarotti has given a concert in his home town's Piazza Grande. It's expensive and booked up well in advance, but crowds sit in the neighbouring bars and listen to the music while watching the show on TV.

Two good venues for live music between Modena and Reggio Emila are **Il Temporock**, Gualtieri, on SS63, **t** Stefania 347 450 6787, *www.temporock.it*, and Vox Club, Via **Vittorio Veneto** 13, Nonantola, **t** (059) 546 979, *www.voxclub.it*.

North of Modena

Carpi

④ Carpi

North of Modena is Carpi, a wealthy, workaholic town with an illustrious past, one of the few small towns in the region worth going out of your way for. It is also one of the few towns not founded by the Romans or earlier. Carpi, named for the groves of hornbeam (*carpinus*) that once stood here, grew up as a fortified settlement under the Lombards in the 8th century. In the Middle Ages Carpi grew into a prosperous city and established a *comune*, but its greatest days came between 1331 and 1525, when it was governed by the Pio family, clever fellows who could keep their little city independent while doing great service as patrons of the arts. Like so many other minor *signori* around Italy, the Pio lost control in the Wars of Italy. After a two-year Spanish occupation, Carpi and its *contado* ended up in the hands of the Este.

The city centre is dominated by the vast **Piazza dei Martiri**, formerly called the *Borgogioioso*. At least once in Carpi you will probably be reminded that this is the third-largest piazza in Italy; whether or not this is true would be hard to say, but it is nearly a thousand feet long, and it leaves an unforgettable impression. With a crowd, receding into the distance it seems like some perspectivist

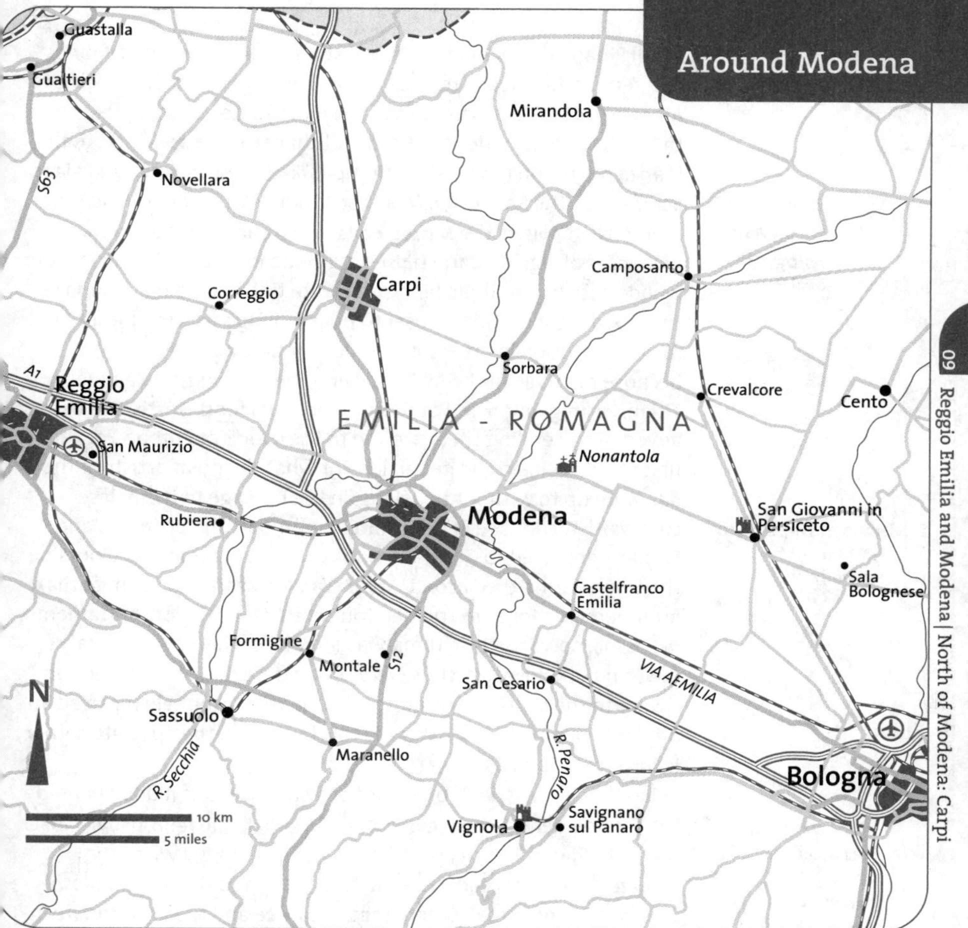

Renaissance painting of the 'ideal city'; without them it becomes positively oceanic, and crossing it on a still Sunday afternoon one feels tempted to stop the lone passer-by and ask for news from land. The piazza is bordered on one side by a long portico, and the view is closed on the short end by the **Cathedral of S. Maria Assunta**, with a sumptuous Baroque façade. Begun by Alberto III, the last and greatest Pio, in 1515, the city didn't get it completely finished and decorated until the 1800s.

Cathedral of S. Maria Assunta
open Mon–Wed, Fri, Sun and hols 7.30–12 and 3.30–7.30; Thurs and Sat 7.30–12.30 and 3.30–7.30

On the other long side stands the 16th-century **Castello dei Pio**. Everyone from the Lombards to the Spanish contributed something to this huge complex, but it was Alberto III who tied it all together with an elegant Renaissance façade. Inside, Carpi keeps its impressive collection of museums, starting with the **Musei Civici**. There is an archaeological section, with finds from the four Terramare villages around Carpi and from Roman times, as well as a

Castello dei Pio
www.comune.carpi.mo.it/musei

Musei Civici
t (059) 649 968; open Thurs, Sat, Sun and hols 10–12.30 and 3.30–7; adm

small Pinacoteca, exhibits on the history of Carpi, ceramics, fabrics and terracotta, but the real reason for coming is to see the rooms of Alberto III's residence, frescoed by Bernardino Loschi and others in the early 1500s. Besides the beautiful chapel, there are works in the Stanza dei Trionfi (a series of 'triumphs' like those in Ferrara's Palazzo Schifanoia), the Salone dei Mori, the Studiolo of Alberto II and other rooms. Next comes the **Museo della Xilografica**, devoted to the woodcuts of Ugo da Carpi (1481–1532), who invented the chiaroscuro woodcut, using multiple blocks to create tinted shading and make the woodcut something closer to painting. Ugo was the father of a major revolution in art – not so much for his own talents, but because he made his living by copying the paintings of Raphael, Titian, Parmigianino and others as woodcuts for the artists to use as advertising, sending them around to the courts of Europe. For the first time, people could get an idea of what the great artists of the day were up to without travelling. In the passage to the palace courtyard, the **Museo al Deportato** remembers the prisoners and civilians deported to Germany from a Nazi camp that stood outside the town during the Second World War. Ask at the museum to make arrangements for a free guided tour; the Campo di Concentramento di Fossoli, now largely in ruins, was the place where most of Italy's Jews and other Nazi victims were kept before their trip to Germany.

Museo della Xilografica
t (059) 649 955; open Thurs, Sat and Sun 10–12.30 and 3.30–7; adm

Museo al Deportato
t (059) 649 978; open Thurs, Sat and Sun 10–12.30 and 3.30–7; adm

Next to the Castello, the pretty 1860 **Teatro Comunale** replaced an original built by Gaspare Vigarini for the Este; in the opposite corner is the old grain market.

Carpi's real treasure is one-third of a church. It sits hidden behind the Palazzo del Pio, the **Pieve di Santa Maria in Castello**, usually just called 'La Sagra'. The city's centre of gravity changed when the Palazzo del Pio was completed in the 1400s, and the *Borgogioioso* was laid out next to it. Before that, the Pieve and the little square in front of it made up the centre. Pieve means a country church, and this one was the nucleus around which Carpi took shape some time in the 8th century. Later on the old walled medieval quarter became known as the 'Castello'; except for the church, almost all of it has disappeared. The first church on this site may have been part of a Roman villa. This was rebuilt in 752 by the Lombard King Aistulf, or Astolfo; the current incarnation was begun around 1120, one of the many churches financed by Countess Matilda of Canossa. After the city was recentred, Signore Alberto III decided to tear the old church down. In the end, however, he left the rear third standing, building a new, plain façade (1514), and incorporating into it the portal from Matilda's church. Other survivors from the original church are the sculptural decoration of the apse, by the followers of Wiligelmo, and the tall, tilted campanile, built in 1221.

Pieve di Santa Maria in Castello
t (059) 688 317; open Thurs 10.30–12.30, Sat and Sun 10.30–12.30 and 4–6.30; no visits during mass

The entrance is through the adjacent **Cappella di Santa Caterina**, with an excellent cycle of quattrocento frescoes on the *Life of St*

Catherine by unknown artists, followers of Giovanni da Modena. Catherine of Alexandria was a favourite subject of medieval Emilian artists; her cult came back with the crusaders. Her story is mostly fairy tale (she was one of the saints tossed out of the book by the Second Vatican Council), and you can follow all the episodes in the frescoes here: Catherine meets the Emperor Maxentius, converts the empress, argues with the pagan philosophers, and is finally martyred on her wheel, while the empress is decapitated; in the background note Mount Sinai, where the saint's supposed relics are still kept in an Orthodox monastery.

In the church proper is the **Cappella di San Martino**, with frescoes by the Ferrarese Antonio Alberti (1424) of the *Adoration of the Magi* and the *Doctors of the Church*. Fragments of medieval frescoes can also be seen around the vaulting of the church, along with two striking sculptural works: a 12th-century *ambone*, the work of a follower of Wiligelmo named Nicolò, and the 1351 *sarcophagus of Manfredo Pio*.

Nonantola and Mirandola

Abbey of Nonantola
t (059) 549 053; open 7.30am–8pm

Museo Diocesiano
t (059) 549 053; open Tues–Sat 9–12.30 and 3–6.30, Sun and hols 3–6.30; adm

Antiquarium
Via Marconi, t (059) 896 555; open Fri–Sun 9.30–12.30 and 3–6, other days by appointment; adm free

Northeast of Modena is the **Abbey of Nonantola**, founded in 752 by King Aistulf's brother-in-law, the abbot Anselmo, rebuilt in the 12th century and suffering various remodellings since. The portal, however, retains its beautiful carving by the workshop of Wiligelmo. The church is dedicated to and contains relics of the 4th-century St Sylvester, pope under Constantine, while the crypt has 64 columns with carved capitals, some as old as the 8th century, and the tomb of another pope, St Adrian III, who died here in 885. The Abbey has two cloisters, and a refectory with frescoes from the 11th and 12th centuries. The **Museo Diocesiano** has medieval reliquaries and documents sent to the abbots by Charlemagne and Otto I. The town of Nonantola also has a small archaeological collection in the **Antiquarium**.

Further north, **Mirandola** is an ancient town that was ruled for four centuries (until 1711) by the Pico family. These names might ring a bell; one of the family was none other than Giovanni Pico della Mirandola, the famous Renaissance philosopher and friend of Lorenzo de' Medici (*see* p.43). In his day the Pico were turning Mirandola into an up-to-date Renaissance town, with one of Italy's first sets of modern fortifications; little of these walls has survived, but Mirandola still has its quattrocento Duomo and its Palazzo Comunale.

Museo Civico
t (059) 896 656

On Via Montanari, the **Museo Civico** has an archaeological collection and a *pinacoteca* with portraits of members of the Pico family.

South of Modena

Maranello and Sassuolo

If you come to Modena to see sports cars, you'll have to make the trip out to **Maranello** and the **Galleria Ferrari** by the factory and testing track, with historic cars, Formula 1 cups and exhibits and films on the car's history: it boasts no fewer than 5,000 race victories around the world since 1940. Enzo Ferrari, who got his start building tractors on his father's farm, moved out to this village during war production in 1943, and promptly got bombed flat by the Allies. Since the rebuilding, Maranello has been Ferrari City, the place where people throughout the town hear the buzz of the cars on the testing track. It's a strange little world: high-tech, but at the same time an anachronistic stronghold of Renaissance-style Italian luxury craftsmanship. Maranello has an Enzo Ferrari Park, and a statue of the founder. Up in the hills south of Maranello, the 11th-century Pieve di Santa Maria Assunta at **Rocca Santa Maria** has some fine Romanesque capitals.

Galleria Ferrari
Via Dino Ferrari 43, **t** *(0536) 943 204, www.galleria.ferrari.com; open June–Sept 9.30–7, rest of year 9.30–6; adm exp*

Between Modena and Maranello, in **Montale Rangone** is the archaeological open-air museum of **Terramara di Montale**. Here around 1600BC, the Terramare people (*see* p.157), built settlements on piles at the edges of lakes. They used bronze tools, buried their cremated dead in communal cemeteries and did their bit for posterity, bringing with them bronze tool-making skills and introducing regular gridplan villages. With reconstructions, archaeological experiments and children's activities, this is a surprisingly lively historical encounter.

Terramara di Montale
t *(059) 532 020, www.parcomontale.it; open April–June and Sept–Oct, Sun and hols 10–7; July–Aug daily 10–7; adm*

Sassuolo, west of Maranello on the Fiume Secchia, is the centre of Italy's flourishing ceramic tile industry. Under the Este it produced rather more artistic ceramics, some of which can be seen at the **Collezione Vistarino**. Though now it's a gritty industrial town, the Este favoured Sassuolo as a summer residence: Francesco I built a palace there, the richly decorated **Palazzo Ducale**, on Piazza della Rosa, with frescoes by Jean Boulanger and Baroque fountains.

Collezione Vistarino
Viale Monte Santo 40, **t** *(0536) 818 111, www.assopiastrelle.it; open Mon–Fri 8.30–12.30 and 2.30–6.30 by appt; closed Aug; adm free*

Palazzo Ducale
Piazza della Rosa; open April–early Nov, Sat 3–6, Sun 10–1 and 3–6, closed 2 weeks Aug; adm

Where to Stay and Eat around Modena

ⓘ Carpi ›
Via Berengario 2, **t** *(059) 649 240, www.carpidiem.it; open Mon–Sat 9.30–12.30 and 3–6, Sun 9.30–12.30*

Carpi and Around ✉ 41012

********Touring****, Via Dallai 1, **t** (059) 681 535, *www.hoteltouringcarpi.it* (€€€€). Modern and by the station, the most comfortable place to stay in Carpi.

******Duomo***, Via Battisti 25, **t** (059) 686 745 (€€€). Just behind the cathedral, this is the only hotel in the centre, but it's comfortable, with parking; air conditioning extra, breakfast included.

L'Incontro, **t** (059) 664 581 (€€€). Five km west of Carpi, on the SS468 to Correggio, this has a huge menu of well-prepared dishes, ranging from the classic *tortellini in brodo* to *carpaccio* of smoked sturgeon (delicious) and pigeon stuffed with *porcini* mushrooms in wine sauce. *Closed Sat lunchtimes and Sun, 1 week Jan and 2 weeks Aug.*

Osteria Bohemia, Via Canale 497 in Soliera, 7km south, **t** (059) 563 041, *www.osteriabohemia.it* (€€€). The interior is infused with heavenly aromas. Also some rooms (€€). *Closed Sun, Mon eve and Aug.*

Teresa Baldini, Via Livorno 32, **t** (059) 662 691 (€€€). Ten km east of Carpi, at San Martino Secchia, is an old-fashioned and welcoming osteria; the *maccheroni al pettine* is perfect, the meats traditionally prepared, and the desserts home-made. *Evenings only; booking required; closed Thurs.*

Nonantola ✉ 41015

Osteria di Rubbiara, Via Risaia 2, **t** (059) 549 019 (€€). Near Nonántola at Rubbiara, this has been in the Pedroni family since 1861. The authentic Modenese cooking is in a very traditional setting. For €30 you'll get whatever's on offer, take it or leave it, but at least one dish such as the omelette or rabbit will come with the family's balsamic vinegar. They also make a huge variety of liqueurs. *Open lunch only exc Fri and Sat eves; closed Tues and 20 days Dec–Jan.*

ⓘ **Nonantola >>**
Palazzo Comunale, Via Marconi 11, **t** *(059) 896 555, www.comune.nonantola.mo.it; open Thurs and Fri 8.30–12.30, Sat and Sun 9–12.30 and 3–6.30*

ⓘ **Mirandola**
Piazza Costituente (0535) 29524, www.comune.mirandola.mo.it

The Modenese Apennines

At weekends, the Modenesi embark on gastronomic voyages into the Apennines: stop at any roadside restaurant (choose the one with the most cars parked outside), and you will find simple meals of smoked meats, cheeses, freshly baked breads and raw vegetables. The meal is named *tigelle* or *crescente* after its distinctive breads – one like a flat, baked muffin, the other of thin dough fried in fat. During the week you won't have to wait for a table.

Into the Mountains

At Sassuolo, you can break away from the flatlands of the Po by heading south into the Apennines, which achieve majestic proportions near the border with Tuscany. The region has perfect updrafts for hang-gliding and sailplanes, especially around **Pavullo** and **Montecreto**. Pavullo is the largest village in the Modenese Apennines, the capital of a little region called the Frignano, where the most astonishing sight is a 100ft cedar of Lebanon in the gardens of the old Palazzo Ducale. To the west, in one of the most inaccessible parts of the mountains, the *partigiani* set up the 'Repubblica di Montefiorino', a free zone that held out for a few months against the Nazis in 1944. In the village of Montefiorino, the **Museo della Repubblica di Montefiorino** tells the whole story with photos, documents and objects from the time.

Museo della Repubblica di Montefiorino
t *(0536) 965 139, istitutostorico@tin.it; open summer daily 10.30–12.30 and 3–6; rest of year Sun, other days by appointment; adm*

In April the emerald-green foothills around **Vignola** are covered with the lacy, rosy-pink blossoms of Vignola's famous cherry trees. These are celebrated in a Cherry Blossom Festival in April, with horse races, bicycle tours, medieval costumes, fair, exhibitions and other events (you can get there from Bologna by way of a special free Cherry Train, the *Treno dei Ciliegi*). Half of Italy's cherries come from Vignola, as did one of Italy's most talented 16th-century architects,

The Modenese Apennines

Rocca di Vignola
t (059) 775 246; open winter Tues–Sat 9–12 and 2.30–6, Sun and hols 10–12 and 2.30–6; summer Tues–Sat 9–12 and 3.30–7, Sun and hols 10–12

Giacomo Barozzi – best known simply as Vignola. He didn't leave anything in his home town, but it does have in its centre one of the best-preserved castles in Emilia-Romagna, the **Rocca di Vignola**. Founded in the 8th century by the abbots of Nonantola, rebuilt with lofty towers in the 13th century, it was improved by the Contrari family in the 15th century, and since 1965 has been owned by a bank, which has financed its complete restoration. A number of rooms retain their frescoes, with rooms of rings and another of doves; the chapel has frescoes by the so-called Maestro di Vignola. The castle often hosts important exhibitions.

Further south, in **Guiglia**, rise the peculiar pinnacles of Rocca Malatina in the **Parco Naturale di Sassi**. Just south of Guiglia don't miss the 11th-century country church, the **Pieve di Trebbio**, with primitive capitals inside.

Sestola

Giardino Esperia
t (0536) 61535, caimo@inwind.it (open mid-June–mid-Sept Tues–Sun 9.30–12.30 and 2–6; July and Aug daily; adm by donation

Museo degli Strumenti Musicali Meccanici
open July–Aug 10–12 and 4–7; adm, free guided tours on Sun

The most striking mountain scenery is up at **Sestola**, a winter and summer resort near the highest peak of the Northern Apennines, Monte Cimone (7,100ft); for a ski report, call **t** (0536) 62350. From Sestola you can visit the pretty glacial **Lago della Ninfa** and the **Giardino Esperia**, planted by the local Alpine club in 1950 at the Passo del Lupo, a botanical frontier, where Alpine and Apennine flowers, trees and herbs grow side by side. Sestola also has the **Museo degli Strumenti Musicali Meccanici**, with calliopes and carillons, barrel organs, automated birds and singing dolls.

Another excursion from Sestola is to **Pian Cavallaro**, and from there to the summit of Monte Cimone for a unique view – on a clear day you can see both the Tyrrhenian and Adriatic seas, and all the way north to the Julian Alps and Mont Blanc. You can also make the ascent from the old village of **Fiumalbo**, just below the Passo Abetone that separates Emilia from Tuscany. Two other mountain lakes are just south of Fiumalbo: **Lago Santo** and **Lago Bacio**, connected by an easy footpath. Not as pretty, but more unusual, is the small **Lago Pratignano**, in the meadows south of Fanano, a little to the east of Sestola. In the spring its banks are strewn with unusual wild flowers and carnivorous plants – bring your waders.

ⓘ Sestola >>
Via Passerini 18, **t** *(0536) 62324*

ⓘ Pavullo
Via Giardini 3, **t** *(0536) 20358*

Where to Stay and Eat in the Modenese Apennines

Vignola ✉ 41058

*****Eden**, Via C. Battisti 49, **t** (059) 772 847, *www.eden-hotel.it* (€€). There's one hotel in cherry town; the rooms are fairly simple but all have TV.

Trattoria Bolognese, Via Muratori 1, **t** (059) 771 207 (€€). Located right in the centre of town, this has a delightful interior courtyard next to a 15th-century castle, where you can feast on excellent *tagliatelle alla bolognese*, accompanied by local Lambrusco. *Closed Fri eve, Sat, and Aug. Booking advisable.*

Sestola ✉ 41029

There are also numerous small hotels in Fiumalbo, especially at Dogana Nuova.

******San Marco**, Via delle Rose 2, **t** (0536) *62330, www.albergosanmarco.it* (€€€). With a pine wood for a backdrop, set in a large 19th-century villa with a panoramic terrace. It has comfortable rooms with air conditioning, a gym and tennis courts in a lovely garden; in the summer it has a restaurant. *Closed Oct and Nov.*

*****Tirolo**, Via delle Rose 9, **t** (0536) 62523, *www.hotel-adas.it/tirolo.htm* (€€). Also has tennis courts and very comfortable rooms. *Open mid-June to mid-Sept and mid-Dec–end Mar.*

****Sport Hotel**, Via delle Ville 116, **t** (0536) 62502, *davidemagnani@libero.it* (€). A pleasant small hotel that's *open all year.*

San Rocco, Corso Umberto I 47, **t** (0536) 62382, *www.hotel-sanrocco.it* (€€€). Lavishly good food; the chef does wonders with vegetables and pasta dishes (try the pecorino cheese with onions and balsamic vinegar or *salsiccia abriaca* – drunken sausage with wine); also tender roast meats. *Closed Mon, May and Oct.*

Bologna

A most peculiar metropolis is Bologna – earnest, erudite and built entirely of good, honest brick. A capital of culture since the Middle Ages, this city has a little bit of everything, all spread beneath an absurd and genial pair of leaning towers. It has been a university town for over a thousand years, which explains a lot of its peculiarities. It is also, by general acclaim, the culinary capital of Italy. And it is unique among the region's cities in having hills within walking distance of the centre.

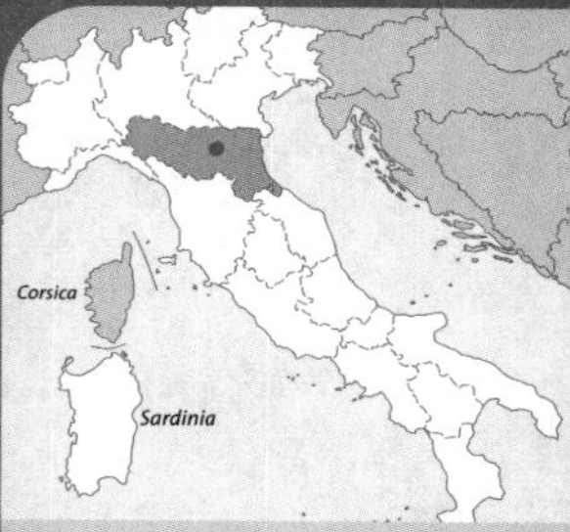

10

See map overleaf

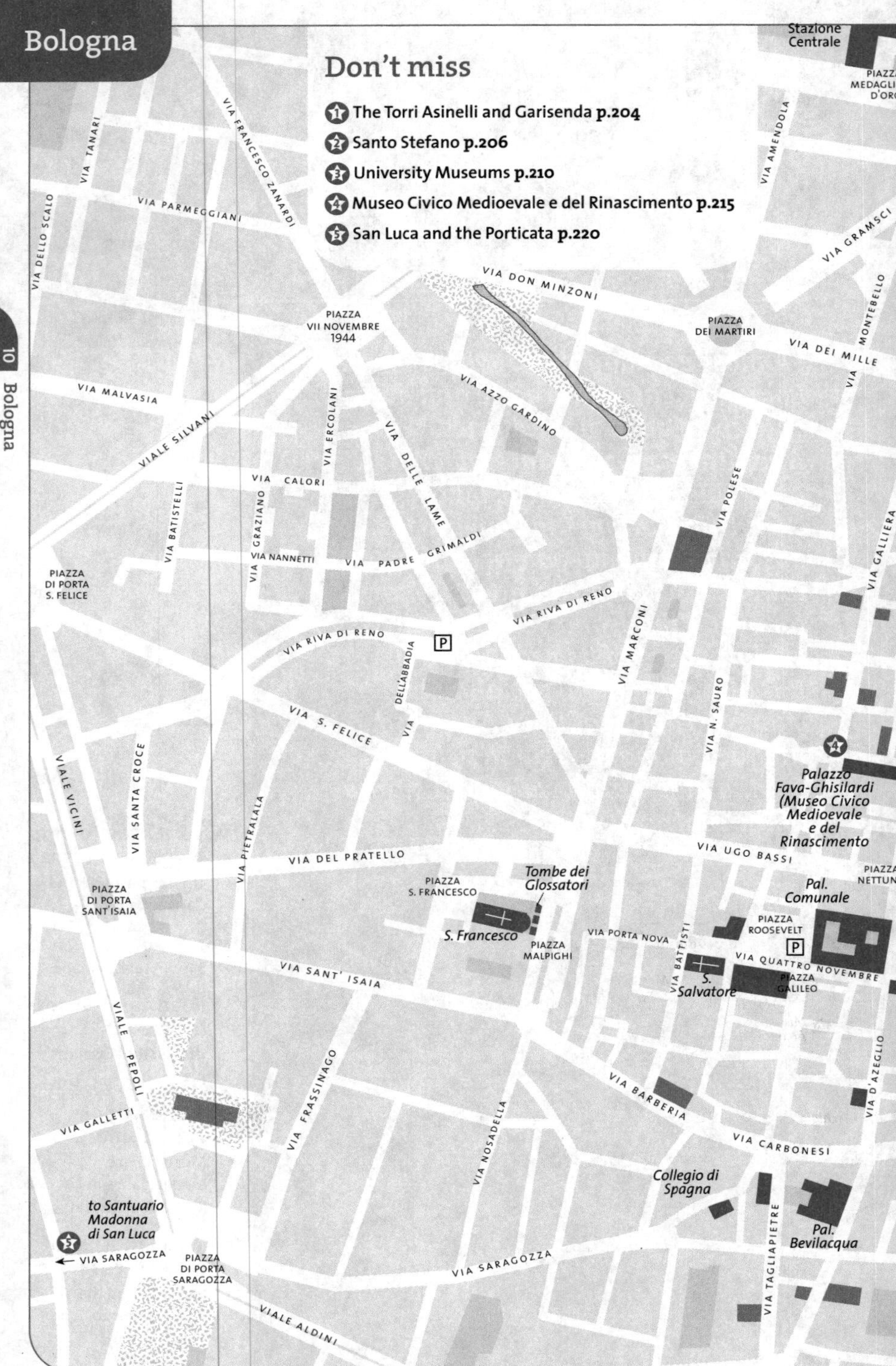

Don't miss
1 The Torri Asinelli and Garisenda p.204
2 Santo Stefano p.206
3 University Museums p.210
4 Museo Civico Medioevale e del Rinascimento p.215
5 San Luca and the Porticata p.220
Stazione Centrale
PIAZZA MEDAGLIE D'ORO
VIA AMENDOLA
VIA GRAMSCI
VIA MONTEBELLO
VIA TANARI
VIA FRANCESCO ZANARDI
VIA PARMEGGIANI
VIA DELLO SCALO
VIA DON MINZONI
PIAZZA VII NOVEMBRE 1944
PIAZZA DEI MARTIRI
VIA DEI MILLE
VIA MALVASIA
VIA ERCOLANI
VIA AZZO GARDINO
VIALE SILVANI
VIA DELLE LAME
VIA CALORI
VIA BATISTELLI
VIA GRAZIANO
VIA POLESE
VIA GALLIERA
VIA NANNETTI
VIA PADRE GRIMALDI
PIAZZA DI PORTA S. FELICE
VIA RIVA DI RENO
VIA MARCONI
VIA DELL'ABBADIA
P
VIA S. FELICE
VIA N. SAURO
VIALE VICINI
VIA SANTA CROCE
VIA PIETRALATA
Palazzo Fava-Ghisilardi (Museo Civico Medioevale e del Rinascimento
VIA DEL PRATELLO
VIA UGO BASSI
PIAZZA NETTUNO
Tombe dei Glossatori
PIAZZA S. FRANCESCO
PIAZZA DI PORTA SANT'ISAIA
Pal. Comunale
S. Francesco
VIA PORTA NOVA
PIAZZA ROOSEVELT
PIAZZA MALPIGHI
VIA BATTISTI
VIA QUATTRO NOVEMBRE
VIA SANT' ISAIA
S. Salvatore
PIAZZA GALILEO
VIALE PEPOLI
VIA FRASSINAGO
VIA BARBERIA
VIA D'AZEGLIO
VIA NOSADELLA
VIA GALLETTI
VIA CARBONESI
Collegio di Spagna
to Santuario Madonna di San Luca
VIA TAGLIAPIETRE
Pal. Bevilacqua
VIA SARAGOZZA
PIAZZA DI PORTA SARAGOZZA
VIALE ALDINI

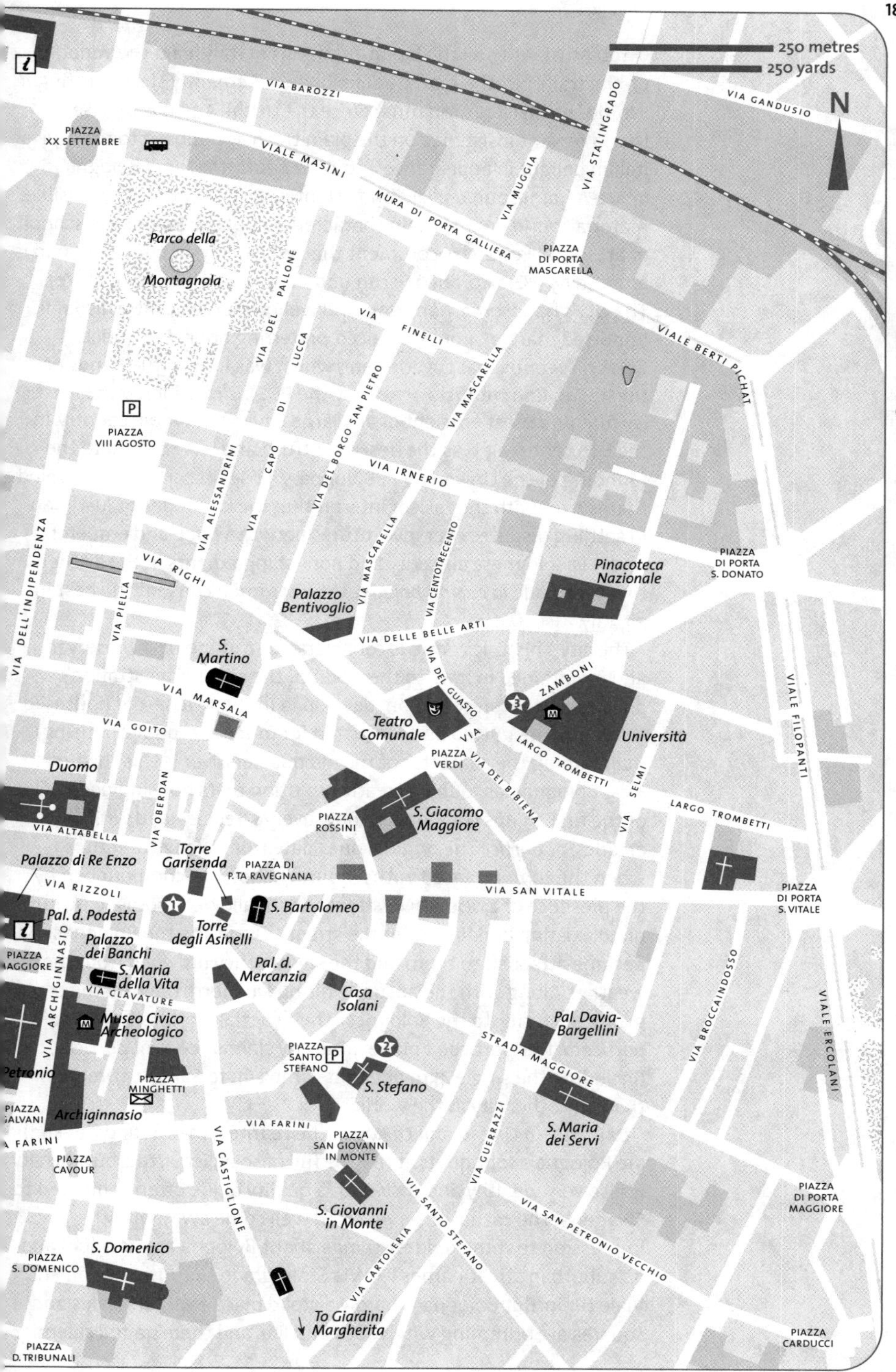
250 metres
250 yards
N
VIA BAROZZI
VIA GANDUSIO
PIAZZA XX SETTEMBRE
VIALE MASINI
VIA STALINGRADO
VIA MUGGIA
MURA DI PORTA GALLIERA
PIAZZA DI PORTA MASCARELLA
Parco della Montagnola
VIA DEL PALLONE
VIA FINELLI
VIALE BERTI PICHAT
VIA DI LUCCA
VIA MASCARELLA
VIA DEL BORGO SAN PIETRO
PIAZZA VIII AGOSTO
VIA CAPO
VIA ALESSANDRINI
VIA IRNERIO
VIA CENTOTRECENTO
VIA DELL'INDIPENDENZA
VIA RIGHI
VIA PIELLA
Palazzo Bentivoglio
Pinacoteca Nazionale
PIAZZA DI PORTA S. DONATO
VIA DELLE BELLE ARTI
S. Martino
VIA MARSALA
VIA DEL GUASTO
ZAMBONI
VIA GOITO
Teatro Comunale
Università
VIALE FILOPANTI
PIAZZA VERDI
LARGO TROMBETTI
VIA DEI BIBIENA
VIA SELMI
Duomo
VIA OBERDAN
VIA ALTABELLA
PIAZZA ROSSINI
S. Giacomo Maggiore
Torre Garisenda
Palazzo di Re Enzo
PIAZZA DI P. TA RAVEGNANA
VIA RIZZOLI
VIA SAN VITALE
PIAZZA DI PORTA S. VITALE
S. Bartolomeo
Pal. d. Podestà
Torre degli Asinelli
Palazzo dei Banchi
PIAZZA MAGGIORE
VIA ARCHIGINNASIO
S. Maria della Vita
Pal. d. Mercanzia
VIA CLAVATURE
Casa Isolani
VIA BROCCAINDOSSO
VIALE ERCOLANI
Museo Civico Archeologico
Pal. Davia-Bargellini
PIAZZA SANTO STEFANO
STRADA MAGGIORE
Petronio
PIAZZA MINGHETTI
S. Stefano
PIAZZA GALVANI
Archiginnasio
VIA FARINI
PIAZZA SAN GIOVANNI IN MONTE
S. Maria dei Servi
PIAZZA CAVOUR
VIA CASTIGLIONE
VIA GUERRAZZI
VIA SANTO STEFANO
S. Giovanni in Monte
PIAZZA DI PORTA MAGGIORE
VIA SAN PETRONIO VECCHIO
S. Domenico
PIAZZA S. DOMENICO
VIA CARTOLERIA
To Giardini Margherita
PIAZZA CARDUCCI
PIAZZA D. TRIBUNALI

'You must write all the beautiful things of Italy,' said the Venetian on the train, but the man from Bologna vehemently shook his finger. 'No, no,' he insisted. 'You must write the truth!' And it is precisely that, a fervent insistence on the plain truth as opposed to the typical Italian delight in appearance and *bella figura*, that sets Bologna apart. A homespun realism and attention to the detail of the visible, material world are the main characteristics of the Bolognese school of art (recall Petrarch's comment that, while only an educated man is amazed by a Giotto, anyone can understand a Bolognese picture). The city's handsome, harmonic and well-preserved centre disdains imported marble or ornate stucco, preferring honest red brick. Bologna's municipal government, which was long in the hands of the Italian Communist Party (now the PDS), is considered the least corrupt and most efficient of any large city in the whole country. In the 11th century it was the desire for truth and law that led to the founding of the University of Bologna, whose first scholars occupied themselves with the task of interpreting the law codes of Justinian in settling disputes over investitures between pope and emperor. And it is Bolognese sincerity and honest ingredients in the kitchen that has made *la cucina bolognese* by common consent the best in all Italy.

The city's historic centre is considered one of the best preserved and maintained in Italy, to the credit of the city administration's policy of 'active preservation', developed in the 1970s – old houses in the centre are gutted and renovated for municipal public housing, maintaining the character of the old quarters. Nor is this the first time Bologna has found a creative solution to its housing needs. One of the first things you notice is how every street is lined with arcades, or *portici*. The original ones date from the 12th century, when the *comune*, faced with a housing shortage compounded by the presence of 2,000 university students, allowed rooms to be built on to existing buildings over the streets. Over time the Bolognesi became attached to them and the shelter they provided from the weather. Along with the absurdly tilting Due Torri, they are the city's soul, its identity; to the Bolognesi, their special world is the *pianeta porticata*, the 'porticoed planet'. The city claims 70km of *portici* (including the single 4km one that climbs up to San Luca), more than any other city in the world.

La Dotta, *La Grassa* and *La Rossa* (the Learned, the Fat and the Red) are Bologna's sobriquets. It may be full of socialist virtue, but the city is also very wealthy and cosy, with a quality of life often compared to Sweden's. The casual observer could well come away with the impression that the reddest things about Bologna are its bricks and its suburban street names like Via Stalingrado, Via Yuri Gagarin and Viale Lenin. But Bologna is hardly a stolid place – its bars, cafés and squares are brimming with youth and life, and there's a full calendar

Getting to Bologna

By Air

Bologna's Guglielmo Marconi airport is to the northwest in the Borgo Panigale; for airport information, **t** (051) 647 9615, *www.bologna-airport.it*. **Aerobus**, the city's airport link, has a *servizio navetta* that runs in a loop, stopping at the arrival and departure terminals, Ospedale Maggiore, Via Ugo Bassi, Via del l'Indipendenza/San Pietro, Via Indipendenza/ Arena del Sole, and the FS Stazione Centrale. They run every 15 min 8am–8pm; there's a timetable available at the tourist office, or call **t** (051) 290 290. Allow an hour for the journey; the traffic can be terrible. There is also a direct service (*servizio diretto*) that runs from the airport to the Fiera district during trade shows (30mins).

Bologna has good **flight connections** with major Italian and European cities. Places you can fly from within Italy include Alghero (Alpi Eagles), Bari (Blu Express), Cagliari (Meridiana), Florence (Austrian), Milan and Rome (Alitalia), Naples (Alpi Eagles and Air One) and Palermo (Meridiana and Myair.com). Other points in Europe with direct flights include London (British Airways from/to Gatwick), Dublin (Aer Lingus), Barcelona (Iberia), Athens (Airone), Frankfurt (Lufthansa), Munich, (Air Dolomiti), Paris (Air France) and Vienna (Austrian). For **Forlì Airport**, *see* p.300.

By Rail

Bologna is one of the prime nodes of the FS rail network, with frequent, fast connections to Venice, Florence, Milan, Ravenna, Rimini and almost everywhere else in Italy from the **Stazione Centrale** in Piazza Medaglie d'Oro, **t** 1478 88088. It is on the north side of the city centre, about a 10–15-min walk from Piazza Maggiore; a number of buses go there. For **Trenitalia** information, **t** 892 021 (from Italy only), *www.trenitalia.com*.

By Bus

The **bus station** (*Autostazione*) is near the FS at Piazza XX Settembre, **t** (051) 245 400, *www.autostazionebo.it*, and has services every hour for Ferrara, Imola, Modena and Ravenna, and less frequent ones to many other destinations in the region. For ATC information, **t** (051) 290 290, *www.atc.bo.it*.

By Road

The motorway (*autostrada*) approaching Bologna skirts around the city to the north in a ring road, the *tangenziale*, which connects up with most major routes. At Bologna the A1 from Milan leaves the Via Emilia and turns south towards Florence, but the A14 continues on to Ravenna and Rimini. The A13 runs north from Bologna to Ferrara and Padua.

Within the *tangenziale* the state roads leading into Bologna connect up with an inner ring road around the city centre, though the SS9/Via Emilia still runs through its middle. The SS64 (Via Stalingrado, inside the *tangenziale*) branches off north for Ferrara, and the SS253 for Ravenna. South of Bologna the SS64 runs to Pistoia and the SS65 to Florence. Since the centre is closed to traffic, you'll be routed around it on the ring of boulevards that follow the course of the demolished city walls.

---

of concerts from rap to jazz to Renaissance madrigals, as well as avant-garde ballet, theatre and art exhibitions. Visitors, though, should be aware that in July and August Bologna can be as exciting as the cheap supermarket salami that bears its name.

History

The area around Bologna was first settled perhaps as early as 1000 BC by the people of the Villanovan culture, who occupied much of north-central Italy; Villanova di Castenaso itself, with the site that gives these people a name, is just outside the city. The Villanovans, once believed to be an Italic people who were conquered by the Etruscans, are now generally accepted simply as an earlier phase of Etruscan culture, before its great economic expansion of the 8th and 7th centuries BC brought it into the mainstream of Mediterranean civilization and opened it to influences from the Greek world. The

Getting around Bologna

Most of Bologna's sights are within easy walking distance of one another, but the city also has an efficient local **bus** system, the ATC. Tickets must be bought before boarding the bus, and are available from *tabacchi*. There are also offices that dispense both tickets and city bus maps and information at the main bus station in Piazza XX Settembre, at a booth outside the railway station on Piazza Medaglie d'Oro, and in the centre at Via IV Novembre 16, and at a new office in Palazzo Re Enzo on via Rizzoli; for information, **t** (051) 290 290. Anyone planning serious museum-hopping might consider the *Giornaliero* (one-day ticket), €3. There is also a City Pass which allows you up to 8 journeys, €6.50.

Bologna's *tangenziale* ring road encircles a typically Italian imbroglio of pedestrian and one-way streets with no place to park. The rules concerning the ZTL (*zona traffico limitato*), which includes most of the city centre, are extremely complex (concerning non-residents, non-catalysed motors, motorbikes, etc.) and they change all the time. If you have a car, the best thing is to leave it in one of the 15 car parks on the periphery, all of which are connected by bus to the centre. There's a big one (free) at the Zona Fiera Nord on Viale Europa. The closer ones (Via Tanari, Via Carracci, Piazza Costituzione, all north of the centre) are pay lots.

If you insist on driving, you may find a parking space in Piazza VIII Agosto, where it is also possible to hire **bicycles** inside the Porta Galliera, at No.7, **t** (051) 630 2015 (*open Mon–Fri 6.30–11 and 12–9, Sat 6.30–11 and 12–3*). For a **taxi** call **t** (051) 372 727 or 534 141.

Etruscans expanded over the Apennines sometime in the 6th century, and founded the town of Velzna *c*. 510 BC.

The finds on display in the Museo Civico Archeologico are sufficient testament to the wealth and sophistication of Etruscan Velzna in the century that followed, even though the city and the rest of the settlements in the Po valley were only frontier outposts of the great Etruscan civilization centred in Tuscany and northern Lazio. The Etruscan world was a collection of city-states, organized in religiously based confederations, and Velzna may have been the chief town of a dodecapolis, or league of twelve cities, similar to that of Tuscany.

Velzna grew quickly and grew fat from trade with the other towns of Italy and Greece, but its good fortune was not to last. In the 4th century everything seemed to go wrong for the Etruscans. While the main cities south of the Apennines were getting battered in trade wars against the Greeks, and beginning to feel the threat from the new power of Rome, the Po valley cities found themselves overwhelmed by invaders from the north, the Celts. The Celtic Boii tribe conquered the region around Velzna *c*. 350, and gave the city its new name *Bononia*. (The Boii also gave their name to Bohemia, whence they had originally come.)

The Celts cared more for poetry, hospitality and other people's cattle than for cities and commerce, and Bononia languished under their control. In the Punic Wars, the Boii and the rest of the Celts sided with Carthage against Rome. Hannibal's army wintered at Bononia in 217. After the Roman victory the Celts of Cisalpine Gaul were doomed. Bononia succumbed to the legions in 189, and was soon after refounded as a Latin colony. For the next six centuries this town had almost nothing to say for itself. With its prime location, at the intersection of the Via Emilia and the Via Cassia, the main road to

Venetia and central Europe, Bononia grew into a prosperous though undistinguished *municipium*, and variously enjoyed the benefits or suffered the vicissitudes of the Roman state. If little is known about the city in this era, it is only because the centre has been continuously occupied through all the centuries since. Even now, central Bologna does not care to change, and opportunities for archaeological excavations are few. A bit of the old Via Emilia, complete with wagon ruts in the stone paving, is visible on the pedestrian underpass beneath Via Rizzoli, and the Roman theatre has been located on Via Carbonesi, almost entirely covered with buildings.

On any map, you can see clearly the extent of Roman Bononia in the grid of rectilinear streets between the Two Towers and Via Nazario Sauro, Via Riva di Reno and Via Farini. In the troubles that accompanied the decline and fall of the Empire, the area west of Via Galliera seems to have been abandoned, and sometime after 300 AD a defensive wall was built around the shrunken town. The town's most important patron saint, St Petronius, was a 5th-century bishop who assumed control of the city and did good work keeping things together in hard times. Like Romagna, and unlike all of Emilia to the west, Bononia was never conquered by the Lombards when they overran Italy in the 570s, and the city remained under the rule of the Byzantine Exarchate of Ravenna until the Lombard King Liutprand finally seized it in 727. They in turn lost it to Charlemagne in 774. There is evidence that the city was thriving even in these depths of the Dark Ages – it was one of the few cities to expand its walls, if only slightly. In the curving streets between the Torre Asinella and Piazza Rossini you can trace on the map the course of an unusual semicircular addition, most likely made in the 8th century.

The Medieval Explosion

All Europe started to revive after the Dark Ages, around the year 1000, and in few places was the sudden upsurge of medieval civilization more pronounced than in Bologna. This previously sleepy and unremarkable community started off the new millennium with a bang, founding one of Italy's first free *comuni* and starting what would become Europe's first university. Bologna had benefited from the new trade fostered in the Po valley by the first great commercial metropolis of western Europe, Venice, and now the city was starting to generate wealth of its own, from trade in wool, linen and hemp (for ropes) as well as luxury manufactures, especially silk. The presence of 2,000 students provided another boost to the economy, and led to a new industry – Bologna was the first city in Italy where books were copied for sale.

In the 1100s Bologna was a boom town on an American scale, with tower-fortresses of the urban nobility zooming up like modern skyscrapers – some 180 of them, more perhaps than any city outside

Florence. By 1200 Bologna, with its 50,000 inhabitants, had become one of the great cities of Europe, surpassed only by Venice, Constantinople, Paris and Milan (Genoa and Palermo were probably about the same size). Thanks to its university it had become the intellectual centre of Italy, and the money was flowing – there were were 242 goldsmiths in the town, compared to only 60 in Rome. Like Modena and Ferrara, medieval Bologna was a city of canals. The most important, now under Via Riva di Reno, powered mills for the city's manufactures and provided a shipping outlet to the Po. The extent to which the city was thriving can be seen in its walls. From the original rectangle of late Roman times, the city expanded to fill a new circuit in the 1100s that was nearly six times the original size (following Piazza Malpighi, Via Marconi, Via Riva di Reno, Via Righi, Piazza Aldovrandi, Via Guerazzi, then down to the Palazzo di Giustizia). Only a century later, the city had quadrupled in size again, and had to build its final wall, now the 4½ mile ring of boulevards (the *Circla*) that encloses the *centro storico* today.

Bologna played its part in the political battles of the time as one of the principal cities of the Lombard League. In the 1200s it was occupied with the typical factional strife, in which the local Guelphs (the Geremei) usually had the better of it over the Ghibellines (the Lambertazzi). The Guelph merchants and nobles helped secure the abolition of serfdom in Bologna's territory by the *Paradisius* law of 1256, and warred continuously with Ghibelline Modena. Bologna defeated that city decisively at the Battle of Fossalta in 1249, capturing the talented Enzo, King of Sardinia and natural son of Emperor Frederick II. Defying custom, Bologna refused to ransom him and kept him locked up until he died in 1272.

Soon after, Bologna formally became part of the Papal States through a legal sleight-of-hand – Pope Gregory X got his supporter Rudolph of Habsburg crowned as Emperor and King of Italy, and in return Rudolph donated sovereignty over Bologna and the Romagna to the papacy. The popes (now in Avignon) attempted to assert their control in 1327, sending Cardinal Bertrand du Pouget to rule the city. He did his best to destroy the *comune*, abolishing most of its offices and functions, while building a fortress at the Porta Galliena to intimidate the citizens. After only six years he had so infuriated the Bolognesi that they ran him out of town. But, as in so many other cities, the inability of the factions ever to behave themselves made the city ready to hand power to a single boss, a *signore*. The first was a banker, Taddeo Pepoli (1337–47), and when he died his sons shocked the Bolognesi by selling the office to the Visconti of Milan.

The city had bigger things to worry about. The Black Death of 1348 carried off a third of the population, a similar rate to that of most Italian cities. Trade was severely disrupted, and the huge spaces enclosed by the newly completed city wall would remain empty for a century or more. Still, Bologna was worth fighting over. The Visconti ruled through their man Giovanni da Oleggio until 1360, when he was forced to relinquish it to the formidable Gil Albornoz, a veteran of the wars against the Moors in Spain who spent a decade leading armies through Italy trying, with considerable success, to re-establish papal control. The Bolognesi found their second spell of papal rule no more palatable than the first, and they regained their independence in a revolt of 1376, setting up a council called the 'Sixteen Reformers of the State of Liberty' to govern them. For a while, it worked just fine. As the economy recovered, the Reformers began an ambitious building programme, including many of the public buildings around Piazza Maggiore and San Petronio, a municipal (not a Church) effort that was intended to be the biggest basilica in the world. Eventually, however, the council and the city came to be dominated by a single family, the Bentivoglio, whose name – which might be translated as either 'Wish-you-well' or 'I-love-you' – contains a good dose of irony either way. Their rule continued the flowering of local culture, despite a sensational family saga of violence, assassination, high-living and questionable legitimacy – the paternity of Annibale Bentivoglio was decided by a throw of the dice. The first Bentivoglio *signore*, Giovanni I, lasted little more than a year before being murdered by a mob (1401–2). His son Anton Galeazzo seized power in 1420, but Pope Martin V eventually forced him out and he too was killed. Another interim of papal predominance and factional strife was resolved in 1445 by bringing Annibale back from exile. He got the knife within a year, but this time the family held on a bit longer. Annibale was followed by another Bentivoglio bastard, Sante (1446–63), and then the energetic, cultivated and thoroughly tyrannical Giovanni II, who lorded it over the city for 43 years.

Despite the patronage of Giovanni, Bologna had little to contribute to the arts of the Renaissance. In painting, sculpture and architecture, the city usually took its cues from Florence, and the greatest works to be seen are all by outsiders: plenty of Tuscans, notably Jacopo della Quercia, Nicolò dell'Arca from Puglia, the dalle Masegne from Venice and Giovanni da Modena.

The Popes Take Over

In 1506 that most warlike and irascible of popes, Julius II, took time off from browbeating Michelangelo and Raphael to bring a big army over the Apennines to vindicate his claims on the Romagna and Bologna. The Bolognesi, who had had their fill of Bentivoglios, were delighted to see him, and in their enthusiasm they sacked and demolished the Bentivoglio Palace and chased Giovanni out of town. It did not occur to them at the time that they had exchanged a weak local despot for a distant and powerful one. By the time it sunk in,

Julius had put an end to Bologna's independence once and for all, and a revolt against him in 1511 was crushed. From then on, the city was ruled by papal legates, with a consultative senate of nobles, and the popes themselves spent several long stays in the city with their court.

In one of these, in 1530, Bologna witnessed a turning point in Italian history. The Emperor, Charles V, insisted on being crowned Holy Roman Emperor in its basilica of San Petronio instead of in Rome, which his troops had mercilessly sacked three years previously. Charles (who had been Emperor for 11 years, but was always too busy for a formal coronation) felt that going to Rome would seem like an act of contrition, and such was the low standing of papal authority that when he told Pope Clement VII that he 'did not need to seek crowns, but that crowns ran after him', the pope could only agree. Charles' double coronation, as Emperor (in San Petronio) and King of Italy (in the Palazzo Comunale), was celebrated with tremendous pomp, but it marked the beginning of three centuries of foreign domination in Italy, and the first symptoms of death for the Renaissance. Luigi Barzini notes that from then on the Italians put away their bright clothes and began to wear black in the Spanish style, as if they were in mourning – just as the Fascisti donned black shirts under Mussolini.

In Bologna it was a great age for palace building, as out of the shadow of the Bentivoglio the other families could once more express themselves. But in many ways the century was a disaster for Bologna. The new totalitarian Church that emerged from the Council of Trent (which briefly held its sessions in Bologna) was determined to control every aspect of Italy's intellectual and artistic life, and the cities under its direct control suffered the most. Carlo Borromeo, the grim Svengali of the Counter-Reformation himself, was briefly Legate, and he set the tone for the years to come. The university, already something of a backwater (like that of Paris, and many other once-great institutions), was now doomed to increasing senility in an atmosphere of book-burnings, intimidation and the exile, incarceration or killing of humanist scholars. The Inquisition arrived in Bologna in 1553. Two years later the authorities locked up Bologna's Jews in the Ghetto, and after they had squeezed every last penny out of them they expelled the lot in 1593.

Ironically, this age was also marked by Bologna's only period of prominence in art, as local talent like the Carracci and Guido Reni defined a new classicizing style in art, one entirely in tune with the dictates of the Counter-Reformation Church. Bologna remained a major art centre for a century, while new churches and monasteries went up all over town. By 1650 there were 96 monastic complexes in Bologna; foreign visitors reported that the city seemed entirely populated by monks and beggars. Times were bad, though never quite as bad as in the papal provinces further south, such as Lazio, Umbria and the Marches, reduced by the misrule of the clerics to utter penury. Bologna still made a sort of living from textiles and hemp, but carrying the weight of the Church and a decadent nobility, and closed off from the new trade routes and technological advances of northern Europe, the city's economic prospects were nil.

For the next 200 years Bologna had practically no history at all. It slumbered peacefully through the 18th century, and through the big shake-up provided by Napoleon. The Bolognesi surprised even themselves when they started Italy's wave of rebellions in 1831, booting out the papal legate who was, however, soon restored by Austrian troops. They revolted again in 1848. In the last year of papal rule, 1858, Bologna finally got a railroad; that, and the new climate of united Italy, helped get the old town going again. The population doubled before the century was out, in a city that was turning into one of Italy's major industrial centres.

Modern Bologna

In the 19th century Bologna was the birthplace of Guglielmo Marconi, who carried out his first experiments with radio at the Villa Grifone, and of the composer Ottorino Respighi (1879–1936), whose music was popularized abroad by his fellow Emilian Arturo Toscanini. It was also at this time that Bologna took the lead in the Italian socialist movement, building strong industrial unions in town and prosperous rural co-operatives on the plains – as well as in enduring the brunt of the Fascist reaction in the 20th century. In 1944 Bologna participated fully in the big wave of courageous strikes meant to slow down the Fascist war effort, and partisan activity in the hinterlands led to brutal Nazi reprisals such as the massacre at Marzabotto. Although it was on the 'Gothic Line', where the Germans held the Allies at bay in 1944–5, and the scene of fervid partisan activity, including pitched battles between the Nazis and partisan brigades around the University and the Ospedale Maggiore, Bologna emerged from the war relatively unscathed.

After the war Bologna's Communists got their chance to run the city, and they made the most of it. An excellent mayor, Giuseppe Dozza, made the city the showcase of the Italian brand of Communism, providing the most honest, efficient and innovative municipal government in the country. Dozza greatly improved public transport and health care, while leading the nation in building new schools, housing and other facilities – even municipal launderettes. The new housing projects may have been 'vomit-coloured cement barracks', as conservative critic Indro Montanelli put it, but that after all was the style of the time, and in the middle of a huge housing crisis the most important thing, as everywhere else in Europe, was getting something built. Nevertheless, the shabby planning that gave the city its distinctly unpleasant band of sprawl is something that Bologna, like most prosperous Italian cities, is going to have to live with for a long time.

Like the rest of Italy, Bologna in the late 1960s and 70s had more than its share of troubles. Italy was making a sharp left turn. While the Communist vote increased greatly in local and national elections, a younger generation was forsaking the PCI for more radical alternatives. The climax of a wave of student agitation in Bologna came in March 1977, when the shooting of a demonstrator by the police led to riots. In these *Anni di Piombo*, the 'Years of Lead', shadowy rightist groups in the armed forces and security police infiltrated and manipulated the so-called 'Red Brigades' and other operations, along with radical rightist groups they controlled directly, into fomenting terrorism throughout the country, with the hope of destabilizing democracy and perhaps even staging a coup. Now that it's all over, most Italians would like to forget all about the *Anni di Piombo*. Others, however, are still trying to get to the bottom of this murky business. There's even a new word, *dietrologia* (the study of who was dietro, or 'behind', the attacks), to describe the endless conspiracy theories and speculation about which national figures and institutions were directly involved. Parliamentary and judicial investigations have established the existence of 'Operation Gladio', in which the infamous P2 'masonic lodge' led by Licio Gelli (a wartime fascist and an officer in the SS at the end of the war, who pulled a lot of strings in Italy for decades afterwards thanks to his co-operation with the CIA) coordinated the terrorist effort, along with the leaders of the Italian secret service, the SID (almost all of whom were P2 members, as were many army chiefs, business leaders and Christian Democrat politicians) and elements in the CIA.

Bologna's Communists, labour leaders and the city itself were prime targets. In 1974 the terrorists blew up a Bologna–Florence train, killing 12 and wounding 105. In 1978 they assassinated Prime Minister Aldo Moro, who favoured bringing the Communists into the government coalition, and two years later made their bloodiest strike ever – the bomb in Bologna's Stazione Centrale that killed 85 people and wounded over 200 on 2 August 1980. Things gradually calmed down after that – the ghouls had made their point. Bologna's earnest Reds soldiered on, despite a national 'reform' that severely limited local government powers in the 1970s. Even the most useful regimes, however, grow old and tired eventually, and in the 1990s many Bolognesi became increasingly discontented with the way their city was moving; a sharp increase in crime and drug addiction, and a general decline in the quality of life were the main concerns (spray-paint graffiti is always an indicator of urban disarray, and Bologna has more of it than almost any Italian city). Many also found the city government becoming too rigid and bureaucratic, and out of touch with the citizens. The 'catastrophe', as local leftists call it, came in the mayoral election of 1998, when a conservative businessman and head of the Chamber of Commerce named Giorgio Guazzaloca squeaked in with 50.69% of the vote.

The right crowed and cackled across Italy. The great Red bastion had capitulated, and in their enthusiasm some even spoke of the election as the 'fall of the Berlin Wall'. Guazzaloca, who is often compared to New York's Rudy Giuliani, has so far not quite been the bogey that leftists feared. He didn't have much of a detailed programme during the campaign, and up to now his most controversial move has been to cut back on the limitations on cars in the *centro storico*, the reversal of a policy that had been expanded since 1972, when Bologna became one of the first cities in Europe to create pedestrian zones and limit traffic in the centre.

Piazza Maggiore

The centre stage of public life, where all Bologna seems to come in the evening, is **Piazza Maggiore** and its antechamber, Piazza Nettuno, graced with the virile and vaguely outrageous **Fountain of Neptune**, 'who has abandoned the fishes to make friends with the pigeons'. The fountain was designed in the 16th century by Tomaso Laureti of Palermo and embellished with sculpture by Giambologna, who despite the name wasn't a Bolognese at all, but Jean Boulogne from Flanders; he spent most of his life in Florence, but this is the work that made his reputation. For company, Giambologna gave 'Il Gigante', as Neptune is familiarly known, an assemblage of putti and mermaids; the vaguely outrageous teenagers that crowd over the fountain at all hours of the day and night came later.

In the corner between the two squares are the adjacent 13th-century **Palazzo di Re Enzo** and the **Palazzo del Podestà**; both host frequent exhibitions, the only times when they are open to the public. The former, facing Neptune's fountain, was built in 1244 and takes its name from the illegitimate son of Emperor Frederick II, the 'King of Sardinia', who was captured by the Bolognesi at the Battle of Fossalta in 1249 and locked up here until he died in 1272. Enzo, a fine soldier and a poet like his father, seems to have been more of a well-guarded guest than a prisoner, spending his time writing troubadour-style love poems and receiving a constant stream of female visitors; an old story says that the first of the Bentivoglio was his bastard son. Bologna's own Ottaviano Respighi wrote a comic opera about him, Re Enzo. The Palazzo del Podestà started from the 1212 Torre dell'Arrengo and grew by additions. It was remodelled in 1484 by Aristotele Fioravanti, who went on to Moscow to design parts of the Kremlin. The corners of the *Voltone*, the big portico facing Piazza Maggiore, contain 16th-century statues of four of Bologna's patron saints (most cities were content with one patron; Bologna, hedging its bets for divine intercession, has eight).

Palazzo Comunale

Palazzo Comunale
open Tues–Fri 9–3; Sat, Sun and hols 10–6.30

Filling the western side of the Piazza Maggiore, the crenellated Palazzo Comunale incorporates the 1287 Casa Accursio (the arcaded section), and the 1425 annexe by Fioravante Fioravanti, father of Aristotele. The Palazzo took on its fortress-like appearance in a rebuilding of 1365, when Cardinal Albornoz had taken over the city for the Church and feared a revolt. Over the main door presides a bronze statue of *Pope Gregory XIII*, the reformer of the calendar and a native of Bologna. Under a canopy to the left is a beautiful terracotta *Madonna* (1478) by Nicolò dell'Arca, a sculptor from Puglia who left his best work in Bologna. The **Sala Borsa**, the old stock exchange on the ground floor which covers remains of a Roman-era public building, has been transformed into a 'Piazza Coperta', a kind of indoor extension of the square to hold exhibitions, office space and the city's new multimedia library, including the English language collection from the British Council. Near the entrance is Bologna's shrine to the Resistance, with photos of all 2,000 of the *partigiani* who died in the war. Also present are the names of all the 'victims of fascist terrorism' who died in the 1980 bombing at the Stazione Centrale.

Museo Morandi
*Piazza Maggiore 6, **t** (051) 203 332, www.museomorandi.it; open Tues–Fri 9–3, Sat, Sun, hols 10–6.30; adm free*

Inside, on the first floor, is the **Sala d'Ercole**, with a statue of Hercules by Alfonso Lombardi and a fresco of the *Madonna del Terremoto* by Il Francia (1505), commissioned after an earthquake struck the city. On the second floor, reached via Bramante's grand staircase, are two museums – the **Collezioni Comunali d'Arte**, which contain works by Bolognese artists, from the medieval Vitale da Bologna and Simone de' Crocefissi to the Carracci and Giuseppe Maria Crespi, and the **Museo Morandi**, devoted to Bologna's greatest modern painter, Giorgio Morandi (1890–1964). He hardly ever left the city and, although friends with Futurists and Metaphysicists in Ferrara, kept to himself, quietly producing some of the 20th century's best paintings. The subject matter – boxes, a vase of flowers – is mundane, but Morandi's fierce gaze transforms it with startling intensity; as Umberto Eco put it, he 'made the dust sing'. There are also landscapes of Grizzana (the nearby village where Morandi spent his summers), portraits, drawings, sculptures, and a reconstruction of his studio.

Behind the Palazzo Comunale is Piazza Roosevelt, with the 1613 **Palazzo Marescalchi** and another seicento palace now housing the Prefettura. Behind these, on Via IV Novembre, is the church of **San Salvatore** (1623), with an impressive interior inspired by the baths of ancient Rome, containing Madonnas by Vitale da Bologna and Simone de' Crocefissi and a striking Mannerist *Marriage of St Catherine* (1534) by Girolamo da Carpi, a work generally acclaimed as his masterpiece. There's electricity in the air in this corner of Bologna. At No.7 Via IV Novembre, you'll notice the plaque for the birthplace of Guglielmo Marconi, while nearby at 2 Via Testoni, Luigi Galvani conducted his famous experiments on electrical impulses in living things – making frogs' legs jump with a jolt of current.

Basilica di San Petronio

Basilica di San Petronio
open daily 7.45–12.30 and 3.30–6; museum closed at time of writing, adm free

Back on Piazza Maggiore, opposite the Palazzo del Podestà, the Basilica di San Petronio, begun by Antonio di Vincenzo (1390), is the largest structure on the square – yet, had the Bolognesi had their way, this temple to their most important patron saint would have been far grander, and even larger than St Peter's in Rome. The Bolognesi constantly remind us that Pope Pius IV himself, in 1565, ordered that the money be spent instead on the university's Archiginnasio (*see* p.203), instead of on municipal prestige. As it is, San Petronio is the fifth-largest church in Italy, and the Pope's decision may have been less maintaining Rome's bragging rights than simple economy. Or it might have been aesthetics; if the models inside are any indication, Pius might well have saved Bologna a very large, marble-coated civic embarrassment. The white and red marble stripes, recalling the city's heraldic colours, only made it up to the level of the portals. Imagine them covering the entire building, and you would have something almost as eccentric as Florence's Duomo, which has been memorably described as 'a cathedral wearing pyjamas'.

Bologna was so miffed by the Pope's decree that in over 400 years it has never even bothered finishing the Basilica's façade. Italian cities have any number of bare, brick-fronted churches, testaments to exhausted ambitions or civic disasters, but this is the most conspicuous. Even staid old Florence felt sufficiently embarrassed finally to tack up a façade for its Duomo in 1888. But not Bologna. Somehow, San Petronio's grimy cliff-face is very Bolognese, a disregard for appearances that says 'Love me as I am.'

The façade does have a remarkable **portal**, with a stately Madonna surrounded by reliefs of Old and New Testament scenes and prophets by Jacopo della Quercia of Siena, begun in 1425. Like Ghiberti's doors to the Baptistry in Florence (for which job della Quercia had been one of the unsuccessful candidates), they are landmarks in the visual evolution of the early Renaissance, and seem strangely modern – almost Art Deco in sensibility. Missing from the front of San Petronio, however, is Michelangelo's colossal bronze statue of Pope Julius II, commissioned by that pope in 1506 after he regained the city for the Papal States. Julius also commissioned a large castle in the centre of Bologna. Both were torn to bits by the population as soon as the Pope's luck changed; and to rub salt into his wounded pride the bronze was sold as scrap to his arch enemy, Alfonso I of Ferrara, who melted it down to cast a great cannon.

The lofty, spacious interior saw the crowning of Charles V as Holy Roman Emperor and, according to local tradition, the conversion of a visiting monk named Martin Luther, who became so nauseated by the papal pomp and pageantry that he decided to go home and start the Reformation. In 1655 the astronomer Cassini traced a meridian on the floor and designed the huge astronomical clock which marks noon and tells the hour of sunrise and sunset with the shaft of light admitted through a small aperture in the vaulting at noon (solar noon, not clock time). The *meridiana* is exactly 1/600,000 of the earth's circumference, and the length of the shadow on it also tells the date. An optical illusion makes the image of the sun look heart-shaped, if you see it at just the right time on certain days of the year; seeing the illusion has always been taken as good luck for newlyweds. The *meridiana* isn't just a toy, though; creating it was serious work that helped determine precisely the movements of the earth, necessary for Pope Gregory's 17th-century calendar reform.

Around the nave you'll see four carved crosses, set atop antique columns. These once marked the four gates leading into the city; according to local legend they were placed there by Petronius, or else St Ambrose, as part of a magic circle that protected the city (actually they are 8th-century, and typical of the crossroads monuments common throughout medieval Emilia). Many of the chapels hold noteworthy works of art. The first on the left has some exceedingly strange (and exceedingly bigoted) frescoes by Giovanni da Modena on the *Triumph of the Church over the Synagogue*. In the fourth chapel (Cappella Bolognini, or dei Re Magi), next to a giant figure of St Christopher, the same Giovanni and his assistants (1415) have filled the entire place with one of the most dramatic, most populous *Last Judgement* scenes ever painted, full of interesting detail: a Heaven painted (quite intentionally) to look like a Church Council, allegorical figures of the Seven Deadly Sins, a Devil with two mouths, one devouring Judas, the other Brutus – sacred and secular treachery seem to be damned equally. To the right of this is a chapel containing an *Annunciation*, with the Virgin by Lorenzo Costa and angel by Il Francia. Two chapels down near the *meridiana*, is Costa's *Madonna with Saints*, and next to that *San Rocco* by Parmigianino.

Over the high altar is the *Tribuna*, designed by Vignola, and behind it a set of intarsia choir stalls. In the right aisle, the sixth chapel from the door has another work of Costa, *St Jerome*; to the right of that is Amico Aspertini's *Pietà*. To the left of the altar is the entrance to the museum, which displays some of the instruments Cassini used to lay out the *meridiana*, and models of some of the grand schemes for the church and its façade.

Via dell'Archiginnasio

The eastern side of Piazza Maggiore is closed by the **Palazzo dei Banchi**, with a long, elegant façade designed by Vignola (1568). The façade was all he needed to do: the project was simply to give a common front to a number of buildings that made up Renaissance Bologna's banking district. Walking through either of the archways in it takes you to the most joyful corner of old Bologna, the little market district that spreads through **Via Pescherie Vecchie** and **Via Clavature**, full of market stands, restaurants and fancy food shops (it's a remnant of the old market that used to fill all of the Piazza Maggiore). On Via Clavature the atmosphere changes quickly with the church of **Santa Maria della Vita** (1690), worth a visit for the terracotta *Lament over the Dead Christ* by Nicolò dell'Arca, a work harrowing in its grief and terror, a 15th-century version of Edvard Munch's *The Scream*.

Museo Civico Archeologico
t (051) 275 7211, www.comune.bologna.it/museoarcheologico; open Tues–Fri 9–3; Sat, Sun and hols 10–6.30; adm free

Next to the Palazzo dei Banchi, facing the great, gloomy wall of San Petronio, is Bologna's excellent **Museo Civico Archeologico**, occupying the building of an old hospital on Via dell'Archiginnasio with the reassuring name of *Ospedale della Morte*. Into its dim and dusty wooden cases is crammed one of Italy's best collections of antiquities – beautifully wrought items from the Iron Age Villanova culture, finely wrought urns and jewellery that clearly show these people as the precursors of the Etruscans. These are followed by artefacts from Etruscan Velzna (the name is usually seen Latinized, as *Felsina*). Velzna may have been a frontier town, compared with the wealthy and cultivated Etruscan metropolises of Tuscany and northern Lazio, but it is richly represented here with funerary art, including a collection of quite spectacular circular tombstones, a form found nowhere else in the Etruscan world, carved with proud warriors or ships; some are more than 10ft in diameter. There is a famous embossed bronze urn, the *Situla di Certosa*, similar to others found in Tuscany. The Etruscans traded through their port of Spina (near Comacchio) with the Greeks, whose Attic vases are one of the highlights of the museum. There are a few items from Gallic *Bononia*, Roman artefacts (a lovely copy of a bust by Phidias of *Athena Lemnia*), and an excellent Egyptian collection.

Archiginnasio
t (051) 276 811, www.archiginnasio.it; open Mon–Sat 9–1.30, closed 2 weeks in Aug

The next long porticoed façade on Via dell'Archiginnasio is the former home of the University, the **Archiginnasio**, its walls covered with the escutcheons and memorials of famous scholars. Bologna's University, though the oldest in Europe, was not provided with a central building until 1565; before then classes were held in public buildings or cloisters. This is the building Bologna got for its money instead of the expansion of San Petronio; the Counter-Reformation popes, always worried about heresy and political opposition, wanted to keep all the intellectuals here in one place where they could keep a close eye on them. After the University expanded to its new

Biblioteca Comunale
t (051) 276 811, www.archiginnasio.it; open Mon–Fri 9–6.45, Sat 9–1.45; closed Sun and first half Aug

quarters in 1803 this became the municipal library, the **Biblioteca Comunale**, which always has a selection of old books, manuscripts, prints and sketches on display. Upstairs, and currently closed for restoration, is the ornate old **anatomical theatre**, shattered by a bomb in the Second World War and painstakingly rebuilt in 1950. The monument in Piazza Galvani in front of the Archiginnasio commemorates Luigi Galvani, the 18th-century Bolognese discoverer of electrical impulses in the nerves who gave his life and name ('galvanize') to physics.

Two Leaning Towers

In the passage under Via Rizzoli (the main street flanking the Piazza Maggiore) you can see the remains of the old Roman Via Emilia, which followed the same route. To the east the end of Via Rizzoli is framed by the beautiful **Piazza Porta Ravegnana**, site of the main gate of the original, Roman-era walls, and Bologna's most familiar landmark, a pair of towers that might have wandered off the set of *The Cabinet of Dr Caligari*. After the initial shock wears off, however, fondness invariably sets in for this odd couple, the Laurel and Hardy of medieval architecture.

The urge for tower-building came with the urbanized nobles of the early Middle Ages. At first, they were quite utilitarian defensive works, a good thing to have in an age when family vendettas were the main subject of the chronicles. Commonly, families would live in little compounds (like the Pepoli, just south of here in Via Castiglione), grouped around towers like these; often an old street gets its name from one noble house that occupied it entirely. Almost from the beginning, in Bologna and other towns, the towers also became status symbols, and families would strive to see who could build the highest. According to legend the Due Torri were built in 1119 in such a competition. The winner, the svelte 318ft **Torre degli Asinelli**, is still the tallest building in Bologna. The *comune* of the 14th century, struggling to establish some kind of law and order among the battling nobles, knocked down these towers whenever they were strong enough to get away with it, and time and poor foundations doomed most of the others.

11 Torre degli Asinelli
open summer 9–6, winter 9–5; adm

The Torre degli Asinelli was probably the champ among such defence towers, although it's only the fifth-highest building of old Italy. It tilts about 7ft out of true, though the 500 steps that lead to the top are more likely to make your head spin than the tilt. The view over Bologna is worth the trouble, however, and the 500 steps will be waiting whenever you feel you're up to the challenge. Its sidekick, the **Torre della Garisenda**, sways tipsily to the south, 10ft out of true; the Garisenda contingent failed to prepare a solid foundation and, when they saw their tower pitching precariously, gave up. In 1360 it became such a threat to public safety that its top was lopped off,

Faulty Tower Tricks

Dante's mention of the Garisenda Tower comes in Canto XXXI of the *Inferno*, when he and Virgil encounter the giant Antaeus frozen in ice at the bottom of Hell:

Qual pare a riguardar la Garisenda
Sotto 'l chinato, quando un nuvol vada
Sovr'essa si, che ella incontro penda

Tal parve Anteo a me, che stava a bada
Di vederlo chinare, e fu tal ora
Ch'i' avrei voluto ir per altra strada.

('...like looking at the Garisenda, under the leaning side, when a cloud comes; so seemed Antaeus to me, about to fall – to see him leaning so, I wished I had taken another path.')

Dante is referring to an illusion that every child in Bologna knows. If you stand underneath the leaning side of the tower when clouds are passing over it against the direction of the tilt, it seems to be falling over on top of you. Try it and see.

leaving only a squat 157ft stump; inscribed on its base you can read what Dante wrote about it in the *Inferno*. Like Pisa's leaning tower, this one needs a lot of care and attention to keep it from tipping over and squashing a large portion of central Bologna; restoration is currently under way and it is closed to the public.

In front of the towers, the **Palazzo dei Drappieri** (1486) is a fine example of the somewhat Florentine, Gothic-windowed style of palaces popular in the days of the Bentivoglio. Walking north from here will take you into a claustrophobic nest of narrow alleys, off Via de' Giudei and Via dell'Inferno, that before 1860 made up Bologna's Jewish **Ghetto**. Jews were segregated here, as in most Italian cities, at the instigation of the Church during the Counter-Reformation. This one was begun in 1555, though in 1593 Pope Clement VIII decided it didn't go far enough, and forced all Jews to leave the Papal State. Later, they gradually trickled back, living in the old Ghetto 'unofficially' and subject to intermittent extortion and persecution by the Papal authorities. On Via Valdonica, their story is told in the **Museo Ebraico**, which for the moment consists mostly of historical displays; they also offer tours of Jewish sites in Bologna, Ferrara and other cities. The museum was an initiative not of Bologna's Jewish community, which currently numbers only about 200 people, but of the regional government. The alleys of the Ghetto contain some interesting medieval relics: the **Casa dei Rampionesi**, a 12th-century house on Via del Carro, and the **Torre degli Uguzzoni**.

Museo Ebraico
t *(051) 291 1280, www.museoebraicobo.it; open Sun–Thurs 10–6, Fri 10–4; adm*

Just to the south of the towers in Piazza della Mercanzia is one of Bologna's finest buildings, the lovely Gothic **Palazzo della Mercanzia** (1384), the medieval merchants' exchange and customs house and now the chamber of commerce; it has an ornate loggia by the architect of San Petronio, Antonio di Vincenzo. Around it, on Piazza della Mercanzia, are houses equally as old; around the corner on Via S. Stefano is the 13th-century **Torre Alberici**.

Palazzo della Mercanzia
t *(051) 609 3111; visits for groups by appointment only*

East of the Centre: The Radial Streets

The east end was the fashionable part of medieval Bologna, and remains so today. So different was this aristocratic corner from the more plebeian San Felice district (west of Via Marconi) that to Dante in the 1300s the people seemed to speak two different languages. From the towers four streets fan out to gates in the eastern walls of the old city. The southernmost of these, **Via Santo Stefano**, begins at the Palazzo della Mercanzia and leads to a quartet of churches, with a cloister and two chapels thrown in, all once part of the monastery of **Santo Stefano**.

27 **Santo Stefano**
t (051) 223 256, www.abbaziasantostefano.it; open daily 9–12 and 3.30–6; adm free

Jerusalem Bononiensis: Santo Stefano

Dedicated to the first Christian martyr, it was founded according to legend by St Petronius, who had visited the hermit-saints of the Holy Land as a youth. Petronius' intent was to reproduce the seven

Santo Stefano

holy sites of Jerusalem, enabling the faithful to make at least a symbolic pilgrimage. Most of the work in this unique complex dates from the 8th–12th centuries, and was considerably altered in modern restorations.

The restorations uncovered the interesting fact that Santo Stefano was built over the site of an ancient religious sanctuary, a temple of the Egyptian goddess Isis (Egyptian religion was extremely popular in the Roman Empire, and promoted by several of the emperors, especially Domitian). Three of the churches of this unique and harmonious Romanesque ensemble face Piazza Santo Stefano. The entrance is through the **Chiesa del Crocifisso**, with a Renaissance pulpit in its façade, begun in the 11th century and containing an ancient crypt below its raised choir; here are the relics of the Bolognese martyrs SS. Vitale and Agricola, discovered by St Ambrose and Bologna's Bishop Eusebius in a Jewish cemetery and brought here in 393. To the left is the entrance to **San Sepolcro**, a strangely irregular polygonal temple, modelled after Jerusalem's Holy Sepulchre and containing the equally curious *Edicola di San Petronio*, a large pulpit adorned with reliefs; in a macabre touch, the saint's bones are visible through a tiny hole at floor level. The circle of columns around it survives from Isis' circular temple, used as a Christian baptistry from the 5th century and rebuilt in its present form in the 11th. Outside the circle, a single column standing alone was claimed as the column to which Christ was bound during his flagellation.

A door behind this column leads directly into **SS. Vitale e Agricola**, Bologna's oldest church, built in the 5th century, with bits and pieces of old Roman buildings and alabaster windows. Beyond it is the **Cortile di Pilato**, in patterned brick with interlacing arches, containing an 8th-century Lombard bathtub that somehow gained the sinister reputation of being the basin in which Pontius Pilate washed his hands. From here you can enter the fourth church, the 13th-century **Trinità**, which may originally have been the east end of a 4th-century church, or a Lombard church of the 800s – like most of the complex, it has been rebuilt and reconfigured so often that scholars have endless opportunity to debate what was what. The Trinità, also called the *Martyrium*, is currently a special chapel of the Bersaglieri, the élite troops of the Italian Army; it contains a wonderful folk-art wooden *Adoration of the Magi* from the 1370s, with the figures painted by Simone de' Crocefissi.

A passage from the Cortile di Pilato leads into the lovely 10th-century **cloister**, with interesting capitals. A room facing it contains the **museum**, with a collection of mostly 14th-century painting, including works by Simone de' Crocifissi, Michele di Matteo (the *Lives of St Stephen and St Petronius*), and a detached fresco of the *Massacre of the Innocents* by Berlinghero di Lucca.

No Jerusalem would be complete without a Mount of Olives, and the small hill to the south of Santo Stefano was called *Monte Oliveto* in the Middle Ages. On top of it, in a picturesque piazza off Via Santo Stefano, **San Giovanni in Monte** was built in 1286 on the site of the original church founded by St Petronius. Largely remodelled in the late 1400s, it contains paintings by Guercino and Lorenzo Costa. The terracotta eagle over the portal is the work of Nicolò dell'Arca.

Strada Maggiore

The most important of the radial streets, the palace-lined **Strada Maggiore**, follows the route of the Via Emilia, passing first in front of the 17th-century **San Bartolomeo**, just behind the Due Torri, notable for its two works by Bolognese masters: Francesco Albani's *Annunciation*, in a chapel on the south aisle, and Guido Reni's *Madonna*. At Strada Maggiore 13, the **Casa Isolani**, which houses the British Council, is one of the best-preserved 13th-century houses left in Bologna, with one of its oldest porticos, supported on wooden beams. At No.44 the 18th-century **Palazzo dei Giganti**, properly the Palazzo Davia-Bargellini, is better known by its nickname, for the two Baroque telamones carved by Gabriele Brunelli around the main entrance. The palace contains the **Museo Civico d'Arte Industriale**, a collection of mostly Bolognese furniture and applied arts from the 16th–18th centuries, and the **Galleria Davia-Bargellini** (also called the 'Quadreria'), housing a small but excellent collection of early Bolognese painting, including works by Simone de' Crocefissi and Antonio Vivarini, as well as Vitale da Bologna's famous smiling *Madonna dei Denti* (the 'Madonna of the Teeth'), perhaps the most characteristic work of the 14th-century Bolognese school. Later paintings include one by the true original of Bologna's Baroque artists, Giuseppe Maria Crespi; the *Giocatori di Dadi* (the 'Dice Players') illustrates his delight in the details of everyday life.

Palazzo dei Giganti
t (051) 236 708; museums open Tues–Sat 9–2, Sun 9–1; adm free

At this point the *portici* of the street intermingle with those of the arcades of the city's Gothic jewel, **Santa Maria dei Servi**, preceded by a lovely *quadroporticus* – Tuscan style, with slender columns and iron braces; one side of it dates from the 1390s, while the rest had to wait until 1855. The church was a little slow too; begun in 1346, it wasn't completed for another two centuries. Inside are fragments of a fresco by Vitale da Bologna, a *Madonna and Saints*, a late work of Crespi and a rare *Madonna* by Giotto's master Cimabue (in the ambulatory) which you'll need to illuminate to see.

Santa Maria dei Servi
open 8–12 and 3.30–8

Via San Vitale

The radial street north of the Strada Maggiore, Via San Vitale, was in the Middle Ages called Via Salaria, the 'salt road', along which that commodity was brought from the salt pans along the Adriatic. Its monuments are two fine palaces of the 16th century, the **Palazzo**

San Vitale
open Mon–Sat 8–12 and 3.30–7.30, Sun 9–12.30 and 4.30–7

Fantuzzi (1538) and the **Casa Franchini**. The church of **San Vitale**, a Romanesque work that originally stood outside the city walls, was rebuilt in the 1800s, but retains a Romanesque crypt and the Renaissance *Capella di Santa Maria degli Angeli*.

Via Zamboni and the University

San Giacomo Maggiore

Conservatorio G. B. Martini
t (051) 221 483, www.conservatorio-bologna.com; open Mon–Sat 9–1; closed Aug

Again starting from the Towers, the Via Zamboni leads shortly to the Piazza Rossini. Rossini, composer of *The Barber of Seville* and *William Tell*, studied from 1806 to 1810 at the **Conservatorio G. B. Martini** on the piazza, and spent much of his life in a nearby palazzo. The Conservatory houses original scores by Mozart, Monteverdi and Rossini and, oddly, a portrait by Gainsborough.

San Giacomo Maggiore
open daily 7–12,30 and 3.30–6.30

Next to the Conservatory, **San Giacomo Maggiore** was begun in 1267 and later enlarged. It was the parish church of the Bentivoglio, who adorned it with art. Giovanni II hired the Ferrarese Lorenzo Costa to paint the frescoes in the Cappella Bentivoglio – the *Triumph of Death*, the *Apocalypse* and a *Madonna Enthroned* – in the midst of Giovanni II and his family. Even allowing for the usual artistic flattery, Giovanni still comes off looking the cultured Renaissance thug. The fresco itself was commissioned in thanksgiving for his escape from hired assassins. The fine altarpiece in the chapel is by Francesco Francia, a native of Bologna, while the high-mounted tomb of *Anton Galeazzo Bentivoglio* (1435), opposite the chapel, is by Jacopo della Quercia. In the other chapels of the ambulatory you can see a polyptych by Paolo Veneziano and an altarpiece of the Crucifixion by Simone de' Crocefissi. San Giacomo continued to accumulate notable works after the Bentivoglio were gone; on the right side of the nave is the Baroque *Cappella Poggi*, entirely decorated and frescoed by Pellegrino Tibaldi, and in a chapel to the right a *San Rocco* by Ludovico Carracci. The **Oratory of Santa Cecilia**, entered from outside the church on Via Zamboni, is frescoed with lively scenes of the *Lives of SS. Valeriano and Cecilia*, by Costa and Francia.

Oratory of Santa Cecilia
open 9.30–1 and 2–6

The Teatro Comunale (*see* p.228), further up Via Zamboni in Piazza Verdi, was built by Antonio Bibiena in 1763 over the ruins of the Bentivoglio Palace, torn down brick by brick by a mob after the family was expelled in 1506. The street to the right of the theatre, Via del Guasto ('of the broken'), got its name from the ruins, which were too extensive to clear and remained here for decades. The Bibiena clan of theatre and stage designers were in demand all over Europe in the 17th and 18th centuries, and did much to popularize the typical Baroque tiers of boxes, which the Teatro Comunale preserves behind its 1933 façade.

The University, and the University Museums

Beyond the theatre is the **University**, which was moved in 1803 from the too central Archiginnasio (where Napoleon's men were worried that the students could cause trouble) into Pellegrino Tibaldi's Mannerist **Palazzo Poggi**. The hall of the palazzo is adorned with Tibaldi's frescoes of *Ulysses* (1549), an early and influential example of Mannerist illusionistic *quadratura* ceiling painting; there are more Mannerist mythological paintings, by Nicolò dell'Abate, in the University Library.

37 University museums
Palazzo Poggi, **t** *(051) 209 9398, www.museopalazzo poggi.unibo.it; open summer daily 10–2, winter Mon–Fri 10–1 and 2–4; adm free exc for exhibitions*

There are a number of small **museums** connected to the university housed in the Palazzo Poggi, including the **Museo Navale**, with collections of early maps and impressive 18th-century model warships (one is nearly 10ft tall); the **Museo di Architettura Militare**, with plans and models of Baroque-era fortifications; and the **Museo Ostetrico**, devoted to obstetrics. The **Museo Aldovrandi** houses the collections of the great Renaissance naturalist Ulisse Aldovrandi (*b.* 1522), who established botany, zoology and entomology as distinct scientific disciplines, and made Bologna an important centre

Bologna the Learned

Bononia Culta was an epithet first given the city by the Roman poet Martial. Nobody has the faintest idea what the Roman-era city did to deserve it, but starting in the 11th century, Bologna did its best to live up to it. The Bolognesi like to claim their university is the oldest in the world, and give it a founding date of 1088, but the matter isn't so clear. All the medieval universities had very informal beginnings, as loose communities of teachers and students; some grew out of cathedral schools that go back to the 800s, and their growth into institutions was gradual and poorly documented. What is certain, though, is that – along with the establishment at Paris – Bologna's was the most important centre of learning in medieval Europe.

Unlike Paris', this one was at first run by the students, not the teachers, and they organized into guilds to maintain their rights. Originally there were four of these, called 'universities' (the original use of the word), though soon these merged into two, the Cismontane for Italians and the Transmontane for all foreigners; later on, each nation had its own guild and building. From the earliest times the student guilds were able to get fixed prices set for their lodgings and books and, since they provided the professors' income directly through fees, they could dispose of incompetent or merely unpopular ones by the simple means of a boycott. The Emperors were usually only too glad to give them a hand, and a decree of 1158 from Frederick Barbarossa even granted them exemption from the legal jurisdiction of the *comune*. Eventually the professors formed guilds of their own; membership in one was the origin of the university degree.

Almost from the beginning, Bologna was known best of all for its studies of the written law. This grew out of the subject of rhetoric, the basis of the education for lawyers and politicians in classical times. In the 1200s the University established faculties of philosophy and medicine. In the latter it was replacing Salerno, where the university was already in decline, and it soon became renowned for it, as the first place in Europe to revive the practice of human dissection. Paris may have had the greater reputation for the liberal arts and theology, but besides medicine Bologna also gradually achieved distinction in the sciences, particularly astronomy.

By this time Bologna had also become a mother of other universities, as groups of students broke away for various reasons to found new schools in Modena, Reggio, Vicenza and Padua. Bolognese masters were also instrumental in staffing the universities of Naples, Palencia, Salamanca and Montpellier, and one alumnus, Vacarius, founded the law school at Oxford in 1144.

for their study. In 1712 the Poggi became the home of the Istituto delle Scienze, founded by Luigi Ferdinando Marsigli with the hope of bringing the new empirical sciences of the day into Bologna and breathing some life into a university that was growing mouldy under papal rule. For the astronomers he built the adjacent observation tower, the **Torre della Specola**, in 1725, where important astronomical work was done in the good old days before street lighting. Now the tower houses the **Museo di Astronomia**, which contains many of the instruments used in the 18th and 19th centuries, a fresco of the constellations and exhibits on the history of astronomy.

Museo di Astronomia
www.bo.astro.it; visits max. 15 people

There's more to see two streets to the north on Via Irnerio. The University's **Botanical Garden** is in fact the second-largest park in the city centre, with a collection of mostly Mediterranean flora, but also such exotica as a fully grown sequoia, as well as a greenhouse for cacti and insectiverous plants. Started by Ulisse Aldovrandi, it is one of the oldest botanical gardens in the world. There is also a botanical museum.

Botanical Garden
open Mon–Fri 8–3, Sat 8–1; botanical museum, open Mon–Fri 9–1

The **Museo della Fisica** (*currently closed*) relates the history of physics with an unusual collection of old scientific instruments and relics, from a lens-making workshop of the 17th century to a model locomotive of 1857. The **Museo di Anatomia Umana Normale** really deserves a visit. Some of 18th- and 19th-century Italy's most talented artists worked in wax, making anatomical models to help in the teaching of medicine; their productions have never been equalled. One of the greatest names of this obscure art, Ercole Lelli, created here full-sized male and female nudes (called 'Adam' and 'Eve') as well as skinless figures that demonstrate the musculature. And no doubt one of the most surprising things you'll see in Bologna is the wax self-portrait of a remarkable woman named Anna Morandi Manzolini, dressed up for a fancy ball and performing brain surgery.

Museo di Anatomia Umana Normale
open summer Tues–Fri 9.30–5.30, Sat and Sun 10–6.30; winter Tues–Sun 9.30–2.30

Museo di Mineralogia
open daily exc Sun 9.30–1; closed Aug

Museo di Antropologia
open Mon–Fri 9–1

Museo di Zoologia
open Mon–Fri 8.30–6.30, Sat and Sun 10–6

Museo di Anatomia Comparata
***t** (051) 209 4248; open Mon–Fri 9–1*

Museo di Anatomia Patologica
*Via Massarenti, **t** (051) 209 7966; open Mon–Fri by appointment*

Museo Anatomico di Animali Domestici
*Via Tolari di Sopra 50, Ozzano Emilia, **t** (051) 209 7952; call ahead; open Mon–Fri on request*

At the end of Via Irnerio, Piazza di Porta San Donato has the **Museo di Mineralogia** with plenty of rocks to show you, along with precious stones, rare minerals and meteorites. Don't think it ends here, for the University has more didactic torture in store behind the Palazzo Poggi at 3 Via Selmi. The **Museo di Antropologia** hasn't a lot to offer – bones and artefacts of prehistoric Italians, and some African masks – while the **Museo di Zoologia** and **Museo di Anatomia Comparata** have the expected ranks of stuffed birds and pinned insects, animal skeletons and a discreet aroma of formaldehyde. Across the ring boulevard, the **Museo di Anatomia Patologica** may prove a little more exciting with its studies of human and animal deformities – either wax models, or the real thing preserved in bottles. Or, for a sobering idea of what Fido looks like under the skin, there's the **Museo Anatomico di Animali Domestici**.

Pinacoteca Nazionale
Via Belle Arti 56, ***t*** *(051) 420 9411, www.pinacotecabologna.it; open Tues–Sun 9–7; adm*

Pinacoteca Nazionale

Set among the university buildings, a block north of Via Zamboni, Bologna's most important art is stored in the Pinacoteca Nazionale, a collection begun by Cardinal Lambertini and expanded after he became Pope Benedict XIV. Most of the first works came from demolished city churches, and plenty more came in when Napoleon suppressed so many of the city's monasteries. Napoleon, as he was wont to do, also stole the best works and moved them to Paris, but, unlike many places, after 1815 Bologna was fortunate enough to get them back. The collections were moved to this old Jesuit monastery in 1816.

The itinerary begins with the 14th-century Bolognese artists, of which that singular painter Vitale da Bologna emerges as the star with his intense *St George and the Dragon* and *Life of St Anthony Abbot* (you'll notice that unlike most of his contemporaries, including Giotto, Vitale knew what a camel looked like). Brilliant colours, a hint of depth, and delight in nature are the rule with Vitale, excepting the grey and sombre *Cristo in Pietà* made in the plague year of 1348. Some of Vitale's approach is reflected in his Bolognese contemporaries: the colourful *Morte della Vergine* of the 'Pseudo Jacopino', and a glowing *Madonna col Bambino* of Simone de' Crocefissi. Giovanni da Modena contributes a *Crocefissione adorata da San Francesco*, and another artist with a distinctive style and a very fine brush, Jacopo di Paolo, a *Crucifixion with saints*. The next room is devoted to 'foreign' painters, and pride of place is taken by the only work of Giotto in Bologna, a polyptych with the *Madonna and saints*. Other foreigners, many of whom had come to Bologna to work on San Petronio, include Lorenzo Monaco, Giovanni Martorelli of Brescia (known for intense, worried-looking saints, as in the *Life of St Anthony Abbot* here), and the Sienese Andrea di Bartolo; from Spoleto, Rinaldo di Ranuccio has a wonderfully stylized Franciscan-style painted crucifix.

Next come three rooms of detached frescoes from Bologna churches. Again Vitale da Bologna stands out, with several works including the *Madonna del Ricamo*, following an old legend where Mary sews the shirt that would be gambled for by the soldiers at the Crucifixion. The Pseudo Jacopino's cinematic *Battle of Clavijo* depicts the climactic fight that saved the last corner of Christian Spain after the 8th-century Arab conquest, when St James (Santiago) came down from heaven to help defeat the Moors. Other exceptional works come from Simone de' Crocefissi, Jacopo da Bologna and Francesco da Rimini, including a *Miracolo di San Francesco*.

The Renaissance section contains more 'foreigners', with fine works of Antonio and Bartolomeo Vivarini and Cima da Conegliano of Venice; it shows the considerable influence of artists from Venice and Tuscany on the local artists present, notably in the big-canvas

Small Fun in the Big Museum

The Italian Renaissance was indeed an exotic fruit, but like most exotic fruits it was sure to go off if not handled carefully. Bolognese art in the late 16th and 17th centuries does have a certain aroma to it. The Counter-Reformation and Italy's loss of political liberty created a quietly traumatized world, one in which a very sophisticated people was reduced to mouthing pious platitudes, with the police and the Inquisition looking over their shoulders. As long as they were careful, Italians could enjoy their last few decades of prosperity. They were impressed by the lavish, solemn spectacles provided by Church and state, and the new art, sanctioned by Rome and commissioned in vast quantities for churches and palaces, seemed an Olympian peak of beauty and elegance.

Something was missing. The Bolognese masters of the new official style, the Carracci and Guido Reni, may have dazzled with their technical perfection, but their innumerable imitators found them a hard act to follow. Bologna in this era has a lot to answer for, and the last rooms of the Pinacoteca will amuse you with a flood of some of the most uninspired painting ever made. Lifeless virtuosity alternates with rare flashes of witless virtuosity, including perhaps the silliest high-fashion *Annunciation* ever, by Bologna's own Pietro Faccini. The thought police of the popes can take most of the credit for this slow strangulation of art, but the Pinacoteca also provides a wonderful glimpse into the sort of people that inhabited this sad, twilight world. *La Famiglia Gozzadini* is a work by the popular portraitist Lavinia Fontana (1552–1602), capturing a prominent family on the cusp of the Renaissance and the Baroque. It's hard to tell whether this strangely Victorian group is an intentional send-up, like Goya's brutally caricaturistic portraits of the Spanish royal family, or Rousseau's *Cart of Père Juniet*, or Grant Wood's *American Gothic*; perhaps there simply wasn't any other way to paint such creatures. The Gozzadini, jowly, smug and overdressed, are horrible enough, though the miserable little family dog steals the show, looking quite the Gozzadini herself in her bracelet and earrings.

virtuosity of Ferrara's Lorenzo Costa and Bologna's 'Il Francia' (Francesco Raibolini, often called here Francesco Francia), the most popular painter in Bologna in the days of the Bentivoglio. There are two small fragments from that elusive master Ercole de' Roberti, including a tearful *Magdalene*, an early work of El Greco, the *Last Supper*, and a *Visitation* of Tintoretto; the most famous painting in the entire museum is probably Raphael's *Ecstasy of St Cecilia*, which the artist sent from Rome to his friend Il Francia. From Emilia-Romagna's Mannerist decades come works by Parmigianino, Pellegrino Tibaldi, Nicolò dell'Abate (scenes from *Orlando Furioso*), and some dependably tepid ones by Il Garofolo, sharing space with Perugino, Giulio Romano and Titian's *Jesus Crucified with the Good Thief*.

The Carracci, who initiated Bologna's move into the forefront of Italian art, get a room to themselves; among the many works present are Ludovico's *Caduta di San Paolo* and *Madonna dei Bargellini*, Annibale's *Madonna di San Ludovico*, and Agostino's *Comunione di San Gerolamo*, one of the most celebrated and influential works of its day. From here it's a short and logical step to the strangely perfect little world of Guido Reni, Bologna's favourite son, who earns the most lavish chamber in the entire museum. Most of his best works are in Rome, but the selection here at least gives a hint of why Reni was once considered one of the greatest painters of all time; even in his own day, his classical precision of line and total command of colour and composition were thought a refreshing advance on the fevered exaggeration of the Mannerists. Highlights include the hypnotic *Triumph of Samson*, the *Massacre of the Innocents*, *Madonna dei Mendicanti* and the *Madonna della Pietà*; and there is a portrait of the artist himself, by Simone Cantarini.

In the rooms that follow, true gems are mixed with a good helping of dross, a fair representation of the age itself. Among the artists to appear are Guercino, Mastaletta (*Rest on the Flight into Egypt*), Domenichino, Francesco Albani, Marcantonio Franceschini, Leonello Spada, Donato Creti (the precociously neoclassical *Sigismonda*) and Giuseppe Maria Crespi (the *Courtyard Scene*). Some of the larger paintings are reserved for the auditorium, the *Aula Didattica* at the end of the itinerary.

San Martino
open daily 8–12 and 4–7

Via Belle Arti, heading back towards the centre, passes several fine palaces, including the 16th-century Palazzo Bentivoglio, built after the family got back on its feet after its loss of power. The street ends at the intersection of Via Mentana; turn left here for **San Martino**, which was built in the early 13th century and remodelled in the 15th. Paolo Uccello painted a fresco here at that time which was believed completely lost until 1981, when a fragment of a *Nativity* was discovered in a chapel of the left transept. The church also contains frescoes by Lippo di Dalmasio and Vitale da Bologna (again, only a fragment), as well as works by Simone de' Crocefissi, Il Francia, Ludovico Carracci and Lorenzo Costa, and a column painted with a formidable *Sant'Onofrio* by the 14th-century Dalmasio di Jacopo. In the first chapel on the left is the *Madonna della Carmine* of Jacopo della Quercia.

North and West of Piazza Maggiore

Duomo di San Pietro
Via dell'Indipendenza; open Mon–Fri 7.30–12 and 4–6.30, Sat 3.30–6.30, Sun and hols 8–12.30 and 3.30–6.30

Via dell'Indipendenza is the main thoroughfare linking the Piazza Maggiore to the station. One block north of Via Ugo Bassi, it passes the **Duomo di San Pietro**, on Via dell'Indipendenza near Piazza Nettuno. Begun in the 10th century, it was remodelled in the Baroque style and, like Venice's old cathedral, was the local symbol of Rome's authority as opposed to that of the municipality, embodied in the basilica of the city's patron saint. As such it received little affection, and it isn't very interesting, unless you are a devotee of St Anne, whose skull is the chief treasure, a gift of Henry VI of England. Also inside are red marble lions from the portal of the original façade, made into stoups, an *Annunciation*, the last work of Ludovico Carracci, and, in the first chapel on the right, a terracotta *Pietà* by Alfonso Lombardi (1522). The leaning Romanesque campanile is a survivor of the original structure, and it's worthwhile strolling past it down **Via Altabella** and its adjacent lanes (especially

Via Sant'Alo and Via Albiroli) for a look at medieval Bologna, with several medieval towers and a number of houses dating from the 13th to the 16th centuries.

The Museo Civico Medioevale e del Rinascimento

4 **Museo Civico Medioevale e del Rinascimento**
t *(051) 203 930; open Tues–Fri 9–3; Sat, Sun and hols 10–6.30; adm free*

The first street on the left north of the cathedral, Via Manzoni, leads to the quattrocento **Palazzo Fava-Ghisilardi**, site of the Museo Civico Medioevale e del Rinascimento, one of the unmissable sights of the city. Before you get to the good stuff, however, you'll have to wade through the delightfully screwy collections of one of Bologna's original 18th-century museums, the **Museo di Naturalia e Artificialia**, which is preserved here for no apparent reason beyond our entertainment (also, as you may have noticed by now, Bologna is a city that never throws *anything* away). There's a mummified baby something, carved ostrich eggs and coconut shells from exotic climes, a smattering of pre-Columbian art, a carved narwhal tusk, and courtesans' slippers from Venice with 18-inch heels (an 18th-century fashion from the harem of the Ottoman sultans).

Once through that, you'll see something that really brings old Bologna back to life – a collection of the tombs of the great doctors of the University. By convention, these would be carved with images of the professors in relief, expounding to a crowd of attentive students. Part of the convention was to make these scenes as lifelike as possible – so many students, with so many faces from over the centuries, earnest, daydreaming or perplexed. Some of the best, from the beginnings of the Renaissance, are by Paolo di Bonaiuto (the *Sepolcro di Lorenzo Pini*), the Tuscan Andrea da Fiesole, and the dalle Masegne brothers (notably the *Arca di Carlo Roberto e Ricardo da Saliceti* of 1403). The dalle Masegne touch is also shown in the statues of *Justice* and *Four Patron Saints of Bologna*, which originally decorated the Loggia della Mercanzia (1391).

Like any good medieval museum, this one has no end of surprising pretty things, such as the mosaic Byzantine *Madonna* from *c.* 1100 made from the tiniest of tesserae. There is an exceptional collection of ivories, a field where medieval sculptors could display their skill in miniature. The best were in Venice and France; here the Venetians of schools like the 14th–15th-century Bottega degli Embriachi, with their trademark spiky foliage borders, compete with French artists who created little coffers for jewellery, and little portable altarpieces for personal devotion, carved with intricate scenes that capture medieval civilization in full flower. Along with the exquisite, there's always a touch of the bizarre, such as the colossal bronze statue of Pope Boniface VIII. This most grasping and arrogant of all popes, whose impostures wrecked the powerful medieval papacy in the early 1300s, commissioned this statue and many like it across Italy, an early sort of political propaganda; Boniface also invented the beehive triple tiara popes used to wear, to show that they were three times mightier than mere kings and emperors.

The collection of sculpture goes on to Jacopo della Quercia's group of the *Madonna and saints*, with flowing draperies that proclaim the Renaissance has arrived (1410); among the later works are a bronze bust of the Bolognese *Pope Gregory XV* by Bernini, and Giambologna's *Mercury*. Bologna had a fine school of miniaturists, and their work is displayed in music books and in the 1361 *Statutes of the Arte dei Merciai* (merchants' guild). There are also collections of armour, ceramics, majolica plates, glass (including spectacular works from Murano – much better than anything they do now) and a 13th-century English cope. In addition, several rooms of the old palazzo are open to the public, with frescoes by all three Carracci and other Bolognese painters showing scenes from the *Aeneid* and classical mythology (*Jason and the Argonauts*).

Next to the museum is a building that you might consider an additional exhibit: the **Casa Conoscenti**, a typical example (and rare survivor) of the house-and-tower complexes of the Middle Ages. Near it you can see the only surviving bit of Bologna's original Roman–Dark Age **city wall**. West of the museum, **Via Galliera** is a street of impressive porticoed palaces, from the days of the Bentivoglio to the 1700s, including the **Palazzo Aldovrandi** (1725), home of one of Bologna's great families, and across the street the cinquecento **Palazzo dal Monte**. Further up is the **Palazzo Felicini**,

Laying Down the Law

Anyone who thinks our contemporary world is overrun with lawyers may be reassured (or depressed) to know that the Middle Ages had it just as bad. Blame it on Bologna, or specifically, on a man named Irnerius, the noble forebear of all the tribe, born in this city around 1055.

Irnerius was hardly the ivory tower sort of scholar. In his day no one could afford such a luxury; there was serious work to be done. In fact Irnerius was a protegé of Matilda of Canossa (*see p.159*); it was she who first convinced him to take up the study of law and then made good use of his talents in diplomatic missions, although after her death Irnerius went over to the other side, serving Emperor Henry V. But both sides had an interest in common: reviving Roman law to replace the many conflicting local codes, such as that of the Lombards in northern Italy, which were commonly based on archaic German tradition and feudal rights. In those days any man had the right to be judged according to the law of his birthplace, residence or station, which might be Lombard law, Byzantine law, or canon law if he was a cleric; the confusions are only too easy to imagine. The growing *comuni*, including Bologna itself, had an even greater interest in reform, since the Germanic codes were made for a rural population, and had nothing useful to say about city rights or the regulation of commerce.

After Irnerius came the 'Four Doctors': Bulgarus, Martinus Gosia, Hugo da Porta Ravennate and Jacobus de Voragine. Legend says they were pupils of Irnerius, though that's probably not true. (It makes a good example of how everything in those times was cast into legend. Another set of legendary 'Four Doctors' was credited with founding the great medical university at Salerno in the same era.) All four were already acting as advisors to Emperor Frederick Barbarossa, following the eternal principle of civilization: where there are smart lawyers, there's power and money too. No profession was a surer road to riches – enough to pay for the most lavish tombs in Bologna – and in the Church, a legal education was the best guarantee of career advancement. In the heyday of the medieval papacy most of the popes started their

careers as canon lawyers. Alexander III (1159–81), one of Bologna's four popes, had been a University *glossatore*; another alumnus, the great Pope Innocent III, may well have been one of his students. Even Thomas Becket, future Archbishop of Canterbury, spent five years in the 1140s studying his glosses in Bologna.

Irnerius' major contribution was a gloss of the Code of Justinian; in other words, he wrote explanations of the difficult points in the margins, along with recommendations of how these 500-year-old laws would apply to modern cases. His successors, who came to be known as *glossatori*, naturally carried this erudite pettifoggery to its logical extreme. By about 1250 ambitious doctors were not only writing glosses, but glosses on the glosses, each identified with the doctor's initial, and occasionally someone would add glosses on these. One scholar complained that the glosses were like a 'multitude of locusts' that literally covered up the text; in this age of expensive hand-copied books, only when all the space on the pages was filled would a new copy be commissioned. One of the doctors entombed here, Francesco Accursio, helped put an end to the confusion with his *Glossa Magna* (1250), a commentary so comprehensive and trenchant that it made the earlier ones obsolete.

Whatever we think of lawyers, some respect is due for an effort that has been called 'the most brilliant achievement of the intellect of medieval Europe'. That intellect, with its passion for order, definition and classification, its reverence for the written word and its relentless chains of logic, eventually made philosophy and science into hidebound scholastic nightmares. But for the law, it was perfect. It sharpened arguments and minds, and turned reason loose on the practical things of this world; some have claimed that it was the greatest factor in setting Western civilization on its dizzying trajectory over centuries to come. For better or worse, the processes and patterns of thought for that civilization were made in Bologna.

from the 1490s; it stands at the corner of Via Riva di Reno, a street that followed the course of the Reno canal. Once lined with mills, this was medieval Bologna's industrial zone.

In its northern reaches, Via dell'Indipendenza reaches the bustling **Piazza VIII Agosto**, old Bologna's cattle market and now the site of a busy, popular, food, clothes and second-hand goods market on Fridays and Saturdays. Just to the north is the attractive **Parco della Montagnola**, the only sizeable public park in the *centro storico*, and the only hill north of the Piazza Maggiore. The Bolognesi take it as a symbol of their love of liberty – it's really a mound of building debris, from the fortresses that stood here and were destroyed by the people on five separate occasions. The pile was covered in earth and landscaped in 1806. Just outside the park on Via del l'Indipendenza is a surviving gate from the 1660s, the grandiose **Porta Galliera**.

San Francesco

San Francesco
open daily 7–12 and 3–7

Via Ugo Bassi, the westerly section of the Via Emilia, runs from Piazza Nettuno past the often frenetic **Mercato Coperto**, shoehorned into the side streets to the north, and then to the narrow and lively Piazza Malpighi, with one of Bologna's old city gates and the lovely Gothic San Francesco, begun in 1236 when St Francis was still alive. Bologna provided one of the fastest-growing and keenest centres of the new order. Francis himself visited twice, and his Bolognese followers invited his disciple St Anthony of Padua down to preach.

In 1796 Napoleon turned the church into a warehouse, and much of its accumulated art was dispersed or destroyed.

The façade, completely rebuilt four years after it was blown clean off the church by Allied bombers in 1944, faces quiet Piazza San Francesco, the football ground of the neighbourhood kids. Inside, the striking, lofty interior, all white with brick piers and vaulting, is characteristic of Bologna's medieval churches. In the left aisle is the *Tomb of Pope Alexander IV*, who died in Bologna in 1410. On the high altar is a beautiful 14th-century marble ancona sculpted by Pier Paolo and Jacobello dalle Masegne (1393), with various saints and wonderfully naturalistic scenes from the life of St Francis.

Around the back of the church on Piazza Malpighi, you can get a look at the great apse of the church with its flying buttresses, rare in Italian churches, along with the very elegant **campanile** added in the 1390s by Antonio di Vincenzo. Facing the street are four of Bologna's unique monuments, the **Tombs of the Glossatori**, little pavilions with pyramidal roofs, raised off the ground on slender columns. These are the memorials to four notable professors of law of the 13th century: Accursio and his son Francesco Accursio, Odofredo Denario and Rolandino de' Romanzi.

South of Piazza Maggiore

From Piazza Maggiore, Via d'Azeglio leads off into one of the quieter parts of old Bologna, eventually reaching the **Palazzo Bevilacqua** (1482), the very picture of a Florentine palace from that era. The Council of Trent, eternally debating the reform of the Church, took refuge here from a plague in Trent in 1547. Behind it, on Via Barberia, the church of **San Paolo Maggiore** is the work of one of Bologna's few interesting Baroque architects, Giovanni Magenta. It contains a major work of one of Bologna's few interesting Baroque sculptors, Alessandro Algardi, a rival of Bernini who spent most of his life in Rome. Besides his sober and eloquent *Decapitation of St Paul*, the church has paintings by Ludovico Carracci, Giacomo Cavedoni and Guercino.

San Paolo Maggiore
open Mon–Sat 8–12 and 4–7, Sun and hols 8.30–1 and 4.30–7

Just north of here, at Via Val d'Aposa 6, is the attractive 15th-century brick and terracotta façade of **Spirito Santo** and, a little to the north of that, a 13th-century tower-house complex called the **Torre dei Catalani**. From San Paolo, Via Collegio di Spagna continues to the **Collegio di Spagna**, the Spanish college founded in 1365 for Spanish students by Cardinal Albornoz, the papacy's top man in Italy while the popes were hiding in Avignon. In the late Middle Ages Bologna had many such colleges, but this one (still officially Spanish territory) is the only one to survive. Cervantes studied here, as did St Ignatius of Loyola.

Collegio di Spagna
t *(051) 330 408, www.bolonios.it; visits by appointment*

San Domenico

San Domenico
open daily 8–12.30 and 3.30–6.30

Behind the Archiginnasio, across Via Farini, Via Garibaldi leads south to San Domenico, built in 1251 to house the relics of St Dominic, founder of the Dominicans, the Order of Preaching Friars. Dominic built a convent on this site and died here in 1221 and, though the exterior and interior of his church have been frequently remodelled (the façade was only added in 1910), it is still one of the great treasure-houses of art in Bologna. Outside, in Piazza San Domenico, are two more **tombs** of noted doctors of the Law, like those of the *glossatori* at San Francesco: those of Egidio Foscherari (1289) and Rolandino de' Passageri (1310).

Inside, the narrow nave only accentuates the effect of a church that is nearly as long as San Petronio. The main attraction is a big chapel in the right aisle, containing the saint's tomb, the spectacular *Arca di San Domenico*. Many hands contributed to this sculptural ensemble, including Nicolò Pisano and his school (including the young Arnolfo da Cambio), who executed the sarcophagus and the beautiful reliefs of the saint's life. Nicolò dell'Arca (Nicolò da Bari, who gained his name and fame from this work) added the cover of the sarcophagus and the statues on top, of Bologna's eight patron saints; Nicolò died before the group was finished, leaving the rest to the 20-year-old Michelangelo, who had to leave Florence during the political turbulence that followed the death of his patron Lorenzo de' Medici. During 1494, when Savonarola, a Dominican who had started his career in this very monastery, was gaining power in Florence, Michelangelo was here sculpting *SS. Petronius and Proculus*. Above all this is an apse fresco by Guido Reni, the *Apotheosis of St Dominic*.

In the opposite chapel, the decorative scheme is a collaborative effort of several Bolognese artists, including Guido Reni, Ludovico Carracci and Francesco Albani. Towards the altar is another matched pair of big chapels. The one the left contains the trecento *tomb of Taddeo Pepoli*, Bologna's trecento boss, by an unknown Florentine artist, and a crucifix by Giunta Pisano (1250), while the one on the right has a painting of *St Thomas Aquinas* by Guercino; next to this is a small chapel with a *Marriage of St Catherine* by yet another Florentine, Filippino Lippi.

Museo di San Domenico
t (051) 640 0411; open Mon–Fri 9.30–12.15 and 3–6.30, Sat, Sun and hols 3–5.30; adm free

Among the other works, look for the early Baroque extravaganzas of Alessandro Tiarini (*St Dominic Resuscitating a Child*) and Leonello Spada (a rather chilling *Burning of the Heretical Books*); behind the high altar is a set of beautiful wooden intarsia choir stalls (1549). To the right of the altar is the entrance to the **Museo di San Domenico**, which contains a good deal of church clutter and a bust of St Dominic by Nicolò dell'Arca.

From Piazza San Domenico, Via Rolandino takes you back north to the shady, lovely **Piazza Minghetti**, a welcome oasis among all the bricks and porticos. The piazza was laid out in the 1870s when the impressive, eclectic **Palazzo delle Casse di Risparmio**, designed by Giuseppe Mengoni, went up on the eastern side. Behind this is **Via Castiglione**, another street of imposing palaces of various centuries. North of the Cassa di Risparmio, towards the Palazzo della Mercanzia and the Due Torri, is one of Bologna's biggest, the **Palazzo Pepoli-Campogrande**, so called from the 'big field' that Taddeo Pepoli, boss of Bologna in 1337–47, had to clear to build it. Taddeo's ancestors in the 1600s still had enough resources to give the palace its present shape. Inside they commissioned some lavish frescoes, including two incredible ceilings with the same theme, the *Triumph of Hercules*: a very florid and busy one by Domenico Canuti (1665), and a more restrained version by Giuseppe Maria Crespi (1691), with *Allegories of the Seasons* in the four corners. A third ceiling has *Alexander Cutting the Gordian Knot*, by Donato Creti (1708). The Pepoli must have been attached to the neighbourhood. Their previous palace, the **Palazzo Pepoli Vecchio**, and the one before that, the 13th-century **Casa Gadda Pepoli**, are right across the street.

Palazzo Pepoli-Campogrande
open by appointment; ask at the Pinacoteca Nazionale, or call ***t*** *(051) 243 249*

South of the Cassa di Risparmio building, Via Castiglione has the **Casa Poeti** and **Casa Cospi** from the 1400s, both with terracotta friezes decorating the façades, and the deconsecrated church of **Santa Lucia**, now the *aula magna* of the University. Carlo Rainaldi, the great Roman Baroque architect, got some early tips here; his father Girolamo designed the church.

The Bologna Hills

Bologna's city centre may not be well endowed with parks and green space, but the city has the good fortune of being built next to a patch of wooded hills, the first foothills of the Apennines. Of course these hills also made the city nearly indefensible after the invention of artillery – but good fortune kept anyone from ever besieging it.

(5) San Luca and the Porticata

San Luca and the Porticata

In the southwestern corner of the *centro storico* is the **Porta Saragozza**, from which begins the portico to beat all porticoes – winding 4km up the Colle della Guardia to the Sanctuary of the Madonna di San Luca, with 666 arches along the way. (If you can't face the whole hike, bus 20 from Via dell'Independenza or Via Ugo Bassi will take you halfway, to the Arco di Meloncello.) About a third of the way there, at Via Casaglia, the portico passes the **Museo Storico Didattico della Tappezzeria** (Historical Museum of Tapestry),

Museo Storico Didattico della Tappezzeria
t *(051) 614 5512, www.iperbole.bologna.it; open Tues–Sun 9–1, Thurs also 3–6; closed Aug; adm*

with a huge collection of woven artefacts from Europe and Asia, and exhibits on how they have been made since the Middle Ages.

According to local legend, the colossal Porticata was built as an act of faith, and the people of Bologna carried the stones by hand to the site. This is actually quite untrue; a more prosaic version says that the city built it to promote its pilgrimage trade by keeping pilgrims out of the rain. That sounds a little fishy too; take it simply as the kind of eccentric embellishment only possible in the Age of Baroque. It took them long enough to build it. Begun in 1674, the Porticata wasn't completely finished until 1793. It does seem to have been intended as a sort of meditational exercise, like the chapels representing the stations of the cross (*Via Crucis*) that were laid out on hillsides around Europe in this era. Beginning at the **Arco di Meloncello** (1732), halfway along the portico, there are 15 rest stops for prayer, corresponding to the 15 Mysteries of the life of the Virgin Mary. Not even Bologna's numerous students of the occult can explain why there are exactly 666 arches (for that matter, one might as well ask why there are 666 panes of glass in the Louvre Pyramid in Paris).

Santuario della Madonna di San Luca

sanctuary church open Mon–Sat 7–12.30 and 2.30–7, Sun 7–7; Oct–Feb till 5, Mar till 6

The **Santuario della Madonna di San Luca** (and if you're walking you'll be glad enough when you finally reach it) was built to house a 'Black Madonna', an icon attributed to St Luke. Another local legend has it that the icon came from the Hagia Sophia in Constantinople. A pious Greek named Theocles had a vision there, in which the Virgin commanded him to remove the icon to the 'sentinel mountain'. He wandered for years with it, before coming to Rome, where he was taken in by a kindly Bolognese senator who told him about the *Colle della Guardia* back home. There doesn't seem to be any truth in this one either. Nobody knows for sure when the icon turned up (it is dated to the 12th century), though this sanctuary seems to have begun as a pilgrim hostel, perhaps in the 11th century, before becoming a pilgrimage destination in its own right. The **sanctuary church** was designed by Carlo Francesco Dotti in 1723. In this age, when the impulse of Baroque architecture was running out of steam, architects often tried to find inspiration by going back to the origins; this church, with its elliptical shape preceded by a curving portico, draws heavily on Bernini's revolutionary churches in Rome, built a century earlier. Still, Dotti had a big problem – making a monument that would make a fitting end to the long pilgrimage walk, and at the same time be a conspicuous landmark, visible from all over Bologna – and his retro creation does the job admirably well. The interior is richly decorated; besides the miraculous icon it contains three paintings by Guido Reni and one by Guercino. From outside, you can look across to some tremendous views of the Apennines.

Colle dell'Osservanza and S. Michele in Bosco

Other famous viewpoints are from the next hill east, the Colle dell'Osservanza (bus no.52 from Piazza Cavour or Via Farini). On the way up, just outside the ring boulevard at Porta San Mamolo, is the church of the **Annunziata**, founded by Orthodox Armenian monks in the Middle Ages and rebuilt in the 1480s. Further up Via del l'Osservanza is the **Villa Aldini**, built on the site where Napoleon admired the panorama of the city skyline, then the church of **Sant'Apollonia di Mezzaratta**, from which many of the trecento frescoes in the Pinacoteca were taken, and finally the **Convento del l'Osservanza**. From there it's a 1km walk to the **Eremo di Ronzano**, a medieval convent for women with a frescoed church from the 1500s. Further south is the big **Parco di Monte Paderno** (also known as Parco di Villa Ghigi), a favourite escape of the Bolognesi (the nos.29 and 30 buses get within 1km of it). Monte Paderno made a big stir in 1603 when Vicenzo Cascariolo, a shoemaker-alchemist, discovered deposits of a luminescent mineral called barite ('Bologna stone'), and claimed he had found the Philosopher's Stone.

On the next hill is **San Michele in Bosco**, in a former Olivetan convent (bus no.30 from Stazione Centrale or Via Ugo Bassi); the church (1523) has a portal by Baldassare Peruzzi, a tomb by Jacopo della Quercia and frescoes by Gerolamo da Carpi and Domenico Canuti; outside it is an unusual frescoed octagonal cloister. The convent is now a hospital, the Istituto Rizzoli, but you should be able to get in to see the impressive 500ft gallery, cleverly designed to create an optical illusion; walk to the far end and look back towards the city, and you can see the Torre Asinelli as if through a telescope.

Peripheral Attractions

Bologna keeps its largest and most beautiful city park out in the southeastern corner of the *centro storico* where few visitors ever see it: the **Giardini Margherita**, named for the much-loved Queen of Italy when the park was laid out in the 1870s; in it is a pretty lagoon with an island in the middle. There's also a reproduction of a 2,800-year-old Villanova-culture round hut on display (perhaps fittingly, since an Etruscan necropolis was discovered in the park itself). Out in the western suburbs (bus nos.14 or 19 from Via Ugo Bassi), the **Certosa** is a medieval Carthusian monastery that has grown, like Ferrara's, into the city's 'monumental cemetery', with acres of grandiose mausolea from the 19th century and the church of **San Girolamo**, with two fine cloisters from the 15th and 16th centuries.

San Girolamo
open winter 8–12 and 2.30–4.45, summer until 5.45

You can get an aerobus (nos.10, 35 or 38 from Stazione FS) to **Bologna Fiere**, the huge grounds northeast of the centre where the city puts on frequent exhibitions and trade fairs. Its centre is dominated by a pair of Japanese Brutalist towers by the noted architect Kenzo Tange, and near the Palazzo dei Congressi is the

Bologna Fiere
***t** (051) 282 111, www.bolognafiere.it*

Galleria d'Arte Moderna
t (051) 502 859, www.galleriadarte moderna.bo.it; open Tues–Sun; adm free

Galleria d'Arte Moderna. The large permanent collection includes works of Morandi, and covers all the trends in Italian art since, from the 'Arte informale' group to the 'Situationists', as well as big-name international artists such as Antoni Tapiès and César, and frequent special exhibitions.

ⓘ Bologna >
*Piazza Maggiore 1, call centre **t** (051) 239 660, http://iat.comune. bologna.it; open daily 9–8*

Tourist Information in Bologna

Bologna's main IAT tourist office is at Piazza Maggiore. Other offices are at the rail station, bus station and airport.

Fire: **t** 115

Police: Piazza Galileo 7, **t** 113. If your car is towed, **t** (051) 371 737.

Ambulance: **t** 118.

Hospital: Ospedale Sant'Orsola, Via Massarenti 9, **t** (051) 636 3111.

24-hour pharmacy: Piazza Maggiore, **t** (051) 238 509 or 239 690. If it isn't open, check the list outside to see which pharmacies are on duty that night, or call **t** 192.

Main post office: Piazza Minghetti, not far from the Archiginnasio (open Mon–Fri 8.15–6.30, Sat 8.15–1), **t** (051) 439 3231.

Lost property: **t** (051) 601 8626.

Markets and Shopping in Bologna

While it has its share of chains, Bologna has no lack of small **boutiques**: Via Rizzoli and Via dell'Indipendenza are the main centres for fashion shops. The more chic outlets can be found in Via Farini, including an arcade of upscale designer shops in Via Clavature and Via d'Azeglio. The most characteristic souvenir of the city, however, is food: the lavish products of the surrounding countryside can be found in abundance at the city's bustling **food markets** at the Mercato Coperto, Via Ugo Bassi 2, and in and around Via degli Orefici, just off the Piazza Maggiore. *Both open mornings Mon–Sat*. **La Piazzola** market and **Mercato della Montagnola** sell clothes and just about everything else in Piazza VIII Agosto and along Via dell'Indipendenza (*open Fri and Sat*); the **Celò Celò Mamanca** market in the Old Ghetto (Via Valdonica and Piazza San Martino) is the place to look for antiques, old lace and old books (*every Thurs exc July and Aug*); the much larger **Mercato di Antiquariato** is held in Piazza Santo Stefano (*2nd Sat–Sun of month exc Jan, July and Aug*).

Bologna's general **food stores** present a dazzling array of delicacies; there's a string of them in the streets around Piazza Maggiore, particularly towards the Two Towers. The old **Paolo Atti & Figli**, Via Caprarie 7 or Via Drapperie 6, **t** (051) 220 425 or 233 349, in business since 1880, sells excellent home-made pasta and pastries. For perfect cheeses, try **Al Regno della Forma**, Via Oberdan 45a. One of the ultimate food shops, **Tamburini**, Via Caprarie 1, **t** (051) 234 726, is famous for its *salumeria* and other gastronomic highlights of Emilia-Romagna.

Sports and Activities in Bologna

Swimming Pools

Bologna has 15 pools, but these two are the most central. Ring first, because they're often fully booked by school groups.

Stadio, Via A. Costa 174, **t** (051) 615 2520 (bus no.14 or no.21).

Sterlino, Via Murri 113, **t** (051) 623 7034 (bus no.13).

Where to Stay in Bologna

The tourist office has a free hotel-booking service, CST, **t** (051) 648 7607 or 800 856 065 (from Italy only, toll free), *www.cst.bo.it*, for 3-star hotels and up (*available Mon–Sat 10–2 and 3–7, Sun and hols 10–2*).

Bologna ✉ 40100

When booking in Bologna, avoid nasty surprises by confirming the price of your room. It's not uncommon for the prices, especially in the top categories, to vary as much as €150 in a hotel, depending on the room, time of year, and what's cooking at Bologna Fiere. All down to the moderate range are air-conditioned. For many of the smaller, lower-category hotels, expect to pay in cash.

Luxury (€€€€€)

*******Grand Hotel Baglioni**, Via del l'Indipendenza 8, **t** (051) 225 445, *www.baglionihotels.com*. In the opulent, centrally located 16th-century Palazzo Ghisilardi-Fava, and so embedded in Bologna's history as to be almost a monument (Morandi's paintings were first exhibited here, in 1914). Antiques line the rooms, and there's an underground garage, baby-sitting service, and a beautiful restaurant frescoed by the Carracci, specializing in authentic Bolognese cuisine, fish and seafood.

******Al Cappello Rosso**, Via Fusari 9, **t** (051) 261 891, *www.alcappellorosso.it*. Another luxurious central hotel, named for the red hat of Cardinal Albornoz who first requisitioned the building to lodge the builders of Bologna's cathedral in 1375. In the 1800s it became an inn proper, and is now one of the city's smartest hotels. Garage, but no restaurant.

******Best Western Hotel San Donato**, Via Zamboni 16, **t** (051) 235 395, *www.hotelsandonato.it*. In the 17th-century Palazzo Malvasia, near the Two Towers, with a loyal clientele who appreciate the location, comfortable rooms and lovely summer terrace. No restaurant.

******Corona d'Oro**, Via Oberdan 12, **t** (051) 745 7611, *www.bolognahotels.it*. Stylish, comfortable hotel occupying an old palazzo dating from 1300 on a narrow cobbled street in the heart of the old city. Some of the 35 rooms still have their original panelled ceilings and frescoes: all have air conditioning, TV and Internet access. With an impressive and spacious newly restored *fin de siècle* reception hall – a delightful setting for the excellent and generous breakfast buffet. Out-of-season prices can drop to the merely expensive. No restaurant. *Closed Aug.*

******Dei Commercianti**, Via Pignattari 11, **t** (051) 745 7511, *www.bolognarthotels.it*. Little hotel in Bologna's 12th-century town hall, near San Petronio and the ritziest shopping streets. All rooms are different – most have balconies; the nicest and priciest rooms, with attic ceilings, ancient beams and the odd fresco, are at the top. Excellent buffet breakfast included. Free bikes are an attractive plus point.

******Holiday Inn City**, Piazza della Costituzione, **t** (051) 41666, *www.holiday-inn.com*. Outside the city walls in the vicinity of the Fiera; with a swimming pool, big American breakfasts and, in summer, poolside barbecues. All rooms were renovated in 2003. Restaurant **La Meridiana** serves international and local cuisine.

******Royal Hotel Carlton**, Via Montebello 8, **t** (051) 249 361, *www.monrifhotels.it*. Ultra-modern palace right in the centre of Bologna, with six floors of deluxe, flamboyant designer rooms. The lobby and bar are strikingly designed, and usefully there's an underground garage. *Closed Aug.*

*****Orologio**, Via IV Novembre 10, **t** (051) 745 7411, *www.bolognarthotels.it*. In a pleasant square beside the Palazzo dei Notai. An atmospheric aged palazzo with a big clock on the façade; cosy rooms with good views of the streets outside. Buffet breakfast included. Free bikes.

*****Palace**, Via Monte Grappa 9/2, **t** (051) 237 442, *www.hotelpalacebologna.com*. In a central, genteely faded handsome old palazzo; try to get one of the large old rooms that haven't changed much since the early 1900s (but note that they now have satellite TV). *Closed Aug.*

*****Regina**, Via Indipendenza 51, **t** (051) 248 878, *www.zanhotel.it*. Modern and quiet, with comfortable rooms. Halfway between the centre and the train station makes this a very handy location from which to explore the city.

*****Touring**, Via Mattuiani 1/2, **t** (051) 584 305, *www.hoteltouring.it*. On the corner of Piazza de' Tribunale and fairly central. Refurbished in 2002, with comfortable rooms including some equipped for disabled customers, good breakfasts, a solarium with views over the city centre and bikes for guests.

Expensive (€€€€)

****Novotel Bologna San Lazzaro**, Via Villanova 31, **t** (051) 600 9229, *www.accorhotels.com*. East of the city, in the *comune* of Castenaso, and close to the *autostrada*. A big, modern complex with a pool, tennis courts, garden and restaurant **La Terrazza,** where you can eat by the pool.

***Best Western Hotel Re Enzo**, Via Santa Croce 26, **t** (051) 523 322, *www.hotelreenzo.it*. Just within the walls south of Via San Felice.

***Donatello**, Via dell'Indipendenza 65, **t** (051) 248 174, *www.hoteldonatello.com*. A fairly typical vintage 1930 hotel near the station, with a variety of air-conditioned rooms, mostly large, comfortable and quiet.

***Roma**, Via D'Azeglio 9, **t** (051) 231 330, *www.hotelroma.biz*. One of Bologna's all-round nicest hotels, located in the medieval *centro storico*, a minute from Piazza Maggiore. Large soundproofed rooms with floral wallpaper and fabrics, and a convenient laundry service and garage.

Moderate (€€€)

***Le Drapperie**, Via Drapperie 5, **t** (051) 223 955, *www.albergodrapperie.com*. In a nest of shopping streets just off Piazza Maggiore. Rooms are small, and the market outside starts up early, but you couldn't be better placed.

***Pedretti**, Via Porrettana 255, Casalecchio di Reno, **t** (051) 572 149, *www.hotelpedretti.info*. Just outside the city in Casalecchio, at the foot of San Luca hill, a 10-min car ride from the airport. Classic old family-run hotel with a deserved reputation for hospitality. Parking, garden, bar and popular local restaurant serving all the Bolognese classics. Ask for one of the quiet rooms at the back. *Closed Fri and 3 weeks in Aug.*

Rossini, Via Bibiena 11, **t** (051) 237 716, *www.albergorossini.com*. Tucked away in the university quarter, with clean, comfortable rooms and very friendly management (some of the en suite rooms are just about in the moderate category, only a few have the benefit of air-conditioning).

Residence Falcone, Vicolo Falcone 24, **t** (051) 330 610, *residence.falcone@tin.it*. Ten good-value, 1- and 2-bedroom apartments, simple and comfortable, popular with opera singers in the season. Ask for the one with its own private garden.

Inexpensive (€€)

Centrale, Via della Zecca 2, **t** (051) 225 114, *www.albergocentralebologna.it*. Another old palazzo in the middle of things in Piazza Maggiore; rooms are simple but pleasant and air-conditioned, and most en suite; some triples available.

*Panorama**, Via Livraghi 1, **t** (051) 221 802, *www.hotelpanoramabologna.it*. Central, clean and friendly. Rooms have TV, but no bath.

*Marconi**, Via Marconi 22, **t** (051) 262 832. Another good choice: welcoming and central. Most rooms have a bath.

Budget (€)

Cheaper accommodation is thin on the ground in Bologna, and you'd do well to book ahead. What exists is mostly centrally located. Check for B&Bs and '*Affittacamere*' at the tourist office or on *http://iat.comune.bologna.it*.

There is one youth hostel, **Ostello Due Torri-San Sisto,** inconveniently located 6km east of the centre on Via Viadagola 5, **t** (051) 501 810, *hostelbologna@hotmail.com*. To get there, take bus 93 from Via Irnerio. IYHF cards are required; 11.30pm curfew.

Eating Out in Bologna

In Italy's self-acclaimed gastronomic capital, eating out is a pleasure whether you plump for a meal at a fancy restaurant or head for one of the city's traditional late-night inns or *osterie*; the *cucina petroniana*, as they call it, rarely disappoints. Besides famous pasta dishes, the city is known for the best pâtés in Italy, for its veal dishes and, of late, for culinary innovations. The Bolognesi do love their restaurants. Even on weeknights in the winter you might find it hard to get a table without a reservation.

Very Expensive (€€€€)

Antica Trattoria del Cacciatore, Via Caduti di Casteldebole 25, **t** (051) 564 203, *www.ristoranteilcacciatore.com*.

Vast establishment north of the centre, near the banks of the river Reno, and founded in the early 1800s for hunters, who would wade there through the shallow river. Well known for its heaving trolleys of delicious *antipasti*, side dishes and desserts that come trundling to your table; with excellent pasta dishes and plenty of game, as well as seafood. Over 300 wines. Dine out on the garden veranda in summer (as long as you've booked – a necessity any time of year). *Open till 3am; kitchen closes at 11pm. Closed Sun eve, Mon, 1st week Jan and 2 weeks Aug.*

Pappagallo, Piazza della Mercanzia 3/c, **t** (051) 232 807, *www.alpappagallo.it*. Bologna's most famous restaurant, in a quattrocento palazzo and named after its brightly painted parrot. The food is Italian with French influences: try the *lasagne Pappagallo* or *tagliatelle alla Bolognese*. Vast wine list. *Booking advisable. Closed Sun and Aug. All credit cards except American Express.*

Battibecco, Via Battibecco 4, **t** (051) 223 298, *www.battibecco.com*. A stone's throw from San Petronio, attracting a lunchtime business clientele. Seafood is the speciality, but there are also vegetarian risottos (with aubergine or *porcini* mushrooms), and dishes such as macaroni with saffron, ham and broad beans. *Closed Sat lunch and Sun.*

Expensive (€€€)

Franco Rossi, Via Goito 3, **t** (051) 238 818. In the heart of town, with a pleasant, friendly ambience that makes every customer feel like a VIP. The focus is on Bolognese traditional specialities – try the *tortellini in brodo* (*tortellini* in broth). Great wines, some by the glass. *Closed Sun exc during the Fair.*

Corte de Galluzzi, Corte Galluzzi 7, **t** (051) 226 481. Atmospheric place in a medieval tower behind the Cathedral, serving original dishes executed with finesse, including plenty of seafood, *tortellini* with black truffles, risotto with *porcini* mushrooms, rabbit glazed in sweet Albana, guinea fowl grilled with mustard and mushrooms, and exquisite desserts. Big wine list, with Italian and French bottles.

Fadiga Bistrot, Via Rialto 23, **t** (051) 269 922. The former owner of La Gallina and La Pernice, talented chef Marco Fadiga presents simple cuisine, with creative flourishes. *Closed Sun and lunchtime.*

Da Cesari, Via de' Carbonesi 8, **t** (051) 237 710 or 226 769, *ristorante@da-cesari.com*. Has been around for more than thirty years, and the ambience has barely altered. Innovative additions have been made to classic Bolognese dishes, so you might find pumpkin ravioli on the menu alongside standards like tripe *alla parmigiana*. *Closed Sun, 1st week Jan, Sat–Sun in July, and all Aug. American Express not accepted.*

Trattoria il Tartufo, Via del Porto 34, **t** (051) 252 662 or 252 494, *www.iltartufotrattoria.com*. Just off Piazza dei Martiri, this family-run trattoria has been pretty popular in town since 1980 thanks to his traditional recipes, based on black truffles and hospitality. Typical items are risotto with truffles, *tortelloni* with artichokes, filled courgettes; rabbit with black truffles or omelette with black truffle, and desserts like *zabaglione* with hot chocolate. *Closed Sun, 2 weeks in July.*

Moderate (€€)

Belle Arti, 14 Via Belle Arti, **t** (051) 225 581, *www.belleartitrattoriapizzeria.com*. Another lively eaterie near the university: splits its menu between the Bolognese and the Mediterranean, with pasta with *cozze* (mussels) or *bottarghe* (fish roe), paella and pizzas, with good home-made desserts, and they stay up weekends until 2am. *Closed Wed and 1 week at the end of Dec.*

Biagi, Via Savenella 9/a, **t** (051) 407 0049, *www.ristorantebiagi.it*. Typical Bolognese cuisine featuring *tortellini*, tagliatelle, *bollito* and *cotoletta alla Bolognese*. Separate room for smokers. *Closed Tues.*

Caminetto d'Oro, Via Falegnami 4, **t** (051) 263 494, *www.caminettodoro.it*. Has the promised fireplace of its name and some of the more unusual of Emilia-Romagna's specialities, especially in the pasta department; good *zuppa inglese* for dessert. *Closed Tues eve, Wed, 1st 10 days Jan and mid-July–end Aug.*

Gigina >

Gigina, Via Stendhal 1/b, **t** (051) 322 300. You need to book a couple of days in advance to dine at this classic and highly renowned Bolognese trattoria, north of the centre and in business since 1956. Traditional, authentically made favourites include lasagne, *tortellini* and tagliatelle, roast guinea fowl and *bollito misto*, and the famous old-fashioned desserts: *torta di riso, zuppa inglese* and *crema fritta. Closed Sat and 3 weeks in Aug.*

Merlò, Via Gombruti 2/d, **t** (051) 239 645. Very popular for its high quality, extensive fish and seafood menu. Meat-eating customers are not neglected either, and this is one place in the city where you can find wild boar on the menu. Try *spaghetti Merlò. Reservations essential for dinner. Closed Sat lunch, Sun, 1st week Jan and first 3 weeks Aug.*

Re Enzo, Via Riva di Reno 79/d, **t** (051) 234 803, *www.ristorantereenzo.it*. Emilian cooking with a touch of Umbria: pasta with Umbrian black truffles, stewed boar, even the famous lentils from Castelluccio; other dishes include venison goulash. Seasonal menus, fixed-price tourist menu lunchtimes only. *Closed Sat lunch, Sun and 3 weeks Aug.*

Rosteria Luciano, Via N. Sauro 19 (north of Via Ugo Bassi), **t** (051) 231 249, *www.rosterialuciano.it*. Combining agreeable old-fashioned service with fine cuisine: *sformato di carciofi, tagliatelle al ragù*, classic *fritto misto* and a good wine list. *Closed Wed, also Sun in Jul and Aug.*

Inexpensive (€)

Cantina Bentivoglio, Via Mascarella 4, **t** (051) 265 416, *www.cantinabenti voglio.it*. Another good wine bar, with vintages great and small, as well as a small menu featuring *bruschetta* and *crostini, pastae fagioli*, traditional tagliatelle and lasagne and some good main dishes. Jazz some nights. *Open 8pm–2am, closed Sun in summer.*

Godot, Via Cartoleria 12, **t** (051) 226 315, *www.godotwine.it*. One of the newer stars in Bologna's culinary firmament: an informal, magnificently stocked wine bar, serving gourmet snacks, lunch and dinner, all made from the finest ingredients to go with a glass or a bottle. Very popular: stays open until 2am. *Closed Sun and 2 weeks in Aug.*

Da Leonida, Vicolo Alemagna 2, **t** (051) 239 742. Popular, elegant trattoria near the Due Torri, where they do everything one could possibly do with *tortellini* and tagliatelle; also the likes of roast pheasant and rabbit with polenta; home-made desserts. *Closed Sun exc during the Fair and 3 weeks in Aug.*

Mariposa, Via Bertiera 12, **t** (051) 225 656, *trattoriamariposa@libero.it*. Typical Bolognese cuisine with *tortellini*, tagliatelle with *ragù* and home-made cakes. *Closed Sun and Mon, and Thurs eve.*

Nuova Epoca, Via Centotrecento 1/b, **t** (051) 222 211, *pizzeria.nuovaepoca@ libero.it*. Wide range of pizzas as well as special pizza-crust sandwiches, packed with delicious fillings. *Closed Sat and Sun lunch and Aug.*

Osteria dell'Orsa, Via Mentana 1, **t** (051) 231 576, *www.osteriadellorsa. com*. In the same area and serving snacks, good sandwiches and salads, as well as some main-course dishes. Also jazz sessions at night. *Open until 1.30am daily.*

Serghei, Via Piella 12, **t** (051) 233 533. This typical little rustic Bolognese family-run trattoria is situated not far from the university. The menu, unchanged for years, features home-made pasta (meat-filled *tortellini* in tasty broth, rocket-filled *agnolotti*), pork cooked in milk, *osso buco*, and a wonderful ricotta tart to finish. *Booking advisable. Closed Sat eve, Sun and Aug.*

Tamburini, Via Caprarie 1, **t** (051) 234 726, *www.tamburini.com*. Self-service restaurant with changing menus; also an excellent place for sampling prepared foods for sale in the shop (at bargain prices). Try the lasagne, *tortellini* and cannelloni. *Closed Sun and a few days in Aug.*

Trattoria Boni, Via Don Luigi Sturzo 22/c–d, **t** (051) 615 4337, *www. trattoriaboni.it*. For those who don't want to go outside the city to find *crescentine*. Well-prepared home-made food, with all the traditional Bolognese specialities such as *pappardelle* with mushrooms and *bollito misto* with Emilian sauces. They also have on offer a popular bargain-price two-course lunch menu that changes daily. *Crescentine available. Thurs, Fri and Sat eves, booking advisable. Closed Sun eve, Mon, 10 days Jan, and 10 days Aug.*

Trattoria-Pizzeria Belfiore, Via Marsala 11, **t** (051) 226 641. A reliable old favourite, with no major surprises but offering good all-round cooking, and pizza. Try for instance *rigatoni alla norcina. Closed Tues.*

Antica Trattoria Spiga, Via Broccaindosso 21/a, **t** (051) 230 063. Just east of the centre off Via San Vitale. Run by the same family since 1933, and still doing well with traditional Bolognese dishes. Try for instance the *tortelloni noci e gorgonzola* or the local speciality *crescentine fritte*, which is available every Wednesday (booking advisable). *Closed Sun, Mon eve and Aug.*

Trattoria da Pietro, Via Falegnami 18, **t** (051) 230 644, *www.astratta.com/bointav/pietro.htm*. In the historic centre, a family-run trattoria that enjoys local renown for its Umbrian and Bolgnese cuisine. Try the polenta and wild boar. *Closed Sun exc during the Fair, Mon, all July and 1 week Dec/Jan. American Express not accepted.*

Trattoria Meloncello, Via Saragozza 240/a, **t** (051) 614 3947. Stop off here if you need fortifying before making the energy-sapping trek up the hill to the Basilica di San Luca. Renowned throughout the city above all for its pasta, which comes as close to melting in the mouth as is possible. There is no written menu to consult here, but the two sisters (who make everything themselves by hand, using carefully selected seasonal ingredients) will patiently explain to diners what's on offer, from the likes of *osso buco* to stuffed squashes. *Booking recommended. Closed Mon eve, Tues, and end July–mid-Aug. All credit cards except Diners and American Express.*

For other budget-priced restaurants, wander round the university area, particularly around Piazza Verdi and Via Belle Arti.

Entertainment and Nightlife in Bologna

Not surprisingly, a thousand-year-old university city like Bologna stays up later than most other Italian cities. People here eat late – often around 10pm – and there are plenty of bars and cafés open till 3am.

During college terms you only have to take a look at the student bars around the university and the posters in their windows to find out about concerts, films, exhibitions, performances and clubs; alternatively check out the listings in Bologna's oddly named local paper, *Il Resto del Carlino* (which does not mean 'the remains of little Charles', as many foreigners suspect, but the change from an old coin called a *Carlino* – when you bought a cigar, instead of change you could have a newspaper).

The local fortnightly *Zero in Condotta* usually has better listings on more youth-orientated events, concerts and so on, and interesting articles if you can read Italian.

One reflection of Bologna's progressive open-mindedness is that it contains the HQ of Italy's largest **gay organization**, Arcigay, and is the only city in the country to have a municipally supported gay centre, the **Cassero**, Via Don Minzioni 18, **t** (051) 649 4416, *www.cassero.it*, which sponsors films and discussions during the week and discos at weekends.

There are several **women's organizations** in the city; **Ufficio Progetto Donna**, Via S. Margherita 13, **t** (051) 271 457, issues lists (*closed Sat and Sun*).

Opera, Classical Music, Theatre and Cinema

The **drama** season at the Teatro Duse, Via Cartoleria 42, **t** +199 107 070, *www.teatroduse.it*, runs from November to May, while **operas, ballet** and **symphonic music** are performed at the Teatro Comunale, Largo Respighi 1, **t** (051) 529 011, *www.comunalebologna.it*, from September to June.

Other **classical music** venues are the Basilica di Santa Maria dei Servi, **t** (051) 261 710, and the Accademia Filarmonica, Via Guerrazzi 13, **t** (051) 554

715, *www.accademiafilarmonica.it*. There's a calendar of special performances (both theatrical and musical) at the Teatro delle Celebrazioni, Via Saragozza 234, **t** (051) 615 3370, *www.teatrocelebrazioni.it*. In summer, there are dance performances and concerts in the Piazza Maggiore. Instead of the usual Italian midsummer shutdown, Bologna's local authorities organize the *Bologna Sogna* festival throughout July and August, featuring concerts, theatre and open-air cinema.

During the winter **movies** are also shown in their original language on Wednesdays at Chaplin, Piazza di Porta Saragozza 5, **t** (051) 585 253, and on Mondays at Adriano, Via S. Felice 52, **t** (051) 555 127. Throughout the year the Nuovo Cinema Lumière, Via Azzo Gardino 65, **t** (051) 219 5311, shows mainly art-house movies. For information about programmes, festivals or repertory cinemas, contact the Cineteca di Bologna, Via Riva di Reno 72, **t** (051) 219 4820, *www.cinetecadibologna.it*.

Cafés and Bars

Bar Rosa Rose, Via Clavature 20, **t** (051) 265 170 *www.rosarose.it*. Popular early-evening meeting point just off the Piazza Maggiore. Sleek and modern.

Caffe del Museo, Via Zamboni 58, **t** (051) 246 620. Popular with students, especially during Thurs all-night Happy Hour when crowds spill out onto the street. *Closed Sun.*

Da Gianni, Via Montegrappa 11, **t** (051) 233 008. Bizarre ice-cream bar with experimental flavours. *Closed Wed and 1 week Dec.*

Kikbar, Via San Donato 66/14, **t** (051) 511 328. Claims to stock every whisky ever made, beginning with 1,300 single malts from Scotland. *Closed Sun and Aug.*

Moline, Via delle Moline 13, near the university, **t** (051) 248 470. Fine *gelati*. *Closed Tues.*

Pasticceria Impero, Via dell' Indipendenza 39, **t** (051) 232 337. A good place to make for at breakfast or later in the day; among other delights, the specialities of the house are *certosini*, cakes with pine nuts, candied fruit, almonds and honey. *Closed Mon.*

Pasticceria Majani, Via dei Carbonesi 5, **t** (051) 234 302. Famous for its *scorza di cioccolata*, and for its *camellini*.

Poco Loco, Via Mezzofanti 18, **t** (051) 392 002. Very popular bar, just outside the *centro storico. Closed Sun.*

La Sorbetteria Castiglione, Via Castiglione 44, **t** (051) 233 257. Ice cream in such flavours as *Edoardo*, a mix of mascarpone and pine nuts in burnt sugar and liqueurs. *Closed Tues.*

Le Stanze, Via del Borgo di San Pietro 1, **t** (051) 228 767. One of Bologna's more unusual cafés, this atmospheric place is housed in a Bentivoglio chapel dating from about 1500. With a small restaurant as well as a bar, it also boasts a library with big soft chairs and exhibition space, and music – modern sounds Mon–Fri, and classical on Sat. *Open daily until 2am. Closed July–Aug.*

Soda Pops, Via Castel Tialto 6, **t** (051) 272 079. Another dungeon-style young place with a live DJ and punch-packing cocktails.

La Torinese, Piazza Re Enzo 1/a, **t** (051) 236 743. A century old and a shrine for hot chocolate and pastries (also restaurant). *Closed Sun.*

Live Jazz, Blues, Rock and Alternative Music

No visitor should leave Bologna without drinking in one of the city's traditional *osterie*; the following places not only serve food, but have live music, and most tend to stay open till late.

Cantina Bentivoglio, Via Mascarella 4, **t** (051) 265 416, *www.cantinabenti voglio.it*. Smart, lively cellar that makes a mellow venue for live acoustic jazz, with snacks or full meals and an endless wine list. *Open till 2am. Closed Sun in summer.*

Capital Town, Via Don Minzoni 5/c, **t** (051) 421 1178, *www.capitaltown.it*. Also a restaurant offering a choice of Italian and Mexican food. *Closed June to end Aug.*

Casa delle Culture e dei Teatri, Via M. E. Lepido 255, **t** (051) 402 051, *www.teatroridotto.it*. Experimental theatre.

Chet Baker Jazz Club, Via Polese 7/a, **t** (051) 223 795, *www.chetbaker.it*.

Intimate, underground jazz bar near Via Marconi: come here for dinner and stay, or later for live jazz (€10 entrance and first drink). *Concerts from Oct to May.*

Officina Estragon, Via Calzoni 6, **t** (051) 365 825, *www.estragon.it*. Near the Fiera. Features weekend ska, hip-hop, reggae, etc. by Italian and foreign bands.

Osteria dell'Orsa, Via Mentana 1, **t** (051) 231 576, *www.osteriadellorsa.com*. Near the university. Beer cellar with jazz twice a week.

Pub Wolf Boomerang, Via Massarenti 118, **t** (051) 342 944, *www.bar-wolf.it*. A good venue for live music, and with no cover charge; jazz, bossanova, tango and folk.

Clubs and Discos

Corto Maltese, Via del Borgo di San Pietro 9/2a, **t** (051) 229 746 *www.cortomaltesediscobar.com*. A perennially popular disco-pub situated near the centre of the city. *Opens at 7pm Tues–Sat and at 9pm Sun–Mon.*

Il Covo, Viale Zagabria, **t** (051) 505 801, *www.covoclub.it*. Disco. *Open from 9pm.*

In summer the ever-generous Bologna city council sponsors inexpensive, open-air **raves**, usually in the outskirts; check posters and listings in the local press.

Palanord, Parco Nord, entrance on Via Michelino. Big winter venue.

Sottotetto Sound Club, Viale Zagabria 1, **t** 338 693 3989. Disco, and live jazz, rock, funk and blues music. *Open Thurs–Sat from 10pm.*

Villa Serena, Via della Barca 1, **t** (051) 615 4447, *www.vserena.it*. Thurs–Sat nights from 9pm all sorts of things go on at Villa Serena, from disco, exhibitions, video and theatre to Las Vegas-style piano-bar music. *Open 8pm–2am.*

Around Bologna

The Northern Plains

A considerable portion of Bologna's prosperity, medieval and modern, is due to la Bassa, the rich, well-watered plain north of the city, laced by rivers, streams and the canals, some of which go back as far as the 13th century. Even when you get beyond the sprawl and small industrial towns that surround the city, it's a monotonous bit of countryside, without any compelling attractions along the way. But if you're passing through...

Northwest on the SS568 for Mirandola and Mantova, **San Giovanni in Persiceto** is famous for its carnival, where each year the people create a parade of lavish allegorical floats. San Giovanni, like many towns around Bologna, has an impressive theatre, the 18th-century Teatro Comunale; the castle, called the Villa Giovannina, has rooms frescoed by Guercino. **Sala Bolognese**, just to the east, has an 11th-century Romanesque church, the Pieve di San Biagio, with an altar carved with a ram's head, recycled from a pagan temple.

Cento, Pieve di Cento, and Bentivoglio

To the north, the Torrente Samoggia divides the twin towns of **Cento** and **Pieve di Cento**. A role as a border town established since the Middle Ages made this a double settlement; even today Cento is in Ferrara province, Pieve di Cento in Bologna's.

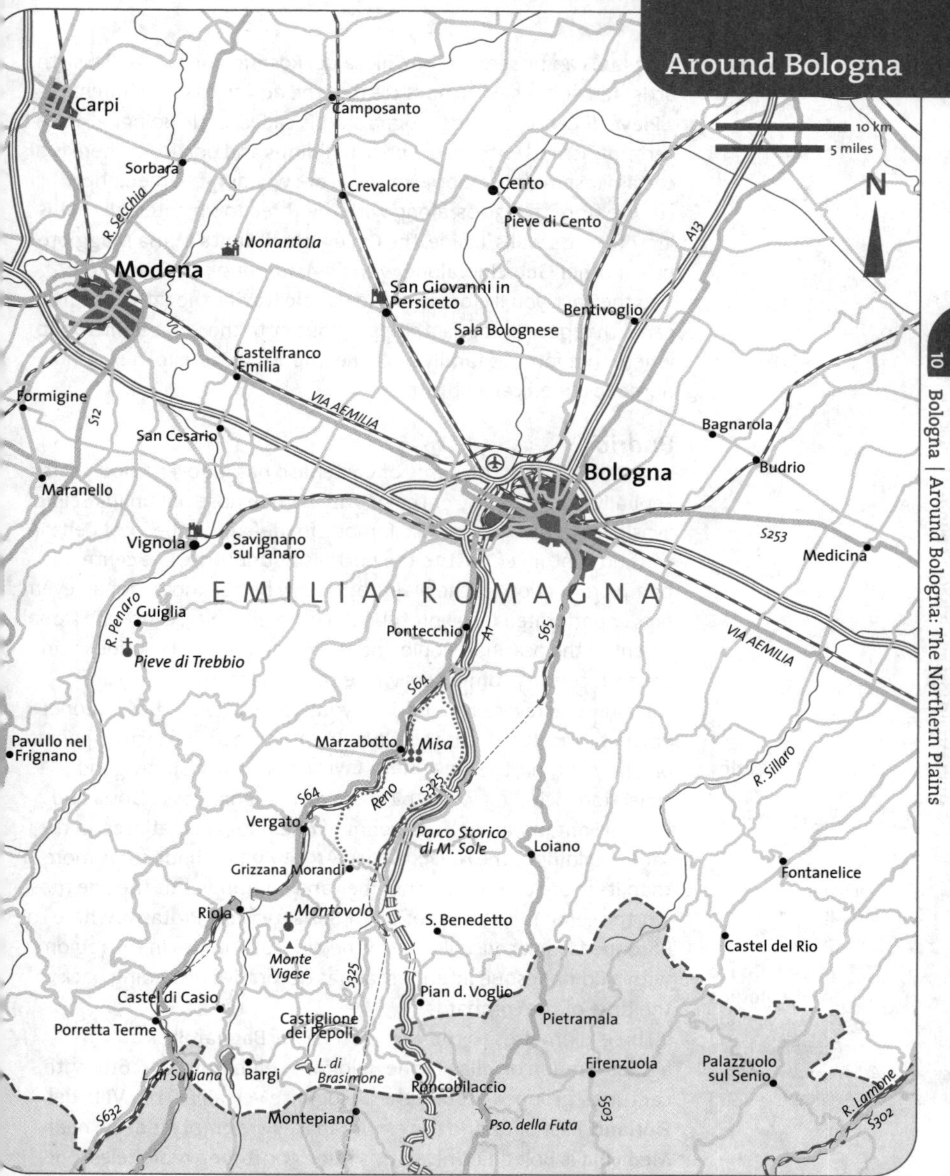

Pinacoteca Civica
Piazza A. Costa 10, Cento, ***t*** *(051) 975 533; open Sat–Sun 9–12 and 3.30–6.30, closed Aug; adm free*

Cento was the birthplace (1591) of the painter Giovanni Francesco Barbieri, better known as Il Guercino ('the squinter'), some of whose work can be seen in the **Casa Provenzali** on Via Provenzali, and in Pieve di Cento in the **Pinacoteca Civica**, which also contains works of other Bolognese artists, including one of the most acclaimed works of Ludovico Carracci, the *Holy Family with St Francis*. Four more Guercino paintings (he came back to spend 19 years in Cento,

1623–42) can be seen in the **Chiesa del Rosario** on Via Ugo Bassi; the artist himself is said to have created the design for the church.

Pieve di Cento, on the Bologna side, is called 'Little Bologna'; little it certainly is, and with its old brick buildings and porticoes there is a certain resemblance. Some of these are wooden-beamed; they survive from the 1300s, along with the three town gates, all that is left of Pieve's walls. Inside, the **Collegiata di Santa Maria Maggiore** has another Guercino, along with an *Assumption* by Guido Reni.

To the east, you'll cross over the **Canale Navile**, the 12th-century canal that gave Bologna a shipping outlet to the Po, at **Bentivoglio**, where that famous family built the imposing **Castello** in 1475, now home to a medical institute.

Budrio

East of Bologna, the name of **Castenaso** has for over 2,000 years kept alive the memory of the mighty Roman nose of Publius Scipio 'Nasica', a general otherwise famous for defeating the local Celts in the 2nd century BC. Just to the north is **Budrio**, once the centre of hemp production on the plains but really better known for an even bigger perforated facial protuberance; here, in 1853, Giuseppe Donati invented the ocarina. People once took ocarinas more seriously; in the 19th century composers wrote sonatas for them. They are certainly still revered in Budrio; if you ever wanted to buy a proper one in terracotta, this is the place. In the Palazzo della Participanza on Via Mentana, the **Pinacoteca Civica** has a surprisingly good collection including works by Vitale da Bologna, Dosso Dossi and Lavinia Fontana, as well as a room of rare books and atlases. In the same building is the **Museo Civico Archeologico**. Budrio has more than its share of Baroque churches and paintings, but the one most worth seeing is just west of town, **SS. Gervasio e Protasio**, where the Baroque façade conceals one of the oldest churches in the region, with a Romanesque interior that has decorative bits going back to the time of the Lombards.

Pinacoteca Civica
*Budrio, **t** (051) 692 8263; open Sun 3.30–6.30, first Sun of month also 10–12.30; by appt Oct–June; adm, includes Museo Civico Archeologico (below)*

Museo Civico Archeologico
open same hours as the Pinacoteca Civica (above); adm included with Pinacoteca ticket

Three kilometres to the west at *frazione* **Bagnarola** is an agglomeration of villas of the Bolognese élite from the 16th–19th centuries, grouped around the 'Bolognese Versailles', the **Villa del Floriano**. East of Budrio the empty spaces are empty indeed; near **Medicina** is Bologna University's huge 500ft-long radio telescope, the **Croce del Nord** – which looks like the head of a garden rake.

Where to Stay and Eat North of Bologna

Pieve di Cento ✉ 40066

Buriani, Via Provinciale 2/a, **t** (051) 975 177, *www.ristoranteburiani.com* (€€€€). Famous family-run restaurant founded in 1967: still maintaining a high-quality cuisine based on the freshest and finest seasonal ingredients; great desserts, great wine list, and a warm, welcoming atmosphere. Try the *tortelloni di ricotta 'burro e oro'*, nettle tagliatelle with ham or the *gran fritto alla Bolognese. Booking essential. Closed Tues and Wed.*

Bentivoglio ✉ 40010

★ Centro Storico >>

***Bentivoglio**, Piazza Carlo Alberto Pizzardi 1, **t** (051) 664 1111, *www.zanhotel.it* (€€€€€). Well-equipped hotel with cosy modern rooms – opposite the castle in a former rope factory 13km north of Bologna and 20km from Ferrara (unfortunately unlike the famous family you can't drift back into town on a canal boat). With a restaurant serving regional cuisine. The restaurant is open to guests only.

Budrio ✉ 40054

Centro Storico, Via Garibaldi 10, **t** (051) 801 678 (€€€). An intimate setting plus beautifully prepared food make this well worth the trip: treats include tiny ravioli filled with Parma ham and potato in a delicate asparagus sauce and gnocchi with saffron, squid and broad beans. Excellent desserts, too. *Closed Sun eve, Mon and Aug.*

South of Bologna: Into the Apennines

The valley of the Reno, south of the city, is one of the prettier parts of the Bologna hills, now more than a little compromised by the presence of the big A1 motorway for Florence. Wealthy Bolognesi used to build their country villas here, and quite a few survive, especially around **Pontecchio**. One of these, the **Villa Griffone**, was the home of Guglielmo Marconi, and it was from here that he sent off the world's first radio signal in 1895. There was only one receiver to pick it up – Marconi's brother had it set up in the hills, and he fired his rifle to tell the inventor it had worked. Today the villa is home to a scientific institute, but you can visit Marconi's colossal **Mausoleum** nearby, built by Mussolini in the middle of the war (1941) in the style of the ancient Etruscans, and the recent **Museo Marconi**.

Museo Marconi
Villa Griffone, **t** *(051) 846 121, www.fgm.it; booked guided tour only*

Farther south the roads for Florence (A1 and SS325) and Pistoia (SS64) split, enclosing between them the **Parco Storico di Monte Sole**, a beautiful wooded area that also contains a major archaeological site, the Etruscan city of **Misa**. That's the archaeologists' name; no one knows what the Etruscans called it when they founded it in the 6th century BC. Aside from the foundations of houses and an acropolis, and a necropolis of squarish stone tombs, there is little to see, and the best of the finds have been taken off to Bologna's Museo Archeologico. The Parco Storico also has room for some Celtic and Roman-era excavations, a big naturist camp (at Ca'le Scope), and plenty of empty farmhouses, currently being restored.

Misa
open daily 8–7

At least a few of the finds from Misa were kept here for the **Museo Etrusco** in nearby **Marzabotto**: bronzes, at which the Etruscans excelled, Greek urns and Etruscan copies, and the reconstruction of part of a building with its painted terracotta decoration. Marzabotto is best known to Italians as the site of the worst Nazi massacre in the country, the equivalent of Lidice in the Czech Republic or Oradour-sur-Glane in France. In 1944 an SS column tore through

Museo Etrusco
Via Porrettana, Marzabotto, **t** *(051) 932 353; open Tues–Thurs 9–1, Fri–Sun 9–1 and 3–6.30; adm*

Emilia-Romagna with the express purpose of brutalizing the population, in order to discourage the Resistance. Here they shot 1,830 people, nearly half Marzabotto's population. That is why there are so many empty houses up in the hills. The victims are remembered in the **Sacrario dei Caduti** in the village.

At the southern edge of the park, the village of Grizzana is now **Grizzana Morandi**, in honour of the painter, who liked to spend his summers here; its houses figure in many of his works. There is a museum, the **Museo Morandi**.

Museo Morandi
Loc. Campiaro 112, **t** *(051) 673 0017; open daily June–20 Aug 4.30–6.30; rest of year by appointment only*

South of Marzabotto, as the SS64 heads into the mountains, **Vergato** was the headquarters of Bologna's 'Captains of the Mountains', who governed the area in the Middle Ages; their restored 14th-century Palazzo dei Capitani stands in the centre.

The next village, little **Riola**, offers two unexpected sights: a Modernist masterpiece and a fairytale castle. First is the concrete and glass church of Santa Maria Assunta, one of the last works of Finnish architect Alvar Aalto (1978); the Rocchetta Mattei, with its rather magical skyline of turrets, loggias and bulbous neo-Moorish domes, was built over a period twenty years by a historian named Cesare Mattei (1850–70). From here you can take the road up Monte Vigese to the 11th-century sanctuary of the **Madonna di Montovolo**, with fragments of frescoes and sculptural work by the Comacene Masters.

Near the Tuscan border is the little spa of **Porretta Terme**, one of the many spots to which Lorenzo the Magnificent of Florence would come to see if it would help his gout (it didn't). The mountain back roads to the east conceal unchanged medieval villages such as **Castel di Casio** and **Bargi**, where they used to make arquebuses. Near the highest peaks on the border are two artificial lakes in lovely settings, both popular recreation areas: **Lago di Suviana** and the smaller **Lago di Brasimone**. From here it's a short hop to the large village of **Castiglione dei Pépoli**, where the elegant sanctuary of the Madonna di Bocca di Rio was built after an appearance of the Virgin Mary to two children in 1480.

Where to Stay and Eat South of Bologna

Porretta Terme ✉ 40046

******Castanea**, Via Roma 5, **t** (0534) 23180, *www.termediporretta.it* (€€€). Large beauty farm, with a sauna, covered pool, gym and disco, all conveniently close to the spa and its park. It has two restaurants, and all rooms are equipped for disabled visitors. Minimum stay 3 nights; full board.

*****Salus**, Via Capponi 8, **t** (0534) 22042, *www.termediporretta.it* (€€). Another beauty farm, this is constructed in the Liberty-style and pleasantly set in the park, a short stroll away from the spa. A good number of the rooms include Jacuzzis. Minimum stay 3 nights; full board.

Ferrara and Ravenna

This is the soggy end of Emilia-Romagna, basting in the marshlands of the Po delta. The moist surroundings, however, have not prevented it from growing two of Italy's most incandescent attractions: Ferrara, the Renaissance art town with a strangely modern edge, and Ravenna of the glittering mosaics, a time capsule of the dying Roman Empire.

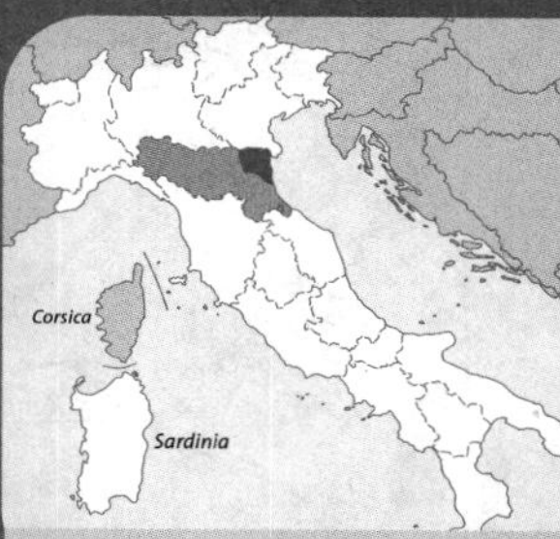

11

See map overleaf

Ferrara and Ravenna

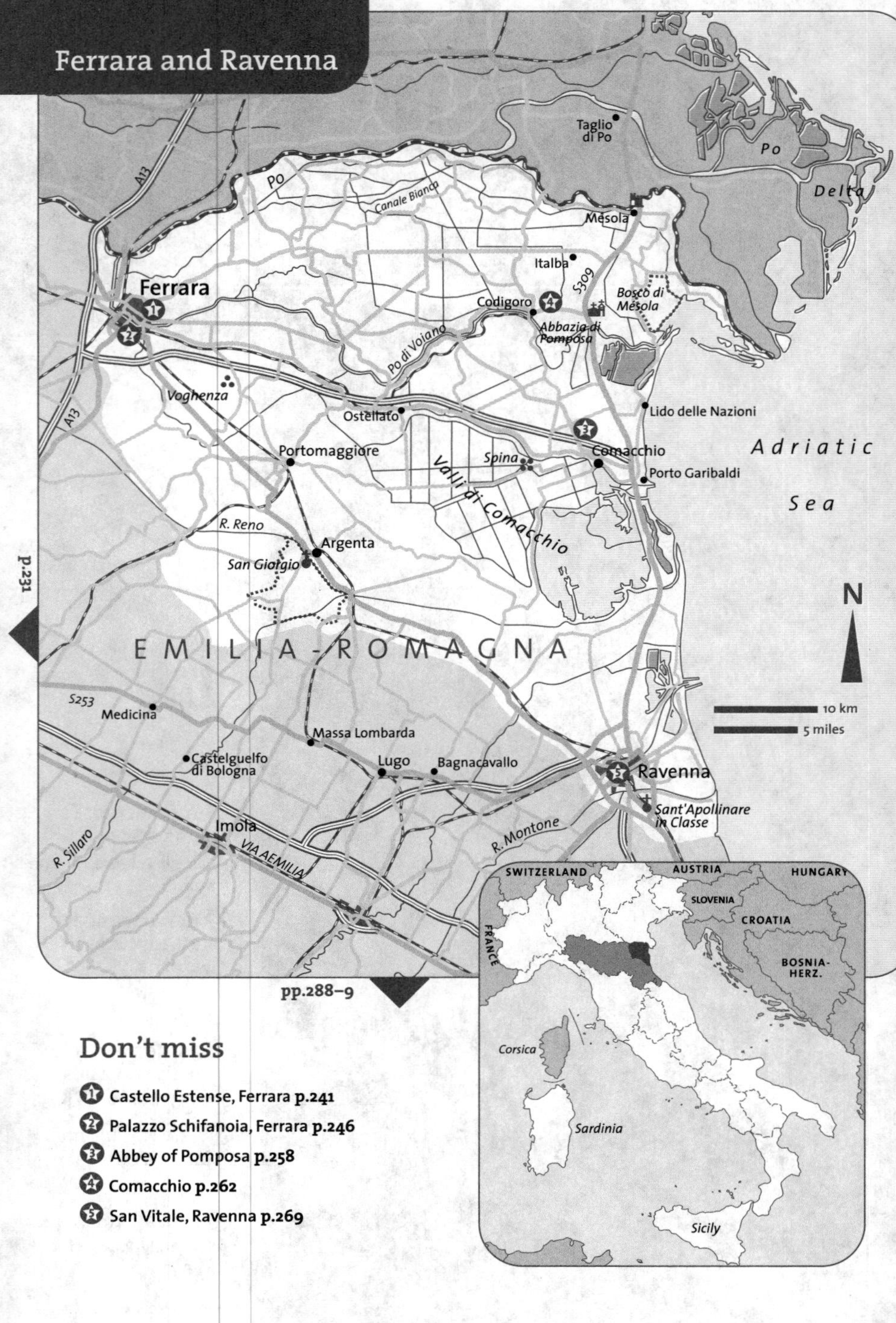

p.231

pp.288–9

Don't miss

1. Castello Estense, Ferrara **p.241**
2. Palazzo Schifanoia, Ferrara **p.246**
3. Abbey of Pomposa **p.258**
4. Comacchio **p.262**
5. San Vitale, Ravenna **p.269**

Ferrara

There's been a certain mystique attached to Ferrara ever since Jacob Burckhardt called it 'the first modern city in Europe' in his classic *Civilization of the Renaissance in Italy*. Whether or not Burckhardt was right can be debated; it is certain that the famous 'additions' to the medieval city in the Renaissance were far too ambitious. Ferrara, even in the most brilliant days of the court of the Este family, never had more than 30,000 citizens – not enough to fill the long streets laid out within the 9km circuit of the walls.

But what was a failure in the Renaissance is a happy success today; if Italian art cities can be said to come and go in fashion, Ferrara is definitely in, popularized by a well-received international campaign to save its uniquely well-preserved walls, and a rebirth of interest in the city's great quattrocento painters. Thanks to the rather tyrannical Este, the charming city enclosed by those walls was one of the brightest stars of the Renaissance, with its own school of art led by the great Cosmè Tura, Ercole de' Roberti, Lorenzo Costa and Francesco del Cossa. Poets patronized by the Este produced three of the Italian Renaissance's greatest epic poems – Boiardo's *Orlando Innamorato* (1483), Ariosto's better-known continuation of the same story, *Orlando Furioso* (1532), and Tasso's *Gerusalemme Liberata* (1581).

History

Ferrara is the youngest of the region's big cities. It may have been Roman *Forum Alieni*, a settlement whose site has never been discovered, but as far as anyone can tell the city had its beginnings in a Byzantine fortified camp, built to control trade on the Po in the 6th century. The first mention of it in the chronicles comes when the Lombards captured it in 753. Ferrara was the first town in the region to set up a *comune*, sometime in the 10th century, though it was occupied soon after by Teobaldo of Canossa; that dynasty controlled it through the days of Countess Matilda, but the city finally reasserted its independence in 1115.

The mighty Po used to wash Ferrara's walls. The factor that built this city, though, has often proved to be one of its biggest problems for, at least in its lower stretches, the Po is a river that just won't stay put. Its main course deserted the city in 1152, though by hard work the Ferrarese were able to keep navigable the little branch of the river that was left them, the Po di Volano, and maintain their status as a port. The medieval city based its economy on river tolls, the salt pans of the Comacchio and the rich agricultural land of the Delta. It was always ruled by one or other of the powerful local dynasties, usually from the Ghibelline Adelardi family or the Guelph Torcelli. The involvement of the great **dukes of Este** (just to the north, in the Veneto) began with Duke Azzo V, who had acquired leadership of the

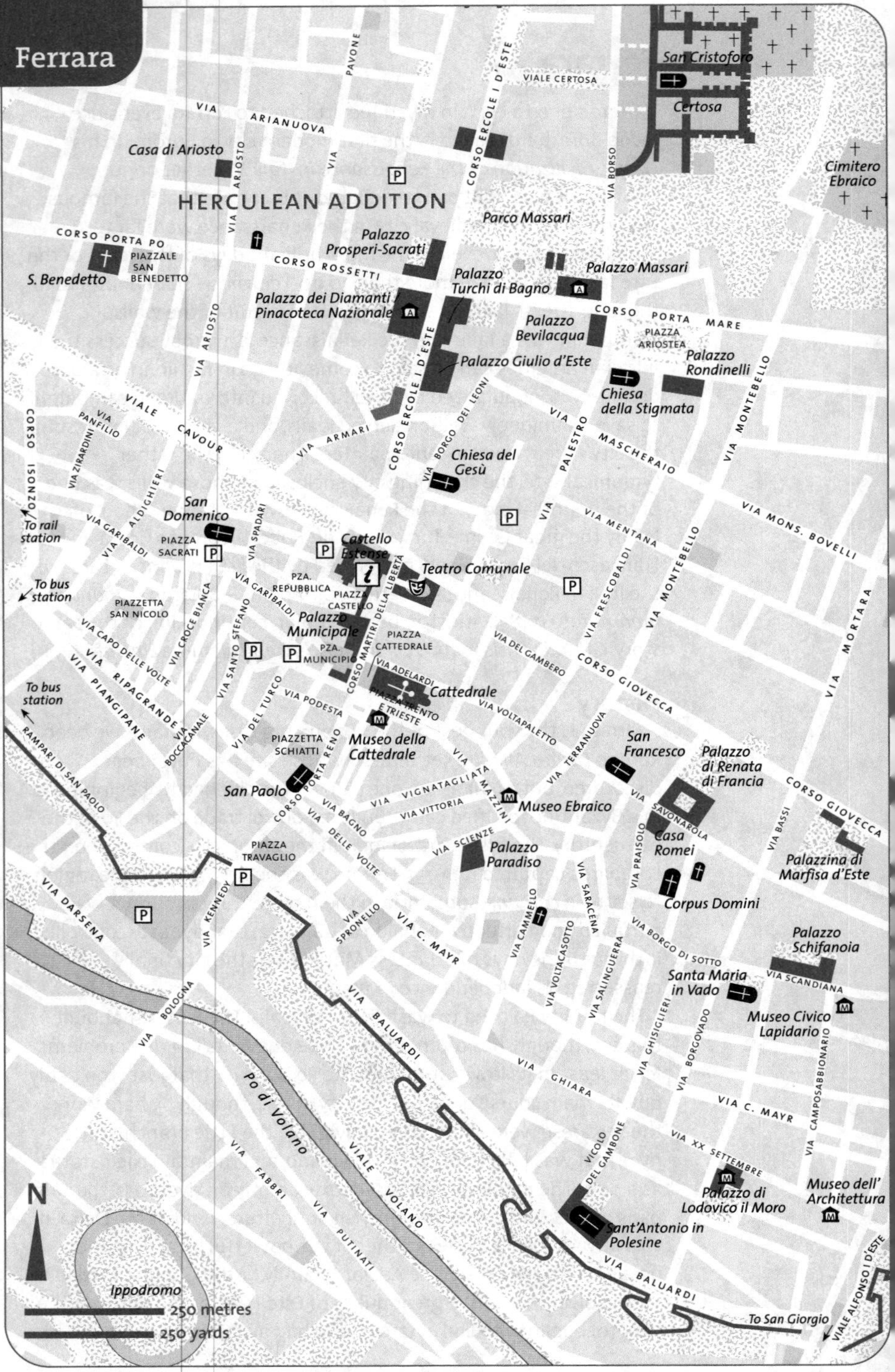

HERCULEAN ADDITION
San Cristoforo
Certosa
Viale Certosa
Cimitero Ebraico
Via Arianuova
Via Pavone
Corso Ercole I d'Este
Casa di Ariosto
Via Ariosto
Via Borso
Parco Massari
Corso Porta Po
Piazzale San Benedetto
S. Benedetto
Palazzo Prosperi-Sacrati
Corso Rossetti
Palazzo Turchi di Bagno
Palazzo Massari
Palazzo dei Diamanti / Pinacoteca Nazionale
Corso Porta Mare
Palazzo Bevilacqua
Piazza Ariostea
Palazzo Giulio d'Este
Palazzo Rondinelli
Chiesa della Stigmata
Via Montebello
Viale Cavour
Corso Isonzo
Via Panfilio
Via Armari
Via Borgo dei Leoni
Via Palestro
Via Mascheraio
Chiesa del Gesù
Via Zirardini
Via Aldighieri
San Domenico
Piazza Sacrati
Via Spadari
To rail station
Via Garibaldi
Castello Estense
Teatro Comunale
Via Mentana
Via Mons. Bovelli
To bus station
Pza. Repubblica
Piazza Castello
Via Martiri della Libertà
Via Frescobaldi
Via Mortara
Piazzetta San Nicolò
Via Croce Bianca
Via Santo Stefano
Palazzo Municipale
Piazza Cattedrale
Via Capo delle Volte
Pza. Municipio
Via Adelardi
Via del Gambero
Corso Giovecca
Via Ripagrande
Via Piangipane
Cattedrale
Piazza Trento e Trieste
Via Voltapaletto
To bus station
Via del Turco
Via Podestà
Via Boccacanale
Museo della Cattedrale
Ramparti di San Paolo
Piazzetta Schiatti
San Francesco
Palazzo di Renata di Francia
San Paolo
Corso Porta Reno
Via Vignatagliata
Via Mazzini
Via Terranuova
Via Bagno
Via Vittoria
Museo Ebraico
Via Savonarola
Via Bassi
Via delle Volte
Via Scienze
Palazzo Paradiso
Casa Romei
Via Praisolo
Palazzina di Marfisa d'Este
Piazza Travaglio
Via Darsena
Via Kennedy
Via Saracena
Corpus Domini
Via Cammello
Via Spronello
Via C. Mayr
Via Voltacasotto
Via Salinguerra
Via Borgo di Sotto
Palazzo Schifanoia
Via Scandiana
Santa Maria in Vado
Museo Civico Lapidario
Via Bologna
Via Baluardi
Via Ghisiglieri
Via Borgovado
Via Camposabbionario
Po di Volano
Via Ghiara
Via C. Mayr
Vicolo del Gambone
Via XX Settembre
Museo dell' Architettura
Palazzo di Lodovico il Moro
Via Fabbri
Via Putinati
Viale Volano
Sant'Antonio in Polesine
N
Ippodromo
250 metres
250 yards
Via Baluardi
To San Giorgio
Viale Alfonso I d'Este

Getting to and around Ferrara

By Rail

Ferrara is on a main rail line from Venice to Bologna, where you can change for other cities in Emilia; there is also a busy line from Ferrara to Ravenna and Rimini. The **railway station** is just outside the city walls, about a kilometre from the city centre (the Este dukes made Ferrara a city of great distances), but you can get in easily on city buses nos.1, 2, 3c, 5 or 9. A separate service, the *FER*, runs from the central station to Ostellato and Codigoro, with buses from there out to the lidos on the coast; for information, **t** (0532) 979 311 or 800 915 030 (*toll free, from Italy only*), *www.fer-online.it*.

By Bus

The **bus station** is near the corner of the Rampari di San Paolo and the Corso Isonzo (city bus 2 connects it with the railway station). A network of lines serves the coast, Bologna, Modena, Ravenna, Cento, Comacchio, Codigoro, Porto Garibaldi and other local destinations: ACFT Punto Bus, **t** (0532) 599 411, *www.acft.it*; they also have an information booth in the railway station (*open daily 7.15am–7.15pm*).

By Road

The main road to Ferrara is the *autostrada* A13 from Bologna to Padua, which passes just west of the city. Alternatively, the SS64 leads from Bologna and the SS16 from Ravenna and on northwards to Rovigo. South of Ferrara a motorway-standard road cuts eastwards off the A13 and SS64 for Comacchio and the Delta. The city has a relatively small *zona traffico limitato*, but you still wouldn't much enjoy **driving** around the narrow streets of the medieval centre; there are **parking** areas there, signposted around Via Garibaldi, but larger and more accessible ones can be found around Via Darsena and Piazza Travaglio at the southern walls.

By Bike

Almost completely flat, Ferrara has a high ratio of **bicycles** to humans. Bikes are available for hire at the *deposito* just outside the train station, **t** (0532) 772 190, or try Itinerando, Via Kennedy, just off Piazza Travaglio, **t** (0532) 202 003.

Guelphs through marriage with the Adelardi. Azzo VI was the most important man in Ferrara before his death in 1212, though after him the Ghibellines reasserted their power with *signori* such as Salinguerra Torelli, who dominated the city from 1222 to 1240, a strong ally (and brother-in-law) of the powerful Ezzelino da Romano, lord of Verona. When the Guelphs seized power again in 1240, they imprisoned Salinguerra and replaced him with Ezzelino's arch enemy, Azzo VII d'Este.

The rise of the Este family made Ferrara a great Guelph city, an outpost of papal power in the north. Azzo's descendants were lords of Ferrara in an unbroken run until 1598. Azzo was succeeded by Obizzo II, a bastard in every sense of the word. Obizzo gutted the rule of law in the city and made himself a tyrant. He abolished the guilds, and threw away Ferrara's profitable control of trade on the Po in return for Venetian support for his ambitions elsewhere; in 1288–9 he extended the family's rule to Reggio and Modena. Gossip had it that Obizzo had murdered his mother, and regularly committed incest with his daughters. Such claims were typical of the political propaganda of the time; they might even have been true.

Later Este proved less villainous than Obizzo, but every one was just as skilled at holding on to power. With great intelligence, and single-minded devotion to keeping the dynasty afloat, they maintained their absolute rule by promoting economic development, granting concessions and reforms when it was prudent to do so, and generally staying in the good graces of their nominal overlords, the popes. The clan also produced some of the most interesting characters of the Renaissance, such as Nicolò II 'the Lame' (1361–88), a friend of Petrarch; his reign saw the revolt of 1385, which led the Este to build the fortified Castello. Alberto V (1388–93) founded the University of Ferrara; Nicolò III (1393–1441) engaged in long wars with neighbouring Padua, with considerable success, though he was more famous as the father of hundreds of children 'on both banks of the Po', and as the villain who terminated one of the tragic love stories of his day – he found that his young wife Parisina and his son by another woman, Ugo, were lovers, and had both of them executed.

The other sons of Nicolò III – Leonello (1441–50), Borso (1450–71) and Ercole I (1471–1505) – met happier fates; ruling in turn, each did his part to promote the city's great cultural flowering. Leonello, a friend of the architect and theorist Leon Battista Alberti, invited the most prominent humanists and artists of the Renaissance to Ferrara (Pisanello, Jacopo Bellini, Mantegna), and cultivated the local painters of the Ferrarese school, one of the most significant collections of artistic talent outside Florence. Borso continued his patronage; he also confirmed Este rule over Reggio and Modena, and was granted the title of Duke of Ferrara by the Pope.

Ferrara was booming, and Ercole I had the huge addition to the city, known as the **Herculean Addition**, designed by his architect Biagio Rossetti. His offspring, Isabella (wife of Francesco Gonzaga of Mantova), Beatrice (married to Lodovico Sforza, *Il Moro*, of Milan), and Cardinal Ippolito, were among the most cultured and influential people of their day. The Duke was a friend and patron of poets, including Ariosto and Matteo Boiardo, whom he made a minister of state. Ercole managed to avoid disaster in a prelude to the Wars of Italy, the 1482–3 'War of Ferrara'. The papacy, which had claimed suzerainty over the Romagna since 1278, offered Ferrara's part of the Po delta (including the rich salt works at Comacchio) to Venice in return for military support against Naples. The Venetians had their excuse to invade the territory, but when Florence, Milan and Spain stepped up to oppose this blatant land grab, Pope Sixtus IV and the Venetians backed down, postponing a pan-Italian conflict.

When the Wars of Italy came, the Este were up to the challenge. Ercole's heir Alfonso I (1505–34) married the beautiful and unjustly maligned Lucrezia Borgia, who ran a brilliant, fashionable court, patronizing Ariosto and Titian, while her husband spent his days casting huge cannons. It was a sort of hobby with him, but Alfonso was no fool. In this dangerous age, cannons were a good thing to have, and his were the finest in Europe. With the guns, and some carefully crafted marriages, Alfonso's skilful diplomacy helped Ferrara avoid invasion, and the Este state emerged from the wars with its independence intact, even though successive popes, Julius II, Leo X and Clement VII, all tried to destroy the Este state.

The son of Alfonso and Lucrezia, Ercole II (1534–59), married Renée, daughter of Louis XII of France, and a Calvinist. She briefly made Ferrara Italy's last centre of Protestant thinkers; she entertained French poet Clément Marot, and even sheltered John Calvin under an assumed name. Eventually relations with Rome became so touchy that she had to be imprisoned and finally sent away.

The last Este Duke of Ferrara, Alfonso II (1559–97), patron of the unstable and unruly poet Torquato Tasso, was considered the best-educated and most courtly ruler of his day, but at the expense of his people. As the ruler of one of the few truly independent small states in Italy, Alfonso needed to lay low and avoid trouble; instead, he entertained extravagant ambitions (he once tried to get himself elected King of Poland). Such adventures, plus the expense of maintaining a glittering court, led to crushingly high taxes and neglect of the city's economy.

Worst of all, from the family's point of view, Alfonso failed to produce a legitimate heir. He tried to name a cousin, Cesare, as his successor, but Pope Clement VIII decreed that he too was illegitimate; by now the Este had few friends either at home or among the neighbouring powers, and there was no way to stop the Pope from taking over Ferrara in 1598. The city was glad to see the last of the family, and it was ruled thereafter by a papal legate (though Cesare continued to rule as Duke of Modena and Reggio, where the popes had no claim; his successors kept the state alive until the time of Napoleon). Without the largesse of the Este, Ferrara rapidly became an artistic backwater, while the cardinals sent as legates plundered the city's treasures to enrich themselves. Under papal rule the economy rapidly foundered while the population declined considerably; visitors in the 1700s reported the city looking almost like a ghost town. After Italian unification Ferrara gradually got back on its feet; agriculture in the Po plain revived, while the city grew into a modest industrial centre. In the 20th century, the modern 'Metaphysical School' of painting (De Chirico, Carrà, De Pisis, Morandi and others) had its origins in the city, inspired at least in part by the great frescoes in the Palazzo Schifanoia.

The City Centre: The Castello Estense

Castello Estense
t (0532) 299 233, www.castelloestense.it; castle residence open Tues–Sun 9.30–5; adm; adm for Torre dei Leoni

At the very centre of Ferrara towers the imposing Castello Estense, its elegant Renaissance towers reflected in the wide moat. It's a queer sort of building, one which doesn't seem to know whether to be a fortress or a palace; in fact it has been both. At once massive and delicate, it is also quite beautiful, the very image of suave and intelligent tyranny. The Castello is also a part of Ferrara's precocious modernist mystique; the Metaphysical painters took it for a kind of existential symbol, and perhaps it was no accident that it inspired so many Victorian factory buildings.

There's no doubt about the Castello's original purpose. It was begun in 1385 after a revolt in May of that year against high taxes in which the tax man, one Tommaso da Tortona, was lynched. After clearing a huge area on the edge of the town wall, Signore Nicolò II laid the first stone for his new stronghold on 29 September – St Michael's Day, he who kicked the rebellious angels out of heaven; the symbolism was undoubtedly not lost on the Ferraresi. The **Via Coperta**, the protected passageway running over the piazza to the old Este palace (now the Palazzo Municipale), gave the dukes a chance to reach the castle in case of further trouble. In the 1400s, under Ercole I, the Este transformed it into part of their residence: its crenellations were replaced by white marble balustrades, and its great halls adorned with art.

The drawbridge, with its counterweights, still seems to be in good working order, but they'll let anybody in now. Inside the courtyard are the city tourist office, some municipal offices and the entrance to the **castle residence**. A few decorated rooms survive in the **ducal apartments**: the best is the *Sala dell'Aurora*, Ercole II's study, with frescoes by Giovanni Settevecchi (*Day and Sunset*) and Bastianino (*Dawn* – Aurora – and *Night*); they collaborated on the charming central fresco of *Time*, surrounded by putti racing chariots drawn by various beasts around a classical racecourse with obelisks. Among the other rooms are the *Camerina dei Baccanali*, and the *Salone e Saletta dei Giochi* – the games rooms, frescoed by Settevecchi with more putti wrestling and swimming, pretending to be gladiators, playing ninepins and a score of other games. The tour includes Renée of France's unadorned **Calvinist chapel** (1590; the ceiling frescoes were added in the 19th century), and the **Torre dei Leoni**, site of the prison where Ugo and Parisina languished before their beheading, and Giulio and Ferrante, brothers of Alfonso I, spent their lives after attempting a conspiracy in 1506. The dukes weren't forgiving. Ferrante died after 34 years in the tower; Giulio came out with a pardon after 53 years, aged 81, walking around Ferrara in perfect health and amusing the people with his old-fashioned, threadbare clothes. The family wasn't known for its modesty either. One part of the original decoration that has disappeared is the 300 portraits of various Este princes, some by famous artists, that once covered almost all the walls.

From the ducal apartments a door leads to the lovely **roof terrace**, with the *Giardino degli Aranci*, a grove of orange trees in huge pots; this ducal fantasy is still kept up, even though they have to bring them indoors each winter. Louis XIV probably got the idea here for his *Orangerie* at Versailles.

Palazzo Municipale

Palazzo Municipale
t (0532) 240 342; open Mon–Fri 9–2 ; visits by appointment

Dukes can take the passageway over to the Palazzo Municipale, but you'll have to go out and cross Piazza della Repubblica (which everyone in Ferrara still calls Piazza Castello), passing the **statue of Savonarola**, the fire-and-brimstone Dominican revivalist who gained control of Florence after the Medici were kicked out in 1494, and convinced the most sophisticated citizens of the Renaissance (in a Ferrarese accent, mind) to give up their treasures to the Bonfire of Vanities; he was a native of Ferrara.

The Palazzo Municipale was begun in 1243, soon after Azzo d'Este seized control of Ferrara, and has been tinkered with ever since; its façade was redone in the 1920s in the picturesque medieval manner. The main entrance facing the cathedral, an arch said to have been the work of Leon Battista Alberti, is adorned with bronze statues of *Nicolò III* on horseback, and *Borso*, smiling on his throne and looking for all the world like Old King Cole; both of these are copies, made after Napoleon melted down the originals to make cannons. The archway leads into a courtyard, now called the Piazzetta Municipale, with a grand Renaissance monumental stair. During business hours, you might be able to get in for a look at the rooms surviving from the days when this was the residence of the Este: the chapel and the *Sala delle Duchesse*, with painted 15th-century decoration.

The Cattedrale

Cattedrale
open Mon–Sat 7.30–12.15 and 3–6.30, Sun and hols until 7.30

It looks, if it looks like anything, a little like an old Mississippi steamboat, come paddling up ol' man Po to moor itself in the piazza. A building as singular in its way as the Castello, the Cattedrale was begun in 1135. The great Wiligelmo, known for his work on Modena Cathedral, and his follower Nicolò both worked on the cathedral at the beginning, though it isn't clear who designed the building or what their original intentions were. When it was finished, sometime before 1300, it had acquired its distinctive box-like shape, massive side gables and a façade with a Gothic false front rising above the level of the church. The upper loggia on the south side is a bit of show-offish Romanesque bravura in the Tuscan manner, with columns variously twisted, zig-zagging or even tied in knots, like those on churches in Lucca. Beneath this, the **Loggia dei Merciai**, the picturesque market portico flanking the cathedral in Piazza Trento e Trieste, was erected in 1473. At the end of this is a lovely candy-striped **campanile**, attributed to Leon Battista Alberti, begun in 1442 and never completed. The last major addition was the apse (1498).

The cathedral's glory is its marble **portico**, guarded by porphyry lions and griffins. Nicolò executed the relief on the tympanum of *St George*, to whom the cathedral is dedicated, killing his dragon, and above it various Old Testament scenes and figures of prophets. Above the portal, a loggia shelters a *Madonna and Child* in terracotta by Cristoforo da Firenze (1427), and above the loggia is a pediment with a magnificent 13th-century scene of the *Last Judgement* by an unknown sculptor. The interior suffered a catastrophic remodelling in 1710, destroying most of its original works of art, and leaving it with a gloomy but somewhat raffish air, helped along by the ranks of glass-bead chandeliers. On the wall over the main door, frescoes by Garofalo of *SS Peter and Paul* survived; to the right of them is a baptismal font from Byzantine times. In the last chapel on the right is a *Martyrdom of St Lawrence* by Guercino, and in the Rossetti apse Bastianino painted a fresco of the *Last Judgement*.

Museo della Cattedrale
t (0532) 244 949; open Tues–Sun 9–1 and 3–6; adm; joint ticket available with Palazzina Marfisa d'Este, Palazzo Schifanoia and Museo Civico Lapidario

Many of the cathedral's displaced works have been moved to the **Museo della Cattedrale**, a small but memorable museum across Piazza Trento e Trieste, on the corner of Via San Martino. Among these are the lovely marble *Madonna of the Pomegranate* by Jacopo della Quercia, some fine 16th-century Flemish tapestries, and two painted organ shutters that rank among the greatest surviving works of Cosmè Tura: an *Annunciation* full of lovely naturalistic detail (even a squirrel), and the remarkable, surreal *St George*, despatching his dragon in a dream landscape. The 12th-century reliefs of the *Labours of the Months*, credited to followers of Parma's Benedetto Antelami, once adorned the cathedral's south door.

Medieval Ferrara

San Domenico
open daily 8.30–12 and 3.30–6

The oldest streets of Ferrara lie between the Castello and the Po, still the shopping district and the liveliest part of town. Behind the Castello is the 1405 church of **San Giuliano**, like the cathedral completely redone inside in the 1700s. One street to the west on Via Spadari is the 1726 **San Domenico**. From here, Via Santo Stefano runs southwards, following the route of a medieval canal; it passes several Renaissance-era houses and the church of **Santo Stefano**, begun in the 11th century and subjected to several later restorations.

San Paolo
open Mon–Fri 8.30–12.30, Sun and hols 8.30–12.30 and 3.30–6.30

Palazzo Paradiso
t (0532) 418 200; open Mon–Fri 9–7.30, Sat 9–1.30; mid-July to mid-Aug Mon–Sat 9–1.30

Three blocks to the east in Piazzetta Schiatti is **San Paolo**, one of the last churches built under Este rule, and still preserving most of its original decoration, including works by Bastianino and Girolamo da Carpi and a fresco in the apse of the *Ascension of the Prophet Elijah* by Scarsellino. The 10th-century campanile, called the **Torre dei Leuti**, is all that's left of an earlier church on this site. Behind the church is a street that has changed its appearance little since the 1300s, the cobbled, atmospheric **Via delle Volte**, named for the vaulted passageways that connect the houses on either side. North, on Via delle Scienze, the **Palazzo Paradiso** (1391) was remodelled in the 1590s to be the home of Ferrara University. Now it is the municipal library, but you can see the university's old anatomical theatre inside, and the original manuscript of *Orlando Furioso*, as well as Ariosto's tomb.

Jewish Museum
Via Mazzini, **t** *(0532) 210 228, www.comune.fe.it/museoebraico; open for guided tours only Sun–Thurs at 10am, 11am and 12pm; adm*

To the north, the **Jewish Museum**, in Via Mazzini, is on the site of three synagogues. Since 1485 the building was the focus of Jewish life in Ferrara; it was purchased by a rich financier from Rome, employed at the Estense court, who left it in his will 'forever for the common use of the Jews'. An interesting collection of objects and documents is now on display. Under the Este, Jews expelled from Spain, Portugal, Germany and the Papal State were welcome in Ferrara, and made up a thriving community. The popes then locked them up in a ghetto around Via Mazzini, beginnning in 1627. Most of Ferrara's Jews were deported in the late stages of the Second World War; only five came back.

Further east, Via Mazzini becomes Via Cammello, passing two 14th-century houses and the 11th-century campanile of **San Gregorio**.

East of the Centre: Churches and Palaces

From behind the cathedral, Via Voltapaletto will take you out to the east end of Ferrara and the first of the city's planned 'additions', laid out under Nicolò III in 1385 (it's a much more pleasant walk than the dull and traffic-plagued main street, Corso Giovecca). At No.11 is the lavishly decorated façade of the **Palazzo Costantini-Contiani**, one of several buildings in Ferrara by Giovan Battista Aleotti, architect of the Farnese Theatre in Parma. Where it crosses Via Terranuova, Voltapaletto changes its name to Via Savonarola, and passes **San Francesco**, another of Rossetti's churches (1494); its huge interior is brightened by terracotta and painted friezes in the nave, the latter by Girolamo da Carpi.

San Francesco
open daily 7.30–11.30 (till 12 Sun and hols) and 3.30–5.30

Casa Romei
open Tues–Sun 8.30–7.30; adm

Next on Via Savonarola is the **Casa Romei**, a fine early Renaissance palace, built for a banker who married one of the Este in 1445. As well as its charming frescoes in the *Sala delle Sibille* and *Sala dei Profeti*, its terracotta fireplaces and the elegant courtyards, there are some expressive detached frescoes moved here from Sant'Andrea and other disused churches, and the rooms are filled with period art and furnishings from other buildings. Across the street, the 1475 **Palazzo di Renata di Francia**, where Renée of France maintained her Protestant circle far from her husband's court, is now part of the University. To the south on Via Pergolato, behind the church of San Girolamo, is the church of **Corpus Domini**, with a rich Baroque interior containing the austere tombs of Alfonso I, Alfonso II and Lucrezia Borgia.

Corpus Domini
open Mon–Fri 9.30–11.30 and 3.30–5.30

Palazzina di Marfisa d'Este
t (0532) 244 949; open Tues–Sun 9–1 and 3–6; adm; joint ticket available with Museo della Cattedrale, Palazzo Schifanoia and Museo Civico Lapidario

North of Via Savonarola, a short walk up Via Ugo Bassi, is the late Renaissance **Palazzina di Marfisa d'Este**, in a garden at Corso della Giovecca 170. It once formed part of a larger complex of buildings, now unfortunately lost, and Marfisa's retreat now seems a bit sad in the busy traffic of the Corso. Marfisa, a friend of Tasso, was beautiful and eccentric, and the subject of several ghost stories; it seems that she enjoyed post-mortem rides through the city at midnight in a wolf-drawn carriage. The interior of her little palace, which once had a colourful majolica pavement, has been admirably restored and fitted with a fine collection of 16th- and 17th-century Tuscan and other Italian furniture, with unusual frescoes on the ceiling. Outside is a loggia with frescoes of two little girls. One is Marfisa; her father Francesco built the palace.

At the end of Corso Giovecca, just before the walls, the big stone arch called the **Prospettiva** was built to close the view down the long straight avenue in 1703.

Palazzo Schifanoia

(2) Palazzo Schifanoia
Via Scandiana, t (0532) 64178, www.artecultura.fe.it; open Tues–Sun 9–6; adm includes Museo Civico Lapidario; joint ticket available with Museo della Cattedrale, Palazzina Marfisa d'Este and Museo Civico Lapidario

It's surprising there's anything left at all. The popes used Ferrara's most famous palace as a tobacco factory, ruining some of the greatest frescoes of the Renaissance, and Napoleon's boys weren't too gentle with it either after they made it a barracks in 1801. *Schifanoia* translates as 'escape from boredom'. Alberto V began this *delizia*, as rural palaces were called, in 1385 in what was then open countryside. It was expanded and redecorated on several occasions, and took its present form in the late 15th century with architectural trim by Rossetti and a stately portal designed by painter Francesco del Cossa, displaying the Este arms.

The reason for visiting is a single bare room, the **Salone dei Mesi**, the 'collective masterpiece of the Ferrarese school', frescoed *c.* 1475 for Borso d'Este by Cosmè Tura, Ercole de' Roberti and Francesco del Cossa, and probably other hands too. Modern criticism usually credits the guiding hand behind this tremendous allegory as Tura's; busy as he was with other commissions for the Este, he left much of the actual painting here to others. The scenes of mythological and allegorical subjects, peopled by amiable 15th-century aristocrats, are believed to have been inspired by Petrarch's *Triumphs* – in each month a different god is seen to 'triumph'. The other inspiration comes from the occult astrology that shaped so much of Renaissance thought and life; running through the centre of the twelve months is a band portraying its sign along with three strange figures for each month on a black background; these represent the decans of the ancient Egyptians, who divided the zodiac into 36 zones of 10 days each, each one ruled by its 'daemon' (*see* p.44).

Of the 12 scenes, only half, March to September, have survived; the rest are damaged beyond restoration or even legibility. The upper band portrays the *Triumph* of each month, while below the decans are scenes of country life, like a medieval Labours of the Months, and the activities of the Este court. Few paintings so successfully capture the quattrocento delight in life and beauty, its vitality and imagination – most famously in the *Triumph of Venus* for the month of April, with a rare Renaissance kiss. Like most of the surviving frescoes, this is attributed to Francesco del Cossa. In much of this painter's work, the figures are posed with an almost superhuman grace, as in the beautiful scene of the pruning of the vines in March, or the enigmatic first decan of that month, a youth holding an arrow and a golden hoop.

The touch of the bizarre here comes not from Tura, none of whose work here seems to have survived, but Ercole de'Roberti, who is credited with most of September, the *Triumph of Vulcan* – weirdly stylized rocks, unlike anything seen in painting before or since, the god's triumphal car drawn by apes, Mars and Venus making love, and a hallucinatory vision of Vulcan's forge attended by dark figures with a single eye in the middle of their foreheads. The palace has several other rooms with surviving decoration, including the 1475 *Sala degli Stucchi*, and houses an eclectic collection of medieval and Renaissance art. There's a good display of bronze medallions, including many by the originator of this Renaissance art and its all-time master, Pisanello (one is of Sigismondo Malatesta's muse Isotta degli Atti). Among a number of fine ivories is an alabaster *Passion of Christ* from a 15th-century sculptor of Nottingham. There are also paintings, including two sombre scenes of decapitations by Scarsellino (*John the Baptist* and *Santa Margherita*).

Museo Civico Lapidario
open Tues–Sun 9–6; adm includes Palazzo Schifanoia; joint ticket available for Museo della Cattedrale, Palazzina Marfisa d'Este and Palazzo Schifanoia

Santa Maria in Vado
open daily 7.30–12 and 3.30–6

Across the street from the Schifanoia, on the corner of Via Camposabbionario, the **Museo Civico Lapidario** is a small collection of Roman-era funeral stones, sculptures and architectural fragments, along with some fine late Imperial sarcophagi. In the opposite direction, on the corner of Via Borgovado, **Santa Maria in Vado** commemorates a miracle of 1171: a priest was offering Communion when blood spurted from the host and splashed up on the vaulting where it can still be seen.

Palazzo di Lodovico il Moro

South of the Schifanoia, the quiet old district around Via XX Settembre is the city's second planned addition, the Addizione di Borso d'Este (1451). Via XX Settembre follows the old course of the Po; the round stones used to pave the streets and in some of the houses came from the dried-up riverbed. At No.124 is the elegant **Palazzo Costabili**, better known as the Palazzo di Lodovico il Moro. Designed by Biagio Rossetti, it was erroneously named after Beatrice d'Este's Milanese husband, though it never belonged to him, but to Antonio Costabili, the Este's ambassador to Milan. It has frescoes by Garofalo;

Palazzo Costabili
Via XX Settembre 124, ***t*** *(0532) 66299; open Tues–Sun 9–2; adm includes Museo Archeologico*

upstairs is an excellent **Museo Archeologico Nazionale**, housing a collection of finds from the ancient necropolis of the Graeco-Etruscan seaport of Spina, near Comacchio, including Attic vases (one of the largest collections of red-figure vases anywhere, some by the noted painters of Athens, as well as Etruscan copies of the Greek work). There is also a splendid gold diadem and two canoes carved from tree trunks in the later Roman period.

Museo dell'Architettura
t (0532) 742 332; open daily 10–1 and 3–6; closed for restoration at the time of writing

If you like Biagio Rossetti's work, just down the street at No.152 you can see the modest house he built for himself, the Casa Rossetti, now home to the **Museo dell'Architettura**.

Sant'Antonio in Polesine

Sant'Antonio in Polesine
open Mon–Fri 9.30–11.30 and 3–5, Sat 9.30–11.15 and 3–4; daily at 7am mass with Gregorian chants; adm by donation

From Via XX Settembre, take Vicolo del Gambone right down to the city wall for one of the best surprises Ferrara has to offer. Few tourists ever make it to the convent of Sant'Antonio in Polesine, but just ring the bell by the door and you're likely to get a complete guided tour from a remarkably learned nun.

Built on an island in the Po before the river changed its course, Sant'Antonio was founded in 1257. It was a cloistered convent, and so the church is divided into a *chiesa esterna* for the public, with a grand Baroque interior including a *trompe l'œil* ceiling by Francesco Ferrari, and a *chiesa interna* for the sisters only, which has three chapels entirely covered with some of the best early painting in Ferrara. The left one, by an unknown follower of Giotto, has the *Early Life of Jesus* on a dark background, where the Three Kings ride on horseback (because he couldn't draw camels); other scenes show a long-haired *Magdalene, St Dionysus* with the sun and moon, and an illustration of the old legend in which Mary hands down her girdle to St Thomas from Heaven. The centre chapel, with vaulting painted in grotesques by Bastianino, has an *Annunciation* by the Ferrarese painter Panetti, and saints from other artists of the 1400s and later. On the right, an unknown 14th-century Bolognese painter added the *Passion*, with Jesus harrowing Hell at the lower right (John the Baptist comes out first), and, in a very rare bit of medieval iconography, Jesus ascending to Heaven on a ladder.

San Giorgio
open daily 7–12 and 3–6.30

Just outside this corner of the walls (through the Porta Romana), and over the Po di Volano, **San Giorgio** was Ferrara's original cathedral until the 12th century; the current building, mostly from the 1400s, houses the sumptuous 1475 *Tomb of Lorenzo Roverella*, Pope Julius II's physician. Also buried here is Cosmè Tura.

The Herculean Addition

North of the Castello Estense stretches the Herculean Addition, laid out by Biagio Rossetti for Ercole I, which more than doubled the size of 15th-century Ferrara. Not long after the fall of the Este dynasty travellers noted that many of the streets here were abandoned and overgrown, and even today they feel somewhat melancholy. Corso Ercole I, extending north from the Castello Estense, was intended as the new district's 'noble street', and it attracted many to build palaces in the area, including the **Palazzo Naselli-Crispi**, by Girolamo da Carpi, just off the Corso on Via Borgo dei Leoni. Next to it, Ferrara's Jesuit church, the 1570 **Chiesa del Gesù** holds paintings by Bastarolo and Giuseppe Maria Crespi, and a painted terracotta group of the *Deposition* where the figures have the faces of Ercole I and members of his court.

Chiesa del Gesù
open Mon–Sat 8–11.30 and 5–7, Sun and hols 7.30–1 and 5–7

Back on the Corso, north of Via degli Armari, is the **Palazzo Giulio d'Este**, built for the fellow who spent his life imprisoned in the Castello, and never got to enjoy it. At the centre of the Addition, where the Corso meets Corso Rossetti/Corso Porta Mare, Biagio Rossetti built three big palaces, the **Palazzo Prosperi-Sacrati**, the **Palazzo Turchi di Bagno**, and the new home of the Este dukes, the **Palazzo dei Diamanti**.

Palazzo dei Diamanti: the Pinacoteca Nazionale

Palazzo dei Diamanti
t (0532) 205 844, www.pinacotecaferrara.it; open Tues, Wed, Fri, Sat 9–2, Thurs 9–7, Sun and hols 9–1; adm

Rossetti's showpiece takes its name from the 8,500 pointed, diamond-shaped stones that stud the façade – diamonds being an emblem of the Este. This unusual building took 74 years to complete, and there's more art in its design than first appear. The little diamonds are not all the same; those on the upper levels are pointed slightly upwards, while the lowest are pointed downwards, in order to reflect as much light as possible. The building as a whole, like the other palaces at this crossroads, was designed to be considered not from straight on, but from the corner angle, highlighting the elegant reliefs and balcony (the Ferraresi called this intersection the '**Quadrivio degli Angeli**'; Rossetti's idea of making a street corner, instead of a piazza, into an urban centrepiece was carried on in Rome's Quattro Fontane and Palermo's Quattro Canti).

The Palazzo houses the **Pinacoteca Nazionale**, a collection mainly of works by the Ferrara school. The museum itinerary doesn't follow a strict chronology. It begins with a private collection maintained intact, the Collezione Vendeghini-Baldi, with fine 14th-century and early Renaissance painting, most of it by painters from elsewhere: Mantegna, Giovanni Bellini, Gentile da Fabriano and Giovanni da Modena, as well as a *Madonna* and *San Petronio* by Ercole de' Roberti (other works by a certain 'Vicino da Ferrara' are also thought to be by de' Roberti).

Next come rooms of Ferraresi from the quattrocento, including several little-known artists with accomplished and distinctive styles: an unknown 'Maestro Ferrarese' and 'Maestro GZ', who contributes a *Trinità* which is reminiscent of Masaccio's famous one in Florence. There's a 'Maestro degli Occhi Spalancati' (Master of the Wide-open

Pleasures of a Moment

Few cities made a greater contribution to the life and art of the quattrocento than Ferrara, but after touring the city, and perusing the great works of the Palazzo Schifanoia and the museums, you may still leave feeling a little unsatisfied. Somehow there should be more.

For an example of why there isn't, consider Cosmè Tura. For one thing, Tura's job as court painter ironically left him little time to paint. The surviving records of the Este show that Duke Borso and Duke Ercole kept him busy designing stage sets, furniture, ceremonial costumes, tableware, cartoons for tapestries, banners, armour for mock tournaments and trappings for the horses, lavish decorations for parties and every sort of luxury trinket. Under Alfonso I and Ercole II, this same job would be taken over by Dosso Dossi, often in collaboration with the great poet Ariosto. He didn't get much chance to paint in Ferrara either.

Such works as Tura and his contemporaries did manage to complete are now dispersed among the museums of Europe and America, while any number of frescoes in Ferrara were doubtlessly wantonly destroyed, like those in the Schifanoia, in the centuries that followed. It is just an example of the indifference that later ages would show towards the real Renaissance of art – the spontaneity, colour and brilliant imagination of the quattrocento, as opposed to the art of virtuosity and authority in the 1500s that the critics came to call the 'High Renaissance'. In the changing tides of taste and fashion, this set of blinkers didn't start to come off until the time of the British pre-Raphaelites and John Ruskin, a century and a half ago.

The loss makes it that much harder to imagine the rarified world of the Este court and its artists. And not only paintings were lost. One reason the Herculean Addition is so big is that it was intended as a spacious, aristocratic district of palaces and parks. The Este were mad about gardens. Besides the orange grove on the roof of their palace, about all that survives of their projects, all the entrances to the city were beautifully landscaped – aesthetic but utilitarian as well, a kind of political propaganda designed to convey the image of a refined, orderly, well-run state. The northern wall was bordered by parks, with avenues designed to frame the towers of the Castello in the distance, and the Castello itself had a big park on its northern side. For anyone arriving by the Po, their introduction to the city would be the dukes' own hideaway, Belvedere Island, with groves and pavilions, fountains and a menagerie.

One of the pavilions was Leonello's legendary Belfiore, a masterpiece of carved wood and stone where Tura and others created a series of paintings of the Muses to inspire the ducal fancy. Nothing remains; two of Tura's magical muses survive in London's National Gallery (one mistakenly called *La Primavera*), and other works from the Belfiore (demolished 1634) have either been wrecked or are scattered round the world. The island itself, like so much else in Ferrara, has disappeared completely, lost between the ambitions of later builders and the shifting courses of the Po.

Eyes) and a 'Maestro degli Occhi Ammiccanti' (Master of the Winking Eyes), painter of a delightful coy *Vergine con il Bambino*; he may have also done the odd *Sepoltura del Cristo* (Burial of Christ), where no one in the picture seems overly concerned about what is taking place. Cosmè Tura weighs in with two *tondi*, the *Giudizio e Martirio di San Maurelio*, originally parts of a predella. Two of the Muses from the lost Belfiore palace have survived, *Erato* and *Urania*, by unknown artists.

From the Ferrarese cinquecento, the sweet Raphaelesque Garofalo (a favourite of the 18th-century critics) surprises with the fantastically complex iconography of his *Antico e Nuovo Testamento* from the church of Sant'Andrea. Other pieces from Ferrara's late Renaissance include works of Bastianino (Sebastiano Filippi), a series of *Fifteen Saints* by Girolamo da Carpi and Garofalo from the monastery of San Giorgio, Dosso Dossi's *Massacre of the Innocents*, and two interesting *City Views* by Girolamo Marchesi.

Later paintings include several works by Scarsellino, one of the last notable artists of the Ferrara school, and some dramatic religious scenes from the late Baroque Uberto and Gaetano Gandolfi. Among the many fine works by non-Ferrarese artists is Carpaccio's *Death of the Virgin*, two landscapes by Hubert Robert, and two works by the little-known Venetian Antonio Maria Marini (*b.* 1668), a *Marina in Barrasca* and *Battaglia su un Ponte*, with a dark strangeness.

Galleria Civica d'Arte Moderna
open only during exhibitions; adm exp

Museo Michelangelo Antonioni
open Tues–Sun 9–1 and 3–6; adm; closed at the time of writing

Museo del Risorgimento e della Resistenza
open Tues–Sun 9–6; adm

For information on all three of the above, call **t** *(0532) 244 949; joint ticket available*

On the ground floor of the palace is the **Galleria Civica d'Arte Moderna**, with a small collection and temporary exhibitions. A building adjacent to the Palazzo houses the **Museo Michelangelo Antonioni**, containing a multimedia fantasy called the 'Enchanted Mountain' designed by the famous director, along with some of his paintings, and the **Museo del Risorgimento e della Resistenza**.

In the western, less-developed half of the Herculean Addition, Corso Biagio Rossetti leads to Rossetti's **San Benedetto** (1496), which was almost completely rebuilt according to original designs after it was bombed in the war. Just to the north on Via Ariosto is the **Casa di Ariosto**, which the poet built for himself. 'Small,' he described it modestly, 'but suited to me.'

Casa di Ariosto
open Tues–Sat 10–1 and 3–6, Sun and hols 10–1; adm free

North of the Quadrivio degli Angeli, Corso Ercole I passes two more Rossetti palaces at Via Arianuova, the **Palazzo Trotti-Mosti** and **Palazzo Guarini Giordani**; both are now part of Ferrara University. A little further on is the last of Ferrara's palaces, the 1913 **Palazzina degli Angeli**, built by a Ferrarese named Adamo Boari who spent his career as one of the leading architects of Mexico City, and came back home in his later years.

Civic Museums of Modern Art

Botanical Garden
open Mon–Fri 9–1, Tues and Thurs till 5; adm free

Musei Civici d'Arte Moderna e Contemporanea
t *(0532) 209 988; open Tues–Sun 9–1 and 3–6; adm; joint ticket available*

Museo Giovanni Boldini e dell'Ottocento
t *(0532) 209 988; open Tues–Sun 9–1 and 3–6; adm; joint ticket available*

To the east of the Quadrivio degli Angeli on Corso Porta Mare, behind the Palazzo Turchi-Bagni, is the University's small **Botanical Garden**. Across the street stands the complex of the **Palazzo Massari**, housing two museums. First is the **Musei Civici d'Arte Moderna e Contemporanea**, dedicated to the Metaphysical School and covering the origins of the movement in Ferrara, though most of the works are by a later painter, Ferrara's Filippo de Pisis, obsessed with still lifes and streetscapes in yellow and grey. Other notable artists present include Arnoldo Bonzaghi and the painter-sculptor Roberto Melli.

Pass through the courtyard, with a sculpture by Man Ray called the *Monument au Peintre Inconnu*, to reach the Palazzina dei Cavalieri di Malta, seat of the Knights of Malta in 1826–34, which contains the **Museo Giovanni Boldini e dell'Ottocento**, dedicated to the works of Ferrara's very own Paris salon painter, a fellow in 'imperial moustaches' who was quite fashionable in the *belle époque*; Verdi dedicated *Otello* to him. Boldini started to be influenced by French modern painting in the 1890s, but he shouldn't have bothered; he was born to paint fancy women in evening gowns. And it was a great age for evening gowns, modelled in his portraits by countesses, an infanta of Spain, and various great ladies of France and Italy. There's a portrait of Degas (and one by Degas of Boldini), and scenes of Montmartre, as well as works of Boldini's followers and contemporaries – near-photographic portraits of vacant faces, and plenty of works that would have been perfect for cigar-box lids; a dissenting paintbrush is wielded by Boldini's eccentric contemporary Gaetano Previati. Extending behind the Palazzo, its gardens have been preserved as central Ferrara's largest park, the **Parco Massari**.

Across from the Palazzo Massari is the only piazza in Rossetti's plan for the Herculean Addition, the spacious and serene **Piazza Ariostea**, embellished with a statue of *Ariosto* set atop a tall column (1883). The Piazza is the site of the city's biggest festival each year, the Palio di San Giorgio, during which it in fact hosts four *palii* – one for boys, one for girls, one for horses and one for donkeys. Rossetti built one of his finest palaces, the arcaded **Palazzo Rondinelli**, on the southern side of the park. On the west side, the **Palazzo Bevilaqua** (1499) was originally Palazzo Strozzi, built by a branch of the great banking family of Florence; between the two palaces is the 1613 **Chiesa della Stigmata**, with a painting of *St Francis* by Guercino inside.

Certosa
t (0532) 205 619, www.amsefc.it/certosa/index.html; open daily 7.30am–7.30pm

Via Borso, a quiet lane lined with colourful flower shops, leads north from here to the **Cimitero Monumentale**, covering a vast expanse in the northeast corner of the walls. The city put the undeveloped land to this use in the early 19th century, incorporating the **Certosa**, a Carthusian monastery founded by Borso d'Este in 1452. Its church of **San Cristoforo**, designed by Rossetti, is embellished with a huge luck-giving *St Christopher*, and contains the tombs of Borso and Marfisa d'Este. Florid 19th-century mausolea and monuments surround the church – Giovanni Boldini gets two of the biggest. Part of the cemetery complex is the **Cimitero Ebraico**, along the walls by Corso Porta Mare, founded in the 17th century when Ferrara had a considerable Jewish population, many of them refugees from Spain; strewn with wild flowers, it is one of the prettiest spots in the city.

The Walls

Ferrara's formidable 9km circuit of red-brick walls, begun under the direction of Rossetti between 1493 and 1505, was one of the prototypes for the new-model fortifications of the Renaissance, designed to withstand artillery assaults. Most of the rest was completed under Alfonso I. Both parts have a moat (which survives in part on the east side), and a low wall with a higher earth embankment behind it, planted with trees to hold it together. They date from the 15th and 16th centuries, and the best stretch is between the eastern end of the Corso Porta Mare and the former Porta degli Angeli, built by Rossetti, on the north side of the city. Cycle paths run along their length, linked with routes into the city and out to the Po.

Activities in Ferrara

Ferrara has its own *Palio* or traditional horse race, every year on the last Sunday in May. It isn't nearly as well known as the one in Siena, but can be more fun (see p.252).

The **Ferrara Buskers' Festival**, **t** (0532) 249 337, *www.ferrarabuskers.com*, is held in the last week in August, when buskers from all over the world come to perform in the streets in the centre of town.

Ferrara Musica, **t** (0532) 202 675, *www.ferraramusica.org*, is an international season of concerts and opera which runs from September to May. Venues include the fine Teatro Comunale.

Ferrara Sotto le Stelle, **t** (0532) 241 194, *www.ferrarasottolestelle.it*, is an alternative-rock music festival held in Piazza Castello during the last week of June and the first three weeks of July.

Where to Stay in Ferrara

ⓘ Ferrara > *in the Castello Estense,* **t** *(0532) 299 303, or Piazza Municipale 11,* **t** *(0532) 419 474, infotur@provincia.fe.it, www.ferraraterraeacqua.it; open daily 9–1 and 2–6*

Ferrara ✉ 44100

Most of Ferrara's hotels are accessible to wheelchair users, except where indicated.

Luxury (€€€€€)

*******Duchessa Isabella**, Via Palestro 70, **t** (0532) 202 121, *www.duchessa isabella.it*. A member of the Relais & Châteaux group. In a magnificent Renaissance palace in the heart of the city. No detail has been overlooked; antiques and crystals furnish the old rooms, some of which still have frescoes by the Ferrara school and coffered ceilings. There's an excellent restaurant, and a lovely private park; guests can use the hotel's bicycles and horse-drawn carriage. *Closed Aug.*

Expensive (€€€€)

******Annunziata**, Piazza Repubblica 5, **t** (0532) 201 111, *www.annunziata.it*. Elegant hotel with big windows overlooking the Castello Estense and very comfortable rooms; with bikes and email services.

******Astra**, Viale Cavour 55, **t** (0532) 206 088, *www.astrahotel.com*. A solidly comfortable, well-furnished hotel on the main street to the station. Also has a fine restaurant.

Moderate (€€€)

******Ripagrande**, Via Ripagrande 21, **t** (0532) 765 250, *www.ripagrandehotel.it*. Memorable hotel in the medieval quarter in the Renaissance Beccari-Freguglia palace. The ground floor has original décor, old brick walls, marble stairs and heavy-beamed ceilings. The 40 rooms above are all modern, equipped with kitchenettes and sitting rooms, air conditioning and TV. There's also a pleasant inner courtyard, where you can have breakfast outside, or dine by candlelight. The restaurant has local cuisine; parking and bicycle hire are other pluses.

******Villa Regina**, Via Comacchio 402, at Cocomaro di Cona, **t** (0532) 740 222, *www.villaregina.it*. An idyllic urban escape within easy reach of the city in a beautiful converted villa situated in a splendid parkland. It has a restaurant too.

*****Europa**, Corso Giovecca 49, **t** (0532) 205 456, *www.hoteleuropaferrara.com*. Verdi stayed in this 17th-century palace near the Palazzo dei Diamanti designed by Biagio Rossetti. Bedrooms are simple but with everything you need including wireless Internet connections; some have frescoes, and the lobby is full of 18th-century antiques; there's also a pretty garden courtyard. Two self-catering apartments and some rooms equipped for disabled people. Parking but no restaurant. They have bikes for rent.

*****Carlton**, Via Garibaldi 93, **t** (0532) 211 130, *www.hotelcarlton.net*. A peaceful, family-run hotel usefully placed near the Duomo with fine rooms with TV, phone and Internet; restaurant and bike rental.

*****Touring**, Viale Cavour 11, **t** (0532) 206 200, *www.hoteltouringfe.it*. Modern hotel placed by the castle has the advantage of an underground car park as well as air conditioning in the rooms.

Inexpensive (€€)

****San Paolo**, Via Baluardi 9, **t** (0532) 762 040, *www.hotelsanpaolo.it*. Pleasantly situated and completely refurbished hotel near the city walls beside Piazza Travaglio, with good rooms and service. Bikes available.

****Santo Stefano**, Via Santo Stefano 21, **t** (0532) 206 924. Bright and pleasant rooms, nearly all of which are en suite. Bikes available. *Not wheelchair accessible.*

Budget (€)

***Casa Degli Artisti**, Via Vittoria 66, **t** (0532) 761 038. The best of the cheapest options: located right in the centre of town, on a quiet side street near the Duomo. Most rooms are without private bathrooms. Not wheelchair accessible.

Ostello Estense, Corso B. Rossetti 24, **t** (0532) 204 227, *hostelferrara@hotmail.com*. Youth hostel in a Renaissance building close to the centre of Ferrara. *Temporarily closed at time of writing but due to re-open.*

Eating Out in Ferrara

Ferrara's most famous dish (the favourite of Lucrezia Borgia) is spicy *salama da sugo* – a sausage that is cured for a year, then gently boiled for about four hours and eaten with a spoon. The bakers of Ferrara are famous for their X-shaped bread, *ciupèta*; little caps of pasta, *cappelletti*, often filled with pumpkin, are another local speciality. When Renée of France came to Ferrara she brought her own vines, the origin of the local viticulture and the delicious *Vino di Bosco*.

Very Expensive–Expensive (€€€–€€€€)

Il Don Giovanni, Corso Ercole I d'Este 1, **t** (0532) 243 363, *www.ildongiovanni.com*. Superb restaurant located in the 18th-century former stock exchange. The menu changes weekly to take advantage of fresh seasonal ingredients: imaginative sea and land food are on offer, often full of delicious surprises in unusual combinations; great desserts, cheese and wine list. *Booking essential. Closed Sun eve and Mon.*

Max, Piazza della Repubblica 16, **t** (0532) 209 309. In town, with tables on the terrace facing the Castello Estense. The best place for fish dishes in Ferrara. Well-prepared seafood, from *antipasti* (*carpaccio* of smoked swordfish), to pasta, to the main course (*sampietro* in a thick clam sauce), followed by chocolate mousse. *Booking advisable. Closed Mon, 1 week Jan and 2 weeks Aug.*

L'Oca Giuliva, Via Boccacanale-di Santo Stefano, **t** (0532) 207 628. Good wine and commendable food, with a traditional menu featuring such items as *pasticcio di maccheroni alla ferrarese*, *salama da sugo* and *cappellacci di zucca*; the other menu changes every two weeks. There is also a list of some 250 wines to choose from. *Booking advisable. Closed Mon, Tues lunch, 2 weeks Sept and 10 days end Dec.*

Quel Fantastico Giovedì, Via Castelnuovo 9 (near Piazza del Travaglio), **t** (0532) 760 570. Intimate, creative restaurant featuring a range of dishes prepared with an effortlessly light touch – you can dine well here on the likes of salmon marinated in herbs, *fritto misto*, steamed prawns or squid stuffed with aubergines in a yellow pepper sauce, and game dishes in season. Save room for dessert – the chocolatey ones especially. The name of the restaurant, 'What a Wonderful Thursday', comes from a story by John Steinbeck. *Booking essential. Closed Wed, late Jan and mid-July–mid-Aug.*

Antica Trattoria Il Cucco >

Moderate (€€)

Antica Trattoria Il Cucco, Via Voltacasotto 3, off Via C. Mayr, **t** (0532) 760 026, *www.trattoriailcucco.it*. This is a rewarding place to indulge in traditional classics on the lines of *cappellacci con la zucca* and, if you book ahead, *salama da sugo* or *pasticcio alla ferrarese* for *secondi*, followed perhaps by *ciambella* and a sweet wine. *Closed Wed.*

Al Brindisi, Via Adelardi, **t** (0532) 209 142, *www.albrindisi.com*. Hidden behind the cathedral. Supposedly the oldest *osteria* in the world (there's been one on this spot since 1453). Now a convivial old wood-panelled *enoteca* with a fine selection of cheeses, *salama da sugo* and other treats. Special tasting, working (lunchtimes only), traditional, vegetarian and shepherds' menus. *Closed Mon.*

Il Testamento del Porco ('the Pig's Will'), Via del Mulinetto 109, **t** (0532) 760 460, *testporco@tin.it*. Just outside the walls by the hippodrome, this is a perennially popular place for typical offerings of Ferrarese cuisine: minestrone, home-made tagliatelle with *porcini* mushrooms; pork in various guises, ostrich and fillet of beef with balsamic vinegar. *Booking advisable. Closed Sat lunch, Sun and mid-Feb–mid-Mar.*

Inexpensive (€)

La Grande Muraglia, Corso Porta Po 172, **t** (0532) 205 445. Good Chinese food is on offer here, but perhaps even more remarkably a glass floor with an aquarium beneath your feet.

Enotria, Via Saraceno 39, **t** (0532) 209 166. One of the fancier *enoteche*, with a fine selection as well as *bruschetta* and *crostini*. *Closed Sun in summer and Mon in winter.*

Entertainment and Nightlife in Ferrara

A university town, Ferrara is quite lively at night. Listings of forthcoming programmes in the cinema and theatre in addition to other events can be found in the local newspaper, *La Nuova Ferrara*.

Bar Ariosto, Piazza Ariostea. The happening place for Ferrara's hip young things.

Caffè Europa, Corso Giovecca 51. A worthwhile stopping place for coffee and delicious pastries.

Centro Storico, handily placed near the Duomo. Bar, with a vast spread of nibbles on offer.

Jazz Club Ferrara, Via Rampari di Belfiore, **t** (0532) 211 573, *www.jazzclubferrara.com*. Wine, food and music.

Around Ferrara

Leaving Ferrara heading east takes you immediately into the flat and watery world of the Po delta. To the southeast, **Voghenza** was Ferrara's predecessor, site of a Roman town that has almost completely disappeared; the bishop's seat was transferred to Ferrara's San Giorgio in the 6th century. Finds from Voghenza's necropoli are kept in the Antiquarium in the nearby castle of **Belriguardo**, built for Nicolò III in 1435. Argenta, on the river Reno to the southeast, has an attractive quattrocento church of San Domenico, now housing a small art gallery, with works by Garofalo, Scarsellino and others. Some towns in Italy were burned by the Germans in the Second World War, but **Argenta** was the only one to be flooded by them, after the Allies had already bombed it to pieces. Just across the river Reno from the town is the tiny Romanesque **Pieve di San Giorgio**, with a carved portal showing *St George* and the

Labours of the Months (1112). All the area around the church is part of the Parco del Delta del Po (*see* p.257). This section, the **Oasi di Campotto**, is one of the last completely untouched wetlands in the Delta, where thousands of birds nest among the water lilies (including the rare black tern); it has been set aside as an important wildlife preserve and is well documented in the environmental and cultural museum **Museo delle Valli d'Argenta**.

Museo delle Valli d'Argenta
t *(0532) 808 058, www.atlantide.net; open Tues–Sun summer 9.30–6; rest of year 9.30–1 and 3.30–6; adm*

Due east of Ferrara, the last town before the coast is **Codigoro**, a friendly, hard-working place where the promenade on the Po di Verano has a Venetian-style Bishop's Palace (Bishop of Comacchio) from the 1700s. Codigoro was the centre for all the land reclamation projects carried out in this part of the Po delta, in medieval times (there's a tower built by the counts of Canossa as part of a water control scheme), and again since 1860; the town has a **Monument to the *Scariolanti***, the 'wheelbarrow-pushers' – all the local men who dug the drainage canals by hand over the decades and made this territory flourish again. A landmark on the outskirts of town is the **Garzaia**, the 'City of the Herons', the gardens of an abandoned sugar factory that has become a favourite nesting spot for hundreds of these birds, who come back each spring; it is now a protected area.

Where to Stay and Eat Around Ferrara

Argenta ✉ 44011

******Villa Reale**, 16a Viale Roiti 16/a, **t** (0532) 852 334, *www.hotelvillareale.it* (€€€). Liberty-style villa converted into a 30-room hotel, in peaceful surroundings only a few minutes from the Oasi di Campotto. Rooms are air-conditioned and comfortable with phone, Internet and TV; no restaurant; wheelchair accessible.

Ostellato ✉ 44020

******Villa Belfiore**, Via Pioppa 27, **t** (0533) 681 164, *www.turismoruralebelfiore.it* (€€€). Between Argenta and Codigoro. Ten rooms in a big house furnished with old Persian carpets and antiques; they also have a pool in the park and a beauty centre. Restaurant with seasonal and vegetarian dishes, and *menu de degustazione*.

★ **Locanda della Tamerice** >

Locanda della Tamerice, Via Argine Mezzano 2, **t** (0533) 680 795, *www.locandadellatamerice.com* (€€€€). Charming, colourful, and one of the top restaurants in the province, headed by renowned chef Igles Corelli. The cold spaghetti with vegetables and shellfish and the *zuppa di pesce* are perfect, and there's a choice of meat dishes and unusual desserts. *Booking essential. Closed Mon, Tues, Wed and 2 weeks Jan.*

Codigoro ✉ 44021

La Capanna da Eraclio, Via per le Venezie 21 (Loc. Ponte Vicini), **t** (0533) 712 154 (€€€€). A particularly welcoming place, run by a family: they do wonderful things to seafood, raw or cooked, or with pasta; try the chef's speciality *anguilla* (eels) '*arost in umad*' and wonderful desserts. *Booking advisable. Closed Wed eve, Thurs and a few weeks Aug–Sept.*

Volano di Codigoro ✉ 41018

*****Hotel Cannevié**, on the Volano road, **t** (0533) 719 103, *www.cannevie.it* (€€). In a big old fisherman's house on a small wetlands nature reserve. With two restaurants: one, **Porticino**, on a little island, has been a fishing house since the 16th century (*closed Tues*). The other, **Restaurant Canneviè**, closes on Mon. Both serve local fish specialities. Bike hire is also available.

The Coast: From the Po to Ravenna

For most people the main attractions along this coast are the Po delta and the magnificent Romanesque Abbey of Pomposa, though there are plenty of Italian family lidos in the vicinity if you're tempted to join the summer ice cream, pizza and parasol brigades.

The Southern Po Delta

Ferrara's portion, the southern half of the Po delta, is only a part of the broad swathe of wetlands that closes the northern end of Italy's Adriatic coast. Other rivers, like the Brenta, pour down from the Alps here too, creating the lagoon of Venice – that city is only 50km away. The Emilia-Romagna stretch of coast begins with **Mesola**, on a branch of the river called the Po di Goro, just south of the main branch.

Mesola's landmark is its **Castello**, the last of the *delizie* of the Este, designed for Alfonso II as a hunting and fishing lodge in 1563 by Giovanni Battista Aleotti and not completed until twenty years later. The unusual structure, a square with four towers set diagonally at the corners, is surrounded by a half-hexagon of arcaded buildings, originally quarters for the Duke's guests; the space between now hosts a busy market on Saturdays. Now a centre for environmental education, the castle often hosts special exhibitions; on the first floor there are rooms decorated with ceramics by the local artist Cesare Laurenti (*d.* 1926).

Parco del Delta del Po
www.parcodeltapo.it

Alfonso II was the first to start draining the marshes south of the Po Delta. Much of the land was planted with rice; a large part of the rest now belongs to the **Parco del Delta del Po**, a regional park that is one of Italy's most important wetlands and a birdwatcher's paradise, especially in spring and autumn: prominent among the 200 species sighted here are flamingos, coots, grebes, herons, a vast assortment of ducks, black-winged stilts, and owls in the wooded sections; the white Camargue horse has also been introduced.

Bosco di Mesola
open Sun and hols only 8am–sunset, Mar–Oct

Part of the primordial coastal pine forest – preserved as the Este's old hunting grounds – survives intact in the **Bosco di Mesola**, now a nature reserve, home to fallow deer, storks, spoonbills and hundreds of other birds. Not far to the west, near Italba, this varied and ever-changing coastline offers something completely different – a marooned 100-acre patch of dunes, once part of the coast, called the **Moraro**.

Excursion boats
*Freccia del Delta, **t** (0533) 999 817; Principessa, **t** (0533) 999 815*

Excursion boats ply the small, narrow canals between the reeds and explore the Sacco di Goro, the mouth of the Po di Goro and the Valle di Gorino, departing from the picturesque fishing hamlets of **Gorino**, **Goro** or **Mesola**. This is also a big area for oysters and their feathered enemies, the oystercatchers.

Down the Coast

The Abbey of Pomposa

The Abbey of Pomposa
t (0533) 719 152; open daily 8.30–7; adm; adm free to church

South of Mesola, the SS309 continues down to the haunting and serene Abbey of Pomposa. Some time in the troubled 6th century the early Benedictines founded their community here, lost among the trackless islets of the Po delta. Besides being relatively safe from invaders, the fertile delta lands also offered shovel-wielding

Getting along the Coast from Po to Ravenna

Buses from Ferrara radiate to the flatlands of the coast. Ferrara's ACFT also run services from Mesola and Codigoro to Ravenna (for information, **t** (0532) 599 411, *www.acft.it*).

Note that there is no convenient bus from anywhere to the Abbey of Pomposa; for that you'll need a car. If you have one, a new fast **road** now leads directly from just south of Ferrara to the beaches past Comacchio. There it meets the coast road, the SS309, between Chioggia and Ravenna. Another, slower road also runs from Ferrara to the coast, the SS495, which passes the Abbey of Pomposa.

Benedictines a chance to work and prosper. Hard work turned to Dark Age opulence in the 10th century, when donations from Emperors Otto I and Otto II gave Pomposa rights in the most valuable property of the region, the salt pans of Comacchio. Things got better; later rulers piled on more rights and donations, and by 1050 Pomposa's abbot was lord of 49 dependent churches and monasteries as well as huge territories in the delta, in and around Ravenna, and as far away as Pavia in Lombardy. By this time the Abbey was a noted centre of culture, with one of the biggest libraries in Italy; in this atmosphere of total tranquillity the monk Guido d'Arezzo invented the modern musical scale in the early 11th century.

Pomposa's fall was just as complete as its ascent. The rise of the medieval *comuni* cut into its power and its revenues, and when floods caused the 1152 shift in the course of the Po they created large areas of swampland around the abbey. By 1340 it was a ghost of its former self, plagued with malaria and ruled by a *commendatore* from outside. Closing a history of a thousand years, the last monks left in 1553, finding a new home at San Benedetto in Ferrara.

The abbey is dwarfed by its great **campanile**, visible for miles around the delta. It was built in 1063 by an architect named Deusdedit and adorned with a unique series of mullioned windows, which progress tier by tier from a narrow slit on the bottom to a grand *quadrifore* (four arches) on top, a brilliant device that adds grace and lightness to the tower. The *patere*, painted majolica medallions that decorate the tower and other parts of the building, are all modern replacements (such things don't wear well); the originals were imported from Tebtunis, a Benedictine monastery in the oasis of al-Faiyum in Egypt that specialized in such ceramics. You'll see others like these in churches all over Italy, especially along the Adriatic coast. Oriental influence here is also shown in the striped Moorish arches of the windows, the blind arcading and the decorative patterns of brick, reminders of just how much early medieval Europe owed to the more advanced art and architecture, both Christian and Muslim, of the Middle East, North Africa and Spain.

The **church**, begun in the 8th century and taking its final form in the 11th, is the heir to the great basilicas of Ravenna, and was probably created by architects and builders from that city, using numerous Byzantine columns, capitals and decorative stonework recycled from earlier buildings. The entrance is through a lovely **atrium**, decorated with patterned brick, reliefs and terracotta in the same manner as the courtyard of Santo Stefano in Bologna. The reliefs' stylization is heavily influenced by the Coptic art of Egypt. Inside the church itself are some ghostly Byzantine-style saints from the original fresco decoration, probably from the 1100s. There are two baptismal fonts, one carved from an early Byzantine capital, the other a strangely primitive work of the 12th century, and a magnificent **pavement**, with maze-like circular designs and mosaic trim, including a strip of fantastical beasts, all done in marble intarsia by artists probably from Ravenna; most of it is 12th-century, though the part nearest the altar is the oldest thing in the abbey, surviving from an earlier church of the 500s.

For all that, the chief glory of Pomposa is its colourful 14th-century **frescoes** that cover nearly all its walls, the most complete and most ambitious fresco cycle of this period in Emilia-Romagna. They were the last major embellishment of the Abbey, added when it was already in serious decline. Many are by Vitale da Bologna, including the faded *Last Judgement* on the west wall, with an imperial dignity and decorum the artist may have picked up from the great works of Ravenna; Vitale is also credited with the *Maestà* (Christ in Majesty, surrounded by a mandorla) in the apse, surrounded by angels and saints, and the scenes below of the *Evangelists*, *Doctors of the Church* and the *Life of Sant'Eustachio*, an extremely popular medieval fairy-tale hagiography – see the saint, a Roman officer, with his famous vision of Christ between the horns of a stag while hunting; his adventures with pirates, lions and wolves; and finally the entire family's martyrdom in a bronze bull with a roaring fire underneath, while Emperor Hadrian looks on.

The frescoes on the walls of the nave, attributed mostly to unknown artists of Bologna, give us the entire *Old Testament*, in the upper band, starting from the right of the altar, and the corresponding stories of the *New Testament* on the lower, with scenes from the *Apocalypse* below them, around the arches, all very much like the scheme that later artists would use in Parma Cathedral. Note the unusual scene of the story of Noah, where the ark is not a normal ship but a perfect cube (as in various esoteric traditions), floating over the ruins of the drowned world.

There are other good frescoes by some of the same artists in the monks' **chapter-house**, including a striking *Crucifixion* on a black background with gilded trim, along with the apostles and various saints, and more in the **refectory**, attributed by some to Giuliano and Pietro da Rimini: a *Last Supper* (where, as often in this region's art, the Apostles sit at a round table), balanced by a scene of the *Miracle of the Abbot Guido* where, dining with a frightened-looking archbishop, Guido calmly turns the water into wine. St Guido Strampiati was abbot here in the mid-11th century and oversaw the building of the tower and the expansion of the abbey church; the archbishop is Geberardo of Ravenna, who was an enemy to Guido throughout his tenure as abbot.

The abbot governed Pomposa from the beautifully austere **Palazzo della Ragione**, built in the 11th century, with the façade substantially altered in the 14th. Originally the palace was connected to the rest of the abbey by other buildings and the whole was surrounded by a high defence wall, now completely disappeared. A **museum** in the Palazzo contains items relating to the monastery, including capitals, architectural fragments and bits of frescoes.

Lidi di Comacchio

The resorts along the sandy **Lidi di Comacchio** begin at the **Lido di Volano** on the other side of the wetlands of the Valle Bertuzzi, where the setting sun ignites the waters in a thousand colours. Valle Bertuzzi is home to a thriving flock of flamingos, one of very few in continental Europe; you can see them nesting from April to October. Of the resorts, the **Lido delle Nazioni** and **Porto Garibaldi** are the most interesting and best equipped. Lido delle Nazioni (in the old days it was called Pialassa, Venetian dialect for 'take it or leave it') has a long artificial lake behind it, a favourite for watersports. Beyond the lake is the beautiful **Spiaggia Romea**, home to a herd of white horses.

Porto Garibaldi's name recalls the defeated hero's refuge here after the fall of the Roman Republic in 1849. He was trying to reach Venice, the only place in Italy still free after the collapse of the revolutionary movements that began in 1848. While hiding in the marshes with Austrian troops on his trail, he lost his pregnant wife Anita, the brave Brazilian woman who fought beside him through his battles on two continents; when she died the Austrians were so close he didn't have time to bury her. There's a monument to Anita along the SS309.

Of all the lidi on this stretch of coast, Porto Garibaldi is the closest to being a real town. It's a salty, somehow endearing place, where the beach crowd, mostly working folk from Bologna and the other cities, shares space with rusty freighters and a big wholesale fish market along the docks of the canal. Between April and September little **cruise boats** depart from the Portocanale into the Delta, most including a fish lunch in the ticket price.

Cruise boats
Andrea Doria,
***t** (0533) 313 514;*
Vichingo,
***t** (0533) 326 272;*
Delfinus,
***t** (0533) 325 102;*
Albatros,
***t** (0533) 325 010*

To the south, Porto Garibaldi merges into **Lido degli Estensi**, a surprisingly beautiful community full of big pine trees and decorated with stone obelisks. This lido tends to be more upmarket, consisting mostly of holiday villas on shady lanes around the beach.

Comacchio: Piccola Venezia

Comacchio

The most important town in the area is **Comacchio**. Famous for its canals and picturesque brick bridges, Comacchio is reminiscent of Venice in its history too. The town grew up in late Roman times, and while the rest of the Roman world was falling apart Comacchio, on an island surrounded by impassable swamps and salt pans, developed into an important port for salt and fish. Between the 7th and 9th centuries it had one of the Adriatic's biggest fleets, and became an important centre for trade. Venice, however, thought that one Venice in the vicinity was enough, and the larger and more energetic town occupied and destroyed Comacchio more than once. In the late 13th century Comacchio fell into the hands of the Este, who made use of its salt trade to pay the soldiers and build *delizie*.

Thanks to the Venetians, nothing is left of Comacchio's ancient glories, but it is still one of the most charming and distinctive towns in the region, and a delight to explore. In the 17th and 18th centuries, thanks to the salt and fish, Comacchio managed the singular achievement of becoming prosperous under papal rule, leaving it with a modest ensemble of Baroque churches and palaces. The centre of town, where the main Via Folegatti crosses the **Canale Maggiore**, has an 1824 clock tower and the 17th-century **Loggia dei Mercanti**, the old grain market. From here the very Venetian Canale Maggiore leads south to the **Ospedale San Camillo**, currently being lengthily restored to house a Museo delle Culture Umane nel Delta del Po. The **Ponte degli Sbirri** ('bridge of the cops', since it led to the papal prison) crosses over to Via Pescheria, home of the fish market and of Comacchio's famous monumental triple bridge, the **Trepponti**, spanning two of the town's canals; a cardinal legate ordered it up from Ravenna architect Luca Danese in 1634.

Santuario di Santa Maria in Aula Regia
open daily 7.30–12 and 3–7

From the **cathedral** (founded 708, current building 1868), Corso Mazzini leads off to the **Loggiato dei Cappuccini**, one of the longest porticos in Emilia-Romagna, 143 arches on marble columns that serve no purpose but to shade your walk to the **Santuario di Santa Maria in Aula Regia**, a wealthy monastery in Comacchio's opulent Dark Ages, though nothing there now is older than 1665.

Much of the area around the town was drained for farmland in the 1940s, but there is still more than enough water about, in the sodden hinterlands called the **Valli di Comacchio**, now mostly part of the Regional Park. Comacchio is famed for its eels, farmed in the Valli – if you're in the area between September and December you can watch the fishermen scoop them up on their way to the sea. Just west of Comacchio stood its ancestor, the ancient Graeco-Etruscan port of **Spina** (now miles from the sea); there's nothing to see here now, but Spina's rich necropolis produced the prize exhibits in Ferrara's archaeology museum.

Tourist Information on the Po Delta Coast

For information on the park, contact **Consorzio del Parco del Delta del Po**, Via Cavour 11, Comacchio, **t** (0533) 314 003, *www.parcodeltapo.it*.

Sports and Activities on the Po Delta Coast

Aster, Piazza Umberto I 33, Mesola 44026, **t** (0533) 993 688, *astermen@yahoo.com*. They guarantee that you'll see at least 60 species of bird in one of their day-long guided tours, and plenty more if you come in late May.

Where to Stay and Eat on the Po Delta Coast

Mesola ✉ 44026

Ca' Laura, Via Cristina 70, Bosco Mesola, **t** (0533) 794 372, *www.calaura.it* (€). A lovely *agriturismo* close to the Delta del Po, ideal for people who like nature, excursions and fitness. Four rooms and one apartment, plus camping.

Lagosanto (near Pomposa) ✉ 44023

Da Pavani, Borgo Fiocinini 13, **t** (0533) 94182 or 900 069 to book a room (€€). Excellent, aromatic seafood (and meat dishes too): feast on gnocchi with crayfish, steamed seafood, or frogs and eels. Eight rooms (€). *Closed Tues eve, 3 weeks in Jan and 2 weeks in June.*

Porto Garibaldi ✉ 44029

Pacifico da Franco, Via Caduti del Mare 10, **t** (0533) 327 169 (€€€€). Oasis of elegance, cordiality and lovely seafood dishes: crêpes filled with prawns and courgettes, exquisite pasta, grilled eel, sea bass; great wines and desserts. *Closed Mon, Sun eve winter, 2 wks Oct.*

Bagno Sole, Viale dei Mille 28, **t** (0533) 327 924, *www.7lidiweb.com/sole* (€€€). Tables indoors or out where you can dine on well-prepared seafood of character: try the *anguilla* (eel), typical of the Comacchio area. *Closed Mon eve, Tues exc summer and 10 days Nov.*

Comacchio ✉ 44022

****Club Spiaggia Romea**, Via dell'Oasi 2, **t** (0533) 355 366, *www.spiaggiaromea.it* (€€€). By the sea at Lido delle Nazioni. Ideal for sports lovers; simple huts in the pines for accommodation, with nearly every conceivable sport, plus bars and disco. Extra charges for horse riding, bike hire, diving and Land-Rover safaris. *Open June–late Sept.*

*****Caravel**, Viale Leonardo da Vinci 56, Lido di Spina, **t** (0533) 330 106 (€€). Relaxing hotel in a garden setting not far from the beach.

*****Logonovo**, Viale delle Querce 109, **t** (0533) 327 520, *www.hotellogonovo.com* (€€). One of many choices on the Lido degli Estensi: medium-sized, modern and 5mins from the sea; with comfortable rooms and a pool.

*****Pineta**, Viale dei Lecci 2, Lido degli Estensi, **t** (0533) 327 956, *www.hotelplazapineta.it* (€€). Typical, friendly, and near the sea; all rooms have TV, air conditioning and balconies. With restaurant. *Open May–Sept.*

Da Vasco e Giulia, Via L. Muratori 2, **t** (0533) 81252, *www.vascoegiulia.it* (€€). Centrally located, most popular trattoria in town: good simple dishes from land or sea. *Closed Mon and Jan.*

ⓘ **Comacchio >>**
*Via Mazzini 4, **t** (0533) 314 154, www.comune.comacchio.fe.it*

ⓘ **Mesola >**
*Castello, **t** (0533) 993 483, www.comune.mesola.fe.it*

ⓘ **Pomposa >**
*in the abbey grounds, **t** (0533) 719 110, www.pomposa.info. Lidi di Comacchio (summer only), Via Ariosto 10, Lido degli Estensi, **t** (0533) 327 464, iatlidoestensi@comacchio.fe.it*

★ **Pacifico da Franco >**

Ravenna

Tucked away among the art towns of Emilia-Romagna there is one famous city that has nothing to do with Renaissance popes and potentates, Guelphs or Ghibellines, sports cars or socialists. Little, in fact, has been heard from Ravenna in the last thousand years. Before then, however, this little city's career was simply astounding – heir to Rome itself, and for a time the leading city of western Europe. For anyone interested in Italy's shadowy progress through the Dark Ages, this is the place to visit.

Getting to and around Ravenna

By Train

Ravenna is not on the main Adriatic railway line, but there are frequent trains from Florence, Venice, Ancona and Bologna (change at Faenza or Ferrara from other cities). The **station** is in Piazzale Farini, on the eastern edge of the old town next to the ship channel, and a short walk from the centre (*disabled assistance available at the station 8am–8pm*). For information, call **Trenitalia, t** 892021 (*toll free, from Italy only*), *www.trenitalia.com*.

By Bus

The **bus station** is nearby, across the tracks from the train station on Via Darsena (a long walk, but there's a *sottopassaggio*, or underpass, under the tracks for a short cut). The no.2 bus from the train station or Piazza del Popolo goes past Theodoric's Mausoleum, otherwise a half-hour walk from the centre. No.60 or 70 goes to Marina di Ravenna. Buses 4 and 44 (but not minibuses 4 and 44) from the station or Piazza del Popolo go to S. Apollinare in Classe and Mirabilandia. Other buses from the train station or from Piazza del Popolo will take you to Classe or any of Ravenna's nearby lidi. For information, call **ATM, t** (0544) 689 900, *www.atm.ra.it*.

By Road

The main road to Ravenna from Bologna and central Italy, the *autostrada* A14 dir, comes to an end just west of the city where it meets the SS16 between Rimini and Ferrara, which skirts round Ravenna. Drivers approaching from the north and west normally come into the city centre along the Via di Roma, its modern main thoroughfare, which crosses the *circonvallazione* or inner ring road.

At the tourist office you can get keys for the free yellow **bicycles** available at four central locations (*service operates Mon–Sat 8.30–7, Sun 10–4*). New **roads** are being built, old ones closed off, and new **parking** areas being established on the periphery in an effort to encourage bike riding, and bring fresh air into the city centre. Be warned, it's a bit of an old, grey miasma, this storied town, and an easy place to get good and lost whether you're walking, driving or riding a bike.

There's a certain magic in three-digit years. History guards their secrets closely, giving us only occasional glimpses of battling barbarians, careful monks 'keeping alive the flame of knowledge' and local Byzantine dukes and counts doing their best to hold things together. In Italy, the Dark Ages were never quite so dark, never the vacuum most people think. This can be seen in Rome, but much more clearly here, in the only Italian city that not only survived but prospered through those troubled times. In Ravenna's churches, adorned with the finest mosaics ever made, such an interruption as the Dark Ages seems to disappear, and you experience the development of Italian history and art from ancient to medieval times as a continuous and logical process.

Imagining Ravenna in its golden age takes some effort. It was Venice before Venice was invented, an urban island in a lagoon with canals for streets; imperial processions through them must have been stunning. Unlike Venice, it was connected to the mainland by causeways; it contained a mixed population of Italians and Greeks, and its greatest ruler was an illiterate German warrior – the history is somewhat complex. The advancing delta of the many small rivers that pour down from the Apennines gradually dried out all Ravenna's magic, at least on the outside, but step inside the city's ancient monuments, including five sites on UNESCO's Heritage List, and you'll see things you can't see anywhere else in the world.

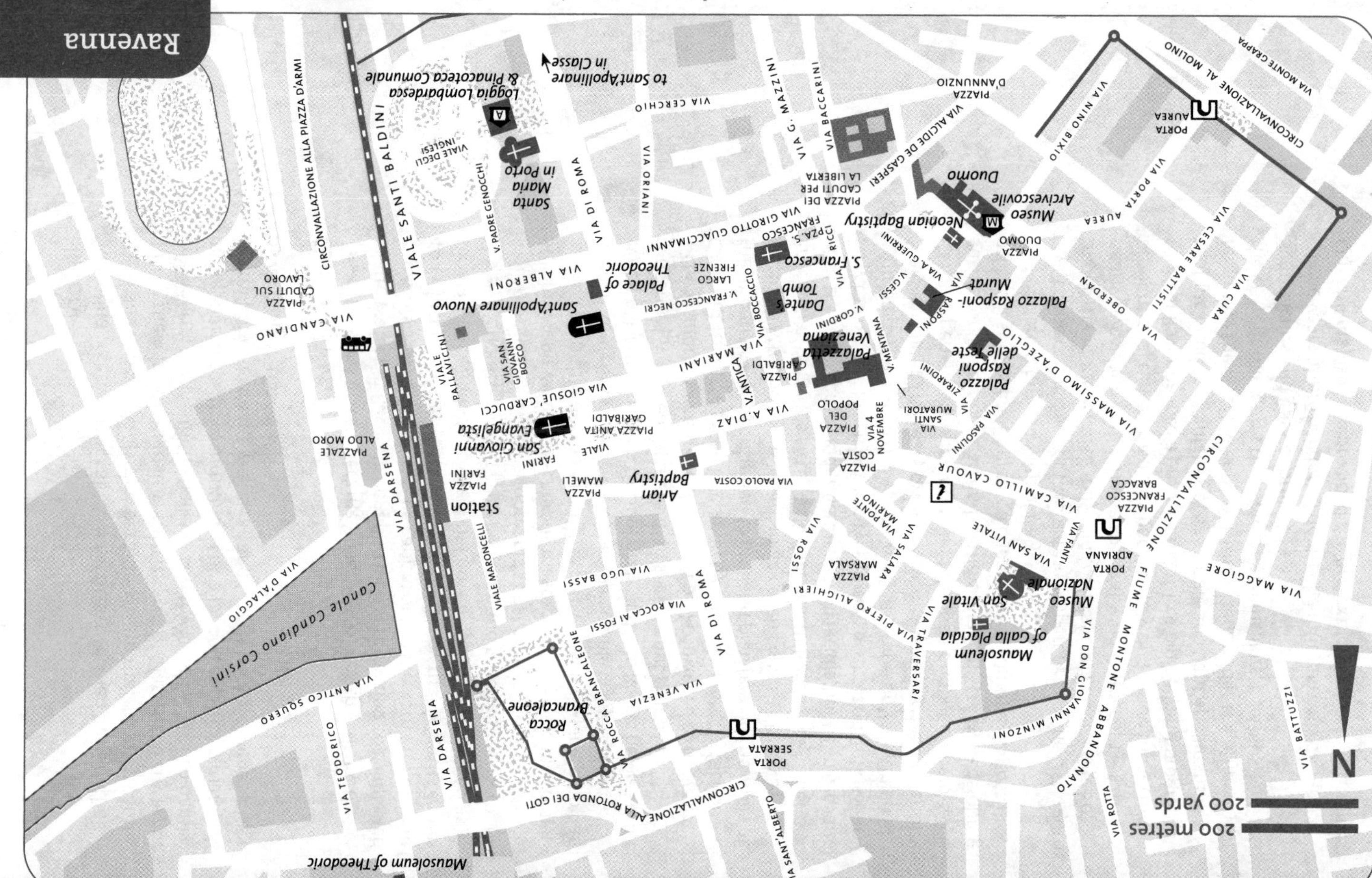
Ravenna
200 metres
200 yards
N
Mausoleum of Theodoric
Rocca Brancaleone
Station
San Giovanni Evangelista
Sant'Apollinare Nuovo
Palace of Theodoric
Santa Maria in Porto
Loggia Lombardesca & Pinacoteca Comunale
to Sant'Apollinare in Classe
Arian Baptistry
Dante's Tomb
S. Francesco
Palazzetta Veneziana
Neonian Baptistry
Duomo
Museo Arcivescovile
Palazzo Rasponi-Murat
Palazzo Rasponi delle Teste
Mausoleum of Galla Placidia
San Vitale
Museo Nazionale
Canale Candiano Corsini
VIA DARSENA
VIA TEODORICO
VIA ANTICO SQUERO
VIA D'ALAGGIO
PIAZZALE ALDO MORO
VIA CANDIANO
PIAZZA CADUTI SUL LAVORO
CIRCONVALLAZIONE ALLA PIAZZA D'ARMI
VIALE SANTI BALDINI
VIALE DEGLI INGLESI
V. PADRE GENOCCHI
VIA ALBERONI
VIA DI ROMA
VIA ORIANI
VIA CERCHIO
VIA G. MAZZINI
VIA BACCARINI
VIA ALCIDE DE GASPERI
PIAZZA D'ANNUNZIO
VIA NINO BIXIO
PORTA AUREA
CIRCONVALLAZIONE AL MOLINO
VIA MONTE GRAPPA
VIA PORTA AUREA
VIA CESARE BATTISTI
VIA CURA
VIA OBERDAN
PIAZZA DUOMO
PIAZZA DEI CADUTI PER LA LIBERTA
VIA GIROTTO GUACCIMANNI
PZA. S. FRANCESCO
VIA RICCI
LARGO FIRENZE
V. FRANCESCO NEGRI
VIA BOCCACCIO
V. GORDINI
V. GESSI
VIA A. GUERRINI
VIA RASPONI
VIA MASSIMO D'AZEGLIO
VIA ZIRARDINI
VIA PASOLINI
VIA SANTI MURATORI
V. MENTANA
VIA 4 NOVEMBRE
PIAZZA DEL POPOLO
PIAZZA GARIBALDI
V. ANTICA
VIA MARIANI
VIA A. DIAZ
VIA GIOSUE' CARDUCCI
VIA SAN GIOVANNI BOSCO
VIALE PALLAVICINI
PIAZZA ANITA GARIBALDI
VIALE FARINI
PIAZZA FARINI
PIAZZA MAMELI
VIA PAOLO COSTA
PIAZZA COSTA
VIA CAMILLO CAVOUR
PIAZZA FRANCESCO BARACCA
CIRCONVALLAZIONE
VIA MAGGIORE
PORTA ADRIANA
VIA FANTI
VIA SAN VITALE
VIA PONTE MARINO
VIA SALARA
PIAZZA MARSALA
VIA ROSSI
VIA PIETRO ALIGHIERI
VIA TRAVERSARI
VIA UGO BASSI
VIA ROCCA AI FOSSI
VIA VENEZIA
VIA ROCCA BRANCALEONE
VIALE MARONCELLI
PORTA SERRATA
CIRCONVALLAZIONE ALLA ROTONDA DEI GOTI
VIA SANT'ALBERTO
VIA DON GIOVANNI MINZONI
FIUME MONTONE ABBANDONATO
VIA ROTTA
VIA BATTUZZI

History

Ravenna, a settlement said to have been occupied by both the Etruscans and the Gauls, first became an important Roman centre during the reign of Augustus. With its port of Classis, the city lay on an important route to the Balkans and the Danube. Set in a nearly impregnable position, surrounded by a lagoon and broad marshes, the military advantage was clear, and Classis became Rome's biggest naval base on the Adriatic.

Capital of Italy

As conditions in Italy became unsettled in the 5th century, the relative safety of Ravenna began to look very inviting to frightened emperors. Honorius moved the capital of the Western Empire here in 402 – just in time, with the invasion of Italy by the Visigoths coming six years later, and Alaric's sack of Rome in 409. The disaster was largely Honorius' fault. In 408 this weak and scheming emperor had foolishly ordered the execution of his best general, the Vandal Stilicho, along with a treacherous massacre of the German soldiers in the legion that defended Italy. He also cashiered Alaric, who had been in Rome's service, and stopped paying his Visigothic army. When Alaric led his men through Italy and into Rome, he was more concerned with feeding them than seeking out plunder.

The Visigoths were soon bought off and convinced to move to Gaul, but Italy had fallen into anarchy while squabbling factions of the Imperial family continued to plot and plan behind the walls of Ravenna. After Honorius' death in 423 such power as the Western Empire had fell to his sister Galla Placidia, ruling as regent along with the army commander Aetius. Galla Placidia built San Giovanni, now the oldest church in the city; she died in 450, and Aetius was murdered by a distrustful young Western Emperor, Valentinian III, four years later. The real power in Ravenna was now held by another German general, Ricimer, who ruled through puppet emperors. His successor Odoacer put an end to the charade in 476 by pensioning off the last Western Emperor, a child named Romulus Augustulus, and declaring himself King of Italy.

With the connivance of the Eastern Emperor Zeno, the Ostrogoths under Theodoric invaded Italy and took Ravenna after a siege of nearly two years. Theodoric (*see* pp.281), who reigned 493–526, brought peace and prosperity back to Italy, and made the fortress town of Ravenna into a proper capital, in a big building programme that included the churches of San Vitale and Sant'Apollinare. His reign saw the last flowering of Latin letters, under the influence of the Ostrogothic king's three famous councillors, Boethius, Symmachus and Cassiodorus.

Nine years after Theodoric's death, the murder of his daughter Queen Amalasuntha provided the pretext for the Eastern Empire's attempt to regain control of Italy. Justinian sent his great general Belisarius into the peninsula in 536, touching off the terrible Greek–Gothic Wars that would consume the country for the next 25 years. Ravenna, taken by trickery in 540, avoided the destruction Belisarius and his successor Narses spread through the rest of Italy, though few other cities were spared. In truth the Dark Ages for Italy began here, brought not by barbarians but by the Byzantine heirs of the Roman Empire, but while the rest of the country lay exhausted and devastated, pampered Ravenna perfected its embellishments. The Byzantines built more churches and more palaces, and the finest mosaic artists of Constantinople came to fix the portraits of Justinian and his consort Theodora on the walls of San Vitale.

All the effort and all the bloodshed proved meaningless when the Lombards overran a wasted Italy in 579. After that, Byzantine rule was limited to a band of central Italy running from Ravenna to Rome, along with some port towns and enclaves in the south. These possessions were reorganized as the 'Exarchate of Ravenna' in the 590s. The Greek exarchs, who were never popular among their new subjects, performed the occasional service in obtaining Constantinople's aid to keep the Lombards at bay throughout their period of rule. While tolerating the exarch's presence, the people of Ravenna came to rely increasingly on their own resources; when help from the east failed to appear, it was their own citizen militia, led by the politically powerful archbishops, that defended the city against invaders.

In the worst of times, the city survived as a sort of cultural time capsule, protected by its own efforts and its surrounding lagoon, still maintaining trade and cultural relations with the east, and carrying on the best traditions of classical culture single-handedly. For a Dark Age, plenty was happening. Some exarchs found the resources to embroil all Italy in war, usually battling against their arch-enemies, the popes in Rome. In the 670s Archbishop Maurus even provoked a short-lived schism in the Church when trying to win ecclesiastic independence for Ravenna.

It was a religious conflict – Iconoclasm, the attempt of Byzantine Emperor Leo III to purify Christianity by destroying the sacred icons – that put an end to the Exarchate. Ravenna revolted against Byzantine rule in 727, the same year the Venetians decided on independence and elected their first doge. While Venice's story was only beginning, Ravenna's days were numbered. With no supplies from the east to see it through a siege, the city fell to the Lombards in 751. Six years later, however, Pepin the Short's Frankish army snatched it away from them, and the city was placed under the rule of the popes. Ravenna declined slowly and gracefully in the following centuries. Venice took over its role as leading port of the

Adriatic as Classis silted up and was abandoned. The newer cities of the Romagna, such as Ferrara and Faenza, assumed a larger role in the region's economy, and even Ravenna's ancient school of Roman law was transferred to Bologna, there to become the seed of Europe's first university.

Polentas and Popes

Despite its declining fortunes, Ravenna managed to rouse itself in 1177, becoming a free *comune* like so many other towns in the Romagna. Originally a strong Ghibelline town, Ravenna crossed over to the Guelphs under Guido 'the Old' da Polenta in 1239. Emperor Frederick II himself came the next year to take back the city for the Ghibellines, and had Guido's father executed. Though his enemies were to hold Ravenna for decades, Guido never gave up. He finally won the city back in 1275, with the aid of the Malatesta of Rimini, inaugurating a period of family rule that was to last for a century and a half.

Already in his eighties, old Guido would still have more troubles to witness. His daughter Francesca, married to Giovanni Malatesta of Rimini, decided she liked his brother Paolo better; Giovanni killed them both when he caught them, in 1283. (The story of Paolo and Francesca would make one of the most touching and famous episodes in Dante, even though that unforgiving poet assigned them both to the Inferno.) In 1290 Guido's own sons locked him up for a time, in a plot to give the city over to the pope, but he regained control of the situation and ruled in relative peace until his death in 1310.

Guido was succeeded by his grandson Guido 'Novello', famous for offering refuge to Dante when a change in Florentine politics made the poet an exile. Dante finished the *Divine Comedy* in Ravenna, and died here in 1321. If he'd lasted a little longer, he might have found enough material for another circle in the Inferno. The first da Polenta had a reputation for honesty and sagacity that often led to their being invited to sort out the affairs of neighbouring cities (a common practice among the *comuni* when the factions could agree on an impartial referee). Guido the Old had once served as *podestà* in Florence, and in 1322 Guido Novello was spending a term as Capitano del Popolo in Bologna when his cousin Ostasio seized the city and murdered Guido's brother, Archbishop Rinaldo, who had been left in charge.

Guido Novello died in exile, and this rogue branch of the da Polenta held on to the city through the reigns of several *signori*, each worse than the last. Ostasio murdered two more close relatives before he was done; his son Bernardino starved his brothers to death after he caught them plotting against him. The next in line, another Guido, was starved to death by his own sons after they overthrew him; after that one of the sons, Obizzo, murdered all the others. It was the Venetians who finally put an end to this family fun. Venice had a commercial stranglehold over Ravenna, and its power and influence in the city steadily increased after 1400. In 1441 the Serenissima threw out the last da Polenta and ruled the city directly.

Ravenna enjoyed a brief period of renewed prosperity which lasted until the popes came back in 1509; the economic decadence brought by papal rule has been reversed only since the 1940s.

Parts of the city were heavily damaged in the Second World War, but in the last few decades, with the construction of a ship channel and new port, the discovery of offshore gas deposits and the introduction of large chemical industries, Ravenna has become a booming modern city – just coincidentally one with a centre full of Byzantine mosaics.

San Vitale

San Vitale
Via San Vitale, near Porta Adriana, the western gate of the centro storico, **t** *(0544) 541 688, www.ravennamosaici.it; open daily Jan–Feb 9.30–5, Mar and Oct 9–5.30, Apr–Sept 9–7; adm joint ticket* *(see p.284)*

At first this dark old church may not seem like much, but as soon as the now-automatic lights come on (a large bag of coins is no longer an essential requirement), the 1,400-year-old mosaics ignite into an explosion of colour. The mosaics of San Vitale, Ravenna's best, are one of the last great works of art of the ancient world, and one of Christianity's first. The octagonal church, begun in 525 during the reign of Theodoric, is itself a fine example of the surprisingly sophisticated architecture from that troubled age. By the time it was finished, in 548, the city was in the hands of Belisarius' Byzantine army; the famous mosaic portraits of Justinian and Theodora can be taken as the traditional imperial style of political propaganda.

Far from being the sorry recapitulation of old building forms and styles you might expect, San Vitale was a breathtakingly original departure in architecture. While the world was falling around their ears, late Roman architects were making revolutionary advances, using complex geometry and new vaulting techniques. In the 6th century it still wasn't entirely settled just what a church was, or what design would be proper for it. Most commonly they took the form of the Roman basilica, a secular building that housed law courts or government offices (Sant'Apollinare Nuovo and Sant'Apollinare in Classe are good examples, along with the early basilican churches of Rome). Central-plan churches had also been popular since the first big imperially sponsored building programme under Constantine, which included such novel works as the Holy Sepulchre in Jerusalem and the 'Golden Octagon' of Antioch; Ravenna's San Vitale was the next step. Their architecture derives from Roman bath complexes, mausolea and perhaps the follies and pavilions of the land-owning élite.

The Mosaics

Either light was born here,
Or reigns here imprisoned

Latin inscription, Sant'Andrea chapel

In Byzantine times the greatest gift an emperor could bestow on any dependent town was a few tons of gold, glass and enamel *tesserae* and an artist. From Justinian's time, the art became almost a trademark of Byzantine civilization. It was not only towns under Byzantine rule that received such favours; probably as part of diplomatic initiatives, you can see the work of Constantinople's mosaicists in Egypt, Sicily and in the mihrab of the Great Mosque of Córdoba.

Before Christianity, mosaics were a favourite Roman medium, but not always taken too seriously. They were usually reserved for the decoration of villas. Some reached the level of fine art (examples are in the Naples museum, the great villa at Piazza Armerina, Sicily, and Antakya in Turkey – ancient Antioch), but more often the productions were on the level of the famous 'Beware of the dog' mosaic in Pompeii, or prophylactic images of Priapus. It was the early Christians, with a desire to build for the ages and a body of scriptures that could best be related pictorially, who made mosaics the new medium of public art in the 6th century. Mostly it was an affair of the Greeks, who still had the talent and the resources for it; we cannot say with absolute certainty, but it's most likely that Greek artists from the court of Constantinople created the celebrated mosaics in the churches and baptistries of Ravenna.

Western Christian art was born here, developing from the simple images – the Good Shepherd and the Cross and Stars – to the iconic Christ in Sant'Apollinare Nuovo and the beautiful scriptural scenes in San Vitale. Never, though, did the early mosaicists turn their back on the idea of art; with the ideals of the ancient world still in their minds, they naturally thought of art and religion as going hand in hand, and found no problem in serving the cause of both. Using a new vocabulary of images and the new techniques of mosaic art, they strove to duplicate, and surpass, the sense of awe and mystery still half-remembered from the interiors of the pagan temples. Try to imagine a church like San Vitale in its original state, with lamps or candles – lots of them – flickering below the gold ground and gorgeous colours. You may see that same light that enchanted the Byzantines – the light of the Gospels, the light from beyond the stars.

Take some time to admire the exterior, with its beautiful interplay of octagons, arches, gables and *exedrae* – pure proportional geometry done in plain solid brick (but for the Greek–Gothic Wars it might have been sheathed in stone). Inside, the curious double capitals on the columns are no design conceit, but an important 5th-century invention; the trapezoidal *impost capital* is specially designed to support the weight of arches. Holding up the second-floor galleries and large octagonal cupola was an unusual design problem; these capitals and the eight stout piers around the dome were the solution. We do not know the name of San Vitale's architects, or whether they were Latins or Greeks, but the year after it was begun, work commenced on the very similar church of SS Sergius and Bacchus in Constantinople, the prototype for the Hagia Sophia 10 years later.

In its structure the great dome in Constantinople owed everything to the little dome of Ravenna: the innovation of the galleries, for example, in which the women were segregated during services, and the elongated apse cleverly combining the central plan favoured by eastern Christians with the basilica form needed for a court's religious ceremonies. Nowhere in what is now Istanbul, however, or anywhere else in the east, will you find anything as brilliant as San Vitale's **mosaics**. Some of the best were undoubtedly lost during the iconoclastic troubles of the 8th century; iconoclasm, however, was fiercely resisted in Italy – it was one of the first causes of the rupture between Ravenna and Constantinople, and between the Roman and Greek churches – and most of Ravenna's art was fortunately spared.

The colours are startling. Almost all the later Byzantine mosaics, in Sicily, Greece and Turkey, are simple figures on a bright gold ground, dazzling at first but somewhat monotonous. There is plenty of gold on the walls of San Vitale, but the best mosaics, in the choir, have deep blue skies and rich green meadows for backgrounds, highlighted by brightly coloured birds and flowers. The two lunettes over the arches flanking the **choir**, each a masterpiece, show the hospitality of Abraham and the sacrifice of Isaac, and the offerings of Abel and Melchizedek, set under fiery clouds with hands of benediction extended from Heaven. These sacrifices are the two events in the Old Testament that prefigure the Transfiguration of Christ. Around the two lunettes are scenes of Moses and Jeremiah; note, above the **lunettes**, the delicately posed pairs of angels holding golden crosses – almost identical to the fanciful figures from earlier Roman art displaying the civic crown of the Caesars, a symbol of the state from the time of Augustus. At the front of the choir the **triumphal arch** has excellent mosaic portraits of the Apostles supported by a pair of dolphins. Look up at the galleries and you will see more fine portraits of the four Evangelists.

The **apse** is dominated by portraits of Justinian and Theodora – mostly, of course, of Theodora, the Constantinople dancing girl who used her many talents to become an empress, eventually coming to wear poor Justinian like a charm on her bracelet. Here she is wearing a rich crown, with long strings of fat diamonds and real pearls. Justinian, like Theodora, appears among his retinue offering a gift to the new church; here he has the air of a hung-over saxophone player, badly in need of a shave and a cup of coffee. His cute daisy slipper steps on the foot (a convention of Byzantine art to show who's boss) of General Belisarius, to his left. The likenesses are good – very like those in Constantinople – suggesting that the artist may have come from there, or at least have closely copied imperial portraits on display at Ravenna.

It can easily be imagined how expensive it was in the 5th century to make mosaics like these. It is said that the Hagia Sophia originally had over four acres of them, and even the treasury of Justinian and Theodora was not bottomless; consequently most of San Vitale remained undecorated until the 17th-century bishops did the dome and the other parts in a not-too-discordant Baroque. The mosaics are such an attraction that you might miss the other features of

San Vitale – including the one under your feet, a **maze** directly in front of the choir. No one knows exactly when it was added, but such mazes were common features of late Roman and medieval churches from Britain to Algeria. No one knows much about their significance either, though their pre-Christian symbolism may have been re-explained as a kind of substitute pilgrimage; the space at the centre was often referred to as 'Jerusalem'. You can walk this one – don't worry, you won't get lost; like all church mazes this one is a single winding path, with no wrong turns or dead ends.

Recently, part of the floor between two piers has been pulled up to reveal the original, an inlaid marble pavement in floral and geometric patterns that is a direct ancestor of medieval pavements in the churches of Tuscany and the south. The lower walls of the church are covered in thin sheets of precious marbles from all over the Mediterranean, much like those of the Hagia Sophia. Also worthy of note is the alabaster 6th-century altar, ancient reliefs of the *Throne of Neptune* and the *Sacrifice of Isaac* near the choir, and the *sarcophagus of Quintus Bonus*, with reliefs of the Magi and Daniel in the lions' den.

Mausoleum of Galla Placidia

Mausoleum of Galla Placidia
***t** (0544) 541 688, www.ravennamosaici.it; open daily Mar and Oct 9–5.30, Apr–Sept 9–7, Nov–Feb 9–4.30; adm joint ticket (see p.284)*

If they tried to make Galla Placidia's life into a Hollywood costumer, no one would believe it. The daughter of Theodosius the Great, last ruler of a united and peaceful empire, she grew up between Constantinople, Rome, Milan and Ravenna amidst the court intrigues that followed his death. She happened to be in Rome when the Visigoths sacked it in 410, and at the age of 18 this princess suddenly became a very valuable bargaining chip in the hands of their leader Alaric. While negotiations were under way to return her, Alaric died, and his young successor Ataulf took his hungry people from impoverished Italy to Gaul, in hopes of finding land and food. Galla Placidia accompanied him on this long and miserable trek, and somewhere along the way the two fell in love.

They were married in 413 at Narbonne, and had a child, named Theodosius, in Barcelona two years later. The emperor, Galla's brother Honorius, was furious, and he may well have arranged Ataulf's assassination in 415. So failed a remarkable chance for German–Italian reconciliation, and possibly the salvation of the Empire. Galla returned to Ravenna the next year, where Honorius forced her into a second marriage, but there were more adventures to come. Galla was still Queen of the Visigoths, and worked faithfully in their interests; as a result of this Honorius banished her in 423. Escaping for Constantinople, she was shipwrecked off Ephesus but miraculously saved. Honorius died the same year, heirless, and Galla sailed right back, this time as regent of the Western Empire, which she ruled for the next 13 years in the name of her son Valentinian.

With such a busy life, Galla might be excused certain failures as a mother. Valentinan turned out a vicious waster, while his sister Honoria was so bad Galla had her locked up in a convent. That didn't stop her – while inside she managed single-handedly to cause the invasion of Italy by the Huns, who had previously been quiet Roman allies. Honoria smuggled out a letter to Attila the Hun, accompanied by a ring, promising to marry him if he would only come down and deliver her.

This small chapel, set in the grounds of San Vitale and originally attached to the neighbouring church of Santa Croce, never really held the tomb of Ravenna's first great patroness – she is buried somewhere near St Peter's in Rome. Nobody has peeked into the three huge stone sarcophagi, traditionally the resting places of Galla Placidia and two emperors, her second husband Constantius and her son Valentinian, and it's anyone's guess who is really inside. Galla Placidia did construct the chapel, and it was probably intended as an Imperial resting place, its relative modesty a demonstration of how much the Western Empire had fallen. It is a small, gabled and cross-shaped building that is almost 7ft shorter than when it was built: the ground level has risen that much in 1,400 years.

The simplicity of the brick exterior, as in San Vitale, makes the brilliant mosaics within that much more of a surprise. The only natural light inside comes from a few tiny slits of windows, made of thin sheets of alabaster that probably came from Egypt. The two important mosaics, on lunettes at opposite ends of the chapel, are coloured as richly as San Vitale. One represents *St Lawrence*, with his flaming grid-iron; the other is a beautiful and typical early Christian portrait of Jesus as the *Good Shepherd*, a beardless, classical-looking figure in a fine cloak and sandals, stroking one of the flock. On the lunettes of the cross-axis, pairs of stags come to drink at the fountain of life; around all four lunettes floral arabesques and maze patterns in bright colours cover the arches and ceilings. Everything in the design betrays as much of the classical Roman style as the nascent Christian, and the unusual figures on the arches holding up the central vault seem hardly out of place. They are *SS Peter and Paul*, dressed in togas and standing with outstretched hands in the conventional pose of Roman senators.

The vault itself, a deep blue firmament glowing with hundreds of dazzling golden stars set in concentric circles, is the mausoleum's most remarkable feature. In the centre, at the top of the vault, a golden cross represents the unimaginable, transcendent God above the heavens. At the corners, symbols of the four *Evangelists* provide an insight into the origins of Christian iconography. Mark's lion, Luke's ox and Matthew's man occupy the places in this sky where you would expect the constellations of Leo, Taurus and Aquarius, 90 degrees apart along the zodiac. For the fourth corner, instead of the objectionable Scorpio (or serpent, as it often appeared in ancient times) the early Christians substituted the eagle of St John.

The mausoleum was originally connected to the church of **Santa Croce**, also built by Galla Placidia, which is closed to the public but you can see through the fence, along with the 9th-century **Santa Maria Maggiore**. After rebuildings, almost nothing is left of these churches from ancient times, except the latter church's **campanile** (also 9th-century), one of the beautiful round towers in the style that is a Ravenna speciality.

Museo Nazionale

Museo Nazionale
t *(0544) 34424; open Tues–Sun 8.30–7.30; adm; joint ticket available (see p.284)*

The medieval and Baroque cloisters attached to San Vitale now house the large collection of antiquities found in Ravenna and Classis. This is a museum worth spending time in, for exceptional works of art like the beautiful 6th-century Byzantine carved screens, and a unique sculpture of *Hercules Capturing the Cerynean Hind*, also 6th-century, perhaps the last surviving piece of art made in ancient times with a classical subject, possibly a copy of an earlier Greek work. An excellent mosaic, recently moved here from a Byzantine palace excavated on Via d'Azeglio, shows Christ as the *Good Shepherd* surrounded by the *Dance of the Seasons*. Beyond these there's a little bit of everything: Etruscan finds from the area, lead pipes and other bits of good Roman plumbing, a boy's linen shirt that has somehow survived from the 6th century, the original bronze cross from the roof of San Vitale, Byzantine forks (they invented them), swords and armour, and no end of coins and broken pots. The detailed and well-labelled coin collection is interesting even to the non-specialist, providing a picture history of Italy from classical times into the early Middle Ages.

Not all of the exhibits are ancient; lovely, intricately carved **ivories** (chests, portable altars and plaques from the Middle Ages and Renaissance) fill an entire room. Most are from France, with charming tableaux of medieval scenes such as tournaments and banquets. There is a good collection of **ceramics** too, not only from Faenza but from other notable Italian centres, such as Castelli, Urbino and Deruta; and a room of **Byzantine icons** from the 14th to the 17th century (it doesn't matter; over time they hardly change at all). Most of these are Italian, a reminder of the long survival of Orthodox communities here; there are works of the Cretan-Venetian school, others from the Veneto, from Russia and even Naples. Cinquecento Italy is represented by a lavishly fancy intarsia cabinet, and by the museum building itself, which includes a domed monumental stair attributed to Bramante. To understand Ravenna and its buildings better, be sure to see the fascinating architectural models of the Neonian baptistry (*see* p.277). The work of a modern Ravenna architect named Raffaello Trinci, its glass cross-sections elaborate the proportions and geometrical theory behind the new architecture of the 6th century, a recasting of ancient sacred geometry that was to have a great influence on the cathedral builders of the Middle Ages, and a greater one on the architects of Islam.

The museum has a recently installed attraction in a separate room, a wonderful set of **frescoes** from the church of Santa Chiara. Once part of a convent closed by Napoleon, the church was later used as a stable and a theatre; the presbytery, with the frescoes, was walled off and forgotten, and they were discovered and detached only recently. All the works (*c.* 1320) are by Pietro da Rimini, the Romagna's greatest painter of the trecento. They include delightful scenes from the vaulting, with the four *Evangelists* paired with four great *Doctors of the Church*: Matthew with Jerome, Mark with Ambrose, John with Augustine and Luke with Pope Gregory the Great. While the Doctors sit puzzling at their desks, surrounded by books, the Evangelists come down, apparently to give them tips on the difficult points of the Scriptures. Among the other frescoes are portraits of *St Francis*, *St Clare* and *St Anthony of Padua*, and two of the loveliest angels of the 14th or any other century.

Look at the inside of the 16th-century **cloister** before you go, built over a lost *quadroporticus* that formed the entrance to San Vitale; among the architectural fragments and sculptures lying about are two huge, stately cedar trees and a sour-faced statue of *Pope Clement XII*.

Ravenna's Centre

The **Piazza del Popolo** at the centre of Ravenna has a Venetian feel to it: the Venetians built it during their brief period of rule, and added the twin columns (like the pair in Venice's Piazzetta San Marco) bearing reliefs by Pietro Lombardo and statues of Ravenna's two patrons, San Vitale and Sant'Apollinare. The Venetians governed from the 1444 **Palazzetta Veneziana**, embellished with Byzantine columns and heavily restored in the 19th century.

North of Piazza del Popolo on Via Ponte Marino, Ravenna has a fine example of a medieval leaning tower, the tall, 12th-century **Torre Pubblica** (or Torre Comunale), now supported by steel struts. Despite the angle of the tower, the windows near the top were built perfectly level. Byron lived for a time in a house in the nearby Via Cavour, during his affair with Countess Teresa Guiccioli. His home now houses the *carabinieri*.

San Francesco and Dante's Tomb

South of Piazza del Popolo, off the colonnaded **Piazza San Francesco**, a modest neoclassical pavilion was built in the 18th century over the **Tomb of Dante**. Ravenna is especially proud of having sheltered the storm-tossed poet in his last years, and the city will gently remind you of it in its street names, its tourist brochures, its Teatro Alighieri and its frequent artistic competitions based on themes from the *Divina Commedia*. Coming here may help explain just what Dante means to Italy; in all the country's more recent wars, for example, groups of soldiers have come here for little rituals to 'dedicate their sacrifice' to the poet's memory. Today there are always wreaths or bouquets brought by all kinds of organizations and private citizens from all over Italy. Beside the tomb is the **Museo Dantesco**, with a collection of paintings, sculptures and books connected with the poet.

Museo Dantesco
t (0544) 30252, www.centrodantesco.it; open Tues–Sun 9–12, in summer also 3.30–6; adm; closed at time of writing but reopening during 2007

The church of **San Francesco**, behind the tomb, was begun in 460, but rebuilt in the 11th century and then thoroughly Baroqued in the 1700s. If the Greek marble columns of the nave look unusually squat, it is because a third of their height is underground. The church has been settling and sinking in the soggy ground for 1,500 years. Some of its beautiful original mosaic pavement is visible through an opening in the floor – under eight feet of water (bring coins for the lighting machine). Also in the church is the 14th-century *tomb of Ostasio da Polenta*, first of the rotten Polentas, and the unusual 1509 *tomb of Luffo Numai*, with advice for the soul from the animal world: a bird whispers 'abstain', while a camel counsels 'endure'. The altar was originally the fine 4th-century sarcophagus of the Archbishop Liberius. In the church itself and the adjacent 'Braccioforte' oratory (behind the iron gate, next to Dante's tomb) there are some fine early Christian sarcophagi.

San Francesco
open daily 7.30–12 and 3–7

Just across Via Ricci is Ravenna's government centre, an ensemble of Mussolini Deco buildings from the 1920s and 30s on a square that after the war was renamed **Piazza dei Caduti per la Libertà**. To the east on Via Mazzini, **Sant'Agata Maggiore** is another church founded by Theodoric, retaining some fine capitals and an unusual *ambo* from the 500s.

Sant'Agata Maggiore
open daily 9–12

The Cathedral: Neonian Baptistry and the Archiepiscopal Museum

Cathedral: Neonian Baptistry and Archiepiscopal Museum
t (0544) 541 688, www.ravennamosaici.it; open daily Jan–Feb 10–5, Mar and Oct 9.30–5.30, Apr–Sept 9–7; Cappella della Santa Vergine del Sudore and Oratorio di Sant'Andrea currently closed; adm joint ticket *(see p.284)*

An earthquake in 1733 wrecked Ravenna's 5th-century **cathedral**, west of the Piazza del Popolo, and there's little to see in the replacement except the surviving medieval pavement, the 6th-century *ambo*, carved with animal reliefs, and the overwrought Baroque **Cappella della Santa Vergine del Sudore**, currently closed for restoration, which contains two fine Byzantine sarcophagi holding the remains of San Barbagiano (a 5th-century monk) and San Rainaldo di Concorezzo (archbishop in 1303, and a defender of the Templars).

The **campanile**, another round tower (10th–11th-century), somehow survived. The disaster also spared the 'Orthodox' or

Neonian Baptistry, named after the 5th-century bishop Neon who commissioned its splendid mosaics. Unlike the Arian Baptistry's (*see* p.280), almost all the decoration here has survived: there is a scene of the *Baptism of Jesus* and fine portraits of the *Apostles* on the ceiling under the dome, while below the eight walls bear four altars and four empty thrones. The *etimasia*, the 'Preparing of the Throne' for Jesus for the Last Judgement, is an odd bit of Byzantine mysticism; interestingly enough, classical Greek art often depicted an empty throne as a symbol for Zeus, only with a pair of thunderbolts instead of a cross.

Some think that the Baptistry is in part older than Neon, built over a chamber of a Roman bath complex. In the 1,500 years or so since its construction, the Baptistry has sunk over 10ft – like everything else on the soggy soil of Ravenna. Its floor was raised through periodic reconstructions; recent excavations have uncovered marble supporting columns down to the bottom. In the side niches are a 6th-century Byzantine altar and a huge, thoroughly pagan marble vase. The marble font, big enough for immersion baptism of adults, is from the 13th century.

The **Museo Arcivescovile**, behind the cathedral, is a small museum that receives few visitors, but this is actually one of the great sights of Ravenna. Its little-known treasures include the ivory *throne of Bishop Maximian*, a masterpiece of 6th-century sculpture, thought to have been a gift from Emperor Justinian, and a 6th-century reliquary, the silver *Cross of Sant'Agnello*. Among the fragments of sculpture and mosaics are works saved from the original cathedral. The large marble disc by the wall, divided into 19 sections, is an episcopal calendar, regulated to the 19-year Julian cycle to allow Ravenna's medieval bishops to calculate the date of Easter and other holy days.

The biggest surprise, however, is finding that the nondescript Archbishop's Palace, in which the museum is located, is in parts as old as anything in Ravenna. A little door at the back leads to a small chapel called the **Oratorio di Sant'Andrea**, currently closed, built around 500 during the reign of Theodoric. The mosaics on the vaults are among Ravenna's best: in the antechamber a fanciful scene of multi-coloured birds and flowers, and an unusual warrior Christ in full Roman armour and wielding the cross like a sword, treading a lion and snake underfoot. In the chapel itself, four angels and the four evangelists' symbols surround Christ's monogram on the dome, and the apse bears a beautiful starry sky around a golden cross, like the one at the Galla Placidia mausoleum. The best mosaics, however, are the excellent portraits of **saints** decorating the arches. Early Christian representations of the saints are often much stronger than the pale, conventional figures of later art. Such portraits as these betray a fascination with the personalities and the psychology of saints; such figures as St Felicitas or St Ursicinus may be forgotten now, but to the early Christians they were not mere holy myths, but near-contemporaries, the spiritual heroes and heroines responsible for the miraculous growth of Christianity, the exemplars of a new age and a new way of life.

Near the cathedral complex on Piazza Kennedy is the 16th-century **Palazzo Rasponi-Murat** (or Spalletti) and adjacent 18th-century **Palazzo Rasponi 'delle Teste'**; behind these, the city is currently restoring the palace gardens and transforming them into a herb garden in the medieval-Renaissance manner, the 'Giardino delle Erbe Dimenticate'.

Down Via Roma

Long, straight Via Roma, a modern thoroughfare that roughly follows one of the *decumani* of the Roman city, is always a welcome sight; it makes this eastern end of Ravenna the only part where you won't be constantly getting lost. (On a map you'll notice the winding streets Via Girolamo Rossi and Via Mazzini, once roughly the course of a stream that divided Ravenna in two. The area to the east, around San Vitale, was the original city, while the part around Via Roma was an expansion of late Imperial times.)

Santa Maria in Porto
open daily 7.30–12.30 and 3.30–7

At the southern end of Via Roma, **Santa Maria in Porto** obviously isn't near the port at all; under Venetian rule this monastery was relocated inside the city walls, and a new church was built in the 1500s. The gloriously ornate façade, one of the final flings of the Baroque and the favourite address of Ravenna's pigeons, was added in the 1780s. Inside are some equally fancy *pietra dura* chapel altars, and a prize relic, claimed as one of the urns from the wedding at Cana – it's really a 2nd-century porphyry vase from Alexandria.

Pinacoteca Comunale
***t** (0544) 482 356, www.museocitta.ra.it; open Tues–Thurs and Sat 9–7, Fri 9–9; adm*

The adjacent cloister, with the elegant early Renaissance **Loggia Lombardesca** facing the Giardino Pubblico behind it, houses Ravenna's **Pinacoteca Comunale**, holding mostly Romagnolo artists from the Middle Ages to the 1700s. Still, the works that stand out are mostly by outsiders: paintings of the Sienese Taddeo di Bartolo and Matteo di Giovanni, a *Crucifixion* by Antonio Vivarini, and Tullio Lombardo's *Funeral Statue of Guidarello Guidarelli*, a 15-year-old who died at Imola fighting for Cesare Borgia. From the late Renaissance and Baroque, there are the works of local painters Luca Longhi and his daughter Barbara (*St Catherine*, a self-portrait), Guercino's *San Romualdo*, full of operatic gesture, the Florentine Cecco Bravo's *Apollo and Daphne*, and some remarkable, almost three-dimensional compositions in chiaroscuro by a little known late Baroque painter from Cattolica, Cesare Pronti.

Palace of Theodoric
t (0544) 34424; open by appointment

Further up Via Roma are the impressive remains of the 6th-century building traditionally called the **Palace of Theodoric**. It doesn't look anything like the *Palatium* in the mosaics of Sant'Apollinare, and the most recent judgement says it was really only the monumental narthex of a lost church; others have speculated that it was a later governmental building of some sort, or even the palace of the Byzantine exarchs. Inside there is a display of mosaics discovered while excavating the area.

Sant'Apollinare Nuovo

Sant'Apollinare Nuovo
t (0544) 541 688, www.ravennamosaici.it; open daily Jan–Feb 10–5, Mar and Oct 9.30–5.30, Apr–Sept 9–7; adm joint ticket (see p.284)

After those of San Vitale, the mosaics of this 6th-century church are the finest in Ravenna. Theodoric built it for the Arians, and after the Byzantine conquest and the suppression of Arianism it was re-dedicated to St Martin. The present name comes from the 9th century, when the remains of Sant'Apollinare were moved here from the 'old' Sant'Apollinare, in Classe. The tall, cylindrical campanile, a style that is a trademark of Ravenna's churches, was added in the 10th century. Unlike San Vitale, Sant'Apollinare was built in the basilican form, with a long nave and side aisles. The two rows of Greek marble columns were probably recycled from an ancient temple. Above them, on walls that lean outwards rather dangerously, are the **mosaics**, begun under Theodoric and completed by the Byzantines, on panels that stretch the length of the church.

On the left, by the door, you see the *City of Classe*, with ships in the protected harbour between twin beacons, and the monuments of the city rearing up behind its walls. On the right, among the monuments of Ravenna, is the *Palatium*, Theodoric's royal palace. The curtains in the archways of the palace replace Gothic notables and probably Theodoric himself, effaced by the Byzantines. Beyond these two urban scenes are processions of martyrs bearing crowns: 22 ladies on the left side, 26 men on the right; the purpose of the black Greek letters on their togas is an utter mystery. The female procession is led by colourful, remarkable portraits of the *Magi* (officially enrolled as Saints of the Church, according to the inscription above), offering their gifts to the enthroned Virgin Mary. Above these panels, more mosaics on both sides portray Old Testament prophets and doctors of the Church, as well as a series of scenes from the life of Jesus. These mosaics, smaller and not as well executed, are from Theodoric's time.

San Giovanni Evangelista

San Giovanni Evangelista
open 7.30–12 and 3.30–6.30

There is another leaning tower – almost as tipsy as the Torre Pubblico – nearby on Viale Farini, two streets up from the railway station. It is the 12th-century campanile of San Giovanni Evangelista, a much-altered church that was begun by Galla Placidia in 425 and is thus the oldest church in Emilia-Romagna; she'd made a vow to the saint to build it if she was saved during her shipwreck off Ephesus, and John came through. Various reconstructions have seen to it that nothing is left of the original mosaics.

Even more than Ravenna's other monuments, this church has had to fight constantly against sinking into the marshy ground; the present pavement covers several earlier ones, and in the 1700s the entire church was disassembled and raised 6ft. Bombings in the last war destroyed the apse and the façade, but some recovered parts of the 13th-century mosaic floor – with scenes of the Fourth Crusade and some fantastical monsters – can be seen in the aisles.

The Arian Baptistry and Santo Spirito

Arian Baptistry
open daily 8.30–7.30; adm free

Just off Via Roma, in a little square between Via Paolo Costa and Via Armando Diaz, the **Arian Baptistry** recalls church struggles of the 5th century. Theodoric and his Ostrogoths, like most of the Germanic peoples, adhered to the Arian heresy, a doctrine that mixed in elements of pagan religion and was condemned by more orthodox Christians as denying the absolute divinity of Christ. Like all heresies, this one is really the story of a political struggle, between Germans and native Italians, and between the Gothic kings and the emperor in Constantinople. Unlike Justinian, a relentless persecutor, the Goths tolerated both faiths. The Arian Baptistry preserves a fine mosaic ceiling, with the twelve Apostles arranged around a scene of the *Baptism of Jesus*. Jesus here is pictured nude, something the orthodox would never have allowed; the old man with the palm branch, across from John the Baptist, represents the river Jordan. The baptistry belonged to the adjacent **Santo Spirito** church (rebuilt in the 16th century), once the Arians' cathedral, while the Athenasians (orthodox) worshipped at what is now the cathedral of Ravenna. Little of the original Santo Spirito is left beyond the columns and capitals and a 6th-century *ambo*.

Santo Spirito
open daily 10–1 and 3–6; closed at time of writing

Mausoleum of Theodoric

Mausoleum of Theodoric
***t** (0544) 684 020; open 8.30–7; adm; joint ticket available (see p.284)*

For the real flavour of the days of the Roman twilight, nothing can beat this compellingly strange, elegant yet half-barbaric building outside the old city. To reach it, head north on Via Roma, past the medieval gate called the Porta Serrata, and turn right on the Circonvallazione alla Rotonda dei Goti. This will take you past the Venetian fortress called the **Rocca di Brancaleone**, which was partially demolished under papal rule and is now part of a city park.

Rocca di Brancaleone
***t** (0544) 36094; open daily 9–7*

The Mausoleum of Theodoric is across the tracks in another small park on Via delle Industrie, near the port. It is totally unlike the other buildings Theodoric built in Ravenna: massive and solid, completely lacking in carved decoration and mosaics, yet quite sophisticated in its design – it is one of the few buildings in Italy

The Barbarian King

The one thing conspicuously missing from the Mausoleum is Theodoric himself. Later Germanic legends said his body had been carried away by Odin's white horse Fafnir to join the warrior heroes in Valhalla. The Italians, however, claimed it was a black horse – the Devil himself – who carried the heretic king down to Hell through the crater of Mount Etna. Modern historians find both these reports somewhat suspicious, and suggest that Theodoric's remains were scattered after Belisarius and his Byzantines captured Ravenna in 540. But the legends of the great king's demise nicely sum up contemporary feelings towards a ruler that the papers, had there been any, would undoubtedly have called 'controversial' in every lead paragraph.

The break-up of the Western Empire was a time of golden opportunity for a man like Theodoric. Born in 454 on the Hungarian plains, the son of the Ostrogothic King Theudemir, Theodoric grew up in the court of Byzantium as a diplomatic hostage, kept to ensure the Ostrogoths didn't break their treaty obligations. Roman culture seems to have made little impression on him; he never even learned to read. Back home in 472, he proved himself a proper Goth by taking his first town (Belgrade) at the age of 18; two years later he was King of the Ostrogoths.

This nation, the most talented and civilized of the Germans, had already created an empire in eastern Europe, and lost it when they were overrun by the Huns. Now, looking for a home, their king allowed the Eastern Emperor Zeno to talk him into moving to Italy, which would be theirs for the taking if they could only do away with Odoacer, a soldier who had demolished the last pretence of Imperial unity by declaring himself King of Italy. Theodoric moved his people, over 100,000 of them, over the Alps in 488, and defeated Odoacer's army in battle. Odoacer holed up in Ravenna, and Theodoric started a siege of the impregnable city that lasted nearly two years. When Odoacer finally surrendered, Theodoric invited him to a banquet, and there he literally sliced him in half with his sword. 'What, didn't he have any bones?' the Goth laughed.

Not a very promising new ruler, the Italians must have thought. But then the barbarian surprised them by settling down and giving them three decades of the most enlightened rule they had known in centuries. Under Theodoric the Kingdom of Italy became a bulwark of strength and stability. Commerce and culture, which had languished in the decadence of the late Empire, both made impressive recoveries. Roads and bridges were repaired, and cities revived. Theodoric worked sincerely to get Germans and Romans to live together in peace, despite Gothic disdain and deep-seated Italian bigotry. An Arian Christian, like all the Goths, he practised a policy few Christians would ever have dreamed of: religious toleration and equality. To help run his government, he selected the finest men of the age from the Roman nobility, the poets Symmachus and Cassiodorus and the philosopher Boethius, who became his chief minister and most trusted adviser.

Not that Theodoric was a friend to the great landowners of the senatorial class. He treated these magnates, who owned nearly everything, and who had bled the Roman economy into penury, to something they had never before experienced – paying taxes. And the next time you hear silly prattle of how the barbarians destroyed Roman culture, think of Theodoric, proclaiming a decree to protect the statues and monuments of Rome from the Romans themselves, who were grinding up the marbles for lime and melting down the bronzes for scrap.

Unfortunately for his historical reputation, and for Italy, Theodoric developed a decidedly bitter and paranoid streak in his old age. He did have his reasons. The jealous emperors in Constantinople, along with most of the senatorial class, hated him and never tired of hatching conspiracies against him. Suspecting everyone close to him, he even had Symmachus and Boethius executed in 525, though he gave the latter enough time in prison to write *The Consolation of Philosophy*.

After Theodoric's death in 526, court intrigues and the underlying mutual mistrust of Italians and Goths had weakened the kingdom enough to give Eastern Emperor Justinian an opportunity to try and conquer Italy. He did, though he inflicted so much damage on it, while exhausting and gravely weakening the Eastern Empire, that civilization would need nearly five centuries to recover. The Gothic kingdom remains one of history's might-have-beens. Perhaps it was just a freak in the complex chronicle of a dying world – though there was a hint of a chance that, had it been left in peace a little longer, the Dark Ages might never have happened.

designed according to the geometrically complex form of the pentagon, which is doubled to make the Mausoleum ten-sided. Some clues in the architecture have led to speculation that the architect came from Syria, but still it may have been an attempt by Theodoric, who built it before he died, to create a specifically 'Gothic' architecture.

The Mausoleum, which in the Middle Ages did service as a church, has two floors. Downstairs there is a cross-shaped chamber of unknown purpose. The second storey, also decagonal though slightly smaller, contains the porphyry sarcophagus, now empty. It is a comment on the times that scholars believe this was a recycled bathtub from a Roman palace. Theodoric was hardly broke, though; he could afford to bring the stone for his tomb over from Istria – and note the roof, a single slab of stone weighing over 300 tons. No one has yet explained how the Goths brought it here and raised it – or why.

Classe: the Basilica of Sant'Apollinare

Basilica of Sant'Apollinare
open Mon–Sat 8.30–7.30, Sun 1–7.30; adm; joint ticket available (see p.284)

In the southern suburbs is another important monument to Ravenna's golden age, at the ruins of Classe, 5km out on the SS9; any local train towards Rimini or the regular bus service (most no.4 or no.44 buses, and no.176, from the train station) can take you there. Sant'Apollinare in Classe, in fact, is literally all that remains of what was once the leading port of the northern Adriatic. The little river Uniti began to silt up Classe's harbour in classical times; when the port ceased to be a Byzantine military base and the funds for yearly dredging were no longer there, the city's fate was sealed. By the 9th century Classe was abandoned. The people of Ravenna presumably carted away most of its stone, and encroaching forests and swamps erased the last traces. Today the former port is a modern industrial suburb, 6km from the sea.

Sant'Apollinare, a huge basilica-form church completed in 549, survived only because of its importance as the burial place of Ravenna's patron. The exterior, in plain brick, is another finely proportioned basilica, with another tall cylindrical campanile. Inside it's almost empty. The beautiful Greek marble columns have well-carved capitals in a unique style. Above them are 18th-century portraits of all Ravenna's archbishops, starting with Sant'Apollinare himself – important to this city where for centuries the archbishops defended local autonomy against emperors, exarchs and popes. There are a number of fine Byzantine sarcophagi around the walls, and a bit of the original pavement, recently recovered, near the altar. The altar itself is made of antique fragments, covered by a Byzantine *ciborium*.

The real attraction, however, is the mosaics in the apse (6th–7th-century), a magnificent green- and gold-ground allegorical vision of the *Transfiguration of Christ*, with Sant'Apollinare in attendance and three sheep in a flower-strewn Mediterranean landscape, representing Peter, James and John, who were with Christ on Mount Tabor. From the front of the church, the mosaic seems to be a gigantic eye. The arch of the apse and the bottom of the mosaic make the almond-shape outline, and the blue circle with the cross on a field of stars the pupil; at the centre of the cross, the tiny circle with the image of Christ makes a third circle, inducing a kind of tunnel vision into the eye. The entire effect seems to have been quite intentional; once you see it, it's utterly hypnotic.

Above the *Transfiguration*, later mosaics (10th-century) on the arch portray a *Christ in Benediction*, up in the multicoloured pastel clouds with symbols of the Evangelists, and lines of sheep proceeding from the gates of Jerusalem and Bethlehem. Below the *Transfiguration*, as at San Vitale, there are figures (6th–7th-century) of four archbishops of Ravenna, including Ursinus, who began the construction of the basilica, and at the ends later mosaics of the sacrifices of Abel, Melchizedek (whose sacrifice in the Old Testament prefigures the Eucharist) and Abraham, opposite the Byzantine Emperor Constantine IV, bestowing privileges on Ravenna's independent church. Archangels Gabriel and Michael appear in Byzantine court dress under a pair of palm trees, the 'tree of life'.

Zona Archeologica di Classe
***t** (0544) 67705; visiting hours at the excavations Mon–Sat 9–7, Sun 9–2; adm*

Elsewhere around Classe there's little to see: bits of Roman road, some foundations. Excavations at the **Zona Archeologica di Classe**, 2km away, along the road to Ravenna, began only in 1961, and continue today. Sant'Apollinare is near the centre of a huge necropolis with some half-million burials. Some interesting things could turn up here in coming years. The area between Classe and the sea is covered with a vast and lovely pine grove, the **Pineta di Classe**, originally planted by the Romans to grow wood for their ships; just south of the town, at Fossa Ghiaia, a road leads to a completely unspoiled expanse of dunes and wetlands on the shore, called **Foce Bevano**.

North of the pines, the Ravenna shore is decorated with a pair of nondescript *lidi*, **Lido Adriano** and **Punta Marina**, merging gradually into Marina di Ravenna at the end of the ship canal, a relaxed port suburb where freighters rub noses with sailboats. There are plenty of seafood restaurants, and what may be Italy's shortest car ferry, a two-minute run across the canal. On the other side, more *lidi* share space with more pine woods: the big **Pineta San Vitale**, which like the Pineta di Classe was planted by the Roman navy.

At the southern edge of the forest, along the road from Porto Corsini to Ravenna, a hut where Garibaldi stayed on his flight to Venice has been restored as a sort of shrine, the **Capanno di**

Garibaldi. Most of this is part of the Po Delta Regional Park; off the SS309, the **Punta di Alberete** is a birdwatchers' haunt, with nature trails through the marshes.

If the children were fidgety through Ravenna's churches and museums, you can drown them here. But if they were good, take them to **Mirabilandia**, 10km south of Ravenna at Savio. Emilia-Romagna's biggest amusement park has lots of rides, a 300ft Ferris wheel, jumping motorcycles, Mayan priests, ice shows, laser shows, 3D films and plenty of ice cream.

Mirabilandia
t (0544) 561 111, www.mirabilandia.com; open April–Sept daily 10–6; July–early Sept till 11pm; adm exp; reduction for children under 1.5m or under 12; children under tall 1m or disabled free

Tourist Information in Ravenna

ⓘ Ravenna >
Via Salara 8, t (0544) 35404 or 35755, www.turismo.ravenna.it; branch at Mausoleo Teodorico, t (0544) 451 539; open daily 9–30–12.30 and 3–6

For the major sights, only a **joint ticket** is available, costing €7.50: this includes San Vitale, Sant'Apollinare Nuovo, Battistero Neoniano and Museo Arcivescovile; a ticket for €9.50 also covers the Mausoleo di Galla Placidia. Two other combined tickets are available, at €5 for the Museo Nazionale and the Mausoleo di Teodorico, and at €6.50 if you add Sant' Apollinare in Classe, although individual tickets are also available for these sights. Although Ravenna's sights have an old tradition of infernally complex opening hours, recent efforts have been made to streamline opening times and, unless otherwise stated, all sights are *open summer daily 9–7; winter daily 9–5.30.*

Shopping and Activities in Ravenna

The **Ravenna Festival** is an important music festival which runs from mid-June–mid-July. Internationally renowned musicians perform concerts, recitals and opera in some of the historic churches and palaces. For information, call **t** (0544) 249 244, *www.ravennafestival.org*.

The craftsmen of Ravenna are trying to revive the art of mosaics, but understandably they're not quite up to Byzantine levels yet. Items range from tacky souvenir plaques to the real thing, in shops and workshops around Via Roma, and on Via Manfredo Fanti near San Vitale. Here, at the **Galleria San Vitale**, you can also take a tour to see how they are made.

Where to Stay in Ravenna

Ravenna ✉ 48100

Luxury (€€€€€)

******Park Hotel Ravenna**, Viale delle Nazioni 181, **t** (0544) 531 743, *www.parkhotelravenna.it*. Big hotel in an early 1900s villa, 10km from the city at Marina di Ravenna, surrounded by pines; most rooms have balconies. There's a pool, tennis courts, and breakfast in the garden, and bicycles for clients who want to pedal into Ravenna or down to the beach. The restaurant **Al Girasole** serves Mediterranean cuisine.

Expensive (€€€€)

******Bisanzio**, Via Salara 30, **t** (0544) 217 111, *www.bizanziohotel.com*. Modern and serene hotel, with 38 rooms, all air-conditioned, and a pretty inner garden. On a quiet street near San Vitale. Continental breakfast included. *Closed 3 weeks in Jan.*

*****Cappello**, Via IV Novembre 41, **t** (0544) 219 813, *www.albergocappello.it*. Located in a 14th-century palazzo reputed to have been the home of Francesca da Rimini. With only seven big and lovely rooms. Charms include frescoes, wood-panelled ceilings, antique fireplaces and an excellent, romantic small restaurant, **La Cucina**, **t** (0544) 219 876 (€€€; open to non-guests). *Hotel open all year; restaurant closed Mon lunch, Sun and Aug.*

Moderate (€€€)

*****Adler**, Via F. Vivaldi 96, **t** (0544) 939 216, *www.adlerhot.it*. A good option along the lido at Classe, with pool. Excellent restaurant with sea view serving local fish dishes. *Open mid-May–mid-Sept.*

★★★**Centrale Byron**, Via IV Novembre 14, **t** (0544) 212 225, *www.hotelbyron.com*. Old favourite, ageing gracefully just off the Piazza del Popolo: air-conditioned, with some very nice rooms and some much plainer ones. No restaurant, but a delightful bar.

★★★**Columbia**, Viale Italia 70, **t** (0544) 446 038, *www.columbiahotel.it*. Beautiful modern hotel in attractive Marina Romea, to the north and a 10min walk from the beach. Air conditioning available in all rooms for €5 supplement. Good restaurant with seafood specialities, swimming pool, solarium and bike rental. *Closed 3 weeks Dec–Jan.*

★ Diana ›

★★★Diana, Via G. Rossi 47, **t** (0544) 39164, *www.hoteldiana.ra.it*. In an 18th-century palace, near the tomb of Galla Placidia. Delightful, comfortable hotel with a charming Baroque lobby and modern facilities in every room from satellite LCD TV to massage armchairs. The delicious breakfast is worth the price; baby-sitting services and bicycles for clients are a bonus.

★★★**Roma**, Via Candiano 26, **t** (0544) 421 515, *www.hotelroma.ra.it*. In a convenient, if not particularly pleasant, location on the other side of the tracks from the railway station. Restaurant with local cuisine such as home-made varieties of pasta.

Moderate (€€)

★★★**Argentario**, Via di Roma 45, **t** (0544) 35555, *www.hotelargentarioravenna.it*. Near the Basilica di Sant'Apollinare and offering pleasant rooms, some in the budget range, all air-conditioned; the big buffet breakfast is extra.

★★**Ravenna**, Viale Maroncelli 12, **t** (0544) 212 204, *www.hotelravenna.ra.it*. Good choice near the station: not all en suite.

★**Al Giaciglio**, Via Rocca Brancaleone 42, **t** 0544 39403, *www.albergoalgiaciglio.com*. Another option, with cheaper rooms without bath, good home cooking in the restaurant, and an inexpensive lunch menu that changes daily; pizza too. *Restaurant closed Sun.*

Hostel Galletti Abbiosi, Via di Roma 140, **t** (0544) 31313, *www.galletti.ra.it*. Very nice hostel in downtown Ravenna, located in a historic building with frescoes on the ceilings. 32 rooms with air conditioning, minibar, phone, TV and safe. Clean and comfortable. Look at the website for last-minute offers.

Budget (€)

There is plenty of budget accommodation but much of it is around the port, a long walk from the centre along Via delle Industrie.

Dante, Via Nicolodi 12, **t** (0544) 421 164, *www.hostelravenna.com*. **Youth hostel** on the east side of the railway tracks, a 10min walk from the station (or take bus no.1). Only the family rooms have a private bathroom. *Open Mar–Dec.*

Eating Out in Ravenna

Very Expensive (€€€€)

Saporetti Trattoria al Pescatore, Via N. Zen 13, **t** (0544) 530 208, *www.ristorantesaporetti.it*. Run by the *simpatico* Saporetti family. Offering delicious seafood (try *sfrappole* with squid and *rucola*) on the Marina di Ravenna; three fixed-price menus available. Dine al fresco in the garden. *Closed Tues, Jan, and Aug.*

Expensive (€€€)

A Casa di Marco, Via Romea Sud 315, **t** (0544) 527 283. Friendly place in Classe serving dishes with a Tuscan feel: *tortellacci* filled with shrimp in a rocket pesto, swordfish, and *amaretto semifreddo* with melted chocolate. *Closed Mon.*

Taverna San Romualdo, Via San t'Alberto 364, **t** (0544) 483 447, *taverna.sanromualdo@libero.it*. Not far from San Vitale. Typically rustic Romagnolo *osteria* serving excellent-value hearty dishes, such as cheese *squaquerone*. Mixed *antipasti* vary according to the season: *tortellacci* stuffed with nettles and served with mascarpone and pine nuts, minestrone flavoured with truffles, octopus stewed with balsamic vinegar and served tepid with rocket and cannellini beans, or a good choice of game in the winter. Also serves some ethnic dishes such as sushi and couscous, local cheese and hams and over 200 types of wine. Desserts are a must: try the nougat *semifreddo* with chocolate sauce. *Closed Tues.*

★ Ca' de Ven >>

Villa Antica, Via Faentina 136, **t** (0544) 500 522, *www.villaantica.it*. Very popular restaurant in the suburbs west of the centre. Formerly 'Tre Spade', it's now under new ownership. Meat and fish menus, plus pizzas. *Closed Tues and mid–end July.*

Moderate (€€)

Capannetti, Vicolo Capannetti 21, **t** (0544) 66681. With an experienced chef who knows what to do with truffles, duck, mushrooms and desserts, though the menu is on the short side. Try the stuffed *tortelli* or rabbit with aromatic vinegar. *Closed Sun eve, Mon, and Jan.*

La Gardela, Via Ponte Marino 3, **t** (0544) 217 147. Small restaurant with air conditioning in the centre of Ravenna. Makes its own *tortelloni*; try *scaloppine* with *taleggio* and rocket, or grilled fish and home-made pasta, and sample the large collection of grappas. Garden in summer. *Closed Thurs, 2 weeks Jan, and 2 weeks Aug.*

Locanda del Melarancio, Via Mentana 33, **t** (0544) 215 258, *www.locanda delmelarancio.it*. Located in a 16th-century palace, offering local cuisine – try the boar with chocolate. Also four rooms (€). *Closed Wed.*

Inexpensive (€)

Ca' de Ven (the 'house of wine'), Via Corrado Ricci 24, **t** (0544) 30163. Enoteca in a beautiful building with painted ceilings, with a huge selection of Emilia-Romagna wines and snacks using local cheeses, hams and sausages. Suitably calm and dark, and a great local favourite, the perfect place to while away an afternoon after a morning with the Byzantines. *Closed Mon.*

Caffè del Teatro, Via Mariani 1. Elegant, light lunches. *Closed Sun.*

La Rustica, Via Alberoni 55, **t** (0544) 218 128, *www.trattoria-larustica.it*. Near the station and practically a museum of country kitchen gear; it's fun speculating just what some of the stuff could be for. Cuisine to match – traditional Romagnolo cooking and especially good home-made pasta dishes. Summer garden. *Booking advisable. Closed Fri and 1 week Nov.*

The Romagna: Imola to Rimini

In a landscape apparently designed by computer, east of Bologna the big towns pop up with precise regularity along the relentlessly straight Via Emilia. They all have their attractions: fine restaurants in Imola, ceramics in Faenza, Forlì's museum and crumbling Mussolini showpieces, and Cesena's Rocca. But this is the place for getting off the straight and narrow – a right turn just about anywhere will take you into a part of the Apennines that is one of this region's hidden treasures, with hill towns like Brisighella, and a little corner of Tuscany that got away.

The whole point of the Via Emilia, of course, is for all the odd bits and pieces of northern Italy to roll down to Rimini, that singular town of Fellini, ghosts and Malatesta weirdness – also the centre of Italy's biggest and most boisterous riviera.

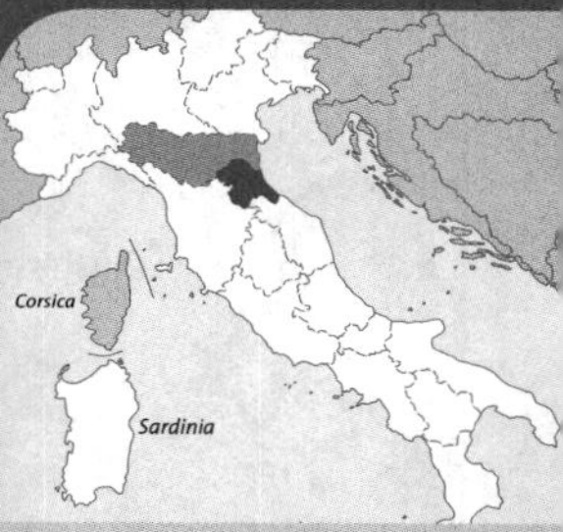

12

1 Faïence in Faenza
International Museum of Ceramics **p.295**

2 Hill-town resort in the Apennines
Brisighella **p.296**

3 Villages of the Tuscan Romagna
Bagno di Romagna **p.302**

4 A museum of sailing ships
Museo Galleggiante, Cesenatico **p.309**

5 Rimini's arcane mysteries
Tempio Malatestiano **p.315**

See map overleaf

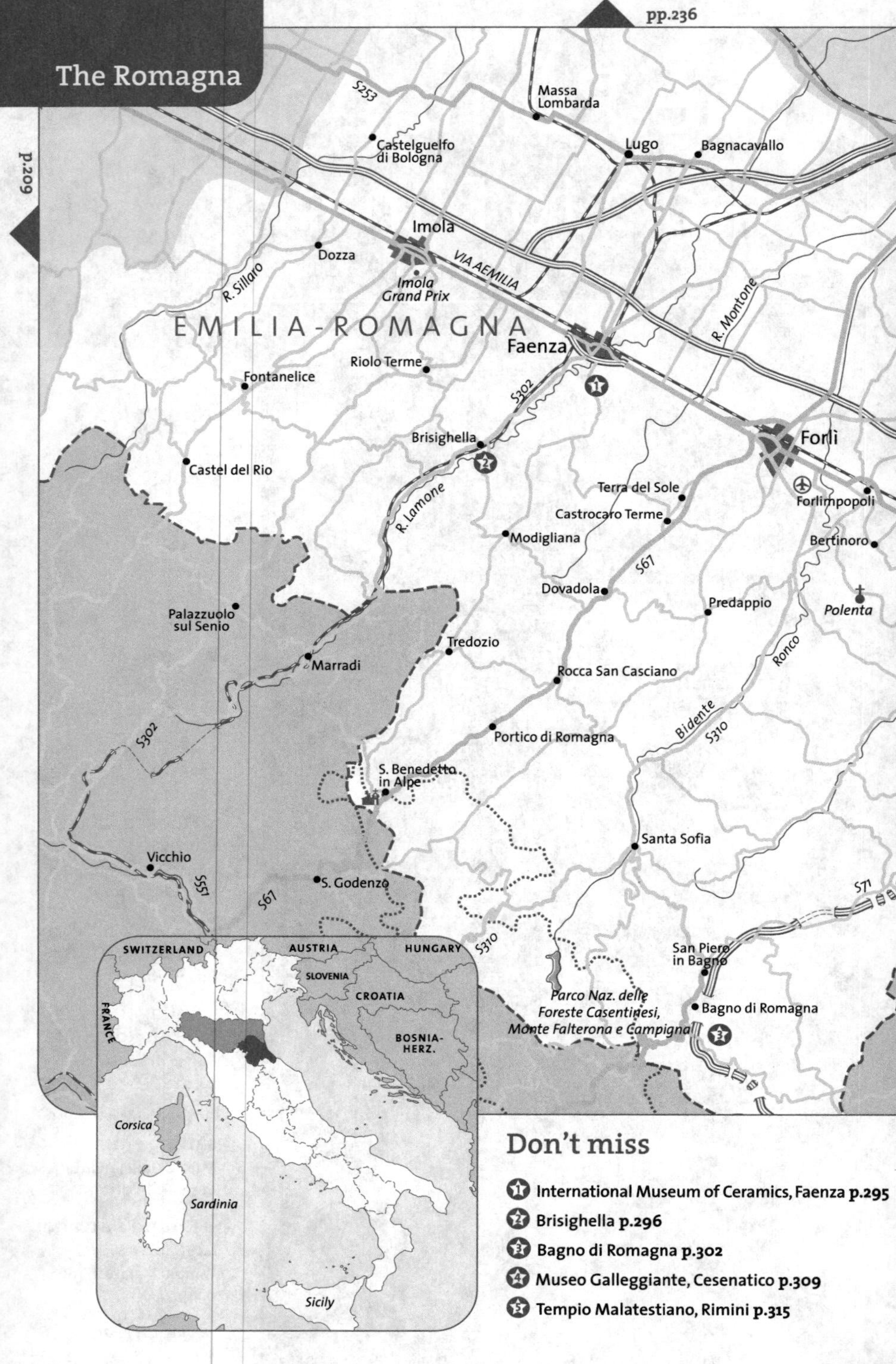
The Romagna
pp.236
p.209
S253
Massa Lombarda
Castelguelfo di Bologna
Lugo
Bagnacavallo
Imola
Dozza
VIA AEMILIA
Imola Grand Prix
R. Sillaro
EMILIA-ROMAGNA
Faenza
R. Montone
Riolo Terme
Fontanelice
S302
Brisighella
Forlì
Castel del Rio
Terra del Sole
Forlimpopoli
Castrocaro Terme
R. Lamone
Modigliana
Bertinoro
S67
Dovadola
Predappio
Polenta
Palazzuolo sul Senio
Tredozio
Marradi
Ronco
Rocca San Casciano
Bidente
S310
S302
Portico di Romagna
S. Benedetto in Alpe
Santa Sofia
Vicchio
S551
S. Godenzo
S67
S71
S310
San Piero in Bagno
Parco Naz. delle Foreste Casentinesi, Monte Falterona e Campigna
Bagno di Romagna
SWITZERLAND
AUSTRIA
HUNGARY
SLOVENIA
CROATIA
FRANCE
BOSNIA-HERZ.
Corsica
Sardinia
Sicily
Don't miss
1 International Museum of Ceramics, Faenza p.295
2 Brisighella p.296
3 Bagno di Romagna p.302
4 Museo Galleggiante, Cesenatico p.309
5 Tempio Malatestiano, Rimini p.315

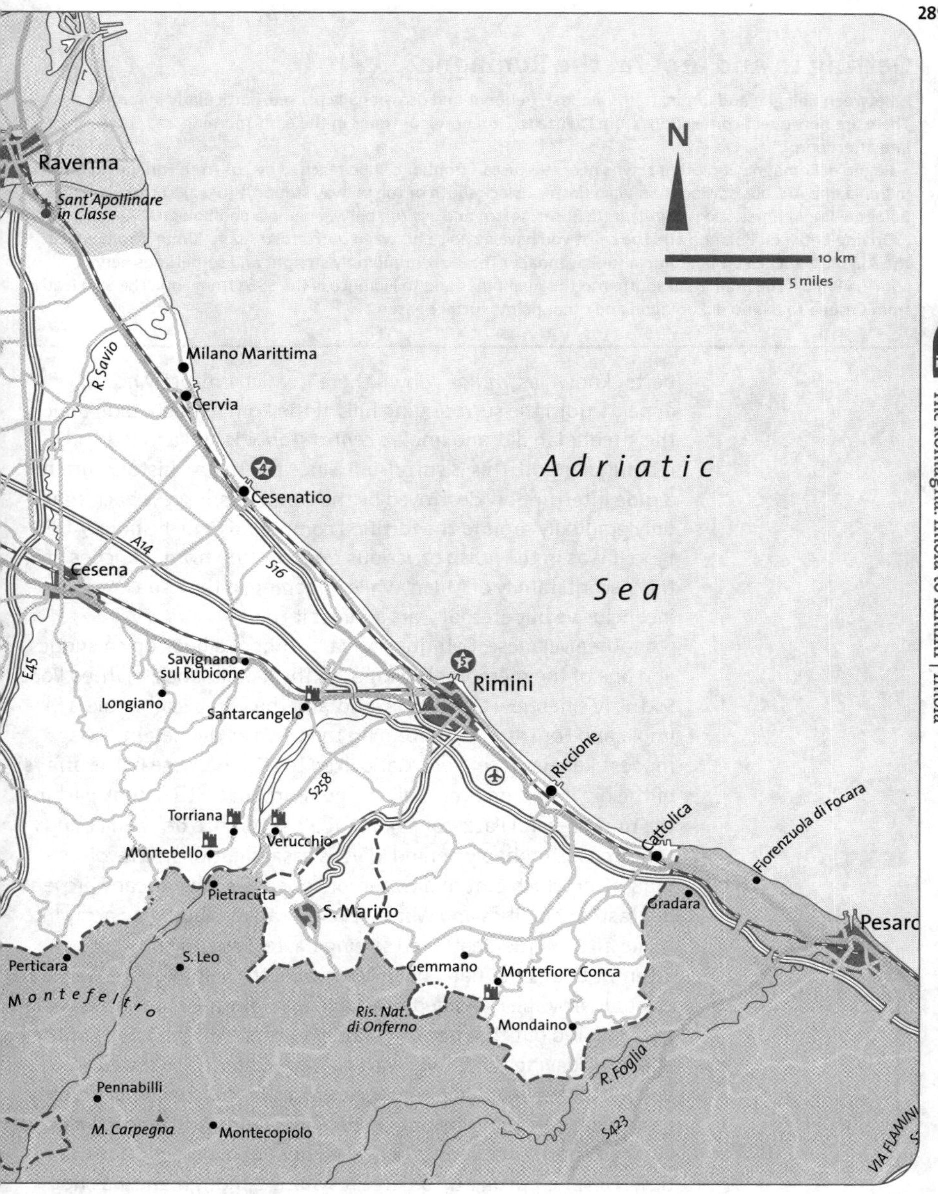

Imola

This proud little city is best known for good food and motor racing, but when you're there Imola will take pains to remind you that it, too, is an art town – but note that most of its sights are officially only open on weekends. Imola grew up on either side of the Via Emilia as the Roman *Forum Cornelii*, although it eventually became

Getting to and around the Romagna

Between Bologna and Rimini **trains** are fast, frequent and occasionally packed, particularly in August. There are now direct connections from Faenza to Florence: four trains in the early morning and three in the late afternoon.

Bagno di Romagna and other towns near the Tuscan frontier can be reached by **bus** from Forlì or Florence. In Imola, the ATC bus station is on Viale Costa, a block south of the railway station, **t** (0542) 22479; for Bologna–Imola times, see *www.atc.bo.it*. Buses 99, 101 and 257 run between Imola and Bologna.

Driving between Bologna and the coast you have a choice between *autostrada* A14 to Rimini (from which the A14 dir branches off near Imola for Ravenna) or the slow, numbingly straight and sometimes nerve-racking SS9/Via Emilia. The main road south into the Apennines and to Florence is the SS67 from Forlì. The SS71 leads from Cesena to Bagno di Romagna and other points further east.

better known as *Imulae* ('down there'), which is exactly how it appears from the surrounding hills. If the Roman name didn't stick, the street plan did, and Imola's *centro storico* is still a mostly tidy rectangular grid. This is surprising, since the town's history suffered a rude interruption: destroyed by the Lombards, it grew back again only gradually, around the fortified compound of its bishops. After 1300 it was in the grasp of various *signori*, often from branches of the Visconti family of Milan, while engaging in the usual inconclusive but eternal wars against its neighbours.

Another Milanese, Caterina Sforza, author of a book on cosmetics and one of the memorable viragos of the Renaissance, married Pope Sixtus IV's nephew Girolamo Riario, and the two became rulers in Imola and Forlì after 1473, running the town at the height of its modest Renaissance glory. Riario liked to stick his nose in the affairs of the big boys, and eventually he got burned for it. He took part in the unsuccessful Pazzi conspiracy against Lorenzo de' Medici, and Lorenzo was probably behind Riario's assassination in a revolt of 1488, after which Caterina was imprisoned. She had already proved her taste for politics and war four years earlier, leading an army into Rome after Sixtus' death and seizing Castel Sant'Angelo in an attempt to ensure that a pope favourable to their interests would be elected. Now she managed to escape and rally her supporters (when they pointed out that her six children were still in the hands of their enemies, leaving the family with no heirs, Caterina reportedly hoisted up her skirts and told the crowd she could still make plenty more). She eventually reconquered all her lands, and enjoyed a good bloody Renaissance vengeance on all her enemies, not for the last time. Despite putting up a fierce resistance, though, she was not able to save her state when Cesare Borgia attacked it in 1499. Caterina got another spell in prison, and then went to live quietly in Florence, where she married a Medici and became the mother of a worthy son, the famous mercenary captain Giovanni of the Black Bands. As for Cesare, after the death of his father, Pope Alexander VI, his little empire went up in smoke, and Imola passed under direct papal rule.

Imola really distinguished itself after Italian unification, as the heart and soul of the Socialist movement. Its radical population elected Italy's first Socialist city government in 1889, seven years after sending the nation's first Socialist deputy to parliament. This was Andrea Costa, a friend of the Russian anarchist revolutionary Bakunin; the two had gone to jail together after the failed revolt of 1874 in Bologna. Though still one of the most solidly left-wing towns in Italy, Imola is better known for its race track, home of the annual San Marino Grand Prix.

Centro Storico and Museums

The centre of Imola, probably occupying the site of the original Roman forum, is the porticoed **Piazza Matteotti**. The **Palazzo Sersanti** here was built for Signore Girolamo Riario in 1480 by an architect named Giorgio Fiorentino. The stretch of Via Emilia west of the Piazza contains some strangely clashing relics of Imola's past, from the belle époque Caffè-Pasticceria Bacchilega on the corner, to the gosh-awful 1936 Mussolinian Casa del Fascio, to the **Farmacia dell'Ospedale** under the porticoes at No.99. This lovely pharmacy, still in business and run by the *comune*, hasn't changed much since its opening in 1766, with its original majolica medicine jars and a beautiful vaulted and frescoed ceiling.

Palazzo Tozzoni
t *(0542) 35856 www.comune.imola.bo.it; open summer Sun 3.15–7.15; winter Sat 9–12 and 2.45–6.45, Sun 2.45–6.45; Mon–Fri 9–12 by appt; adm; joint ticket available for Rocca Sforzesca, Pinacoteca Comunale and Palazzo Tozzoni*

Museo Diocesano
t *(0542) 24362; open Tues and Thurs 9–12 and 2–5; other days by appointment; adm free*

South of Via Emilia, on Via Garibaldi, the **Palazzo Tozzoni** will give you a rare chance to see how a prominent family lived in the 18th century. Built in 1738, it has conserved most of its original decorations and furnishings (lots of ornate stucco and gilding) as well as the family's collections of paintings, prints, books, coins and archaeological finds. In the neoclassical 18th-century **cathedral** on Via Don Bughetti you can pay your respects at the tomb of Imola's patron San Cassiano, a 3rd-century schoolteacher whose martyrdom was particularly unpleasant: he was stabbed with the pens of his pagan students. There's a small collection of paintings from Imola's churches, along with medieval illuminated books and Baroque carriages, in the **Museo Diocesano** across the street in the Bishops' Palace.

Museo Archeologico Naturalistico G. Scartabelli
closed for restoration; collections are housed in Convento San Francisco

Pinacoteca Comunale
t *(0542) 602 609; open Sat and Sun 3–6; adm; joint ticket available for Rocca Sforzesca, Pinacoteca Comunale and Palazzo Tozzoni*

Back on the Via Emilia, just north of the cathedral, Imola's Palazzo dei Musei contains the **Museo Archeologico Naturalistico G. Scartabelli**, mostly rocks and minerals and a little archaeology. Just behind it on Via Sacchi, the **Pinacoteca Comunale** has a number of detached frescoes and a painted processional standard from Venice, all from the 1400s; a *Madonna della Misericordia* attributed (by the Imolesi at least) to Raphael; and three works of Lavinia Fontana, including a surprising pagan *Scena del Sacrificio*; as well as local artists of the 19th and 20th centuries.

To the east of the museum on Via Cavour, the **Palazzo Calderini** is the very picture of a Florentine palace of the quattrocento, with its rusticated ground floor, counterpoised by a graceful second storey with characteristic Florentine double windows.

Rocca Sforzesca

Rocca Sforzesca
t (0542) 602 609, www.comune.imola.bo.it; open summer Sat 9–12 and 3–7, Sun 3–7; winter Sat 9–12 and 2.30–6.30, Sun 2.30–6.30; also Mon–Fri 9–12 by appointment; adm; joint ticket available for Rocca Sforzesca, Pinacoteca Comunale and Palazzo Tozzoni

Zoo Acquario
t (0542) 24180, www.zooacquario.it; open Tues–Sat 9–12 and 4–7, Sun 9.30–12 and 4–7; closed Mon, Sun in July and 3 wks Aug; adm

Imola's landmark, the impressive Rocca Sforzesca in the southwest corner of the old town on Via Garibaldi, owes its current appearance, refined and low-slung, to a 15th-century rebuilding by the Duke of Milan, Galeazzo Sforza; parts of the earlier castle were retained inside the new walls. Though the model for many similar castles throughout the Romagna and beyond, it didn't hold out for long against Cesare Borgia in 1499. Cesare had an expert on fortifications with him, a certain Leonardo da Vinci; he drew a town plan of Imola, made for improving the defences, that is now at Windsor Palace. Recently restored, the Rocca houses a museum of arms and ceramics discovered during the work.

Near the station on Via Aspromonte, the **Zoo Acquario** is the region's biggest aquarium, with an impressive stock of tropical fish, sharks, snakes and turtles.

ⓘ Imola >
Via Mazzini 14, t (0542) 602 207, www.comune.imola.bo.it or www.stai.it

Where to Stay and Eat in Imola

Imola ✉ 40026

********Molino Rosso****, Via Statale Selice 49, **t** (0542) 63111, *www.molinorosso.it* (€€€€€). Imola's most luxurious hotel, outside the centre of town on the road to the A14, formerly the site of an old mill. The hotel has big, quiet, well-equipped rooms, nice bathrooms; tennis courts, swimming pool, beach volleyball, football pitch, billiards and bikes are available for guests. Its 300-seat restaurant organizes fine cookery courses.

*****Il Maglio**, Via Statale Selice 26/a, **t** (0542) 642 299, *www.hotelilmaglio.it* (€€€). In the same area as the Molino Rosso but much smaller: arranged with 39 rooms and a family suite on three floors this family-owned hotel is modern, comfortable and air conditioned, with a good restaurant.

*****Ziò**, Viale Nardozzi 14, **t** (0542) 35274, *www.hotelzioimola.com* (€€€). Closer to the centre: very comfortable hotel located on a quiet street but close to the international Formula One circuit. Rooms are comfortable enough, with phone, minibar, satellite TV and air conditioning.

*****Moderno**, Via XX Settembre 22, **t** (0542) 23122 (€€). With seven simple rooms (no air conditioning) right in the centre of things, and there is also an excellent restaurant. *Closed 1st week June.*

San Domenico, Via G. Sacchi 1, **t** (0542) 29000, *www.sandomenico.it* (€€€€). Shrine to gastronomes around the world for the past three decades. The holy temple of Italian culinary traditions offers a constantly changing menu, sublimely prepared, with the lightest and most delicate of touches. It has a slightly dated 1970s dining room, fresh and wonderful food, and an exquisite, credit-card-shattering wine list. Tasting menus available. *Closed Sat lunch in summer, Sun, Mon and some days in Jan and Aug.*

Osteria del Vicolo Nuovo, Vicolo Coldronchi 6, **t** (0542) 32552, *www.vicolonuovo.it* (€€€). In a 17th-century cellar, serving delicious modern dishes based on local traditions: cheese soufflé with *porcini* mushrooms, duck with orange, rabbit roasted in San Giovese wine, tongue with *salsa verde*, an assortment of vegetarian dishes, and delicious cheeses. Tasting menu. Kitchen open late: special menu after 11pm. *Booking advisable. Closed Sun, Mon and July–late Aug.*

È Parlaminté, Via G. Mameli 33, **t** (0542) 30144, *parlaminte@katamail.com* (€€). A cheerful, family-run favourite in Imola; everyone comes to eat *passatelli in brodo* or *baccalà*, and discuss affairs of the day – the name means 'the parliament'. *Booking advisable. Closed Mon, and Sun eve; May–Aug all Sun.*

La Tavernetta, Via Tito Speri 6, off the Via Emilia Ovest, **t** (0542) 22339 (€€). Another very popular spot, offering a wide choice of dishes including seafood and roast boar and *tortelli* with pumpkin and mustard. *Closed Mon and Aug.*

Dozza

Rocca Malvezzi-Campeggi
t *(0542) 678 240; open summer Tues–Sat 10–12.30 and 3–6.30, Sun and hols 10–1 and 3–7.30; winter Tues–Sat 10–12.30 and 2.30–5, Sun and hols 10–1 and 2.30–6; adm*

Enoteca Regionale Emilia-Romagna
t *(0542) 678 089, www. enotecaemilia romagna.it; open summer Tues–Fri 9.30–1 and 2.30–6.30, Sat 10–1 and 3–6.30, Sun 10–1 and 3–7; winter Tues–Fri 9.30–1 and 2.30–6.30, Sat–Sun 10–1 and 2.30–6, Sun 10–1 and 3–6.45*

Biennale Muro Dipinto
t *(0542) 678 116, www.murodipinto.it*

Museo della Guerra
t *(0542) 95554, www.museoguerra-casteldelrio.it; open Sun and hols 2–6; other days by appointment; adm*

ⓘ Dozza >
Via XX Settembre 51, **t** *(0542) 678 052, www.comune.dozza.bo.it*

Caterina Sforza was also the ruler of Dozza, a handsome medieval hill town south of the Via Emilia a few kilometres back towards Bologna. She rebuilt the asymmetrical castle and massive tower, a smaller version of Imola's Rocca called the **Rocca Malvezzi-Campeggi**, standing over a deep moat. In 1529 Pope Clement V granted the castle to the Malvezzi-Campeggi of Bologna, who converted it in part to a stately residence. When they died out in 1960, the castle became the property of the *comune*. There is a handsome loggia with finely carved castles, and some of the rooms contain antiques, tapestries and family portraits, but the main allure is the cellars, home of the **Enoteca Regionale Emilia-Romagna**, a treasure-trove where you can sample 600 of the region's wines.

Dozza itself is decorated with bright murals, the result of the wall-painting festival, the **Biennale Muro Dipinto**, held in biennually in September in odd-numbered years. Sketches for the paintings, and some that have been detached from the walls, are on display in the Rocca.

South of Imola on the SS610, almost on the Tuscan border, **Castel del Rio** has yet another Renaissance castle, the 1504 Castello Alidosi, which houses the **Museo della Guerra**, with exhibits from local Second World War campaigns. The family who built the castle are also responsible for the beautiful Ponte Alidosi over the Fiume Santerno, an 'ass-back' (*schiena d'asino*) stone bridge with a single 120ft arch.

Where to Stay and Eat in and near Dozza

Dozza ✉ 40050

******Monte del Re**, Via Monte del Re 43, **t** (0542) 678 4000, *www.montedelre.it* (€€€€€). Refined hotel in a 13th-century Franciscan convent and park in hills just above Dozza. Stylish furnishings, big beds, mod cons and air conditioning keep the rooms from being too monastic in tone. Flowers and antiques brighten the public rooms. Fabulous swimming pool, winter garden and restaurant, serving good regional and international cuisine.

*****Canè**, Via XX Settembre 27, **t** (0542) 678 120, *www.ristorantecanet.net* (€€€€). Located right in the *centro storico* with en suite rooms refurbished in 2004 with TV, air conditioning and Internet. The main attractions here are the restaurant (€€) and its summer garden terrace; the ravioli and *pollo alla diavola* are legendary. *Closed Mon and Jan.*

Le Bistrot, Via Calanco 5, **t** (0542) 678 580 (€€). Another good dining choice, situated just outside the walls. It offers light and delicious versions of the regional cuisine – such as strudels of ricotta and greens, *culatello* with a sauce of pine nuts, rocket and balsamic vinegar, ravioli in asparagus and courgette sauce, and stuffed, deboned rabbit. They also have eight rooms. *Booking advisable. Closed Tues, Feb and July.*

Castelguelfo di Bologna (north of Dozza) ✉ 40023

******Locanda Solarola***, Via Santa Croce 5, **t** (0542) 670 102, *www.locandasolarola.com* (€€€€). A welcoming place to stay, this is pleasantly placed in a beautiful green meadow. Every room is charming and different in character, and each individually furnished with antiques, and comfortably equipped, with minibar and TV. Garden, swimming pool in summer, billiards room, bicycles, a reading room and pretty restaurant (which is also open to non-guests). Bologna is only 28km away. *It only has 15 rooms, so book ahead. Closed Jan and 1 week Aug.*

Locanda dell'Agnese, Via Larga 1, **t** (0542) 53321, *www.locandadellagnese.it* (€€). A popular family-run *locanda*, this has seven simple rooms (€) in addition to its renowned restaurant serving local cuisine such as *tortelloni* with ricotta cheese, butter and sage, or pig's liver. Excellent cheese and desserts. *Booking advisable. Closed Mon.*

Faenza

'Faïence ware' was born here in Faenza in the 16th century with the invention of a new style of majolica: a piece was given a solid white glaze then rapidly, almost impressionistically, decorated with two tones of yellow and blue. It caused a sensation, and was in such demand throughout Europe that Faenza became a household name.

Ceramics, Ceramics, Ceramics

Ente Ceramica
Corso Mazzini 92,
***t** (0546) 21145,*
www.enteceramica.it

Today Faenza has regained much of its 16th-century renown as a ceramics centre. There are 500 students enrolled in its *Istituto d'Arte per la Ceramica* and experimental laboratory, as well as some 60 artists from around the world who run workshops in the town. The **Ente Ceramica** has changing exhibits of their work, and issues a list of studios that you may visit and buy from. Particularly worth seeing are *Carlo Zauli*, Via della Croce 6; *Ivo Sassi*, Via Bondiollo 11; *Mila Donati*, Corso Saffi 44; *La Vecchia Faenza*, Via S. Ippolito 25; *Ceramiche Cortese*, Corso Mazzini 49; *Goffredo Gaeta*, Via Carena 3; and the *Consorzio Ceramiche*, Via Pietro Borlotti, next to the cathedral. Among several buildings and palaces adorned with majolica the best is the Liberty-style Palazzo Matteucci in the main street, Corso Mazzini.

Every year from September to October Faenza hosts an international ceramics exhibition; the theme is contemporary in odd years, and antique in even ones.

Museo Internazionale delle Ceramiche
Viale Baccarini 19, **t** *(0546) 697 311, www.micfaenza.org; open summer Tues–Sun and hols 9.30–7; winter Tues–Thurs 9.30–1.30, Fri–Sun and hols 9.30–5.30; adm*

The **Museo Internazionale delle Ceramiche**, north of the centre, was founded in 1908 and restored after its bombing in the War. It houses a magnificent collection of ceramics, centred on 16th- and 17th-century Italian works; pieces from Faenza adorned with giraffe-necked Renaissance ladies were typical nuptial gifts. There are some fine Liberty-style pieces by Domenico Baccarini and Francesco Nonni, and downstairs reveals an excellent collection of international ceramic art, including pieces by Picasso, Matisse, Chagall and Rouault.

Outside of the plates, Faenza is a shabby old town, but it does have a grand centrepiece, the adjacent squares **Piazza del Popolo** and **Piazza della Libertà**: these are at their best during the **markets**, held three mornings a week on Tuesdays, Thursdays and Saturdays. Faenza's public buildings face each other on the Piazza del Popolo, the medieval **Palazzo del Municipio**, with a façade added in the early 20th century, and the 13th-century **Palazzo del Podestà**. Linking the piazza to Piazzetta Nenni is a lovely double portico from the 1600s, the **Voltone della Molinella**, with its fresco constantly lit. On Piazza della Libertà, the unfinished Renaissance **Duomo** has some good Renaissance sculpture in its severe white interior, notably in the *Capella di San Savino*, with a beautiful marble arca sculpted with reliefs by the Tuscan Benedetto da Maiano, and some ceramic work from a real master – Andrea della Robbia of Florence, who did the colourful tondo over the altar with the arms of Faenza's Renaissance rulers, the Manfredis. There are also plenty of Baroque touches, including a bizarre flying figure of *Death* looming out from the pier nearest the altar.

Palazzo Milzetti
Via Tonducci, **t** *(0546) 26493; open Mon–Sat 8.45–1.30, Thurs 2.15–4.30; adm*

Pinacoteca Comunale
Via Severoli, **t** *(0546) 660 799; open Sat–Sun 10–7; adm free*

Faenza was one of the more forward-looking towns of the Papal State in the 1700s, and it has a number of buildings in the neoclassical style imported from Enlightenment France. The finest of these is the **Palazzo Milzetti** on Via Tonducci, south of Corso Mazzini. Completed in 1802, it contains some fine rooms with painted and stucco decoration influenced by the recently discovered ruins of Pompeii; there is also some esoteric Masonic symbolism that would have got the Milzettis into trouble with the Inquisition – but when they built it Faenza was under the rule of Napoleon. The **Pinacoteca Comunale** on Via Severoli contains a good collection of paintings by Romagna artists, sculpture by Alfonso Lombardi, and some works formerly attributed to Donatello.

North of Faenza

The Ravenna plain north of Faenza is a fertile and hard-working agricultural area, and home to a number of big market towns, none of which will detain you for very long. **Massa Lombarda** gets its name from the Lombard refugees who settled here in the 1250s, fleeing from the depredations of the horrible Ezzelino da Romano of

Verona; the church of **Santa Maria in Fabriago**, just north of town, has a 9th-century Ravenna-style round campanile.

Lugo, like the Lugo in Spain and so many other cities across Europe (Lyon, Laon, Loudon, Leiden), gets its name from the Celtic god Lugh, their equivalent of Mercury or Hermes. Despite its ancient foundation (Neolithic finds here go back over 5,000 years), Lugo's sights are limited to the 16th-century Rocca and the 1783 Paviglione, an arcaded market square that once functioned as the region's market for silkworms.

Nobody knows about the name of **Bagnacavallo** ('horse-bath'), but this town has the distinction of having once been the property of Sir John Hawkwood, the English mercenary captain of the 1300s whose monument you can see in Florence's Duomo. It also has a unique elliptical piazza, the porticoed 1758 Piazza Nuova, and a 7th-century church just outside town, the **Pieve di San Pietro in Sylvis**, with some frescoes of the 14th-century Rimini school.

South of Faenza: Brisighella

② Brisighella

Rocca
t (0546) 83129; open mid-April–mid-Oct Tues–Sat 10–12 and 3.30–7, Sun and hols 10–12 and 3.30–7.30; rest of year Sat 2.30–4.30; adm; Torre dell'Orologio, open Sat 4–7, Sun and hols 11–12.30 and 4–7; also Tues–Sat, 4–7 in summer; adm

Museo Civico
t (0546) 85777; open 15 April–15 Oct Fri–Sun 10–12 and 3.30–7.30; rest of the year Sat 3–6.30, Sun 10–12 and 3.30–6.30; adm

Museo del Lavoro Contadino
t (0546) 85777; open 15 Oct–15 Apr Sat 2.30–4.30, Sun 10–12 and 2.30–4.30; rest of year Tues–Fri 10–12 and 3.30–7, Sat–Sun 10–12.15 and 3.30–7.30; adm

Some 12km outside Faenza on the Florence road, Brisighella is a charming village and thermal spa in the Lamone valley with an unforgettable skyline. The sharp cliffs overhead are crowned by the splendid golden brick towers of the 12th-century **Rocca**, originally a respectable guard tower (1290) with a clock slapped on its front in the 18th century. Brisighella traditionally produced much of the clay fired in Faenza's kilns – next to the village you can see the gashes left in the hills by the old quarries. So precious was this cargo borne by the village's mule caravans that a protected, elevated passageway, the **Via degli Asini** (Mule Road), was built through the centre of town. In case of attack it could be sealed up at either end. There's a small picture collection in the **Museo Civico**, on Piazza Marconi, which includes the works of a local Art Nouveau poster artist named Giuseppe Ugonia.

In the Rocca, accessible by car or a short climb up from the town, you can visit the **Museo del Lavoro Contadino**, with a collection devoted to the region's traditional peasant culture, life and work. The castle, built in 1310 by the Manfredi of Faenza, took its present form under the Venetian occupation of 1503–9. In the first decade of the Wars of Italy, Venice had taken advantage of the confusion to snatch territories from all its neighbours; almost every power in Italy, led by Pope Julius II, ganged up on her in the League of Cambrai of 1508. Venice was lucky to survive and keep most of its empire intact in the nine-year struggle that followed; all the Venetian possessions in the Romagna were lost.

The terme and the hotels are in the lower town, across the tracks by the river. On the southern edge of town there's a brick Romanesque church, the 9th-century **Pieve del Thò**, incorporating parts of ancient Roman buildings.

Pieve del Thò
open Sun mornings only

Much of the area around Brisighella, and as far as the coast, makes a good example of the kind of landscapes you'll see in patches all down Italy's Adriatic side: not especially high hills, but curiously jagged and jumbled ones, where the back roads boom up and down like rollercoasters – the kind of country favoured by Italy's famously masochistic weekend cyclists.

Unless you come straight from Faenza, you'll have to take roads such as these to get to **Modigliana**, hidden away in the valley of the Marenzo. Modigliana has a sweet medieval centre, with lots of bridges and houses overlooking the river; it is entered by the **Tribuna**, a grandly picturesque bridge-gate built under Florentine rule. Above the town stands the ruined **Roccaccia** – as its name implies even the Modiglianesi find this castle more silly than picturesque, with half its tower (divided vertically) fallen away. In **Tredozio**, south of Modigliana, the 18th-century **Palazzo Fantini** is known for its Italian garden; in summer it is used for concerts and plays.

Palazzo Fantini
t (051) 330 095 for information on concerts and plays in summer

Shopping and Activities in Faenza and Brisighella

Faenza's traditional ***palio*** takes place on the last Sunday in June.

As a resort town, Brisighella does its best to keep visitors busy. Around the last week of June it hosts an elaborate **Medieval Festival**, with music, games, feasts, plays and more; it also offers plenty of sporting activities.

Faenza doesn't have a monopoly on **ceramics** – several workshops still operate in Brisighella.

There's a weekly **antiques market** on Friday evenings in the summer (besides the usual Wednesday morning **food and produce** market), and a number of craft shops in addition to the places selling ceramics.

Where to Stay and Eat in Faenza and Brisighella

ⓘ **Faenza >**
Piazza del Popolo 1, t (0546) 25231, prolocofaenza@racine.ra.it, www.prolocofaenza.it

Faenza ✉ 48018

******Hotel Vittoria**, Corso Garibaldi 23, **t** (0546) 21508, *www.hotel-vittoria.com* (€€€€). In the centre of town: attractive hotel with 19th-century furnishings and the occasional frescoed ceiling; rooms are large and air-conditioned, plus a laundry service. It has a restaurant too.

******Cavallino**, just outside Faenza at Via Forlivese 185, **t** (0546) 634 411, *www.hotel-cavallino.it* (€€). Situated a short drive away at Via Forlivese: with a garage, garden and restaurant, and offering bicycles to clients who want to pedal into town. Rooms have all the facilities you would expect, and four have hydro-massage. Very good buffet breakfast; restaurant which prides itself on home-made pasta.

For cheaper accommodation, there are now many *affittacamere* (rooms for rent) in private houses. Call the tourist office for details.

Le Volte, Corso Mazzini 54, **t** (0546) 661 600, *paladinivincenzo@tin.it* (€€). Near the Pinacoteca, and hidden away in old wine cellars beneath an arcade called the Galleria Gessi in a 15th-century palace. Surrounded by antique furniture: specialities include *tortelloni al radicchio*, duck breast roasted with cabbage and pepper, or rack of lamb in a herb crust. *Booking advisable. Closed Sun, end July–mid-Aug, 1 week Jan.*

Enoteca Astorre, Piazza della Libertà 16, **t** (0546) 681 407, *www.enotecaastorre.it* (€). Beside the Duomo, and offering a rewarding array of regional and further-flung Italian wines accompanied by *bruschetta*, *piadine* and tasty snacks; they also do full meals and two-course lunches with good Romagna-style starters.

La Pavona, Via Santa Lucia 45, **t** (0546) 31075, *www.buongusto.net/lapavona* (€). Reasonably priced trattoria on the edge of town (down Corso Saffi, and 800m past the bridge). With an outdoor pergola; the large menu features home-made pasta and local dishes from *antipasto* to dessert, with lots of vegetarian dishes, and mushrooms and truffles in autumn. They also have an excellent wine list. *Closed Tues, and a few weeks from end Sept.*

ⓘ **Brisighella >**
Piazzetta Porta Gabolo 5, **t** *(0546) 811 66, iat.brisighella@racine.ra.it, or iat.brisighella@provincia.ra.it; open summer only*

★ **Gigiolè >**

Brisighella ✉ 48013

Brisighella has become something of a pilgrimage destination for gourmets, thanks to the lead of the Gigiolè, and to the town's qualities of olive oil.

★★★★**Gigiolè**, Piazza Carducci 5, **t** (0546) 81209, *www.gigiole.it* (€€€). In the centre of Brisighella. The excellent restaurant (€€€) has long been a mecca for foodies. The *raison d'être* continues to be the superb food created by a chef who has done detailed research into Romagna's medieval culinary traditions – bean and spelt soup, a classic *borlonga*, filled with greens and cheese; ravioli stuffed with rabbit and mint, chestnut-flour pasta with *porcini* mushrooms, and a rich dessert cart with dishes such as pomegranate mousse. *Restaurant closed Sun eve and Mon. Booking essential.*

★★★**Valverde**, Via Lamone 14, **t** (0546) 81388, *www.hotelvalverde.com* (€). Modern, good hotel in a garden setting by the river near the baths; rooms with phone, TV and balconies. It also has a restaurant with tourist menus featuring local cuisine.

The tourist office can lead you to a number of attractive *agriturismo* choices in the area:

★★★★**Relais Torre Pratesi**, Via Cavina 11, **t** (0546) 84545, *www.torrepratesi.it* (€€€€). A few kilometres south of the village – follow the signs for Fognano and Zattaglia-Riolo Terme. In a 15th-century tower on a hill in open countryside, and with an adjoining farmhouse, both of which have been carefully restored to create a luxurious *agriturismo*. Four of the rooms are in the tower, and all are well equipped. With superb views, swimming pool and bikes, with excellent opportunities for walking, mountain biking, horse riding, golf at the nearby La Torre course and and a good restaurant for guests with traditional local dishes. *Closed much of Jan.*

La Felce, Via Monte Mauro 8/b, **t** (0546) 73989, *www.agriturismolafelce.it* (€). Ten kilometres from Brisighella, this delightful *agriturismo* is a good base for enjoying peaceful rural surroundings. It comprises comfortable apartments, with kitchen and air-conditioning. *Open Mar–Sept; weekends only during the rest of the year.*

Valpiana, Via Tura 7, **t** (0546) 88067, *www.agriturismovalpiana.it* (€). Up in the hills, with facilities for cycling, horse riding, hunting and fishing, also a few rooms and a restaurant with an evocative atmosphere; they speak English. *Open Mar–Dec.*

Trattoria di Strada Casale, Fraz. Strada Casale 22, **t** (0546) 88054 (€€€). Remo Camurani and Andrea Spada offer superb creative food based on the finest ingredients with a menu that changes every day, and a fabulous five-course fixed-price *menu degustazione*. Try ravioli with local cheese or veal with anchovy sauce and capers. *Booking advisable. Open weekday eves only; also open for lunch on Sat and Sun; closed Wed, 20 days Jan, 10 days June and 10 days Sept.*

Cantina del Bonsignore, Via Recuperati 4a, **t** (0546) 81889 (€€). Atmospheric trattoria in the *centro storico* in the wine cellar of the *monsignore's* palace. Dine wonderfully well on delicacies such as poppy-seed ravioli, sheep's milk cheese with currants and pine nuts and a *tortino di polenta* with *porcini* mushrooms. *Booking strongly advisable. Open eves only, Sept–May*

Sun and hols too; closed Thurs, 2 weeks Aug and 2 weeks Sept.

La Grotta, Via Metelli 1, **t** (0546) 81829 (€€). In a cave, as its name suggests, though there's nothing troglodyte about the food. The chef and owner is Yasuhiro Endo from Japan. Local cuisine is mixed with oriental flavours and revised with creativity. *Closed Mon lunch and Tues.*

Osteria di Porta Fiorentina, Via Naldi 20, **t** (0546) 81517 (€). Good for wine and snacks (cheese, *salumi*, salads, etc.). *Open eves till 2am; closed Wed.*

Forlì

The *Forum Livii* on the Via Emilia was elided over the centuries into Forlì, a city of over 100,000 that has been around for two thousand years without calling attention to itself in any way – a rare achievement in Italy, and one that puts it on the list with the likes of Terni and Frosinone as one of the nation's most obscure provincial capitals. The city did produce one outstanding Renaissance painter, Melozzo da Forlì, but the only frescoes he left in town were blasted to bits in the war. From a distance Forlì seems a smaller version of Bologna: an old sprawling *centro storico* with not two tilted towers but two good straight ones sticking up. The first is the tall medieval Torre Civica on the **Palazzo del Municipio**; another victim of Allied bombing, it was entirely rebuilt in the 1970s. The Municipio stands on the central Piazza Aurelio Saffi, across from the 1932 **Palazzo della Posta**, an introduction to Forlì's one little secret. Benito Mussolini was born in nearby Predappio, and he favoured his home area with monuments and public buildings. Being a Duce, he could get away with doing this on a massive scale, and he left Forlì an open-air museum of Mussolinian architecture.

Abbazia di San Mercuriale
t *(0543) 25653, donquinto@tin.it; open daily 6.30–late eve; adm by donation; adm for the tower*

Standing diagonally from Mussolini's post office is the striking 12th-century **Abbazia di San Mercuriale**, named for the city's patron and first bishop, a great persecutor of pagans in the 4th century. This isn't Forlì's cathedral, but the site of its first church and long a Benedictine monastery. From its original structure there's Forlì's other landmark tower, the 235ft **campanile** (1180), and a lunette of the Magi by the school of Antelami on the main portal; the interior, repeatedly renovated from the 17th to the 19th centuries, has little to show but the lovely quattrocento *tomb of Barbara Manfredi*, an ocean of preposterous painting, and a row of rocking-horses installed to keep the children entertained during mass.

Museo Archeologico e Pinacoteca Melozzo degli Ambrogi
t *(0543) 712 606; open Tues–Sat 9–1.30, Tues and Thurs also 3–5.30; adm free; closed for restoration*

Corso della Repubblica leads eastwards to the worthy **Museo Archeologico e Pinacoteca Melozzo degli Ambrogi**. This offers a rare chance to see (minor) paintings by Fra Angelico outside Tuscany, as well as works by local artist Marco Palmezzano (an *Annunciation*), Il Francia, Francesco del Cossa and others, plus Flemish tapestries, ethnographic exhibits and ceramics. Pride of place is held by Antonio Canova's marble *Hebe*, as rarefied a neoclassical fantasy as you could ask for. The nearby **Santa Maria dei Servi** on Piazza Morgagni merits

Getting to Forlì

Forlì's Luigi Ridolfi **airport** is Bologna's second airport, **t** (0543) 474 990, *www.forliairport.com*. It has flights to London Stansted, Paris and Frankfurt, as well as domestic services. The airport is 6km from the rail station; buses run every 20mins. It is also connected to Bologna, Ravenna and Rimini by frequent **buses** and **trains**.

a stop for the finely sculpted *tomb of Luffo Numai* (1502) and a frescoed chapel of the 1300s.

West of Piazza Saffi, the **Duomo** on Corso Garibaldi was completely rebuilt in 1841; note the painting inside of 15th-century firemen. At the southern corner of the city centre stands Forlì's castle, the picturesque 15th-century **Rocca di Ravaldino**. This was another possession of Caterina Sforza, the place where she made her heroic stand against the rebels and displayed her virtue in public (*see* p.290).

Rocca di Ravaldino
t (0543) 34264; open for temporary exhibitions, festivals, concerts and other events

Out in the eastern suburbs, just south of the village of Carpinello, stands an unusual round Renaissance temple, the **Santuario di Santa Maria delle Grazie** (1500), constructed in honour of a holy hermit named Pietro Bianco, who had once been a pirate. His tomb and other sculptures are attributed to Agostino di Duccio.

Santuario di Santa Maria delle Grazie
t (0543) 61732; open during mass, at 11am in spring or 9am in summer; other times by appointment only

Città del Duce

We promised you Mussolini Deco, and you'll find it at the eastern edge of the centre, on and around **Piazza della Vittoria**, centre of an entire district laid out between 1925 and 1932 called the *Città del Duce*. Plenty of nonsense has been written about architecture and design under the Fascist regime. But for the inscriptions and pasted-on fasces and slogans, Mussolini's architecture was no more 'authoritarian' than that of Paris in the 1930s, or the works of the New Deal in the USA. A little Bauhaus, a little Chicago World's Fair, and a discreet touch of travertine Roman monumentalism are the main ingredients, with recurring conceits like the open porticos of tall square columns, seen all over Italy. The entire ensemble is highly evocative, a reminder of just how much Fascism, like the Baroque, depended on mass spectacles and settings appropriate to them.

It's ironic that Italy built far better under Mussolini than it ever has under democracy since 1945. But though the Fascist era produced some exceptional buildings and plans, none of them are here in Forlì. Some individual buildings strive to impress, like the huge **Aeronautical Academy** on the Piazza (now a school); others can only amuse, like the dilapidated Fascist youth group building behind it (now a cinema). North of the Piazza the Duce built a grand boulevard towards the station lined with more of the same, now called **Viale della Libertà**.

Where to Stay and Eat in Forlì

Forlì ✉ 47100

******Principe**, Via Bologna 153, **t** (0543) 702 065, *info@hotelprincipe.net* (€€€€). Just outside the centre. Air-conditioned, modern rooms with TV and ADSL; bike rental; restaurant serving good land- and seafood.

******San Giorgio**, Via Ravegnana 538/d, Loc. Pieve Acquedotto, **t** (0543) 796 699, *www.hotelsangiorgioforli.it* (€€€€). Classic 1960s-style hotel stylishly renovated in 2006; 8km east of town, so you'll need a car.

*****Vittorino**, Via Baratti 4, **t** (0543) 21521, *h.vittorino@libero.it* (€€). In the centre; with small and simple rooms; also has a restaurant.

La Casa Rusticale dei Cavalieri Templari, Viale Bologna 275, **t** (0543) 701 888, *osteriadeitemplari@libero.it* (€€€). In a house built as a Templar lodge in the 13th century which went through various incarnations as a church and farmhouse. Now it's the place for delicious local cuisine: *piadine*, home-made pasta dishes and classic Romagnoli *secondi*. *Closed Sun and Mon.*

Osteria del Medio, Via G. Saffi 7, **t** (0543) 30598 (€€). Near the Pinacoteca, this serves local specialities such as potato cake with asparagus sauce, home-made pasta, mushrooms, cheeses and hams. *Closed Tues and Wed lunchtime.*

ⓘ Forlì > *Piazzetta XC Pacifici 2, in the municipal offices,* **t** *(0543) 712 435, www.turismoforlivese.it; closed Wed and Sun afternoon; there is also an IAT office at the airport*

Into the Apennines

South of Forlì there are three principal routes into the Apennines, each passing through pretty mountain valleys. Thank Mussolini that they are in this book at all; most dictators fill their birthplaces with big buildings, but the Duce went a step further and gave his home province something other politicians can only dream of: a little bit of Tuscany. In 1923 he redrew the frontiers, and gave what had been known since the early Middle Ages as the 'Tuscan Romagna' to Forlì.

Some of the best scenery here is in the Montone valley, along the main SS67 from Forlì to Florence. Tuscany once began only 8km from Forlì, at **Terra del Sole**, a planned Renaissance town begun in 1564 by the Archduke of Tuscany, Cosimo de' Medici. Cosimo was consolidating his realm after conquering Siena in 1555, and the city-fortress of Terra del Sole, 'Sun Land', was designed to remind the pope that Cosimo was no pushover: built as a military and administrative centre in the form of a perfect rectangle, Terra del Sole is surrounded by low thick walls that would repel the artillery of the day; a star-shaped castle guards each of the two gates.

Museum of Mankind and the Environment **t** *(0543) 766 766, museo@terradelsole.org; guided tours June–Sept Tues, Thurs, Sat and Sun at 4, 5 and 6; Oct–May Tues, Thurs and Sun at 3, 4 and 5; adm*

In the centre of Terra del Sole is the Palazzo Pretorio, HQ of the commissioners of the Medici's Romagna province, and now the tourist office and **Museum of Mankind and the Environment**. On the first Sunday in September the two sides of town, the Florentine and the Roman, compete in the Palio of Santa Reparta, which goes back to the mid-16th century. Not far from Terra del Sole is the small spa of **Castrocaro Terme**. The hilltop **Fortezza di Castrocaro**, which dates from the 10th century, was abandoned for 300 years but has been restored, and has medieval weaponry and furniture. It provides an evocative setting for concerts, plays, falconry and archery displays,

Fortezza di Castrocaro **t** *(0543) 769 541, www.proloco-castrocaro.it; open June–Sept Thurs–Sat, 4–8pm, Sun and hols 10–1 and 4–8; Oct–May Thurs–Sat 3–7pm; Sun and hols 10–1 and 3–7pm, closed Jan–Feb except weekends; adm*

and a medieval festival in mid-June. Ruined medieval castles haunt the next towns of Dovadola and Rocca San Casciano.

The narrow alternative route just to the east (SS9 ter) passes through the Sangiovese wine country around **Predappio**, where Mussolini was born in 1883, the son of a socialist blacksmith, and where his remains were reburied in the local cemetery in 1957, near those of his wife Rachele; his modest mausoleum has become a shrine for Italy's small population of retrograde blackshirts. Mussolini made his home village the seat of the local *comune* and embellished it with public buildings, leaving the old *comune*, Predappio Alta, alone beneath its overgrown castle, where, the **Cà de Sanzvès** is the place to taste the local ruby-red 'blood of Jove'.

Cà de Sanzvès
open daily 10–12 and 3–midnight; closed Tues

As you head into the mountains, old Florentine associations are thick on the ground. Dante's beloved Beatrice spent several summers in the very pretty old medieval town of **Portico di Romagna**; the Portinari house where she stayed can still be seen in the main street. Near the Tuscan frontier the 9th-century abbey in **San Benedetto in Alpe** sheltered Dante after his unsuccessful bid to return to Florence from exile (*Inferno*, Canto XVI, 94–105). San Benedetto is on the edge of the **Parco Nazionale delle Foreste Casentinesi, Monte Falterona e Campigna** that covers the mountainous border between Romagna and Tuscany. Established in 1993 and crisscrossed by ancient paths, its deep majestic silver firs and century-old beeches shelter eagles, wolves, roe deer, red deer, fallow deer and mouflons, introduced from Sardinia in 1870. In San Benedetto, you can hire horses to explore the region's valleys, especially the lovely **Valle dell'Acquacheta** with its bucolic, stepped waterfall. The rapid Brusia river is popular with canoeists and kayakers; this is a marvellous area for hill-walking.

The main SS310 from Forlì continues into the scenic Upper Bidenta valley. There are ski facilities in the valley at Monte Campigna, near the old Tuscan town of **Santa Sofia**, home of the national park headquarters in Romagna. To the south are the **Lago di Ridracoli** and its dam, and the Romagna Aqueduct, in the midst of a heavily forested region, inaccessible by car. South of the lake, inside the Foresta di Lama (property of Florence cathedral for hundreds of years), lies the reserve of **Sasso Fratino**, a very rare section of primordial woodland untampered with since the last Ice Age.

Lago di Ridracoli
park information office, ***t*** *(0543) 971 375; open weekends only*

Bagno di Romagna

Bagno di Romagna

Bagno di Romagna (1,500ft) and **San Piero in Bagno**, 3km away, both have thermal and mud baths, and are popular summer resorts. Bagno di Romagna, like the rest of this area, was part of Tuscany from the 9th century, when Pope Adrian II granted the lands to the Bishop of Arezzo. In 1453 it came directly under the rule of the Florentines, who encrusted the façade of the 14th-century **Palazzo**

dei Capitani with a big set of Medici balls (the spheres on their escutcheon; since the Medici were originally pharmacists, their Florentine opponents called them the 'pills') and the marble coats of arms of former captains. Among the illustrious Renaissance visitors who came to take the waters were several of the Medici family and Benvenuto Cellini.

Besides the Palazzo dei Capitani (now a tourist information centre), Bagno is full of old Florentine touches and palazzi. The chapels of the Romanesque **Basilica of Santa Maria Assunta** contain an impressive collection of Florentine art: on the high altar, a beautiful triptych by Neri di Bicci of the *Assumption and Saints* (1468); a terracotta of *Sant'Agnese* by Andrea della Robbia; a lovely *Madonna*, attributed to the early 15th-century Maestro di Sant'Ivo; a *Nativity* from the same century by the Maestro del Tondo Borghese; a *Madonna and Saints* by Michele di Rudolfo del Ghirlandaio; and a

Crucifixion by the early 18th-century Florentine Gherardini. Even the bicarbonate-alkaline and sulphurous waters which gush out at 45°C are Florentine, at least according to the locals: it is rain that fell 700 years ago, and that seeped deep into the earth to pick up heat and its special mineral qualities before gushing back to the surface.

Back on the Via Emilia: Forlimpopoli, Bertinoro and Around

All of **Forlimpopoli** postdates 1360, the year that papal legate Cardinal Albornoz decided to make the rebellious town an example *pour encourager les autres* and razed it to the ground. In its place he built a fat-towered **Rocca** on the Via Emilia and attempted to rename the town Salvaterra. But over the next 20 years the survivors of the attack drifted back, and in 1380 the pope confirmed the position of the old ruling family, the Ordelaffi, who took over the castle. In the 19th century the town council demolished the huge central tower and made one of the rooms in the surviving towers into the municipal theatre. The theatre itself was the scene of Forlimpopoli's second dramatic moment in history, in 1851, when one of the many bandits who terrorized the Papal State, the notorious 'Ferryman' Stefano Pelloni, boldly interrupted a performance to demand from the audience 'a contribution of 40,000 *scudi*'. Today the Rocca houses the **Museo Civico**, complete with a small archaeological collection.

Museo Civico
open Sat 4.30–6.30, Sun 10–12 and 4–6; adm free

Another road heads south for **Bertinoro**, a medieval town famous for its wine and hospitality. The wine is Albana, and there's a wonderful story someone concocted that the town got its name when Galla Placidia drank some of this nectar out of a primitive wooden mug and declared: 'O wine, you are so good I could *drink you in gold!*' ('*ber-ti in oro*'). The hospitality was such in old Bertinoro (now, this story is true) that the noble familes constantly squabbled over who would have the privilege of hosting guests. The solution was to erect a column in front of the 14th-century **Palazzo Comunale** and hang it with rings, one belonging to each family; the ring to which a stranger tethered his horse decided which family would be his host. The column was removed in 1570, but in 1922 its foundations were rediscovered and it was re-erected as it was, complete with iron rings. The **Rocca di Bertinoro**, dating back to the 11th century, has been much altered during the course of its history and by its many different owners; from the 16th century on it was the palace of the local bishops. It has now been restored and contains an institute devoted to the restoration of old clerical regalia.

Rocca di Bertinoro
t (0543) 446 500; open by appointment only

Nearby **Polenta**, stronghold of the famous family of that name who ruled medieval Ravenna, has a fine 9th-century Byzantine-Romanesque basilican church, **San Donato**; often restored, it still has its finely sculpted original capitals.

San Donato
open daily 8.30–12.30 and 2–6.30

ⓘ Bagno di Romagna >>
Via Fiorentina 38, t (0543) 911 046, www.bagnodiromagna turismo.it

ⓘ Castrocaro Terme >
Viale Marconi 81, t (0543) 767 162, iat@comune.castrocaro termeeterradelsole.it

★ Grand Hotel Terme Roseo >>

ⓘ Bertinoro >
Piazza della Libertà 1, t (0543) 469 213, www.comune. bertinoro.fo.it

ⓘ Parco Nazionale delle Foreste Casentinesi
Monte Falterona e Campigna community headquarters: Via Nefetti 3, Santa Sofia, t (0543) 971 297, www. parcoforestecasentinesi.it

Where to Stay and Eat in the Forlì Apennines

Castrocaro Terme ✉ 47011

*****Ambasciatori**, Via Cantarelli 10, **t** (0543) 767 345, *www.hotel ambasciatoricastrocaro.com* (€€). Welcoming place near the spa and its park: pool, gym, tanning beds, sauna, massage room, solarium and bicycles as well as a bar and restaurant.

La Frasca, Via Matteotti 38, **t** (0543) 767 471, *www.lafrasca.it* (€€€€). The same hotel's excellent gourmet restaurant, offering some of the most stunning *cucina Romagnola* you'll find. You could opt for one of the four *menus di degustazione*. Superb wine list. *Booking advisable. Closed Tues, first half of Jan and second half of Aug.*

Antica Osteria degli Archi, Piazzetta San Nicolò 2, **t** (0543) 768 281 (€€€). Wonderfully romantic restaurant with a beautiful terrace. Specializes in meat dishes but seafood and vegetarian options also delicious. *Closed Mon and a few days Jan.*

Bertinoro ✉ 47032

Fattoria Paradiso, Via Palmeggiana 285, **t** (0543) 445 044, *www.fattoriaparadiso.it* (€€). Handsome wine estate in the hills 2km from Bertinoro. Simple, attractive *agriturismo* rooms, all wheelchair accessible, in a 15th-century farmhouse; pool and restaurant serving traditional dishes.

Belvedere, Via Mazzini 7, **t** (0543) 445 127, *www.belvedere-ristorante.com* (€€). Dine on a terrace with a wonderful view while feasting on creative cuisine including vegetarian and macrobiotic options. Lovely desserts and a good choice of Romagna wines. *Closed Wed, Thurs lunch in winter and three weeks in Jan.*

Portico di Romagna ✉ 47010

******Al Vecchio Convento**, Via Roma 7, **t** (0543) 967 053, *www.vecchioconvento.it* (€€). Small, charming and very welcoming haven up a scenic if narrow winding road and based in a 19th-century building, furnished here and there with antiques. Its restaurant uses organic ingredients.

Bagno di Romagna ✉ 47021

******Hotel Tosco Romagnolo**, Piazza Dante Aligheri 2, **t** (0543) 911 260, *www.paoloteverini.it* (€€€€€). Peaceful, modern, charming place to relax, with a garden on the banks of a *torrente*, tennis and a rooftop pool, and one of Italy's most enchanting restaurants, **Paolo Teverini** (€€€€), offering a delightful special menu based on Tuscan and Romagna country traditions. *Restaurant closed Mon, Tues except in Jul and Aug; closed 2 weeks in Jan.*

******Euroterme**, Via Lungo Savio 2, **t** (0543) 911 414, *www.euroterme.com* (€€€). On the edge of town: big and modern and offering health and beauty treatments. They can also organize trails, horse-riding and bikes. *Closed Jan–mid-Apr; minimum stay 3 nights.*

******Grand Hotel Terme Roseo**, Piazza Risasoli 2, **t** (0543) 911 016, *www.termeroseo.it* (€€€). Occupies the palace of the Counts Biozzi. The hotel has a spa-water heated pool, gym, garden and solarium. Shiatsu massage, beauty treatments, bioenergetic gymnastics and auricular reflexotherapy (whatever they might be) are also on offer, along with the usual mudpacks. *Minimum stay 3 nights.*

Ca' Di Gianni, Via Ca' Di Gianni 159, **t** (0543) 903 421, *www.cadigianni.it* (€€). Farmhouse in the forest above San Piero with a few rooms, a restaurant and a large riding stable. Three *menu di degustazione* offer a taste of local traditional cooking.

****Al Tiglio**, Via Lungo Savio 7, **t** (0543) 911 032 (€). Simple but providing a nice bed and shower. Restaurant with a choice of local dishes.

***Locanda Gambero Rosso**, Via Verdi 5, Bagno, **t** (0543) 903 405, *locanda.gamberorosso@libero.it* (€). At San Piero in Bagno: family run and very hospitable with simple rooms with en suite bath, and an excellent restaurant (€€) serving typical Apennine cuisine – *cucina povera*, as it's called, but delicious, especially when prepared with excellent local ingredients. In the autumn, don't miss the mushroom and truffle omelette. *Closed Mon.*

Cesena

Cesena, now perhaps best known as the site of the European Trotting Championships in August, is almost as big as Forlì, and shares with it the honour of provincial capital. Originally a Roman fortress town, the city had more than its share of turmoil in the 14th–15th centuries. Ruled by the Ordelaffi of Forlì, it was taken over by Cardinal Albornoz in 1357. Papal rule was so oppressive that the people rose up in 1377 against the Breton troops of the papal legate Robert of Geneva, killing hundreds. In revenge, thousands of citizens were killed or forced into exile by the pope's army; Cesena was sacked and the castle burned. At the end of the year Cesena fell into the hands of the Malatesta, although it was decades before the city recovered.

The last of the line, Domenico Novello (ruled 1429–65), was the city's great benefactor, promoting the university there and founding in 1452 the **Biblioteca Malatestiana**. Located next to the beautiful cloister of San Francesco, the Biblioteca was designed by Matteo Nuti and inspired in part by Cosimo de' Medici's famous library at San Marco in Florence. This one, however, has survived in nearly mint 15th-century condition, preserving the front door, desks, lecterns and the priceless collection of manuscripts collected by Novello and his doctor, Giovanni di Marco da Rimini. Novello also hired Matteo Nuti to repair the **Rocca Malatestiana**, which still dominates the town from above, and to link it to the centre of town. Later improvements were carried out by Cesare Borgia, who made Cesena the capital for his ambitions in the region, which endured as long as his papa was the one with a capital P. It later served as a papal fortress and prison, and has been restored to house a museum of the fortress itself and a museum devoted to traditional country life and agricultural techniques.

Biblioteca Malatestiana
t *(0547) 610 892, www.malatestiana.it; open Mon–Sat 9–12.30 and 4–7, Sun and hols 10–12.30; adm*

Rocca Malatestiana
entrance at Via degli Ordelaffi 2, ***t*** *(0547) 356 327, iat@comune.cesena.fc.it; open Tues–Sat 9–12 and 4–7, Sun 9–12 and 3–7; adm*

There's another Rocca Malatestiana in **Longiano**, to the east, just south of the Via Emilia, a residential castle piled on top of the town, where Carlo Malatesta died in 1423. It now houses the **Fondazione Tito Balestra**, named for Longiano's 20th-century poet, who was a collector of modern art: there are works by De Pisis, Mafai and Rosai and 1,800 pieces by Mino Maccari.

Fondazione Tito Balestra
t *(0547) 665 850, www.fondazionetitobalestra.org; open Sat and Sun 10–12 and 3–7, other times by appointment*

Between Cesena and Rimini at **Savignano** the road crosses a poor excuse for a stream that most authorities accept as the shadowy Rubicon, the dividing line between Cisalpine Gaul and what was then considered Italy, which Julius Caesar crossed with his army in 49 BC, thereby defying the Senate and declaring his intention to take over the Roman state. Today it acts as a separating line between respectable Emilia-Romagna from the international beach Babylon of Rimini.

Where to Stay and Eat in Cesena

ⓘ **Cesena >**
Piazza del Popolo 11,
t (0547) 356 327,
www.comune.cesena.fc.it

Cesena ✉ 47023

****Casali**, Via B. Croce 81, **t** (0547) 22745, *www.hotelcasalicesena.it* (€€€€). Traditional, luxurious, the nicest hotel in Cesena.

Osteria Michiletta, Via Fantaguzzi 26, **t** (0547) 24691, *www.osteriamichiletta.it* (€€). The oldest *osteria* in town and very popular. Good, healthy dishes, based on vegetables and freshly ground wheat and other cereals. There are also meat dishes on offer. *Closed Sun, 2 weeks Jan and 2 weeks Aug.*

Donini per la Gola, Via Corte Dandini 10, *www.doniniperlagola.it*, **t** (0547) 21875 (€). Right in the centre: come here for simple and genuine dishes; also take-away food. *Closed Tues, Sun.*

The Adriatic Riviera

Seen by the aliens from their spaceships, this must be one of the most unusual and enticing sights of Europe. Welcome to Linear City – forty miles long and a few blocks deep, a mass of compacted (and mostly quite attractive) urbanity, with the SS16 on one side and a solid line of beach on the other. It's the place where Italians come because their grandparents did, where Germans come to look for Italians, the British come to fill shopping trolleys with British gin, and Russians finally get a chance to wear their designer sunglasses. On any given night in August, over 100,000 of them will be sitting down to *tagliatelle al ragù* in their *pensioni* and thinking that life is pretty damn sweet.

There's no place like it. And right in the middle is the surprising city of Rimini, home of one of the most beguiling monuments of the Renaissance and a vortex for weirdness of all kinds, from genuine haunted castles, to hallucinogenically kitschy roadside attractions, to the sovereign and independent Republic of San Marino.

Ravenna to Rimini

From Ravenna and Classe the long stretch of small resorts that began at Comacchio straggles on towards Rimini. The various tiny lidi are slow-paced, if packed with families in the summer. The lidi nearest Ravenna – Lido di Classe and Lido di Savio – suffer somewhat from industrial pollution, but there has been a big effort to keep the beaches clean. None is a really good choice for a long stay, though all are quite convenient for a day on the beach if you're passing through.

The pine woods continue down to the first big centre on the coast, **Cervia-Milano Marittima**, with 9km of sugar-fine sand, all immaculately groomed by an endless row of bathing concessions. Before baking bodies on the beach became big, Cervia earned its living through 'white gold' or salt, which made it a prize from the time of the ancient Greeks, who founded the first town here –

The Adriatic Riviera

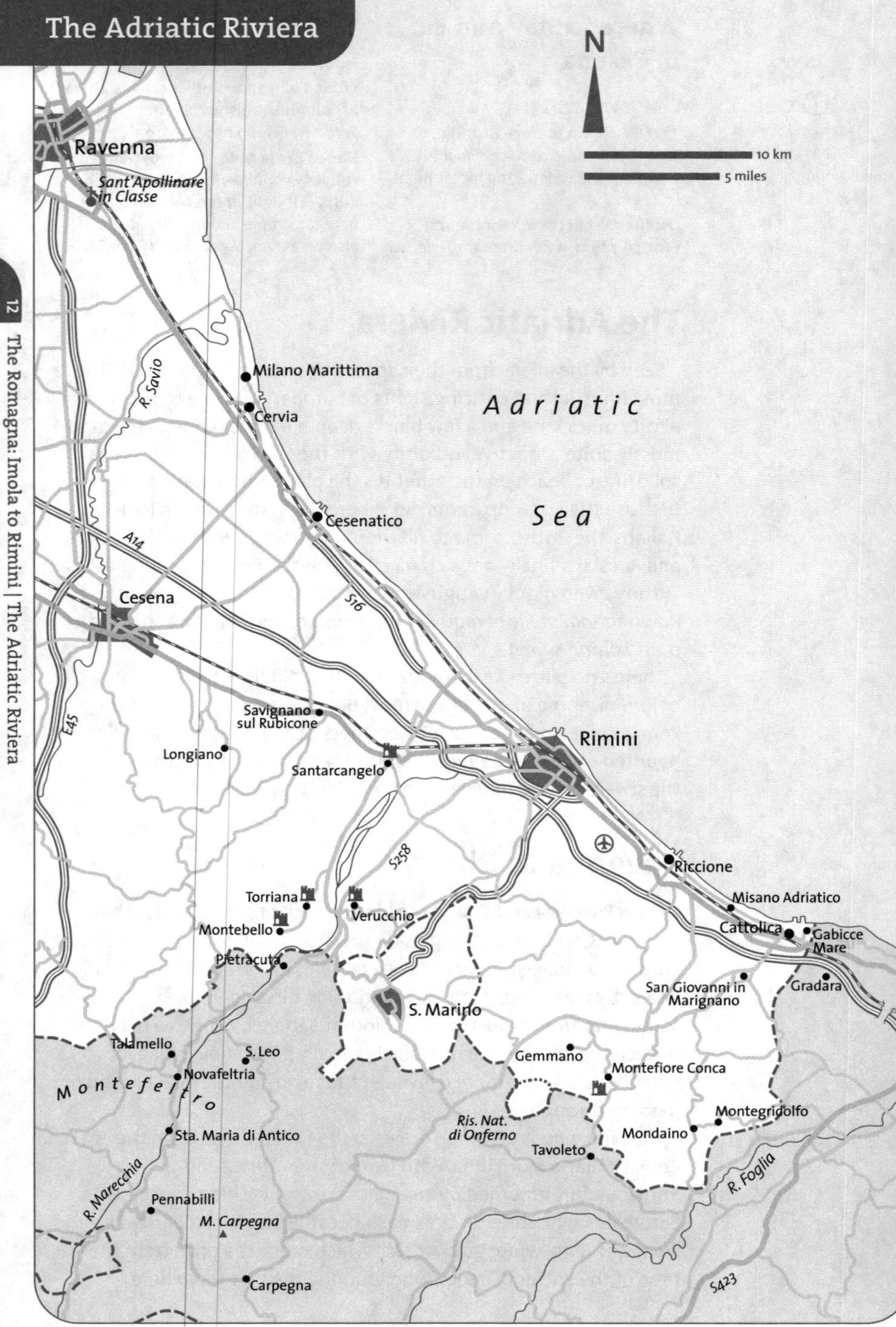

Ficocle, which was destroyed by Exarch Theodore in 709. The Venetians influenced it or controlled it outright from the 13th century to 1509 – in 1445 they even inaugurated a 'Marriage to the Sea' on Ascension Day, modelled after their famously arrogant ceremony in Venice. After 1509 Cervia made money for the pope, who insisted that his states use his costly product and no one else's. The vast salt warehouses, dating from 1691 and 1712, and the quadrangle of salt workers' houses in the *centro storico* are still intact, as are the salt pans; they still produce piles of the stuff, and form the southern extent of the Po Delta Park, attracting their share of migratory birds. The mineral-rich waters of the pans are also used therapeutically at a spa, the **Terme di Cervia**.

Next down the coast, **Cesenatico** was founded in 1302 by Cesena as its port, although it too would spend much time under the Venetians until 1509. The secret of its success is the **Porto-Canale**, a pretty, canal-like harbour, improved in 1502 by Leonardo da Vinci for Cesare Borgia; the bridge is marked by two columns erected by the Venetians. Today the harbour is home to one of the most important fishing fleets on the Adriatic, and to the unusual open-air **Museo Galleggiante della Marineria**, a floating maritime museum of traditional (and rather beautiful) fishing and trading boats used in the northern Adriatic. There are no opening hours or admission charges: the boats with their colourful sails raised are simply displayed in the canal during the warm months.

★ Museo Galleggiante della Marineria
t *(0547) 79264, www.museomarineria.eu; always open; adm free*

ⓘ Cervia >
Viale dei Mille 65, **t** *(0544) 974 400, www.comunecervia.it/turismo; open Apr–Sept*

ⓘ Milano Marittima >
Via Giacomo Matteotti 39/41, **t** *(0544) 993 435, iatmilanomarittima@comunecervia.it*

Where to Stay and Eat on the Adriatic Riviera

Cervia-Milano Marittima ✉ 48015

******Grand Hotel Cervia**, Lungomare Grazia Deledda 9, **t** (0544) 970 500, *www.grandhotelcervia.it* (€€€€). Pretty, pink Liberty-style hotel with old-fashioned décor and all mod cons. Every room has balcony, TV, minibar, phone and air conditioning. There's a private beach, plus a garden, solarium and sauna.

*****Genzianella**, Viale Roma 85, **t** (0544) 970 442, *www.emmehotels.com* (€€). Near the centre, with games, and access to Cervia's golf course. Rooms with TV, phone, minibar, fan and wireless Internet.

*****Santiago**, Viale 2 Giugno 42, **t** (0544) 975 477, *www.hotelsantiago.it* (€€). In a quiet spot near the sea, with a pretty garden.

Al Teatro, Via XX Settembre 169, **t** (0544) 71639, *www.ristorantealteatro.it* (€€€). The classic place to dine in Cervia: seafood rules. Try the *gnocchetti teneri agli scampi. Menu degustazione* at €50. *Closed Mon, 20 days Jan and 20 days Sept.*

E' Cantinon, Via XX Settembre 28, **t** (0544) 977 078, *www.ilcantinone.com* (€€). Converted old wine shop, with big fireplace and rustic atmosphere. The home-made pasta is especially good, as are freshly made *piadine* and *salumi* and grilled meats. *Booking advisable. Eves only; closed Mon and part of Feb and Sept.*

Casa delle Aie, Via Ascone 4, **t** (0544) 927 631 (€€). Jovial establishment serving rigorously traditional Romagnolo specialities in an 18th-century house; on a summer's evening don't be surprised if people burst into song. Try the excellent *piadina* and home-made pasta. *Wheelchair* accessible. *Open eves plus Sun lunch; closed Wed (exc Aug) and Nov.*

ⓘ **Cesenatico >** *Via Roma 112,* **t** *(0547) 673 287, www.cesenatico.it/turismo*

Cesenatico ✉ 47042

*****Britannia**, Viale G. Garducci 129, **t** (0547) 672 500, *www.hbritannia.it* (€€€€). Refined early 1900s villa by the sea with a big flowery terrace, a pool and olive grove leading down to a private beach. Rooms include all creature comforts, and there's a good restaurant with panoramic sea views, open to guests only. *Open April–late Sept.*

*****Grand Hotel**, Piazza Andrea Costa 1, **t** (0547) 80012, *www.grandhotel.cesenatico.fo.it* (€€€). Romantic hotel by the sea established in 1929. Rooms are well-equipped and air conditioned, although not all are en suite; facilities include an attractive pool, garden terrace and private beach, tennis courts and a restaurant serving dishes from Romagna and other regions. Check the website for special offers. *Closed mid-Oct–April.*

La Buca, Corso Garibaldi 41, **t** (0547) 82474, *www.labucaristorante.it* (€€€). Best seafood in town. *Closed Mon and 3 weeks Oct.*

Capo Nero, Viale Carducci, Bagno 14, Valverde, **t** (0547) 82279 (€€). South of the centre in Valverde and offering fine dining in a garden by the beach in summer, including a range of good meat and seafood dishes, and pizza in the summer, though you pay extra for the location. *Closed Tues and all Oct.*

Osteria del Gran Fritto, Corso Garibaldi, **t** (0547) 82474, *www.labucaristorante.it* (€€). Next to La Buca, and run by the same owners. The main, in fact the only, *secondo* on the menu is a *gran fritto dell'Adriatico*. Very popular; bookings not accepted. *Closed Mon and 3 weeks Oct.*

Osteria dei Poeti, Viale dei Mille 55, **t** (0547) 82055 (€). Friendly, charming place with food to match – lots of seafood, but other enjoyable dishes as well. Try for instance the *monopiatto – antipasto*, which has first and second courses all on the same plate. Cheeses come with a Sardinian touch – arbutus honey or rose-petal jam. *Open eves only until 3am; closed Mon.*

Rimini

At first glance Italy's biggest resort may strike you as strictly cold potatoes, a full 15km of peeling skin and pizza, serenaded by the portable radios of ten thousand teenagers and the eternal whines and giggles of their little brothers and sisters. To many Italians, however, Rimini means pure sweaty-palmed excitement. In the 1960s, following the grand old Italian pastime of *caccia alle svedesi*, a staple of the national film industry was the Rimini holiday seduction movie, in which a bumbling protagonist with glasses was swept off his feet by some incredible Nordic goddess, who was as bouncy as she was adventurous. After many complications, embarrassing both for the audience and the actors, it could all lead to true love. For the bumbling protagonists of real life, whether from Milan or Munich, all this may only be wishful thinking but they still come in their millions each year to what has now been dubbed 'the Beach of Europe.'

As a resort Rimini has its advantages. Noisy as it certainly is, it's a respectable, family place, relatively cheap for northern Italy, convenient and well organized. Also, tucked away behind the beachfront is a genuine old city, much damaged in the Second World War, but inviting, and offering one four-star Renaissance attraction.

Getting to and around Rimini

Regular international and domestic flights fly into Rimini's **Federico Fellini airport**, **t** (0541) 715 711, *www.riminiairport.com*, behind the beaches at Miramare. Frequent buses run from the airport to the rail stations, with train connections to Bologna and Ravenna.

On this stretch of coast, the FS Adriatic **rail** line works almost like a tram service, with lots of trains and stops near the beaches in all the resorts.

Rimini city **buses**, Via Dante 42, **t** (0541) 300 533, *www.tram.rimini.it*, run regularly in summer, carrying people up and down the long beach strip. As well as individual tickets, an 'Orange Ticket' is available, giving unlimited travel within Rimini and the whole area between Bellaria, Santarcangelo and Riccione (24 hours for €3, three days for €5.50 or eight days for €11). From the rail station in Rimini, on Piazzale Cesare Battisti, there are also buses to most nearby towns, including San Leo, Verucchio and San Marino. For **taxis**, **t** (0541) 50020.

Cultural day-trippers who shudder at the thought of Rimini's beach madness can dip in easily – the Tempio Malatestiano is only a 10-minute walk from the station.

History

Settlements around Rimini go back to the late Neolithic period, but when the site of the city itself was still swamps, sand bars and lagoons, the modest metropolis of this area was the little village of Verucchio, up on the hills to the southwest. The Villanova people lived here for centuries, and maintained a trading station at the mouth of the river Marecchia. By the 5th century BC, there was enough solid ground on the coast for people to start gradually drifting down from the hills. The Villanovans were succeeded by the Umbrians, an Italic people who had expanded into parts of the Romagna Apennines, and later by the Celts, who seem to have been busy traders here.

The area was one of Rome's first conquests in Cisalpine Gaul, after their victory at the Battle of Sentinum (Sassoferrato) in 295 BC. The founding of *Ariminium*, the first Roman colony north of the Apennines (268), had been a matter of some controversy in the Senate; it was a sign of Rome's resolve to conquer all of Cisalpine Gaul. The opening of the Via Emilia in 218 made Ariminium the natural port for all the trade of the new region, and the city grew along with it, throwing off its colonial status to become a full-fledged *municipium* in 90 BC. A rude interruption came in the Civil Wars – Ariminium sided with the populist Marius, and got thoroughly sacked by the victorious conservative general Sulla – but this setback was soon overcome. In 49 BC the city picked the right horse, siding with Julius Caesar when he passed through on his way to power in Rome, and in the next century Ariminium became one of the more opulent towns of northern Italy, with an amphitheatre nearly as big as Rome's Colosseum. Ariminium shared in the general late Imperial decay of Italy, and it must have been hit hard in the various barbarian invasions and in the Greek–Gothic Wars, when it changed hands several times; records are scarce. The victorious Byzantines made it the capital of a new 'Pentapolis', a province of five maritime cities (with Fano, Pesaro, Senigallia and Ancona in the

Marches), ruled by a duke subject to the exarch at Ravenna, and it fell to the Lombards in 751 along with Ravenna. By 1000 the city had shrunk to a tiny part of its Roman-era extent, a few streets around Piazza Cavour.

A *comune* was founded at some unknown date, and Rimini started to grow again with a little help from Mother Nature – the river Marecchia changed its course to flow right under the city's walls, providing a convenient new port to replace the old one that had silted up. Under the *comune*, the leading official of the city was called the *Pater civitatis*. This office, and control of the city, became so identified with a single powerful family that they eventually took it as a family name – the Parcitadi. Medieval Rimini followed the usual path of the Italian cities: it built a Palazzo Comunale, made plenty of money, fought continually with its neighbours, grew dramatically and built a new set of walls (1330). It did show at least two eccentricities. It was unshakeably Ghibelline, and in the 1200s it had a large population of Cathars – the Manichaean heretics who flourished in southern France before the Albigensian Crusade. In northern Italy they were called Patarenes, but they suffered the same Church pogroms and eventual extinction.

The Headache Family

The Malatesta started out as Lords of Verucchio, Ghibelline backwoods barons who often supported Rimini in its wars. They moved into the city in 1216, and the greatest of the line, Malatesta da Verucchio ('Headache from Hump'), became a political power in the 1240s. In 1248, after Emperor Frederick's defeat at Parma, he saw his chance to ride a big wave. He defected to the Guelph camp, and while Guelphs were winning control all over northern Italy he managed to seize power in Rimini with the aid of the Church and neighbouring Guelph cities. The coup did not come off without resistance – fifty years of it, in fact, but Malatesta was up to the challenge on every occasion, and settled the issue once and for all in 1295 by arranging a formal ceremony of reconciliation with the Parcitadi and the other Ghibellines, and then attacking them the same night while they slept. This redoubtable old warrior continued to run the city until 1312, when he was over 100, just like his neighbour and ally Guido 'the Old' da Polenta of Ravenna, whom he outlived by two years.

Malatesta left enough sons to keep control until 1334: Malatestino the Cross-eyed, Giovanni the Lame and Paolo the Fair, among others (Paolo was the lover of Francesca in Dante's famous story; Giovanni the deceived husband who did them both in). When the last of them were finally overthrown, it was another Malatesta who managed it: cousin Pandolfo, called Guastafamiglia, the 'family-wrecker', and his sons. As usual in Italy, bloody politics and great art were tripping hand in hand. While the Malatesta were having their fun, their city spawned one of the finest schools of trecento painting in Italy, including the great Pietro da Rimini.

After Guastafamiglia came Galeotto Malatesta (1364–85), succeeded by the only gentleman in the whole dynasty, Carlo, who presided over 44 years of prosperity and relative peace until his death in 1429. His time marked the height of Malatesta power and prestige; another branch of the family ruled Bergamo and Brescia in Lombardy. Carlo's nephew and successor Galeotto Roberto was more interested in piety and meditation than in ruling a city-state, and naturally all his neighbours took advantage of him, led, also naturally, by other Malatestas (another branch of the family, ruling at Pesaro). When a revolt broke out in the city, Roberto could only pray. But the Malatestas hadn't gone soft just yet. His younger brother Sigismondo, aged 14, raised some loyal troops and won control of the situation. Roberto packed himself off to a monastery two years later, and young Sigismondo slipped into his chair as *signore*.

Sigismondo Pandolfo Malatesta has gone into the books as one bad hombre. According to the great but sometimes credulous historian Jakob Burckhardt: 'The verdict of history...convicts him of murder, rape, adultery, incest, sacrilege, perjury, and treason, committed not once, but often.' Burkhardt adds that his frequent attempts on the virtue of his children, both male and female, may have resulted from 'some astrological superstition'. In 1462 Pope Pius II accorded him a unique honour – a canonization to Hell. The Pope, who was behind most of the accusations, can be excused a little exaggeration. He wanted Sigismondo's land, and resorted to invoking supernatural aid and earthly propaganda when he couldn't beat him at war. For Sigismondo was one of the great mercenary captains of the Renaissance, and he took part in almost every conflict of the time; though at first the commander of the papal armies, he eventually switched sides and warred against the popes and their new champion, the 'ideal Renaissance prince' Federico da Montefeltro, the fellow who built the 'ideal Renaissance palace' at nearby Urbino (Federico, if the truth be told, was no sweetheart either, but once you start on Renaissance gossip there's no end to it).

Modern historians give Sigismondo better reviews, finding him on the whole no more pagan and perverse than the average Renaissance *signore*, and less so than many popes. Certainly, he was an able and intelligent ruler and a great patron of the arts, who brought Leon Battista Alberti, Piero della Francesca and Agostino di Duccio to work on his wonderful Temple. A long career as a successful and occasionally treacherous mercenary does not win many friends, though, and when the crisis came in his fight against the implacable Pius II, Sigismondo was on his own. By 1463 he had lost all his lands, and was allowed to keep only the city of Rimini; nearly bankrupt, he was forced to hire out his services as a mercenary again for the last five years of his life, two of which were spent fighting in Greece in the service of the Venetians. His son Roberto, called 'Il Magnifico', followed in his footsteps as a soldier, and inherited some of his talent; he also mended fences by marrying Federico da Montefeltro's daughter. After winning a battle for Pope Sixtus IV in 1481, he was given a hero's welcome in Rome, after which he quite unaccountably died, most likely from poison.

The last of the Malatesta was a real rotter, the oppressive and violent Pandolfo IV. When the Wars of Italy began in 1494, Malatesta rule became increasingly precarious. Not only was the papacy still out to get the family, but the Riminesi, nobles and commoners alike, were becoming increasingly weary of them. Cesare Borgia, in the service of his father Pope Alexander VI, seized the city in 1500, and though Pandolfo briefly won it back twice, in 1522 and 1527, the game was up. Papal rule proved as calamitous in Rimini as it was in that other citadel of the Renaissance, Ferrara; few places suffered as much from the last struggles of the Wars. Famine in 1529 killed off a quarter of the population, and a French army ravaged the countryside as late as 1559.

From Last Resort to First Resort

The only notable events in Rimini's history for the next two centuries were the severe earthquakes that hit the city in 1672 and 1786. Nineteenth-century Rimini was a basket case, even by the standards of the Papal State, but its people played their part in the Risorgimento, joining the rebellion of 1831 and even staging one of their own in 1845. Recovery, though perhaps no one realized it, had already begun two years earlier from a most unexpected source – that worthless expanse of sand running along the Adriatic shore. Sea bathing had its origins as a medical cure, and a local doctor helped establish Italy's first *Stabilimento Balneare* in 1843. By the 1890s people were beginning to suspect that it might be fun, too. In the booming economy of the 1900s, the period when Italians really started to enjoy life again for the first time since the 1400s, beaches were the craze among the upper and middle classes; Rimini's famous Grand Hotel went up in 1908.

Working people got to join in, ironically, under Mussolini, who mandated paid vacations and discount holiday rail fares, and whose *Dopolavoro* ('after work') organization built big holiday complexes on the beaches for railroad men and factory workers and their families. After the war Rimini continued as a favourite of Italian families, and it also began to attract sun-seekers from all over Europe. Its latest metamorphosis has taken place only in the last ten years or so. Today you'll see as many signs in Russian as in English or

German around the beaches. The fall of the Iron Curtain made it possible for Czechs, Poles, Russians, Hungarians and everyone else in Eastern Europe to get out for a holiday again, and only one place was close, friendly and relatively inexpensive. They only add to the charm of the biggest, funkiest, most unpretentious and most cosmopolitan lido in Europe. Rimini is an up-and-coming place, full of confidence and more future-oriented than most Italian cities. Already it is starting to convert its prosperity into the rehabilitation of its historic centre and some striking new architecture outside it, notably Paolo Portoghesi's Hotel Savoia on the lido, a new courts complex on Via Flaminia Conca, a marina-hotel project on the Porto Canale, and the Fiera, a huge trade fair in the suburbs meant to rival Bologna's.

The Tempio Malatestiano

Tempio Malatestiano
t (0541) 24244; open Mon–Sat 8–12.30 and 3.30–6.30, Sun 9–1 and 3.30–7

Old Rimini was the home town of the late Federico Fellini, and you may recognize some of the street scenes from *Amarcord* – not filmed here, but meticulously reproduced at Cinecittà in Rome. For the fact that there is any *centro storico* to see at all, thank Italian determination and *dov'era com'era* spirit. During 369 separate bombing raids during 1943–4, 82 per cent of Rimini's buildings were hit, possibly the highest proportion in Italy, and half of these were completely destroyed or damaged beyond repair. When the Allies took the city they found it a ghost town; nearly the entire population had fled for safety to San Marino or elsewhere in the hills. Some special angel (though not necessarily a Christian one) seems to have been watching over the city's unique Renaissance monument, the eclectic and thoroughly mysterious work that has come to be known as Tempio Malatestiano: old photos show it standing almost alone in a field of ruins. Though badly damaged, the Tempio found another unlikely angel after the war – southern US dime-store magnate Samuel Kress, whose foundation brought the nickels and dimes of Dixie to the rescue. A more thorough rehabilitation and cleaning, inside and out was completed more recently, and the Tempio is looking as bright and new as it did to Sigismondo and Isotta.

Whatever Sigismondo's personal habits, he was an educated man and a good judge of art. To transform this unfinished 13th-century Gothic Franciscan church into his Temple he called in Leon Battista Alberti to redesign the exterior and Agostino di Duccio for the reliefs inside. The project that began in the 1440s as a simple chapel soon grew into the reconstruction of the entire building, as Alberti encased the church in a new exterior wall of Istrian marble. Slow in building, due to Sigismondo's many distractions and perennial lack of funds, the Temple was never completed. Work stopped completely in 1461, a disastrous time in which the *signore* was excommunicated and beset with enemies on all sides. Alberti's intentions for the completed building can be seen in a medal minted for Sigismondo at the

Tempio Malatestiano

1 Tomb of Sigismondo Malatesta
2 Arca degli Antenati (Tomb of the Ancestors)
3 Chapel of the Ancestors
4 Memorial Chapel
5 Chapel of the Children
6 Chapel of the Liberal Arts
7 Statue of St Sigismund
8 Chapel of the Angels
9 Reliquary Cell (Piero della Francesca fresco)
10 Giotto's Crucifix
11 Tomb of Isotta degli Atti
12 Chapel of the Planets

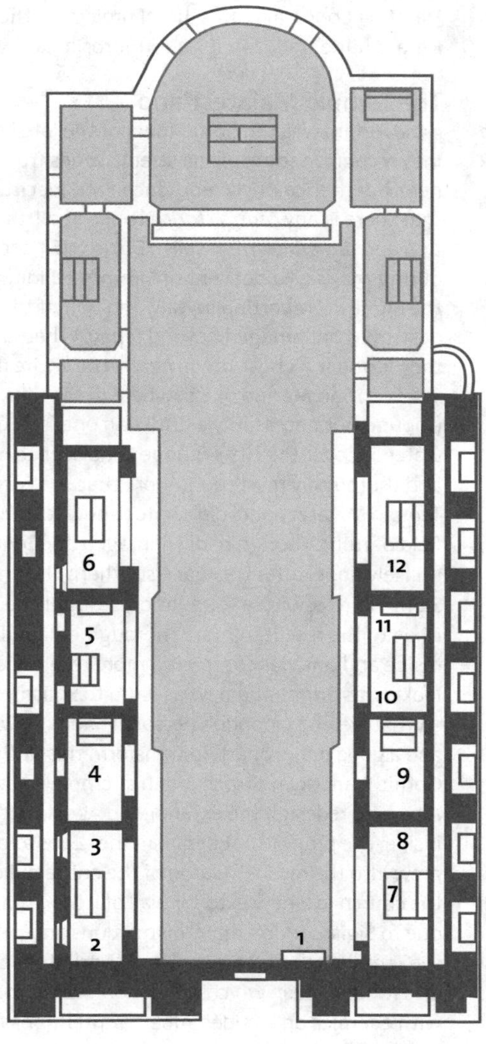

beginning of its construction. A second-storey arch was to have been built over the portal (as in the architect's Sant'Andrea in Mantova); the gable-like pediment around it would have been rounded, and the entire work would have been dominated by a great dome, as wide as the building itself and more than doubling its height.

Scholars have been puzzling for centuries over just what sort of temple Sigismondo had in mind. Though the Temple has been used as Rimini's cathedral since 1809, it is hardly a Christian building; frequent lame attempts to claim it as such run up against the near-total absence of Christianity anywhere in its decoration, which celebrates astrology and the liberal arts amidst an enchanted forest of allegories, putti and enigmatic symbols and mottoes. Pope Pius himself, in his long list of accusations against Sigismondo, mentioned 'the building of a pagan temple'. Some have tried to explain the work as a temple to Sigismondo's muse, Isotta degli Atti, his longtime mistress and third wife, who is buried here along with Sigismondo. But it goes deeper than that. One of the *signore*'s court scholars, Roberto Volturio, mentioned in his writings that the entire Temple was full of symbols that would proclaim the doctrines of arcane philosophy to the learned, while remaining hidden to vulgar folk. That, unfortunately, includes all of us; whatever secret Neo-Platonic philosophy was current at Sigismondo's court is probably lost forever (*see* pp.42–4).

Alberti's unfinished exterior, grafting Roman arcades and pilasters on to the plain Franciscan building, grievously feels the lack of the upper storey of the façade, and the planned cupola that might have tied the composition together. The big arches on the sides were meant to hold sarcophagi of notable men; only a few were ever used, including one on the right side that holds the remains of the Greek philosopher Gemisthos Plethon, which Sigismondo brought back from Mistra in the Peloponnese. Inside, four pairs of chapels hold the Temple's major feature, the **sculptural reliefs** made by Agostino – among the greatest works of the Renaissance. These are mostly on the pilasters on the edges of the chapels, above the recurring devices of the decorative scheme: the omnipresent monograms S and I, for Sigismondo and Isotta, together like a dollar sign, and plenty of elephants, the Malatesta heraldic symbol.

In the left aisle, the first chapel contains figures of the classical sibyls and prophets, along with the *Arca degli antenati* (Tomb of the Ancestors) and reliefs of *Minerva* and the *Triumph of Scipio*. The third is decorated with quite strange reliefs of children, and the fourth with allegories of the *Liberal arts and sciences*. On the right, just inside the door is the *Tomb of Sigismondo*. The first chapel has reliefs of putti or angels, while the second has the famous fresco by Piero della Francesca (1451) of *Sigismondo and his Patron St Sigismund*, an obscure Vandal King of Burgundy. Sigismondo got the Medici in

Florence to send Piero up to him, and this revolutionary artist gave him the first work of the Florentine Renaissance style north of the Apennines. Paintings of a ruler and his patron saint were common, but nothing like this calm, naturalistic one.

In the next chapel a painted crucifix by Giotto is the only surviving work from the original decoration of San Francesco. Giotto had been commissioned to decorate the entire church early in the 1300s, and other works of his may well have been destroyed by Sigismondo's rebuilding. His crucifix shares the space with the *Tomb of Isotta degli Atti*, by Matteo de'Pasti. The pilasters on this side contain some of Agostino's finest work, in the allegorical panels of the planets and signs of the zodiac; note especially the enchanting Moon – Cynthia in her silver car – and a scene of 15th-century Rimini beneath the claws of the Crab, the city's natal sign and also Sigismondo's.

Piazza Tre Martiri

Even 10 years ago the centre of Rimini was a dowdy, dusty place, but the change since then has been dramatic. Most of its old buildings have been rehabilitated, and some of the streets themselves have got a new look. **Via IV Novembre**, in front of the Malatesta Temple, and the nearby **Piazza Tre Martiri** have been pedestrianized and given a striking new pavement and streetlights: unabashedly modern, but fitting in remarkably well with the historic surroundings, it could be a model for any other city in Europe. The Piazza occupies the site of the Roman forum, and fragments of the arcades of ancient buildings can still be seen built into some of the walls. The landmark **Torre dell'Orologio** was rebuilt in 1759 from an existing clock tower of the 1500s. Piazza Tre Martiri is apparently haunted: in the 13th century the Knights Templars had one of their most important commanderies here and witches were later burned in the Piazza. In the 1920s and 30s Rosicrucians, Theosophists and Mesmerizers gathered to hold seances. In the 1950s and 60s Italy's foremost mediums, Luciano and Serina Rossi, set up here, and by the 1970s Rimini had so many bizarre sects that it challenged Turin as Italy's capital of the occult.

Roman Souvenirs

The other street running through the Piazza was the main street, the decumanus of old Ariminium, now called **Corso d'Augusto**, with relics of the Roman city at either end. The well-preserved **Arch of Augustus** at the southern end (27 BC), was a monumental gateway in the city walls, built to honour the first emperor and to mark the meeting of the Via Emilia, the Via Popilia and the Via Flaminia. The small busts flanking the entrance are *Jupiter* and *Apollo*, and *Minerva* and *Neptune*. From here, Via Bastioni Orientali runs eastwards to another Roman relic, the **Anfiteatro**, of which only the foundations remain. Built in the reign of Hadrian, in AD 138, this temple of gore and Roman vileness was used for barely a century; in the unsettled 3rd century, when Italian cities started to build walls, Rimini's incorporated the amphitheatre as a defensive bastion. In the Middle Ages most of its stones were carried away for other buildings, and the site itself was covered with houses until excavations in the 1920s.

At the northern end of Corso d'Augusto is the five-arched **Bridge of Tiberius** of AD 21, a fine work badly patched up after damage in the Greek–Gothic wars; the Goths, under siege, had partially demolished it in an unsuccessful attempt to keep out Belisarius' army. A few streets further over the bridge, the church of **San Giuliano** contains a painting of that saint's martyrdom, the last work of Paolo Veronese. From here towards the sea, along the **Porto Canale**, stretches Rimini's colourful fishing port.

Piazza Cavour and the Rocca Sismondo

Near the bridge, Piazza Cavour, site of the markets on Wednesday and Saturday mornings, is decorated with a lovely marble **fountain** of 1543, a graceful old market arcade called the **Pescheria**, and a glowering statue of Pope Paul V. This was the early medieval centre of town, before Rimini grew back to fill its Roman street plan. The **Palazzo dell'Arengo** has been Rimini's town hall since 1207; an arch connects it to the adjacent **Palazzo del Podestà**, built in the 1300s. The name is a bit misleading, since in the 1300s there were no more imperial *podestàs* – only Malatestas. Under the arch, note the stone with all Rimini's standard measures and brick sizes engraved on it, dated 1544. Both of these palazzi had to be substantially rebuilt after the War. The bombs totally gutted the **Teatro Galli** on the narrow end of the piazza, one of the last bits of war damage to be redeemed; they're still working on it now.

Rocca Sismondo
t (0541) 29192; open for temporary exhibitions only

Behind the Theatre stands the bulky castle of the Malatestas, the **Rocca Sismondo** (or Sigismondo), which grew out of the family's original complex of houses, begun when Malatesta da Verucchio moved into the city in 1216. Built by Sigismondo in 1446, and possibly designed by Brunelleschi, the great architect of quattrocento Florence, the castle was sold at a knockdown price by the last of the Malatesta, Pandolfo IV, to Cesare Borgia after he lost control of the city. Since then it has lost all its Renaissance graces to partial demolitions in the 17th and 19th centuries (the popes used it as a prison); you can see how it originally looked in Piero della Francesca's painting in the Tempio Malatesta. The relief elephant over the gate, Sigismondo's symbol, survives, though little else does.

Museo delle Sguardi
t (0591) 751 224, www.comune.rimini.it; open Tues–Fri 10–1, Sat–Sun and hols 10–1 and 4–4; adm

In Covignano, the Palazzo Alvarado is a truly extraordinary museum, the **Museo delle Sguardi**. Delfino Dinz Rialto, a diplomat and explorer who died in 1979, spent much of his life travelling and living among the traditional cultures of the world. Dinz Rialto had a good eye for art, and along the way he built up an excellent collection from the most diverse sources, with over 3,000 pieces of ancient and modern art from Africa, Oceania and the Americas. Some of the standouts are the ritual equipment for a New Guinea 'spirit house', entire tree trunks carved into drums from New Hebrides, and someone who will probably be familiar to anybody from around the Caribbean – a Yoruba figure of Shango, the god of Santería, portrayed here in his original African form as a thunder god with a double axe.

Sant'Agostino
Via Cairoli; open Mon–Sat 9–12 and 3.30–5.30 (till 6.30 in summer), Sun and hols 7.45–12.30 and 3–6

Not many of the works of the trecento 'school of Rimini' can still be seen in the city, but some of the best are in **Sant'Agostino** just off Piazza Cavour. Works such as the *Storia della Vergine* by an unknown painter (attributed by some to Giovanni da Rimini) show the influence of Giotto in many ways, not least of which is the use of simple architectural fantasies for backgrounds, making such scenes as the *Presentation at the Temple* into self-contained dreamlike worlds. Other frescoes, including an enthroned *Virgin* and a *Christ with Mary Magdalene*, are by another anonymous painter called the 'Maestro dell'Arengo'.

Across the Corso: Museo della Città

Museo della Città
*Via L. Tonini 1, **t** (0541) 21482, www.comune.rimini.it; open Tues–Sat 10.30–12.30 and 4.30–7.30, Sun and hols 4.30–7.30; July and Aug Tues also 9–11pm; adm, free on Sun*

East of the Corso di Augusto, an old Jesuit monastery on Piazza Ferrari now houses the Museo della Città. At the entrance are Roman mosaics with exotic African scenes (a favourite subject of mosaic art in homes), and one with a view of Ariminium's port. Inside is a Pinacoteca with a number of works by the Riminese school of the 1300s, including parts of a *Last Judgement* detached from Sant'Agostino. Also present are works of Rimini's most accomplished seicento painter, Guido Cagnacci, as well as two by Guercino and one by Guido Reni (*San Giuseppe*), the colourful *Pala di San Vicenzo Ferrer* by Ghirlandaio and his workshop, and a wonderful *Pietà* by Giovanni Bellini, with angel children commiserating instead of Mary. This work was Sigismondo's last commission, and Bellini finished it just before the *signore* died in 1468. Just outside the museum, the big fenced hole in Piazza Ferrari was the home of a Roman-era doctor, discovered by chance; the excavation has been going on for over 10 years now, but they have turned up paintings and mosaics, as well as the doctor's surgical instruments, and the city hopes some day to make the site into a museum.

Cineteca del Comune di Rimini
*Via Gambalunga 27, **t** (0541) 704302, cineteca@comune.rimini.it; open Mon–Fri 2–7, Sat 8–1*

Nearby on Via Gambalunga is a place that figured prominently in the personal mythology of Federico Fellini, the **Cinema Fulgor**, where the director was introduced to the fantasy world of film. Now the building has become the **Cineteca del Comune di Rimini** with a film library especially devoted to films about Rimini or made by Riminese directors; it also houses drawings by Fellini.

I Remember

The futile, frustrated Hollywood fantasies in the Cinema Fulgor are a key scene in *Amarcord*, Fellini's portrait of provincial Italy in the 1930s. On one level, the film is about Rimini; the comic characters, all masterfully sketched by a born caricaturist, were based on real people, and many of the vignettes apparently really did happen, from the madman in the tree screaming 'I want a woman!' to the passing of the ocean liner *Rex*. A Romagnolo dialect poet, Tonino Guerra, collaborated on the script, and the film is chockful of lyrical local colour, from the early shots of the *fogarazza*, the burning in March of the witch of winter, to the collective fantasies about romantic sheiks in the Grand Hotel. The familiarity is increased by Fellini's jocular messing about with the traditional role of audience and director: on several occasions a pedantic lawyer tries to give a tour of Rimini while Fellini himself blows raspberries and throws snowballs at him from behind the camera. But from the beginning, everything is suspect: it's the village idiot who introduces the film, casting doubts on all that follows. For Fellini the autobiographical details were incidental; *Amarcord*, he insisted, did not mean 'I remember' (*mi ricordo*), as everyone interprets it, but was rather 'like a brand of *aperitivo*' made of many things blended together. In an interview he gave called 'The Fascism Within Us', Fellini explained that one of his reasons for making the film came from his conviction that *Amarcord*'s dominant themes of adolescence and fascism are:

the permanent historical seasons of our lives; adolescence of our individual lives, fascism of our national life. That is, this remaining children for eternity, this leaving responsibilities for others, this living with the comforting sensation that there is someone who thinks for you (and at one time it's mother...another time Il Duce, another time the Madonna...); and in the meanwhile, you have this limited, time-wasting freedom which permits you only to cultivate absurd dreams – the dream of the American cinema, or the Oriental dream concerning women; in conclusion, the same, old, monstrous out-of-date myths that even today seem to me to form the most important conditioning of the average Italian.

According to Fellini, what ultimately binds *Amarcord*'s hapless characters is confusion and ignorance; all of Rimini, in fact, is shown to be in a state of arrested development. Unlike Bertolucci and other Italian directors with a political agenda, Fellini doesn't demonize the Fascists in his film or allow his Italian audience to dismiss them as brutal perverts, as something alien to themselves; his bumbling, clownish blackshirts are as misguided as everyone else. The frequent scenes of fog and smoke not only give *Amarcord* its dreamy air, but symbolize the ignorance and alienation (at one point the fog is so thick the grandfather can't even find his own door). An enigmatic motorcyclist goes around and around; a peacock, the symbol of vanity, appears in the snow; the priest and the teachers misinform and misguide.

'The pretext of being together is always a levelling process. People stay together only to commit stupid acts,' said Fellini, and the several occasions in the film when his slightly crazy and frustrated but individually innocuous characters gather together – for the bonfire, for the Fascist holiday of 21 April, or to greet the Fascist bigwig – are when they become disquieting and truly imbecilic, caught up in the ritual, void of individual responsibility, and capable of any madness.

If anyone in Rimini is on to the real intentions of their favourite son, they do not seem to hold it against him. The best caricaturists can't help making the humanity of their subjects shine through. And the director himself, for all the typical sardonic scolding of his interviews, was incapable of making his home town and its people seem anything but perfectly endearing.

Museo del l'Aviazione
Via S. Aquilina 58, ***t*** *(0541) 756 696, www.museoaviazione.net; open summer daily 9–7; winter Sat–Sun and hols 10–5; adm*

Museo Nazionale del Motociclo
see overleaf

Outside the *centro storico*, there's a vast **Museo dell'Aviazione** with over 40 planes, mostly fighter planes from various wars, plus Clark Gable's, as well as a display of pilots' uniforms, photos and medals. The **Museo Nazionale del Motociclo** has some 200 vintage motorcycles and a big library for aficionados.

Some Beach Statistics

Rimini may have set up the very first sea-bathing establishment in Italy in 1843, but today the subject makes the city's holiday barons

Museo Nazionale del Motociclo
Via Casalecchio 58/n, **t** *(0541) 731 096, www.museomotociclo.it; open daily 10–12.30 and 3–7; adm*

Fiabilandia
Rivazzurra di Rimini, **t** *(0541) 372 064, www.fiabilandia.it; open April–mid-July and Sept 10–7, mid-July–Aug 10–10, Oct Sun 10–6; adm*

Italia in Miniatura
bus 8 from Rimini station; **t** *(0541) 736 736, www.italiainminiatura.com; open end Mar–end July and 2nd week Sept to 1st week Oct 9.30–6.30; end July to 1st week Sept 9–12 midnight; rest of year Sat–Sun and hol weekends 9–sunset; adm*

and the hotel consortium mildly uneasy. 'There's room for everybody,' they say, and in a way they're right. The resort has 15km of broad beaches, and about 1,600 hotels with some 55,000 rooms. At the usual resort ratio, that means about 85,000 beds. It could be a problem in the really busy season. If all the beds are full – plus another 25,000 day-trippers, campers and holiday apartment tenants – that makes 110,000 souls, or 7,333 per kilometre of beach front. There are other things to do in Rimini, fortunately, but with only 5½ inches of shore per bum, if everyone hits the water at the same time the results could be catastrophic.

This really need never happen. Many of these people at any given time will be in Rimini's 751 bars, 343 restaurants, 70 dance halls and discos, 49 cinemas, 14 miniature golf courses, seven *luna parks* (funfairs) and 3 bowling alleys. There really is something for everybody – plenty of sailing schools and wind-surfing schools, three dolphin shows and half a dozen water parks.

Other attractions include **Fiabilandia**, an amusement park for the little ones. North of town on the coast road, towards Viserba there's **Italia in Miniatura**, which, besides mouse-sized cathedrals and castles, offers you performing bears, action-packed go-karts and 'bumper boats'.

ⓘ Rimini >
Piazzale Cesare Battisti, **t** *(0541) 51331, www.riminiturismo.it, infomarinacentro@comune.rimini.it*

Piazza Fellini 3, **t** *(0541) 56902*

Airport, **t** *(0541) 378 731, iataeroporto@libero.it*

Tourist Information in Rimini

In summer, at least, it's positively difficult to remain uninformed, as Rimini and its suburbs have as many information offices as ice-cream stands. The **main tourist office** is at Piazzale Cesare Battisti, next to the station, and there is another large office on the **beach** at Piazza Fellini. Next to both of these there are offices of the **Promozione Alberghiera**, the **local hotel association** and **accommodation service** (*see* below). There are five more information desks along the 15km beach, and in the Municipio, on Piazza Cavour, there is a city information office, plus one at the **airport**.

Where to Stay in Rimini

Rimini ✉ 47900

A holiday in Rimini often means a standard package. Expect a modern room with a balcony, pleasant but rather unimaginatively furnished; in the high season you'll probably have to take half-board, which will probably be unfortunate. You may as well take pot luck at the **Promozione Alberghiera**, Piazza Tripoli 8, **t** (0541) 391 172, *www.promozionealberghiera.it*, or in the railway station, Piazzale Fellini 3, **t** (0541) 53399, the local hoteliers' association, and let them find you a vacancy. They also have four other well-marked offices around town, as well as in Bellaria, **t** (0541) 340 060, and Riccione, **t** (0541) 693 628.

People do not come to Rimini for scenery, charming inns or fine cuisine, but for the crowd and the endless possibilities for fun that go with it. If that sounds good to you, make sure to get a place in the centre where the action is. The places mentioned below are close to both the beach and the town.

Luxury (€€€€€)

*******Grand Hotel**, Via Ramusio 1, Parco F. Fellini at Marina Centro, **t** (0541) 56000, *www.grandhotelrimini.com*. The imposing turn-of-the-20th-century palace of dreams which helped make

Rimini what it is today. Young Federico Fellini was fascinated with the grand hotel, and it gets a starring role in *Amarcord* (though a hotel nearer Rome played the part). Indecently luxurious, rooms glittering with well-polished brass, and enormous crystal chandeliers. The only hotel in Rimini with its own dance orchestra, as well as a park, pool and private beach, tennis, and fitness centre, restaurant (€€€€) and a bar where you can drink a Fellini cocktail.

****__Ambasciatori__, Viale Amerigo Vespucci 22, **t** (0541) 55561, *www.hotelambasciatori.it*. Brash and modern building set just back from the sea and designed to attract a youngish crowd, rooms with air conditioning, TV, phone and minibar, and a private beach.

****__Milton__, Via C. Colombo 2, **t** (0541) 54600, *www.hotelmilton.com*. In a residential area right on the beach with elegant, completely soundproofed rooms, good restaurant, and a garden bar, pool, fitness and beauty centre, tennis courts and bicycles for guests.

****__Le Meridien__, Lungomare Murri 13, **t** (0541) 396 600, *www.lemeridien.com*. New building by architect Paolo Portoghesi, right in the centre and capturing the elegance of the old days with a modern twist; private beach, garage, pool and solarium.

***__Le Rose__, Viale Regina Elena 46, **t** (0541) 308 711, *www.lerosesuitehotel.com*. Just in from the beach: mini-apartments for two to five people with kitchenettes, as well as a pool and gym, and access to tennis.

Expensive (€€€€)

****__Hotel Ambassador__, Via Regina Elena 86, **t** (0541) 387 207, *www.ambassadorrimini.com*. Built in the early 1900s just in from the sea, with a shady garden and pool; rooms are simple; price includes buffet breakfast; restaurant with meat and seafood specialities.

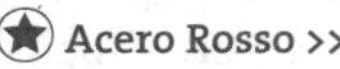

Acero Rosso >>

__Hotel Card__, Via Dante 50, **t (0541) 26412, *www.hotelcard.it*. Completely refurbished rooms, situated close to the Tempio Malatestiano and the rail station.

Moderate (€€€)

***__Villa Lalla__, Viale Vitorio Veneto 22, **t** (0541) 55155, *www.villalalla.com*. Midway between the *centro storico* and the beach. Pleasant, medium-sized hotel from the 1950s, with big rooms, and nice extras – bicycles, solarium, library and videotheque, excursions and kids' activities. *Restaurant open June–mid-Sept.*

***__Esedra__, Viale Caio Duilio 3, Marina Centro, **t** (0541) 23421, *www.esedrahotel.com*. Handsome remodelled seaside villa dating from the 1890s, with 53 spacious up-to-date rooms, surrounded by a garden and pool; room price includes a sauna and gym, and a big buffet breakfast. *Closed 2 weeks in Dec.*

Inexpensive (€€)

***__Napoleon__, Piazzale C. Battisti 22, **t** (0541) 27501, *www.napoleonrimini.it*. Pleasant hotel vintage 1973, rooms with big bathrooms, air conditioning, minibar, phone and TV; bicycles and laundry service. Near the station.

***__Hotel New Primula__, Viale Trento 12, **t** (0541) 23712, *www.hotelnewprimula.it*. Also well situated and comfortable. *Closed Nov–Feb.*

***__Saxon__, Via Cirene 36, **t** (0541) 391 400, *www.hotelsaxon.135.it*. Central, pleasant and friendly, but it has no restaurant.

Budget (€)

__Primavera__, Viale Lagomaggio 113, **t (0541) 380 206, *www.hotelprimavera.info*. Good position; comfortable rooms. Special offers on web site.

Jammin', Viale Derna 22, **t** (0541) 390800, *www.hosteljammin.com*. A youth hostel just a few steps from the old city centre, the station and the beach. Has 15 wheelchair-accessible rooms, and takes up to 55 people. Free use of bikes. *Open May–mid-Nov.*

Eating Out in Rimini

Expensive (€€€)

Acero Rosso, Viale Tiberio 11, **t** (0541) 53577, *www.acerorosso.it*. Rimini's surprise gourmet experience: supremely elegant restaurant just outside the historic centre with a choice of three *menu di degustazione*:

fish, meat, or vegetarian, all well prepared, and followed by masterful desserts. Summer garden. Good-value lunch menus, and a decent wine list. *Booking for dinner advisable. Closed Sun eve, Mon exc summer, and late July–mid-Aug.*

Dallo Zio, Via S. Chiara 16, **t** (0541) 786 747, *www.ristorantedallozio.it*. Seafood palace in the old town, offering marine lasagna, fishy vol-au-vent, stuffed squid and other surprises; popular with locals and tourists alike. *Open eves, all day Sat and Sun, closed Mon except in summer. American Express not accepted.*

Lo Squero, Lungomare Tintori 7, **t** (0541) 53881. Near the Grand Hotel, with an outdoor terrace overlooking the beach: shellfish are a speciality. *Closed Tues except summer, Nov and Dec.*

Taverna degli Artisti, Viale Vespucci 1, **t** (0541) 28519, *www.tavernadegliartisti.com*. Known for its colourful menu including seafood, pizzas, light pasta openers and something unexpected – a little *degustazione* of whisky; they have almost every brand from around the world. *Closed Wed.*

Moderate (€€)

Osteria Il Quartino, Via Coriano 161, **t** (0541) 731 215, *www.ilquartino.it*. In an old farmhouse on the edge of Rimini (take the Via Flaminia). Dine very well – not on seafood but the likes of *tagliata* and *ragù antico* and ravioli Parma-style, filled with herbs, and other regional delights like lamb, rabbit and guinea fowl. *Closed Tues.*

Osteria del Canevone, Via Tonini Luigi 34, **t** (0541) 29693, *www.osteriadelcanevone.it*. Located in a 16th-century palace in the heart of the *centro storico*, offering experimental recipes from Veneto and Romagna. Try *primi piatti* and *strozzapreti* with sausage. Elegant atmosphere and good service. *Closed Tues and Aug.*

4 Moschetteri, Via S. Maria al Mare, just off Piazza Ferrari, **t** (0541) 56496. Almost perfect trattoria in the centre. Excellent pizza and pasta, and a menu of Romagna favourites that changes every day. *Closed Tues.*

Osteria de Borg, Via Dei Forzieri 12, **t** (0541) 56071. Small *osteria* in the San Giuliano area with a summer garden. For a change from seafood and pizza, try the imaginative menu of soups, *tortellini* stuffed with carrot or *strozzapreti* with broccoli and spicy sausage. *Closed Mon and 2 weeks July.*

Rimini Key, Piazzale B. Croce, **t** (0541) 381 445. One of many tempting and cheap pizzerias along the seafront.

Inexpensive (€)

Caffè del Teatro, Piazza Cavour 6, **t** (0541) 781 528. You can watch Rimini go by from the glassed-in terrace, over an inexpensive lunch; try the *spiedini di mazzancolle*. *Open until 8; closed Sun.*

La Mi Mama, Via Poletti 32, **t** (0541) 787509, *www.lamimama.it*. Formerly the Osteria Saraghina's: new young owners Marco, Massimiliano and Mirko conjure up food based on the old Romagna traditions. *Piadina* and home-made pasta are a must; try also the desserts. *Closed Mon exc summer.*

More Beaches: Riccione to Cattolica

Holiday madness continues in a big way through the string of resorts south of Rimini and east of San Marino. **Riccione**, **Misano Adriatico** and **Cattolica** are all huge places, and in the summer they can be as crowded and intense as Rimini itself. They're really more or less suburban extensions of Rimini, and there's no great reason to see them for themselves. Trendy Riccione, the 'Green Pearl of the Adriatic', is Romagna's newest resort and perhaps the most family-oriented, with its long beach, gardens and the now pedestrian-only Viale Ceccarini for fashionable *passeggiatas*. Its **Museo del Territorio**, however, goes way back, with a collection of fossils and remains of

Museo del Territorio
*Viale Lazio 10, **t** (0541) 600113, museo@comune.riccione.re.it; open Sept–20 June Tues–Sat 9–12, Tues, Wed and Fri also 3–6; 21 June–end Aug Tues–Sat 9–12, Tues, Wed and Fri also 9–11pm*

the elephants, rhinoceroses, bears and giant stags that once frolicked in the valley of the Conca, followed by Palaeolithic, Neolithic and Roman finds.

South of Riccione, at the mouth of the river Conca, **Cattolica** was founded as a station along the Via Flaminia. Its first famous seaside tourist was Lucien Bonaparte, Napoleon's brother, and the rest is history. Some of this, along with a collection of traditional fishing boats, is installed in the **Museo della Regina**.

Museo della Regina
Via Pascoli 23, t (0541) 831 464; open summer Tues 9.30–12.30, Wed–Fri and Sun 4.30–7 and 8.30–11pm; winter Tues–Sat 9.30–12.30, Fri–Sun 3.30–7; closed Mon

In **San Giovanni in Marignano**, just inland from the fast food of Cattolica, frankfurters and hamburgers have a special meaning; the villagers are known to everyone else in the Romagna as the *Mangiatedeschi*, the 'German-eaters'. The people of San Giovanni do not care to commemorate in this ancient tradition. It started when two women living in these parts lured in and wolfed down 17 Goths in 539 (according to the Byzantine historian Procopius); it was the middle of the Greek-Gothic Wars, and times were hard. Perhaps they were hard to digest, for the villagers didn't try another one for 1,300 years; an Austrian soldier was apparently cut up and stewed in 1859. And such was the wartime hunger in 1944 that several retreating Germans met a similar fate. Or so they say.

Where to Stay and Eat in and around Riccione

ⓘ Riccione >
Piazzale Ceccarini 10, **t** *(0541) 693 302, iat@comune.riccione.rn.it*

Riccione ✉ 47838

*******Grand Hotel Des Bains**, Viale Gramsci 56, t (0541) 601 650, *www.grandhoteldesbains.com* (€€€€€). Established in 1908 and as lavish as they come, decorated with stuccoes, mirrors and opulent furnishings, yet with every modern amenity, including private beach, outdoor and indoor pools and fitness centre.

*****Dory**, Viale Puccini 4, t (0541) 642 896, *www.hoteldory.it* (€€€€). Near the sea and offering more than most for your money – beach cabins and sunbeds, big buffet breakfasts, bicycles, videos, a gym, beauty and fitness centre and sauna, and sea excursions. Rooms, which have phone, TV, minibar and modems, offer a variety of comforts, from the basic to the 'orchid rooms' with queen-sized beds and fancy baths. Bikes for rent.

*****Adlon**, Viale G. D'Annunzio 104, t (0541) 643 550, *www.adlon.it* (€€€). On the beach, hospitable and family-run, and ideal for families with children, with games, baby-sitting services and kitchen access for parents; free bikes, windsurfers and a gym come in handy if they're older. Rooms are big; most have balconies on the sea. *Closed Nov–mid-Mar.*

*****Marzia**, Viale De Amicis 18, t (0541) 642 323, *www.hotelmarzia.net* (€€€). Another very comfortable choice, in a quiet corner surrounded by a garden; the big rooms are light-filled and all have balconies; there's a pool, beach cabins, sauna and good restaurant; air conditioning available for extra.

Azzurra, Piazzale Azzarita 2, t (0541) 648 604, *www.ristoranteazzurra.com* (€€€). With a beautiful seaside terrace and the freshest vegetable and seafood cuisine, often in delightful combinations: pasta with scampi, courgette flowers and pecorino cheese, or turbot with potatoes, capers, olives and baby tomatoes. *Open until 2am.*

Il Casale, Viale Abruzzi 7, t (0541) 604 620, *www.ilcasale.net* (€€). A change from seafood: set back from the seaside madness, with another delightful terrace for lazy lunches over seasonal menus with dishes such as pasta half moons with asparagus or steak. *Open until midnight. Closed Mon in winter.*

Misano Adriatico > Viale Platani 22, **t** (0541) 615 520, iat@comune.misano-adriatico.rn.it

Locanda I Girasoli >

Cattolica > Via Matteotti 46, **t** (0541) 963 341, iat@cattolica.net

Trampolines, Lungomare della Repubblica 18, t (0541) 600 702, *www.trampolines.it* (€€). Huge and popular for a snack, pizza or full meal, featuring all the favourite Italian munchies from *crostini* to *bruschetta* to *piadine*, also pizza, fish dishes and meat. *Open until 1am; closed Tues exc summer and Nov–Feb.*

Misano Adriatico ✉ 47843

Locanda I Girasoli, Misano Monte, Via Ca' Rastelli 13, t (0541) 610 724, *www.locandagirasoli.it* (€€). One of the most delightful places around here. Far from the scent of sun cream, with eight comfortable country-style rooms in a 19th-century house surrounded by olive trees and sunflowers. There's a heated pool, children's playground, tennis courts, and a restaurant (open to non-guests, but book) serving delicious home cooking which may make it hard to get down to the beach.

Cattolica ✉ 47841

*****Splendid Club House**, Viale Carducci 84, t (0541) 961 520, *www.hotelsplendidcattolica.com* (€€€). Next to the beach; in a range of styles and prices, some rooms with kitchenette, and apartments near the sea. It also has a fitness centre, evening entertainment, kids' activities and a big seaside terrace.

*****Maxim**, Via Facchini 7, t (0541) 962 137, *www.hotelmaxim.it* (€€€). Well-endowed hotel, where many of the 66 pleasant rooms (with balconies, TV and minibar) have sea views. Sauna, heated pool, whirlpool and gym; big buffet breakfast included in the price. *Closed Oct–mid-Mar.*

Il Granaio, Via R. Fabbro 18, t (0541) 957 205 (€€). Just inland at San Giovanni in Marignano. Occupies an ancient granary and serves unusual but tasty dishes; good wine list too. *Closed Tues and 2 weeks Aug.*

Entertainment and Nightlife in and around Riccione

Music, Theatre and Cinema

The tourist office publishes *Instantaneo*, with detailed information on what's on in the area. Throughout the season art exhibitions cater for rainy days, and the city of Fellini with its 14 cinemas also hosts a series of film events – themed festivals, cartoon seasons and open-air extravaganzas – centred on the semi-official Rimini Film Festival in May. In late summer and autumn Rimini stages the **Sagra Musicale Malatestiana**, a festival of classical music, **t** (0541) 26239.

The nearby town of Santarcangelo holds an annual **theatre festival** in July, packed with innovative work, **t** (0541) 626 185, *www.santarcangelofestival.com*.

Clubs and Discos

Rimini and its perhaps even more in-vogue neighbour Riccione make up the undisputed clubland capital of Italy, a magnet for ravers from all over Italy and abroad.

On summer weekends crowds descend from all the cities within a 200km radius, and on mornings-after the road back to Bologna is often scattered with the battered cars of partygoers who didn't make it home.

For listings and information on clubs, one-nighters and anything else coming up, check Il *Resto del Carlino* and the magazine *Chiamami Città*, or search for posters. The main place for cruising the clubs is along the seafront, from about 10pm onwards, though there's also another little knot of activity in Rimini away from the beach in Covignano. If you get fed up with walking, a night bus runs along the whole length of the seafront between Riccione and Bellaria, and to Covignano.

Pascià, Via Sardegna 30, Riccione, **t** (0541) 697 844, *www.pasciariccione.it*. Large, stylish venue offering a mix of house, soul, techno and Euro-dance. *Open Wed and Fri–Sun.*

Paradiso, Via Covignano 260, **t** (0541) 751 132, *www.paradisoclub.com*. Very fashionable club, with a regular diet of Euro-dance, but also special events and all musical styles. *Open Fri–Sun.*

Rimini Rimini Rimini, Via Antiche Fonti Romane 97, Covignano, **t** (0541) 752 053, *www.riminiriminirimini.it*. Shows, food, culture and dancing in an entertainment park for adults and children.

Inland from Rimini

The seven *comuni* behind Rimini belong to the Valmarecchia, the crossroads between the Romagna, the Marche, Tuscany and the little Republic of San Marino – a jumble of hills and valleys and towns, with the sea never far away. The Malatesta built a number of castles to protect their flanks from their many enemies, and perhaps it shouldn't come as a surprise, considering Sigismondo's special status in Hell, that most of them have ghostly legends attached to them.

Santarcangelo di Romagna

Just 10km behind Rimini on the slopes of Monte Giove, Santarcangelo di Romagna is named after a 6th-century Byzantine chapel dedicated to St Michael. It has an important handicrafts tradition and a steep, labyrinthine *centro storico* under its foursquare **Malatesta castle**, one of several that claims to have witnessed the immortal indiscretion of Francesca da Polenta and Paolo Malatesta (*see* p.268); on moonless nights a female ghost is said to shuffle nervously about, although people think she is really the second wife of Paolo's lame brother Giovanni. The rest of the village is an antidote to the big resort, dedicated to the old traditions of Romagna: at Via Battisti 13 is a 17th-century fabric print shop, still in business. The **Museo Etnografico degli Usi e Costumi della Gente di Romagna** has a collection of artefacts related to traditional crafts – wine, shoes, iron, cloth-printing and musical instruments, farming, milling and popular theatre, with 80 puppets. Besides the ghost, Santarcangelo has another mystery: the two hundred artificial **caves** in the cliffs of Monte Giove, most with long access tunnels, ending in circular rooms. What were they for? Guesses range from Celtic or Mithraic places of worship to cellars for the local Sangiovese. There are legends of a huge golden treasure, stored away and guarded by ghosts that you can hear if you stay in there at night and press your ear to the ground.

Malatesta castle
t (0541) 620 832, sig.ma@flashnet.it; open 1st Sat of month 1.30–5.30; other days by

Museo Etnografico degli Usi e Costumi della Gente di Romagna
Via Montevecchi 41, t (0541) 624 703, www.metweb.org; open Tues, Thurs, Sat and Sun 10.30–12.30 and 3.30–5.30; Wed and Fri 10.30–12.30; summer daily 10.30–12.30 and 4.30–7; adm

Santarcangelo caves
t (0541) 624 537; open by appointment

Torriana and Montebello

Known unpleasantly as *Scorticata*, 'the Flayed', until Mussolini renamed it in the 1920s, **Torriana** was another key defence point in the Valmarecchia; a jagged 13th-century tower and later Rocca defend the natural sheer bulwark that rises behind the town; the story goes that Galeotto Malatesta, the same who killed his wife Francesca and brother Paolo, was himself murdered in the citadel's underground passages. But another ghost, one of the best documented phantoms in Italy, as a matter of fact, haunts Torriana's second and better preserved **Castello di Montebello**. Built on its steep cliff in the 12th century by Malatesta da Verucchio, the castle

Castello di Montebello
t (0541) 675 180, www.castellodimontebello.com; open summer Tues–Sun 2.30–7 and 10.30pm–12 midnight; winter Sat–Sun 2.30–6 and 10.30pm–12 midnight; adm

was given in 1464 by Pius II to the Counts di Bagno, and they held on to it until the 18th century; there's a guided tour that takes in antiques and paintings belonging to the counts, and a wine cellar with tastings in the adjacent 11th-century church, which was converted into an armoury. The ghost is named Azzurrina. She was the little albino daughter of a captain of the guard, who vanished one stormy night in the late 14th century, and who allegedly returns on the night of the summer solstice every five years or so (lately it's during election years) to play in the castle. RAI (Italian State Radio and Television) spent one evening recording the sounds – a ball bouncing on the flagstones, skipping, a child's laughter in a thunderstorm, and the bells tolling midnight. But there are no bells anywhere near the castle. If you come for a tour on a summer evening, they play the recording to spook visitors.

From Montebello a footpath leads to the **Santuario di Sajano**, on another rocky spur; this too was originally a castle, and keeps a round Byzantine tower from that period. The restored sanctuary has three 17th-century altars, some late Byzantine elements, and a miraculous 15th-century Madonna who draws crowds of pilgrims on 15 August.

Verucchio

Medieval Verucchio (from the Latin *verrucula*, or hump) is an attractive hill town, built like Torriana high on a rocky spur over the Valmarecchia, a naturally defensive spot that attracted settlers in Villanovan times. In the traumatic years of Greek and Gothic battles, it became a place of refuge; the fortress, rebuilt in the 10th century, became the cradle of the Malatesta clan with its first big shot, Malatesta il Centenario, the father of the famous Paolo and Giovanni. His descendant Sigismondo made Verucchio one of his chief citadels to keep an eye on the coast and Montefeltro, adding new walls and gates and the tower of the **Rocca Malatestiana**. In later years it had a number of rulers, including at one point a lute-player named Giovanni Maria, before it fell to the papal administrators. In the town centre, the **Collegiata** was rebuilt in the 19th century, but keeps older art from the town's other churches: two precious wooden crucifixes, one by the 14th-century Rimini school and the other by the 15th-century Venetian Nicolò di Pietro.

Rocca Malatestiana
t *(0541) 670 222, iat.verucchio@iper.net; open April–Sept daily 9.30–12.30 and 2.30–7.30; Oct–Mar Sat 2.30–6.30, Sun and hols 10–1 and 2.30–6; adm*

Between 1960 and 1975, archaeologists brought to light hundreds of tombs in the Villanovan necropolis, dating from the 9th–7th centuries BC. The chemical nature of Verucchio's soil is such that the grave goods are astonishingly well preserved, and suggest a society of 'shepherd kings' who kept flocks, occasionally made war on each other, and traded amber between the Adriatic and Tuscany. The evidence for this '*civiltà verucchiese*' may be seen in the **Museo Civico Archeologico Villanoviano**, housed in a former Augustine monastery

Museo Civico Archeologico Villanoviano
t *(0541) 670 222, www.comunediverucchio.it/museo; open summer daily 9.30–12.30 and 2.30–7.30; winter Sat 2.30–6.30, Sun 10–1 and 2.30–6; adm*

outside the Porta Sant'Agostino at the lower end of town. There are burial urns, unusual ceramics, fancy gold fibulas, amber discs, weapons and helmets, parts of a wooden inlaid throne and even woollen fabrics. Further down in the valley, St Francis is said to have stayed in a hut, where he performed several miracles, one of which was planting his staff in the ground and finding it had taken root overnight; this is said to be the tremendous 700-year-old cypress that still grows in the cloister of the **Convento di San Francesco**, the oldest Franciscan foundation in Emilia-Romagna. The church has a pretty door, a trecento fresco by the Rimini school, and a carved choir from the 15th century.

ⓘ **Santarcangelo >**
Via C. Battisti 5,
***t** (0541) 624 270,*
iat@comune.santarcangelo.rn.it,
www.iatsantarcangelo.com

ⓘ **Verucchio >>**
Piazza Malatesta 22,
***t** (0541) 670 222,*
iat.verucchio@iper.net,
www.comunediverucchio.it

Where to Stay and Eat Inland from Rimini

Santarcangelo ✉ 47824

******Della Porta**, Via A. Costa 85, **t** (0541) 622 152, *www.hoteldellaporta.com* (€€€). Two old mills converted into a charming small hotel. Air-conditioned rooms are furnished with country antiques, and some of the ceilings have *trompe-l'œil* frescoes. Sauna and solarium; baby sitting.

Palazzo Marcosanti, Via Ripa Bianca 411, **t** (0541) 629 522, *marcosanti@inyourlife.com* (€€€). Five kilometres south of Santarcangelo in Sant'Andrea di Poggio Berni. Two double rooms in a 12th-century castle, once owned by the Malatesta, then by other noble families. Excellent meals. *Advance bookings only.*

La Sangiovesa, Piazza Balacchi 14, **t** (0541) 620 710, *www.sangiovesa.it* (€€€). The most picturesque place to dine. The *piadine* and pasta dishes are home-made with stoneground flour from a nearby mill. The menu changes with the season, but is firmly Romagnolo, down to the *ciambella* at the end; the adjacent *osteria* has a fine selection of regional wines and good *salumi*, cheeses and other tasty bits. *Booking advisable. Eves only until 1am; closed Mon.*

Torriana ✉ 47825

Il Povero Diavolo Osteria e Locanda, Via Roma 30, **t** (0541) 675 060, *www.ristorantepoverodiavolo.com* (€€€). One of the most picturesque places to dine near Rimini. The innovative couple in the kitchen seduce diners with excellent *salumi*, five kinds of home-made bread, delicate yet flavourful pasta dishes, a wide choice of Italian and foreign cheeses, and splendid wines; you can also dine in the subterranean *osteria*, or just have *piadine*, cheese and wine. Includes five rooms with lovely views. *Menu degustazione. Booking advisable. Open eves only except Suns and hols; closed Wed in winter, and 3 weeks Jan.*

Pacini, Via Castello di Montebello 5, **t** (0541) 675 410, *www.ristorantepacini.com* (€). Next to the castle. Featuring the hearty delights of Romagna; good home-made *salumi*, pasta and meat dishes, rabbit and truffles. *Closed Wed (exc July–Aug) and Jan.*

Verucchio ✉ 47826

Le Case Rosse, Via Tenuta Amalia 141, Loc. Villa Verucchio, **t** (0541) 678 123, *www.tenutaamalia.com* (€€). Six *agriturismo* rooms on a wine estate by a golf course named after Amalia, the wife of Britain's George IV, who spent time here. Besides golf – it's just a few metres from Rimini's golf club – Le Case Rosse offers riding, mountain bikes, and three fine restaurants.

Casa Zanni, Via Casale 171, **t** (0541) 678 449, *www.casazanni.it* (€€). One of Romagna's best-known trattorias, founded in 1919 by Antonio Zanni, a miner who opened up an eatery, serving meals to those in need – a tradition his grandchildren continue to this day. Delicious *piadine* and grilled meats are cooked while you watch; also excellent *salumi* and house wine. You can also buy the local products in the shop. *Closed Tues exc summer.*

San Marino

As a perfect counterpart to the sand-strewn funfair of Rimini, just 23km inland you may visit the world's only sovereign and independent roadside attraction. Before Rimini became the Italian Miami Beach, the 26,000 citizens of San Marino had to make a living peddling postage stamps. Now, with their medieval streets crowded with day-trippers, the San Marinesi have been unable to resist the temptation to order some bright medieval costumes, polish up their picturesque mountain villages, and open some souvenir stands and 'duty-free' shops. Their famous stamps, though nothing like the beautifully engraved numbers of 50 years ago, are still prized by collectors, and recently the country has begun to mint its own coins again after a lapse of 40 years; nevertheless the citizens of San Marino, who may just have the highest average income in Europe, still make their living almost entirely from tourism.

The World's Smallest Republic

Also the world's oldest republic. According to legend San Marino was founded as a Christian settlement on the easily defensible slopes of Monte Titano by a stonecutter named Marinus, fleeing from the persecutions of Diocletian in the year AD 310. 'Overlooked', as the San Marinesi charmingly put it, by the empire and various states that followed it, the little community had the peace and quiet to evolve its medieval democratic institutions; its constitution in its present form dates from 1243 when the first pair of 'consuls' was elected by a popular assembly. The consuls are now called Captains Regent, but little else has changed in 700 years. Twice, in 1503 and 1739, the Republic was invaded by papal forces, and independence was preserved only by a little good luck. Napoleon, passing through in 1797, found San Marino amusing, and half-seriously offered to enlarge its boundaries, a proposal that was politely declined. It felt secure enough to offer shelter to Garibaldi, his wife Anita and 1,500 of his followers, fleeing Rome after the fall of the republic of 1849, with an Austrian army in pursuit; when the Austrians surrounded San Marino, demanding their expulsion, Garibaldi dissolved his army in the night and made a run for the coast before dawn. Since then, the republic has been an island of peace, taking in refugees in the Second World War.

Entering San Marino from Rimini at the village called **Dogana**, 'customs' (though there are no border formalities now), you pass through a string of villages, merging together along the ferociously built-up main road, with plenty of 'factory outlet' shops for fashions and other goods to take advantage of the tourist trade. San Marino, no midget like the Vatican City, is all of 12km long at its widest extent. At the foot of Monte Titano (one of the mountains the

Getting to and around San Marino

On weekdays there are eight, and on holidays six Bonelli, **t** (0541) 372 432, *www.bonellibus.com*, and Benedettini, **t** (0549) 903 854, *www.bus.it/benedettini*, **buses** to San Marino from Rimini's train station. There's a **funicular** up from Borgo Maggiore to San Marino town (*winter 8am–6.30pm; early July 8am–9pm; mid-July–early Sept 8am–1am*). If you do take the long climb up to the town, there are a few **parking** areas (with meters) well signposted around the edges. Trying to drive through the town would be folly.

---

mythological Titans piled up to reach heaven, to overthrow the gods), is **Borgomaggiore** (also called **San Marino**), the largest town, with most of the shops and the citadel of the republic. This is a steep medieval hill town carefully preserved in aspic – one where you can walk past a modest house on a side street bearing a plaque that says it is the Command of the Militia, or the State Ministry of Culture and the Environment. Not everything is as old as it looks: the **Palazzo del Governo,** full of Ruritanian guardsmen in brass buttons and epaulettes, is a reconstruction of 1894 with a recent restoration by Gae Aulenti. Here the Grand Council meets and the Captains Regent have their offices, while other rooms are full of San Marino memorabilia. The same hours apply to the **Museo e Pinacoteca di San Francesco**, in a 14th-century convent on Via Basilicus, and to the (rebuilt) medieval **tower fortresses** on the three peaks that give San Marino its famous silhouette (famous to philatelists anyhow), long the symbol of the republic. The first, **Rocca Guaita**, was restored in 1500 and used as a prison; the second, **Rocca Cesta**, on the highest peak of Monte Titano, contains weapons from the 12th to the 19th centuries; the third, **Rocca Montale**, can only be seen from outside. Then there's a cheesy batch of **private museums** – Medieval Criminals, Torture, Reptiles, Curiosities and Waxworks – and the **Collezione Maranello Rosso**, devoted to post-1950 Ferrari 250s.

Palazzo del Governo
t (0549) 885 370, www.museidistato.sm; open winter daily 8.45–5; summer daily 8–8; adm includes entrance to Palazzo Pubblico

Museo e Pinacoteca di San Francesco
t (0549) 885 132, www.museidistato.sm; open winter daily 8.45–5; summer daily 8–8; adm

Over the Border: San Leo

San Leo, on the western side of San Marino in the Marche, was according to legend founded by a companion of Marinus, but lost its independence long ago. The rough-walled, 9th-century church called the **Pieve** is worth a look, but San Leo's real attraction is the **castle**, built for the Montefeltro dukes in the 15th century. Like their famous palace at Urbino (only an hour away), this fortress is a perfect representative Renaissance building, balanced, finely proportioned in its lines, a building of intelligence and style. Also it is impregnable, hung on a breathtakingly sheer cliff. Once this mountain held a temple of Jupiter; as *Mons Feretrius* (referring to Jove's lightning) it gave its name to the Montefeltro family. A later fortress on this site was briefly 'capital of Italy' in the 960s, during the reign of King Berengar II. Now there is a small picture gallery in the castle and the dismal cell where the popes kept one of their most famous prisoners, Count Cagliostro, until he went raving mad and died.

San Leo castle
t 800 553 800, musei.san-leo@provincia.ps.it; open winter daily 9–6; summer daily 9–8; adm

Tourist Information in San Marino

ⓘ **San Marino >** *Ufficio di Stato per il turismo, Conrada Omagnamo 20, **t** (0549) 882 914, www.visitsanmarino.com.*

The tourist office is in the centre of town. For hotel bookings, try Consorzio San Marino 2000, Via Piana 103, **t** (0549) 995 031, *www.sanmarino2000.sm*

Where to Stay and Eat in San Marino

San Marino ✉ 47031

San Marino has become accustomed to entertaining tourists, and being so close to Rimini has turned out to be an unexpected windfall. The euro is accepted everywhere, but make sure you don't get too many San Marino coins in change; back in Italy they will only buy souvenirs. It isn't a bad place to stop if you can resist the charms of the Rimini lido.

****Titano**, Contrada del Collegio 31, **t** (0549) 991 006, *www.hoteltitano.com* (€€€€). Restored century-old building on San Marino's citadel, in the middle of the old town. Half the rooms have great countryside views. There is also a good restaurant with a terrace.

****La Rocca**, Salita alla Rocca 34, **t** (0549) 991 166 (€€). Not far away, with a TV in each of its 10 rooms, a pool, and balconies with a view. *Closed Nov.*

Locanda dell'Artista, Via del Dragone 18, Loc. Montegiardino, **t** (0549) 996 024, *www.locandadellartista.com* (€€€). Offers traditional dishes of the little republic, including some vegetarian ones, with home-baked bread and sweets. *Open eves only; closed Mon and Nov.*

Buca San Francesco, Piazzetta Placito Feretrano, **t** (0549) 991 462 (€€). Best restaurant in the centre. Soups, *tortellini* and *scallopine alla sanmarinese* are worth picking out in particular; the pasta is home-made. *Closed Fri in winter and mid-Oct to mid-Nov.*

East of San Marino, South of Cattolica

Riserva Naturale di Onferno *t (0541) 984 694, www.grottedionferno.it; guided tours of the main cave and surrounding woods July–Aug Sat–Sun 10.30am–12 midnight, April–June and Sept Sat–Sun 3–6, Mar and Oct Sun 3–6, Nov–Feb Sun 2.30–4.30; adm; torch and helmets are supplied; same hours for the Museo Naturalistico*

Rocca Malatestiana *t (0541) 980 035, utmontefiore@email.it; open May–June and Sept daily 10–12 and 3–7; July–Aug 10–12 and 3.30–7.30; Oct–Apr 10–12 and 2.30–6.30; adm*

Down on the border of the Marche, 44km from Rimini, **Gemmano** has the province's most striking natural site, the karstic ravines and caves of the **Riserva Naturale di Onferno**. Once these were the gates of Hell, but in 1810 a bishop of Rimini, offended to have such a thing in his diocese, changed the first letter of Inferno to an O. The caves, explored for the first time only in 1960, mark the outer edge of the world's largest gypsum vein, running under the Apennines, and has peculiar eroded breast-like formations hanging from the roof, known as the *mammelloni*. Because of temperature inversions they emit vapours in the evening, especially in winter: these were for centuries considered an ominous sign of hellish activity, along with the bats who simply adore the place – there are over 3,000, belonging to six different species. Three nature paths have been laid through the reserve, suitable for mountain bikes, which can be hired on the spot; maps are supplied. In Piazza Roma you can learn more about the local natural history in the **Museo Naturalistico**, in the 11th-century San Colomba church.

On the highest rock in the Valconca is **Montefiore Conca** and another **Rocca Malatestiana**, this one impressive in its sobriety, with sheer naked walls built in the form of a single massive tower in the early 14th century; it made such an impression on Giovanni Bellini that he used it in at least two of his backgrounds. It was reputedly impregnable, but under Sigismondo's son Giovanni it fell to the family's arch enemy Federico da Montefeltro (though only because he had managed to bribe some of the guards). Under the popes the castle's career took a curious turn when it was given, along with the city of Fano, to pay off a debt to Constantine Comnenos, a descendant of the Byzantine emperors and Prince of Macedonia. Constantine lived in the castle until he died in 1530, but afterwards the fortress, now militarily out of date, was neglected and ruined by earthquakes. It was completely restored in 1950: the Malatesta arms are still in place over the gate; the largest room is vaulted and frescoed with fragments of battle scenes by Jacopo Avanzi. Other rooms contain an impressive collection of fossils and minerals. The local priest has gathered together some 3,500 items from the Second World War, when this part of the world was on the Eastern Gothic Line: the collection, the **Reperti II Guerra Mondiale** is in the parish house.

Reperti II Guerra Mondiale
***t** (0541) 980 045; open by appointment on Sun afternoons*

Then there's **Montegridolfo**, a handsome medieval fortified village right on the border with the Marche that has been restored after years of total abandonment. It provides a convenient destination for coach tours, offering a tastefully done, measured teaspoon of the quaint and old, but no ghosts.

For these you have to continue on a bit, to **Mondaino**, a picturesque medieval burg wrapped in its walls with a pretty semicircular piazza in the centre. It was famous in Etruscan times for a temple dedicated to Diana and the numerous deer (*daino*) that roamed its slopes. Its Malatesta castle is haunted by yet another pair of unhappy lovers, who were run through by a jealous husband's sword. For years they sighed, lamented, shook their chains and scared people to death, but so many paranormal addicts came to hear them that they declared, through a medium, that they were fed up and moved their ectoplasm elsewhere. The castle now houses more solid relics in their stead: an important **Museo Paleontologico**. Some five to ten million years ago in the Miocene period, when the Adriatic dried up, thousands of fish perished in the mud at the bottom of the sea. They were preserved in the strata of Mondaino's sedimentary rock; fine examples are on display here, along with leaves and birds' feathers and wings, teeth belonging to the *Procarcharodon megalodon*, a 100ft-long ancestor of the shark, and the oddball 'mummy fish'.

Museo Paleontologico
***t** (0541) 981 674, infomondaino@mondaino.com; open Mon–Sat 9–12, Sun and hols 10–1 and 3–6; adm by donation*

Nearly all the Malatesta castles have legends about mysterious underground passages, and recently a real one was found here, a long, steep secret tunnel running down from the castle to the river. Mondaino has another attraction as well: a **Mediterranean arboretum**, with 5,780 plants and trees.

Mediterranean arboretum
*Via Pieggia 6, **t** (0541) 25777, www.arboreto.org; open by appointment only*

Where to Stay and Eat in Montegridolfo

Montegridolfo ✉ 47873

****Palazzo Viviani, Via Roma 38, t (0541) 855 350, *www.montegridolfo.com* (€€€€€). Variety of suites, apartments and double rooms with all conveniences, scattered through the ruler's palace and medieval buildings in the village centre. The complex includes a swimming pool as well as an elegant restaurant.

Osteria dell'Accademia, Via Roma 20, **t** (0541) 855 335, *masalvi@libero.it* (€€). Restaurant with a panoramic terrace, adjacent to the Palazzo Viviani, and especially recommendable. Try for instance the *zuppa rustica del Montefeltro*, or polenta and truffles. *Booking advisable. Closed Mon–Fri in winter and 2 weeks Jan.*

Language

The fathers of modern Italian were Dante, Manzoni and television. Each played its part in creating a national language from an infinity of regional and local dialects; the Florentine Dante, the first to write in the vernacular, did much to put the Tuscan dialect into the foreground of Italian literature. Manzoni's revolutionary novel, *I Promessi Sposi*, heightened national consciousness by using an everyday language all could understand in the 19th century. Television in the last few decades has performed an even more spectacular linguistic unification; many Italians still speak a dialect at home though.

Perhaps because they are so busy learning their own beautiful but grammatically complex language, Italians are not especially apt at learning others. English lessons, however, have been the rage for years, and at most hotels and restaurants there will be someone who speaks some English. In small towns and out of the way places, finding an Anglophone may prove more difficult. The words and phrases below should help you out in most situations, but the ideal way to come to Italy is with some Italian under your belt; your visit will be richer, and you're much more likely to make some Italian friends.

Note that in the big northern cities, the informal way of addressing someone as you, *tu*, is widely used; the more formal *lei* or *voi* is commonly used in provincial districts.

Pronunciation

Italian words are pronounced phonetically. Every vowel and consonant except 'h' is sounded. The stress usually (but not always!) falls on the penultimate syllable. Accents indicate if it falls on the last syllable (as in *città*); accents serve no other purpose, except to distinguish between *e* (and) and *è* (is).

Consonants

Consonants are the same as in English, with the following **exceptions**:

c when followed by an 'e' or 'i' is pronounced like the English '*ch*' (*cinque* thus becomes cheenquay).

g is also soft before 'i' or 'e' as in *gira* (jee-rah).

z is pronounced like '*ts*'.

Look out too for the following **consonant combinations**:

sc before the vowels 'i' or 'e' become like the English '*sh*' as in *sci*, pronounced 'shee'.

ch is pronounced like a 'k', as in *Chianti*, 'kee-an-tee'.

gn is pronounced as '*nya*' (thus *bagno* is pronounced ban-yo).

gli is pronounced like the middle of the word *million* (so *Castiglione* is pronounced Ca-steel-yoh-nay).

Vowels

a is pronounced as in English *father*.

e when unstressed is pronounced like 'a' in *fate*; when stressed it can be the same or like the 'e' in *pet*.

i is like the 'i' in *machine*.

o has two sounds, 'o' as in *hope* when unstressed, and usually 'o' as in *rock* when stressed.

u is pronounced like the 'u' in *June*.

Useful Words and Phrases

yes *sì*
no *no*
maybe *forse*
I don't know *Non (lo) so*
I don't understand (Italian) *Non capisco (l'italiano)*
Does someone here speak English? *C'è qualcuno qui che parla inglese?*
Speak slowly *Parla lentamente*

Could you help me? *Potrebbe aiutarmi?*
Help! *Aiuto!*
Please *Per favore*
Thank you (very much) *Grazie (molte/mille)*
You're welcome *Prego*
It doesn't matter *Non importa*
All right *Va bene*
Excuse me *Permesso/Mi scusi*
I'm sorry *Mi dispiace*
Be careful! *Attenzione!/Attento!*
Nothing *Niente*
It is urgent! *È urgente!*
How are you? *Come sta/stai?*
What is your name? *Come si chiama?/ ti chiami?*
Hello *Salve* or *ciao* (both informal)/ *Buongiorno* (formal)
Good morning *Buongiorno*
Good afternoon/evening *Buonasera*
Goodnight *Buonanotte*
Goodbye *ArrivederLa* (formal), Arrivederci/Ciao (informal)
What do you call this in Italian? *Come si chiama questo in italiano?*
What? *Che?*
Who? *Chi?*
Where? *Dove?*
When? *Quando?*
Why? *Perché?*
How? *Come?*
I am lost *Mi sono perso/persa (male/female)*
I am hungry/thirsty *Ho fame/sete*
I am tired *Sono stanco/stanca (male/female)*
I feel unwell *Mi sento male*
Leave me alone *Lasciami in pace*
good *buono*
bad *cattivo*
well *bene*
badly *male*
hot *caldo*
cold *freddo*
slow *lento*
fast *rapido*
up *su*
down *giù*
big *grande*
small *piccolo*
here *qui*
there *lì*
too (excessively) *troppo*
lots/a lot *molto*
OK *d'accordo*
Is that OK with you? *ti* (formal: *le) va bene?*
That's OK, thanks *Va bene così grazie*
I'm OK (I don't need any) *Io sono a posto*
address *l'indirizzo*

Time

What time is it? *Che ore sono?*
day *giorno*
week *settimana*
month *mese*
morning *mattina*
afternoon *pomeriggio*
evening *sera*
yesterday *ieri*
today *oggi*
tomorrow *domani*
soon *fra poco*
later *dopo, più tardi*
It is too early/late *È troppo presto/tardi*
spring *la primavera*
summer *l'estate*
autumn *l'autunno*
winter *l'inverno*

Months

January *gennaio*
February *febbraio*
March *marzo*
April *aprile*
May *maggio*
June *giugno*
July *luglio*
August *agosto*
September *settembre*
October *ottobre*
November *novembre*
December *dicembre*

Days

Monday *lunedì*
Tuesday *martedì*
Wednesday *mercoledì*
Thursday *giovedì*
Friday *venerdì*
Saturday *sabato*
Sunday *domenica*

Numbers

one *uno/una*
two *due*
three *tre*

four *quattro*
five *cinque*
six *sei*
seven *sette*
eight *otto*
nine *nove*
ten *dieci*
eleven *undici*
twelve *dodici*
thirteen *tredici*
fourteen *quattordici*
fifteen *quindici*
sixteen *sedici*
seventeen *diciassette*
eighteen *diciotto*
nineteen *diciannove*
twenty *venti*
twenty-one *ventuno*
thirty *trenta*
forty *quaranta*
fifty *cinquanta*
sixty *sessanta*
seventy *settanta*
eighty *ottanta*
ninety *novanta*
hundred *cento*
one hundred and one *centuno*
two hundred *duecento*
one thousand *mille*
two thousand *duemila*
million *milione*

Transport

airport *aeroporto*
customs *dogana*
bus stop *fermata*
bus/coach *autobus/pullman*
railway station *stazione ferroviaria*
train *treno*
platform *binario*
taxi *tassì/taxi*
One ticket to ... *Un biglietto per ...*
one way *semplice/andata*
return *andata e ritorno*
first/second class *prima/seconda classe*
seat *posto*
reserved seat *posto prenotato*
I want to go to... *Desidero andare a...*
How can I get to...? *Come posso andare a...?*
Do you stop at...? *Si ferma a...?*
Where is...? *Dov'è/Dove sono...?*
Where does it leave from? *Da dove parte?*
How far is it to...? *Quanto siamo lontani da...?*
What is the name of this station? *Come si chiama questa stazione?*
When does the next ... leave? *Quando parte il prossimo...?*
How long does the trip take? *Quanto tempo dura il viaggio?*
How much is the fare? *Quant'è il biglietto?*
Have a good trip! *Buon viaggio!*
near *vicino*
far *lontano*
left *sinistra*
right *destra*
straight ahead *sempre diritto*
north/south/east/west *nord/sud/est/ovest*
crossroads *incrocio*
fork, junction *bivio*
street *strada*
road *via*
square *piazza*
bicycle/motorbike *bicicletta/motocicletta*
petrol *benzina*
diesel *gasolio*
garage *garage*
car hire *noleggio macchina*
driver *guidatore, autista*
motorbike/scooter *motocicletta/Vespa*
This doesn't work *Questo non funziona*
map/town plan *carta/pianta*
breakdown *guasto*
driving licence *patente di guida*
speed *velocità*
danger *pericolo*
parking *parcheggio*
no parking *sosta vietata*
narrow *stretto*
bridge *ponte*
toll *pedaggio*
slow down *rallentare*

Shopping, Services, Sightseeing

I would like... *Vorrei...*
How much is it? *Quanto costa?*
open *aperto*
closed *chiuso*
cheap *a buon prezzo*
expensive *caro*
bank *banca*
entrance *ingresso*
exit *uscita*

hospital *ospedale*
money *soldi*
credit card *carta di credito*
newspaper *giornale*
pharmacy *farmacia*
police station *commissariato*
policeman *poliziotto*
post office *ufficio postale*
shop *negozio*
supermarket *supermercato*
tobacco shop *tabaccaio*
WC *toilette, bagno, servizi*
Men *Signori, Uomini*
Women *Signore, Donne*

Useful Hotel Vocabulary

I'd like a double room, please *Vorrei una camera doppia (matrimoniale), per favore*
I'd like a single room *Vorrei una camera singola*
...with/without bath *...con/senza bagno*
...for two nights *...per due notti*
We are leaving tomorrow morning *Partiamo domani mattina*
Is breakfast included? *È compresa la prima colazione?*
May I see the room, please? *Posso vedere la camera?*
Is there a room with a balcony? *C'è una camera con balcone?*
There isn't (aren't) any hot water, soap, light, toilet paper, towels *Manca/Mancano acqua calda, sapone, luce, carta igienica, asciugamani*
May I pay by credit card? *Posso pagare con carta di credito?*
May I see the room, please? *Vorrei vedere la camera, per coretsia*
May I see another room please? *Per favore potrei vedere un'altra camera?*
Fine, I'll take it *Bene, la prendo*
Is breakfast included? *E' compresa la prima colazione?*
What time do you serve breakfast? *A che ora è la colazione?*
How do I get to the town centre? *Come posso raggiungere il centro città?*

Glossary

acroterion decorative protrusion on the rooftop of an Etruscan, Greek or Roman temple. At the corners of the roof they are called *antefixes*.

ambones twin pulpits (singular: *ambo*), often elaborately decorated.

ambulatory an aisle around the apse of a church.

atrium entrance court of a Roman house or early church.

badia an abbey or abbey church.

baldacchino baldachin, a columned stone canopy above the altar of a church.

basilica a rectangular building, usually divided into three aisles by rows of columns. In Rome this was the common form for law courts and public buildings, and Roman Christians adapted it for early churches.

borgo from the Saxon *burh* of S. Spirito in Rome: a suburb or village.

***bucchero* ware** black, delicately thin Etruscan ceramics, usually incised or painted.

campanile a bell tower.

camposanto a cemetery.

cardo transverse street of a Roman *castrum*-shaped city.

cartoon the preliminary sketch for a fresco or tapestry.

caryatid supporting pillar or column carved into a standing female form; male versions are called *telamones*.

castrum a Roman military camp, always neatly rectangular, with straight streets and gates at cardinal points. Later the Romans founded cities in this form.

cenacolo fresco of the Last Supper, often on the wall of a monastery refectory.

chiaroscuro the arrangement or treatment of light and dark areas in a painting.

ciborium a tabernacle, often large and free-standing; or used in the sense of a *baldacchino*.

comune commune, or commonwealth, referring to the governments of the medieval free cities. Today denotes local government.

condottiere the leader of a band of mercenaries in late medieval and Renaissance times.

confraternity a religious lay brotherhood, often serving as a neighbourhood mutual-aid and burial society, or following some specific charitable work.

contrapposto the dramatic but rather unnatural twist in a statue, especially in a Mannerist or Baroque work, derived from Hellenistic and Roman art.

convento a convent or monastery.

decumanus street of a Roman *castrum*-shaped city parallel to the longer axis, the central, main avenue called the Decumanus Major.

dodecapolis a federation of the twelve city-states; a common form of religious or political organization in ancient times (as with the Etruscans).

duomo cathedral.

ex voto an offering (a terracotta figurine, painting, medallion, silver bauble, or whatever) made in thanksgiving to a god or Christian saint.

forum the central square of a Roman town, with its most important temples and buildings. The word means 'outside': the original Roman Forum was outside the city walls.

frazione (abbreviated fraz.) a subdivision of a modern Italian *comune* (town, city or village), usually an outlying settlement or suburb; sometimes called a *locazione*.

fresco wall painting, the most important Italian medium of art since Etruscan times. It isn't easy. First the artist draws the *sinopia* (q.v.) on the wall, then this is covered with plaster, but only a little at a time, as the paint must be on the plaster before it dries. Leonardo da Vinci's endless attempts to find clever short-cuts ensured that little of his work would survive.

Ghibellines (see *Guelphs*) one of the great medieval parties, the supporters of the Holy Roman Emperors.

gonfalon the banner of a medieval free city; the *gonfaloniere*, or flag-bearer, was often the most important public official.

graffito originally, incised decoration on buildings, walls, etc.; only lately has it come to mean casually scribbled messages in public places.

Greek cross in the floor plans of churches, a cross with equal arms. The more familiar plan, with one arm extended to form a nave, is called a Latin Cross.

grisaille painting or fresco in monochrome.

grotesques carved or painted faces used in Etruscan and later Roman decoration; Raphael and other artists rediscovered them in the 'grotto' of Nero's Golden House in Rome, and they became popular in Renaissance decoration.

Guelphs (see *Ghibellines*) the other great medieval faction, supporters of the Pope.

intarsia decorative inlaid wood or marble.

Liberty style the Italian name for Art Nouveau (from London's Liberty department store).

locazione see *frazione*.

loggia an open-sided gallery or arcade.

lunette semicircular space on a wall, above a door or under vaulting, filled by either a window or a mural painting.

mandorla in medieval art, an almond-shaped aura surrounding figures of Christ in Majesty.

matroneum the elevated women's gallery around the nave of an early church.

narthex the enclosed porch of a church.

naumachia a mock naval battle, like those staged in the Colosseum.

palazzo not just a palace, but any large, important building.

palio a banner, and the horse race in which city neighbourhoods contend for it in their annual festivals. The most famous is Siena.

Pantocrator Christ 'ruler of all', a common subject for apse paintings and mosaics in areas influenced by Byzantine art.

pietra dura rich inlay work using semi-precious stones.

pieve a country or village parish church.

pluteo screen, usually of marble, between two columns, often highly decorated.

podestà in medieval cities, an official with mostly judicial duties sent by the Holy Roman Emperors; their power, or lack of it, depended on the strength of the *comune*.

popolo in the medieval *comuni*, this meant not 'the people' in general, but the middle classes, organized in a body to protect their interests and led by a Capitano del Popolo. The poorer classes were the *popolo minuto*.

predella smaller paintings on panels below the main subject of a painted altarpiece.

presepio a Christmas crib.

putti naked small children, a popular motif for decoration since the 1400s, that developed into the flocks of cherubs that infested much of Italy in the Baroque era.

quadratura illusionistic style of painting, invented in Rome and perfected in mid 16th-century Bologna, that uses painted architectural elements in perspective to create imaginary space behind a wall or above a ceiling.

quadroporticus an enclosed rectangular portico, like a quadrangle or cloister, that leads to the main entrance of a church; common in early medieval churches.

quattrocento the 1400s – the Italian way of referring to centuries (duecento, trecento, quattrocento, cinquecento, seicento, etc.).

rocca a fortress.

sinopia the layout of a *fresco* (q.v.), etched by the artist on the wall before the plaster is applied.

stele a vertical funeral stone.

stigmata a miraculous simulation of the bleeding wounds of Christ, appearing in holy men.

telamon see *caryatid*.

thermae Roman baths.

tondo round relief, painting or terracotta.

transenna marble screen separating the altar area from the rest of a church.

triptych a painting, especially an altarpiece, in three sections.

trompe l'œil art that uses perspective effects to deceive the eye – for example, to create the illusion of depth on a flat surface (see *quadratura*).

tympanum a semicircular space, often with a painting or relief, above a church portal.

voussoir one of the stones of an arch.

Further Reading

Alighieri, Dante, *The Divine Comedy* (plenty of good translations). Few poems have ever had such a mythical significance for a nation. Anyone serious about understanding Italy and its world view will need more than a passing acquaintance with Dante.

Bassani, Giorgio, *The Garden of the Finzi-Continis* (Quartet Books, 1989). Emilia-Romagna's best-known contemporary writer spun this tale partly from his experiences growing up Jewish in wartime Bologna. Much of his other work evokes the region, including *Five Stories of Ferrara* (1956).

Burckhardt, Jacob, *The Civilization of the Renaissance in Italy* (Harper & Row, 1975). The classic on the subject (first published in 1860), the mark against which scholars still level their poison pens of revisionism.

Burke, Greg, *Parma: A Year in Serie A* (Witherby, 1998). A quite unusual book, of interest mostly to soccer fans but containing some insights on Parma and Italian life in general.

Clark, Kenneth, *Leonardo da Vinci* (Penguin).

Fellini, Federico, *Fellini on Fellini* (Da Capo Press, 1996). A collection of the great director's writings and letters, and some boyhood memories of Rimini.

Gardner, Edmund Garratt, *Dukes and Poets in Ferrara: A Study in the Poetry, Religion and Politics of the 15th and Early 16th Centuries* (Haskell, 1982). Ferrara in its golden age, concentrating on literature.

Ginsborg, Paul, *A History of Contemporary Italy: Society and Politics 1943–1988* (Penguin, 1990). A good modern account of national events since the fall of Mussolini.

Gioffrè, Rosalba and Gabriella Ganugi, *Emilia Romagna* (Flavours of Italy Series, New Holland, 1999). A celebration of Italy's top food region, with lots of recipes.

Hale, J.R. (ed), *A Concise Encyclopaedia of the Italian Renaissance* (Thames & Hudson, 1981). An excellent reference guide, with concise, well-written essays.

Leonardo da Vinci, *Notebooks* (Oxford, 1983).

Levey, Michael, *Early Renaissance* (1967) and High Renaissance (1975; both Penguin). Old-fashioned accounts of the period, with a breathless reverence for the 1500s – but still full of intriguing interpretations.

Meier, Barbara, *Verdi* (Life and Times Series, Haus Publishing, 2003) A short biography.

Murray, Linda, *The High Renaissance* and *The Late Renaissance and Mannerism* (Thames and Hudson, 1977). Excellent introductions to the period; also Peter and Linda Murray, *The Art of the Renaissance* (1963).

Procacci, Giuliano, *History of the Italian People* (Penguin, 1973). An in-depth view from the year 1000 to the present.

Richards, Charles, *The New Italians* (Penguin, 1995). Observant, amusing study of life in Italy during and since the political upheaval and financial scandals in the early 1990s.

Rosenberg, Charles, *The Este Monuments and Urban Development in Renaissance Ferrara* (Cambridge University Press, 1998). The story of this precocious mini-Florence in its greatest days.

Sidoli, Richard Camillo, *The Cooking of Parma* (Rizzoli, 1996). Not only recipes, but a fond recollection of village life and traditions.

Symonds, John Addington, *A Short History of the Renaissance in Italy* (Smith, Elder, 1893). A condensed version of the authority of a hundred years ago, but still makes fascinating reading today.

Vasari, Giorgio, *Lives of the Painters, Sculptors and Architects* (Everyman, 1996). Readable, anecdotal accounts of the Renaissance greats by the father of modern art history.

Index

Main page references are in **bold**. Page references to maps are in *italics*.

4th edition published 2007

Cadogan Guides
2nd Floor, 233 High Holborn,
London WC1V 7DN
info@cadoganguides.co.uk
www.cadoganguides.com

The Globe Pequot Press
246 Goose Lane, PO Box 480, Guilford,
Connecticut 06437–0480

Cover photographs: © Cephas Picture Library/Alamy; © Marina Spironetti/Alamy
Introduction photographs: p.1 © FAN travelstock/Alamy; p.2 © David Noton Photography/Alamy; p.3 © Lebrecht Music and Arts Photo Library/Alamy; p.6-9 © Bologna Turismo; p.9 © John Ferro Sims/Alamy; p.10 © Marina Spironetti/Alamy, © Bologna Turismo, © Lebrecht Music and Arts Photo Library/Alamy; p.11 © CubolImages srl/Alamy; p.12 © Slim Plantagenate/Alamy; p.13 © Sara Gray/Getty; p.14-16 © Bologna Turismo; p.16 © WILLIAM HUME/Alamy; p.16 © guichaoua/Alamy
Maps © Cadogan Guides, drawn by Maidenhead Cartographic Services Ltd

Art Director: Sarah Gardner
Managing Editor: Antonia Cunningham
Editor: Tim Locke
Assistant Editor: Nicola Jessop
Proofreading: Daphne Trotter
Indexing: Isobel McLean
Updater: Gabriella Cursoli

Printed in Italy by Legoprint
A catalogue record for this book is available from the British Library
ISBN 978-186011-350-5

The author and publishers have made every effort to ensure the accuracy of the information in this book at the time of going to press. However, they cannot accept any responsibility for any loss, injury or inconvenience resulting from the use of information contained in this guide.

Please help us to keep this guide up to date. We have done our best to ensure that the information in this guide is correct at the time of going to press. But places and facilities are constantly changing, and standards and prices in hotels and restaurants fluctuate. We would be delighted to receive any comments concerning existing entries or omissions. Authors of the best letters will receive a Cadogan Guide of their choice.